Contents

T5-DHD-926

CONTENTS

■ THE AMERICAS
Quiescent Inflation Allows US Growth 130

Experts from Oxford Analytica, Oxford

Year of Rising Risk for Argentina..............................133

Experts from Oxford Analytica, Oxford

The Range of Country @ratings in the Americas ...136

Sylvia Greisman and Olivier Oechslin, *Coface Country Risk and Economic Studies Department, Paris*

■ ASIA
Uninterrupted Growth for China..................................200

Experts from Oxford Analytica, London

The Range of Country @ratings in Asia 203

Sylvia Greisman and Pierre Paganelli, *Coface Country Risk and Economic Studies Department, Paris*

■ THE MIDDLE EAST AND NORTH AFRICA
Saudi Regime to Weather Insurgency..........................270

Experts from Oxford Analytica, London

The Range of Country @ratings in the Middle East and North Africa.................273

Sylvia Greisman and Catherine Monteil, *Coface Country Risk and Economic Studies Department, Paris*

■ SUB-SAHARAN AFRICA
Succession Dominates in South Africa 338

Experts from Oxford Analytica, Oxford

The Range of Country @ratings in Sub-Saharan Africa 341

Sylvia Greisman and Bernard Lignereux, *Coface Country Risk and Economic Studies Department, Paris*

Acknowledgements

The publisher wishes to thank the Oxford Analytica and Coface country risk and short-term experts (Nathalie Ballage, Thierry Lefevre, Jean-Louis Daudier, Dominique Fruchter, Bernard Lignereux, Catherine Monteil, Olivier Oechslin, Pierre Paganelli, Jean-François Rondest and Yves Zlotowski) who have contributed to *The Handbook of Country Risk 2005*.

Our thanks are also extended to Stanley Glick (Lingua Franca), Govind Bhinder (FEAT – Financial and Economic Authors and Translators) and Coface's Communication Department.

Risks for Growth... and Payments

François David, *Chairman, Coface*

Economic recovery and improved company solvency materialized in 2004 as we expected. However, with growth spreading to all industrialized countries, it clearly slowed in the second half, particularly in Japan and Europe. Several factors undermined European growth, dragging economic activity in that region down: the euro appreciation against the dollar, increased oil prices and very limited economic-policy leeway. Overall, 2004 performance was mixed for industrialized countries, except the United States. However, it was exceptionally good in emerging countries, which generally benefited from strong demand, high raw material prices and low-risk premiums in financial markets.

Company solvency withstood the second half slowdown relatively well in 2004. Cash positions bolstered by increased turnover, low inflationary pressures and favourable financing terms partially offset the growing pressure on margins resulting from raw material price increases. Payment behaviour was thus generally good. Credit risk nonetheless seems to have clearly bottomed out. The decline in payment-incident frequency slowed late in the year reflecting the less dynamic growth outlook for industrialized countries.

In 2005, the world growth slowdown should only moderately exacerbate credit risk, provided, however, there are no major shocks concerning the two main risk factors: oil prices and the dollar exchange rate. Barrel prices could remain near the average registered in 2004. With demand still strong, shortage risks have remained substantial due to the limited reserve production available and OPEC's policy of avoiding excessively sharp declines in dollar-denominated prices. Meanwhile, downward pressure on the US currency should persist amid limited prospects for reductions in US fiscal and current account deficits. Although the most likely scenario calls for gradual increases in US interest rates, a sudden tightening of monetary policy in response to a dollar collapse will remain possible. That would doubtless affect the remarkable improvement in company solvency registered in the past two years and have a substantial negative impact on economic activity in the United States as well as in emerging countries.

Barring a major shock, growth should nonetheless only slow moderately in 2005. Regional disparities should persist, however, with emerging Asian countries, primarily China, remaining the most dynamic economic focal point. Conversely, Europe will continue to contend with declining competitiveness in a less buoyant context linked to the world demand slowdown.

The Outlook for 2005–2006

Jonathan Reuvid, *Senior Editor, GMB Publishing*

Only an optimist, viewing the closing months of 2004 and peering ahead into the crystal ball of 2005–2006, could say that the world is a safer place politically or economically than a year ago. That is not to say that there are no glimpses of light at the ends of tunnels or silver linings in dark clouds, but the general prognostication is hardly encouraging.

Last year we took a different approach to providing a broad brush analysis of the global geopolitical and geoeconomic environments. It would be tasteless this year to liken the shifts and conflicts within and between the two to 'movements of the tectonic plates', as we have done in the past. The catastrophic fallout of the Indian Ocean tsunami is too recent. However, the message from the analogy is reinforced. There are major threats to international security and the world economy which, if unattended, could wreak extensive man-made havoc. In this introduction we will focus as much on the threats as on the opportunities and begin with the present state of international security.

■ RISKS TO INTERNATIONAL SECURITY

A year ago we concluded that, on balance, the benefits of living with US political hegemony outweighed the risks. That view was based on a promising outlook both for Afghanistan and for the outcome of the regime change in Iraq following the intervention of the United States and its coalition of the willing. Today, that verdict seems less safe. Although underlying tensions remain, the presidential election in Afghanistan yielded a positive result and was judged as sufficiently democratic by international observers. However, the success of the elections in Iraq is only a first step towards democracy.

The Middle East

Whatever the merits of the case for the invasion of Iraq, and with that splendid gift of 20:20 vision, which all commentators possess in abundance, it is clear that the White House totally underestimated the manpower needed to secure the country after its technically awesome display of electronically guided hardware had achieved military victory. Like distance learning, distance warfare achieves lasting results only if supported by sufficient face-to-face engagement. That basic tenet was well understood in the previous Gulf War; unfortunately this President Bush and Defence Secretary Rumsfeld chose not to heed seasoned military opinion. As a result, the United States and its allies face the prospect of maintaining a more than peacekeeping presence in Iraq for an indeterminate period against insurgents employing the full range of terrorist tactics against the civilian population as well as alien forces. Abuse of Iraqi prisoners by US soldiers, and now it seems by British soldiers too, has weakened the case that this was a liberating army. So long as allied troops are required to remain, as they must for the foreseeable future until armed insurgency is banished, many Iraqi citizens will inevitable view them as an army of occupation.

The White House tells us that the world is a safer place as a result of the regime changes in Afghanistan and Iraq and it is true that there have been no comparable atrocities by al-Quaeda in the United States or Europe since the horrifying attacks of 9/11. National security has been greatly strengthened throughout the West, so it is difficult to tell whether the non-recurrence of violence reflects reduced opportunity or enfeeblement of the terrorist organization itself. There is little published evidence for the public to confirm that the war on terror is being won and intelligence agency reports are no longer accorded the respect that they once carried.

Among the significant political events of 2004, President Bush's re-election to office with a clear mandate for a second four-year term ranks high. His inauguration speech with its single thread mission statement of the 'expansion of freedom in all the world' cannot be faulted for lack of ambition but rings global warning bells, particularly in the Arab world. However, with the exception of Iran, oil-rich Arab states are unlikely to feel much individual anxiety.

Prime Minister Blair, President Bush's principal apologist abroad, has assured us that the President has learned that the best way to pursue his foreign policy is through diplomacy in harmony with his allies and there were echoes of a fresh focus on diplomacy in the confirmation hearing of incoming Foreign Secretary Condoleeza Rice before the US Senate committee. During the extended period of US presidential electioneering, EU foreign ministers, led by France, Germany and the United Kingdom, were given implicit approval to negotiate an agreement with Iran to contain its nuclear capability but there is no certainty that the United States will continue to cut them much slack on an issue that it perceives to be the leading threat to international security.

Indeed, the growing difference of opinion between the White House and those same leaders of the EU preparing to relax the embargo on arms sales to China suggests that the president intends to maintain a firm grip on all foreign affairs issues that might affect US foreign policy – in this case the United States' underwriting of Taiwan's national security and sovereignty.

The acid test of the US Administration's resolve to achieve peace diplomatically or, if necessary, with physical intervention remains the Middle East – specifically the Palestine–Israel conflict. The election of Mahmoud Abbas as Yasser Arafat's successor in a relatively free election with a robust majority has brought a ray of hope that the 'road map' to peace could be unrolled; however, Israel insists that Abbas shows that he can achieve the binding agreement of Palestine's two resident terrorist groups to abandon violence, or their suppression, before it will engage in negotiations with him. Hopefully, without the electoral pressures of the domestic US pro-Israel lobby, President Bush will find the strength to ride herd on Israel's Prime Minister, Ariel Sharon, in a genuine search for long-term peace even if Abbas cannot clear the first hurdle.

The global perspective

President Chirac offers an alternative to US hegemony with his multipolar strategy. This approach has the conceptual attraction of giving the EU a key role in determining a consensual foreign policy common to both the United States and the EU. Logically, there should be additional poles: the Arab League, perhaps, and an Asian pole in which China and India would be key participants. This strategy was one of the drivers for President Chirac's support for the opening of negotiations with Turkey to join the EU, representing a first step towards a European alliance with Islam. Paradoxically, the *entente* with Turkey has strengthened opposition to the draft EU Constitution both in France and in some other enlarged EU member states. A rejection of the Constitution, either in the French referendum this year or by any of the other 24 states, could mean that the EU, as the principal polar ice floe in the president's strategy, may suffer a dose of 'global warming'.

No other alternative to the US domination of foreign affairs is in sight. Having shown itself ineffectual in 2003 when put to the test, the UN has not regained its former influence. After a shaky start, the UN humanitarian agencies have performed reasonably well in response to the tsunami catastrophe of 26 December 2004, but that is not enough. The multinational panel of wise men reviewing UN functions and its structure has already identified proposals for reorganization and it is to be hoped that action on their final report will be taken swiftly, preferably to coincide with the appointment of the next director general.

The second major threat to global security – North Korea's nuclear capability under the government of Kim Jong Il – seems to have subsided for the time being thanks to the efforts of China as moderator in a protracted multinational dialogue. One by-product of Western intelligence agency disinformation over weapons of mass destruction (WMD) in the case of Iraq has been to devalue the WMD threat generally. That may be a mistake, but for the time being we should be content that Kim remains sulking in his tent.

■ OTHER POLITICAL ISSUES

Elsewhere, the news has been mixed. A welcome truce in the warring factions of Sudan could mean that there will be genuine relief for its starving and oppressed population in 2005. Conversely, the situation in Congo seems intractable and it is difficult to detect any strands of realistic hope within the present conflict.

Europe

In Europe, three developing situations hold centre stage. The first is the new political order in Ukraine following Viktor Yushenko's democratic election as president after the first election, which he and his supporters successfully challenged both on legal grounds and through a three-week peaceful campaign on the streets of Kiev. The first election results were finally declared invalid by the Ukraine Supreme Court, which also upheld the outcome of the second election. At one point in the dispute, a less than peaceful replay of the regime overturns in Central and Eastern Europe 15 years ago seemed imminent but the Ukrainian institutions, not least the Supreme Court, proved robust and the democratic process was maintained. The electoral outcome is not clear-cut and Yushenko will need tangible economic support from the EU to demonstrate the advantages of EU association if he is to win over the supporters of the displaced Viktor Yanukovich who believe that the former alignment with Russia should continue.

If the change of government in Ukraine represents a silver lining, then the increased concentration of power seized by Vladimir Putin, Russia's president, in the course of 2004 is certainly a black cloud.

The effective nationalization of the principal operating assets of Yukos, Russia's major oil company, by means of an enforced sale by tender to state-owned interests, was not just the punishment of an oligarch or the reasonable action necessary to recover unpaid taxes, but a strong indication that the Kremlin is slipping back towards a command economy. If this trend is confirmed, inward investment to Russia will inevitably start to dry up.

The third major development in Europe is, of course, the draft EU Constitution on which a series of referenda before ratification will be held, starting in June 2005. As already suggested, the agreement by EU leaders to enter negotiations with Turkey for future membership or association is likely to have a negative effect. In theory, if just one of the 25 member states rejects the Constitution it will not be enacted by the others, and among those committed to a referendum there are several countries – in particular the United Kingdom – where a 'yes' will be difficult to secure. What happens if there is no unanimity is more than a moot point. Constitution aficionados suggest that those countries failing to ratify should retire from the EU; others suggest that the Council of Ministers should attempt to agree a modified Constitution and that the ratification process should be repeated all over again. A more attractive solution already under discussion might be for those who ratified the Constitution and those who rejected it to agree to differ with a restructure of the EU in the form of concentric circles. The inner circle would adopt the Constitution with those not already members joining the euro zone; the outer circle would continue to observe the present body of EU law, its rules and regulations regarding trade, competition and environmental law and all but the most controversial social measures, which have passed into law recently. Some outer circle members might argue for exclusion from the Common Agricultural Policy, which fails to meet the interests and circumstances of diverse members. Under this scenario the outer circle could accommodate, in time, both Turkey and Ukraine as full members.

Asia

In Asia, the new found *détente* between India and Pakistan is holding, although progress towards *entente* on the key issue of Kashmir is sure to be slow. General Pervez Musharraf's decision to stay in power as president while retaining control of the army is understandable in view of the continuing threat to his country's security from the terrorists allied to al-Quaeda resident in Pakistan, but hardly conforms to President Bush's template for democratic government.

Africa

The development needs of Sub-Saharan Africa are usually presented either as an economic issue demanding massive financial aid or as an urgent humanitarian need to address the below-subsistence level poverty and HIV/AIDS pandemic that ravages so many countries. But there are uncomfortable political issues too.

Multinational companies are eager to exploit the oil and gas opportunites of the west coast of Sub-Saharan Africa, especially Nigeria, identified in the overview of Sub-Saharan Africa later in this book, and there are international mineral extraction companies with similar interests in the Republic of South Africa (RSA) and elsewhere. But business prospects in other Sub-Saharan African countries are hardly enticing. Most economies start from such low levels of economic activity that it is hard to envisage how they could grow and prosper as in Asia, where the strong domestic work ethic and business entrepreneurship have generated startling GDP growth over the past 40 years. Nor are the business risks considered acceptable where there is no rule of law and the carapace of dictatorship is barely concealed by a veneer of para-democracy.

The RSA itself, the powerhouse of the region's economy, is a model for both democratic and economic development. However, its influence has been undermined by President Mbeke's state of denial regarding the HIV/AIDS virus and his tacit support for the misrule of President Mugabe of neighbouring Zimbabwe – a different kind of virus that has laid his country to economic waste.

These factors, to which aspiring world statesmen often avoid drawing attention but which are deeply distasteful to many, will inhibit the renewed mission in 2005 to extract more aid for Africa from donor nations.

◼ THE WORLD ECONOMY IN 2005–2006

As usual, Oxford Analytica reviews thoroughly the economic outlook for each of the regions in the overviews that follow, while the economy and risk factors of each country are analysed individually in depth in the body of the book. This introduction focuses on the economic interaction of the regions comprising the greater part of the global economy and the underlying imbalances that pose risks for its future. That does not mean that the economic impact of the oil-producing states of the Middle East and the Caspian region are negligible or that the mineral production of South America is insignificant – the continuing growth of the Chinese economy is heavily dependent on both – but the relevance of Sub-Saharan Africa (which accounts for only 6 per cent of world oil production) is barely relevant and the financial crises of the Argentinian and other debt economies offer a continuing drain on, rather than contribution to, global wealth.

The US economy – motoring on

As 2004 drew to a close, fears for a serious slowdown receded and GDP growth for 2005 through 2006 is widely forecast to run at 3.5–4.0 per cent against 4.3 per cent in 2004. Corporate profits are expected to grow rather more slowly in 2005 than the 15.7 per cent rate achieved in 2004, but moderate output growth will ensure that there are no adverse consequences for exports from US trading partners.

This benign scenario is predicated on the US government and the Federal Reserve continuing to contain inflation. The core PCE inflation rate is rising modestly but the Federal Reserve's policy of gradual tightening is expected to achieve an average annual inflation rate of around 2.5 per cent in 2005, marginally below that of 2004.

Doubts about the future of the US economy centre on the low propensity to save and the massive federal deficit. As Oxford Analytica points out, personal savings are at an all-time low while consumer credit, household and mortgage debt all stand at dangerously high levels. However, the debt mountain is underpinned by household assets at a level five times as large as total GDP. No significant changes in taxation are likely during the second Bush Administration unless inflation starts to spiral.

The federal fiscal deficit is now at the level of 4 per cent of GDP and the current account deficit is approaching 6 per cent of GDP which, according to economic theory, is unsustainable in the long term and currently contributes to the dollar's weakness. So far, US bond yields have remained stable but any significant increase would spark off mortgage rate rises, curtail consumer spending and lower GDP growth introducing an inevitably dampening effect on world trade.

At the end of the third quarter of 2004, the United States registered a negative current balance for the preceding 12 months of US$603 billion, of which a large part is due to the current account deficit on its trade with China (U$1,124 billion in 2004). From 1 January 2005, the global quotas on the export of textiles and clothing from China have been removed and the impact on US, as well as EU, imports is expected to be considerable. The WTO estimates that China could seize half the world market in this sector – about twice its current share. Against this background the US trade deficit is unlikely to narrow in the next two years unless a marked slowdown of the economy takes root in 2006 under the circumstances described above.

It is at this point that the longer-term US economic outlook and, as such, also that of the world economy becomes inextricably entwined with that of China. US pressure on China to revalue its renminbi or remove its peg to the US dollar as an effective means of addressing its foreign trade imbalance continues to mount. However, there is no immediate prospect for renminbi revaluation and, in its robust response to US critics, the People's Bank of China points to its savings rate of more than 40 per cent, compared with less than 2 per cent in the United States, as evidence of US profligacy.

Asia's century

Last year we highlighted the growing impact of China on the world economy and 2004 saw dramatic evidence of China's emergence as a world economic superpower. Loose talk about a 'hard landing' for the Chinese economy has melted away, as so often in the past. Again, the government under President Hu Jintao showed that it still controls the levers of macroeconomic management, this time supplementing direct measures of restraint with the use of conventional monetary policy. GDP growth for the year is estimated at above 9 per cent and is expected to march forward through 2005 and 2006 at no less than 8.5 per cent. It has become clear that the pattern of global manufacturing has shifted irrevocably and, looking ahead, that the key question for manufacturers worldwide is how China will change the world economy rather than the converse. China's incremental exports are moving further up the value chain as the capital equipment and technology that boosted Chinese imports since WTO entry are translated into production capacity. The two landmark events of WTO accession and the smooth transfer of power to China's fourth generation leadership at the beginning of 2003 have undoubtedly accelerated and strengthened progress.

In foreign trade, China achieved a full-year positive trade balance of US$32 billion for 2004, the highest since 1998 in spite of fulfilling its WTO obligations to lower import tariffs. China is estimated to have overtaken Japan in 2004 in terms of trade volume, becoming the world's third largest trading nation after the United States and Germany.

Reasons why China will not address the issue of its undervalued currency in the short term are twofold. First, China needs to complete the restructuring of its banking system; it has now made a sound start with the reorganization of the 'Big Four' state-owned banks in anticipation of the further opening-up of the industry to foreign banks in 2007. Second, China plans to have liberalized about 70 per cent of the 43 items in its capital account within four to five years which will make the renminbi a virtually convertible currency. Any significant early adjustment to the currency is considered dangerous to the overall economy.

The growing foreign exchange reserves that China is accumulating, reported at US$609.9 billion at the end of 2004 and largely invested in US government securities, are not entirely comfortable for China. For the time being, they help to support the US economy but when the renminbi is revalued, US dollar reserves will correspondingly depreciate. Therefore, the deployment of reserves into acquisitions abroad is an attractive alternative to bonds; growing Chinese outward investment was another phenomenon of 2004. In December, the purchase of IBM's personal computer business by Lenovo, China's top computer company, gave notice that China is in the market to acquire foreign assets and leading brands. The most recent investment report of the United Nations Conference of Trade and Development (UNCTAD) rates China as fifth in the league of countries from which investment is expected to come over the next two years.

Foreign direct investment (FDI) into China continues to accumulate. In 2003, total contracted FDI increased by 38 per cent. By October 2004, FDI at US$52 billion had already exceeded the whole of the previous year and is likely to continue rising for the next few years so long as revaluation is judged to be a medium-term certainty.

Elsewhere in Asia, excluding those countries whose economies have been stricken by the demands of reconstruction following the tsunami disaster, the economic outlook remains favourable. India is powering ahead in China's footsteps as the next developing economic giant, although the business model is somewhat different.

Japan recovered quite strongly in 2004 with 3.2 per cent GDP growth but is projecting less vibrant growth of only 1.6 per cent for 2005. Its budget deficit remains uncomfortably high at 6.5 per cent of GDP, but the current account balance on foreign trade was almost US$168 billion in surplus for the 12 months to end-November 2004 and is expected to grow at a similar rate in 2005. Other APEC countries achieved GDP growth rates approaching or above 5 per cent in 2004 and all are continuing to benefit from the strong export of raw materials and some capital goods and technical products to China.

Europe

Our selective *tour d'horizon* concludes with commentary on Europe, specifically the EU and the euro area. With the exception of Austria, all of the original EU-15 countries are forecasting lower GDP growth for 2005 than in 2004. Only Austria, Belgium, Spain, Sweden and the United Kingdom are expecting growth of more than 2 per cent in 2005. For the euro area as a whole there are signs of a fresh slowdown, with GDP growth fading from 1.8 to perhaps 1.6 per cent in 2005, consumer price inflation moderating from 2.1 to 1.8 per cent and the growth in industrial production registering just 0.5 per cent year-on-year in November 2004.

However, there are more hopeful signs within the euro area from Germany whose economic health is fundamental to its successful performance. Driven by the increase in the trade-weighted exchange rate of the euro, the German corporate sector has undergone intense restructuring and has managed to reduce the gap in its unit labour costs from the euro-zone average. The German labour market has proved far more flexible than the prophets of doom warned and manufacturing companies in headline industries are shedding labour and, in some cases, even cutting nominal wages. For 2005, German industry has secured an untypically modest wage agreement, and even the 35-hour week, a bastion of trade union policy, seems to be negotiable in some sectors.

The euro's strength against the US dollar in 2004 (and thereby against the Chinese renminbi too) has caused some euro-area members, particularly France and Italy, to bring strong pressure on the European Central Bank (ECB) for intervention. By contrast, German exports again showed robust growth of 5 per cent in 2004 despite the negative impact of the stronger euro. The currency effects in Germany's case may have been delayed by increased hedging or by the fact that a high proportion of its 'investment goods' are sold on price-covered forward contracts.

Nevertheless, EU foreign trade has been affected by the impact of the euro area's deficit with China that soared to US$48.1 billion in the first ten months of 2004. For the whole EU the deficit with China was US$73.4 billion. The euro area outcome represents a year-on-year increase of 23 per cent and contrasts with its surplus with the rest of the world.

Outside the euro-area, the UK economy is showing signs of weakness at the beginning of 2005 after a long run of more positive growth. GDP growth is now expected to decline in 2005 from 3.2 to 2.4 per cent and unemployment and consumer prices to rise marginally. The budget deficit at the end of 2004 is calculated at 3.3 per cent of GDP, still lower than France or Germany but above the current EU criterion. At the end of the third quarter of 2004, the 12-month current account balance was in deficit by US$47.4 billion. No tightening of the economy is expected in advance of the general election, currently forecast for May 2005.

The marked contrast between the growth economies of the CEE-8 that joined the EU at the end of 2003 and those of the EU-15 noted a year ago persists. All of the eight achieved GDP growth of 3.3 per cent or more in 2004 and look for continuing growth in 2005. Poland and the three Baltic states all grew by more than 5.7 per cent in 2004 and anticipate only slightly lower rates of growth in 2005. Encouragingly, the high fiscal deficits of the Visegrad countries are in decline. Crucial to their future prosperity are continuing gains in labour productivity that will attract technology-intensive FDI to offset current account deficits. In this respect, as in the export climate, they are suffering increased competition from China and India. The Asian impact is indeed pervasive.

The @rating System

In 2000, Coface introduced the first worldwide insurable company rating scheme. The @rating system assesses the ability of a company to meet its business obligations vis-à-vis customers and suppliers. International businesses can now log on to www.cofacerating.com or any of the national websites (eg www.cofacerating.fr) and access the three following rating systems:

@rating credit opinion indicates the recommended credit exposure for a company using a very simple assessment scale (1 @ = 20,000 euros, 2 @ = 50,000 euros, 3 @ = 100,000 euros, etc). Credit exposure arising from BtoB credit transactions is insurable by Coface. An @rating credit opinion is assigned to some 44 million companies worldwide, reflecting Coface's dual expertise in corporate information and credit insurance.

@rating score, which was launched in October 2002 by Coface and Coface Scrl, measures a company's default risk over one year. It comprehensively and accurately rates 4.5 million large, medium and small-sized French companies. @rating score is used not only by different sized companies but also by financial institutions looking to develop a rating system that complies with new banking regulations (McDonough ratio).

Measuring credit risk among companies is an important exercise when addressing not only traditional needs (bank loans to firms, BtoB credit and market credit) but also emerging needs created by new instruments such as loan securitizations and new banking solvency regulations (McDonough ratio). While scepticism over accounting practices persists, companies and banks have an even greater need for reliable tools to benefit from the recovery while keeping risks under control.

Country @rating, another of Coface's key achievements, allows people and businesses engaged in international trade to strengthen the security of their transactions. It continuously tracks a series of indicators for 151 countries, evaluating political and institutional factors, growth vulnerability, the risk of foreign currency shortage, the ability of a government to meet its international obligations, external over-indebtedness, the risk of a systemic crisis in the banking sector and payment behaviour for short-term transactions. An aggregate rating is assigned to each of the 151 countries monitored on the basis of seven risk categories. As in the approach used by rating agencies, there are seven different rating grades from A1 to A4, B,C and D. The definition of country @ratings is provided overleaf.

Country @rating Definition

Economic liberalization has led to a boom in BtoB trade, with 70 per cent of accounts being settled by short-term instruments. It is therefore vital to assess the risk associated with such transactions. Country @rating addresses this need by evaluating the extent to which a firm's financial commitments in a given country are influenced by that country's economic, financial and political prospects. Log on to **www.cofacerating.com** to access country @rating, the supplement to company @rating.

A1 The steady political and economic environment has positive effects on an already good payment record of companies. Very weak default probability.

A2 Default probability is still weak even in the case when one country's political and economic environment or the payment record of companies is not as good as in A1-rated countries.

A3 Adverse political or economic circumstances may lead to a worsening payment record that is already lower than the previous categories, although the probability of a payment default is still low.

A4 An already patchy payment record could be further worsened by a deteriorating political and economic environment. Nevertheless, the probability of a default is still acceptable.

B An unsteady political and economic environment is likely to affect further an already poor payment record.

C A very unsteady political and economic environment could deteriorate an already bad payment record.

D The high risk profile of a country's economic and political environment will further worsen a generally very bad payment record.

Oxford Analytica

Our corporate goal: *to be the information industry standard for strategic analysis of geopolitical, macroeconomic and social developments.*

Founded in 1975, *Oxford Analytica* is an international consulting firm providing business and political leaders with timely analysis of worldwide political, economic and social developments.

Oxford Analytica acts as a bridge between the world of ideas and the world of enterprise. One of its major assets is an extensive international network that draws on the scholarship and expertise of over 1,000 senior members at Oxford University and other leading universities around the world, as well as think-tanks and institutes of international standing.

Clients of *Oxford Analytica* are able to integrate the judgements drawn from this unparalleled resource into their own decision-making process. Clients include multinational corporations, major banks, national governments and international institutions in more than 40 countries.

Global strategic analysis

Sectoral Overview

Sylvia Greisman and Dominique Fruchter
Coface Country Risk and Economic Studies Department, Paris

Sector @ratings measure the average level of non-payment risk associated with companies in individual economic sectors. A rating reflects the influence of the economic outlook and average company financial situation on payment behaviour in short-term commercial transactions in a particular sector. To determine sector @ratings, Coface combines three types of measurements:

- the vulnerability of economic conditions in the sector, which reflects the influence of market prospects, price levels and production costs on company solvency;
- company financial solidity in the sector, which reflects the capability of companies to cope with economic downturns;
- payment experience on transactions payable in the short term as reflected by Coface databases.

Coface establishes sector @ratings on ten levels ranging from A+ for the lowest risks to D for the highest. Sector @ratings are complementary to @rating credit opinions on companies and country @ratings.

Range of sectoral risks

HIGHEST RISK

D

C-

C   Clothing/Air transport

C+   Textiles

B-   Computers/Construction

B   Telecommunications

B+   Car industry

A-   Mechanical engineering/Paper/Mass distribution

A   Chemicals/Electronics/Steel

A+   Pharmaceutical

LOWEST RISK

SECTORAL RISK PANORAMA

The quality of risks improved significantly in most sectors in 2004. However, the improvement stalled late in the year mainly because of flagging economic prospects in several sectors.

In 2005, continued increases in raw material prices, affecting company production costs and margins, should accompany a moderate world demand slowdown. Moreover, regional disparities in demand dynamism and competitiveness terms will remain crucial factors. The predominantly favourable situation in emerging Asian markets has thus benefited most sectors, in contrast, for example, to sagging European growth that could slow further under the effect of reduced competitiveness resulting from a further euro appreciation.

- In that context, companies in several sectors, including pharmaceuticals (rated A+), steel (A), chemicals (A), electronics (A), as well as mass distribution (A-) and mechanical engineering (A-), have benefited from sound financial situations and buoyant markets permitting them to cope with fierce competition or, in the case of electronics, a demand slowdown. The average risk level in those A-rated sectors has been low.
- The car industry (rated B+), telecommunications (B) and computers (B-) sectors have been subject to stiff competition in many regions amid slower demand growth. Construction (B-), with a nonetheless very regional, even national, market should experience a slowdown after years of euphoria in many countries while sluggish conditions

should persist in Germany and Japan. Average payment risk in B-rated sectors has been moderate.

- Representing a higher risk level, companies in textiles (rated C+) and the clothing sector (C) will have to cope with the end of the Multifibre Arrangement, with demand focusing increasingly on standardized, low-priced products. An already high level of risk could deteriorate further for producers in industrialized and some emerging countries. In a completely different area, air transport (C) still has to contend with continued high oil prices undermining the solvency of the weakest companies. Payment risks in those C-rated sectors have been at disquieting levels.

Sectors rated A+, A, A-: The economic environment has been good in the sector and has had a positive influence on the company financial situation. Payment experience has been satisfactory. Default probability has been low on average.

■ PHARMACEUTICALS (A+)

The market outlook has remained good despite a sales slowdown. Company payment behaviour has been satisfactory, generally underpinned by healthy financial situations even if the impact of generic sales and increasing cost of therapeutic risk could ultimately undermine performance in the sector.

World pharmaceutical product sales have continued to grow although at a less robust pace than in the past (up 7 per cent expected on average between 2004 and 2007 against 10 per cent previously). That slower growth should particularly concern brand drugs due to increasing international competition and the development of generics. Moreover, facing aging populations and increasing health spending, all developed countries have been giving preference to less costly copies. Laboratories have been working to develop strategies for putting new successor drugs rapidly on the market to replace drugs with expired patents, notably bestsellers like anti-cholesterol and anti-ulcer products. In that context, new

concentrations will be likely in the sector for the purpose of reaching critical size and amortizing R&D spending.

North America, representing the largest consumer region by far (50 per cent of world sales), has continued to drive the market. However, US laboratories have particularly suffered from patent expiry and increasingly aggressive competition from some generic producers. Meanwhile, new drug launches and research productivity have been in decline. Besides generics, increased therapeutic risk has recently hurt certain laboratories, compelling them to withdraw leading medicines, which affected their financial performance in 2004.

In Europe, sales growth has varied by country (from up 3 per cent to up 8 per cent in 2004). European laboratories have been faring relatively well with the generic phenomenon less widespread than in the United States and more subject to regulation. To cope with the problem, European actors have been pursuing economies of scale through mergers (Sanofi-Aventis). In 2005, new drug launches could buoy sales growth.

Although Japan remains an important market, its growth has been more moderate and its profitability lower due to price cuts imposed by authorities.

In Latin America, the market has been growing strongly without, however, returning to prevailing pre-2000 levels.

■ STEEL (A)

The continuing higher levels of world demand and prices have been buoying steelmakers' financial health. Payment incidents have concerned non-integrated processors and distributors that have had difficulties passing price increases on to customers.

Steel consumption should rise an additional 5 per cent in 2005, after a 9 per cent increase in 2004, despite the relative slowdown of the Chinese growth. After posting a record performance in 2004, steelmakers will continue to benefit from that buoyant environment in 2005 and will increase their prices sharply starting in the first quarter (about 20 per cent). Facing a persistent, virtually worldwide shortage, large steelmakers have been

Steel output
— European Union (15)
— USA
— Asia

increasing their production capacity. Furthermore, concentration, acquisition, alliance and delocalization strategies are being implemented, for example, the merger of Ispat, LNM and the US ISG to form the world's largest steelmaker group, Mittal Steel, surpassing Arcelor in production capacity terms. Other actors may envisage similar groupings, particularly medium-sized producers like Corus (The Netherlands), Severstal (Russia), Riva (Italy), SSAB (Sweden) and so on.

In the **United States**, insufficient supply to meet demand could again put high pressure on prices in 2005. The highpoint of the cycle has nonetheless been approaching. Furthermore, the still-expected cooling off of Chinese demand and the prospective construction of new mills could ultimately help ease price pressure.

In **Europe**, increased demand and higher prices have spurred a marked improvement in the financial situation of actors in the sector in 2004. The situation in 2005 will depend on trends in user sectors including the car industry, construction and household appliances. For exports, the strategy now calls for delocalizing production of standard semi-finished products to mining countries (Brazil and Australia) and keeping in Europe only higher value-added products more apt to withstand price competition.

In **Asia**, Chinese demand has continued to grow although at a slower rate. In 2004 **China** will have consumed 28 per cent of world steel and, according to the WTO, its share will reach 33 per cent in 2008. The Chinese economy's soft landing, after measures taken by the government early in the year, has only had a limited effect on the quantities of steel consumed. To meet their needs, Chinese steelmakers have been increasing the number of partnerships and acquisitions. The signing of long-term contracts with suppliers has been providing

them with supply guarantees even if that may entail sacrificing negotiating leverage on basic metal prices in case of a trend reversal.

In **India**, where consumption has been increasing very rapidly (up 6 per cent to 7 per cent a year), the South Korean group Posco, allied with the BHP natural resources group, has been envisaging development of a gigantic steel complex in the state of Orissa in eastern India where mineral reserves are abundant.

In **Japan**, steelmakers just registered their fifth consecutive year of strong production. Strong demand from carmaking, shipbuilding and electrical construction has been offsetting a weak building market. Driven by other Asian countries, exports have remained robust. In the face of dynamic demand and prices, steelmakers have been currently proceeding with modernization of their production facilities that should permit them to rapidly increase production.

■ CHEMICALS (A)

Overall, the situation of the chemicals sector improved markedly in 2004 in line with the expansion of world industrial activity. Company financial health improved despite increased raw material costs. In 2005, the trend should remain positive despite a certain slowdown of business activity and the persistent pressure on margins exerted by high raw material prices.

Demand has continued to grow very rapidly in Asia, particularly in China, which has benefited regional chemists, especially Japanese companies although their home market has been much less dynamic.

In the **United States**, producers registered a 6 per cent increase in business activity in 2004, thanks notably to strong domestic demand. Increases in production and capacity utilization have contributed to a sharp improvement in their financial situation despite higher energy and raw material costs. Even if production only increases 3.5 per cent in 2005, their earnings will continue to improve with the US dollar depreciation reducing the pressure of imports. They will nonetheless have to deal with criticism concerning environmental protection that will ultimately lead to increased production costs.

In Europe, the improvement has been both less pronounced and more precarious as the sector's dynamism has been resting solely on exports with domestic sales remaining tentative. Business activity will thus only increase 2.6 per cent in 2005 after 2.4 per cent in 2004. The dollar's decline will impede exports and exacerbate import pressure. Moreover, increased input prices, even reduced by the euro appreciation, will continue to be imposed on basic chemical producers, who will pass on the increases to the downstream industry. Those companies concerned downstream, confronted with sluggish demand and stiff competition, will have greater difficulty passing such increases on to their customers. Finally, the coming changes in European regulations in the REACH (Registration, Evaluation and Authorization of Chemicals) framework could lead to higher charges and accelerate the process of discontinuing selected low value-added products.

■ ELECTRONIC COMPONENTS (A)
Economic conditions in the world electronic component sector stabilized at a very high level, above the previous cycle's peak reached in 2002. However, the current activity peak now seems to have passed. Moreover, increased price competition has been squeezing company margins.

World semi-conductor deliveries rose about 20 per cent in 2004 after 18 per cent in 2003, allowing the industry to return to the level reached prior to the bursting of the bubble. However, growth sagged significantly in the second half of the year. Shipments will decline slightly in 2005. That slowdown will reflect manufacturers' prudence in the face of their increased stocks and a prospective downturn of demand for 'traditional' computers, mobile telephony terminals (respectively 40 per cent and 20 per cent of the total user market) and telecommunications network equipment.

Steady demand for laptop and pocket computers, personal organizers, measurement and control instruments, medical applications and consumer electronics (20 per cent of the total market with camcorders, digital cameras, flat-

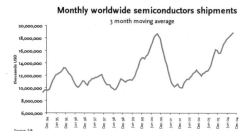

Monthly worldwide semiconductors shipments
3 month moving average

Source: SIA

screen televisions) has apparently not sufficed to restore confidence. It is true that substantial new production capacity will come into play after the massive investments made by Asian, US and European industrialists locked in fierce competition.

The slowdown will be more pronounced in Europe and in the United States than in the Asia Pacific region because of the increasing delocalization of production, particularly for consumer products, toward that region.

■ MECHANICAL ENGINEERING (A-)
The sector benefited last year from the worldwide company investment recovery. However, the drop in new orders registered in the last months of 2004, coupled with the expected world growth slowdown, would suggest that activity will slow in 2005. Moreover, increased production will not necessarily result in a corresponding increase in earnings. Margins can sometimes be squeezed between rising prices for intermediate products, notably steel, and stiff price competition on standardized products, exacerbated by exchange rate fluctuations. Payment behaviour should, however, remain relatively good.

In the United States, domestic sales and exports of machinery registered robust growth in 2004, bearing out the recovery of capital goods investment in construction, agriculture, raw material extraction, metallurgy and turbines. Sales price increases accompanied the increased demand but without returning to the levels that prevailed during the boom in the 1990s. The slowdown expected in 2005 will be limited in scale due to favourable exchange rates, with domestic sales remaining at satisfactory levels.

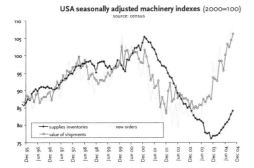

USA seasonally adjusted machinery indexes (2000=100)
source: census

Legend:
- supplies inventories
- value of shipments
- new orders

In Europe, 2004 marked the return of a positive economic trend in the sector, notably in Germany, underpinned particularly by exports, which offset an essentially sluggish domestic market. However, companies, in particular smaller companies, continued to suffer from insufficient profitability resulting from the pressure on margins caused by unfavourable trends on steel prices and exchange rates. A slowdown should develop in 2005 with exports affected by the euro's continued strength and sagging world demand.

In Japan, the economic recovery begun in 2003 continued in 2004 thanks to both an investment upturn in large Japanese companies and the dynamism of exports (over a third of sales) to regional countries and the United States. In 2005, the domestic investment slowdown and unfavourable exchange rates could affect economic activity.

■ PAPER/CARDBOARD (A-)

After four difficult years, market conditions improved for paper thanks notably to the beneficial effects of world growth on demand and prices for paper products. The improvement in company finances has been less substantial, thus affecting payment behaviour. The margin for growth is still substantial, with the sector remaining below the peaks in business activity and prices reached in 2000.

In North America, the sector has benefited both from an earlier start on recovery and a higher growth rate as well as from better control over prices resulting from a recent concentration process. Forestry developers have benefited from sharp price rises linked to single-family-dwelling sector dynamism. Heavy debt, often resulting from takeovers of competitors, has nonetheless been burdensome. Canadian companies have, moreover, been contending with the Canadian dollar's appreciation and duties on their wood exports to the United States.

In Europe, despite a significant increase in their production, companies have been struggling to improve their margins due to difficulties in imposing sufficiently high price increases, notably for printing and writing papers. In the coming months, however, the disparity with their US counterparts could diminish.

In emerging regions, the Asian papermaking sector has benefited from the region's dynamism. Brazilian and Chilean pulp producers have benefited from the high levels of world demand and prices for pulp.

■ MASS DISTRIBUTION (A-)

The economic upturn has apparently already ended even with the market remaining below the peak reached in 2000. Although the outlook is still generally bright, the sector has been contending with pressure from discounters, the hegemony of a few major players and liberalization of the legislative and regulatory framework.

It has also continued to face marked national disparities attributable at once to household consumption levels, trade regulations and the competitive situation. However, the regional and world presence of the sector's major players has tended to mitigate the sometimes-contradictory effects of national characteristics on company finances.

The North American market has benefited from the continued dynamism of household consumption. However, a slowdown is under way, due notably to high petrol prices and a disappointing labour market. Moreover, fierce competition has continued to mark the sector with Wal-Mart omnipresent in all sales formats and regions. That situation has spurred continuation of the concentration process as evidenced by the recent K-mart/Sears merger.

Japanese mass distribution has benefited from a moderate household consumption recovery. The market still offers substantial development potential. The Daiei group's current difficulties have nonetheless raised many questions. Should it be subject to a takeover by its competitor Aeon, the resulting entity would be too powerful to allow other local actors to survive. Even Wal-Mart (United States) and Tesco (United Kingdom), solidly established in Japan, would have trouble competing.

In Europe, the financial health of actors in the sector has remained dependent on household demand dynamism. Germany, Italy, Portugal and The Netherlands have been sensitive markets. In The Netherlands, the Casino subsidiary, Laurus, has experienced difficulties. In Italy, the Rinascente chain, also in difficulty, has been up for sale with the food branch already taken over by Auchan. The German market has continued to suffer from a lack of confidence by households confronted with unemployment and uncertainty about the outlook for social security. That unfavourable context has been fanning price competition, exacerbated by the strong position of independent discounters (eg Aldi, Lidl); to the detriment of traditional supermarkets and mini-markets. Groups that have been in difficulty include Karstadt-Quelle and Spar (ITM group).

In Central European markets, the earnings performance of large Western groups that have recently set up local operations has not always lived up to expectations due to too narrow a consumer base, positioning being still poorly suited to local tastes or living standards and an overcrowded market.

Performance has been much better in Asia (excluding Japan) thanks to buoyant economic conditions, good adjustment to local characteristics and partnerships with local actors.

Sectors rated B+, B, B-: In an essentially favourable economic environment, although not safe from short-term deterioration with negative repercussions on the company financial situation, payment behaviour is generally correct and default probability acceptable.

■ CAR INDUSTRY (B+)

The overall market outlook has been improving slightly. Financially, major car and parts makers partly avoided increasing raw material prices (steel, plastic and others) in 2004 thanks to contracts, often multi-year, linking them to suppliers. However, renegotiation of those contracts in 2005 will eat away at margins. The situation has generally been much more difficult for second-tier parts manufacturers, generally linked to suppliers by short-term contracts, whose more limited size denies them negotiating leverage. Moreover, raw materials represent a larger proportion of their cost of production.

That general trend nonetheless encompasses large regional disparities.

In the **United States**, sales have stabilized at a high level. European carmakers' market share has declined to the benefit of their Asian competitors while the US carmaker share appears to have stabilized. Promotional campaigns and Daimler Chrysler's improved fortunes with its new models going down well have allowed that stabilization. The downside has been reduced earnings performance not entirely offset by revenues from financial services. Soaring costs of medical coverage for active and retired staff along with losses generated by their European operations, currently being restructured, have also had a negative impact. That weakness has been ill timed, particularly as the consumption slowdown, rising interest rates and increasing cost of petrol could have a negative effect on sales in 2005. The 'sport utility vehicle' (SUV) segment – by far the most profitable – has been very vulnerable due to high petrol consumption. Prudence will be in order for carmakers and their suppliers, resulting in production stoppages to avoid any increase in stocks.

In **Europe**, despite a sharp late-year rebound, the market expanded little in 2004, with an identical trend likely in 2005. However, this gloomy picture particularly concerns local carmakers with the notable exception of BMW, while their Asian counterparts are enjoying robust sales. The overall stabilization of sales has come at the wrong time with new production capacity about to come into play in Central Europe (notably Slovakia), existing factories only operating at three-quarters of capacity on average and several carmakers already suffering greatly. Furthermore, the strong euro has been handicapping exports, which has increasingly prompted carmakers to set up industrial operations worldwide.

In Japan, production has been rising due to increased sales in the United States (with that region generating two-thirds of Japanese carmaker earnings), Europe and the rest of Asia, which have been offsetting the domestic market stagnation.

In China, sales have sagged markedly (up 15 per cent in 2004 after being up 80 per cent in 2003) due to consumer credit restrictions imposed by authorities. Despite a large reservoir of potential buyers, that trend has developed just when domestic and foreign carmakers have been massively expanding their production capacity at the risk of exacerbating price competition.

In Latin America, sales have continued to improve in the south, notably Brazil, benefiting European and US carmakers with local operations, even though their margins still suffer from the pressure affecting domestic prices and from surplus capacity. The Mexican market has continued to develop rapidly thanks to more favourable local conditions, a more varied product offer and development of financing possibilities.

■ TELECOMMUNICATIONS (B)

The equipment sales recovery initiated in 2003 already seems to be giving signs of petering out with the level prevailing in 2000 still well out of reach. Despite emergence of stiff Asian competition, the company financial situation has remained satisfactory.

Network equipment manufacturers benefited greatly in 2004 thanks to an accelerated expansion of rapid internet connections worldwide and recovery of investments linked to the development of third generation (3G) technology by mobile telephony operators. The improved market conditions have even benefited optical equipment, which had particularly suffered after the technological bubble burst. However, the situation of historic European and US equipment

manufacturers has remained difficult with a moderate slowdown expected in 2005, and continued overcapacity and competition remaining fierce. While most companies survived the crisis, new ones have emerged in Asia benefiting from their booming regional market and proving to be particularly aggressive in other emerging markets.

Despite a downturn, mobile telephony handset sales increased, reaching 670 million units in 2004. In industrialized countries, two main factors have been driving purchases: equipment replacement and a desire to avail of new functions, such as picture-taking or those derived from computers, like email and personal agendas.

Sales growth in emerging regions like Asia, Latin America, and Central and Eastern Europe has been robust. However, competition has stiffened, due notably to the ascendancy of Asian manufacturers, particularly Korean, with a substantial lead in advanced handsets. That has been putting pressure on the prices and margins of European and US manufacturers with a further slowdown of sales expected in 2005 (up 8 per cent).

Market conditions have been generally favourable for operators. In Western Europe, long-standing players have consolidated their financial situation and posted good earnings performance allowing them to begin investing again in their 3G mobile telephony networks. They succeeded in stemming the decline of fixed-telephony revenues thanks to their simultaneous presence in mobile telephony and development of highspeed internet services such as ADSL, which, to fend off competition from alternative operators, has increasingly included television and telephony. Their domination of markets and networks has warranted the intervention of national regulatory bodies, which monitor wholesale and retail prices.

In North America, the four Bell companies have also been contending with the decline of fixed telephony, which they have also attempted to withstand by offering packages including telephony, highspeed internet and television; three of the 'Bells' have also been compensating for losses through their mobile telephony activities. However, they have to contend with the presence of three other independent national mobile telephone operators (of which two, Nextel and Sprint, are currently in the process of merging), a vast number of regional or virtual operators and, cable operators well established as internet service providers.

■ CONSTRUCTION (B-)

World economic conditions have remained favourable in the sector. The residential segment could stabilize in certain countries, whereas a recovery has developed in public works and non-residential construction. Companies' financial health has remained satisfactory. The sectoral trend is nonetheless very dependent on national specificities.

In the United States, residential construction has remained very dynamic. However, the continued tightening of monetary policy, the disappointing employment trend, the now high proportion of homeowner households and the large stock of rental housing available could lead to a slowdown in 2005. The decline will only be limited due to the favourable demographics and will essentially concern low-cost housing in certain districts. Renovation of old housing should continue to expand. Meanwhile, the recovery of non-residential construction and public works that began in the second half of 2004 should gain momentum in 2005. Improvement in local fiscal sanitation should allow spending to resume on consolidation, transport and the environment, whereas private operators will resume spending on energy delivery and communications networks.

In Japan, a revival has been developing in private non-residential construction where business activity, which had stagnated for several years, could increase 6 per cent during the current fiscal year. Dynamism has been manifest for factories and sales areas. That recovery has notably been linked to the fact that order-givers have been able to purchase land at competitive prices in recent years. Meanwhile, private residential construction has also been recovering. Conversely, public works have remained in the doldrums due the poor state of public sector finances.

In Europe, the overall situation has been improving in the sector. Although the residential

United States
New one-family home sales

source: Department of Commerce

segment could begin to stall in 2005, the recovery already under way in public works will continue and the non-residential trend should become positive again. Beyond this overall situation, marked disparities have remained between countries. In the United Kingdom, the now very high levels of prices and household debt, coupled with the rising cost of credit, seems to be getting the best of the housing segment's dynamism.

In Germany, the construction sector has continued its long decline and will continue to do so until the overcapacity accumulated in the East disappears. The residential segment is still suffering from the effects of high unemployment and uncertainties about the outlook for incomes. The non-residential segment has continued to suffer from the high office-space vacancy rate with public works affected by the deterioration of public sector finances.

■ COMPUTERS (B-)

World economic conditions prevailing in the computer sector have stabilized at a satisfactory level, although not rediscovering the euphoria that prevailed until 2000.

Companies operating in industrialized countries are no longer replacing their equipment and software as often as before, with their annual rate of PC replacement dropping from 35 per cent to 20 per cent. The upsurge of buying in emerging regions has not been able to offset that phenomenon due to the disproportion of volumes between emerging and industrialized regions. Moreover, the very competitive environment has been affecting company margins.

World personal computer sales could begin to sag in 2005 after increasing 12 per cent in volume and 6 per cent in value in 2004, more or less as they did in 2003. That outlook is notably attributable to a lack of novelty in both components and software, the slowdown in purchasing by US consumers and federal government and in equipment replacement already undertaken by companies.

Laptop sales (about 40 per cent of PC sales) should continue to register dynamic growth, as should servers, personal organizers, multifunction printers and flat screens.

Growth will remain very dynamic in emerging regions (Asia, Latin America, Central and Eastern Europe and the Middle East), moderate in Western Europe and North America and weak in Japan.

Despite increased deliveries, rising component prices and competitive pressure on sales prices, notably at the low end, have resulted in shrinking margins at once for assemblers, subcontractors and distributors.

Sectors rated C+, C, C-: In a very uncertain sectoral environment combined with a very vulnerable company financial situation, payment behaviour is poor with default probability disquietingly high.

■ TEXTILES AND CLOTHING (C+ AND C)
The situation has remained difficult for both textiles and clothing. In industrialized countries, those two sectors should suffer even more from imports from emerging countries after discontinuation of the Multifibre Arrangement in January 2005, with the difficulties compounded by increased raw material costs and euro/dollar exchange rate fluctuations. In that context, companies have been struggling to improve their financial situation and solvency. Payment incidents, already frequent, have been increasing.

The largest groups have continued to massively delocalize production facilities to low-cost countries whereas smaller companies have been closing one after the other. The price pressure they have been subject to has been compelling them to reduce their margins and limit investment and production-tool modernization.

Although not prohibiting customs duties or possible recourse to safeguard measures,

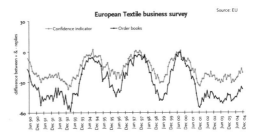

European Textile business survey — Source: EU

discontinuation on 1 January 2005 of import quotas (extended in 1995 under WTO auspices) will spur further delocalizations and imports. The consequences will be numerous. Based on the recent status of quotas, the impact should be greatest on 'basic' articles. Their average purchase price could decline without it being clear whether the importer, retailer or consumer will benefit most.

That opening to competition will constitute a major challenge, not only for industrialized countries but also for those in the Mediterranean region, Eastern Europe, Central America and South Asia, as well as for Caribbean, Pacific and Indian Ocean island nations. Sheltered by quotas, the latter countries succeeded in developing substantial textile exports and, to survive now, they will, in particular, have to exploit any geographical proximity to large markets.

Conversely, China and India should benefit fully from the new context, due to their particularly competitive production conditions, notably vast reserves of low-cost labour. According to WTO estimates, China's market share should triple in the United States (to reach 50 per cent) and double in Europe (to 30 per cent).

■ AIR TRANSPORT (C)
The economic recovery initiated in the second half of 2003 continued in 2004 and should firm up in 2005, marked by increased air traffic, a rising number of international tourist arrivals and overnight stays in hotels. However, higher fuel prices have been cancelling out the positive impact of the better market trend.

In 2004, world air passenger traffic finally exceeded the level reached in 2001. Better control over seating capacity made possible by the disappearance and regrouping of companies has permitted improving the average load factor to 75 per cent. However, despite the restructuring and cost reduction programmes undertaken since 2001, the upsurge of kerosene prices, spurred by soaring oil prices, has postponed a return to profitability for airlines. The International Air Transport Association (IATA) has estimated that losses suffered by its members should reach US$4.8 billion overall in 2004, which would bring the cumulative deficit to over US$35 billion since 2000.

Most of the losses have been suffered by North American companies, particularly affected by the dollar depreciation and the impossibility of passing fuel price increases on to ticket prices due to the weakness of the domestic traffic recovery and fierce competition from low-cost carriers (30 per cent of domestic traffic). Many local companies have been benefiting from Chapter XI bankruptcy law protection.

Comparatively, Asian companies have been in a much more favourable situation, benefiting from surging regional traffic and much better earnings performance from the outset. The fortunes of European companies have varied widely, although buoyed by the favourable impact of the euro appreciation on fuel prices and by a sharp recovery of traffic allowing them to pass on cost increases more effectively. They have been contending with low-cost carriers, which have compelled them to build alliances (British Airways and Iberia) or merge (Air France and KLM), restructure their product and service offer and continue cutting costs.

World Economy Will Weather the Weak Dollar

Experts from Oxford Analytica, Oxford

The US current account deficit at 6 per cent of GDP in 2004 reached a level somewhat inconsistent with a stable currency in OECD experience. A weak dollar might now help to resolve the problem; the balance of probability favours an orderly resolution. The IMF, among others, has for the past two years warned European, US and Asian policymakers to coordinate an exit from worsening global imbalances lest the currency markets do it for them.

KEY INSIGHTS

→ Euro-area and Japanese growth should fall only slightly short of OECD projections of 1.9 per cent and 2.1 per cent respectively, and US growth should meet or exceed the OECD projection of 3.3 per cent.

→ The mid-1980s saw the most recent serious inflation-adjusted, broad trade-weighted dollar depreciation. Yet real global GDP growth decelerated by only 0.3 percentage points in 1986 and accelerated in both 1987 and 1988. The global economy should similarly cope with a dollar devaluation in 2005.

→ A more competitive currency could put the US business community back in the fight to push through overdue trade talks such as the WTO Doha Round and the Free Trade Area of the Americas.

This now seems closer at hand, although the process will be more gradual and the consequences less catastrophic than commonly feared. Stronger currencies in Europe and Asia will enhance household wealth. Notwithstanding serious constraints on household spending – particularly in the euro-area – this wealth effect should, at the margin, provide some lift to domestic demand. With consumption constituting the largest component of GDP by expenditure, even a small lift can have meaningful GDP implications. The opposite effect will be less pronounced in the United States. Although household savings will increase, the impact will be tempered by a stronger contribution from net exports and a boost from declining oil prices. Lower oil prices and still-abundant global production capacity should also prevent dollar weakness from stoking enough inflationary pressure to force a faster-than-anticipated tightening of US interest rates.

A benign rebalancing requires Asian currency appreciation, and this too seems closer at hand. As the US broad currency adjustment needed to resolve its external deficit is so large, this does not mean a relaxation of pressure on the euro and other laissez-faire currencies. Even with a 15 per cent Asia-wide revaluation, by the end of 2005, the dollar would still reach 1.5 to the euro, and the yen 91 to the dollar.

MID-1980s REPRISE?

The mid-1980s saw the most recent serious inflation-adjusted, broad trade-weighted dollar depreciation when the annual average rate of the dollar fell 25 per cent between 1985 and 1988, half of it in the first year and half spread between the subsequent two years. Yet real global GDP growth decelerated by only 0.3 percentage points in 1986. Growth accelerated in both 1987 and 1988, by 0.3 and 0.9 percentage points respectively, to 4.5 per cent (compared with 4.1 per cent in 2004). The global economy should similarly cope with a dollar devaluation in 2005. As in the mid-1980s, it could be aided by a significant decline in oil prices.

Although global GDP growth will be slower in 2005 than in 2004 – which saw the strongest global growth performance in 14 years – euro-area and Japanese growth should fall only slightly short of OECD projections of 1.9 per cent and 2.1 per cent respectively. US growth should meet or exceed the OECD projection of 3.3 per cent.

LIQUIDITY FEARS

Moderate Federal Reserve tightening is in prospect, and should help reduce liquidity concerns. The Federal Reserve reduced interest rates by 550 basis points in the aftermath of the burst investment bubble of 2000. Atlantic economies absorbed this expansion with large nominal currency appreciations, but East Asian economies fought it with large dollar reserve purchases. In the process, they vastly expanded what economist Ed Leamer calls 'supermoney' – US base money and demand deposits, plus global foreign exchange reserve balances. This surge in liquidity has pushed a wide variety of assets to valuations that look high by historical norms. OECD house prices, subinvestment grade debt, exotic sovereign bonds and a variety of commodities have all been lifted by the tide of liquidity.

This makes an inflationary surge particularly unwelcome, as it could provoke a rise in interest rates sufficient to test these valuations. Although some classes of asset will wilt under a generally rising Federal Funds rate, a crash is unlikely because interest rates will not spike. Sceptics might argue that a change in East Asian currency policy could spell the end of easy liquidity and low inflation. If East Asia allows a regional revaluation (eg of 15 per cent), and if the region's exporters prove able to defend this revaluation (rather than pricing to market), then 40 per cent of US trade would become 15 per cent more expensive. Yet the dollar exchange rate pass-through to consumer prices is weak, with importers likely to push cost pressures down the value chain rather than lose US market share.

DOLLAR

In 2003 the central banks of Japan and China spent nearly US$400 billion to support the dollar. Japan spent another US$140 billion during the first quarter of 2004 but has been absent since. The United States has instead been importing capital from countries enjoying increased export income from rising commodity prices. Oil prices boosted export incomes of Gulf economies by US$50 billion in 2004. Russia's foreign exchange reserves increased by over US$50 billion during the past 12 months. With commodities prices cooling, and Asian central banks on the sidelines, by December the dollar had fallen to new lows against the euro and several Asian currencies enjoyed modest rallies.

The lack of emphasis on fiscal tightening in Washington signals the Bush Administration's comfort with a weaker dollar. Only if dollar weakness significantly drives up bond yields will it react. That could take the form of a token commitment to reduce the deficit combined with explicit support of trading partners' reserve growth. Only when global reserves growth begins more convincingly to fuel global inflation will the limits of this policy be reached. Such a scenario is unlikely in 2005, although serious US fiscal deterioration would speed its arrival.

RESERVES CONFUSION

Commentaries on threats to the dollar often highlight the dollar's status as a reserve currency. Much of this is confused, insofar as it is assumed that central banks manage their reserves to maximize risk-adjusted returns. On this basis, the dollar's decline could risk its status as a reserve currency as central banks seek to avoid capital losses. Yet, for many export-oriented economies, reserves are denominated in dollars because the dollar exchange rate is the crucial one for trade, and intervention to target that rate necessarily yields a high (and growing) proportion of dollar-denominated reserves. Exchanging dollar-denominated reserve assets for assets in another currency, eg euros, would simply add more dollars to the foreign exchange market, accentuating its weakness. Insofar as this counteracts the policymaker's priority of minimizing exchange-rate losses in competitiveness, it makes little sense.

Although it will entail losses on central bank reserves, a weaker dollar will have the overlooked but still important benefit of rejuvenating US support for trade liberalization. The late-1990s WTO talks in Seattle foundered on a variety of issues (culminating in developing-country alarm at US President Clinton's promotion of labour provisions), but it is little wonder that US business was not energized to push them through as it had done in previous trade rounds. The dollar appreciated 20 per cent on an inflation-adjusted, broad trade-weighted annual average basis in the second half of the decade. A more competitive currency could now put the business community back in the fight to push through overdue trade talks such as the WTO Doha Round and the Free Trade Area of the Americas.

CONCLUSION

Global growth in 2005 will fall short of the 2004 rate of 4.1 per cent by as much as one percentage point, but will be achieved in spite of a correction in the dollar, which sets the stage for a smaller US current account deficit. Wealth effects from stronger currencies should aid European and Asian domestic demand, offsetting some of the loss in US net imports.

Oil Could Drift Toward US$30

Experts from Oxford Analytica, Oxford

The oil price remains an important determinant of global economic growth. Prospects for oil prices in 2005 depend upon the view taken on the causes of the high prices experienced in 2004.

KEY INSIGHTS

→ Assuming geopolitics do not provide a shock, oil prices will average above, but close to, US$30 (Brent terms).

→ Oil demand will remain healthy but will not repeat the exceptional growth of 2004. Global economic growth will slow and a mild winter appears to be in store for the northern hemisphere.

→ Long-term investment is insufficient, and it seems clear that Saudi Arabia has decided to seek price stability at a level over US$30.

There are two schools of thought:

1. Cyclical. Demand growth at 2.64 million barrels per day (b/d), of which China accounted for over 800,000 b/d, is the highest since 1978. It has been driven by very strong global economic growth coupled with strategic stockpiling on fears over stability in the Middle East. On the supply side, non-OPEC (outside of the CIS) has disappointed as projects have been delayed due to shortages in the service industry. Political factors have taken out production at various points from Venezuela, Iraq, Nigeria and Norway. Hurricane Ivan cost 1.2 million b/d in September, and even as of December 2004, production was down over 200,000 b/d. Although there has not been physical shortage, inventories have been at very low levels

historically, and spare capacity in OPEC fell from some 6 million b/d at the start of 2002 to less than 500,000 b/d as of early December 2004. Hedge funds and commodity funds have also been key influences.

2. Structural. Structuralists point to the fact that, after spending most of 1986–2002 between US$18 and US$21, the back-end of the forward curve over five years moved above US$30 in 2004. This change is argued to reflect growing concern that the industry, long living on previous investments, has now reached a point where capacity in all stages of the value chain is tight and is likely to remain so for some time. In short, the industry is suffering from insufficient investment. The international oil companies are returning funds to shareholders and finance ministries are starving the national oil companies of funds. Assessing future prospects requires identifying which elements of the cycle will continue to give price strength, and assessing what exactly the structural changes have been.

CYCLICAL FACTORS

Although oil demand will remain healthy in 2005, it will not repeat the exceptional growth of 2004. Global economic growth will slow and a mild winter appears to be in store for the northern hemisphere. The International Energy Agency (IEA) forecasts demand growth of 1.4 million b/d in 2005. At the same time, non-OPEC will show more strength in supply. The IEA expects growth of 1.7 million b/d including OPEC, compared with 1.5 million b/d in 2004. Russia and the Caspian are expected to be major contributors to this increase along with deepwater Mexican Gulf and Canadian heavy oil.

If OPEC is to manage the market and defend a high price, it must cut production in 2005 (although it is worth remembering this was also the consensus view at this time in 2003, which proved wrong). It appears that fourth-quarter 2004 will see an unseasonal stock build. The forward market has been in contango (ie forward prices exceed spot prices) since 5 November. This implies plentiful supply and gives refiners an incentive to hold physical stocks instead of paper. It also gives no incentives in the paper markets to rebuild long positions. OPEC, at over 30 million b/d in October 2004, was producing at its highest level since 1979. However, the IEA estimates the call on OPEC to be only 28 million b/d and 26.5 million b/d in the first and second quarters of 2005 respectively.

Cyclical factors thus point to prices in 2005 coming down from the 40s to the lower 30s. The paper markets seem to agree on this, with the non-commercial players cutting their net long positions to the lowest for a year. However, the market remains highly vulnerable to the loss of any major exporter. Although OPEC capacity is expected to creep up in 2005, the lack of much spare capacity remains a worry. There is also concern that capacity expansions face problems caused by the natural decline of mature fields accounting for over 1 million b/d loss of capacity plus delays to project approval and, in many cases, problems with foreign company involvement.

STRUCTURAL FACTORS

There are solid grounds for concern that there will be insufficient investment by the oil companies and by the service industries whose margins have been squeezed by the post-merger 'super giants' and the use of e-commerce. A more serious and immediate structural change concerns Saudi Arabia's oil pricing policy. Since 1986, Saudi Arabia has pursued a policy of maintaining stable oil prices at relatively low levels in an effort to encourage a reversal of the move out of oil created by the oil price shocks of the 1970s. However, it now seems likely that during the course of this year a decision has been taken to maintain stability but at much higher prices – probably over US$30. There are several reasons behind this move:

- Dollar weakness means the high dollar price is not reflected in its purchasing power.
- The Kingdom is desperate for revenues as its burgeoning population creates serious economic and, thus, political strains.
- The strategy of low prices to encourage a return to oil has been consistently undermined as consumer governments impose ever greater sales taxes on the final product price. This practice is developing even outside the OECD, where it has been common for years.
- The US Federal Reserve Chairman, Alan Greenspan, has publicly said that the world economy and the United States can comfortably live with US$30 oil.

CONCLUSION

Assuming geopolitics do not provide a shock, oil prices (in Brent terms) in 2005 will average closer to US$30 than to the high-30s of 2004. OPEC will be in control and will only lose it if it is exceptionally unlucky or incompetent. However, constraints on investment in capacity mean that this price is likely to rule for many years to come. The US$19 average price of the 1990s will not be revisited.

Europe

1

Euro-area Economy Set to Disappoint

Experts from Oxford Analytica, Oxford

The modest improvement in economic performance in 2004 is set to continue in the coming year, driven in large measure by continued – if less vigorous – expansion in global production and trade. However, there is no sign of a dynamic cyclical upswing. The forecast recovery of the euro-area economies in 2004 will be fulfilled with an outcome of about 1.9 per cent real GDP growth. This represents welcome relief to a region that had experienced growth rates of below 1 per cent in both 2002 and 2003. However, it remains disappointing in comparison with all other major regions of the world, which are set to exceed European growth figures by a considerable margin.

KEY INSIGHTS

→ The recovery of corporate investment will be a key test of the improvement in the potential of domestic euro-area demand; there is a strong danger that outcomes will be lower than general expectations.

→ Any further depreciation of the dollar against the euro could move the ECB and other central banks to intervene to support the dollar. However, this will be ineffectual in the absence of US fiscal restraint.

→ Weaker-than-forecast performance in the first two quarters of 2005 could galvanize some euro-area member states into increasing the pressure for substantial changes to the Stability and Growth Pact (SGP), leading to likely divisions within the Council of Economics and Finance

Ministers of the European Union (ECOFIN) and between ECOFIN and the ECB.

More significantly, confidence in the continuation of a strong cyclical recovery next year on a global level and of modest growth in the euro-area has been shaken by the rise in world oil prices and by the appreciation of the euro against the dollar:

● This has persuaded most public and private forecasters to reduce their estimates for euro-area growth in 2005 to between 1.9 per cent (OECD and ECB) and 2 per cent (autumn report from the leading German economic research institutes). Thus, growth in 2004 and 2005 remains below the accepted threshold (2.0–2.5 per cent), above which there is likely to be an improvement in employment levels.

● Both national-level and European Commission business and consumer confidence indicators suggest an overall weakening in expectations for 2005. Purchasing managers' indices this autumn strengthened the mood of uncertainty.

● In this context, even the revised forecasts still look over-optimistic. A more likely outcome for 2005 is slightly below that of 2004, with a possible deterioration in output growth in the first two quarters.

CAUSES OF EURO-AREA FRAGILITY

The euro-area is bedeviled by a persistent asymmetry of demand, whereby growth has become increasingly dependent on exports and where private consumption, state consumption and private investment have been growing very modestly, if at all.

Euro area: Economic prospects

Indicator	Annual growth (%)					
	2000	2001	2002	2003	2004e	2005f
Real GDP	3.5	1.5	0.8	0.6	1.9	1.9
Private consumption	3.0	0.8	0.6	1.0	1.3	1.6
Government consumption	1.9	2.2	3.1	1.7	1.6	1.2
Gross fixed capital formation	4.7	-0.5	-2.7	-0.6	1.1	3.1
Exports	12.2	2.5	1.7	0.1	6.2	4.5
Net exports	0.6	0.7	0.6	-0.7	0.5	0.2

e = estimate, f = forecast
Source: ECB Monthly Reports, Autumn Report of Germany's Leading Economic Institutes, November 2004.

- With GDP growth averaging 1.6 per cent between 2000 and 2004, private consumption has grown annually by only 1.3 per cent, government consumption by 2.1 per cent, investment by a very low annual average of 0.2 per cent and exports by 4.5 per cent.
- In those years where export growth has dipped (2002 and 2003), there has been no compensatory growth in any of the other demand factors, notwithstanding the short-lived rise in state expenditure in 2002.
- In all other respects, the pattern of growth mirrors the pattern of export growth. This uneven pattern is set to continue, even though private consumption may pick up somewhat next year.

Aggregate domestic demand conceals significant variations between euro-area countries, with stronger performance in some smaller economies as well as in Spain. However, core economies – most notably Germany and Italy, which alone account for 47 per cent of total euro-area GDP – have experienced a persistent weaknesses of all three domestic demand components.

1. Consumer timidity. Household demand weaknesses derive from a number of factors:

continuing insecurities about long-term employment prospects; low increases in real net income over an extended period; and additional cost burdens on households, ranging from higher energy bills to surcharges for health care (notably in The Netherlands and in Germany). Consumer confidence showed little improvement in 2004 and a worsening of expectations for 2005. This pessimism is also reflected in a renewed deterioration of overall retail confidence ratings.

A longer-term problem derives from the fact that the population of the euro-area (and wider Europe) is set to decline in the next quarter-century. The consumption patterns of the increasing group of older citizens are less dynamic than those of less numerous younger generations.

2. Uncertain investment. The very weak showing of investment levels reflects persistent uncertainty about the long-term commitment of companies to locations for investment where labour and infrastructure costs are high and where the advantages of market proximity are in part neutralized by the prospect of stagnating private consumption. The marked European preference for outsourcing labour-intensive elements of production and service provision underscores the reluctance to extend capacity. The forecast recovery of investment from 1.1 per cent growth in 2004 to 3.1 per cent growth in 2005 cannot be seen as a foregone conclusion, despite indications of increased order books for investment goods.

3. Constrained government. State consumption is constrained both by weak revenue streams, above all in the core economies, and by the pressure to consolidate budgetary commitments within the framework of the SGP (currently under review). Although the SGP's targets and the budgetary targets of individual states are being consistently missed, the spirit of it remains deflationary and apathetic to anticyclical state measures. State consumption is therefore set both to grow weakly in 2005 and to compound the continuing weaknesses of domestic demand.

EXPORT RISKS

Export demand has been lifted this year by the acceleration of world trade, notably by the continuing investment boom in China and in Central and Eastern Europe, but also by the marked recovery of key Latin American economies, home to many subsidiaries of European companies. However, the continued appreciation of the euro against the dollar is clearly a problem, and the increased competitiveness of US exporters could put pressure on key euro-area exporters, notably in investment goods.

Indeed, the exchange rate fluctuations of the dollar in the 1980s and in more recent years do show a strong correlation between nominal exchange rates and export growth rates. With rising US deficits, there is a clear danger that a continuing dollar depreciation will choke back euro-area export growth. Although such depreciation might lead to some form of coordinated intervention by central banks, it is doubtful whether this would have a substantial – or sustainable – effect in the absence of concerted action by the United States to address its deficit problems.

MONETARY POLICY

Strong M3 growth and a rate of inflation – 2.2 per cent in November – that continues to remain above the ECB's target of 'close to but below' 2.0 per cent make a continuation of the Bank's policy stance very likely. Indeed, credit conditions remain benign with near-zero real interest rates. In the absence of a marked improvement in domestic demand, there is no reason to believe that corporate borrowing for investment would be boosted by an easing of refinancing rates.

Recent ECB utterances have confirmed suspicions that there has been little consideration of a cut in interest rates, with policymakers concentrating on their anti-inflation mandate in the context of what the Bank has described as a 'worrisome' short-term outlook for inflation and 'upside risks' over the medium term. Although this will not prevent further pressure from euro-area government figures for a looser monetary policy, particularly if the euro appreciates further against the dollar, there is little expectation that such calls would be heeded.

CONCLUSION

The euro-area's domestic demand weaknesses are set to continue in 2005 and beyond. Even a strong upturn in export demand – unlikely given global growth prospects and the current exchange rate environment – will not generate growth sufficient to improve employment prospects.

CEE–8 Economies Set for Steady Growth

1

Experts from Oxford Analytica, Oxford

There are strong grounds for optimism as the CEE–8 countries enter their first full year as EU members. While China- or even Celtic-type GDP growth paths are implausible, the region exhibits a robust GDP trajectory that promotes convergence toward EU income levels. The economic prospects for the CEE–8 in 2005 are broadly favourable.

KEY INSIGHTS

→ A favourable long-term economic outlook, including growth of close to 4.6 per cent in 2005, reflects increasing domestic and foreign investment, rising intraregional trade, expanding world market shares and deepening structural reforms.

→ Sustaining that path requires continued improvements in labour productivity, accelerated infrastructural development and greater macroeconomic discipline.

→ The main risks to growth in 2005 are, however, external – in particular growth in the CEE–8's key EU-15 markets, dollar decline, still-high commodity prices and heightened competition for foreign direct investment (FDI).

Real GDP growth in the region in 2005 should be close to the World Bank's forecast of 4.6 per cent. This is down from 2004's projected 5.0 per cent, and lower than projected growth rates in South Asia and Asia-Pacific. However, it surpasses Latin America's anticipated growth rate and well exceeds those of the United States, the euro-area and Japan.

Moreover, a number of factors – increasing domestic and foreign investment rates, rising intra-regional trade, expanding world market shares and deepening EU-mandated structural reforms – bode well for CEE's long-term growth path.

Sustaining that path depends on:

● continued gains in labour productivity to offset wage growth and bolster the region's capacity to attract technology-intensive FDI;

● accelerated infrastructural development to enhance the region's allure as a manufacturing and distribution platform for servicing the pan-European market; and

● heightened macroeconomic discipline to facilitate monetary integration in the ERM-II countries and lay the foundation for eventual euro-area membership for the others.

CEE–8: Real GDP growth (%)

	2003	2004e	2005f	GDP 2004 (US$ billion)
Poland	3.8	5.8	5.1	230
Czech Republic	3.1	3.3	3.4	103
Hungary	2.9	3.5	3.7	98
Slovak Republic	4.2	4.8	4.3	40
Slovenia	2.3	3.9	4.1	33
Lithuania	9.0	7.0	7.0	22
Latvia	7.5	6.5	6.0	13
Estonia	5.1	5.8	5.4	11

e = estimate, f = forecast
Source: IMF WEO, September 2004

■ **Key risks**

The primary threats to CEE–8 growth in 2005 stem less from policy deficiencies than from adverse developments in the global economy:

1. **EU-15 slowdown.** Owing to the EU's preponderant role in the export-dependent CEE–8 economies, a fall in the EU–15's already modest growth level would likely force a downward recalibration of CEE–8 growth prospects in 2005.

2. **Euro appreciation.** Recent shifts in the dollar/euro exchange rate raise particular concerns over 2005 growth prospects in the CEE–8 countries that have entered or will soon enter ERM-II in preparation for early euro-area membership – Estonia, Lithuania and Slovenia should be joined by Latvia in early 2005. Thus far, low inflation rates and strong productivity growth have preserved the export competitiveness of these countries despite real currency appreciation. However, a dramatic rise in the euro in 2005 could potentially have damaging repercussions for the small accession countries anchored to the common currency.

3. **Interest rates.** An expected steady rise in US interest rates will raise the debt servicing costs of CEE–8 countries like Poland that carry dollar-denominated debt.

4. **FDI competition.** FDI in the CEE–8, which declined during the year preceding accession, is expected to rebound in 2005 as lump-sum automotive ventures in the Czech Republic and Slovakia ramp up and multinationals that entered in the 1990s launch 'second wind' investments.

However, the CEE–8 economies confront mounting competition from larger emerging markets (notably China and, to a lesser degree, India) in bidding for FDI. Indeed, several prominent electronics manufacturers (Flextronics, IBM and Philips) have vacated sunk investments in the CEE–8 and moved production to China. Facing the latter country's insurmountable scale and labour-cost advantages, the CEE–8 countries must leverage their core assets – strong human capital, high quality infrastructures and geographical centrality in the pan-European market – to sustain the FDI inflows essential for the region's long-term development.

5. **Inflation.** The CEE–8 experienced a small bump in inflation during the first and second quarters of 2004, reflecting the impact of accession-related price increases and the surge in global commodity prices. Inflationary pressures in Poland prompted the central bank to raise interest rates. However, inflation peaked at just 4.5 per cent even in Poland, and mostly subsided to the lower single digits elsewhere in the region as 2005 approached. Latvia exhibits the region's highest inflation rate (7.7 per cent), creating potential glitches in its planned switch from a special drawing right (SDR) to euro peg early next year.

The main inflationary risk facing the CEE–8 in 2005 emanates from price increases in fuel and raw materials, upon which the resource-poor CEE countries are heavily dependent. However, this risk is mitigated by euro appreciation for those countries in ERM-II (which boosts purchasing power over dollar-denominated commodities) and strong monetary discipline in the Central European countries that cannot achieve early euro-area entry.

6. **Wage growth.** Although positive for household living standards, rapid wage growth in the CEE–8 countries threatens their ability to compete with China and others for FDI. However, productivity gains have thus far served to neutralize these wage increases and maintain regional competitiveness. The anticipated recovery of FDI in 2005 – a significant share of which is destined for industrial automation and other technology-intensive spheres – augurs positively for CEE's productivity growth path.

7. **Fiscal deficits.** The high fiscal deficits of the Visegrad countries are declining. Poland's fiscal deficit is expected to fall from 5.7 per cent in 2004 to 3.9 per cent of GDP in 2005. The Czech Finance Ministry projects a 2005 deficit of 4.7 per cent, while Slovak authorities predict a deficit of 3.8 per cent. Deficit spending remains problematic in Hungary, whose 2004 deficit will reach 6.5 per cent

of GDP. Social welfare and pension reforms planned by the Gyurcsany government may fail to lower the deficit to the targeted 4.7 per cent in 2005.

Beyond the imperative of keeping budget deficits on a downward track, the Visegrad countries face the political and economic challenges of systemic reforms of their public sectors, which are largely relative to the Baltic states and exhibit pervasive inefficiencies and poor quality services.

8. Current account deficits. Befitting their status as low- to middle-income economies with high import demand for advanced capital equipment, raw materials and other products unavailable locally, the Baltic states exhibit large current account deficits (21 per cent of GDP in Estonia, 17 per cent in Latvia, 10 per cent in Lithuania). These are likely to decrease in 2005 as Baltic export shares rise. However, the developmental profile of the three countries – small, open, resource-poor economies at intermediate levels of industrial development – presages large structural imbalances in their current accounts in coming years, underscoring the importance of continued inflows of foreign portfolio investment and FDI to finance the deficits.

The current account deficits of the Visegrad countries range in the low–middle single digits, demonstrating increased demand for CEE exports in the EU single market. Hungary again emerges as the regional outlier, with a current account deficit approaching 10 per cent in 2004, which in light of its recent falloff in FDI has provoked concerns about the sustainability of its external financial position. Hungary's ability to reverse these trends in 2005 hinges on its ability to boost high value-added exports to the EU-15 and restore its reputation as a preferred locale for manufacturing-related FDI.

CONCLUSION

With a few exceptions the CEE-8's macroeconomic fundamentals are sound, encouraging the inflows of foreign portfolio investment needed to finance their external deficits. FDI is poised to rebound, signaling the CEE-8's continued evolution as a favoured site for multinationals seeking to penetrate the EU market. These countries' chief vulnerabilities – shifts in exchange rates, spikes in global commodity prices, increases in US interest rates – mirror their growing integration into the global economy.

1

The Range of Country @ratings in Europe

Sylvia Greisman, Jean-Louis Daudier, Dominique Fruchter and
Yves Zlotowski
Coface Country Risk and Economic Studies Department, Paris

COUNTRY @RATING SCALE

The regional rating is the average of the country risk @ratings weighted according to the share of each country in the regional GDP.

Country @ratings measure the average level of short-term non-payment risk associated with companies in individual countries. A rating reflects the influence of a particular country's economic, financial and political outlook on financial commitments of local companies. It is thus complementary to @rating credit opinions on companies.

The solvency of Western European companies recovered gradually during 2004, as expected given the improvement in risk quality anticipated at the beginning of the year. That improvement does seem to have peaked, however, and the situation could become more difficult in 2005.

Companies in Western Europe, especially those in the euro zone, face a dual challenge: loss of competitiveness arising from the euro appreciation against the US dollar and weaker external demand. Although good results obtained during 2004 should enable them to cope with a less buoyant environment, profitability issues can be expected, especially among companies in countries whose growth has until now depended on healthy exports. Consequently, Germany, Italy, The Netherlands and Portugal are still rated A2, with Italy and Portugal negatively watchlisted.

Conversely, in Central Europe, quality of risk continues to improve in the context of the accession of 10 new countries to EU membership. The main upgrade concerns Poland, where stronger growth and improved corporate payment behaviour have prompted a rating change to A3. Continued strong growth has also made it possible to upgrade Estonia (A2), Lithuania and Latvia (both A3) and to positively watchlist Bulgaria (presently rated B).

Average risk levels across the Community of Independent States (CIS) have been stable although remaining significantly higher than those in emerging countries.

In **Western Europe**, economic activity improved markedly in the first half of 2004. That was, however, followed by a more sluggish period starting in summer. After raw material prices surged, the continuing dollar depreciation gradually affected competitiveness in the euro zone. Unemployment, concerns about the outlook for social safety net and unpredictable oil prices eroded consumer and investor confidence. In 2005, any durable euro appreciation against the dollar could have an adverse effect on growth in the euro zone, with domestic demand apparently unable to pick up the slack for exports and the ability of

PAYMENT INCIDENTS INDEX
(12 months moving average - base 100: World 1995)

— Western Europe
— Central and Eastern Europe

governments to stimulate the economy limited by budget deficits. A scenario of economic recovery will thus be unlikely before the second half of 2005. The situation will continue to vary widely by country, however.

Rapid growth has continued in Central Europe, fuelled by both investment and exports. The growth differential with respect to Western Europe, the main trading partner, has not narrowed. The outlook for 2005 has remained bright, despite a hesitant economic context in the West. Nevertheless, that growth has been generating few jobs and, for many countries, imbalances between public and external accounts remain significant. Many new EU members will only be in a position to join the euro zone at the end of the decade given the fiscal adjustments needed.

Further east, the economic and financial situation in Russia has remained favourable. Although the country has been benefiting from high oil prices, increased centralization of power and disruptions of the business climate marked 2004.

Reflecting the robust growth, payment behaviour has generally improved, although that will not preclude occasional non-payment incidents in weak sectors of those economies with restructuring still in process.

■ **Countries rated A1**

Very stable political and economic conditions favourably influence generally good company payment behaviour. Moreover, a satisfactory legal framework ensures protection of creditors and the effectiveness of collection procedures. This generally favourable environment nonetheless does not exclude either disparities in growth or occasional risks of payment default.

In France growth recovered sharply in 2004. After a dynamic start, however, economic activity sagged during the year. Growth should again slow moderately in 2005. Consumption should be sluggish due to concerns about unemployment and the social safety net, while energy costs could still put pressure on household purchasing power. The euro appreciation could impede export growth. Equipment renewal needs and the bright outlook in certain domestic markets, such as building and public works, will continue to spur productive investment.

The reconstitution of company cash positions over the past year has permitted gradual improvement in payment behaviour, although little further improvement will be likely in the less favourable environment expected in 2005.

In the United Kingdom dynamic consumption buoyed by higher salaries, new public sector jobs and a wealth effect generated by increased property values all contributed to strong growth in 2004. However, the slowdown observed late in the year should persist in 2005. Tighter monetary policy and the stabilization of property prices will limit household cash flow and consumption.

Consequently, the economy will be more export-driven, with exports benefiting from the sterling depreciation against the euro.

The low Coface payment incident index and a drop in bankruptcies would suggest that the difficulties encountered by British industry have been easing. The slowdown in domestic demand may, however, cause a moderate rise in non-payment incidents on the part of companies dealing mainly with the domestic market.

In Spain strong growth continued throughout 2004, driven by the buoyancy of the consumer market and building sector. Conversely, industrial investment, exports and tourism performed disappointingly. In 2005, less dynamic domestic demand should lead to a growth slowdown. Consumption and housing expenditure should lose momentum. Exports and tourism will be affected both by erosion of their price competitiveness and a downturn in key markets. Corporate investment, however, may well accelerate, with infrastructure expenditure remaining buoyant.

The generally favourable economic climate has had a positive effect on company solvency. However, sectors such as textiles, footwear, home appliances and car parts manufacturing are particularly vulnerable to competition from Asia and Eastern Europe.

■ **Countries rated A2**

Default probability is still weak even in the case when one country's political and economic environment or the payment record of companies is not as good as in A1-rated countries.

In Germany an already modest recovery lost momentum in the third quarter of 2004. A brisk increase in industrial exports was not sustained because of sagging external demand. In 2005, growth should stay at about the same level. Exports are expected to progress less rapidly due to stabilization of worldwide demand and the negative impact of the euro, although they will still remain the main economic driver.

The frequency of non-payment incidents has, however, fallen, reflecting improvement in the company financial situation where increased productivity has improved profit margins. Nevertheless, this chiefly concerns companies that focus on exports or that have production facilities abroad, and the situation will remain shaky in the

COFACE MAP OF COUNTRY @RATINGS

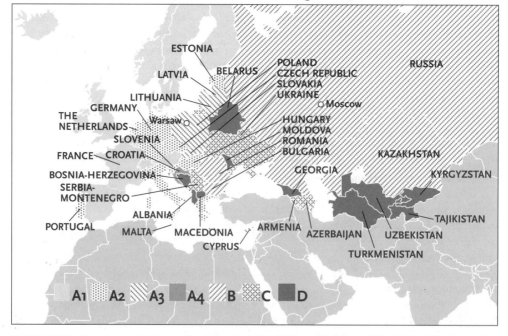

relatively unfavourable environment likely to prevail in 2005.

In Italy (negative watchlisted) growth should increase only slightly in 2005. Exports, for example, will suffer from the euro appreciation and stabilization of external demand. In this relatively unfavourable context, productive investment will progress at an insufficient rate to ensure replacement of obsolete equipment, and the large fiscal deficit will hinder government efforts to restart the economy.

With economic upturn unlikely, risk levels should generally stay high. The Coface payment incident index should remain above average, and may even increase further. Companies in the textile, electronics and printing sectors have remained weakest.

Growth firmed up in the Czech Republic in 2004, with exports and investment picking up the slack for consumption. The economy's dynamism should persist in 2005 owing to steady FDI inflows and rising production capacities in the car industry provided the economic situation does not deteriorate significantly in the EU, especially in Germany. The Czech public deficit has remained

high, and efforts to stabilize the budget must continue. Moreover, increased revenues paid to foreign investors partly offset improvements in the trade balance. Nevertheless, the need for external financing is still low with respect to export revenues, privatizations should further increase the inflow of direct investment and foreign debt has remained moderate.

In Hungary, following an upturn in 2004 fuelled by a sharp increase in investment and a surge in exports, economic activity should remain buoyant in 2005 thanks to robust domestic demand spurred by public spending in the run-up to elections. Nevertheless, the country has continued to suffer from serious external and internal imbalances. Budget excesses and increasing public debt have called into question the validity of the medium-term convergence programme submitted by the Hungarian government to the EU. In parallel, continuing external deficits have increased financing needs nonetheless being met more effectively with FDI picking up. However, the country's insufficient foreign exchange reserves will limit its ability to withstand a liquidity crisis.

COFACE MAP OF MEDIUM- AND LONG-TERM COUNTRY RISK

■ **Countries rated A3**

Adverse political or economic circumstances may lead to a worsening payment record that is already lower than the previous categories, although the probability of a payment default is still low.

Growth in Poland accelerated in 2004, reflecting both a surge in exports and strengthening of domestic demand. This context has contributed to restoring company solvency. The economy should sag in 2005 because of the exchange rate appreciation, which should limit the progress of sales abroad, and because investment will be hindered by higher interest rates and uncertainties regarding the buoyancy of European demand and changes in the local political situation. Improving public accounts and keeping public debt in check have remained crucial challenges. However, good export performance has made it possible to keep the current deficit down. Nevertheless, with foreign debt amortization increasing financing needs and with FDI covering a quarter of those needs, the country will remain dependent on financial markets.

In Slovakia, reforms put in place in recent years in preparation for accession to the EU have meant marked improvement in the economic and financial situation. FDI inflows have reinforced growth potential and spurred a surge in exports. Although the public sector deficit has remained significant, buoyant trade and welfare spending reform should allow the country to meet Maastricht fiscal criteria more rapidly than its major neighbours and join the euro zone in 2009. Risk factors mainly concern the exchange rate appreciation and growing dependency on the car industry.

■ **Countries rated B**

An unsteady political and economic environment is likely to affect further an already poor payment record.

In Russia the financial situation has remained favourable and there has been a rise in domestic investment, which has boosted economic activity. Although growth has remained robust, the economy has remained too dependent on raw material sectors, making it highly vulnerable to fluctuations in oil prices. Moreover, the competitiveness of the manufacturing sector may suffer from the real appreciation of the rouble. In the political arena, the recentralization of power, which favours the presidency, has continued. That weakening of countervailing powers has made the nation's politics highly dependent on its leader. The repercussions of the Yukos affair recalled the fact that respect of property rights still cannot be taken for granted. The affair also prompted new capital outflows. The banking liquidity crisis in summer 2004 underlined the weakness of a sector still badly in need of radical reform. Although company solvency has been improving, financial accountability is still limited with creditor protection remaining ineffective.

In Bulgaria (positive watchlisted) buoyant growth, continued budget discipline and active management of public sector foreign debt have all contributed to a marked improvement in the nation's solvency. In 2004 investors welcomed the final stages of negotiations on EU accession (with membership planned for early 2007) and conclusion of a new IMF confirmation agreement. FDI has increased accordingly. The main risk factors are still the size of the current deficit (linked to a surge in domestic demand) and insufficient progress made on reforms, especially those designed to improve the business environment.

Economic activity has remained buoyant in Romania, spurred by export dynamism and robust domestic demand. The downside of that dynamism has been an increase in the current account deficit. However, increasing direct investment and significantly less costly loans from abroad have made it possible to finance that deficit without too much difficulty as evidenced, for example, by the comfortable level of the country's exchange reserves. The authorities must nonetheless pursue their efforts to reduce public deficits and thereby keep external imbalances in check. Following the opposition victory in the December 2004 presidential election, it has fallen to a new government coalition to secure EU membership for Romania. In that regard, commitments to fighting corruption, ensuring judicial independence and reducing government subsidies have remained essential.

Albania

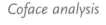

Population (million inhabitants)	3.2
GDP (US$ million)	4,835
GDP per capita (US$)	1,511

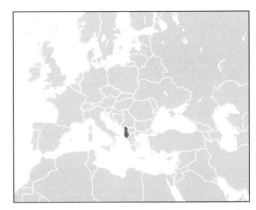

Coface analysis

Short-term: **D**

Medium-term:
Very high risk

RISK ASSESSMENT

Economic performance improved markedly in recent years thanks to policies implemented by government authorities under IMF-approved programmes.

Despite bright prospects further out, the economy is still too centred on the services sector with industry and exports struggling to get off the ground. That explains the persistence of a large current account deficit that increased expatriate workers' remittances have not been sufficient to offset. That situation is mainly attributable to poor infrastructure and an inadequate institutional framework, which have impeded development of the private sector and FDI. Progress on reforms has continued to lag, notably in the legal area, effective application of laws and protection of property rights.

Meanwhile, Albania has remained one of Europe's poorest countries. Politically, electoral reform has stalled and rivalries at the head of the ruling Socialist Party ultimately caused it to break up, undermining the prime minister's position. Legislative elections are due in 2005.

MAIN ECONOMIC INDICATORS

US$ millions	2000	2001	2002	2003	2004[(e)]	2005[(f)]
Economic growth (%)	7.3	7.6	4.7	6.0	6.2	6.0
Inflation (%)	0.0	3.1	5.2	2.4	3.4	3.0
Public sector balance (%GDP)	−9.2	−8.2	−6.7	−4.5	−6.5	−5.0
Exports	255	305	330	447	567	750
Imports	1,076	1,332	1,485	1,783	2,168	2,398
Trade balance	−821	−1,027	−1,155	−1,336	−1,601	−1,648
Current account balance (%GDP)	−7.4	−6.2	−9.0	−7.6	−7.5	−7.3
Foreign debt (%GDP)	31.8	28.2	24.4	22.9	20.0	20.9
Debt service (%Exports)	2.2	2.3	3.8	2.7	3.4	4.8
Foreign exchange reserves (in months of imports)	4.8	4.9	4.9	4.7	4.4	4.4

e = estimate, f = forecast

Armenia

Population (million inhabitants)	3.1
GDP (US$ million)	2,367
GDP per capita (US$)	764

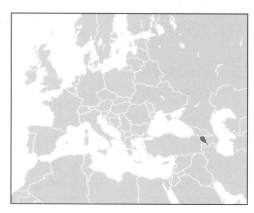

Coface analysis

Short-term: **C**

Medium-term:
Very high risk

RISK ASSESSMENT

Growth has remained very robust thanks to a steady precious and semi-precious metal export sector (over 50 per cent of exports) and strong domestic demand. The commercial and construction sectors have been driving the economy. The country has also been pursuing monetary stabilization, which has permitted bringing inflation and the public sector deficit under control. Armenia has benefited from steady IMF and World Bank support. Its financial situation has been gradually improving. The still-high current account deficit has been declining thanks to export dynamism and a high level of inward private transfers. Even though debt service has been limited, the country has remained very dependent on multilateral institutions for financing.

Although very economically integrated with Europe and developing strategic relations with the United States, Armenia is still Moscow's privileged partner in the Caucasus. The Russian troops stationed on Armenian soil, Russia's virtual total control over the energy sector, and the many Armenian workers employed in Russia have all been factors underpinning a strategic partnership likely to persist and grow stronger.

Domestically, the opposition has continued to contest the legitimacy of President Robert Kotcharian (elected in March 2003 and strengthened by his camp's victory in the May 2003 legislative elections). Recurrent political tensions and a hardly favourable business environment have thus been deterring foreign investment.

MAIN ECONOMIC INDICATORS

US$ millions	2000	2001	2002	2003	2004[(e)]	2005[(f)]
Economic growth (%)	6.0	9.6	12.9	13.9	9.0	8.0
Inflation (%)	0.4	2.9	2.0	8.6	3.0	3.0
Public sector balance (%GDP)	−6.4	−3.8	−0.5	−4.3	−2.0	−2.7
Exports	310	342	505	678	771	856
Imports	773	773	883	1,112	1,205	1,292
Trade balance	−463	−431	−378	−434	−434	−436
Current account balance (%GDP)	−14.5	−13.4	−8.9	−9.5	−8.6	−7.9
Foreign debt (%GDP)	46.3	45.0	42.7	43.4	38.1	35.2
Debt service (%Exports)	10.6	9.7	10.5	11.6	6.5	6.5
Foreign exchange reserves (in months of imports)	3.9	3.6	3.7	4.1	3.7	3.7

e = estimate, f = forecast

Austria

Population (million inhabitants)	8.1
GDP (US$ million)	253,100
GDP per capita (US$)	31,300

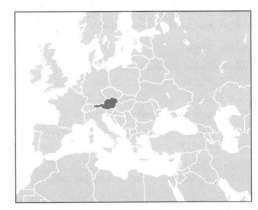

Coface analysis   Short-term: **A1**

RISK ASSESSMENT

An export upturn attributable to surging capital goods shipments to Central and Eastern European countries and to the increased supply of spare parts to German exporters spurred a moderate economic recovery in 2004. The increased number of tourists from new EU member countries and continuation of the public infrastructure–construction programme also had a positive effect. Household consumption, meanwhile, suffered from the effects of the tougher rules adopted for the retirement and health insurance regimes.

Economic activity will gain momentum in 2005. With exports continuing to post satisfactory growth, household consumption and, to a lesser extent, investment will accelerate thanks to lower income tax on households and reduced corporate tax on companies. Due to robust domestic demand and the tax reductions, external and public deficits will widen.

The weak growth registered from 2001 to 2003 ultimately caused a sharp increase in company bankruptcies (over 10 per cent in 2004), notably smaller companies and those in the construction, restaurant and business services sectors. The Coface payment incident index has nonetheless remained below the world average. With economic conditions continuing to improve, the company financial situation should also improve and the number of bankruptcies should stop growing in 2005. The reduction of employer taxes and social contributions should contribute to that result.

MAIN ECONOMIC INDICATORS						
%	2000	2001	2002	2003	2004(e)	2005(f)
Economic growth	3.4	0.7	1.2	0.8	1.8	2.3
Consumption (var.)	3.9	1.0	−0.1	0.6	1.6	2.4
Investment (var.)	12.2	1.3	−4.3	10.0	4.9	5.5
Inflation	2.0	2.3	1.7	1.3	1.8	1.7
Unemployment rate	4.7	4.8	5.5	5.7	5.6	5.8
Short-term interest rate	4.4	4.3	3.3	2.3	2.0	2.2
Public sector balance (%GDP)	−1.6	0.1	−0.4	−1.3	−1.4	−2.0
Public sector debt (%GDP)	69.4	70.2	71.9	69.7	67.1	68.1
Exports (var.)	10.5	6.8	3.8	1.4	7.1	6.9
Imports (var.)	10.1	5.0	−0.2	4.8	6.5	7.5
Current account balance (%GDP)	−2.5	−1.9	0.4	−0.4	−0.6	−1.1

e = estimate, f = forecast

PAYMENT AND COLLECTION PRACTICES

■ Payment

Bills of exchange and cheques are neither widely used nor recommended, as they are not always the most effective means of payment. To be valid, bills of exchange must meet strict criteria. This deters business people from using them. Cheques need not be backed by funds at the date of issue, but must be covered at the date of presentation. Banks generally return bad cheques to their issuers, who may also stop payment on their own without fear of criminal proceedings for misuse of this facility.

Bills of exchange and cheques are more commonly employed for repayments where the counterparties have agreed to their use.

Conversely, SWIFT transfers are widely used for domestic and international transactions and offer a cost-effective, rapid and secure means of payment.

■ Debt collection

As a rule, the collection process begins with the debtor being sent a demand for payment by registered mail, reminding the debtor of his or her obligation to pay the outstanding sum plus default interest in accordance with the sales agreement.

Where there is no interest rate clause in the agreement, the rate of interest applicable from 1 August 2002 is the Bank of Austria's base rate, calculated by reference to the European Central Bank's refinancing rate, marked up by eight basis points.

For claims that ´are certain, liquid and uncontested, but below 10,000 euros (formerly 130,000 Austrian schillings), creditors may seek a fast-track court injunction (*Mahnverfahren*) from the district court by submitting a pre-printed form.

An amendment to the code of civil procedure (ZPO), in force since 1 January 2003, allows creditors to seek a fast-track injunction for claims of up to 30,000 euros. Under this procedure, the judge serves the debtor with an order to pay the outstanding amount, plus legal costs. If the debtor does not appeal the injunction (*Einspruch*) within two weeks of service of the ruling, the order is enforceable relatively quickly.

A special procedure (*Wechselmandantverfahren*) exists for unpaid bills of exchange under which the court immediately serves a writ ordering the debtor to settle within two weeks. Should the debtor contest the claim, the case will be tried through the normal channels of court proceedings.

Where no settlement can be reached, or where a claim is contested, the last remaining alternative is to file an ordinary action (*Klage*) before the district court (*Bezirksgericht*) or the regional court (*Landesgericht*) depending on the claim amount or the type of dispute.

A separate commercial court (*Handelsgericht*) exists in the district of Vienna alone to hear commercial cases (commercial disputes, unfair competition suits, insolvency petitions, etc).

During the preliminary stage of proceedings the parties must make written submissions of evidence and file their respective claims. The court then decides on the facts of the case presented to it, but does not investigate cases on its own initiative. At the main hearing, the judge examines the evidence submitted and hears the parties' arguments as well as witnesses' testimonies.

An enforcement order can usually be obtained in first instance within about 10–12 months.

PAYMENT INCIDENTS INDEX
(12 months moving average - base 100 : World 1995)

Azerbaijan

Population (million inhabitants)	8.2
GDP (US$ million)	6,090
GDP per capita (US$)	743

Coface analysis

Short-term: **C**

Medium-term:
High risk

RISK ASSESSMENT

The country's economic and financial situation has been very good, benefiting from increased oil production spurred by very ample foreign investment flows into hydrocarbon production and transport. The BTC pipeline linking Azerbaijan to a Turkish port on the Mediterranean coast is one of the major construction projects under way. High barrel prices have spurred an increase in exports in value terms. Although the country has been running record current account deficits, the volume of imports is attributable to the energy sector's development with financing needs covered by foreign investment inflows that should continue unabated.

The economy's hydrocarbon focus is not without risk considering the very slow pace of modernization of other sectors. With revenues so dependent on the oil sector, public sector financial management will be precarious. Moreover, the economy's raw material export base has hardly been conducive to reforms as evidenced by the lagging pace of compliance with IMF agreement conditions.

Politically, Ilham Aleev, son of the former leader who headed the country since independence, assumed the highest office in October 2003 after contested elections. The new president's authority has been gradually firming up as he imposes loyal followers. Wealth from oil export revenues has been spreading poorly in society, which could breed discontent in segments of the population. Moreover, rapid resolution of the dispute with Armenia over Nagorny Karabakh will be unlikely.

MAIN ECONOMIC INDICATORS						
US$ millions	2000	2001	2002	2003	2004[(e)]	2005[(f)]
Economic growth (%)	11.1	9.9	10.6	11.2	10.0	12.0
Inflation (%)	2.2	1.5	3.2	3.4	3.5	5.0
Public sector balance (%GDP)	−0.6	0.9	−0.5	−2.0	−0.8	−0.8
Exports	1,877	2,046	2,305	2,655	3,414	4,739
Imports	1,539	1,465	1,823	2,723	3,458	4,080
Trade balance	338	581	482	−68	−44	659
Current account balance (%GDP)	−3	−1	−13	−28	−33	−24
Foreign debt (%GDP)	22.6	21.1	21.3	21.1	20.7	19.0
Debt service (%Exports)	4.9	5.3	5.0	4.5	4.0	3.6
Foreign exchange reserves (in months of imports)	3.5	3.5	2.8	1.9	1.8	1.8

e = estimate, f = forecast

Belarus

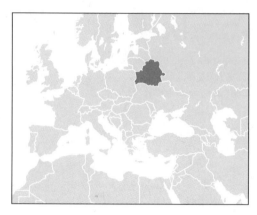

Population (million inhabitants)	9.9
GDP (US$ million)	14,304
GDP per capita (US$)	1,445

Coface analysis

Short-term: **D**

Medium-term:
Very high risk

RISK ASSESSMENT

Growth should slow due to low industrial investment attributable to a lack of company restructuring. With companies often remaining under government control, they still operate in a Soviet-like environment. The agricultural sector, dominated by collective farms, has been staying afloat thanks to government subsidies. Although checked by the price-control system, inflation has nonetheless remained among the highest in the CIS. As for the banking system, government authorities have dictated its credit policy, which would suggest a high level of non-performing loans. Finally, the country's foreign currency liquidity situation has been strained as evidenced by the very low level of currency reserves. Lacking access to financial markets, Belarus' foreign debt ratios have remained at modest levels.

The domestic political situation has undergone no notable change. After a referendum in October 2004 with the outcome contested by international observers, President Loukashenko may seek re-election in 2006 and should thus dominate the political scene for several more years. A scenario of political and economic reform will hardly be likely since, even ostracized on the international scene, Belarus' president can always count on Russia's backing. Although a monetary union could come into effect in 2006, progress on the Russia–Belarus Union project has been very limited.

MAIN ECONOMIC INDICATORS

US$ millions	2000	2001	2002	2003	2004[(e)]	2005[(f)]
Economic growth (%)	5.8	4.7	5.0	6.8	4.8	3.5
Inflation (%)	168.6	61.1	34.8	25.4	21.8	22.0
Public sector balance (%GDP)	−1.0	−2.9	−1.9	−1.1	−3.0	−3.0
Exports	6,641	7,334	7,965	10,010	10,419	10,596
Imports	7,525	8,141	8,879	11,085	11,909	12,263
Trade balance	−884	−807	−914	−1,075	−1,491	−1,666
Current account balance	−323	−435	−378	−451	−748	−925
Current account balance (%GDP)	−2.5	−3.5	−2.6	−2.6	−3.5	−3.8
Foreign debt (%GDP)	15.9	19.7	21.2	19.6	18.3	18.8
Debt service (%Exports)	4.2	3.4	4.1	4.6	3.3	3.3
Foreign exchange reserves (in months of imports)	0.6	0.5	0.6	0.5	0.3	0.3

e = estimate, f = forecast

Belgium

Population (million inhabitants)	10.4
GDP (US$ million)	301,900
GDP per capita (US$)	29,100

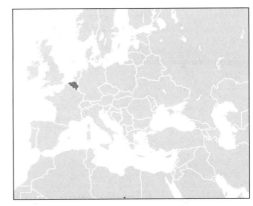

Coface analysis Short-term: **A1**

STRENGTHS

- Located in the heart of Europe's major industrial region, Belgium is the hub of many road, port and rail communication channels.
- The multiculturalism and multilingualism spurred by the country's proximity to a variety of countries and the presence of European and international institutions have facilitated both the entry of foreign companies and trade relations in general.
- The country has been near fiscal equilibrium for several years.

WEAKNESSES

- Belgium's regionalized political organization, whether for institutions or, more recently, political parties, has reduced national competences thereby complicating matters in reducing regional disparities.
- The opening of the economy resulting from the domestic market's narrowness has made it largely dependent on foreign demand.
- Labour market rigidity has contributed to keeping unemployment high, notably by a low employment rate for less-skilled and older workers.
- A balanced budget has not permitted sufficiently reducing public sector debt, which the government has been struggling to get below the 100 per cent of GDP threshold and which must imperatively come down in view of the aging population.

RISK ASSESSMENT

Growth accelerated in 2004, driven by robust intermediate-product exports. That dynamism has had a favourable impact on employment and household consumption. However, company investment has not really recovered.

A slight economic slowdown is expected in 2005 with world demand likely to sag. Nonetheless, increased production capacity utilization rates with exports remaining dynamic should spur an investment recovery. Despite tax cuts, consumption should continue to suffer from the purchasing power stagnation resulting from energy product price increases not considered by wage-indexing mechanisms. Meanwhile, after several years of equilibrium, the slightly negative public sector balance will still not permit the country to begin significantly reducing public debt.

In a more buoyant economic context, the Coface payment incident index has continued to decline. Only textiles, clothing, furniture and tanning have remained very risky. The payment situation also deteriorated recently in chemicals. The slowdown expected in 2005 should remain moderate and not lead to a significant deterioration of payments.

19

MAIN ECONOMIC INDICATORS

%	2000	2001	2002	2003	2004(e)	2005(f)
Economic growth	3.7	0.9	0.9	1.3	2.6	2.3
Consumption (var.)	3.4	0.7	0.3	2.2	2.2	2.1
Investment (var.)	4.6	3.6	−3.8	−1.9	1.2	3.5
Inflation	2.7	2.4	1.6	1.5	1.8	1.6
Unemployment rate	6.9	6.7	7.3	7.9	7.7	7.6
Short-term interest rate	4.4	4.3	3.3	2.3	2.1	2.3
Public sector balance (%GDP)	0.1	0.5	0.0	0.2	−0.1	−0.4
Public sector debt (%GDP)	115.0	113.5	110.4	104.9	100.7	98.0
Exports (var.)	8.2	1.8	1.3	1.7	5.6	5.1
Imports (var.)	8.3	1.0	1.0	2.1	5.6	5.6
Current account balance (%GDP)	3.9	3.9	5.7	4.2	3.6	3.6

e = estimate, f = forecast

MAIN ECONOMIC SECTORS

■ **Construction**

Residential renovation and construction, buoyed by still-low mortgage rates and an expected increase in housing prices, drove activity in the sector in 2004. In 2005, growth should benefit from steady residential sector demand and the investment programme initiated by the Walloon region for renovation of 36,000 public housing units. A shortage of skilled labour could nonetheless undermine that growth. Due to soaring steel prices, however, companies have hardly been able to improve their margins and bankruptcies have been increasing in the sector.

■ **Chemicals**

Growth generally slowed in 2004, particularly in several segments including paint and varnish, plastic material, rubber and cosmetics where prices also fell. Sales prices for drugs have been subject to increasing pressure from the public health insurance system, which thus hopes to reduce its deficit. Only prices for basic chemicals have increased sharply spurred by higher oil prices. In 2005, the sector should again post good growth despite a less bright outlook for exports. Oil prices and environmental pressures could, however, affect company earnings and deter investment.

■ **Textiles**

In 2004, the very moderate increase in Belgian textile production failed to meet expectations prompted by the European and world economic recovery. Competition from Turkey and China along with the euro appreciation affected prices and exports. Investment thus fell again, except in technical textiles. Although the situation should be much the same in 2005, in the medium term the elimination of quotas will force Belgian textiles to focus on more value-added products.

■ **Information and communication technologies**

In 2004, the telecommunications sector improved further thanks notably to the growth of broadband mobile services and the internet. Operators have nonetheless limited their investments since the bubble burst. As for computer equipment, the sector benefited from renewal of some existing installations and a brighter business outlook. The market for printers, laptops and flat screens has continued to trend up. IT services have been gradually recovering. In 2005, the sector's growth will remain very dependent on company investment.

■ Car industry

Improved economic conditions and the automobile trade fair held in Brussels in early 2004 permitted the sector to recover and to outperform the large European countries. Although carmakers have continued to restructure their production facilities in Europe, Belgium – thanks to reorganizations already undertaken – should not suffer too much from new waves of redundancies. The approximate 300 Belgian companies subcontracting for carmakers have been subject to price pressure with their leeway limited by very restrictive contracts. The trend in the sector will depend on the new tax regulations for company cars and the confidence level of households. Moderate growth will be likely.

PAYMENT AND COLLECTION PRACTICES

■ Payment

The bill of exchange is a common means of payment in Belgium. In the event of default, a protest may be drawn up through a bailiff within two days of the due date whereby the bearer can initiate proceedings against the bill's endorsers.

The National Bank of Belgium publishes a list of protests that can be consulted by the public at the office of the clerk of the commercial court and in some business and financial newspapers (*Journal des protêts, Echo de la Bourse*). Such publication is as an effective means of pressuring debtors to settle disputes because of the possibility that they might be refused credit by banks and suppliers.

Cheques are commonly used, but to a lesser extent than bills of exchange. Issuing uncovered cheques is a criminal offence. The Belgian public prosecutor's office is frequently willing to press criminal charges for claims over 5,000 euros (formerly about 200,000 Belgian francs). Uncovered cheques (like protested drafts) are equivalent to an acknowledgement of debt and, when needed, can be used to obtain an attachment order.

Although bank transfers are the fastest means of payment (all major Belgian banks use the SWIFT system), they do not offer a foolproof guarantee of payment as the transaction is very much dependent on the buyer's good faith. They should, therefore, be used where background financial information on the buyer is available to the seller.

■ Debt collection

Out-of-court collection begins with the debtor being sent a demand by registered letter for settlement of the outstanding principal, plus late interest or application of a penalty clause (*clause penale*) provided for in the terms and conditions of sale.

In the absence of a prior contractual agreement, interest on an unpaid invoice is automatically applicable from the day following the due date at a six-monthly rate set by the Ministry of Finance based on the European Central Bank's refinancing rate plus seven basis points (the 2 August 2002 Act on 'combating late payments in commercial transactions' in force since 7 August 2002).

Summary proceedings resulting in an injunction to pay in respect of claims under 1,860 euros (formerly 75,000 Belgian francs) fall within the sole jurisdiction of a justice of the peace. They must be supported by a document drawn up by the debtor pointing to the undisputed nature of the claim. But owing to their excessive formalism, summary proceedings are little used. Moreover, they require a lawyer's signature.

Where debtors refuse to settle amicably or fail to respond to a formal demand, creditors can initiate ordinary proceedings against them whereby they are summoned to appear before the court of first instance or, for overdue commercial payments, the competent commercial court. For undisputed claims, rulings are usually delivered either immediately from the bench or within a month of the final hearing.

For disputed claims, proceedings can take up to two years (especially in the event of an appeal). However, under the Belgian code of civil procedure the judge may set a deadline for the submission of arguments and evidence at the request of the parties.

The Bankruptcy Act of 8 August 1997 (amended by the law of 4 September 2002) and the

Composition Act of 17 July 1997 – both of which came into force on 1 January 1998 – recognize retention of property rights in specific cases and circumstances. For instance, an action for recovery is only admissible if initiated before the registered list of admitted debts is drawn up (*procès-verbal de vérification de créances*).

Another safeguard benefiting creditors is the right granted to sellers of moveable property stipulated under article 20-5 of the 16 December 1851 mortgage law. That right concerns all durable goods employed directly in an industrial, commercial or craft activity and generally considered as 'real estate' by incorporation or economic destination. A creditor may act on this right during a five-year period, a debtor's bankruptcy notwithstanding, provided he or she has registered certified true copies of invoices with the clerk's office of the commercial court in the debtor's district of residence, within 15 days of delivery of the goods.

PAYMENT INCIDENTS INDEX
(12 months moving average - base 100 : World 1995)

Bosnia and Herzegovina

Population (million inhabitants)	4.1
GDP (US$ million)	5,599
GDP per capita (US$)	1,366

Short-term: **D**

Medium-term:

Coface analysis **Very high risk**

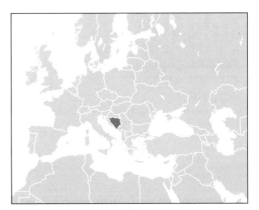

RISK ASSESSMENT

Much progress has been made since the 1995 Dayton agreement with the presence of a peacekeeping force, IMF backing and debt cancellation. GDP and exports have grown markedly. The currency board regime has become firmly entrenched and prices have stabilized with the banking sector now privatized and the public sector deficit down sharply. Moreover, the country has replenished its foreign exchange reserves.

The near-term economic outlook is still bright. Investment, strengthening foreign demand and construction of new infrastructure should buoy growth. Major risk factors have nonetheless persisted. The current account deficit will be difficult to sustain in the medium term, particularly with international financial aid declining and with private remittances and capital repatriation constituting volatile flows of funds. Moreover, the social and political environment has hardly been conducive to reform implementation. The country has continued to suffer from high unemployment, a shaky government coalition of nationalist parties and its complex structure.

MAIN ECONOMIC INDICATORS						
US$ millions	2000	2001	2002	2003	2004[(e)]	2005[(f)]
Economic growth (%)	5.5	4.4	5.5	3.5	5.1	5.7
Inflation (%)	5.0	3.2	0.3	0.1	0.9	1.7
Public sector balance (%GDP)*	−16.5	−10.5	−7.3	−3.0	−3.4	−2.1
Exports	832	870	1,046	1,407	1,715	1,937
Imports	2,547	2,701	3,122	3,845	4,322	4,532
Trade balance	−1,715	−1,831	−2,076	−2,438	−2,607	−2,595
Current account balance (%GDP)	−13.1	−16.2	−18.5	−17.4	−15.8	−14.8
Foreign debt (%GDP)	58.8	48.2	42.2	34.0	32.8	31.2
Debt service (%Exports)	4.3	3.8	5.3	5.1	4.4	4.5
Foreign exchange reserves (in months of imports)	2.1	5.0	4.5	5.0	4.4	4.3

*excluding grants

e = estimate, f = forecast

23

Bulgaria

Population (million inhabitants)	8
GDP (US$ million)	15,486

Short-term: **B**

Medium-term:

Coface analysis **Moderately high risk**

STRENGTHS

- Reform implementation, disciplined fiscal policy and active debt management have permitted consolidating the economic situation and markedly improving government solvency.
- The banking sector has emerged strengthened from the 1996–1997 crisis.
- The country enjoys multilateral institution backing and completed the formal negotiating process with the EU.
- The country benefits from skilled labour.
- It has attracted substantial direct investment inflows.

WEAKNESSES

- Strong imports spurred by a credit upsurge have been generating substantial current account imbalances.
- Although declining, the foreign debt burden has remained relatively high.
- Much progress is still needed on structural reforms notably concerning the business environment.
- Such progress will be necessary to ensure continued steady capital flows and improve a particularly rigid foreign exchange regime (currency board).
- The level of development has remained low and the savings rate insufficient.

RISK ASSESSMENT

Steady growth, continued fiscal discipline and active management of public external debt have permitted markedly improving government solvency. In 2004, investors responded favourably to the end of EU membership negotiations with admission scheduled for 2007 and to conclusion of a new IMF stand-by arrangement. This favourable response is evident from the growth of FDI. Both the large current account deficit attributable to surging domestic demand and the lagging pace of reforms, notably to improve the business environment, will constitute the main risk factors.

Despite institutional deficiencies and the government coalition's unpopularity, political risk has remained manageable. Current economic policy should persist after the July 2005 legislative elections, whatever their outcome.

In a favourable context, some sectors like textiles, mobile telephony or mass distribution have been posting good performance. Nonetheless, significant late payments have continued to mark overall company payment behaviour.

MAIN ECONOMIC INDICATORS

US$ millions	2000	2001	2002	2003	2004(e)	2005(f)
Economic growth (%)	5.4	4.1	4.9	4.3	5.3	5.5
Inflation (%)	10.3	7.4	5.8	2.3	6.7	5.3
Public sector balance (%)	−0.6	−0.6	−0.9	−0.4	0.5	0.0
Unemployment rate (%)	16.4	19.5	16.8	12.7	n/a	n/a
Exports	4,825	5,113	5,692	7,439	9,220	10,300
Imports	6,000	6,693	7,287	9,912	12,110	13,530
Trade balance	−1,176	−1,581	−1,595	−2,474	−2,890	−3,230
Current account balance	−679	−984	−827	−1,487	−1,700	−1,800
Current account balance (%GDP)	−5.4	−7.2	−5.3	−7.5	−7.0	−6.7
Foreign debt (%GDP)	88.9	78.2	72.1	66.4	58.7	60.1
Debt service (%Exports)	13.5	16.0	11.7	7.6	11.9	8.5
Foreign exchange reserves (in months of imports)	4.8	4.5	5.5	5.7	5.4	5.3

e = estimate, f = forecast

CONDITIONS OF ACCESS TO THE MARKET

■ Market overview

A country counting roughly 8 million inhabitants whose standard of living – while below the 25-member EU average – is rising steadily, Bulgaria has seen its per capita GDP increase from US$1,220 in 1997 to US$2,004 in 2003. There are widespread income disparities, however. The average monthly wage in 2003 was US$160; 80 per cent of Bulgarians live in hardship if not poverty and 5 per cent earn more than the European average.

■ Means of entry

The country functions as a market economy. The banking sector has been privatized, whereas the government monopolies in energy and telecommunications have been dismantled and their privatization almost completed.

Customs duties on industrial products from the EU were abolished in 2002. French companies enjoy intellectual and industrial property protection under a bilateral agreement concluded on 28 November 2003.

■ Attitude towards foreign investors

The country is extremely open to foreign investment. Foreign direct investment at the end of June 2004 totalled US$8,179 million. Annual foreign investment inflows at the end of 2004 amounted to US$3 billion, compared with US$1.4 billion in 2003. The government is very well disposed to foreign investors and spares no effort to facilitate their ventures in the country.

OPPORTUNITY SCOPE

Breakdown of domestic demand (%GDP + imports)
- Private consumption   43
- Public consumption   11
- Investment   13

Exports: 53% of GDP   Imports: 60% of GDP

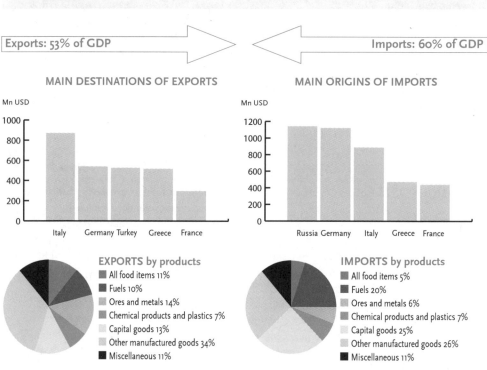

MAIN DESTINATIONS OF EXPORTS

Mn USD

Italy | Germany | Turkey | Greece | France

MAIN ORIGINS OF IMPORTS

Mn USD

Russia | Germany | Italy | Greece | France

EXPORTS by products
- All food items 11%
- Fuels 10%
- Ores and metals 14%
- Chemical products and plastics 7%
- Capital goods 13%
- Other manufactured goods 34%
- Miscellaneous 11%

IMPORTS by products
- All food items 5%
- Fuels 20%
- Ores and metals 6%
- Chemical products and plastics 7%
- Capital goods 25%
- Other manufactured goods 26%
- Miscellaneous 11%

STANDARD OF LIVING / PURCHASING POWER

Indicators	Bulgaria	Regional average	DC average
GNP per capita (PPP dollars)	7030	8313	4601
GNP per capita (USD)	1770	2535	1840
Human Development Index	0.796	0.805	0.684
Wealthiest 10% share of national income	23.7	30	32
Urban population percentage	68	68	45
Percentage under 15 years old	15	17	30
Number of telephones per 1000 inhabitants	368	257	120
Number of computers per 1000 inhabitants	52	84	37

Croatia

Population (million inhabitants)   4
GDP (US$ million)   22,436

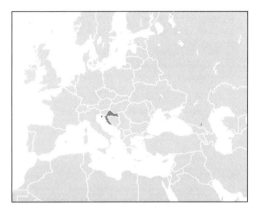

Short-term: **A4**

Coface analysis   Medium-term:
Moderately high risk

STRENGTHS

- With the new government continuing the policy of cooperation with international institutions pursued by its predecessors, the EU has decided to initiate membership negotiations with the country in early 2005.
- Reforms have strengthened market confidence.
- Although declining, foreign investment has permitted restructuring part of the economy.
- Croatia has great tourist potential.

WEAKNESSES

- The persistence of large fiscal and current account deficits has continued to hamper the economy, causing a marked increase in the public and foreign debt burden.
- The contribution of foreign investment to covering financing needs has been insufficient, thus increasing the country's dependence on borrowing abroad.
- Rapid admission of the country to the EU will depend on continued pursuit of reforms and cooperation with the International Criminal Court.

RISK ASSESSMENT

After a period of overheating linked to credit expansion, the economy registered a slight slowdown. The main risk factor concerns the persistence of high fiscal and current account deficits, which have caused a marked increase in debt amid weak foreign direct investment inflows. Croatia has nonetheless registered a comfortable level of currency reserves. Furthermore, the pursuit of reforms and the prospect of EU membership within the decade should permit the country to retain favourable conditions of access to capital markets and attract more investors. Finally, the new government, after prompting fears due to its nationalist past, has continued the policy of cooperation pursued by its predecessors with international institutions. However, the war crimes tribunal in The Hague regrets the government's ambiguous position on transferring suspected war criminals.

CONDITIONS OF ACCESS TO THE MARKET

■ Market overview

Of an estimated population of 4.44 million, 1.53 million are employed. The average unemployment rate was 17.2 per cent in August 2004. Average take-home pay, estimated at 556 euros in July 2004, rose by 5.8 per cent over the previous year against a background of price stability.

MAIN ECONOMIC INDICATORS						
US$ millions	2000	2001	2002	2003	2004[(e)]	2005[(f)]
Economic growth (%)	2.9	4.4	5.2	4.3	3.8	3.5
Inflation (%)	6.2	4.6	1.7	1.8	2.4	2.5
Public sector balance (%GDP)	−6.5	−6.8	−4.8	−6.3	−4.5	−3.7
Unemployment rate (%)	22.6	22.0	22.3	19.2	n/a	n/a
Exports	4,567	4,759	5,004	6,290	7,290	7,660
Imports	7,771	8,860	10,652	14,210	16,330	17,100
Trade balance	−3,204	−4,101	−5,649	−7,920	−9,040	−9,440
Current account balance	−440	−593	−1,896	−1,684	−1,700	−1,650
Current account balance (%GDP)	−2.4	−3.0	−8.3	−5.8	−5.1	−4.7
Foreign debt (%GDP)	60.0	57.1	67.6	82.1	78.4	82.6
Debt service (%Exports)	19.2	19.5	26.5	20.0	16.6	19.2
Foreign exchange reserves (in months of imports)	4.1	4.8	5.0	5.3	4.8	4.8

e = estimate, f = forecast

Imports, whose rise has been somewhat slowed by the central bank's credit tightening measures, are normally exempt from prior approval, except for products governed by international agreements (arms, gold, works of art, etc) or subject to public health restrictions (foodstuffs, etc). Under the most favoured nation system, applicable since WTO accession, customs duties continue to be lowered. The European Union Council of Ministers granted candidate-country status to Croatia on 18 June 2004 and accession negotiations are supposed to start in early 2005.

For industrial products, 68 per cent of tariffs are 5 per cent or less. The average tariff for agri-foodstuffs should have been gradually cut to 16.4 per cent by 2005, but the government has asked for transition status and for the deadline to be put back to 2007.

All means of payment are used in Croatia. For private purchases, credit cards are more widely used than cheques, which are not all that common. Cash payment often attracts a 10 per cent discount. Money orders can be used to settle government invoices. For business transactions, the most widely used instruments are bank transfers, bank guarantees confirmed by a foreign bank and cheques drawn against a recognized local bank.

■ **Attitude towards foreign investors**
Croatian law guarantees foreign investors equality of treatment with locals, despite a small number of practical difficulties. The uncertainty surrounding land and property rights creates a climate of insecurity that the judicial system is struggling to address (lengthy court procedures, non-enforcement of court orders, lack of independence of the judiciary). Between 1993 and the second quarter of 2003, FDI amounted to US$9.28 billion, and to US$425 million for the six first months of 2004. The three leading investors over the last 10 years are Austria (24.89 per cent), Germany (21.01 per cent) and the United States (16.37 per cent). France accounts for 1.57 per cent of FDI (US$146 million).

■ **Foreign exchange regulations**
The national currency, the kuna, is not convertible outside the country. Foreign companies must open a foreign currency account and a kuna account to do business in the country.

The central bank (HNB) has adopted a slightly overvalued floating exchange rate for the kuna, which it regulates by intervening on the currency market. At 17 November 2004, the exchange rate was 7.56 kunas to the euro.

OPPORTUNITY SCOPE

Breakdown of domestic demand (%GDP + imports)
- Private consumption   39
- Public consumption   14
- Investment   17

Exports: 46% of GDP   Imports: 55% of GDP

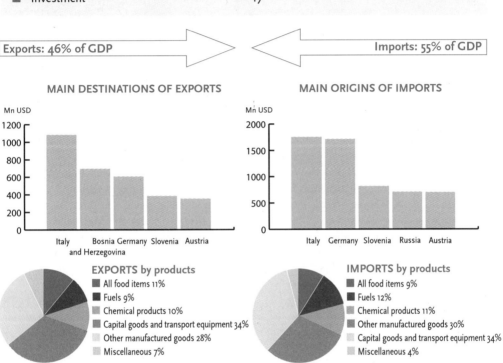

MAIN DESTINATIONS OF EXPORTS

Mn USD

Italy · Bosnia and Herzegovina · Germany · Slovenia · Austria

EXPORTS by products
- All food items 11%
- Fuels 9%
- Chemical products 10%
- Capital goods and transport equipment 34%
- Other manufactured goods 28%
- Miscellaneous 7%

MAIN ORIGINS OF IMPORTS

Mn USD

Italy · Germany · Slovenia · Russia · Austria

IMPORTS by products
- All food items 9%
- Fuels 12%
- Chemical products 11%
- Other manufactured goods 30%
- Capital goods and transport equipment 34%
- Miscellaneous 4%

STANDARD OF LIVING / PURCHASING POWER

Indicators	Croatia	Regional average	DC average
GNP per capita (PPP dollars)	10000	8313	4601
GNP per capita (USD)	4540	2535	1840
Human Development Index	0.830	0.805	0.684
Wealthiest 10% share of national income	24.5	30	32
Urban population percentage	59	68	45
Percentage under 15 years old	16	17	30
Number of telephones per 1000 inhabitants	417	257	120
Number of computers per 1000 inhabitants	174	84	37

Cyprus

Population (inhabitants)	765,000
GDP (US$ million)	9,131
GDP per capita (US$)	11,936

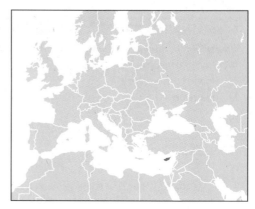

Short-term: **A3**

Medium-term:

Coface analysis   **Low risk**

RISK ASSESSMENT

After a period of decline, growth recovered in 2004, buoyed by domestic demand and the revival of tourism. That revival, in conjunction with private consumption and construction sector investment, should contribute to a slight upturn in 2005. Real per capita income has continued to rise and has now reached a level above 80 per cent of the Europe-of-25 average. Unemployment has remained very low with inflation still under control. Meanwhile, the country has been engaged in a process of harmonizing its legislation with that of the EU, which it joined (for the Greek portion) in May 2004.

Despite those successes, risk factors have persisted. The Cypriot economy is still very vulnerable to external shocks due to its small size and open economy. A significant slowdown in Europe or upsurge of tensions in the Middle East would have serious repercussions on growth. Moreover, public sector debt (over 70 per cent of GDP) has been above the Maastricht threshold. The country must thus notably strengthen the competitiveness of its products and services and bring the consolidation of public sector finances to a successful conclusion.

Little progress will be likely in the near future on settlement of the Cyprus question considering the rejection of the Annan plan. However, new initiatives could now emerge with the EU having decided to begin accession negotiations with Turkey.

MAIN ECONOMIC INDICATORS						
US$ millions	2000	2001	2002	2003	2004(e)	2005(f)
Economic growth (%)	5.0	4.1	2.1	1.9	3.2	3.5
Inflation (%)	4.1	2.0	2.8	4.1	2.1	2.5
Public sector balance (%GDP)	−3.1	−3.0	−3.6	−6.4	−4.8	−2.9
Exports	951	975	855	955	1,097	1,274
Imports	3,557	3,553	3,703	4,090	5,110	5,773
Trade balance	−2,606	−2,577	−2,847	−3,134	−4,014	−4,499
Current account balance (%GDP)	−5.4	−3.4	−4.4	−3.4	−4.2	−3.7
Foreign debt (%GDP)	48.8	55.6	59.7	48.8	43.9	40.2
Debt service (%Exports)	6.3	7.5	7.6	6.5	5.7	5.1
Foreign exchange reserves (in months of imports)	3.3	4.4	5.7	5.4	5.0	4.8

e = estimate, f = forecast

Czech Republic

Population (million inhabitants)	10
GDP (US$ million)	69,514

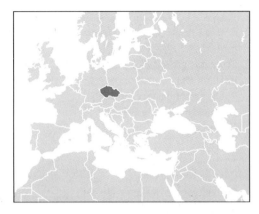

Short-term: **A2**

Medium-term:

Coface analysis **Low risk**

STRENGTHS

- With a high-potential productive apparatus, the country's work productivity has been increasing sharply.
- The country has posted the highest levels of FDI per capita in Central Europe.
- Foreign exchange reserves have remained at comfortable levels and the foreign debt burden has been moderate.
- The country's EU accession has bolstered its economic stability.

WEAKNESSES

- The public sector deficit has been exacerbated by banking sector restructuring costs.
- The Czech economy has remained dependent on the economic fortunes of its main trading partners.
- The current account deficit has remained large due notably to increased earnings paid to foreign investors.
- The pace of reforms could slow if the populist parties win the 2006 elections.

RISK ASSESSMENT

Growth firmed up in 2004, with exports and investment partly picking up the slack for consumption. Although that improvement has not prevented occasional payment defaults in the weakest sectors, the Coface company payment incident index has nonetheless remained near the world average.

The economic dynamism should persist in 2005 amid improvement in the labour market, steady FDI inflows, increased production capacity in the car industry and continued growth of sales abroad. Forecasts could suffer, however, from an economic downturn in the EU (notably Germany), a loss of competitiveness due to the exchange rate appreciation or possible flagging efforts by authorities particularly on consolidation of public sector finances.

Although shrinking significantly, the current account deficit has remained relatively large if only because of increased repatriation of earnings by foreign owned companies. External financing needs have nonetheless remained low in relation to export revenues with privatizations likely to boost FDI inflows further and the foreign debt burden remaining moderate.

EUROPE

MAIN ECONOMIC INDICATORS						
US$ billions	2000	2001	2002	2003	2004[e]	2005[f]
Economic growth (%)	3.3	2.6	1.5	3.1	3.8	4.1
Inflation (%)	3.9	4.7	1.8	0.1	2.8	2.4
Public sector balance (%GDP)	−4.2	−5.0	−6.7	−6.2	−7.0	−5.9
Unemployment rate (%)	9.0	8.5	9.2	9.9	9.6	n/a
Exports	29.1	33.4	38.3	48.6	68.8	83.4
Imports	32.2	36.4	40.5	51.1	69.7	84.3
Trade balance	−3.1	−3.1	−2.2	−2.5	−0.9	−0.9
Current account balance	−2.7	−3.3	−4.2	−5.6	−4.8	−5.0
Current account balance (%GDP)	−4.9	−5.4	−5.6	−6.2	−4.7	−4.1
Foreign debt (%GDP)	38.4	36.7	36.6	38.8	38.5	35.1
Debt service (%Exports)	13.2	9.8	9.1	6.9	6.1	4.4
Foreign exchange reserves (in months of imports)	3.8	3.7	5.4	4.9	3.9	3.5

e = estimate, f = forecast

CONDITIONS OF ACCESS TO THE MARKET

■ **Means of entry**

The Czech Republic entered the customs union when it joined the EU on 1 May 2004. As a result, there are no tariff or non-tariff barriers to products imported from the EU.

■ **Attitude towards foreign investors**

The government pursues a proactive investment promotion policy, mainly via the investment promotion agency, Czechinvest. Start-ups and schemes to modernize or extend existing plant and machinery for the purposes of creating new production lines are eligible for grants. To qualify, companies must invest a minimum of 200 million koruna (6.3 million euros) over three years, or 100 million koruna (3.15 million euros) if their activity is based in a high-unemployment region. Newly formed entities pay no corporation tax for ten years, while existing entities are granted ten-year partial tax exemption.

The new law also provides for other forms of assistance, including job creation subsidies, training allowances and infrastructure development grants. Moreover, companies investing in the so-called 'strategic' services sector (software development,

e-solutions research, high-tech equipment repairs, telephone services, audit and consultancy) are now eligible for government subsidies, provided they invest a minimum of 30 million koruna (1 million euros) over three years, create 50 new jobs during this period and meet Czech environmental standards.

Firms investing in the so-called 'technology' zones – ie R&D centres for the design and development of innovative goods in the high-tech sector – are also eligible for government subsidies. Qualification criteria in this case are less strict: minimum investment of 15 million koruna (470,000 euros) and the creation of at least 15 jobs over three years.

■ **Foreign exchange regulations**

The Czech koruna is fully convertible. Business transactions are usually settled by bank transfer in euros or korunas. The bulk of payments between companies doing business together on a regular basis are made by SWIFT transfer and pass off smoothly. However, for initial business transactions or large orders, it is advisable to use documentary credit (payable by the buyer's bank upon presentation of proof of export by the seller).

PAYMENT AND COLLECTION PRACTICES

■ Payment

Bills of exchange and cheques are not widely used, as they must be issued in accordance with certain criteria to be valid.

For unpaid and protested bills of exchange (*směnka cizí*), promissory notes (*směnka vlastní*) and cheques, creditors may access a fast-track procedure for ordering payment under which, if the judge admits the plaintiff's application, the debtor has only three days to contest the order against him or her.

Bank transfers are by far the most widely used means of payment. Leading Czech banks – after successive phases of privatization and concentration – are now linked to the SWIFT system, which provides an easier, quicker and cheaper method for handling domestic and international payments and to the CERTIS interbank clearing system for local payments.

Inspired by EU regulations, a new payment systems law in force since 1 January 2003 sets the rules for transferring funds in the enlarged European area and empowers the Czech National Bank (Česká Národni Banka) to ovesee local use of electronic payment instruments.

■ Debt collection

It is advisable, as far as possible, not to initiate recovery proceedings locally because of the country's cumbersome legal system, the high cost of legal action and lengthy court procedures – it takes almost three years to obtain a writ of execution due to a lack of judges properly trained in the rules of the market economy and proper equipment.

After service of final demand for payment supported by proof of debt elicits no response from the debtor, creditors are advised to seek an out-of-court settlement based on a schedule of payment, preferably drawn up by a public notary, accompanied by an enforcement clause that allows them, in case of default by the debtor, to go directly to the enforcement stage, after the court admits the binding nature of that document.

Where creditors have significant proof of claim (unpaid bills of exchange or cheques, acknowledgement of debt, etc), they may obtain an injunction to pay (*platební rozkaz*) under a fast-track procedure, which may take from three months to a year depending on the workload of the courts, but which does not necessitate a hearing as long as the claim is sufficiently well founded.

Where a debtor contests an injunction within 15 days of its service, an ordinary procedure will then apply with the parties subsequently summoned to one or more hearings to be heard and produce evidence. The judge will then decide whether to throw out the plaintiff's application or order the debtor to pay principal and costs.

Ordinary proceedings are partly in writing, with the parties filing submissions accompanied by all supporting case documents (original or certified copies), and partly oral with the litigants and their witnesses heard on the main hearing date.

Any settlement reached between the parties during these proceedings and ratified by the court is tantamount to a writ of execution, in the event of non-compliance at a later date.

Commercial disputes are heard by civil courts (district courts and regional courts) since the abolition, in January 2001, of the only regional commercial courts existing in Prague, Brno and Ostrava.

To speed up enforcement of court orders (with over 400,000 cases pending enforcement by end June 2002), a new body of bailiffs (*soudní exekutor*), endowed with less formal enforcement powers, was created in May 2001 and has been gradually improving enforcement.

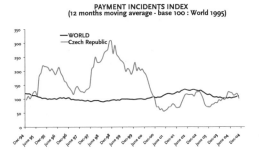

PAYMENT INCIDENTS INDEX
(12 months moving average - base 100 : World 1995)

OPPORTUNITY SCOPE

Breakdown of domestic demand (%GDP + imports)

Private consumption	32
Public consumption	13
Investment	17

Exports: 65% of GDP

Imports: 67% of GDP

MAIN DESTINATIONS OF EXPORTS

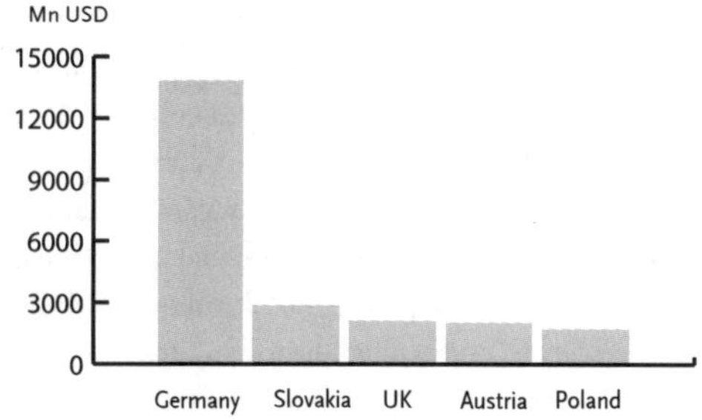

Mn USD
15000
12000
9000
6000
3000
0
Germany
Slovakia
UK
Austria
Poland

MAIN ORIGINS OF IMPORTS

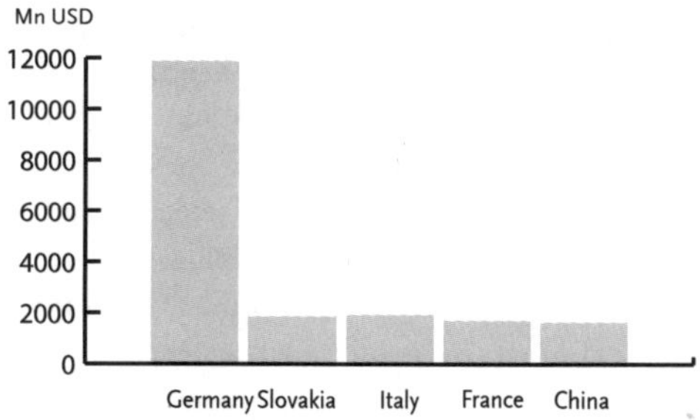

Mn USD
12000
10000
8000
6000
4000
2000
0
Germany
Slovakia
Italy
France
China

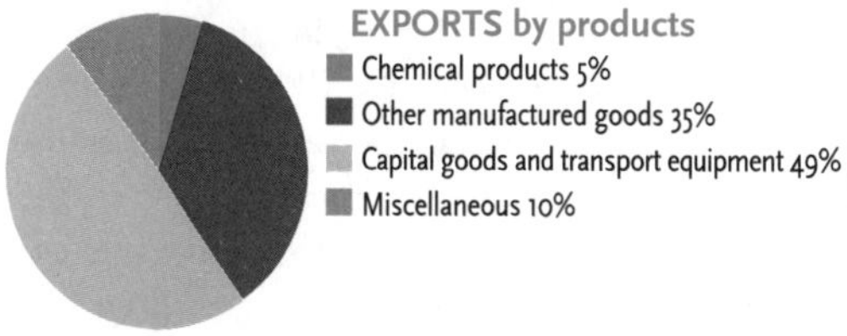

EXPORTS by products
Chemical products 5%
Other manufactured goods 35%
Capital goods and transport equipment 49%
Miscellaneous 10%

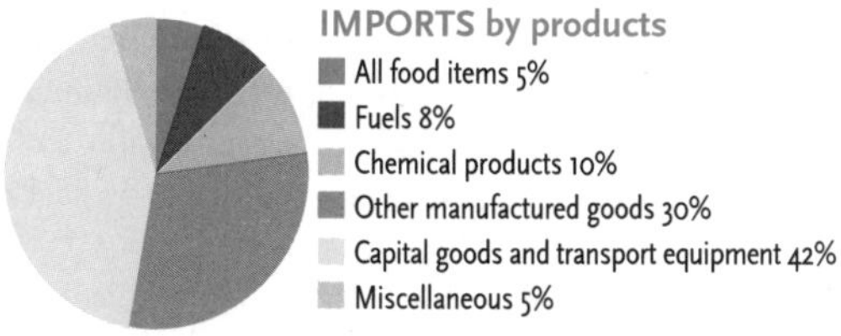

IMPORTS by products
All food items 5%
Fuels 8%
Chemical products 10%
Other manufactured goods 30%
Capital goods and transport equipment 42%
Miscellaneous 5%

STANDARD OF LIVING / PURCHASING POWER

Indicators	Czech Republic	Regional average	DC average
GNP per capita (PPP dollars)	14920	8313	4601
GNP per capita (USD)	5480	2535	1840
Human Development Index	0.868	0.805	0.684
Wealthiest 10% share of national income	22.4	30	32
Urban population percentage	75	68	45
Percentage under 15 years old	16	17	30
Number of telephones per 1000 inhabitants	362	257	120
Number of computers per 1000 inhabitants	177	84	37

Denmark

Population (million inhabitants)	5.4
GDP (US$ million)	212,300
GDP per capita (US$)	39,400

Coface analysis   Short-term: **A1**

RISK ASSESSMENT

Growth accelerated in 2004. Tax reductions and low interest rates buoyed household consumption. Residential property investment expanded strongly thanks to the introduction of more attractive financing terms. Industrial investment also recovered.

Growth should remain robust in 2005. Although the effects of tax incentives on domestic demand will peter out, improvement in the job market could pick up the slack in spurring household spending. Exports, benefiting from an increasing focus on the most dynamic European and Asian markets, should make further moderate gains despite the Danish krone's appreciation. The government will again run a public sector surplus thanks to the tight monetary and fiscal policy it has pursued. Furthermore, inflation will remain at a relatively low level.

Although increasing in the past 12 months by 5 per cent, the number of bankruptcies is still not very high. The Coface payment incident index eased in 2004, remaining substantially below the world average. That trend should persist in 2005.

MAIN ECONOMIC INDICATORS						
%	2000	2001	2002	2003	2004(e)	2005(f)
Economic growth	2.8	1.6	1.0	0.5	2.4	2.4
Consumption (var.)	−0.7	−0.2	0.6	0.8	3.3	2.5
Investment (var.)	6.6	6.9	4.2	−1.1	3.7	2.7
Inflation	2.9	2.3	2.4	2.1	1.3	1.9
Unemployment rate	4.4	4.3	4.6	5.6	6.3	5.6
Short-term interest rate	4.9	4.6	3.5	2.4	2.2	2.4
Public sector balance (%GDP)	2.5	2.8	1.6	1.2	1.5	1.6
Public sector debt (%GDP)	54.3	53.8	54.1	49.5	44.0	42.0
Exports (var.)	13.4	4.4	4.8	0.0	2.3	3.6
Imports (var.)	13.5	3.4	7.3	−0.6	3.5	3.3
Current account balance (%GDP)	1.5	3.0	2.0	2.7	2.8	2.8

e = estimate, f = forecast   35

PAYMENT AND COLLECTION PRACTICES

■ Payment

Like the cheque, the bill of exchange is not frequently used in Denmark. Both are an embodiment and, therefore, an acknowledgement of debt.

Accepted but remaining unpaid bills and cheques are legally enforceable instruments that exempt creditors from obtaining a court judgment. In such cases, a judge–bailiff (*Fogedret*) is appointed to oversee enforcing attachment. First, however, the debtor is summonsed to declare his or her financial situation for the purposes of determining ability to repay the debt. It is a criminal offence to make a false statement of insolvency.

Bank transfers are the most commonly used means of payment. All major Danish banks use the SWIFT network – a rapid and efficient international funds transfer service.

■ Debt collection

Out-of-court collection begins with the creditor or his or her legal counsel sending debtor a final demand for payment by registered or ordinary mail in which the latter is given ten days to settle the principal amount, plus any interest penalties provided for in the agreement.

Where there is no such clause, the rate of interest applicable to commercial agreements contracted after 1 August 2002 is the Danish National Bank's benchmark (lending rate or *udlånsrente*) in force on 1 January or 1 July of the year in reference, plus seven basis points.

It should also be noted that, where the due date for payment is not complied with, any settlement or acknowledgement of debt negotiated at this stage of the recovery process is directly enforceable, on condition that an enforcement clause is duly included in the new settlement or agreement.

For claims that are not settled out of court, creditors usually engage a lawyer to defend their interests, even though Danish law allows plaintiffs

and defendants direct representation in court. Unlike other countries, Denmark has only one type of legal professional: lawyers (ie there are no notaries, barristers, bailiffs-at-law, etc).

Where debtors fail to respond to a demand for payment or where the dispute is not serious, creditors may obtain, usually after three months of proceedings, a judgment following an adversarial hearing or a judgment by default ordering the debtor to pay, within 14 days, the principal amount plus court fees and, where applicable, a proportion of the creditor's legal costs.

Complex or disputed claims of up to 1 million Danish krone are heard by the court of first instance (*Byret*). The proceedings at this level are predominantly oral, rather than written. Claims above this amount are heard by one of two regional courts: the Vestre Landsret in Viborg or the Østre Landsret in Copenhagen. The proceedings here involve a series of preliminary hearings, in which the parties present written submissions and proofs, and a plenary hearing, in which the court hears witness testimonies and the parties' arguments.

Denmark does not have a system of commercial courts outside the Copenhagen area, which has a maritime and commercial court (*Sø-og Handelsretten*) presided over by a panel of professional and non-professional judges who have jurisdiction over insolvency actions as well as commercial and maritime disputes.

PAYMENT INCIDENTS INDEX
(12 months moving average - base 100 : World 1995)

Estonia

Population (million inhabitants)	1
GDP (US$ million)	6,507

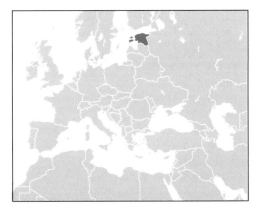

Short-term: **A2**

Medium-term:

Coface analysis   **Low risk**

STRENGTHS

- The economic opening and liberalization policy has produced a broad consensus.
- Estonia boasts one of Central Europe's most business-friendly environments, and its economic performance has been among the region's best.
- That climate has been conducive to rapid modernization of industry and to redirecting foreign trade towards Scandinavian markets.
- The banking system has remained sound.
- Public sector debt has been low.

WEAKNESSES

- Growth has depended on international economic conditions due to Estonia's very open trade policy.
- The import content of exports linked to subcontracting activities has been partly responsible for the current account deficit's size, which has made the economy more vulnerable to external shocks.
- The domestic savings rate has remained low in relation to investment.
- The foreign debt burden has remained high.

RISK ASSESSMENT

Growth accelerated in 2004, driven by domestic demand and buoyed by technology sector exports. The economy should remain dynamic in 2005 thanks to the firmness of the telecommunications market and economic conditions in Scandinavian countries, which are Estonia's main trading partners.

Despite strong sales growth abroad, however, large external account imbalances have persisted, reflecting the buoyant domestic demand and the fact that the subcontracting industry has been importing the main inputs it needs for production.

Despite appreciable FDI inflows, the foreign debt burden should remain high. Debt service has nonetheless remained at moderate levels due to favourable borrowing terms.

Politically, the rivalries within the government coalition should have only limited effect on the conduct of economic policy, which should remain focused on the need to continue the process of economic harmonization with the EU. The country took another step by joining the European exchange rate mechanism in June 2004 (while retaining the currency board system) with the goal of adopting the single currency.

CONDITIONS OF ACCESS TO THE MARKET

■ Market overview

At purchasing power parity, per capita GDP in 2003 was, according to some estimates, 11,000 euros – the highest among the Baltic states. The average wage at end 2003 was 431 euros, up 9.4 per cent on 2002.

MAIN ECONOMIC INDICATORS

US$ millions	2000	2001	2002	2003	2004[(e)]	2005[(f)]
Economic growth (%)	7.8	6.4	7.2	5.1	5.9	6.0
Inflation (%)	4.0	5.8	3.6	1.3	2.9	3.1
Public sector balance (%GDP)	−0.6	0.4	1.1	2.4	0.2	−0.3
Unemployment rate (%)	13.7	12.6	10.3	10.0	8.1	7.3
Exports	3,311	3,360	3,532	4,603	6,159	6,899
Imports	4,080	4,148	4,621	6,183	7,850	8,716
Trade balance	−768	−789	−1,089	−1,580	−1,691	−1,817
Current account balance	−294	−339	−717	−1,199	−1,201	−1,198
Current account balance (%GDP)	−5.4	−5.7	−10.2	−13.2	−11.0	−9.7
Foreign debt (%GDP)	54.7	55.7	60.2	70.5	69.8	69.4
Debt service (%Exports)	6.5	7.5	9.1	10.7	10.2	10.4
Foreign exchange reserves (in months of imports)	2.1	1.7	1.9	2.0	1.7	1.6

e = estimate, f = forecast

■ **Means of entry**

Estonia's programme to develop a market economy is founded on an ultra-liberal trade policy. The country joined the EU on 1 May 2004. Until 2000, there were no import duties. Since 1 July 2002, Estonia has applied the EU's common external tariff on non-EU goods. Trade with EU countries is exempt from customs duties. Excise duties are levied on certain products without any distinction between domestic and imported goods. Estonia administers a system of non-tariff barriers based on automatic licensing for some products (wines and spirits, lubricants, medicines). The same licensing rules apply to domestically produced goods. There are no ceilings.

The country's standards legislation does not contain any restrictions of note that might serve to protect local industry. Although down payments are advisable for initial business transactions, 30- or 60-day credit is the most widely used method of payment. Credit cover is advisable. The Estonian banking industry is perfectly sound. The two leading banks are owned by Swedish banks and account for 85 per cent of the country's banking assets.

■ **Attitude towards foreign investors**

Since September 1991, Estonia has had a foreign investment law that provides for simple and non-discriminatory company registration procedures. A foreign company may hold a 100 per cent stake in a local company. There is no special incentive scheme and foreigners are accorded the same treatment as nationals in matters of direct taxation. There are no restrictions on the repatriation of profits after tax, dividends or proceeds from the sale or liquidation of an investment. Estonia has signed a mutual investment promotion and protection agreement as well as a dual taxation agreement with France, both of which are in force. Income tax and corporation tax are levied at a flat rate of 26 per cent. Plans are under way to gradually cut this to 20 per cent. Retained earnings have been exempt from tax since 1 January 2000.

One of the country's assets for foreign investors is its highly qualified yet cheap labour. Social security contributions, borne entirely by employers, amount to 33 per cent of wages, including 13 per cent for health insurance and 20 per cent for pensions. An unemployment contribution – 0.5 per cent of an employee's wage borne by the employer and 1 per cent by the employee – was introduced on 1 January 2002. A pension fund, the second pillar of the country's pension system, was launched on 1 April 2002.

■ **Foreign exchange regulations**

With a parity of 8 kroon to the deutschmark that has remained unchanged since its launch in June 1992, the Estonian kroon is freely convertible and consequently enjoys *de facto* parity with the euro (1 euro = 15.64664 kroon). Estonia has abolished exchange controls and local banks accept accounts in both local and foreign currency. Estonia joined

ERM-II in June 2004 – the last stage before the adoption of the euro, which will take place, in all likelihood, on 1 January 2007.

OPPORTUNITY SCOPE

Breakdown of domestic demand (%GDP + imports)

- Private consumption 30
- Public consumption 10
- Investment 16

Exports: 84% of GDP | Imports: 94% of GDP

MAIN DESTINATIONS OF EXPORTS

Mn USD

Finland Sweden Russia Latvia UK

MAIN ORIGINS OF IMPORTS

Mn USD

Finland Russia Germany Sweden Italy

EXPORTS by products
- All food items 12%
- Agricultural raw materials 9%
- Fuels 5%
- Chemical products 5%
- Other manufactured goods 39%
- Capital goods and transport equipment 28%
- Miscellaneous 2%

IMPORTS by products
- All food items 12%
- Fuels 7%
- Chemical products 9%
- Other manufactured goods 29%
- Capital goods and transport equipment 38%
- Miscellaneous 5%

STANDARD OF LIVING / PURCHASING POWER

Indicators	Estonia	Regional average	DC average
GNP per capita (PPP dollars)	11630	8313	4601
GNP per capita (USD)	4190	2535	1840
Human Development Index	0.853	0.805	0.684
Wealthiest 10% share of national income	28.5	30	32
Urban population percentage	69	68	45
Percentage under 15 years old	17	17	30
Number of telephones per 1000 inhabitants	351	257	120
Number of computers per 1000 inhabitants	210	84	37

Finland

Population (million inhabitants)	5.2
GDP (US$ million)	160,800
GDP per capita (US$)	30,900

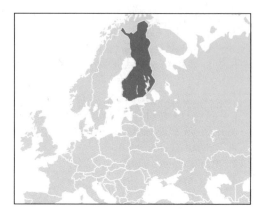

Coface analysis   Short-term: **A1**

RISK ASSESSMENT

Growth accelerated in 2004. Investment recovered after several years of contraction, buoyed by improved company earnings. Exports grew moderately despite Nokia's poor sales performance. Only household consumption slowed with its growth nonetheless remaining above the European country average.

In 2005, economic activity should consolidate. Household demand and housing investment will benefit from new tax breaks facilitated by sound public finances, still-low interest rate levels and the wage increases expected with the renewal of the national biennial agreement on wages scheduled for February 2005. Exports should register a more significant recovery provided Nokia continues to restore its market share in mobile telephony handsets and euro appreciation does not excessively affect paper product sales.

Finnish companies withstood the 2003 economic slowdown relatively well, thanks notably to their solid financial situation. Based on continued strong growth, payment incident frequency should remain far below the world and European averages in 2005.

MAIN ECONOMIC INDICATORS

%	2000	2001	2002	2003	2004[(e)]	2005[(f)]
Economic growth	5.4	1.0	2.3	2.1	2.9	2.9
Consumer (var.)	3.2	1.7	1.7	4.5	2.8	2.8
Investment (var.)	6.8	9.7	−7.1	−7.6	2.7	3.0
Inflation	3.0	2.7	2.0	1.3	0.5	1.1
Unemployment rate	9.8	9.1	9.1	9.1	8.9	8.5
Short-term interest rate	4.4	4.3	3.3	2.3	2.0	2.2
Public sector balance (%GDP)	7.1	5.2	4.2	2.6	2.3	2.1
Public sector debt (%GDP)	53.5	51.8	50.8	51.5	51.0	51.0
Exports (var.)	19.4	−0.8	5.2	1.2	3.2	4.1
Imports (var.)	16.3	0.6	1.7	3.0	1.7	2.1
Current account balance (%GDP)	7.4	7.2	7.6	4.1	4.3	4.3

e = estimate, f = forecast

PAYMENT AND COLLECTION PRACTICES

■ Payment

Bills of exchange are not commonly used in Finland because, as in Germany, they signal the supplier's distrust of the buyer. A bill of exchange primarily substantiates a claim and constitutes a valid acknowledgment of debt.

Cheques, also little used in domestic and international transactions, only constitute acknowledgement of debt. However, cheques that are uncovered at the time of issue can result in the issuers being liable to criminal penalties. Moreover, as cheque collection takes a particularly long time in Finland (20 days for domestic cheques or those drawn in European and Mediterranean coastal countries, 70 days for cheques issued outside Europe), that payment method is not recommended.

Conversely, SWIFT bank transfers are increasingly used to settle commercial transactions. Finns are familiar with this efficient method of payment. When using this instrument, sellers are advised to provide full and accurate bank details to facilitate timely payment, which, it should not be forgotten, is ultimately dependent on the buyer's good faith.

DEBT COLLECTION

Out-of-court collection begins with the debtor being sent a final demand for payment by registered or ordinary mail in which he or she is asked to pay the outstanding principal together with any contractually agreed interest.

In the absence of an interest rate clause in the agreement, interest automatically accrues from the due date of the unpaid invoice at a rate equal to the Central Bank of Finland's (Suomen Pankki) six-monthly rate, calculated by reference to the European Central Bank's refinancing rate, plus seven basis points (Interest Act Amendment, effective since 1 July 2002).

The Interest Act (Korkolaki) of 20 August 1982 already required debtors to pay up within contractually agreed timeframes or become liable to interest penalties.

For documented and undisputed claims, creditors may resort to the fast-track procedure resulting in an injunction to pay (suppea

haastehakemus). This is a simple written procedure based on submission of whatever documents substantiate the claim (invoice, bill of exchange, acknowledgement of debt, etc). Creditors do not need a lawyer to initiate such an action.

The reform of civil procedure, enacted on 1 December 1993, requires plaintiffs to submit all supporting documents and evidence substantiating a claim before the debtor is asked to provide, in response, a written statement explaining his or her position.

During the preliminary hearing, the court bases its deliberations on the parties' written submissions and supporting case documents. Thereafter, the litigant's arguments are heard.

Where the dispute remains unresolved after this preliminary hearing, plenary proceedings are held before the court of first instance (Käräjäoikeus) comprising one to three presiding judges depending on the case's complexity. During this hearing, the judges examine the documentary evidence and hear the parties' witnesses before rapidly delivering their verdict. The average timeframe for obtaining a writ of execution is ten months.

Commercial cases are generally heard by civil courts, although a 'Market and Competition Court' (Markkinatuomioistuin) located in Helsinki has been in operation as a single entity since 1 March 2002. This court is competent to examine fraudulent business practices, denounce unfair trading, investigate corporate mergers, deliver prohibition orders against such practices and slap fines on offenders.

Note that under contract law, the term of limitation has been reduced to three years since 1 January 2004 and will apply retroactively to contracts already in force.

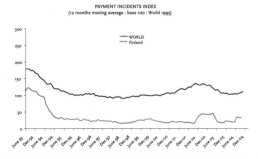

PAYMENT INCIDENTS INDEX
(12 months moving average - base 100 : World 1995)

France

Population (million inhabitants)	62.4
GDP (US$ million)	1,757,500
GDP per capita (US$)	28,600

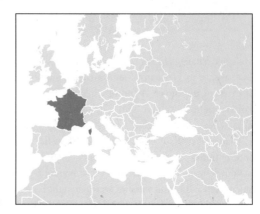

Coface analysis　　　　Short-term: **A1**

STRENGTHS

- The workforce is skilled and work productivity high.
- The quality of transport, water and energy infrastructure is good.
- Energy policy has permitted the country to reduce its dependence on oil and limit the impact of high oil prices.
- Reforms have been initiated to bring fiscal and social security-system deficits under control.

WEAKNESSES

- Growth has been insufficient to reduce unemployment, which has been severely affecting consumption and social security-system accounts.
- The need to contain deficits has limited the leeway to stimulate the economy.
- The means devoted to research and innovation have remained insufficient.
- Low demographic growth has been undermining the long-term outlook and keeps constant pressure on pension financing.

RISK ASSESSMENT

A sharp growth recovery marked 2004. The low cost of credit and a wealth effect generated by property prices spurred household consumption in the first half. Company exports and investment recovered; nevertheless, the revival gradually lost some of its impetus during the year.

Economic growth should weaken moderately in 2005. Consumption should remain affected by household fears about employment and the outlook for the social safety net while energy costs could undermine their purchasing power again. Exports could be hit by the euro appreciation versus the US dollar. Equipment renewal needs and the still-favourable outlook in certain domestic markets, such as building and public works, will continue to

spur productive investment. Despite tight fiscal policy, it will nonetheless be difficult to bring the public deficit back to about 5 per cent of GDP, which will leave the government with little leeway for any economic stimulatory measures.

Bankruptcies rose 4 per cent in 2004. Improvement in company cash positions nonetheless permitted very gradual improvement in payment behaviour although a less favourable context in 2005 could slow this development. Certain sectors particularly sensitive to raw material price fluctuations bear watching, notably transportation and plastics technology. With elimination of quotas imminent, the textile situation has remained a source of concern.

MAIN ECONOMIC INDICATORS

%	2000	2001	2002	2003	2004(e)	2005(f)
Economic growth	4.2	2.1	1.1	0.5	2.1	1.8
Consumption (var.)	2.9	2.8	1.8	1.7	2.1	2.0
Investment (var.)	9.7	3.1	−3.7	−1.6	2.9	4.5
Inflation	1.8	1.8	1.9	2.2	2.2	1.9
Unemployment rate	9.4	8.7	9.0	9.7	9.8	9.7
Short-term interest rate	4.4	4.3	3.3	2.3	2.1	2.3
Public sector balance (%GDP)	−1.4	−1.5	−3.3	−4.1	−3.6	−3.1
Public sector debt (%GDP)	66.2	64.9	68.7	71.2	68.2	68.6
Exports (var.)	13.4	1.9	1.7	−2.6	3.4	3.9
Imports (var.)	15.2	1.6	3.3	0.3	7.7	6.7
Current account balance (%GDP)	1.4	1.7	1.0	0.4	−0.2	−0.3

e = estimate, f = forecast

MAIN ECONOMIC SECTORS

Steel

Steel production should increase by only 2 per cent in 2005. Strong world demand should continue to sustain prices, which should permit absorbing high production costs. With delocalized production, the Arcelor group should take advantage of strategically located operations to limit the effects of surging raw material prices and shipping costs and benefit from the more dynamic markets. The 5 per cent production increase in 2004 resulted from strong external demand and dynamic domestic investment in residential building that will persist in 2005. Flat products intended for passenger cars should benefit from moderate demand whereas demand for those intended for heavy goods vehicles and public works equipment should increase.

Chemicals

Excluding pharmaceuticals, chemicals industry growth declined again in 2004 with the situation particularly difficult for plastics technology affected both by surging raw material prices and delocalizations. Pharmaceuticals production, however, rose 7.5 per cent. Conditions in the sector should improve in 2005, buoyed by still-high external demand and strengthening domestic demand. Overall, production should increase by 2 per cent in volume in the sector.

Building and public works

The sector performed exceptionally well in 2004 with building permits increasing 20.8 per cent and new housing construction the highest registered in 20 years. Growth of rental property investments spurred by the Robien Act and development of urban renewal programmes, as well as low interest rates, contributed to that performance. Non-residential building continued to decline but at a more moderate pace thanks to the good financial shape of local communities and the launch of the 'Hospital 2007' programme. In the public works sector, the positive trend has persisted thanks to major transport infrastructure projects and increases in work on roads and motorways. Increased raw material prices have triggered slippage on costs contributing, in part, to building price increases. Despite a slight slowdown in recent months, the sector should grow another 2–2.5 per cent in 2005, driven notably by the growth of new housing and steady civil engineering performance.

Textiles and clothing

Textile and clothing production declined by 10 and 22 per cent respectively in 2004, undermined by a growing household consumption trend towards low-price imported products and by an export decline attributable to the euro appreciation.

Markets in Europe have thinned out with the clothing sector's massive delocalization. Companies in the sector have been finding it increasingly difficult to leverage their creativity in a price-oriented market. Sales of autumn–winter collections have been disappointing with the sector's performance likely to contract again in 2005.

■ Mechanical engineering

In 2004, French mechanical engineering resumed slow growth (up 1.7 per cent in volume), driven mainly by domestic demand. However, export growth was below the 3 per cent rise expected. After the renewed optimism observed in late 2004, prospects for 2005 have generally appeared disappointing with companies still suffering from very large cost increases they cannot pass on in sales prices. Moreover, the euro's strength has increased the pressure on export prices. Increasing numbers of companies have thus been delocalizing their production to low production-cost countries. The light-work materials segment has remained dynamic due to the building boom while precision mechanics has stabilized. However, companies have been concerned by the tendency of most industrialists to revise their projects downward.

■ Car industry

In France, passenger car registrations stagnated in 2004 (down 3 per cent for French brands). The overall market could come to a standstill in 2005. Car manufacturers and parts makers, squeezed between rising production costs and a stagnant market, have been banking on variety and growth differentials between their various industrial facilities. Some improvement is expected but not before autumn.

PAYMENT AND COLLECTION PRACTICES

■ Payment

Albeit with stiff competition from bank cards, the cheque has essentially remained the most widely used payment instrument in France, representing 31 per cent of payment operations, or nearly half the volume handled by payment systems in value terms.[1] For cheques remaining unpaid over 30 days from the date they were first presented for payment, the beneficiary may immediately obtain an enforcement order (without need of further procedural act or cost) based on a certificate of non-payment provided by his or her banker after a second unsuccessful presentation of the cheque for payment and where the debtor has not provided proof of payment within 15 days of formal notice to pay served by a bailiff (article L 131–73 of the monetary and financial code).

Bills of exchange, a much less frequently used mode of payment than cheques, have been in virtually constant decline although total volume have remained steady in value terms year on year. Bills of exchange are attractive for companies insofar as they may be discounted or transferred, thus providing a valuable source of short-term financing. Moreover, they allow creditors to bring legal recourse in respect of exchange law (*droit cambiaire*) and are particularly suitable for successive instalment payments.

Although lagging behind cheques, the number of bank transfer operations has continued to increase every year, gaining 3 per cent in 2003 and representing 15 per cent of all script payments or 35 per cent of the volume handled by payment systems in value terms.[1]

Bank transfers can be made within France or internationally via the SWIFT network, which offers a reliable platform for timely payment subject to mutual trust and confidence between suppliers and their customers.

■ Debt collection

Since the new economic regulations law of 15 May 2001, commercial debts automatically bear interest from the day after the payment due date shown on the invoice or specified in the commercial contract. Unless the terms and conditions of sale stipulate interest rates and conditions of application, the applicable rate will be the European Central Bank's refinancing rate, increased by seven percentage points. Formal notice to pay nonetheless

44

[1] Source: Bank of France, report, 2003 financial year.

remains a precondition for creditors to take any legal action.

Where a debt results from a contractual undertaking and is undisputed, creditors may obtain an injunction to pay (*injonction de payer*). This relatively straightforward system does not require creditors to argue their case before the appropriate commercial court (the court having jurisdiction in the district where the debtor's registered offices are located) and enables them to rapidly obtain a court order to be served thereafter by a bailiff.

A summary procedure (*référé-provision*) offers a rapid and effective means of debt collection, even in routine cases, provided the claims are not subject to dispute. However, the presence of an attorney is required at the proceedings to represent the creditor in court.

If a claim proves to be litigious, the judge competent to rule on special urgency (*juge des référés*) evaluates whether the claim is well founded.

As appropriate, the judge may then declare him- or herself incompetent and invite the plaintiff to seek a ruling on the substance of the case through the formal court process.

Formal procedures of this kind permit having the validity of a claim recognized by the court, a relatively lengthy process lasting about a year or more owing to the emphasis placed on the adversarial nature of proceedings and the numerous phases involved in the French procedural system: submission of supporting case documents, written submissions by the litigants, examination of the types of evidence, various recesses for deliberations, etc.

If justified by a claim's size and the uncertain solvency of the debtor, legal action may include a petition to obtain an attachment order on available assets and thereby protect the plaintiff's interests pending completion of the proceedings and enforcement of the court's final verdict.

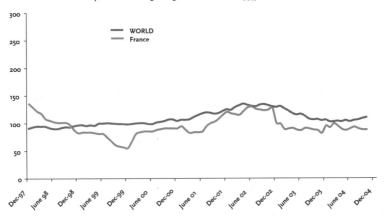

PAYMENT INCIDENTS INDEX
(12 months moving average - base 100 : World 1995)

Georgia

Population (million inhabitants)	5.2
GDP (US$ million)	3,396
GDP per capita (US$)	653

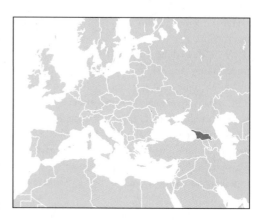

Short-term: **D**

Medium-term:
Very high risk

Coface analysis

RISK ASSESSMENT

The March 2004 legislative elections consolidated the power of the new president, Mikhail Saakachvili, swept into office in January 2004. The new administration has nonetheless been contending with a difficult political legacy. Domestically, the government and institutions have been sorely weakened. Despite a reassertion of authority over Adjara, Georgia's territorial integrity is still in jeopardy with Abkhazia and South Ossetia remaining *de facto* autonomous republics.

Internationally, the new president has sought closer relations with the EU and United States while remaining intent on improving relations with Russia. There have nonetheless been recurring tensions with Moscow, which has maintained a military presence in the country and is supporting Abkhazia's and South Ossetia's aspirations for independence. An unspoken rivalry between Washington and Moscow (with US military advisors present in Georgia) to gain influence in the Caucasus region has stoked the country's recurrent instability.

Economically, the robust growth has largely represented a catch-up phase after several years of economic decay buoyed, moreover, by construction of oil and gas pipelines extending from Azerbaijan to Turkey. However, the economy has shown little diversification with its base of companies too concentrated. Moreover, the grey market is reportedly among the largest in the CIS. Financially, the country has enjoyed IMF backing and signed a rescheduling agreement with Paris Club creditors in July 2004. In any case, the financial situation should remain very dependent on multilateral organizations.

MAIN ECONOMIC INDICATORS

US$ millions	2000	2001	2002	2003	2004[(e)]	2005[(f)]
Economic growth (%)	1.9	4.7	5.5	8.6	10.0	12.0
Inflation (%)	4.0	4.7	5.6	4.8	5.0	5.6
Public sector balance (%GDP)	−4.0	−2.0	−2.0	−2.5	−1.6	−0.6
Exports	584	473	553	650	691	740
Imports	982	959	992	1,265	1,461	1,535
Trade balance	−398	−486	−439	−615	−770	−795
Current account balance (%GDP)	−4.4	−6.5	−6.0	−9.9	−13.0	−12.5
Foreign debt (%GDP)	52.0	53.5	54.8	47.1	46.5	46.9
Debt service (%Exports)	14.4	15.4	17.8	13.5	14.3	14.3
Foreign exchange reserves (in months of imports)	0.9	1.4	1.6	1.3	1.2	1.4

e = estimate, f = forecast

Germany

Population (million inhabitants) 82.5
GDP (US$ million) 2,401,900
GDP per capita (US$) 29,100

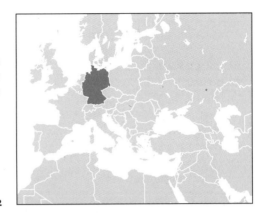

Coface analysis   Short-term: **A2**

STRENGTHS

- The German economy has benefited from the admission of Central and Eastern European countries to the EU.
- Industrial exports have remained competitive, contributing to formation of a substantial current account surplus.
- Extensive unionization and company 'codetermination' have fostered social cohesion (although sometimes resulting in slow decision making).
- The compromise reached by the government and opposition should permit pursuing the Agenda–2010 reforms intended to increase labour market flexibility and restore the social security system's financial equilibrium.

WEAKNESSES

- Aging demographics have been a drag on growth and constitute a challenge for the social safety net.
- The gap between West and East has persisted.
- The public sector has been running large structural deficits.
- A still insufficiently profitable banking sector could increase the cost and selectivity of credit, particularly for smaller businesses.
- The construction and public works sector has continued to suffer for the excesses that followed reunification and from reductions in public investment spending.

RISK ASSESSMENT

An already moderate recovery began weakening in the 2004 third quarter with the robust industrial export growth, on which the economic upturn has been completely dependent, unable to sustain itself amid slowing external demand. Growth will continue at a slow pace in 2005. Although remaining the principal economic driver, exports should grow more slowly due to stabilization of world demand and the negative impact of the euro appreciation. Industrial machinery and equipment investment should finally begin recovering due to progressive saturation of production capacities in export sectors. Conversely, public sector deficits should continue to impede public investment spending; the high vacancy rate in office space is depressing commercial construction. Household spending should finally show some life thanks to an improving employment picture and pent-up demand for durable goods.

Prudence will nonetheless still be in order amid still-high unemployment, uncertainty about future prospects for the social safety net, and the increasing number of agreements between unions and employers calling for wage moderation in exchange for job security. Tax cuts should thus inflate savings and not make wiping out the public sector deficit any easier. Reducing that deficit will require a freeze on spending and civil service remuneration, reduction of subsidies to public

MAIN ECONOMIC INDICATORS

%	2000	2001	2002	2003	2004[e]	2005[f]
Economic growth	3.1	1.0	0.1	−0.1	1.6	1.3
Consumption (var.)	2.2	1.8	−0.7	0.0	−0.7	0.7
Investment (var.)	7.7	−3.3	−7.2	−0.6	−0.4	2.5
Inflation	1.4	1.9	1.3	1.0	1.7	1.5
Unemployment rate	7.3	7.4	8.2	9.1	10.5	10.5
Short-term interest rate	4.4	4.3	3.3	2.3	2.0	2.2
Public sector balance (% GDP)	1.3	−2.8	−3.5	−3.8	−3.8	−3.4
Public sector debt (% GDP)	60.9	60.5	62.8	65.3	66.5	67.5
Exports (var.)	14.2	6.1	4.1	1.8	8.5	5.5
Imports (var.)	11.1	1.4	−1.6	3.9	6.5	5.1
Current account balance (% GDP)	−1.4	0.1	2.1	2.3	3.4	3.3

e = estimate, f = forecast

institutions and securitization of pension claims on the post office and Deutsche Telekom.

The Coface payment incident index has been ebbing to the level before the black 2001–2003 period. Company bankruptcies stabilized in 2004. That attests to the improved financial situation of companies whose margins have recovered due to productivity gains resulting notably from delocalization of the most labour intensive activities and from wage moderation. The improvement has concerned mainly companies with an export focus or production facilities abroad and, very marginally, the construction, public works, wood and distribution sectors due to their domestic focus.

MAIN ECONOMIC SECTORS

■ Computers
In 2004, demand notably increased for computers and servers due to, among other reasons, the recovery of long-postponed business investment. However, the digital-consumer and software product markets have benefited from the highest growth potential. For the entire sector, growth should again be moderate in 2005. The distribution network has been subject to major upheavals with many mergers and acquisitions and the ascendancy of average-size diversified distributors, notably diversified towards accessories and components, which derive their strength from rapid stock turnover and proximity to customers.

■ Construction
Investment in construction suffered a 3 per cent decline in 2004 affecting at once residential, commercial and public construction. The causes include the prudence of households, persistence of a housing surplus in eastern regions, extensive vacant office space in large cities and the poor shape of public sector finances. In 2005, business activity should only shed about 1 per cent. With commercial (office and commercial space) and institutional construction continuing to decline, housing construction will stabilize – doubtless in connection with the scheduled end of the public aid programme.

■ Printing and paper
The printing situation improved after four sluggish years with prices stabilizing and the players generally envisaging 2005 with optimism. Paper production increased in 2004 thanks essentially to higher foreign demand. Nonetheless, the increased tonnage did not result in a corresponding increase in sales with substantial overcapacity dragging prices down. The expected improvement in the graphics industry should benefit papermakers.

1

Distribution

The sector has remained confronted with stagnating household consumption. Food-product distribution has suffered relatively less than other segments like textiles or furniture. Hard discount has continued to exert great pressure, notably on traditional department stores. The market should evolve towards increased concentration and internationalization of major players.

Car industry

Weak European demand and stiff international competition, notably Asian, have not been the sole causes of the pressure on German carmakers. Increased raw material costs (metal, plastic) have severely squeezed margins to such an extent that drastic cost-cutting measures will be inevitable.

PAYMENT AND COLLECTION PRACTICES

Payment

Standard payment instruments such as bills of exchange and cheques are not used very widely in Germany. For Germans, a bill of exchange implies a precarious financial position or distrust on the part of the supplier.

Cheques are not considered a payment as such but a 'payment attempt'. As German law ignores the principle of covered cheques, the issuer can cancel payment at any time and on any ground. Bounced cheques are therefore fairly common.

Bills of exchange and cheques clearly do not seem to be effective payment instruments even though they entitle creditors to access a fast-track procedure for debt collection.

Bank transfer (*Überweisung*), by contrast, remains the prevalent means of payment. Leading German banks are connected to the SWIFT network, which enables them to provide a quick and efficient funds transfer service.

Debt collection

The recovery process begins with the debtor being sent a final demand for payment, via ordinary or registered mail, reminding the debtor of his or her obligations. The law on 'speedier matured debts', in force since 1 May 2000, states that, where the due date is not specified in the conditions of sale, the customer is deemed to be in default if he or she does not pay up within 30 days of receipt of the invoice or a demand for payment, and is liable to interest penalties thereafter.

From 1 January 2002, the benchmark default interest rate is the Bundesbank's six-monthly base rate, calculated by reference to the European Central Bank's refinancing rate, plus eight percentage points for retailers or commercial companies and five percentage points for consumers (non-commercial).

If payment or an out-of-court settlement is not forthcoming despite this approach, the creditor must initiate court proceedings. If the claim is not disputed, the creditor can seek an injunction to pay (*Mahnbescheid*) through a simplified and inexpensive procedure involving the use of pre-printed forms and resulting in a writ of execution fairly quickly. Foreign creditors must file their claim with the Schöneberg court in Berlin, which, after examining the claim, may deliver an injunction to pay. The debtor is given two weeks to pay up or challenge the ruling.

Ordinary legal proceedings tend to be oral, with the judge reaching a decision on the arguments presented by both parties present in court. If the case is contested, the judge hears the litigants or their lawyers and asks them to submit any evidence deemed relevant by the judge, which the judge alone is then authorized to assess. The adverse parties are requested also to submit a pleading memorandum outlining their claims within the specified time limit.

Once the claim has been properly examined, a public hearing is held at which the court hands down a well-founded judgment.

The reform of civil procedure, enacted on 1 January 2002, is designed to give all German citizens quick and effective access to law. The new measures encourage parties to attempt conciliation before resorting to legal action and give the district courts (*Amtsgerichte*) stronger powers. They also require the majority of cases to be settled in first instance, either through an out-of-court settlement or through a court decision. The appeal court's role is limited to verifying whether a case involves a question of principle or necessitates revision of the law in order to ensure 'consistent jurisprudence'.

PAYMENT INCIDENTS INDEX
(12 months moving average - base 100 : World 1995)

Greece

Population (million inhabitants)	11
GDP (US$ million)	172,700
GDP per capita (US$)	15,700

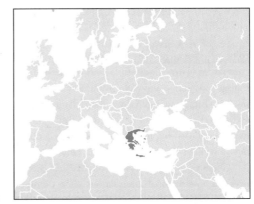

Coface analysis   Short-term: **A2**

RISK ASSESSMENT

After a very dynamic period, the domestic demand slowdown registered since the 2004 second half should persist in 2005. Investment, notably in a construction sector stimulated by preparations for the Olympic Games and low interest rates, is no longer able to play a locomotive role in the economy. The Olympics have nonetheless spurred capital-equipment and infrastructure modernization, which should bolster company competitiveness. Consumption should remain firm (up 3 per cent), although below the dynamism registered in 2004, buoyed by tax cuts and higher real wages. Public sector finances still constitute the main weakness. With the Games having cost 7 billion euros instead of the expected 4.6 billion euros, foreign debt has continued to rise and the public deficit has been increasing dangerously (exceeding 5 per cent of

GDP in 2004 with 3.5 per cent likely in 2005). Containing the phenomenon will necessitate major fiscal adjustments and implementation of measures to reduce public spending while financing the priority reforms programmed by the government in health and education. Although interest rates will rise, they will not exceed 4 per cent and inflation will remain above the European average.

In that context, special attention should be paid to how company financial health evolves, notably in the tourism sector, with the disappearance of several factors linked to the Games and after a disappointing 2004 season. Weaknesses have also persisted in some sectors like clothing, textiles and wood, as well as fruit and vegetables. Although the Coface payment incident index has remained well below the world average, the situation could worsen in 2005.

MAIN ECONOMIC INDICATORS

%	2000	2001	2002	2003	2004(e)	2005(f)
Economic growth	4.5	4.3	3.6	4.5	3.8	3.0
Consumption (var.)	2.2	2.8	3.1	4.2	3.8	3.0
Investment (var.)	9.4	8.5	6.2	16.2	7.0	5.0
Inflation	2.9	3.7	3.9	3.4	3.2	3.1
Unemployment rate	11.2	10.5	10.2	9.5	8.9	8.8
Short-term interest rate	4.4	4.3	3.3	2.3	2.1	2.2
Public sector balance (% GDP)	−4.1	−3.7	−3.7	−4.6	−5.3	−3.5
Public sector debt (% GDP)	114.0	114.7	112.5	109.0	112.0	109.5
Exports (var.)	14.1	−1.0	−7.7	1.0	5.9	6.9
Imports (var.)	15.1	−5.2	−2.9	4.8	7.3	5.9
Current account balance (% GDP)	−8.7	−9.7	−7.6	−6.5	−6.2	−5.8

e = estimate, f = forecast

PAYMENT AND COLLECTION PRACTICES

■ PAYMENT

Bills of exchange are widely used by Greek companies in domestic and international transactions and, along with promissory notes, have not been subject to stamp duty since 1 January 2002. In the event of payment default, a protest certifying the dishonoured bill must be drawn up by a public notary within two working days of the due date.

Cheques, on the other hand, are less widely used in international transactions. For domestic transactions, the practice is to use cheques as a credit rather than payment instrument. Post-dated cheques endorsed by several creditors are fairly common. Furthermore, issuers of dishonoured cheques may be liable to prosecution if a complaint is lodged.

Promissory letters (*hyposhetiki epistoli*) are another means of payment widely used by Greek companies in international transactions. They are a written acknowledgement of an obligation to pay issued to the creditor by the customer's bank committing the maker to pay the creditor at a contractually fixed date. Although promissory letters are a sufficiently effective instrument in that they constitute a clear acknowledgement of debt on the part of the buyer, they are not deemed a bill of exchange and so fall outside the scope of the exchange law (*droit cambiare*).

SWIFT bank transfers are used to settle a growing proportion of transactions and offer a quick and secure method of payment.

■ Debt collection

The recovery process commences with the debtor being sent a final demand for payment by registered mail reminding the debtor of his or her payment obligations, including any interest penalties that may have been contractually agreed or, failing this, those accruing at the legal rate of interest.

Under a presidential decree passed on 5 June 2003, interest is due from the day following the date of payment fixed in the commercial agreement at a rate, unless the parties agree otherwise, equal to the European Central Bank's refinancing rate plus seven basis points.

Creditors may seek an injunction to pay (*diataghi pliromis*) from the court via a lawyer under a fast-track procedure that generally takes one month from the date of lodging of the petition and, for undisputed claims, results in immediate enforcement of the court order, which generally does not have suspensive effect. To do so, creditors must submit documentary evidence equivalent to an acknowledgement of debt by the customer or a bill of exchange, such as an accepted and protested bill, an unpaid promissory note or an unpaid promissory letter, an acknowledgement of debt established by private deed, or an original invoice featuring the goods sold as well as the buyer's signature certifying receipt of delivery.

Based on competence thresholds in effect since 1 October 2003, a justice of the peace (*Eirinodikeio*) hears claims up to 12,000 euros. Above that amount, a court of first instance presided by a single judge (*Monomeles Protodikeio*) hears claims not exceeding 80,000 euros. A panel of three judges (*Polymeles Protodikeio*) is set up to hear larger claims.

Where creditors do not have a written acknowledgement signed by the debtor, or where the claim is disputed, the only remaining alternative is to obtain a summons under ordinary proceedings. Such litigation generally takes over a year, or even two years, depending on the backlog of cases in each jurisdiction, the complexity of the action and whether it requires extensive evidence – such as examination of all the documents related to a commercial transaction – and obligatory witness testimonies.

PAYMENT INCIDENTS INDEX
(12 months moving average - base 100 : World 1995)

Hungary

Population (million inhabitants)	10
GDP (US$ million)	65,843

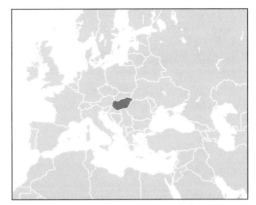

Coface analysis

Short-term: **A2**

Medium-term:
Low risk

STRENGTHS

- Hungary is one of Central Europe's most advanced countries on reforms.
- Its financial system is among the region's most developed.
- The country's admission to the EU has bolstered its political and economic stability with the new objective being adoption of the euro by 2010.
- Its very high quality labour force has helped attract foreign investors.
- Hungary is well positioned geographically in the centre of Europe.

WEAKNESSES

- Opening the country's economy has made it dependent on the economic fortunes of its main EU trading partners.
- Its fiscal deficit has remained high with the public sector debt burden increasing.
- External accounts have been suffering from structural imbalances due notably to the restructuring process.
- Doubts prompted by the high level of the 'twin deficits' (fiscal and current account) along with relatively high foreign debt have constituted a constraint.

RISK ASSESSMENT

After an upturn in 2004, spurred by a sharp investment recovery and increased exports, economic activity should continue at a sustained pace in 2005 buoyed by domestic demand stimulated in a pre-electoral context. The country has nonetheless continued to run substantial internal and external imbalances. Fiscal slippage and growing public sector debt have called into question the validity of the medium-term convergence programme the government submitted to the EU. Efforts on fiscal adjustment will have to continue to permit joining the euro zone by 2010. Meanwhile, persistent external deficits have generated higher financing needs with the country's capacity to cover those needs nonetheless improving slightly due to an FDI upturn. Although its increasing debt service obligations have not given cause for concern, the country's insufficient currency reserves would limit its capacity to withstand a liquidity crisis. However, in the run-up to legislative elections in 2006, the new government (in office since October 2004) may tend to give priority to its political objectives over deficit reduction or reform implementation.

The Coface payment incident index has remained below the world average. The chemical, wood, consumer electronics and household appliance sectors have continued to perform well with agriculture, construction, textiles and paper contending with a difficult situation.

MAIN ECONOMIC INDICATORS

US$ billions	2000	2001	2002	2003	2004(e)	2005(f)
Economic growth (%)	5.2	3.8	3.5	2.9	4.1	4.3
Inflation (%)	9.8	9.1	5.3	4.7	6.9	4.6
Public sector balance (%GDP)	−3.0	−4.4	−9.2	−6.2	−5.5	−5.1
Unemployment rate (%)	6.4	5.7	5.8	5.9	n/a	n/a
Exports	28.8	31.0	34.7	43.3	53.3	60.5
Imports	31.8	33.3	36.8	46.6	56.9	64.4
Trade balance	−2.9	−2.2	−2.1	−3.3	−3.6	−3.9
Current account balance	−3.8	−2.9	−4.4	−7.5	−8.6	−8.9
Current account balance (%GDP)	−8.1	−5.6	−6.8	−9.0	−8.7	−8.4
Foreign debt (%GDP)	65.0	63.7	62.0	67.1	62.2	62.6
Debt service (%Exports)	15.2	13.8	13.3	14.4	12.2	14.7
Foreign exchange reserves (in months of imports)	3.4	3.0	2.6	2.5	2.1	1.9

e = estimate, f = forecast

CONDITIONS OF ACCESS TO THE MARKET

■ Means of entry

With EU membership, the last tariff peaks (foodstuffs) have been abolished. Nevertheless, some non-tariff barriers survive here and there in the form of licensing procedures (cattle breeding). Consumer goods are subject to few barriers since rules were harmonized. However, exporters should note that there is a fairly expensive and lengthy registration procedure for cosmetics. Public procurement procedures at times lack transparency. However, a new EU-compliant public procurement law was passed on 1 May 2004.

■ Attitude towards foreign investors

Investment in Hungary is unrestricted, regardless of source of funding and size of foreign shareholding. The system of tax incentives was revised in 2002 to bring it into line with EU competition and public subsidies law. The new system of investment assistance is based on three types of incentive: tax exemption, new direct grants and investment-friendly administrative procedures. The decline in FDI since 2003 has led the new Gyurcsany government to rethink the system of incentives for foreign investment in line with community rules. Restrictions on the acquisition of secondary residences by EU nationals and EU-incorporated firms are to be lifted no later than May 2009. Hungary has also obtained a transition period until May 2011 to relax its ban on foreign acquisition of farmland and forests. While the arrangements of this transition, in theory, allow EU farmers to purchase land for their activity in Hungary under certain conditions, in practice they make it difficult to acquire farmland.

■ Foreign exchange regulations

Since the widening of the forint's fluctuation band to +/−15 per cent in May 2001, the Hungarian currency has fluctuated, rising until January 2003 but falling in June and again in December 2003. Due to the interest rate policy pursued by the central bank, the forint is and has for several months been at its highest level in the fluctuation band (1 euro = 244 forints at mid-November 2004).

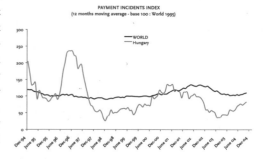

PAYMENT INCIDENTS INDEX
(12 months moving average - base 100 : World 1995)

PAYMENT AND COLLECTION PRACTICES

■ Payment

Bills of exchange and cheques are not commonly used as their validity depends on compliance with several formal issuing requirements. For dishonoured and protested bills and cheques, creditors nonetheless have recourse to a summary procedure to obtain an injunction to pay.

The promissory note *in blanco* (*üres átruházás*), which involves an incomplete payment deed when issued, and a complement of missing elements upon cashing, is much less common than in Poland.

Bank transfers are by far the most common payment method. After successive phases of privatization and concentration, the main Hungarian banks are now connected to the SWIFT network, which provides low-cost, flexible and speedy processing of domestic and international payments.

■ Debt collection

It is advisable, where possible, to avoid taking legal action locally due to the formalism and high cost of legal procedures and lengthy court proceedings: it takes almost two years to obtain a writ of execution due to the lack of judges with adequate training in market economy practices and proper equipment. Service of a demand for payment accompanied by proof of debt reminds the debtor of his or her obligation to pay the outstanding sum plus any accrued interest.

Since 1 May 2004, interest is due from the day after the payment date stipulated in the commercial contract and, unless otherwise agreed by the parties, the applicable rate will be the National Bank of Hungary's (Magyar Nemzeti Bank) base rate plus seven basis points.

It is advisable to seek an amicable settlement based on a payment schedule drawn up by a public notary, which includes an 'enforcement clause' that allows creditors, in case of default by the debtor, to go directly to the enforcement stage, subject to acknowledgement by the court of that document's binding nature.

With positive proof of debt (acknowledgement of debt, unpaid bill of exchange, dishonoured cheque, etc), creditors may obtain an injunction to pay (*fizetézi meghagyás*) via a summary procedure nonetheless as costly as ordinary proceedings. The summary procedure permits the judge – if he or she considers the petition justified – to grant an injunction without hearing the defendant, enjoining him or her to pay the principal and legal costs within 15 days of service of the ruling (or within three days for an unpaid bill of exchange).

Ordinary proceedings are partly in writing, with the parties filing submissions accompanied by all supporting case documents (original or certified copies), and partly oral, with the litigants and their witnesses heard on the main hearing date.

At any stage of such proceedings and where possible, the judge may attempt conciliation between the parties. It is relatively common practice to issue a winding-up petition against the debtor immediately to prompt a speedier reaction or payment.

Commercial disputes are heard either by local courts (*Helyi Bíróság*), acting in a commercial capacity, or by regional courts (*Megyei Bíróság*),) depending on the size of the claim.

OPPORTUNITY SCOPE

Breakdown of domestic demand (%GDP + imports)
- ■ Private consumption   40
- ■ Public consumption   7
- ■ Investment   14

Exports: 64% of GDP   Imports: 67% of GDP

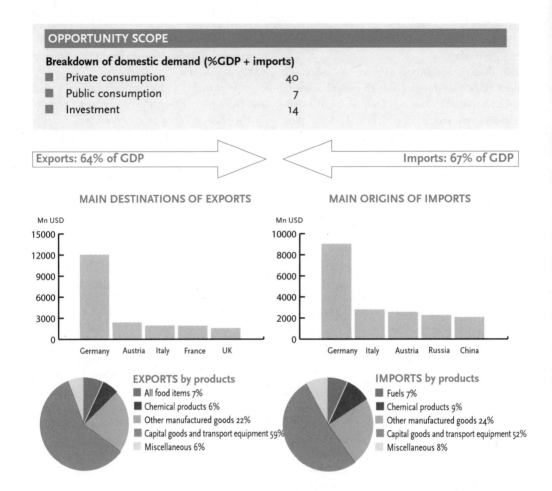

MAIN DESTINATIONS OF EXPORTS

Mn USD

Germany, Austria, Italy, France, UK

MAIN ORIGINS OF IMPORTS

Mn USD

Germany, Italy, Austria, Russia, China

EXPORTS by products
- ■ All food items 7%
- ■ Chemical products 6%
- ■ Other manufactured goods 22%
- ■ Capital goods and transport equipment 59%
- ■ Miscellaneous 6%

IMPORTS by products
- ■ Fuels 7%
- ■ Chemical products 9%
- ■ Other manufactured goods 24%
- ■ Capital goods and transport equipment 52%
- ■ Miscellaneous 8%

STANDARD OF LIVING / PURCHASING POWER

Indicators	Hungary	Regional average	DC average
GNP per capita (PPP dollars)	13070	8313	4601
GNP per capita (USD)	5290	2535	1840
Human Development Index	0.848	0.805	0.684
Wealthiest 10% share of national income	22.8	30	32
Urban population percentage	65	68	45
Percentage under 15 years old	17	17	30
Number of telephones per 1000 inhabitants	361	257	120
Number of computers per 1000 inhabitants	108	84	37

Iceland

Population (inhabitants)	289,000
GDP (US$ million)	10,600
GDP per capita (US$)	36,500

Coface analysis Short-term: **A1**

RISK ASSESSMENT

The economy continued to expand in 2004, fuelled by robust consumption, tourism development and investment in the aluminium and hydroelectricity sectors. Housing construction, stimulated by favourable financing terms, also reached record levels.

Growth will remain strong in 2005, still driven by buoyant domestic demand. Declining unemployment, a wealth effect linked to the continued rise of housing prices, and tax reductions will again spur household spending. Still-favourable real interest rates and the recent mortgage-market liberalization will buoy housing investment. However, the current account deficit should widen further with imports of consumer and capital goods still growing strongly and sea products, aluminium and ferrosilicon exports maintaining a moderate upward trend resulting from rising prices and decelerating world demand. Amid accommodating fiscal policy, it will be up to the central bank to check overheating by tightening monetary policy.

The current economic upturn has benefited companies notably in the fishing and marine products sector despite higher fuel prices. Their earnings have been improving with their debt denominated in foreign currency easing thanks to continued low interest rates and the Icelandic kronur's appreciation.

MAIN ECONOMIC INDICATORS

%	2000	2001	2002	2003	2004(e)	2005(f)
Economic growth	5.7	2.2	−0.5	4.1	5.5	5.9
Consumption (var.)	4.0	−3.8	−1.0	6.6	7.0	9.3
Investment (var.)	14.9	−15.1	−22.6	25.9	27.0	29.0
Inflation	5.1	6.4	5.2	2.1	3.2	3.5
Unemployment rate	2.3	2.3	3.3	3.4	3.1	2.6
Short-term interest rate	11.2	11.0	8.0	5.0	6.1	7.8
Public sector balance (% GDP)	2.5	0.3	−0.4	−1.5	0.5	2.1
Public sector debt (% GDP)	41.9	47.4	43.6	41.5	37.5	32.5
Exports (var.)	5.0	7.7	3.6	0.3	7.5	6.7
Imports (var.)	8.0	−9.0	−2.5	9.7	13.0	16.0
Current account balance (% GDP)	−10.1	−4.0	1.1	−4.1	−6.4	−10.9

e = estimate, f = forecast

Ireland

Population (million inhabitants)	4
GDP (US$ million)	152,100
GDP per capita (US$)	38,100

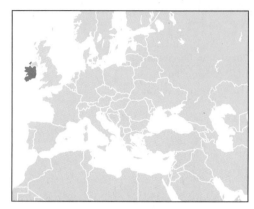

Coface analysis   Short-term: **A1**

RISK ASSESSMENT

Benefiting from a recovery of investment in computer and electronic equipment, notably in the United States and Asia, growth strengthened in 2004. The first beneficiaries were exports, mainly to those regions (20 per cent to the United States alone), and company investment – very dependent on the activity of US multinationals in the high technology sector with local operations.

Economic activity will retain its dynamism in 2005 without, however, matching the double-digit growth rates of the last decade. Barring a sudden downturn in a still-tense property market, household consumption should gain further momentum buoyed by the arrival of new immigrants, employment and income growth, bolstered at once by much lower inflation and the favourable outcome of the autumn 2004 wage negotiations undertaken in

the triennial national wage agreement framework. Exports, mainly comprising high value-added products, will remain dynamic despite now high labour costs and the euro appreciation. The virtual equilibrium of public sector finances resulting from the economic growth and property tax proceeds has permitted gradually remedying public service and infrastructure deficiencies that could otherwise ultimately deter foreign investment.

Although the improved economic conditions resulted in a sharp decline in bankruptcies in 2004, they nonetheless remained commonplace in several sectors including road transport, printing and clothing as well as in construction where buoyant demand resulted in development of overcapacity. In 2005, continued economic dynamism and the low Coface payment incident index augurs well for persistence of that trend.

MAIN ECONOMIC INDICATORS						
%	2000	2001	2002	2003	2004(e)	2005(f)
Economic growth	9.9	6.0	6.1	3.6	4.6	4.9
Consumption (var.)	8.5	5.2	2.6	2.6	3.0	3.8
Investment (var.)	5.3	−7.3	1.3	2.6	5.1	4.4
Inflation	5.3	4.0	4.7	4.0	2.3	2.5
Unemployment rate	4.3	3.9	4.4	4.6	4.4	4.1
Short-term interest rate	4.4	4.3	3.3	2.3	2.0	2.2
Public sector balance (%GDP)	4.4	0.9	−0.2	0.2	−0.3	−0.8
Public sector debt (%GDP)	38.3	36.1	32.4	32.1	31.0	31.0
Exports (var.)	20.4	8.5	5.7	−0.9	6.0	8.0
Imports (var.)	21.3	6.7	3.4	−2.3	5.4	7.9
Current account balance (%GDP)	−0.4	−0.7	−1.3	−1.4	−1.1	−0.4

e = estimate, f = forecast

PAYMENT AND COLLECTION PRACTICES

■ Payment

Bills of exchange are little used in domestic commercial transactions and only occasionally used in international trade. The cheque, defined as 'a bill of exchange drawn on a bank and payable on demand', is more widely used for commercial transactions, but does not provide a foolproof guarantee as issuing a bouncing cheque is not a criminal offence.

On the other hand, SWIFT bank transfers are widely used, as they are quick and efficient.

Payment orders issued via the website of the client's bank are a rapidly growing instrument.

■ Debt collection

The collection process usually begins with the debtor being sent a final demand, or 'seven-day' letter, by registered mail asking him or her to pay the principal along with any contractually agreed default interest. Where there is no specific interest clause, the rate applicable to commercial contracts concluded after 7 August 2002 (Regulation number 388, 2002) is the benchmark rate, ie the European Central Bank's refinancing rate, in force before 1 January or 1 July of each year, marked up by seven basis points and calculated on a daily percentage.

For claims of 1,270 euros (formerly 1,000 Irish punt) or more, creditors may threaten debtors with a statutory demand for the winding up of their business if they fail to pay up within 21 days of a final demand for payment being sent to them (21-day notice). Thereafter the debtor is regarded as insolvent (Companies Act 1963, amended in 1990, section 214).

Irish law and the Irish legal system are mainly founded on British 'common law' inherited from the past, although separate national legislation has subsequently been developed.

In ordinary proceedings, creditors who hold material evidence of their claim (contractual documents, acknowledgement of debt, unpaid bills of exchange) may seek a summary judgment from the court where their claim is not contested. This allows them to obtain a writ of enforcement more quickly. If a debtor fails to respond to a civil summons before the district court or a civil bill before the circuit court, the creditor may obtain a judgment by default based on the submission of an 'affidavit of debt' without a court hearing.

An affidavit of debt is a sworn statement that substantiates the outstanding amount and the cause of the claim. It bears a signature attested by a notary or an Irish consular office.

Cases are heard by either a district court, a circuit court or the High Court in Dublin, depending on the amount of the claim. Similarly, each court may hand down a summary judgment where justified by the circumstances of the petitioner's claim. Where defendants answer a summons but refuse to settle their debt, rather formal plenary proceedings are instituted in which the court gives equal importance to the case documents submitted by the parties and barristers' arguments as to the oral evidence presented at the main hearing.

For claims brought before the district courts (ie below 6,348.69 euros, formerly 5,000 Irish punt), there is a simplified written procedure, but the accent is mainly on hearing respective litigants' witnesses.

PAYMENT INCIDENTS INDEX
(12 months moving average - base 100 : World 1995)

Italy

Population (million inhabitants)	57.5
GDP (US$ million)	1,468,300
GDP per capita (US$)	25,300

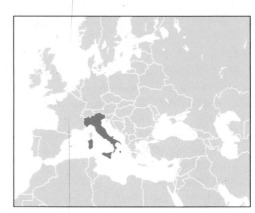

Coface analysis   Short-term: **A2**

STRENGTHS

- The 'Pact for Italy' adopted in 2002 by government authorities, labour and management should permit pursuing labour market reform while improving social policy effectiveness.
- Several large Italian groups (such as Generali, ENI, Finmeccanica and Benetton) undergoing or finishing their restructuring have begun to grow again at rates not reached in years.
- Privatizations have changed the economic environment and liberalization of several sectors (eg energy, telephony) has imbued it with new dynamism by fostering competition.
- Despite some delays, savings and efficiency gains resulting from civil service reform should gain momentum, particularly in a more stable political context.

WEAKNESSES

- Progress on pension and health system reform has been insufficient in view of the low birth rate and rapidly aging population. Public accounts have remained structurally in deficit, which has prevented significantly reducing the imposing public debt burden.
- The underground economy, notably in southern regions, has remained substantial with its integration only proceeding very gradually despite recent incentive measures.
- Economic disparities between the country's northern and southern regions have remained too great with the south still lacking the resources that would permit it to overcome its longstanding handicaps.
- Traditional regional networks of smaller companies have been suffering from stiff competition in their specialities, such as textiles, and a lack of resources to innovate.
- The economy has been suffering from insufficient specialization on high-technology content products.

RISK ASSESSMENT

After two years of stagnation, economic activity improved slightly in 2004. Despite the euro appreciation, exports benefited moderately from more buoyant world demand and improved competitiveness due to easing inflation. However, cancellation of the income tax reductions, necessitated by the deterioration of public finances, contributed to keeping consumption down. The investment recovery registered in the first half proved to be only temporary.

Growth should only improve slightly in 2005. Despite reduced tax schedules, household consumption should remain sluggish, particularly due to persistent uncertainty about the outlook for the social safety net. The euro appreciation and

MAIN ECONOMIC INDICATORS

%	2000	2001	2002	2003	2004[(e)]	2005[(f)]
Economic growth	3.2	1.7	0.4	0.4	1.3	1.5
Consumption (var.)	2.8	0.8	0.4	1.2	1.3	1.4
Investment (var.)	8.8	1.0	−0.1	−4.7	3.3	2.7
Inflation	2.6	2.3	2.6	2.8	2.2	2.1
Unemployment rate	10.7	9.6	9.1	8.8	8.6	8.5
Short-term interest rate	4.4	4.3	3.3	2.3	2.1	2.5
Public sector balance (%GDP)	−0.7	−2.7	−2.5	−2.7	−3.0	−3.5
Public sector debt (%GDP)	124.5	122.0	121.5	120.9	110.7	110.1
Exports (var.)	9.7	1.6	−3.4	−3.9	3.7	3.0
Imports (var.)	7.1	0.5	−0.2	−0.6	2.6	3.0
Current account balance (%GDP)	−0.6	−0.1	−0.8	−1.4	−1.0	−1.1

e = estimate, f = forecast

stabilization of European and world demand will hamper exports, especially in the traditional textile segment. In that lacklustre context, productive investment will increase at a rate not sufficient to remedy the obsolescence of equipment. Only construction investment should maintain relatively high growth due to the firmness of the residential property market. Meanwhile, the size of the fiscal deficit, which has reached 3.5 per cent of GDP, will limit any possibility for the authorities to stimulate the economy.

The Coface payment incident index for Italian companies has remained above the world average and, moreover, has continued to deteriorate, reflecting the increase in the number of bankruptcies of nearly 9 per cent in 2004. Bearing in mind the lack of prospects for improved economic conditions, the level of risk should remain high in 2005 with companies in the textile, electronics and printing/publishing sectors remaining weakest.

MAIN ECONOMIC SECTORS

■ Food

After an improvement in early 2004, a trend towards production and price stabilization marked the second half of the year. That trend should persist in 2005, especially given the appreciable risk that strained relations with mass distribution players will result in increased price pressure.

■ Car industry

Registrations stagnated in 2004. The Fiat group has been struggling to protect its market share in Italy and Europe (7.4 per cent in 2004) and lagging in implementing restructuring measures.

■ Electronics and electrical engineering

Operators have been troubled by the generally poor outlook of a sector handicapped by the substantial ground Italy needs to make up in research and high-technology services. Pressure on costs has been very intense. Only products intended for transportation equipment and certain industrial equipment have been benefiting from more buoyant markets.

■ Mass distribution

With the exception of hard discount, which has given no sign of weakening, mass distribution has suffered from the consumption slowdown. Promotional campaigns have become increasingly commonplace. However, the price war has inevitably been squeezing margins and resulting in continued restructuring exemplified by Auchan's recent takeover of the Rinascente chain.

■ **Steel/metallurgy/mechanical engineering**

The growth of Italian steel production matched the EU average with an increase of slightly more than 5 per cent in 2004. The metallurgy segment has benefited from an upward trend, reflected by the dynamism of production prices. Conversely, mechanical engineering business could suffer from raw material price trends, notably for steel, and from the gloomy outlook for equipment purchases by companies, except equipment intended for the building industry.

■ **Textiles and clothing**

The sector's production has remained shaky. Spending on clothing has continued to decline in the budgets of households often seeking low prices. Beyond uncertainty about a possible demand recovery, the problem of competition from Asian countries has been increasing in the more-standardized product segments and the pressure should increase with the end of quotas in 2005. The many delocalizations have been hitting the sector hard.

PAYMENT AND COLLECTION PRACTICES

■ **Payment**

Trade notes (*cambiali*) are available in the form of bills of exchange or promissory notes. *Cambiali* must be duly accepted by the drawee and stamped locally at 12/1,000 of their value or at 6/1,000 if stamped beforehand in France. In case of default, they constitute *de facto* enforcement orders as the courts automatically admit them as a writ of execution (*ezecuzione forzata*) against the debtor.

Signed bills of exchange are a fairly secure means of payment but are rarely used on account of the high stamp duty, the somewhat lengthy cashing period and the drawee's fear of damage to his or her reputation caused by the recording and publication of protested unpaid bills at the chambers of commerce.

Cheques too are in widespread use since the legislation on cheque amounts was relaxed in April 1990. However, to be cashed abroad, they must bear the wording *non trasferibile* and include the date and place of issue.

Bank vouchers (*ricevuta bancaria*) are not a means of payment, but merely a notice of bank domicile drawn up by the creditor and submitted by the creditor to his or her own bank for presentation to the debtor's bank for the purposes of payment (the vouchers are also available in electronic form, in which case they are known as *Ri.Ba. elettronica*). Courts may accept bank vouchers, if signed by the buyer, as acknowledgement of debt. However, they do not have the force of a writ of execution.

Bank transfers are widely used (90 per cent of payments from Italy are made by bank transfer), and in particular SWIFT transfers, as they are considerably faster than ordinary transfers. The bank transfer is a cheap and secure means of payment once the contracting parties have established mutual trust.

■ **Debt collection**

As elsewhere, an out-of-court settlement is always preferable to legal action. Demands and telephone dunning are quite effective, as are on-site visits that provide an opportunity to restore dialogue between supplier and customer, and so to conclude a settlement.

Settlement negotiations focus on payment of the principal, plus any contractual default interest that may be provided for in writing and accepted by the buyer. Where there is no such agreement, the rate applicable to commercial agreements concluded after 8 August 2002 (Decree-Law of 9 October 2002) is the six-monthly rate set by the Ministry of Economic Affairs and Finance by reference to the European Central Bank's refinancing rate, increased by seven basis points.

Failing an out-of-court settlement with the customer, the type of legal action taken will depend on the type of documents justifying the claim.

In the case of *cambiali* notes (bills of exchange, promissory notes) and cheques, creditors may obtain a writ of execution in the form of a demand for payment (*atto di precetto*) delivered by a bailiff prior to attachment of debtor's property.

Creditors may obtain an injunction to pay (*decreto ingiuntivo*) by way of a fast-track procedure if they can produce written proof of their claim. That permits them to avoid taking ordinary legal action to establish their right to payment, a process still considered slow despite the civil procedure reform adopted in May 1995. Ordinary proceedings can take up to two years, although creditors may obtain, in first instance, a provisional payment order that serves as a writ of execution.

PAYMENT INCIDENTS INDEX
(12 months moving average - base 100 : World 1995)

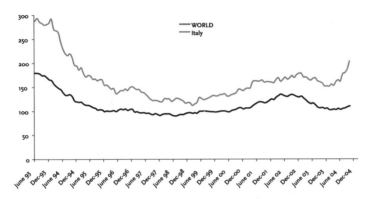

Kazakhstan

Population (million inhabitants)	15
GDP (US$ million)	24,637

Short-term: **B**

Medium-term:

Coface analysis **Moderately high risk**

STRENGTHS

- The country has a wealth of natural resources, such as oil and metals.
- Pipeline construction (operational like CPC linking Kazakhstan to the Black Sea, or in the project stage as with the one that will go to China) will permit sharp increases in crude exports.
- For its size, Kazakhstan is the CIS country that has attracted the most FDI.
- Good relations with Russia, China and Western countries have been factors in the country's development and political stability.

WEAKNESSES

- Economic conditions and public sector accounts will ultimately be vulnerable to raw material prices.
- The focus on raw materials has been impeding industrial sector development.
- President Nazerbaev's regime has hardened its stance in the face of ascendant political opposition.
- Relations with foreign investors (essential in developing the energy potential) have sometimes been tense.

RISK ASSESSMENT

The economy has continued to post excellent performance with growth remaining high. External accounts have benefited from the high oil prices and increased production volume (up 13 per cent a year since 2000). Moreover, higher individual incomes have stimulated domestic demand. Direct investment inflows, with a large proportion going to crude exploitation and transport, have also been substantially buoying growth. That investment should continue to represent about 5 per cent of annual GDP in coming years. The real exchange rate appreciation, typical of natural resource-exporting economies, could however impede the diversification efforts essential for more balanced growth.

Financially, fiscal policy has remained tight with inflation remaining essentially under control despite rapid expansion of the money supply and with debt ratios trending down. Considering the appetite of Kazakh banks and companies for international financing, however, the rapid increase of the resulting debt nonetheless bears watching.

The political situation has been stable. The elites and regional powers could nonetheless call into question the domination of the clan in power. In any case, the current president should continue to dominate the political scene and seek re-election for a new six-year term in the elections coming in 2006.

MAIN ECONOMIC INDICATORS

US$ millions	2000	2001	2002	2003	2004[(e)]	2005[(f)]
Economic growth (%)	9.8	13.5	9.8	9.2	9.4	8.0
Inflation (%)	9.8	6.4	6.6	6.8	6.5	6.0
Public sector balance (%GDP)	-0.8	2.7	3.0	2.3	1.6	1.1
Exports	9,468	9,124	10,027	13,233	20,900	25,200
Imports	6,848	7,607	7,726	9,144	13,900	16,000
Trade balance	2,620	1,517	2,301	4,089	7,000	9,200
Current account balance	768	-896	-862	-200	1,200	1,600
Current account balance (%GDP)	3.7	-4.9	-3.9	-0.6	2.9	3.2
Foreign debt (%GDP)	69.3	82.8	82.3	74.8	63.7	38.0
Debt service (%Exports)	25.9	26.4	25.9	21.6	23.2	23.2
Foreign exchange reserves (in months of imports)	2.8	2.9	3.4	4.5	4.0	4.0

e = estimate, f = forecast

CONDITIONS OF ACCESS TO THE MARKET

■ Market overview

Some 13 years after gaining independence on 16 December 1991, Kazakhstan has yet to complete its reform programme, despite its 'good pupil' image. A candidate for WTO accession, the country is riddled with corruption, bureaucracy, an inefficient tax system and glaring social cleavages. However, it has made great strides in public sector privatization – albeit in somewhat untransparent conditions – and trade liberalization. Other signs of progress are the volume of net FDI at the end of 2003 (US$18 billion) and the country's growing foreign trade surplus driven by strong oil, mineral and metal exports.

■ Means of access

Despite its designation as a market economy by the EU in 2000 (and by the United States in 2002) and its mildly protectionist policies, landlocked Kazakhstan remains a difficult place in which to do business. Customs duties continue to fall, with the average rate standing at below 7.8 per cent. There is also 15 per cent non-refundable VAT calculated on the customs value. However, customs clearance is marred by illegal practices and tariff peaks persist. A number of products are also subject to certification. The fact that certificates from non-CIS countries are not valid in Kazakhstan significantly slows down import formalities. Foreign businesses should make allowance for corruption, even though it is not systematic.

■ Attitude towards foreign investors

At the end of 2003, Kazakhstan had the biggest volume of FDI in the CIS after Russia. Foreign investor interest is driven by the country's oil and gas reserves and undeniable political stability. The new law of January 2003, however, strengthens the government's interventionist powers during a downturn. The introduction of ever higher oil and gas taxes in early 2004 could hamper the influx of FDI. Generally speaking, the sustained improvement in the country's economic situation, which is extremely vulnerable to international economic trends and fluctuations in the price of oil, has increased tensions between the state and foreign investors as the government becomes aware of the country's potential. Paradoxically, this realization seems to make it increasingly difficult to do business with government and semi-public bodies. The private sector and the retail trade, on the other hand, are flourishing after three years of strong economic growth. However, experience shows that investors would do well to take every legal precaution before entering into joint venture agreements with local partners.

OPPORTUNITY SCOPE

Breakdown of domestic demand (%GDP + imports)

Private consumption	41
Public consumption	8
Investment	18

Exports: 47% of GDP

Imports: 46% of GDP

MAIN DESTINATIONS OF EXPORTS

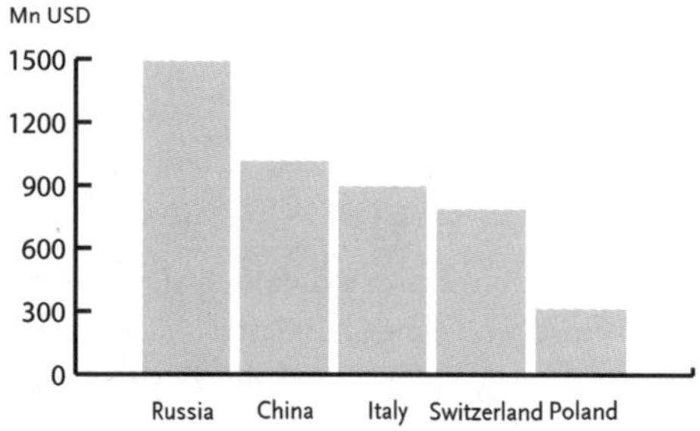

Mn USD
1500
1200
900
600
300
0
Russia
China
Italy
Switzerland
Poland

MAIN ORIGINS OF IMPORTS

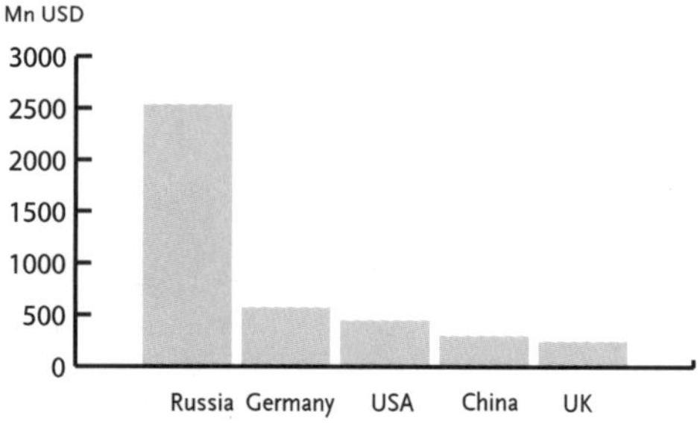

Mn USD
3000
2500
2000
1500
1000
500
0
Russia
Germany
USA
China
UK

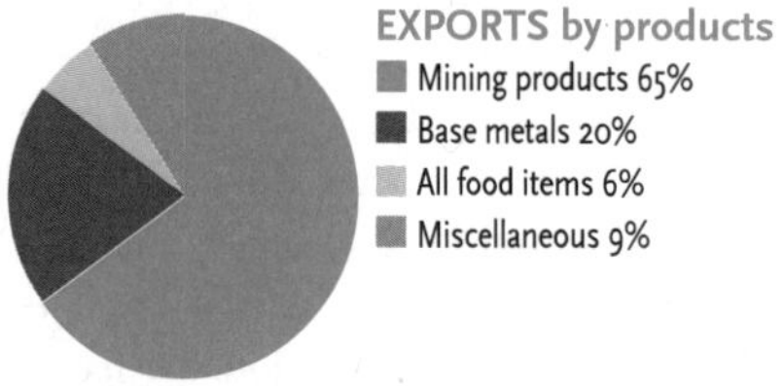

EXPORTS by products
Mining products 65%
Base metals 20%
All food items 6%
Miscellaneous 9%

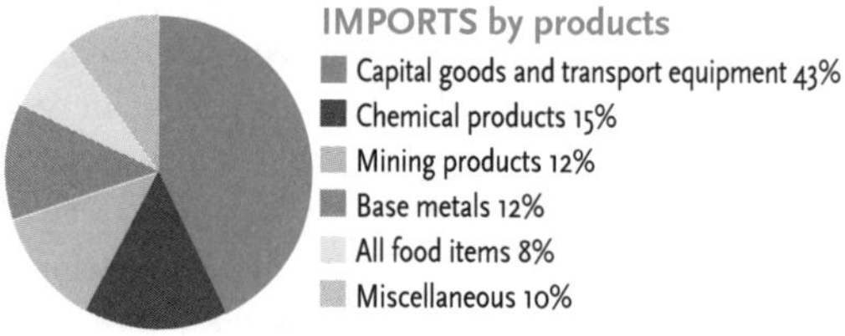

IMPORTS by products
Capital goods and transport equipment 43%
Chemical products 15%
Mining products 12%
Base metals 12%
All food items 8%
Miscellaneous 10%

STANDARD OF LIVING / PURCHASING POWER

Indicators	Kazakhstan	Regional average	DC average
GNP per capita (PPP dollars)	5630	8313	4601
GNP per capita (USD)	1520	2535	1840
Human Development Index	0.766	0.805	0.684
Wealthiest 10% share of national income	24.2	30	32
Urban population percentage	56	68	45
Percentage under 15 years old	25	17	30
Number of telephones per 1000 inhabitants	130	257	120
Number of computers per 1000 inhabitants	n/a	84	37

Kyrgyzstan

Population (million inhabitants)	5
GDP (US$ million)	1,603
GDP per capita (US$)	321

Coface analysis

Short-term: **D**

Medium-term:
Very high risk

RISK ASSESSMENT

Kyrgyzstan has been posting high growth, buoyed by increased gold production – the country's main source of wealth representing 34 per cent of exports, notably to the Swiss market. Start-up of precious metal production in two new mines by 2006 augurs well for growth. Moreover, macroeconomic stabilization has continued with the country benefiting from IMF backing.

The financial situation has nonetheless remained tense. The foreign debt burden still does not seem very sustainable with debt ratios, although gradually declining, remaining too high. Support from multilateral institutions has thus remained essential. Moreover, 44 per cent of inhabitants live below the poverty line, particularly in the farming sector whose performance has been weak and which still represents 35 per cent of national output. Finally, the level of corruption has been among the highest in the Commonwealth of Independent States.

Internationally, President Askar Akaev has maintained his balanced policy between the great powers. He has hosted a US base since the Afghanistan military campaign and a Russian military base, since October 2003, that has become permanent. He has concurrently maintained military cooperation with China. Domestically, the regime has appeared less authoritarian than those of its Central Asian neighbours. President Akaev may nonetheless not relinquish power in 2005, his stated intention to do so notwithstanding. In that context, the upcoming elections could cause relative political instability.

MAIN ECONOMIC INDICATORS

US$ millions	2000	2001	2002	2003	2004[(e)]	2005[(f)]
Economic growth (%)	5.3	5.4	0.0	6.7	6.0	5.0
Inflation (%)	9.6	3.7	2.0	5.0	5.0	5.0
Public sector balance (%GDP)	−9.2	−5.1	−5.5	−5.2	−4.3	−4.0
Exports	510.9	480.3	498.0	590.0	629.0	660.0
Imports	506.9	440.3	552.0	673.0	749.0	822.0
Trade balance	4	40	−54	−83	−120	−162
Current account balance (%GDP)	−6.6	−3.3	−3.9	−2.7	−3.9	−5.4
Foreign debt (%GDP)	111.0	111.2	108.6	100.6	89.8	90.6
Debt service (%Exports)	22.5	28.0	26.0	20.0	0.0	20.0
Foreign exchange reserves (in months of imports)	4.4	4.0	4.3	4.8	5.4	5.2

e = estimate, f = forecast

Latvia

Population (million inhabitants)	2
GDP (US$ million)	8,406

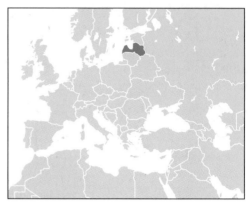

Short-term: **A3**

Coface analysis

Medium-term:
Quite low risk

STRENGTHS

- The country has played a pivotal role in East–West trade and benefited from a skilled workforce.
- On average, since 1996, Latvia has posted the highest growth rate among new EU member countries.
- The exchange rate peg and sensible economic policy have favoured the country's economic stability.
- That context has attracted FDI and facilitated the country's EU accession.
- Public sector debt has remained low.

WEAKNESSES

- A substantial wealth gap with the EU-15 still has to be bridged.
- Substantial external account imbalances have been a subsidiary effect of the efforts on investment.
- The country has remained dependent on Russia for transit business, notably involving energy products.
- The short-term and, consequently, foreign debt burdens have been substantial.
- Government instability has slowed the pace of reforms.

RISK ASSESSMENT

Economic activity remained strong in 2004, driven by still-robust domestic demand. Growth should nonetheless sag in 2005 with employment and real wages growing more slowly, which should undermine consumer spending. Credit expansion could also stall with companies and households seeking to limit their indebtedness. Investment linked to EU accession should nonetheless continue, enhancing Latvia's long-term growth potential.

The size of the current account deficit, fuelled primarily by surging imports, has been the main risk factor. That imbalance will remain large in 2005, especially with increased port capacity in Russia apt to affect transit business. However, moderate direct investment inflows, multilateral loans and bank borrowing should continue to cover that deficit. That borrowing has mainly consisted of large short-term deposits by non-residents. The scale of that type of debt has generated some vulnerability, which nonetheless has to be put in perspective with those deposits mainly invested abroad in quality liquid assets that have shown little sensitivity to regional crises.

Politically, chronically weak government coalitions have not jeopardized the broad lines of economic policy.

MAIN ECONOMIC INDICATORS

US$ millions	2000	2001	2002	2003	2004[(e)]	2005[(f)]
Economic growth (%)	6.9	8.0	6.4	7.5	7.5	5.5
Inflation (%)	2.6	2.5	1.9	2.9	6.2	4.2
Public sector balance (%GDP)	-3.0	-2.0	-2.4	-1.6	-1.5	-2.0
Unemployment rate (%)	14.6	12.8	11.6	10.3	n/a	n/a
Exports	2,058	2,216	2,576	3,171	3,726	4,222
Imports	3,116	3,567	4,020	5,169	6,171	6,721
Trade balance	-1,058	-1,351	-1,444	-1,998	-2,445	-2,499
Current account balance	-495	-732	-602	-956	-1,314	-1,289
Current account balance (%GDP)	-6.4	-8.9	-6.5	-8.6	-10.5	-9.7
Foreign debt (%GDP)	61.0	67.7	75.7	82.6	87.2	95.6
Debt service (%Exports)	20.3	19.6	19.2	17.0	15.8	15.0
Foreign exchange reserves (in months of imports)	2.5	3.1	3.0	2.6	2.3	2.2

e = estimate, f = forecast

CONDITIONS OF ACCESS TO THE MARKET

■ **Market overview**

The Latvian market is open and highly competitive and there are no special protectionist measures in place. A WTO member since February 1999, Latvia is among the ten new countries that joined the EU on 1 May 2004. The next stage is entry into the EMU, which is scheduled for 2008.

■ **Means of entry**

Since EU accession, Latvia has been applying the common external tariff, along with the import restrictions applicable in all the other member states. The country's intellectual property laws are, at times, unsatisfactory. Depending on relations with the customer, pre-payments are common, as are 30- to 45-day documentary credit and bank transfers. Payments can be made in lats or in foreign currency. The euro has overtaken the dollar as the leading currency of payment, with 57.6 per cent of imports denominated in euros during the first quarter of 2004, compared with 24.2 per cent in dollars. There are no restrictions on capital transfers. Information on the creditworthiness of Latvian companies can be obtained from the credit information firm IGK BALT, a local subsidiary of Coface IGK Holding.

■ **Attitude towards foreign investors**

The country is open to foreign investors, with FDI accounting for 5 per cent of GDP in the first quarter of 2004. After cutting corporation tax from 19 per cent in 2003 to 15 per cent in 2004, Latvia has one of the lowest corporation tax rates in the enlarged EU. The new Labour Code, adopted in 2002, is in line with European directives. Social security contributions in general amount to 33.09 per cent of wages, with 26.09 per cent borne by the employer and 9 per cent by the employee. A bilateral double taxation treaty has been in force since 1 May 2001.

■ **Foreign exchange regulations**

Pegged to the special drawing rights since February 1994, the lat's value fluctuates in tandem with the currencies comprising the special drawing rights. In the first half of 2004, the lat fell against the euro and rose against the dollar. At 3 November 2004, the exchange rate was 1.48 euros to the lat. There are no foreign exchange controls in Latvia.

The Latvian Central Bank planned to join ERM-II – with simultaneous pegging of the lat to the euro – on 1 January 2005 before adopting the euro definitively on 1 January 2008. However, the latest inflation and current account deficit figures have led it to contemplate a postponement of this timetable. The fall of the government on 28 October 2004, triggered by the no-confidence vote during the first reading of the 2005 draft budget in parliament, makes such an outcome increasingly likely.

OPPORTUNITY SCOPE

Breakdown of domestic demand (%GDP + imports)

Private consumption	40
Public consumption	13
Investment	17

Exports: 45% of GDP → ← Imports: 56% of GDP

MAIN DESTINATIONS OF EXPORTS

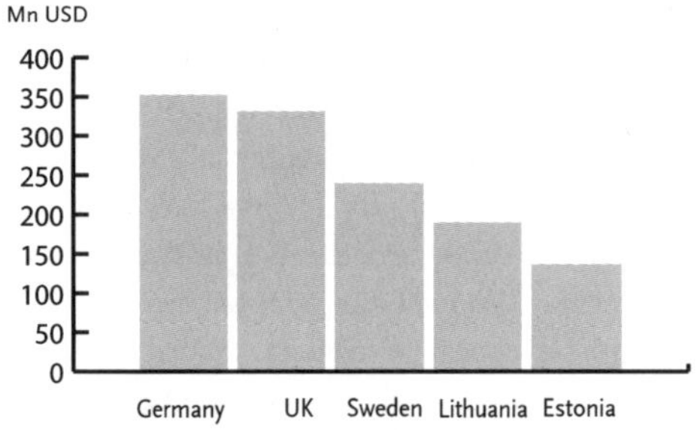

Mn USD
400
350
300
250
200
150
100
50
0
Germany
UK
Sweden
Lithuania
Estonia

MAIN ORIGINS OF IMPORTS

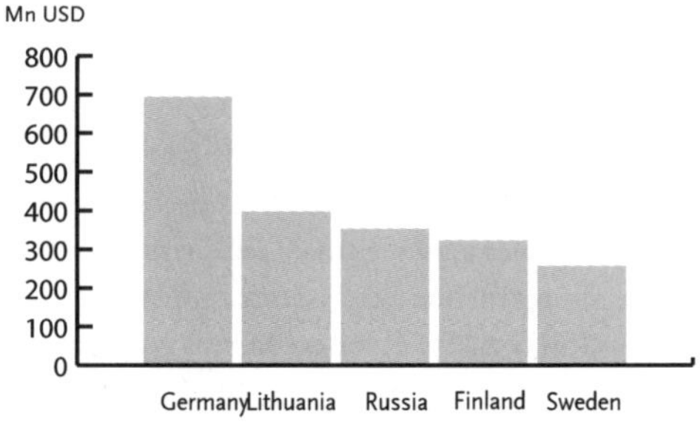

Mn USD
800
700
600
500
400
300
200
100
0
Germany
Lithuania
Russia
Finland
Sweden

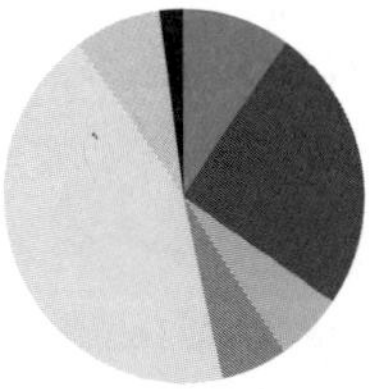

EXPORTS by products
- All food items 10%
- Agricultural raw materials 25%
- Capital goods and transport equipment 8%
- Chemical products 6%
- Other manufactured goods 44%
- Ores and metals 6%
- Miscellaneous 2%

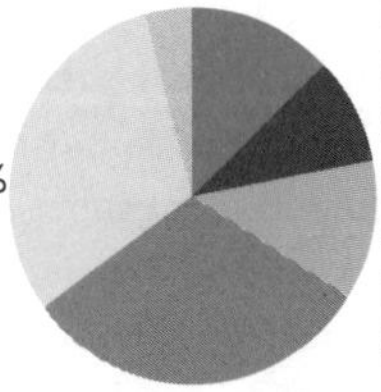

IMPORTS by products
- All food items 13%
- Fuels 9%
- Chemical products 12%
- Capital goods and transport equipment 31%
- Other manufactured goods 31%
- Miscellaneous 4%

STANDARD OF LIVING / PURCHASING POWER

Indicators	Latvia	Regional average	DC average
GNP per capita (PPP dollars)	9190	8313	4601
GNP per capita (USD)	3480	2535	1840
Human Development Index	0.823	0.805	0.684
Wealthiest 10% share of national income	25.9	30	32
Urban population percentage	60	68	45
Percentage under 15 years old	16	17	30
Number of telephones per 1000 inhabitants	301	257	120
Number of computers per 1000 inhabitants	172	84	37

Lithuania

Population (million inhabitants)	3
GDP (US$ million)	13,796

Coface analysis

Short-term: **A3**

Medium-term:
Quite low risk

STRENGTHS

- In just a few years, the country has transformed its economy and proven capable of meeting the challenges of EU accession.
- Sensible macroeconomic policy and the litas–euro peg should facilitate adoption of the single currency.
- With a skilled workforce and low payroll costs, the country has also benefited from its favourable geographic situation.
- The population's ethnic homogeneity has been a stability factor.

WEAKNESSES

- Lithuania has remained vulnerable to external shocks due to its large external financing needs, mainly generated by external account imbalances.
- The litas appreciation could undermine the country's competitiveness.
- Short-term debt has been high in relation to currency reserves.
- The country has much ground to make up in combating corruption, improving civil service capacity, reforming pensions and restructuring agriculture.

RISK ASSESSMENT

Domestic demand has remained the main growth driver. The economy should continue to expand strongly in 2005 with higher real wages and an improved employment situation spurring private consumption and with low interest rates buoying investment. However, economic activity could suffer from a possible interruption of the oil supply from the Russian company Yukos, the majority shareholder of Lithuania's main exporter, the Mazeikiu Nafta refinery.

Government authorities are hoping to join the European Monetary Union rapidly with the country having joined the ERM-II exchange rate mechanism in June 2004. In that context, the government will have to pursue prudent fiscal policy with the central bank continuing to defend price stability under the currency board.

The robust domestic demand has nonetheless resulted in an upsurge of imports and marked increase in the current account deficit. Although FDI has been covering a relatively limited proportion of external financing needs, the country has enjoyed access to capital markets in favourable conditions. Moreover, even if the stock of foreign debt has increased substantially, it has stabilized in relation to GDP thanks to the strong growth.

Politically, the succession of weak government coalitions has seriously impeded the legislative process. However, economic policy has remained unchanged in its broad lines.

MAIN ECONOMIC INDICATORS

US$ millions	2000	2001	2002	2003	2004(e)	2005(f)
Economic growth (%)	3.9	6.4	6.8	9.7	6.7	6.4
Inflation (%)	1.0	1.3	0.3	−1.2	1.2	1.8
Public sector balance (%GDP)	−2.8	−2.0	−1.2	−1.8	−2.7	−2.5
Unemployment rate (%)	16.4	17.4	13.8	12.4	n/a	n/a
Exports	4,050	4,889	6,028	7,658	8,850	9,740
Imports	5,154	5,997	7,343	9,362	11,050	12,300
Trade balance	−1,104	−1,108	−1,315	−1,704	−2,200	−2,560
Current account balance	−675	−574	−721	−1,278	−1,830	−2,030
Current account balance (%GDP)	−5.9	−4.7	−5.1	−7.0	−8.5	−8.4
Foreign debt (%GDP)	42.7	43.6	44.1	45.4	46.3	46.6
Debt service (%Exports)	19.3	32.6	37.1	18.5	17.1	18.0
Foreign exchange reserves (in months of imports)	2.5	2.7	3.3	3.6	3.7	3.4

e = estimate, f = forecast

CONDITIONS OF ACCESS TO THE MARKET

■ Market overview

Purchasing power has been rising steadily for several years on the back of strong economic growth. The average wage in mid-2004 was about 350 euros. Lithuania's economic development is driven partly by investment and mainly by household spending against the background of a buoyant and highly competitive mass retail sector.

■ Means of entry

Since its entry into the EU on 1 May 2004, Lithuania is part of the single European market. It is now a very open market where only excise duties and levies on products such as alcoholic beverages and oil remain in force. Certain products may be imported only by holders of an ad-hoc licence, but the conditions for obtaining such licences have been greatly relaxed, particularly for alcoholic beverages. The ban on beef imports has been lifted. A new EU-compliant public procurement law has been in force since early 2003. However, the administrative machinery needs to be cranked up for the purposes of enforcement.

Standards harmonization has made great headway and it is not difficult to obtain the relevant certificates so long as the products comply with a European standard. Competition law is also in line with EU criteria. For payments, short-term credit is increasingly used and has all but replaced pre-payment and documentary credit.

■ Attitude towards foreign investors

Foreign investors are treated on an equal footing with Lithuanian nationals and there are no cases of discrimination. Lithuania remains attractive to foreign investors largely because of its 15 per cent corporation tax. Foreign investors may freely repatriate profits, income and dividends derived from their activities upon meeting their tax obligations. The workforce is highly skilled and wage costs are low. The service sector offers the highest wages. Employer and employee social security contributions – payable to the country's social security agency, Sodra – are 31 per cent and 3 per cent of gross wages respectively.

Foreign investors generally appreciate the overall business climate in Lithuania. A combination of factors makes the country attractive: proper regulatory framework, low taxation, good infrastructure, skilled labour and low labour costs.

■ Foreign exchange regulations

The Lithuanian currency, the litas, has been tied to the euro at a fixed rate (1 euro = 3.4528 litas) since

1 February 2002. Numerous Lithuanian firms hold euro-denominated accounts. Lithuania entered ERM-II in June 2004 and plans to join the euro zone in mid-2006 or early 2007.

OPPORTUNITY SCOPE

Breakdown of domestic demand (%GDP + imports)
- Private consumption   39
- Public consumption   13
- Investment   14

Exports: 54% of GDP   Imports: 60% of GDP

MAIN DESTINATIONS OF EXPORTS

Mn USD — UK, Russia, Germany, Latvia, Denmark

MAIN ORIGINS OF IMPORTS

Mn USD — Russia, Germany, Italy, Poland, UK

EXPORTS by products
- Processed food items 11%
- Mineral products 19%
- Chemical products and plastics 9%
- Capital goods 26%
- Other manufactured goods 25%
- Miscellaneous 10%

IMPORTS by products
- Processed food items 8%
- Mineral products 18%
- Chemical products and plastics 14%
- Capital goods 34%
- Other manufactured goods 16%
- Miscellaneous 10%

STANDARD OF LIVING / PURCHASING POWER

Indicators	Lithuania	Regional average	DC average
GNP per capita (PPP dollars)	10190	8313	4601
GNP per capita (USD)	3670	2535	1840
Human Development Index	0.842	0.805	0.684
Wealthiest 10% share of national income	24.9	30	32
Urban population percentage	69	68	45
Percentage under 15 years old	18	17	30
Number of telephones per 1000 inhabitants	270	257	120
Number of computers per 1000 inhabitants	110	84	37

Luxembourg

Population (inhabitants)	452,000
GDP (US$ million)	27,000
GDP per capita (US$)	60,100

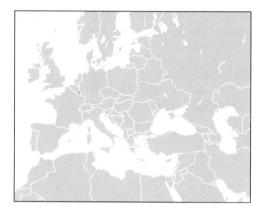

Coface analysis Short-term: **A1**

RISK ASSESSMENT

The recovery that began end-2003 gained momentum in 2004. Exports of goods and services benefited from strong world demand for steel products and from the recovery of services linked to the upturn of financial markets. Private consumption benefited from the renewed confidence of households with the labour market coming back to life, particularly in the financial sector. Disinvestment has ceased due to housing market dynamism buoyed by low interest rates and also to increased capital spending by companies.

Growth will remain robust in 2005 with a slight industrial export slowdown likely to be offset by a sharp rise in public spending, facilitated by the virtual absence of public deficits and debt, as well as by substantial reserves accumulated in good years. Household and company spending should strengthen provided conditions improve further in the financial sector, whose economic weight has remained decisive.

Bankruptcies continued to decline in 2004 (down about 5 per cent). The situation has been improving in all industrial sectors, notably steel, and has remained good in retail. The improvement has been slimmer in civil engineering where housing dynamism has been offsetting the poor performance of public works and commercial construction affected by overcapacity. The favourable economic conditions, in conjunction with a low Coface payment incident index, augurs well for continuation of that trend in 2005.

MAIN ECONOMIC INDICATORS

%	2000	2001	2002	2003	2004[e]	2005[f]
Economic growth	9.0	1.5	2.5	2.9	4.2	4.3
Consumption (var.)	4.6	5.1	3.2	1.6	2.1	2.9
Investment (var.)	−2.2	10.5	0.4	−3.9	5.0	6.5
Inflation	3.8	2.4	2.1	2.5	2.9	2.4
Unemployment rate	2.6	2.6	3.0	3.8	4.2	4.2
Short-term interest rate	4.4	4.3	3.3	2.3	2.0	2.2
Public sector balance (%GDP)	6.4	6.2	2.4	0.8	−0.6	−1.0
Public sector debt (%GDP)	5.5	5.5	5.7	5.3	5.7	5.7
Exports (var.)	17.3	1.8	−0.6	1.8	6.5	5.7
Imports (var.)	15.4	3.7	−2.6	1.6	6.3	5.9
Current account balance (%GDP)	13.7	9.0	11.8	8.2	9.0	10.0

e = estimate, f = forecast

PAYMENT INCIDENTS INDEX
(12 months moving average - base 100 : World 1995)

1

Macedonia

Population (million inhabitants)	2
GDP (US$ million)	3,791
GDP per capita (US$)	1,896

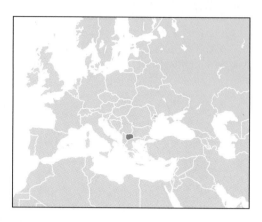

Short-term: **D**

Medium-term:

Coface analysis   **Very high risk**

RISK ASSESSMENT

Poor industrial-production performance prompted the slowdown registered in 2004 despite the improvement achieved in other sectors. In 2005, economic growth should accelerate albeit amid the constraint caused by political uncertainty and restrictive economic policy. With authorities having succeeded in stabilizing public sector accounts, the government's new economic programme to be negotiated with the IMF should focus more on implementing reforms, particularly in the legal and health areas.

Meanwhile, large external account imbalances have persisted. Although exports have benefited from the European recovery and initiation of

investment programmes, they still cover only 60 per cent of imports, which have been growing faster than sales abroad, due notably to the increasing cost of oil. Moreover, the country continues to depend on international financial aid due to insufficient FDI, deterred by high political risk and an unfavourable business environment.

The social situation has remained tense due the high level of unemployment. Interethnic tensions – between the Slavic majority and Albanian minority – could re-emerge despite the failure of opponents of the decentralization law (final key element in the 2001 Ohrid peace agreement) in the November 2004 referendum. Finally, dissension within the government could impede the reform process.

MAIN ECONOMIC INDICATORS						
US$ millions	2000	2001	2002	2003	2004[(e)]	2005[(f)]
Economic growth (%)	4.5	−4.5	0.9	3.1	1.0	4.0
Inflation (%)	5.8	5.3	2.4	1.2	−0.2	1.0
Public sector balance (%GDP)	1.8	−7.2	−5.6	−1.6	−2.2	n/a
Exports	1,321	1,155	1,112	1,359	1,601	1,709
Imports	2,011	1,682	1,917	2,211	2,704	2,889
Trade balance	−690	−526	−804	−852	−1,103	−1,180
Current account balance (%GDP)	−2.0	−7.1	−9.4	−6.0	−9.6	−9.3
Foreign debt (%GDP)	41.5	41.3	40.7	37.5	37.2	37.4
Debt service (%Exports)	8.7	14.6	11.5	10.0	10.0	8.4
Foreign exchange reserves (in months of imports)	3.5	4.4	3.9	4.1	3.5	3.4

e = estimate, f = forecast

Malta

Population (inhabitants) 397,000
GDP (US$ million) 3,623
GDP per capita (US$) 9,126

Short-term: **A3**

Medium-term:

Coface analysis   **Low risk**

RISK ASSESSMENT

Economic growth recovered in 2004, fuelled mainly by exports, notably electronic and pharmaceutical products. Investment has continued to trend up, particularly in manufacturing and construction. However, private and public consumption have stalled: private spending under the effect of reduced household disposable income attributable to deterioration of the employment market and higher inflation and public spending due to the government's efforts to reduce a large fiscal deficit and public sector debt representing about 70 per cent of GDP.

Despite tourism revenues, the current account deficit has remained high due to increased oil costs and capital goods purchases. However, official financial aid, especially from the EU, linked to infrastructure projects, has supplemented capital inflows, thereby permitting Malta to keep foreign exchange reserves at comfortable levels.

With the Maltese lira currently pegged to a currency basket (including the euro for 70 per cent), Malta envisions joining the European exchange rate mechanism in 2005.

MAIN ECONOMIC INDICATORS						
US$ millions	2000	2001	2002	2003	2004(e)	2005(f)
Economic growth (%)	6.4	−1.2	2.2	−1.7	1.0	1.8
Inflation (%)	2.4	2.9	2.2	1.3	2.9	2.2
Public sector balance (%GDP)	−5.5	−5.2	−6.2	−9.7	−5.2	n/a
Exports	2,479	2,002	2,254	2,505	2,775	2,935
Imports	3,232	2,568	2,668	3,194	3,756	3,951
Trade balance	−754	−566	−414	−689	−981	−1,016
Current account balance (%GDP)	−13.2	−4.6	−1.2	−6.0	−6.2	−4.3
Foreign debt (%GDP)	88.7	70.8	92.4	86.2	71.3	70.8
Debt service (%Exports)	4.1	5.6	4.5	5.4	5.2	5.1
Foreign exchange reserves (in months of imports)	3.5	4.9	6.3	6.5	6.2	6.4

e = estimate, f = forecast

Moldova

Population (million inhabitants)	4.3
GDP (US$ million)	1,624
GDP per capita (US$)	378

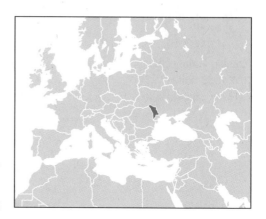

Coface analysis

Short-term: **D**

Medium-term:
Very high risk

RISK ASSESSMENT

Economic growth has been accelerating, buoyed by firm demand from Moldova's main trading partners, Russia, Romania and Ukraine. Household spending has also been driving the economy, spurred by the high level of private transfers from workers residing abroad. The recovery has nonetheless been very shaky with the country remaining specialized in low value-added food products (22 per cent of GDP and 40 per cent of exports). Economic conditions have thus remained dependent on exogenous factors such as food prices and weather. Low investment and an unfavourable business climate have been seriously impeding the economy's diversification.

Although monetary and fiscal policy has remained prudent, as evidenced by the public sector's limited deficit, the country's financial situation is still very tense with a large current account deficit and an excessive debt burden for Europe's poorest economy. However, Moldova cannot count on steady international financial community backing due to the communist government's reluctance to pursue needed structural reforms. Moreover, government authorities have been facing recurrent conflict with the opposition in a country very divided over the country's future: either closer relations with the EU or continued membership of the CIS. Political debate could become even more polarized with elections scheduled in 2005. Furthermore, the recent upsurge of tensions with authorities of the quasi-autonomous Transnistria region (12 per cent of the territory) has been another source of political instability.

MAIN ECONOMIC INDICATORS

US$ millions	2000	2001	2002	2003	2004[(e)]	2005[(f)]
Economic growth (%)	2.1	6.0	8.0	6.0	8.0	5.0
Inflation (%)	18.5	6.0	4.0	18.0	8.0	8.0
Public sector balance (%GDP)	−1.4	−0.3	−0.9	0.2	−0.7	−0.7
Exports	477	567	660	806	1,040	1,100
Imports	771	880	1,038	1,429	1,808	1,900
Trade balance	−294	−313	−378	−622	−768	−800
Current account balance	−125	−78	−56	−142	−148	−151
Current account balance (%GDP)	−9.6	−5.2	−3.3	−7.1	−5.5	−5.4
Foreign debt (%GDP)	92.3	80.0	76.5	70.0	51.9	50.0
Debt service (%Exports)	14.1	14.9	16.8	9.4	11.2	11.0
Foreign exchange reserves (in months of imports)	2.7	3.0	3.0	2.5	2.3	2.4

e = estimate, f = forecast

The Netherlands

Population (million inhabitants)	16.2
GDP (US$ million)	512,700
GDP per capita (US$)	31,600

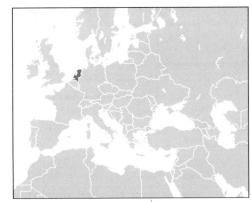

Coface analysis   Short-term: **A2**

RISK ASSESSMENT

After a period of recession, the country experienced only a weak recovery developed in 2004 and buoyed by an export upturn amid more vivid world demand. Domestic demand has been flat, however, with tighter fiscal policy, the rapid rise of unemployment and the resulting loss of purchasing power spurring savings to the detriment of consumption.

Growth should remain sluggish in 2005. Easing inflation notwithstanding, stagnant purchasing power and fears about employment will continue to deter household spending. Amid slowing world growth, exports will suffer further from a lack of price competitiveness due to high labour costs and the euro appreciation. Facing sluggish demand, companies will limit themselves to replacement investments. Confronted with a public sector deficit reaching 3 per cent of GDP, the government will continue to pursue its policy of reducing spending via new measures like freezing civil service wages, toughening rules on access to unemployment benefits, reforming the health insurance system and limiting retirements before age 65.

Persistence of a sluggish economic environment has combined with the deterioration of company competitiveness. Although the Coface payment incident index has worsened as a result in recent months, it has nonetheless remained far below the world average. Bankruptcies have continued to increase although at a more moderate pace – up 4 per cent in 2004. The growth outlook affords little hope for improved company solvency in 2005.

MAIN ECONOMIC INDICATORS

%	2000	2001	2002	2003	2004[(e)]	2005[(f)]
Economic growth	3.5	1.4	0.6	−0.9	1.2	1.3
Consumption (var.)	3.5	1.4	1.3	−0.9	0.2	1.0
Investment (var.)	1.0	−2.7	−6.5	−3.2	0.5	2.0
Inflation	2.3	5.1	3.9	2.2	1.4	0.9
Unemployment rate	3.0	2.5	2.9	4.1	5.3	5.8
Short-term interest rate	4.4	4.3	3.3	2.3	2.1	2.6
Public sector balance (%GDP)	2.2	0.0	−1.6	−3.2	−3.0	−2.8
Public sector debt (%GDP)	66.7	62.1	62.1	63.2	65.2	67.2
Exports (var.)	11.3	1.6	0.8	0.0	6.0	5.4
Imports (var.)	10.5	2.2	0.8	0.6	3.9	5.0
Current account balance (%GDP)	2.0	1.9	2.5	2.9	2.7	2.9

e = estimate, f = forecast

PAYMENT AND COLLECTION PRACTICES

■ Payment

Bills of exchange are rarely used in the Netherlands because it is not standard business practice to do so. As in Germany, they signal mistrust on the part of the supplier and so are incompatible with the climate of trust needed to maintain a stable business relationship.

Cheques too are little used. They are an unreliable means of payment as they can be cashed only if covered. Consequently, issuing an uncovered cheque is not a criminal offence and those on the receiving end of a bounced cheque incur rather high bank charges.

Under Dutch law, bills of exchange and cheques serve mainly to substantiate the existence of a debt.

By contrast, bank transfers ('Bankgiro') are by far the most common means of payment. All leading Dutch banks use the SWIFT network, which offers a cheap, flexible and quick international funds transfer service.

Centralizing accounts, based on a centralized local cashing system and simplified management of fund repatriation, are also widely used.

■ Debt collection

The collection process begins with the debtor being served with a formal demand for the payment of principal plus accrued interest. This is followed, where necessary, by the service of a summons via a bailiff or solicitor.

Where the sales agreement makes no mention of the interest rate, from 1 December 2002 the rate of interest applicable is the European Central Bank's refinancing rate, marked up by seven basis points. The rate in force before the first day of the six-monthly period concerned applies throughout that period.

In the absence of payment or an agreement, creditors may engage a local lawyer to initiate legal proceedings. The Dutch legal system allows lawyers to act as both barristers and solicitors: as solicitors they practise within the jurisdiction of their registration, whereas as barristers they may plead cases before any court in the country.

Before initiating legal proceedings, effective

pressure can be brought to bear on a debtor by means of a winding-up petition. For undisputed claims, this can be obtained without much difficulty, provided the creditor produces evidence of payment default. Such petitions are filed in a civil court (there being no commercial courts), but require the existence of a second claim of any kind (commercial, alimony, tax debt and so on) in order to be admissible.

Ordinary proceedings in which both parties are heard are for the most part based on written submissions. They consist of a simplified procedure being brought before a district court (*kantongerecht*) for claims under 5,000 euros (formerly 10,000 guilders). Larger claims are heard by a court of first instance *(Rechtbank)*, whereby both parties argue their case via written submissions. Unless the parties expressly request the right to make oral arguments, which is rarely the case, the judge bases his or her ruling on the principal case documents submitted by the parties after they have appeared in court (most notably to seek an amicable settlement).

For complex cases requiring special examination, the judge will follow a more formal procedure based on the examination of each litigant's brief and counter-briefs. In such matters, the judge will carefully assess the parties' compliance with the general terms and conditions of sale appearing on invoices and purchase orders, since they form the legal framework of the commercial contract and thus play a crucial role in the proceedings.

Finally, recourse to arbitration is common in the Netherlands. Most arbitration bodies work in specific fields and arbitrators are often selected from among specialist lawyers. Arbitral awards tend to be based on equity rather than on legal considerations.

PAYMENT INCIDENTS INDEX
(12 months moving average - base 100 : World 1995)

Norway

Population (million inhabitants)	4.6
GDP (US$ million)	220,900
GDP per capita (US$)	48,400

Coface analysis Short-term: **A1**

RISK ASSESSMENT

Non-oil economic activity rebounded in 2004 thanks to dynamic household consumption. Households benefited from a sharp interest rate decline, appreciation of property assets and increased purchasing power attributable to low inflation. Investment linked to the oil sector, housing and services was also very robust.

Growth will remain dynamic in 2005. Although household spending will doubtless slow amid the expected interest rate increases, the downturn will be mild since it will be largely offset by wage increases resulting from the growing tensions in the labour market and by substantial reserve savings.

Exports will increase at the same rate as last year with traditional merchandise sales offsetting stabilization of oil revenues. Meanwhile, very ample tax revenues deriving from oil will continue not only to feed the 'Fund for the Future' but also to transform the general fiscal deficit into a surplus conducive to tax reductions and increased public spending.

The economic upturn has resulted in a marked improvement in the company situation as evidenced by a decline of bankruptcies registered in 2004 of approximately 13 per cent. That situation should persist in 2005 considering the low Coface payment incident index.

MAIN ECONOMIC INDICATORS

%	2000	2001	2002	2003	2004(e)	2005(f)
Economic growth	2.8	2.7	1.4	0.4	3.2	3.0
Consumption (var.)	3.9	1.8	3.6	3.8	4.3	4.0
Investment (var.)	−4.1	−4.1	−4.5	−6.5	4.0	4.0
Inflation	3.1	3.0	1.3	2.5	0.6	1.8
Unemployment rate	3.4	3.6	3.9	4.5	4.4	4.1
Short-term interest rate	6.7	7.2	6.9	4.1	1.8	2.0
Public sector balance (%GDP)	15.0	13.7	9.1	8.3	8.8	9.1
Public sector debt (%GDP)	30.0	29.2	35.7	35.2	36.5	32.5
Exports (var.)	4.0	5.0	0.1	1.2	2.3	2.4
Imports (var.)	2.7	0.9	2.3	2.2	6.5	3.5
Current account balance (%GDP)	14.9	15.5	12.9	12.9	14.0	13.0

e = estimate, f = forecast

PAYMENT AND COLLECTION PRACTICES

■ Payment

Bills of exchange and cheques are neither widely used nor recommended, as they must meet a number of formal requirements in order to be valid. In addition, creditors frequently refuse to accept cheques as a means of payment. As a rule, both instruments serve mainly to substantiate the existence of a debt.

Conversely, promissory notes (*gjeldsbrev*) are much more common in commercial transactions and offer superior guarantees when accompanied by an acknowledgement of debt from the buyer as, in the event of default, such an admission allows the beneficiary to obtain a writ of execution from the competent court (*Namrett*).

Bank transfers are by far the most widely used means of payment. All leading Norwegian banks use the SWIFT network, which offers a cheap, flexible and quick international funds transfer service.

Centralizing accounts, based on a centralized local cashing system and simplified management of fund transfers, are also fairly widely used.

Electronic payments, involving the execution of payment orders via the website of the client's bank, are rapidly gaining popularity.

■ Debt collection

The collection process commences with the debtor being sent a demand for the payment of the principal amount, plus any contractually agreed interest penalties, within 14 days. Where an agreement contains no specific penalty clause, interest starts to accrue 30 days after the creditor serves a demand for payment and, since 1 January 2004, is calculated at the Central Bank of Norway's (Norges Bank) base rate, in effect on 1 January and 1 July of the relevant year, increased by seven percentage points.

In the absence of payment or an agreement, creditors may go before the Conciliation Board (*Forliksrådet*), an administrative body presided over by non-professional judges, to obtain a quick an inexpensive ruling. In this event, they must submit documents authenticating their claim, which should be denominated in Norwegian kroner. The Conciliation Board then summons the debtor at short notice to acknowledge or dispute the claim before hearing the parties, either in person or through their official representatives (*Stevnevitne*). At this stage of proceedings, lawyers are not required.

If a settlement is not forthcoming, the case is referred to the court of first instance for examination. However, for claims found to be valid, the Conciliation Board has the power to hand down a decision, which has the force of a court judgment.

Where a defendant fails to respond to the arbitrator's summons or appear at the hearing, the Board passes a ruling in default, which also has the force of a court judgment.

More complex or disputed claims are heard by the court of first instance (*Byret*). The plenary proceedings of this court are based on oral evidence and written submissions. The court examines the arguments and hears the parties' witnesses before delivering a verdict.

Norway does not have a system of commercial courts, but the probate court (*Skifteret*) is also competent to rule on insolvency proceedings.

PAYMENT INCIDENTS INDEX
(12 months moving average - base 100 : World 1995)

Poland

Population (million inhabitants)	39
GDP (US$ million)	189,021

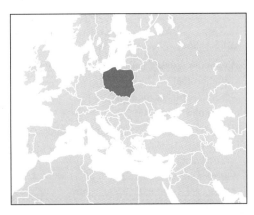

Short-term: **A3**

Medium-term:
Quite low risk

Coface analysis

STRENGTHS

- The economy has been growing strongly, buoyed by export dynamism and an investment recovery.
- Poland's admission to the EU has enhanced the growth outlook.
- Foreign debt ratios have remained sustainable.
- Moderate short-term debt and still-comfortable currency reserves will limit the country's vulnerability to a crisis of confidence.

WEAKNESSES

- A large public sector deficit is still hampering the country.
- Despite improvement in the trade balance, external financing needs have remained appreciable.
- The private sector's foreign currency debt has increased sharply in recent years.
- A weak government coalition and social tensions have been complicating matters in conducting economic policy and pursuing reforms.

RISK ASSESSMENT

Growth accelerated in 2004 reflecting both an export upsurge, fuelled by the past zloty depreciation and increased productivity, and a strengthening of domestic demand. That dynamic context spurred improvement in company solvency with the Coface payment incident index dropping sharply in consequence.

The growth rate should be more moderate in 2005 due to appreciation of the exchange rate, which would limit sales growth abroad, and an investment recovery affected by higher interest rates, as well as doubts about the dynamism of European demand and developments in the domestic political situation.

Improving government finances and limiting the growth of public sector debt have remained crucial challenges. However, the firmness of exports has permitted limiting the current account deficit. Amortization of foreign debt has nonetheless been increasing financing needs with foreign direct investment covering only a quarter of those needs, which has kept Poland dependent on financial markets.

Although weak, the social democratic government should persevere until the June 2005 parliamentary elections with a political changeover then likely to result.

MAIN ECONOMIC INDICATORS

US$ billions	2000	2001	2002	2003	2004[(e)]	2005[(f)]
Economic growth (%)	4.0	1.0	1.4	3.8	5.8	5.0
Inflation (%)	10.2	5.5	2.0	0.8	3.5	3.5
Public sector balance (%GDP)	−2.6	−5.1	−6.3	−6.1	−7.1	−6.6
Unemployment rate (%)	15.1	17.4	20.0	20.0	n/a	n/a
Exports	35.9	41.7	46.7	61.0	80.7	92.3
Imports	48.2	49.3	54.0	66.7	86.5	98.4
Trade balance	−12.3	−7.7	−7.2	−5.7	−5.8	−6.1
Current account balance	−10.0	−5.3	−5.0	−4.1	−5.5	−6.9
Current account balance (%GDP)	−6.0	−2.8	−2.6	−2.0	−2.3	−2.5
Foreign debt (%GDP)	41.7	38.7	44.3	50.0	44.7	40.6
Debt service (%Exports)	12.4	23.3	14.6	16.0	11.9	11.5
Foreign exchange reserves (in months of imports)	5.2	4.9	5.1	4.8	3.8	3.4

e = estimate, f = forecast

CONDITIONS OF ACCESS TO THE MARKET

■ **Market overview**

As of 1 January 2004 the minimum gross wage is 824 zlotys (190 euros); the average wage at the end of 2004 was 2,400 zlotys (about 560 euros).

■ **Means of entry**

Sweeping reforms in the laws and regulations governing market access have brought Poland closer into line with EU standards. On 1 May 2004, Poland dismantled all customs barriers vis-à-vis the EU. Transitional measures, however, remain in force for pharmaceutical companies (licences) and medical equipment and instruments. It will take time before market access in Poland, especially in the agri-food sector, is free from restrictions.

■ **Attitude towards foreign investors**

Drawing on the country's clear competitive edge, the Polish government has so far attracted US$73 billion in FDI. The privatization programme, funded to the tune of 60 per cent by foreign investors, shows signs of picking up after three sluggish years. Many leading companies in the energy, petrochemicals, heavy industry, defence, food and transport sectors are still waiting to be sold through IPOs or private placements.

The economic freedom act of July 2004 places foreign persons and companies on an equal footing with Polish nationals and firms. It also reduces the number of concessions, permissions and registration formalities, while simplifying company incorporation procedures through the creation of a one-stop shop. Safeguards for foreign investors have been strengthened and there are now no restrictions on the repatriation of dividends. However, the shortcomings of the administrative machinery – transparency, red tape and, in some cases, corruption – endure. Administrative and, above all, court procedures remain lengthy and complex.

■ **Foreign exchange regulations**

The zloty's exchange rate is determined by the market with a central parity set daily by the National Bank of Poland. The zloty has been fully convertible since 1 October 2002.

PAYMENT AND COLLECTION PRACTICES

Payment

Bills of exchange and cheques are not widely used, as they must meet a number of formal issuing requirements in order to be valid. Nevertheless, for dishonoured and protested bills and cheques, creditors may resort to a fast-track procedure resulting in an injunction to pay.

Until now, cash payments were commonly used in Poland by individuals and firms alike, but under the Freedom of Business Activity Act (*Ustawa o swobodzie działalności gospodarczej*) of 2 July 2004, which came into force on 21 August 2004, companies are required to make settlements via a bank account for transactions exceeding the equivalent in zlotys of 15,000 euros. This measure aims to counter fraudulent money laundering.

One highly original instrument is the *weksel in blanco*, an incomplete promissory note bearing only the term *weksel* and the issuer's signature at the time of issue. The signature constitutes an irrevocable promise to pay and this undertaking is enforceable upon completion of the promissory note (amount, place and date of payment) in accordance with a prior agreement between issuer and beneficiary. *Weksels in blanco* are widely used, as they also constitute a guarantee of payment in commercial agreements and the rescheduling of payments.

Bank transfers are by far the most widely used means of payment. Leading Polish banks – after an initial phase of privatization and a second phase of concentration – use the SWIFT network, which offers a cheap, flexible and quick domestic and international funds transfer service.

Debt collection

It is advisable, as far as possible, not to initiate recovery proceedings locally due not only to the cumbersome formalities and the high cost of legal action but also to the country's lengthy court procedures: it takes almost two years to obtain a writ of execution due to the lack of judges adequately trained in the rules of the market economy and proper equipment.

Serving a demand for payment, accompanied by proof of debt, reminds the debtor of his or her obligation to pay the outstanding sum, plus any accrued interest. From 1 January 2004, interest may be claimed as of the 31st day following delivery of the product or service, even where the parties have agreed to a longer payment time. The legal interest rate will apply from the 31st day until the contractual payment date; thereafter, in the case of late payment, the higher tax penalty rate will be applicable.

It is advisable to seek an amicable settlement based on a payment schedule drawn up by a public notary, which includes an 'enforcement clause' that allows creditors, in the event of default by the debtor, to go directly to the enforcement stage, subject to acknowledgement by the court of the binding nature of this document.

Creditors may seek an injunction to pay (*nakaz zaplaty*) via a fast-track and less expensive procedure, provided they produce positive proof of debt (bill of exchange, cheque, unpaid *weksel in blanco*, acknowledgement of debt, etc). If the judge is not convinced of the substance of the claim – a decision he or she alone is empowered to make – he or she may refer the case to full trial.

Ordinary proceedings are partly in writing, with the parties filing submissions accompanied by all supporting case documents (original or certified copies), and partly oral with the litigants and their witnesses heard on the main hearing date. At such legal proceedings, the judge is required, as far as possible, to attempt conciliation between the parties.

Commercial disputes are generally heard by the commercial courts (*sąd gospodarczy*), which fall under the jurisdiction of either district courts or regional courts (*Voïvodies*) depending on the size of the claim.

PAYMENT INCIDENTS INDEX
(12 months moving average - base 100 : World 1995)

OPPORTUNITY SCOPE

Breakdown of domestic demand (%GDP + imports)

■ Private consumption   50
■ Public consumption   15
■ Investment   15

Exports: 28% of GDP   Imports: 31% of GDP

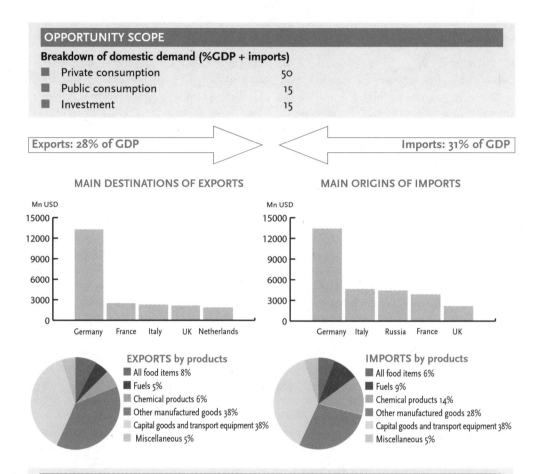

MAIN DESTINATIONS OF EXPORTS

Mn USD
Germany, France, Italy, UK, Netherlands

MAIN ORIGINS OF IMPORTS

Mn USD
Germany, Italy, Russia, France, UK

EXPORTS by products
■ All food items 8%
■ Fuels 5%
■ Chemical products 6%
■ Other manufactured goods 38%
■ Capital goods and transport equipment 38%
■ Miscellaneous 5%

IMPORTS by products
■ All food items 6%
■ Fuels 9%
■ Chemical products 14%
■ Other manufactured goods 28%
■ Capital goods and transport equipment 38%
■ Miscellaneous 5%

STANDARD OF LIVING / PURCHASING POWER

Indicators	Poland	Regional average	DC average
GNP per capita (PPP dollars)	10450	8313	4601
GNP per capita (USD)	4570	2535	1840
Human Development Index	0.850	0.805	0.684
Wealthiest 10% share of national income	27.4	30	32
Urban population percentage	63	68	45
Percentage under 15 years old	19	17	30
Number of telephones per 1000 inhabitants	295	257	120
Number of computers per 1000 inhabitants	106	84	37

Portugal

Population (million inhabitants) 10.4
GDP (US$ million) 146,800
GDP per capita (US$) 14,100

Coface analysis   Short-term: **A2**

RISK ASSESSMENT

After a recession year, the Portuguese economy registered a modest recovery in 2004, buoyed in the first half by strengthening domestic demand largely fuelled by preparations for the European football championships. A slowdown nonetheless developed thereafter.

Growth will only improve slightly in 2005. Private consumption should increase, buoyed by reduced unemployment. Despite the euro appreciation, exports will benefit from a partial recovery of company competitiveness attributable to easing inflation. Productive investment will

increase in consequence. The public sector financial situation will remain shaky. Without consensus policy, the fiscal deficit will remain above 3 per cent of GDP despite exceptional proceeds from privatizations.

The company situation has only been improving gradually under the combined effect of the recovery of domestic demand and exports. However, in the more competitive context resulting from EU enlargement and expiration of the Multifibre Arrangement, significant risks have persisted in sectors like textiles, clothing and car-industry subcontracting.

MAIN ECONOMIC INDICATORS						
%	2000	2001	2002	2003	2004[(e)]	2005[(f)]
Economic growth	3.4	1.6	0.4	−1.2	1.4	1.9
Consumption (var.)	2.9	1.2	1.0	−0.5	2.0	2.2
Investment (var.)	4.4	0.8	−4.9	−9.8	2.4	4.7
Inflation	2.9	4.3	3.6	3.3	2.4	2.2
Unemployment rate	4.0	4.0	5.0	6.3	6.8	6.3
Short-term interest rate	4.4	4.3	3.3	2.3	2.1	2.4
Public sector balance (%GDP)	−2.9	−4.4	−2.7	−2.8	−3.9	−3.3
Public sector debt (%GDP)	61.4	65.1	68.1	70.3	71.5	69.9
Exports (var.)	7.8	1.0	2.0	4.0	5.2	5.3
Imports (var.)	5.5	1.1	−0.3	−0.9	4.7	5.7
Current account balance (%GDP)	−10.9	−9.5	−6.7	−5.1	−4.8	−4.4

e = estimate, f = forecast

87

PAYMENT AND COLLECTION PRACTICES

■ Payment

Bills of exchange are widely used for commercial transactions in Portugal. In order to be valid, however, they are subject to stamp duty whose rate is set each year in the country's budget. The current rate of stamp duty is 0.5 per cent of the amount of the bill, or a minimum of 1 euro. A bill of exchange is generally deemed independent of the contract to which it relates.

While creditors, in the event of payment default, are not required to issue a protest notice before bringing an action to court, such a notice can be used to publicize payment default and pressure the debtor to honour his or her obligations, albeit belatedly.

Cheques too are widely used. They are payable on presentation and subject to the minimum stamp duty that is borne by the bank. It is no longer an offence to issue uncovered cheques as a guarantee for staggered payments.

In the event of default, cheques, bills of exchange and promissory notes offer effective guarantees to creditors as they are enforceable instruments in law and entitle holders to initiate executory proceedings. Under this process, creditors may petition the court to issue a writ of execution and notify the debtor of such an order. Where the debtor still fails to pay up, creditors may request the court to issue an attachment order against the debtor's property.

SWIFT bank transfers, which are both flexible and efficient, also account for a growing proportion of payments.

■ Debt collection

Out-of-court collection starts with the debtor being sent a final demand for the payment of the principal amount, plus any default interest that may have been agreed between the parties, within eight days. Save as otherwise provided in the agreement, from 18 February 2003, the rate of interest applicable is the European Central Bank's refinancing rate marked up by seven basis points. The Ministerial Order of April 1999, which set the legal default interest rate at 12 per cent for commercial debt,

remained in force until 30 September 2004. The order on 31 August 2004, applicable on 1 October 2004, states the default interest, set now by decree of the Treasury Department, will be published in the *Diario da Republica* in the first fortnight of January and July each year.

Since 19 March 2003, the fast-track procedure (injunction to pay – *injunção*) applicable to commercial claims considered uncontested and whatever the amount involved must be heard by the court in whose jurisdiction the obligation is enforceable.

For disputed claims, creditors may initiate formal and costly declarative proceedings (*acção declarativa*), lasting a year or more, to obtain a ruling establishing their right to payment. They must then initiate enforcement proceedings (*acção executiva*) to enforce the court's ruling.

Under the revised code of civil procedure introduced in January 1996, any original deed established by private seal (ie any written document issued to a supplier) in which the buyer unequivocally acknowledges his or her debt is henceforth deemed an instrument enforceable by law. This provision aims to encourage buyers to comply with contractual undertakings and offers creditors a safeguard against protracted legal action. As Portugal does not have commercial courts (other than those in Lisbon and Oporto, which deal with insolvency proceedings, dissolution of companies and protection of industrial property), civil courts (*Varas Cíveis*), presided over by a collegial panel of three judges, hear large commercial claims exceeding 14,963.94 euros (formerly 3 million escudos).

PAYMENT INCIDENTS INDEX
(12 months moving average - base 100 : World 1995)

Romania

Population (million inhabitants)	22
GDP (US$ million)	45,749

Short-term: **B**

Medium-term:

Coface analysis   **Moderately high risk**

STRENGTHS

● Romania boasts an appreciable domestic market.

● Its labour force is skilled and low cost.

● Its EU accession, planned for 2007 or 2008, has enhanced its economic outlook.

● Public and external debt levels have been reasonable with foreign exchange reserves at comfortable levels.

WEAKNESSES

● The country's increased external financing needs have correspondingly increased its dependence on foreign capital.

● Sustaining strong growth and market confidence will depend on pursuit of reforms (privatizations, subsidy system, labour code, anti-corruption measures, legal system, bankruptcies).

● The lack of a clear parliamentary majority could undermine the new government.

RISK ASSESSMENT

Economic activity has remained strong, buoyed by export and domestic demand dynamism. The growth of wages and credit has notably been underpinning buoyant consumption and investment. In those favourable economic conditions, sectors like textiles, pharmaceuticals, mass distribution or car and car-part manufacturers have been demonstrating above-average dynamism. However, late payments by companies have remained commonplace.

A widening current account deficit has been a subsidiary effect of that dynamism. However, FDI, which has been increasing, and borrowing abroad, whose cost has declined significantly, have permitted financing that deficit without major

difficulties as attested by the comfortable level of currency reserves. Authorities will nonetheless have to continue their efforts to reduce public sector deficits to permit controlling external imbalances.

After the opposition victory in the December 2004 presidential elections, a new government coalition will be responsible for securing Romania's EU accession. Although the previous government succeeded in concluding the accession negotiations, the country had to accept a safeguard clause that could delay its admission for a year, normally scheduled for January 2007. Brussels notably expects Romania to meet its commitments on combating corruption, legal system independence and reduction of government subsidies.

MAIN ECONOMIC INDICATORS

US$ billions	2000	2001	2002	2003	2004(e)	2005(f)
Economic growth (%)	2.1	5.7	5.0	4.9	6.5	5.2
Inflation (%)	45.7	34.5	22.5	15.3	11.8	8.3
Public sector balance (%GDP)(*)	−8.7	−7.9	−5.2	−5.3	−3.3	−2.4
Unemployment rate (%)	10.5	8.6	8.1	7.2	6.5	6.3
Exports	10.4	11.4	13.9	17.6	24.3	29.4
Imports	12.1	14.4	16.5	22.2	29.5	35.0
Trade balance	−1.7	−3.0	−2.6	−4.5	−5.2	−5.7
Current account balance	−1.4	−2.2	−1.5	−3.3	−3.9	−4.1
Current account balance (%GDP)	−3.7	−5.5	−3.3	−5.8	−5.5	−5.1
Foreign debt (%GDP)	32.2	34.2	38.7	40.2	36.1	35.4
Debt service (%Exports)	14.0	16.9	15.8	15.5	12.2	10.2
Foreign exchange reserves (in months of imports)	3.2	3.8	4.4	4.1	4.2	3.5

*general government deficit + public energy-sector losses   e = estimate, f = forecast

CONDITIONS OF ACCESS TO THE MARKET

■ Market overview

The pace of EU accession negotiations initiated in 2000 accelerated these past two years with Romanian authorities taking strides to bring them to a conclusion before end-2004. The wrapping up of the last two chapters of established community policy and practice (competition and justice) was nonetheless coupled with a safeguard clause that could be activated should Romania fail to meet its commitments. Progress towards liberalizing the Romanian market (trade and foreign investment) continues to be brisk. Almost 70 per cent of the country's foreign trade is carried out with the EU. In its last progress report the EU commission concluded that Romania now has a viable market economy. However, restructuring the agricultural and agri-food sectors remains one of the most difficult challenges facing the country.

■ Means of entry

Goods can be traded freely as import–export licences are required for only a handful of products (eg foodstuffs, used equipment). Imports of beef from countries with reported cases of BSE are now admitted under certain conditions set out in the animal and public health certificate (RO VFA OCT 02). Certain farm products are protected by customs duties that vary between 9 per cent and 45 per cent. However, there is a provision for waiving duties on products imported under a quota system. Customs duties on industrial products imported from the EU have been phased out in stages in accordance with the Association Agreement concluded in 1995.

New means of payment such as bank transfers and bills of exchange have been adopted. Cheques are virtually non-existent. The use of charge cards is spreading gradually. When dealing with clients for the first time, it is advisable to use documentary credit for payments. Documents against payment/acceptance are also used. Some large banks offer factoring services. The banking sector restructuring programme is at an advanced stage. Leasing is enjoying a boom in the industrial and capital goods sectors. Payment prior to shipment is frequently accepted, and recommended, in Romania.

■ Attitude towards foreign investors

The law of July 2001 defines the legal framework for foreign investment in excess of US$1 million and enshrines the principle of non-discrimination between foreign and domestic investors. It also regulates SME investments. Foreign investment schemes over US$10 million are eligible for special benefits. Since August 1993, all profits can be freely transferred. The new constitution, voted recently, permits land ownership by foreigners, provided they set up a company.

■ Foreign exchange regulations

Romanian importers have immediate access to foreign exchange through their banks. Business persons and private individuals can open foreign currency accounts with approved Romanian and foreign banks. Romanian and foreign business persons are allowed to hold and freely dispose of all their foreign currency earnings. Only leu deposits by non-residents are still forbidden, although all restrictions on capital accounts are due to be lifted by April 2005.

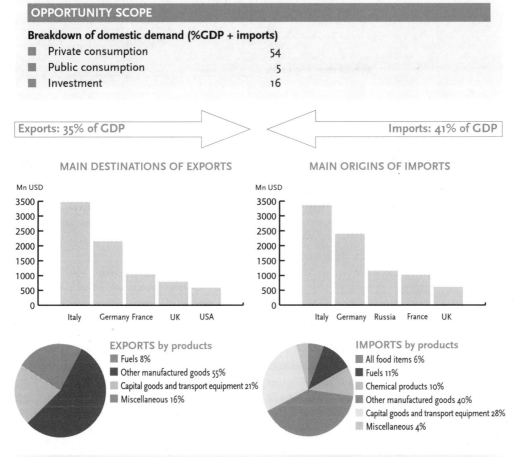

OPPORTUNITY SCOPE

Breakdown of domestic demand (%GDP + imports)

■ Private consumption	54
■ Public consumption	5
■ Investment	16

Exports: 35% of GDP   Imports: 41% of GDP

MAIN DESTINATIONS OF EXPORTS

Mn USD

Italy, Germany, France, UK, USA

MAIN ORIGINS OF IMPORTS

Mn USD

Italy, Germany, Russia, France, UK

EXPORTS by products
- Fuels 8%
- Other manufactured goods 55%
- Capital goods and transport equipment 21%
- Miscellaneous 16%

IMPORTS by products
- All food items 6%
- Fuels 11%
- Chemical products 10%
- Other manufactured goods 40%
- Capital goods and transport equipment 28%
- Miscellaneous 4%

STANDARD OF LIVING / PURCHASING POWER

Indicators	Romania	Regional average	DC average
GNP per capita (PPP dollars)	6490	8313	4601
GNP per capita (USD)	1870	2535	1840
Human Development Index	0.778	0.805	0.684
Wealthiest 10% share of national income	23.6	30	32
Urban population percentage	55	68	45
Percentage under 15 years old	17	17	30
Number of telephones per 1000 inhabitants	194	257	120
Number of computers per 1000 inhabitants	69	84	37

Russia

Population (million inhabitants)	144
GDP (US$ million)	346,520

Short-term: **B**

Medium-term:

Coface analysis **Moderately high risk**

STRENGTHS

- Russia boasts many natural resources and a skilled labour force.
- Its regional and nuclear power status has strengthened since Vladimir Putin took office.
- Many reforms have been legislated.
- The political stability resulting from the federal government's reassertion of authority over the federation, parliament and the oligarchies has begun to influence economic behaviour.

WEAKNESSES

- Dominated by raw materials, the economy has remained vulnerable to world price swings with pressure on the real exchange rate hampering national production.
- The industrial sector is not very open to foreign investment, which has remained very limited.
- Conflicts of interests of economic and regional actors often block implementation of reforms adopted.
- Reforms on property rights and company financial transparency are still not enough to improve the business environment.

RISK ASSESSMENT

The financial situation has remained good thanks to continued current account and public sector surpluses and large currency reserves. That dynamic is not attributable solely to oil prices: tax reform has been successful and fiscal policy has become more transparent. There also has been an increase in domestic investment very beneficial to the economy.

The recovery has nonetheless been shaky with the economy's dependence on raw material sectors making it very vulnerable to swings in barrel prices. Moreover, the lack of foreign investment could limit the extraction sector's expansion. Meanwhile, the manufacturing sector's competitiveness could suffer from the real rouble appreciation.

Politically, the recentralization of power in favour of the presidency has been gaining momentum, justified by the upsurge of terrorism.

That weakening of all countervailing powers has made the political process dependent on the highest office. The shock waves generated by the Yukos affair have provided a reminder that the struggles over the control of energy assets have remained a current reality and that respect for property rights is still inconsistent. That affair has also triggered new capital outflows.

Meanwhile, the banking sector's liquidity crisis in summer 2004 revealed the weakness of a sector where radical reform is still pending. In any case, legislated changes have had some difficulty becoming part of an economic reality still marked by a weak regulatory and institutional framework for the market economy. Although the solvency of companies has been improving in a more buoyant economic environment, their financial transparency has remained limited with protection for creditors still ineffective.

MAIN ECONOMIC INDICATORS

US$ billions	2000	2001	2002	2003	2004[(e)]	2005[(f)]
Economic growth (%)	10.0	5.1	4.7	7.3	7.5	6.5
Inflation (%)	20.2	19.0	15.0	12.0	10.4	8.4
Public sector balance (%GDP)	1.2	2.7	1.4	1.7	2.5	2.5
Exports	91.2	86.5	90.9	114.6	143.0	144.5
Imports	31.4	40.7	49.0	60.0	78.0	88.0
Trade balance	59.8	45.8	42.1	54.3	65.5	56.2
Current account balance	44.2	30.0	27.5	29.0	34.5	22.0
Current account balance (%GDP)	17.0	9.8	8.0	6.7	5.9	3.3
Foreign debt (%GDP)	53.3	42.3	41.6	41.5	33.7	31.7
Debt service (%Exports)	21.5	20.2	19.4	15.3	15.3	17.7
Foreign exchange reserves (in months of imports)	5.1	5.7	6.8	8.6	8.8	9.0

e = estimate, f = forecast

CONDITIONS OF ACCESS TO THE MARKET

■ **Means of entry**

Reforms undertaken in such varied fields as customs, taxation, land ownership and administration aim to bring Russia's economic mechanisms into line with international standards and practices. The reforms should help promote the exchange of goods and strengthen investor confidence. Only their continued and proper implementation, which the prospect of Russia's WTO accession should serve to speed up, will significantly enhance the business climate and boost foreign investor confidence.

Since January 2001, Russia has carried out a series of customs reforms designed to lower and unify customs duties. Despite these improvements, customs clearance remains a difficult exercise due to ongoing customs reorganization and rigid customs clearance procedures. The new customs code, which came into force on 1 January 2004, seeks to remedy this situation, in particular by reducing clearance times and setting in place simplified clearance procedures. However, as its provisions are still to be fully enforced, it will only be possible to evaluate its benefits in the longer term.

■ **Attitude towards foreign investors**

Despite macroeconomic restructuring, the economic situation remains precarious and calls for wider structural reforms. Banking sector reform has hardly begun; infrastructure development, particularly as far as the energy sector is concerned, requires considerable investment; and the legal environment for business lacks credibility and needs greater transparency.

Tax reforms have resulted in across-the-board tax cuts: the standard rate of corporation tax has been lowered to 24 per cent; the standard rate of personal income tax has been reduced to 13 per cent; sales tax has been abolished since 1 January 2004; and VAT has been cut from 20 per cent to 18 per cent. Plans are underway to reduce the single welfare tax from 35.6 per cent to 26 per cent by 2005 and further cut VAT from 18 per cent to 16 per cent in 2006.

A new land ownership law, in force since 30 October 2001, authorizes the sale of urban, industrial and commercial land, but not farmland. It gives foreign businesses and nationals almost the same property rights as Russians, including the ownership of land in all but a few cases. A series of reforms designed to streamline investment regulations were carried out in early 2001. The measures simplify licensing, investment registration (via a one-stop shop) and product certification. The growing awareness in the last few years of the usefulness of intellectual property protection has resulted in the introduction of better legal safeguards (eg amendments to the brands and denominations of origin act passed on 16 December 2002 and amendments to the law on copyright and related rights signed by President Poutine on 20 July 2004). However, only proper implementation of the new provisions will help combat the alarming level of infringement.

Although there has been a marked improvement in investment legislation, some negative signs are starting to emerge. For instance, since autumn 2002 the foreign business community has been subjected to unnecessary red tape to obtain visas and work permits. The Yukos affair, whose outcome is still unknown, casts doubts over the uniform application of the law, particularly in respect of the strategic sectors. Concerns so far are more marked among Russian investors than foreigners.

■ **Foreign exchange regulations**

Exchange controls were relaxed in 2001. The threshold for converting earnings, usually generated in dollars, into roubles was lowered from 75 per cent to 50 per cent on 1 January 2002 and then to 30 per cent under the law on exchange regulations and controls passed on 18 June 2004, which also provides for the phasing out of the conversion obligation.

OPPORTUNITY SCOPE

Breakdown of domestic demand (%GDP + imports)
- Private consumption — 41
- Public consumption — 14
- Investment — 17

Exports: 35% of GDP → ← Imports: 24% of GDP

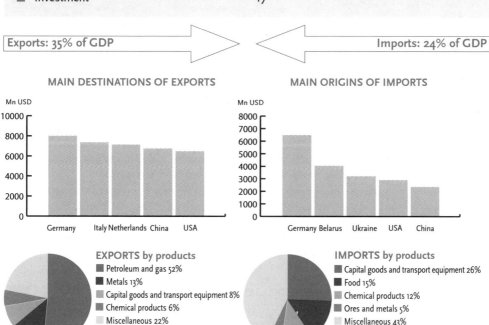

MAIN DESTINATIONS OF EXPORTS

Mn USD

Germany · Italy · Netherlands · China · USA

MAIN ORIGINS OF IMPORTS

Mn USD

Germany · Belarus · Ukraine · USA · China

EXPORTS by products
- Petroleum and gas 52%
- Metals 13%
- Capital goods and transport equipment 8%
- Chemical products 6%
- Miscellaneous 22%

IMPORTS by products
- Capital goods and transport equipment 26%
- Food 15%
- Chemical products 12%
- Ores and metals 5%
- Miscellaneous 43%

STANDARD OF LIVING / PURCHASING POWER

Indicators	Russia	Regional average	DC average
GNP per capita (PPP dollars)	8080	8313	4601
GNP per capita (USD)	2130	2535	1840
Human Development Index	0.795	0.805	0.684
Wealthiest 10% share of national income	36	30	32
Urban population percentage	73	68	45
Percentage under 15 years old	17	17	30
Number of telephones per 1000 inhabitants	242	257	120
Number of computers per 1000 inhabitants	89	84	37

Serbia and Montenegro

Population (million inhabitants)	8
GDP (US$ million)	15,681

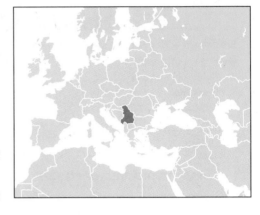

Short-term: **C**

Coface analysis

Medium-term:
Very high risk

STRENGTHS

- The political normalization and reforms undertaken since October 2000 have permitted the country to earn broad support from international financial institutions and improve its economic and financial situation.
- Restructuring the foreign debt, despite its still-significant size, has improved the country's solvency.
- The workforce is skilled and low cost.

WEAKNESSES

- Production has remained low after a decade of disinvestment and conflict.
- An obsolescent productive apparatus amid strengthening domestic demand has pushed the current account deficit to very high levels.
- Restructuring costs and social needs have been weighing on public sector finances.
- The reform process has stalled since mid-2003 due to political instability amid persistent challenges to the country's territorial integrity.

RISK ASSESSMENT

Growth resumed in 2004, thanks to a recovery of farm production and the steadiness of manufacturing and services. The economy should remain strong in 2005 provided foreign demand (notably from Italy and Germany) does not weaken significantly.

However, macroeconomic stability has remained shaky. Disinflation has eased due to rapid wage growth and increased oil prices. External account imbalances have been worsening with export growth remaining insufficient in relation to imports. The foreign debt burden should thus remain significant despite the debt restructuring agreement concluded with London Club creditors.

In that context, Serbian authorities have been letting the dinar depreciate and discussions with the IMF have been focusing on the need to pursue restrictive economic policy. The Fund has also insisted on the need to speed up the pace of reforms involving privatizations as well as those concerning improvement of efficiency in state-owned enterprises.

Politically, Western chancelleries welcomed the victory of an enthusiastic partisan of EU and NATO accession in the Serbian presidential election in June 2004. However, the country's cooperation with the International Criminal Court for former Yugoslavia has not improved and the minority coalition in Serbia has remained weak and divided.

MAIN ECONOMIC INDICATORS

US$ millions	2000	2001	2002	2003	2004[(e)]	2005[(f)]
Economic growth (%)	5.2	5.3	3.8	2.0	6.0	5.0
Inflation (%)	69.9	91.1	21.2	11.2	9.4	10.4
Public sector balance (%GDP)	−2.9	−1.4	−4.5	−4.2	−3.4	−2.4
Unemployment rate (%)	25.9	31.3	28.9	34.5	n/a	n/a
Exports	1,923	2,003	2,412	2,732	3,245	3,802
Imports	3,711	4,837	6,320	7,510	9,763	10,446
Trade balance	−1,788	−2,834	−3,908	−4,778	−6,518	−6,644
Current account balance	−339	−528	−1,383	−1,859	−2,834	−2,906
Current account balance (%GDP)	−3.9	−4.6	−8.8	−9.4	−12.7	−12.3
Foreign debt (%GDP)	132.5	103.2	75.5	72.2	57.6	54.0
Debt service (%Exports)	1.4	2.1	3.0	6.2	12.1	13.3
Foreign exchange reserves (in months of imports)	1.4	2.5	3.7	4.8	3.6	4.0

e = estimate, f = forecast

OPPORTUNITY SCOPE

Breakdown of domestic demand (%GDP + imports)
- Private consumption   62
- Public consumption   13
- Investment   11

Exports: 21% of GDP

Imports: 44% of GDP

MAIN DESTINATIONS OF EXPORTS

Mn USD

Italy   Germany   Austria   France Netherlands

MAIN ORIGINS OF IMPORTS

Mn USD

Germany Italy   Austria Slovenia Greece

EXPORTS by products
- Food and tobacco 21%
- Manufactured goods 30%
- Various finished products 15%
- Miscellaneous 34%

IMPORTS by products
- Fuels and lubricants 17%
- Manufactured goods 20%
- Machinery and equipment 26%
- Miscellaneous 37%

STANDARD OF LIVING / PURCHASING POWER

Indicators	Serbia & Montenegro	Regional average	DC average
GNP per capita (PPP dollars)	n/a	8313	4601
GNP per capita (USD)	1400	2535	1840
Human Development Index	n/a	0.805	0.684
Wealthiest 10% share of national income	n/a	30	32
Urban population percentage	52	68	45
Percentage under 15 years old	20	17	30
Number of telephones per 1000 inhabitants	233	257	120
Number of computers per 1000 inhabitants	27	84	37

Slovakia

Population (million inhabitants)	5
GDP (US$ million)	23,682

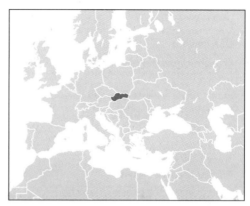

Coface analysis

Short-term: **A3**

Medium-term:
Quite low risk

STRENGTHS

- Admission to the EU has bolstered the country's economic and financial situation.
- FDIs, both greenfield and those linked to privatizations, have enhanced the economic potential.
- Foreign currency reserves have been at comfortable levels.
- Implementation of social spending reforms has been rapid.

WEAKNESSES

- Public sector financial imbalances have persisted.
- The Slovak koruny's appreciation could undermine the country's competitiveness.
- Foreign debt has remained relatively high in relation to GDP.
- The unemployment rate is still high.

RISK ASSESSMENT

Reforms implemented in recent years with the prospect of admission to the EU have notably permitted improving the country's economic and financial situation. FDI inflows have strengthened the growth potential and spurred a sharp increase in exports, which has permitted limiting external financing needs.

Although the public sector deficit has remained appreciable, the economy's firmness along with social spending reforms should permit the country to meet Maastricht criteria – more rapidly than its neighbours – by 2007 and join the euro zone by 2009. Foreign debt ratios have been improving with foreign exchange reserves staying at comfortable levels.

Political risk has eased markedly although dissension has persisted within the reform coalition in power with continued high unemployment stoking social tensions.

Risk factors mainly concern the exchange rate appreciation and a growing dependence on the car industry.

In that favourable economic context, company solvency has generally remained good with the Coface payment incident index remaining at risk levels below the world average. The situation has nonetheless still been difficult in some branches like food, textiles and health. Conversely, the car industry, energy and mobile telephony have retained their great dynamism.

MAIN ECONOMIC INDICATORS

US$ millions	2000	2001	2002	2003	2004$^{(e)}$	2005$^{(f)}$
Economic growth (%)	2.0	3.8	4.4	4.2	4.9	5.0
Inflation (%)	12.0	7.1	3.3	8.6	7.7	3.4
Public sector balance (%GDP)	−3.8	−6.0	−5.7	−3.6	−3.5	−4.0
Unemployment rate (%)	18.6	19.2	18.5	17.5	n/a	n/a
Exports	11,870	12,631	14,365	21,838	28,300	33,500
Imports	12,786	14,766	16,497	22,479	29,330	35,060
Trade balance	−917	−2,135	−2,131	−641	−1,030	−1,560
Current account balance	−622	−1,678	−1,832	−155	−610	−1,270
Current account balance (%GDP)	−3.1	−8.0	−7.6	−0.5	−1.5	−3.0
Foreign debt (%GDP)	53.4	54.0	54.5	55.6	48.4	49.5
Debt service (%Exports)	17.4	14.3	12.3	13.5	7.9	6.7
Foreign exchange reserves (in months of imports)	3.2	2.9	5.4	5.3	4.7	4.6

e = estimate, f = forecast

CONDITIONS OF ACCESS TO THE MARKET

■ Market overview

The job situation in the country remains alarming with high unemployment and wide regional disparities. Despite substantial wage increases in 2003–2004, the average monthly wage is a mere 350 euros. Following the completion of banking sector reorganization and the partial privatization of the gas and electricity supply companies, the ongoing privatization of the Slovak electricity utility (SE) and the water supply company marks the last stage in the liberalization of Slovakia's economy. Although the expanding consumer goods market clearly provides many business opportunities, capital goods supply and industrial joint ventures (subcontracting, manufacturing under licence and, above all, joint start-ups) offer the greatest growth prospects.

■ Means of entry

Customs duties on industrial products have been lifted, but agricultural products do not qualify for exemption and continue to bear duty. Residual barriers linked to certification and technical standards are gradually being dismantled as Slovakia moves closer towards compliance with EU integration criteria. The Slovak customs code has adopted in full the European harmonized code,

with a common external tariff applicable to non-EU countries and intra-EU procedures (declaration of traded goods) applicable to trade with other member states. The most widely used means of payment are SWIFT transfers, bills of exchange and documentary credit. Disputes and litigation are relatively rare.

■ Attitude towards foreign investors

Slovakia's liberal legislation permits investors to wholly own a local company. A 34 per cent stake constitutes a blocking minority. The law establishes equality of treatment between Slovak and foreign investors. The Slovak Investment and Trade Development Agency (SARIO) is more proactive than before in the development of Slovak industrial areas. The new government has just lifted restrictions on foreign shareholdings in the so-

PAYMENT INCIDENTS INDEX
(12 months moving average - base 100 : World 1995)

called strategic sectors (energy, etc). This will help boost FDI in the country.

■ **Foreign exchange regulations**
The Slovak koruny, which enjoys fairly stable parity with the euro, is freely convertible but rarely traded abroad. Since the abolition of exchange controls and the introduction of a new banking law, international commercial settlements are conducted with greater ease.

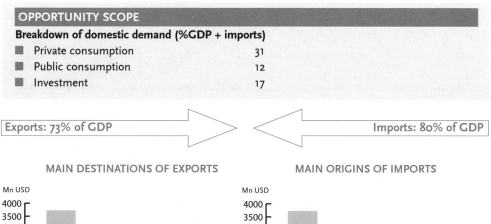

OPPORTUNITY SCOPE

Breakdown of domestic demand (%GDP + imports)

■ Private consumption	31
■ Public consumption	12
■ Investment	17

Exports: 73% of GDP ➡ ⬅ Imports: 80% of GDP

MAIN DESTINATIONS OF EXPORTS

Mn USD

(Germany, Czech Republic, Italy, Austria, Hungary)

MAIN ORIGINS OF IMPORTS

Mn USD

(Germany, Czech Republic, Russia, Italy, France)

EXPORTS by products
- ■ Fuels 6%
- ■ Chemical products 7%
- ■ Other manufactured goods 39%
- ■ Capital goods and transport equipment 39%
- ■ Miscellaneous 9%

IMPORTS by products
- ■ All food items 5%
- ■ Fuels 13%
- ■ Chemical products 10%
- ■ Other manufactured goods 28%
- ■ Capital goods and transport equipment 38%
- ■ Miscellaneous 5%

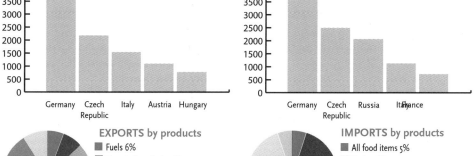

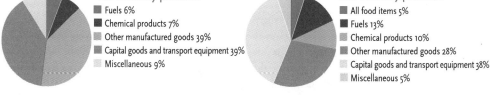

STANDARD OF LIVING / PURCHASING POWER

Indicators	Slovakia	Regional average	DC average
GNP per capita (PPP dollars)	12590	8313	4601
GNP per capita (USD)	3970	2535	1840
Human Development Index	0.842	0.805	0.684
Wealthiest 10% share of national income	20.9	30	32
Urban population percentage	58	68	45
Percentage under 15 years old	19	17	30
Number of telephones per 1000 inhabitants	268	257	120
Number of computers per 1000 inhabitants	180	84	37

Slovenia

Population (million inhabitants) 2
GDP (US$ million) 21,960

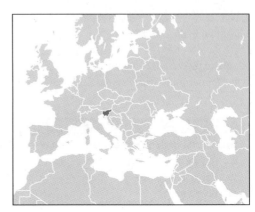

Coface analysis

Short-term: **A2**

Medium-term:
Low risk

STRENGTHS

- The economy has been prosperous and stable.
- EU accession has enhanced the country's medium-term outlook.
- Public sector finances and external accounts have remained sound.
- Slovenia boasts the highest level of wealth in Central Europe.
- The country is ethnically homogeneous.

WEAKNESSES

- Small in size and open, Slovenia's economy has remained dependent on the international situation.
- The country has to contend with increased competition from other emerging countries.
- Foreign debt has been relatively high in relation to GDP.
- Reforms still need to be taken further (privatization, promotion of competition, labour market flexibility).

RISK ASSESSMENT

The economy recovered in 2004 with a sharp upturn in the run-up to EU accession. Growth should remain strong in 2005 amid steady private consumption and fixed investment. Moreover, the country has been participating in the European exchange rate mechanism since June 2004, which should contribute to bringing down inflation that has remained above the European average.

Although the faster growth of imports in relation to exports has resulted in an enlarged trade deficit, the current account has stayed nearly in balance due to development of sales of transport services and tourism. Even though external financing needs have been growing due mainly to increased debt amortization, debt service has remained reasonable in relation to export revenues. Moreover, FDI inflows should pick up if the government finalizes major privatizations.

Despite a majority change after the October 2004 legislative elections, the prospect of the country's rapid admission to the EMU should continue to guide economic policy. Slovenia has already met most Maastricht criteria.

MAIN ECONOMIC INDICATORS

US$ millions	2000	2001	2002	2003	2004(e)	2005(f)
Economic growth (%)	3.9	2.7	3.3	2.5	3.9	4.0
Inflation (%)	8.9	8.4	7.5	5.6	3.5	3.2
Public sector balance (%GDP)	−1.3	−1.3	−1.5	−1.4	−1.7	−1.6
Unemployment rate (%)	7.0	6.4	6.3	6.7	6.7	6.4
Exports	8,808	9,343	10,473	12,928	15,357	17,241
Imports	9,947	9,962	10,716	13,552	16,523	18,488
Trade balance	−1,139	−619	−243	−624	−1,166	−1,247
Current account balance	−548	31	375	15	−83	−99
Current account balance (%GDP)	−2.9	0.2	1.7	0.1	−0.3	−0.3
Foreign debt (%GDP)	45.8	47.5	48.8	53.0	56.1	58.9
Debt service (%Exports)	9.0	14.1	12.5	14.7	15.2	15.8
Foreign exchange reserves (in months of imports)	3.3	4.4	6.4	6.2	4.9	4.5

e = estimate, f = forecast

CONDITIONS OF ACCESS TO THE MARKET

■ Means of entry

Public tenders are open to EU firms in principle. Non-tariff barriers include fairly arbitrary enforcement of certification rules and standards and excessive food inspections and plant health tests by customs, which were introduced in 2001 and 2002. There is nevertheless progress towards greater harmonization with EU criteria every day. SWIFT transfers are a common means of payment. Many Slovenian companies settle their invoices through deferred payment arrangements, thanks to their creditworthiness and good credit rating. Debt collection firms are efficient, but court procedures are generally slow. Lack of local financing on competitive terms (rates and duration) hampers the operations of both Slovenian and foreign businesses and explains the increasing reliance on foreign loans.

■ Attitude towards foreign investors

Investment is unrestricted, except in armaments, compulsory pension funds and health insurance. However, there are no special incentives for foreign investment. Government approval is required to acquire over 25 per cent of a Slovenian company with a capital of 800 million tolars or more (approximately 4 million euros). Foreign companies enjoy equal access to tax-free trade areas in Maribor,

Celje and the fast-expanding port of Koper. Market access is more or less unrestricted, although in a number of sectors (retail, locally manufactured consumer goods, financial services, pharmaceuticals) Slovenian companies fiercely resist foreign competition. Tax audits of companies are often carried out in a questionable manner and result in litigation. There remains a woeful lack of transparency in the way public tenders are conducted, with public opinion supporting cartels in public works and construction, telecommunications, etc. However, the situation is fast changing as the country comes under ever greater pressure to comply with EU integration criteria.

■ Foreign exchange regulations

The tolar is a floating and fully convertible currency with its central rate set at 239,640 since its entry into ERM-II in June 2004. The currency is due to be integrated into the euro in 2007.

PAYMENT INCIDENTS INDEX
(12 months moving average - base 100 : World 1995)

Breakdown of domestic demand (%GDP + imports)

- ■ Private consumption   35
- ■ Public consumption   13
- ■ Investment   15

Exports: 58% of GDP   Imports: 56% of GDP

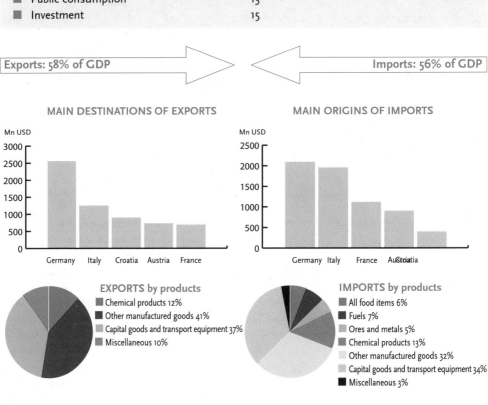

MAIN DESTINATIONS OF EXPORTS

Mn USD

Germany, Italy, Croatia, Austria, France

MAIN ORIGINS OF IMPORTS

Mn USD

Germany, Italy, France, Austria, Croatia

EXPORTS by products
- ■ Chemical products 12%
- ■ Other manufactured goods 41%
- ■ Capital goods and transport equipment 37%
- ■ Miscellaneous 10%

IMPORTS by products
- ■ All food items 6%
- ■ Fuels 7%
- ■ Ores and metals 5%
- ■ Chemical products 13%
- ■ Other manufactured goods 32%
- ■ Capital goods and transport equipment 34%
- ■ Miscellaneous 3%

STANDARD OF LIVING / PURCHASING POWER

Indicators	Slovenia	Regional average	DC average
GNP per capita (PPP dollars)	18480	8313	4601
GNP per capita (USD)	10370	2535	1840
Human Development Index	0.895	0.805	0.684
Wealthiest 10% share of national income	21.4	30	32
Urban population percentage	49	68	45
Percentage under 15 years old	15	17	30
Number of telephones per 1000 inhabitants	506	257	120
Number of computers per 1000 inhabitants	301	84	37

Spain

Population (million inhabitants)	41.9
GDP (US$ million)	838,600
GDP per capita (US$)	20,500

Coface analysis   Short-term: **A1**

STRENGTHS

- Public sector accounts have been in balance thanks to social security account surpluses resulting from employment growth, and to legislation prohibiting territorial public institutions from running deficits.
- Public infrastructure investments, still benefiting from European aid, have continued, permitting the country to upgrade its out-of-date communications networks.
- Although Spain has remained a premium tourist destination, it will have to improve the quality of services offered to meet competition from low-cost destinations.
- Close ties with much of the Americas and use of a common language will continue to constitute major advantages.

WEAKNESSES

- Even with immigration, weak demographics will undermine a shaky health insurance and pension system, which, moreover, has provided little protection.
- Labour legislation has remained too inflexible despite reforms undertaken, which has contributed to keeping structural unemployment high.
- Low productivity, wage indexation and European monetary policy unsuited to Spain's case have generated inflationary pressures and affected the country's competitiveness.
- Dissemination of high technology and spending on research and development have been insufficient to permit a transition to the higher value-added products and services needed to meet Asian and Eastern European competition.

RISK ASSESSMENT

Public and private consumption, as well as construction, sustained growth dynamism in 2004. Conversely, industrial investment, exports and tourism underperformed.

In 2005, growth should slow due to less dynamic domestic demand. Household consumption and housing spending should sag. High household debt, slower job creation and persistent inflationary pressures will offset increased social spending, continued negative real interest rates and a wealth effect linked to property

appreciation. Lagging company investment, which has been affecting productivity, could nonetheless recover with infrastructure spending remaining robust. However, foreign trade will still have a negative impact on growth. Slowdown in imports will not be enough to offset the persistent lacklustre exports and tourism affected by both erosion of their competitiveness and unfavourable trends in the main markets.

As evidenced by the Coface payment incident index, the good economic climate has been generally benefiting company solvency. However,

MAIN ECONOMIC INDICATORS

%	2000	2001	2002	2003	2004[(e)]	2005[(f)]
Economic growth	4.4	2.8	2.2	2.5	2.6	2.2
Consumption (var.)	4.1	2.8	2.9	2.9	3.2	2.3
Investment (var.)	7.9	3.4	−1.3	3.3	3.5	5.6
Inflation	3.5	2.8	3.6	3.1	3.0	2.9
Unemployment rate	11.0	10.5	11.4	11.3	10.9	10.8
Short-term interest rate	4.4	4.3	3.3	2.3	2.0	2.2
Public sector balance (%GDP)	−0.8	−0.3	−0.1	0.4	−1.1	−0.4
Public sector debt (%GDP)	67.3	63.5	61.3	59.4	58.4	57.0
Exports (var.)	10.1	3.6	1.2	2.6	4.9	5.0
Imports (var.)	10.5	3.9	3.1	4.8	7.9	5.9
Current account balance (%GDP)	−3.4	−2.8	−2.4	−2.8	−4.0	−3.9

e = estimate, f = forecast

sectors like textiles, shoes, household appliances or even car industry subcontracting have been particularly vulnerable to Asian and Eastern European competition. Meanwhile, companies involved in building vacation homes (concentrated on Mediterranean shores) could suffer from a market downturn caused by high prices and the pound sterling's sharp decline.

MAIN ECONOMIC SECTORS

■ Computers

Services and software have been growing faster than hardware. Although personal computer sales, particularly of laptops, increased in volume, they fell in billing terms due to the price decline. The sector has suffered from the fact that company and household high-technology investments have remained below the European average despite the lagging technology level of their equipment. Companies have nonetheless been in good health, although recently created manufacturers and assemblers bear close watching.

■ Paper/cardboard

After growing weakly in 2003 and the first half of 2004, the sector has benefited from an acceleration linked to a continued good domestic economic context conducive to price increases. Insufficient production in relation to domestic consumption has resulted in continued capacity increases in a sector presenting no particular risks.

■ Chemicals

Besides the giant Repsol and subsidiaries of foreign groups, the sector comprises many smaller companies. Growth has been higher than elsewhere in the European chemicals sector due to the persistent dynamism of domestic demand and recovery of international demand. Despite the impact of rising oil costs, largely passed on in sales prices, sector companies have been posing no particular problems.

■ Textiles

Besides Inditex and Mango, the sector comprises smaller companies severely buffeted by the US dollar's decline and Asian competition, which would explain the numerous company closings and bankruptcies. The downstream industry (with spinning, weaving and ennoblement) as well as small clothing companies have been weak whereas large clothing companies have proven capable of delocalizing facilities and developing integrated organizations that include distribution.

Steel

Spanish steel increased production (up 6 per cent) and prices in 2004 thanks to the domestic market's expansion and the reduction of quantities available in an international market contending with Chinese demand. With companies unable to pass on high raw material prices to customers, their earning did not improve in the same proportion. That situation will persist in 2005.

Car industry

Outside subsidiaries of foreign car and parts makers, the sector has remained fragmented. About 650 companies manufacturing equipment, parts and accessories have remained completely dependent on their customers. They have been suffering from rising steel costs that they cannot entirely pass on. However, domestic market dynamism (registrations up 10 per cent in 2004) has permitted increasing sales.

Distribution

Spanish-owned groups have posted faster growth than subsidiaries of foreign distributors doubtless due to the large number of store openings. Due to regulatory constraints, the creations have mainly been supermarkets and self-service discount stores. This sector has presented no particular risks.

PAYMENT AND COLLECTION PRACTICES

Payment

The bill of exchange is frequently used for commercial transactions in Spain. In the event of default, it offers creditors certain safeguards, including access to the new 'exchange procedure' (*juicio cambiario*) introduced by the recent civil procedure rules under which, based on his or her appraisal of the documents submitted, a first instance judge (*juzgado de primera instancia*) may order a debtor to pay within ten days and have his or her property attached. Where a claim is contested, a court hearing is held to examine both parties' arguments and a judgment handed down within ten further days of the hearing.

Widely accepted though somewhat difficult to obtain, the bill of exchange guaranteed by a bank limits the risk of payment default by offering creditors additional recourse to the endorser of the bill.

The cheque, which is less widely used than the bill of exchange, offers similar legal safeguards under the 'exchange procedure' (*procédure cambiaire*) in the event of default.

The same is true of the promissory note (*pagaré*), which, like the bill of exchange, is an instrument enforceable by law. However, defaults on this instrument are not recorded in the RAI (*Registro de Aceptationes Impagadas*), an official register of official bad debts where banks and other financial institutions may check a company's payment record before extending credit.

SWIFT bank transfers, widely used by Spanish banks, are a quick, fairly reliable and cheap instrument, provided the purchaser, in good faith, orders payment. If the buyer fails to order a transfer, the legal remedy consists in instituting ordinary proceedings for non-payment of the invoice.

Debt collection

To speed up court procedures and modernize the obsolete code of civil procedure dating back to February 1881, new rules of civil procedure (*Ley de Enjuiciamento Civil*) were introduced on 8 January 2001. The rules cut the time taken up by litigation significantly and give oral arguments priority over written submissions – the cornerstone of the previous system – even though the authentication of large numbers of documents remains a requirement.

PAYMENT INCIDENTS INDEX
(12 months moving average - base 100 : World 1995)

Where sellers cannot reach an amicable settlement with a buyer, they may enforce their right to payment through the new civil procedure (*juicio declarativo*), divided into ordinary proceedings (*juicio ordinario*) for claims over 3,000 euros (formerly 500,000 pesetas) and oral proceedings (*juicio verbal*) for claims under 3,000 euros.

The aim of the new procedure is to speed up delivery of enforcement orders by reducing and simplifying the stages of the old procedure.

In addition, commercial claims under 30,000 euros (formerly 5 million pesetas) now benefit from a more flexible special procedure (*juicio monitorio*) initiated with a pre-printed form addressed to the judge of first instance (*juzgado de primera instancia*) who may, after reviewing supporting documents, order the debtor to pay within 20 days.

This innovative law, essentially consistent with judicial practice in other European countries, notably by introducing a summary procedure, has been progressively gaining acceptance as it breaks with the tradition of formalism acquired by the Spanish judiciary over several decades.

Sweden

Population (million inhabitants)	9
GDP (US$ million)	301,600
GDP per capita (US$)	33,700

Coface analysis   Short-term: **A1**

RISK ASSESSMENT

In 2004, the Swedish economy resumed strong growth, fuelled by a marked export recovery, notably in the car industry, pharmaceuticals and telecommunications. Meanwhile, relatively weak import growth permitted Sweden to develop a comfortable trade surplus.

In 2005, the economy should slow moderately with exports hampered by the Swedish krona's appreciation against a euro already very strong itself. However, domestic demand should contribute more to growth amid increased household consumption and residential investment, facilitated by the possibility of borrowing at low interest rates and new tax breaks. Industrial investment should also begin to increase

again considering the high production capacity utilization rates and the improved company financial situation. Meanwhile, despite fiscal surpluses, the government has been striving to stem the growth of public spending in anticipation of the substantial costs that an aging population should generate in coming years.

In that relatively favourable context, bankruptcies decreased in 2004 (down 7 per cent). Although the Coface payment incident index rose in recent months, it has nonetheless remained below the world average. Vigilance will be in order with traditionally nettlesome sectors like wood and clothing as well as sectors that are big hydrocarbon users.

MAIN ECONOMIC INDICATORS

%	2000	2001	2002	2003	2004[(e)]	2005[(f)]
Economic growth	4.4	1.2	2.0	1.7	3.3	2.8
Consumption (var.)	5.0	0.4	1.4	1.9	2.3	2.7
Investment (var.)	8.2	−2.9	−7.0	−2.7	3.1	5.5
Inflation	0.9	2.4	2.2	1.9	0.6	1.4
Unemployment rate	4.7	4.0	4.0	4.9	5.7	5.2
Short-term interest rate	4.0	4.0	4.1	3.0	2.4	3.2
Public sector balance (%GDP)	5.1	2.9	−0.3	0.2	0.5	0.5
Public sector debt (%GDP)	64.2	63.2	62.1	61.9	58.4	58.4
Exports (var.)	11.1	0.4	1.0	5.3	10.7	7.0
Imports (var.)	11.5	−2.6	−1.9	5.0	6.9	9.3
Current account balance (%GDP)	4.1	4.4	5.3	6.4	6.9	6.4

e = estimate, f = forecast

PAYMENT AND COLLECTION PRACTICES

■ Payment

Bills of exchange and promissory notes are neither widely used nor recommended as they must meet a number of formal requirements in order to be valid. Just as the rules for issuing cheques have become more flexible, so the sanctions for issuers of uncovered cheques have been relaxed in recent years.

Conversely, use of the SWIFT system by Swedish banks provides a secure, efficient and fairly cheap domestic and international funds transfer service. However, as payment is dependent on the buyer's good faith, sellers are advised to take great care to ensure that their bank account details are correct if they wish to receive timely payment.

■ Debt collection

As a rule, the collection process begins with the debtor being sent a final demand by registered mail asking him or her to pay the principal amount together with any contractually agreed interest penalties. Where there is no specific interest clause in the contract, the rate of interest applicable from 1 July 2002 is the Bank of Sweden's (Sveriges Riksbank) six-monthly benchmark rate (*reporäntan*), plus eight basis points.

Under the Swedish Interest Act (*räntelag*, 1975, last amended in 2002), interest starts to accrue 30 days after the invoice date or after a demand for payment is sent to the debtor by registered mail.

Where claims meet certain requirements – denominated in Swedish krona, certain, liquid and indisputable – creditors can obtain an injunction to pay (*Betalningsföreläggande*) within more or less four months from the Enforcement Service, set up on 1 January 1992.

This Enforcement Service (Kronofogde-myndigheten) may order a debtor to settle the claim or justify late payment within two weeks. If the debtor fails to respond after one month, the Service issues a writ of execution at the creditor's request. While formal, this system offers a relatively straightforward and quick remedy in respect of undisputed claims and has greatly freed up the courts. Creditors are not required to engage a lawyer but, in some circumstances, would be well advised to do so.

Where claims are disputed or where buyers fail to enter into an agreement to pay, the Enforcement Service has no jurisdiction. Creditors must obtain legal remedy through the ordinary court process by bringing their claims before a court of first instance (*Tingsrätt*). It should be noted that civil courts also have jurisdiction to hear commercial disputes.

Proceedings involve a preliminary hearing in which the judge attempts to reconcile the parties after examining their case documents, evidence and arguments. If the dispute remains unresolved, the proceedings continue with written submissions and oral arguments until the main hearing, where the accent is on counsels' pleadings (defence and prosecution) and examination of witnesses' testimonies. In accordance with the 'immediacy of judgment' principle, the court bases its decision exclusively on the evidence presented at the trial.

It takes about 10–12 months on average to obtain a writ of execution in first instance, bearing in mind that there is a widespread tendency in Sweden to appeal against judgments.

PAYMENT INCIDENTS INDEX
(12 months moving average - base 100 : World 1995)

Switzerland

Population (million inhabitants)	7.3
GDP (US$ million)	321,800
GDP per capita (US$)	43,900

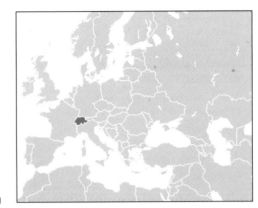

Coface analysis   Short-term: **A1**

STRENGTHS

- Switzerland's central position in Europe, excellent infrastructure, discreet and efficient financial services, political and social stability, moderate taxes and quality of life have attracted investors.
- A flexible labour market, high skill levels and multilingualism have ensured high participation rates and low unemployment compared with neighbouring countries.
- The international operations of large industrial and financial groups have permitted remedying for the narrow domestic market and declining growth.
- With a few adjustments, the social safety net should permit coping with the aging population.

WEAKNESSES

- Non-member status outside the EU, even tempered by bilateral agreements, has tended to limit competition and sustain resistance to change.
- Despite adoption of legislation intended to make the domestic market more flexible and establish better control over cartels, the competitiveness of economic actors, notably in regulated sectors like agriculture or energy, has remained inadequate.
- Pursuit of consensus among the representatives of the four parties within the federal government and frequent recourse to popular votes have impeded reforms.
- There are substantial local disparities and overlap of responsibilities between the confederation and cantons.

RISK ASSESSMENT

In 2004, the economy resumed moderate and balanced growth, underpinned by all national product components. Household consumption registered a marked upturn with exports benefiting from increasing demand for capital goods and financial services. Investment recovered after several years of decline.

In 2005, economic activity will decelerate very slightly since exports, which represent nearly half of GDP, could suffer from a slowdown in Western Europe, which constitutes the destination of over 60 per cent of sales. The investment dynamism will be difficult to sustain. Only household consumption will grow a little amid easing unemployment.

The better economic conditions have spurred improvement in the Coface payment incident index, borne out by a marked slowdown in company bankruptcies: up 9 per cent expected in 2004 against up 13 per cent in 2003. That downturn is particularly significant since it encompasses a decline in industry and stabilization in construction. Only commerce (notably textiles, automobiles and furniture) suffered a sharp deterioration doubtless linked to the many companies started in that sector.

MAIN ECONOMIC INDICATORS

%	2000	2001	2002	2003	2004[(e)]	2005[(f)]
Economic growth	3.6	1.0	0.3	−0.4	1.8	1.7
Consumption (var.)	2.3	2.0	0.3	0.5	1.7	1.8
Investment (var.)	5.0	−2.1	−2.2	−1.7	5.5	3.3
Inflation	1.6	1.0	0.6	0.6	0.8	1.3
Unemployment rate	2.5	2.5	3.1	4.0	3.9	3.6
Short-term interest rate	3.2	2.9	1.1	0.3	0.6	1.6
Public sector balance (%GDP)	2.6	0.2	−0.2	−1.1	−2.7	−1.9
Public sector debt (%GDP)	51.2	51.4	55.4	56.7	57.0	56.5
Exports (var.)	12.2	0.2	−0.2	0.0	5.0	4.0
Imports (var.)	9.6	3.2	−2.8	1.4	5.5	6.0
Current account balance (%GDP)	12.9	8.0	8.4	13.2	12.5	12.0

e = estimate, f = forecast

MAIN ECONOMIC SECTORS

■ **Building and public works**

In 2004, business expanded thanks to the housing segment's good performance. However, the other segments (public works and commercial construction) remained flat. Amid continued stiff competition, prices and earnings are still under pressure. The trend should be similar in 2005 nonetheless with an upturn developing in sales-area construction.

■ **Tourism**

A three-year downturn ended in 2004 thanks to the return of US and Asian tourists and a business-travel recovery. However, German and Swiss tourists remained discreet. Business should improve again in 2005, although more slowly, due to the US dollar's decline and sagging transcontinental tourism not offset by resumption of domestic tourism.

■ **Watchmaking**

In 2004, the sector benefited from renewed Japanese and US tourism and the dynamic economic conditions in those regions, which account for nearly half of sales. The move upmarket and growing sales contribution of emerging countries has had a favourable impact. In 2005, business should remain robust with the dollar's decline having little impact on an affluent clientele.

■ **Chemicals and pharmaceuticals**

For chemicals, a branch where exports absorb virtually all production, the excellent world industrial activity trend in 2004 could only be beneficial. That situation should persist in 2005. The dollar decline will not matter much, mitigated by the resulting impact on raw material costs and the mainly European focus of sales. Pharmaceuticals activity, with little sensitivity to economic or currency fluctuations, will remain robust.

■ **Industrial equipment**

This export sector (75 per cent of production exported, a third of which goes to Germany) benefited fully from the world industrial investment recovery. However, performance could drop in 2005 amid a possible company spending slowdown in Europe and the higher cost of steel.

■ **Retail trade**

The sector benefited from an improved consumption trend in 2004 that should persist in 2005. The concentration process has continued with concomitant closings of small stores and with the arrival of foreign companies intensifying competition and consumers increasingly giving preference to shopping malls and extended store hours.

Food industries

The better domestic and European economic conditions generally benefited companies in the sector. However, cheese and chocolate makers have been struggling to halt the erosion of their market share abroad due to high prices and the competition's move upmarket. They have also been suffering in their own market, recently opened to European competition. Faced with a saturated domestic market, sector actors can only rely on quality products and sales growth abroad; growth is, nonetheless, hampered by prices 50 per cent higher on average than those of their European counterparts.

PAYMENT AND COLLECTION PRACTICES

Payments

Bills of exchange and cheques are not commonly used owing to prohibitive banking and tax charges; the stamp duty on bills of exchange is 0.75 per cent of the principal amount for domestic bills, and 1.5 per cent for international bills. Similarly, commercial operators are particularly demanding as regards the formal validity of cheques and bills of exchange as payment instruments.

SWIFT bank transfers are the most commonly used payment system. Most Swiss banks are connected to the SWIFT network, which facilitates rapid and effective payments.

Debt collection

The Swiss legal system presents technical specificities, as follows:

- The existence of an administrative authority (eg Office des Poursuites et des Faillites, or Betreibungs und Konkursamt) in each canton, which is responsible for executing court orders and whose functioning is regulated by federal law. Interested parties may consult or obtain extracts of the Office's records.
- Specific rules for legal procedure prevail in each canton (there are 26 different codes of civil procedure), which sometimes vary greatly depending on the legal doctrine that has inspired them. As such, before instigating actions, plaintiffs should ensure that their counsel is familiar with the law of the concerned jurisdiction as well as the language to be used before the court (French, German or Italian). These two key constraints hamper the swift course of justice and a project to harmonize these various procedures is under review.

The debt collection process commences with the issuing of notice to pay by ordinary mail or registered letter (thus enabling interest penalties to be charged). This gives the debtor two weeks in which to pay the principal amount, plus – unless otherwise agreed by the parties – interest penalties equivalent to the bank rate applicable in the place of payment.

In the absence of payment, the creditor will submit a duly completed and signed petition form (*réquisition de poursuite*) to the Office des Poursuites et des Faillites (Enforcement and Bankruptcy Office), which then serves the debtor with a final order to pay within 20 days.

While very easy to use by creditors, that procedure nonetheless permits debtors to oppose the order within ten days of being served, without having to provide grounds. In such cases, the only alternative for creditors is to seek redress through the courts.

Conversely, where a seller holds unconditional proof of debt signed by the buyer (any original document in which the buyer recognizes his or her debt, bill of exchange, cheque, etc), the seller may request the temporary lifting of the debtor's opposition (*main levée de l'opposition*) without having to appear before the court. This is a summary procedure, quick and relatively easy to obtain, in which the court's decision is based upon the documents submitted by the seller.

Once this lifting order has been granted, the debtor has 20 days in which to refer the case before the judge to obtain the debt's release (*libération de dette*) and, in turn, obtain an executory order. That entails initiating a formal procedure, with a written phase and an oral examination of witnesses during court hearings, lasting from one to three years depending on the canton involved. Legal costs vary widely depending on the rates charged by the various cantons.

Once the court hands down a final ruling, the Office des Poursuites et des Faillites delivers an execution order or, in the case of traders, a winding-up petition (*commination*). In all cases, the law decides which measure – execution order or winding-up petition – is applied.

Either a court of first instance or a district court hears legal procedures. Commercial courts, presided over by a panel of professional and non-professional judges, exist in four Germanic cantons: Aargau, Berne, Saint Gall and Zurich.

Once an appeal has been lodged with the cantonal court, as a last recourse for claims exceeding 8,000 Swiss francs, cases are heard by the only federal court of justice, the Swiss Federal Court (Schweizerisches Bundesgericht) in Lausanne.

PAYMENT INCIDENTS INDEX
(12 months moving average - base 100 : World 1995)

Tajikistan

Population (million inhabitants)	6.3
GDP (US$ million)	1,212
GDP per capita (US$)	192

Short-term: **D**

Medium-term:

Coface analysis **Very high risk**

RISK ASSESSMENT

Growth has remained robust, buoyed by dynamic Kazakh and Russian demand and steady aluminium and farm production, those two sectors together representing 78 per cent of total exports. However, that robust economic activity has largely been due just to a catch-up phase after a very severe recession in the 1990s. Moreover, the foundations of that performance have been shaky. Company restructuring has been limited and the predominant role of raw materials has made the economy vulnerable to weather conditions and world price fluctuations.

Improvement in external accounts (thanks notably to increased inward private transfers),

coupled with relatively tight economic policy, has bolstered the country's financial situation with debt ratios tending to ease. However, a high poverty rate has made the country very dependent on bilateral and multilateral financing.

Politically, President Rakhmonov and his party have a tight grip on power with change unlikely. Meanwhile, the country has nonetheless remained flanked by the great powers. With the country still very near to Moscow both militarily (an agreement was signed in June 2004 on the establishment of a Russian military base) and commercially, it has also maintained good relations with the United States, as evidenced by Washington's position as its primary donor.

MAIN ECONOMIC INDICATORS						
US$ millions	2000	2001	2002	2003	2004$^{(e)}$	2005$^{(f)}$
Economic growth (%)	8.3	10.2	9.1	10.2	8.5	7.5
Inflation (%)	60.6	12.5	14.5	13.7	7.0	5.0
Public sector balance (%GDP)	−0.6	−0.1	−0.1	0.9	−0.4	−0.5
Exports	788	652	699	799	869	943
Imports	834	773	823	1,004	1,095	1,192
Trade balance	−46	−121	−124	−205	−226	−249
Current account balance (%GDP)	−6.5	−7.1	−2.7	−1.3	−2.0	−2.2
Foreign debt (%GDP)	129.0	98.4	82.3	64.7	61.0	59.1
Debt service (%Exports)	9.6	25.2	22.9	18.2	13.4	14.8
Foreign exchange reserves (in months of imports)	2.1	1.9	1.8	1.9	2.3	2.8

e = estimate, f = forecast

Turkmenistan

Population (million inhabitants)	4.8
GDP (US$ million)	7,672
GDP per capita (US$)	1,598

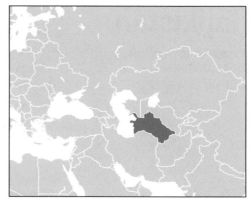

Short-term: **D**

Medium-term:

Coface analysis **Very high risk**

RISK ASSESSMENT

The hydrocarbon sector still dominates the economy with gas representing 60 per cent of exports and oil and oil products 26 per cent. Landlocked and very dependent on Russia in market-access terms, the country's relations with Moscow have been improving. An agreement now links it to Russia for its gas deliveries (signed in 2003 for 25 years) and Gazprom is involved in the Turkmen joint venture responsible for gas exports to Ukraine, Turkmenistan's primary market.

Steady raw material prices and favourable developments in the gas sector have permitted the country to post high growth rates – although inflated by official statistics. Even if the deteriorated

condition of gas pipelines has been limiting capacity to transport gas to Russia, the economy's focus on energy exports has bolstered the economic and political strategy pursued by President Niazov since independence in 1991. No economic liberalization whatsoever will thus be likely with massive subsidies to non-hydrocarbon exporting sectors and price controls continuing to pass for economic policy.

Moreover, liberalization will be no more likely in the political arena with the regime remaining very authoritarian. Unpredictable measures, frequent purges and a cult of personality have been making a 'palace revolution' a possible scenario.

MAIN ECONOMIC INDICATORS

US$ millions	2000	2001	2002	2003	2004(e)	2005(e)
Economic growth (%)	17.6	15.9	8.1	7.7	7.0	7.0
Inflation (%)	7.4	11.7	7.8	2.7	4.0	4.0
Public sector balance (%GDP)	−0.3	0.6	−10.0	−10.0	−9.0	−8.0
Exports	2,508	2,623	2,862	3,468	4,000	4,000
Imports	1,742	20,108	1,832	2,502	3,000	3,000
Trade balance	766	−17,485	1,030	966	1,000	1,000
Current account balance (%GDP)	8.4	1.7	6.5	4.6	4.0	4.0
Foreign debt (%GDP)	44.3	28.8	22.4	18.0	17.8	16.6
Debt service (%Exports)	14.2	17.3	35.0	37.0	36.0	36.0
Foreign exchange reserves (in months of imports)	9.2	1.2	15.0	10.0	8.8	9.1

e = estimate, f = forecast

Ukraine

Population (million inhabitants)	49
GDP (US$ million)	41,477

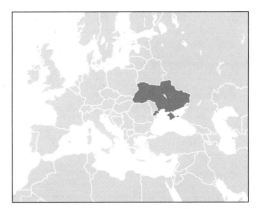

Short-term: **C**

Coface analysis

Medium-term:
High risk

STRENGTHS

- Ukraine has been benefiting from transit fees levied on Russian gas exports to Western Europe.
- The economy is relatively diversified (food sector, heavy and light industries).
- Bordering the EU, the country is strategically positioned.

WEAKNESSES

- Responsible for 40 per cent of exports, the metal sector has been suffering from substantial obsolescence of capital equipment.
- Ukraine has remained dependent on Russia for energy inputs and a large proportion of metal exports.
- Political instability has been impeding economic reforms, which has kept foreign investment at very low levels.

RISK ASSESSMENT

Economic conditions have been very buoyant and the current account has remained in surplus, permitting a sharp improvement in the external financial situation. Thanks to initiation of tax reforms, fiscal policy has remained relatively restrictive. The country's debt ratios have improved substantially with a long-tense currency liquidity situation now satisfactory.

With its very pronounced specialization in metals and a low investment rate, Ukraine's economic performance is shaky. It will depend on continued tax reform and improvement in the legal framework in general.

The 2004 presidential elections at the end of 2004 marked a watershed. The victory of Viktor Yushenko could permit restarting the reform process (and notably reactivating the IMF programme) and consolidating the country's ties to the EU. However, the geographic, linguistic and religious factors dividing the population, the importance of oligarchies and vested interests and the Russian neighbour's preponderant economic and political influence could sustain recurrent political instability.

MAIN ECONOMIC INDICATORS

US$ billions	2000	2001	2002	2003	2004[e]	2005[f]
Economic growth (%)	5.9	9.2	5.2	9.4	11.8	6.0
Inflation (%)	25.8	6.1	−0.6	8.2	11.5	9.0
Public sector balance (%GDP)	2.1	−1.5	0.2	0.1	−3.0	−1.0
Exports	15.7	17.1	18.7	23.7	32.9	34.0
Imports	14.9	16.9	18.0	24.0	30.0	33.2
Trade balance	0.8	0.2	0.7	−0.3	2.9	0.7
Current account balance	1.5	1.4	3.2	2.9	6.3	3.0
Current account balance (%GDP)	4.7	3.7	7.5	5.8	9.0	4.1
Foreign debt (%GDP)	33.1	26.6	24.0	21.9	19.2	15.7
Debt service (%Exports)	10.4	6.7	5.4	6.3	6.4	4.8
Foreign exchange reserves (in months of imports)	1.0	1.8	2.5	3.0	4.2	4.3

e = estimate, f = forecast

CONDITIONS OF ACCESS TO THE MARKET

■ **Market overview**

Economic growth is driven by rising exports of steel, chemicals, machinery and capital goods. The automotive and construction sectors are expanding. Despite these good indicators, however, Ukraine is still not considered a market economy by international organizations on account of its discriminatory practices.

■ **Means of entry**

Market access remains a problem in Ukraine mainly due to the maintenance of tariff and non-tariff barriers. Despite the entry into force of a new customs code in January 2004, customs practices are often at variance with the law. Tedious product certification procedures put a brake on exports. Even European ISO certification is deemed inadequate by the Ukrainian certification authorities. Apart from the over-zealous manner in which companies are audited by the tax authorities and red tape, the main problem remains the delay in VAT refunds. Because of this, the IMF suspended the standby loan granted to Ukraine in March 2004. The electoral promises made during the presidential campaign have led several government departments to multiply checks. Finally, the absence of proper bankruptcy laws does not inspire

confidence in the country's payment procedures and system of export credits. On the other hand, the government has taken steps to gradually reduce VAT from 20 per cent to 15 per cent with effect from 1 January 2005 and cut corporation tax from 30 per cent to 25 per cent and eventually to 20 per cent in 2005. These measures give a much-needed fillip to the process of reforms under way. Ukraine has also stepped up intellectual property protection but its efforts in this regard are judged to be unsatisfactory by the international community – so much so that this issue remains a stumbling block to progress in negotiations with the WTO.

■ **Attitude towards foreign investors**

The proceeds from privatization in 2004 amounted to nearly 8 billion hryvnia, rather easily beating the forecast of 2.13 billion hryvnia. The privatization programme involved the sale by public tender of shares in large industrial groups, government monopolies and strategic companies such as the metal giant Krivoriszhtal. Despite the will to bring new shareholders into Ukrainian companies, tendering procedures and the award of licences remain untransparent and usually favour local companies to the detriment of foreign ones. The new civil and commercial codes attempt to provide a better investment environment (intellectual property protection, bankruptcies, commercial agreements), but contradictions between the two codes undermine enforcement. The special economic areas have attracted more Ukrainian companies than foreign ones. At 1 January 2004, 554 projects totalling US$2,671 million had been completed, including US$845 million with foreign investment. There is nevertheless growing interest in Ukraine among European investors, including those from the new EU member states. While the business climate clearly needs to be improved, the economic boom in this country of 48 million and new neighbour of the EU is leading numerous foreign firms to take a closer look at this market.

1

OPPORTUNITY SCOPE

Breakdown of domestic demand (%GDP + imports)
- Private consumption — 37
- Public consumption — 13
- Investment — 13

Exports: 56% of GDP → ← Imports: 52% of GDP

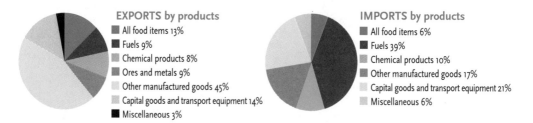

MAIN DESTINATIONS OF EXPORTS

Mn USD

Russia, Turkey, Italy, Germany, China

EXPORTS by products
- All food items 13%
- Fuels 9%
- Chemical products 8%
- Ores and metals 9%
- Other manufactured goods 45%
- Capital goods and transport equipment 14%
- Miscellaneous 3%

MAIN ORIGINS OF IMPORTS

Mn USD

Russia, Turkmen-istan, Germany, Poland, USA

IMPORTS by products
- All food items 6%
- Fuels 39%
- Chemical products 10%
- Other manufactured goods 17%
- Capital goods and transport equipment 21%
- Miscellaneous 6%

STANDARD OF LIVING / PURCHASING POWER

Indicators	Ukraine	Regional average	DC average
GNP per capita (PPP dollars)	4800	8313	4601
GNP per capita (USD)	780	2535	1840
Human Development Index	0.777	0.805	0.684
Wealthiest 10% share of national income	23.2	30	32
Urban population percentage	68	68	45
Percentage under 15 years old	17	17	30
Number of telephones per 1000 inhabitants	216	257	120
Number of computers per 1000 inhabitants	19	84	37

United Kingdom

Population (million inhabitants)	59.4
GDP (US$ million)	1,795,000
GDP per capita (US$)	30,200

Coface analysis   Short-term: **A1**

STRENGTHS

- Despite re-emergence of a deficit, the public sector financial situation has remained satisfactory with low debt and continued compliance with the rule calling for equivalence between debt contracted and investments made over a given cycle.
- Moderate taxes, procedural simplicity and access to the Anglo-Saxon world have contributed to making the country a preferred destination worldwide for FDI.
- With traditional industries in decline, higher value-added sectors like speciality chemicals, pharmaceuticals, aeronautics and electronics have been developing rapidly.
- Unemployment has been relatively low thanks partly to labour market flexibility and employment agency efficiency.

WEAKNESSES

- After a euphoric period for residential property, risks of a trend reversal have been looming due to a large and mainly variable-rate household debt burden.
- The dichotomy between the still-dynamic services and housing sectors and traditional industries going downhill has not been facilitating the Bank of England's task in setting interest rates.
- Public services like transportation, health and education have been struggling to fulfil their role despite substantial public financing devoted to them; overall productivity has been showing the effects.
- The difficult peace process in Northern Ireland has remained a nettlesome problem for authorities.

RISK ASSESSMENT

Spending dynamism sustained by wage growth, public sector job creation and a wealth effect linked to property appreciation spurred robust economic expansion in 2004. In that buoyant environment, companies began to invest again.

Growth will weaken in 2005. Although interest rates have stopped rising and fiscal policy has remained accommodating, the slowdown that began at the end of 2004 should continue – the result of past monetary policy tightening and stabilization of property prices, which have limited the refinancing capacity of households. Already over-indebted, households should substantially reduce their spending in favour of savings. Economic growth will thus depend more on exports, which will benefit from the pound sterling depreciation against the euro. In that context, productive investment will only grow moderately.

The low Coface payment incident index and decline of company bankruptcies would suggest that the difficulties experienced by British industry have been gradually easing even though the household spending slowdown could be

MAIN ECONOMIC INDICATORS

%	2000	2001	2002	2003	2004[(e)]	2005[(f)]
Economic growth	3.9	2.3	1.8	2.2	3.2	2.5
Consumption (var.)	4.6	2.9	3.3	2.3	3.1	2.0
Investment (var.)	4.8	1.8	0.9	−1.1	6.0	3.8
Inflation	0.8	1.2	1.3	1.4	1.5	1.7
Unemployment rate	5.5	5.1	5.2	5.0	4.8	4.8
Short-term interest rate	6.1	5.0	4.0	3.7	4.9	5.0
Public sector balance (%GDP)	3.9	0.7	−1.5	−3.5	−2.9	−2.7
Public sector debt (%GDP)	45.9	41.2	41.5	42.0	43.5	43.5
Exports (var.)	9.4	2.9	0.1	0.1	2.3	5.8
Imports (var.)	9.1	4.9	4.1	1.3	4.7	4.6
Current account balance (%GDP)	−2.1	−1.8	−1.8	−2.7	−2.6	−2.4

e = estimate, f = forecast

problematic for textile production and retail trade, food or the car industry. High raw material costs will be a further handicap, notably for metallurgy and mechanical engineering, which should nonetheless benefit from more robust exports and the pound sterling depreciation against the euro.

MAIN ECONOMIC SECTORS

■ Distribution

In 2004, sales benefited from improved access to credit and the wealth effect resulting from the appreciation of property values. Successive interest rate hikes by the central bank ultimately stemmed indebtedness and household spending. Among the various players, distributors of electronic equipment and home electronics will continue to perform well in 2005, clothing has been going downhill, and food has been enduring severe price competition between the giants – Tesco, Asda (owned by Wal-Mart), Sainsbury's and recently-merged Morrison–Safeway. To hold their prices, those companies have not hesitated to exert increasing pressure on suppliers.

■ Steel

The growth of Chinese demand in 2004, pushing prices sharply up, radically improved the steelmakers' situation, permitting them to return to high profitability, especially the Anglo-Dutch firm, Corus. That favourable trend should continue in 2005. The steelmakers' new challenges are now to sustain raw material supplies on the best terms and to absorb higher shipping costs. Downstream, however, many players have been suffering from their inability to pass on higher steel costs in their sales prices.

■ Car industry

The pressure on the major world players has remained intense as they continue to pursue their cost-cutting policies. The outcome of the steel-supply contract renegotiations with steelmakers could have a significant impact on 2005 vehicle prices. The United Kingdom's situation has been gloomy with registrations stagnating and the delocalization menace looming more than ever. The shutdown of three Jaguar factories was recently announced. The last remaining British carmaker, MG Rover, has been struggling to develop partnerships in China to strengthen its position. Parts manufacturers, already contending with tight margins, have also continued to face difficulties due to high steel prices and international competition.

1

■ **Construction**

The United Kingdom's construction industry should hold its own with the likely residential construction slowdown offset by good earnings prospects in other segments. Government spending, intended to improve public services in transportation, health and education has buoyed construction of infrastructure and commercial premises. Property prices could undergo a sharp adjustment after the euphoria of recent years. The chronic housing shortage in the United Kingdom will nonetheless continue to underpin demand with the shortage of skilled workers and building land impeding implementation of projects.

■ **Computer equipment and telecommunications**

The computer equipment market's dynamism attests to the desire of companies to replace their existing computers and servers dating back to the pre-2000 boom. Both public initiatives, auch as equipping schools, and private preferences, notably for laptop models, have been fuelling demand. For telecommunications operators, growth should remain robust in 2005. Their financial constraints notwithstanding, they will have to upgrade their aging networks to handle third and fourth generation technologies. The question of system security has also been taking on growing importance due to the upsurge of bank fraud via the internet. Competition is still fierce with tight margins for companies.

PAYMENT AND COLLECTION PRACTICES

■ **Payment**

Cheques are widely used but do not provide real security as non-payment of a cheque is not a criminal offence (cheques do not have to be covered when issued). The drawer of a cheque may stop payment at any time. Cheques can be presented for cashing a second time under the RDPR (Refer to Drawer Please Re-present) option.

The bill of exchange, while rare in commercial transactions, is used in special cases.

If a foreign bill remains unpaid at maturity, it must be protested. Centralized accounting helps reduce costs and cashing times.

Bank transfers, particularly via the SWIFT network, are regularly used for domestic and international settlements. Leading British companies also use two other highly automated interbank transfer systems – BACS (Bankers' Automated Clearing Services) and CHAPS (Clearing House Automated Payment Systems).

■ **Debt collection**

Debt collection agencies or solicitors handle the recovery of overdue payments, which begins with the issue of a reminder. Under the Late Payment of Commercial Debts (Interest) Act 1998, small companies are entitled – from 1 November 1998 – to demand default interest from large companies, both public and private. This law, introduced in successive stages with the last stage coming into effect on 7 August 2002, now permits all commercial companies to bill interest in cases of late payment. Save as otherwise provided between the parties, the applicable rate of interest is the Bank of England's base rate (dealing rate) plus eight basis points.

A creditor initiates the legal collection process by lodging a 'claim form' with the competent legal authority.

Summary judgments, while speedier to obtain during ordinary proceedings, are more difficult to obtain by the claimant on claims contested by the defendant. The reform of the judicial process (or the Lord Woolf reform), which saw the introduction of new Civil Procedure Rules with effect from 26 April 1999, is considered by lawyers to be a major breakthrough in dealing with disputed claims.

The new rules of procedure have gradually cut litigation time as parties can seek ways of coming to a settlement either directly or through mediation (ie ADR: Alternative Dispute Resolution).

123

Devices to speed up proceedings include the establishment of three separate 'tracks' – small claims track, fast track, and multitrack – based on the size of the claim and the drawing up of a timetable of hearing dates by the courts.

Judgments are enforced either through conventional methods (service by bailiff, attachment of debtor assets with subsequent auction) or more directly for claims exceeding £750 by formally serving a statutory demand for payment. Then, after expiry of a 21-day period and without settlement, transaction or provision of a payment guarantee, the creditor may file a winding-up petition with the court.

To elicit a speedier reaction or payment by debtors, the statutory demand procedure may be used in some cases to collect uncontested claims directly without obtaining a prior ruling.

PAYMENT INCIDENTS INDEX
(12 months moving average - base 100 : World 1995)

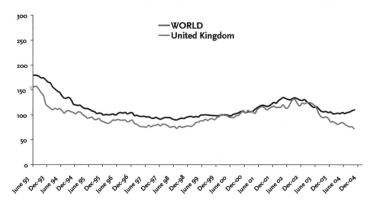

Uzbekistan

Population (million inhabitants)	25
GDP (US$ million)	7,932

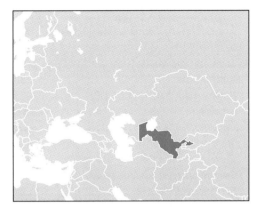

Short-term: **D**

Coface analysis

Medium-term:
Very high risk

STRENGTHS

- Uzbekistan boasts natural wealth, mainly cotton and gold.
- The country has sought to diversify towards other raw materials (oil and gas) and industry (cars).
- As the Commonwealth of Independent States' most populous Central Asian country with some 25 million inhabitants, it constitutes an attractive market.
- The country, which has hosted US bases since the military operations in Afghanistan, has become a top strategic focus.

WEAKNESSES

- The country's main sources of wealth are subject to exogenous factors (world prices, climate).
- The weakness of reforms has been an obstacle to continuing support from multilateral institutions.
- Centralized decision making and the state-controlled economy have impeded growth.
- Although Islamism has been repressed, the causes of its expansion (notably social) have persisted.

RISK ASSESSMENT

The country's financial situation has benefited from improvement in cotton and gold prices with the current account posting high surpluses. Debt ratios have been essentially trending down with tight fiscal policy easing sovereign risk.

Uzbekistan has nonetheless remained very vulnerable in several ways. Growth has been shaky due to a lack of reforms in the cotton sector, which has affected yields. Moreover, the business climate has remained unfavourable to the private sector. Reforms directed at opening the economy have

been very limited or have remained toothless. Stiff trade restrictions, for example, accompanied the soum's transition to convertibility.

Politically, risks of destabilization have been substantial. The hold of President Islam Karimov's regime on the organs of political power has certainly brought some stability. However, repression of the Islamic faith has tended to eliminate all forms of opposition. Moreover, the terrorist risk has remained high with social tensions stoking severe frustrations among the population.

MAIN ECONOMIC INDICATORS						
US$ millions	2000	2001	2002	2003	2004[(e)]	2005[(f)]
Economic growth (%)	3.3	4.1	3.1	1.5	2.5	2.5
Inflation (%)	48.5	58.2	24.4	7.7	14.0	10.0
Public sector balance (%GDP)	−2.4	−1.3	−1.9	0.1	−2.3	−1.4
Exports	2,935	2,740	2,510	3,240	3,829	3,846
Imports	2,441	2,554	2,186	2,405	2,876	3,108
Trade balance	494	186	324	835	953	738
Current account balance	216	−113	116	882	846	556
Current account balance (%GDP)	1.6	−1.6	1.5	9.1	7.9	4.9
Foreign debt (%GDP)	24.5	31.4	60.0	54.3	42.6	39.2
Debt service (%Exports)	25.7	25.8	23.4	24.8	23.7	23.7
Foreign exchange reserves (in months of imports)	6.1	5.4	6.2	7.8	7.0	6.5

e = estimate, f = forecast

CONDITIONS OF ACCESS TO THE MARKET

■ Market overview

Uzbekistan signed Article 8 of the IMF charter on 15 October 2003 and at the same time declared full convertibility of its currency. This has been followed by slow but steady changes in trade regulations, which fall short of full freedom of access to the market. That is why Uzbekistan is not yet an easy market for foreign firms, especially small and medium-sized ones. The volume of trade is small and imports are limited to basic foodstuffs such as sugar, oil and flour. Big companies, though, can find business opportunities if they arrange appropriate project funding. To rein in its debt, the government has decided to act on the advice of international financial institutions and limit the sovereign guarantee facility to genuine priority areas. The country's debt servicing capacity, in fact, is restricted by volatile export revenues based mainly on cotton and gold. The absence of a government guarantee makes it difficult, though not impossible, to mount projects. International organizations like EBRD, Asian Development Bank (ADB) and IBD are ready to assist projects intended to open market access and develop the private sector. However, decision making is slow and there are frequent price reviews because of exchange rate movements. This makes it all but impossible to do without exchange risk cover.

An Uzbek Chamber of Commerce has been set up to facilitate relations between Uzbek and foreign firms and limit all too frequent state intervention. There is also a European business group responsible for advising and assisting European firms and helping the Uzbek government to open market access.

■ Means of entry

Market access is the focus of regulatory and legislative reforms, along with the opening up of the foreign exchange market for the national currency. Currently all sectors are open, except the strategic ones. There are no special restrictions on imported consumer and capital goods. The recommended means of payment remains the irrevocable and confirmed letter of credit. Payments in hard currency are no longer limited by the currency's convertibility, but by the shortage of foreign exchange at the banks of prospective customers. Firms based in Uzbekistan, however, usually manage to obtain foreign exchange in less than a month.

■ Attitude towards foreign investors

Uzbek legislation offers investors safeguards against discrimination, nationalization and expropriation, while authorizing unrestricted repatriation of profits and capital. The only problem is the availability of foreign exchange. Red tape remains the biggest obstacle, but legislation on this issue is under review.

Uzbekistan is privatizing its enterprises and a list of companies for sale has been drawn up. However, the majority of these enterprises have either filed for insolvency or exist only on paper. For takeovers, the rule is to get foreign investors to renew the production apparatus, although they are not required to retain existing staff. In strategic sectors, such as cotton and its derivatives, gold, energy and aeronautics, foreign shareholdings are capped at 40 per cent, with the Uzbek government retaining a majority stake. Uzbekistan is a member of the Islamic Development Bank and receives assistance from major multilateral financial institutions (eg ADB, World Bank).

■ Foreign exchange regulations

The currency is fully and freely convertible as of 15 October 2003. However, the country manages its currency flows with a great deal of caution. This may help to avert a crisis and control inflation, but it is not conducive to sweeping currency liberalization. The exchange rate seems to have steadied. The main problem faced by firms conducting business or making an investment is the shortage of foreign exchange. It takes on average less than a month to obtain foreign exchange.

OPPORTUNITY SCOPE

Breakdown of domestic demand (%GDP + imports)
- Private consumption — 43
- Public consumption — 14
- Investment — 15

Exports: 38% of GDP ⟶ ⟵ Imports: 34% of GDP

MAIN DESTINATIONS OF EXPORTS

Mn USD

Russia   Ukraine   Italy   Tajikistan   Poland

MAIN ORIGINS OF IMPORTS

Mn USD

Russia   Germany   South Korea   Kazakhstan   USA

EXPORTS by products
- Cotton fibre 20%
- Energy 10%
- Capital goods and transport equipment 10%
- Miscellaneous 61%

IMPORTS by products
- Capital goods and transport equipment 44%
- Plastics and derivatives 13%
- All food items 10%
- Miscellaneous 33%

STANDARD OF LIVING / PURCHASING POWER

Indicators	Uzbekistan	Regional average	DC average
GNP per capita (PPP dollars)	1640	8313	4601
GNP per capita (USD)	310	2535	1840
Human Development Index	0.709	0.805	0.684
Wealthiest 10% share of national income	22	30	32
Urban population percentage	37	68	45
Percentage under 15 years old	35	17	30
Number of telephones per 1000 inhabitants	66	257	120
Number of computers per 1000 inhabitants	n/a	84	37

The Americas

Quiescent Inflation Allows US Growth

Experts from Oxford Analytica, Oxford

US GDP at US$11.8 trillion accounts for more than a quarter of the world economy. US domestic demand growth has provided much of the fuel for global growth in the current cycle. Recent recessions have been so brief (averaging seven months for the 1990 and 2001 recessions) that observers assume the economy has a strong propensity for growth.

KEY INSIGHTS

→ Dollar weakness notwithstanding, subdued inflation should allow the Federal Reserve to continue its policy of gentle and incremental tightening.

→ The recovery in profitability and attendant high liquidity should help firms step up capital spending.

→ Social security reforms could boost long interest rates if they set the stage for a major expansion of the fiscal deficit.

During the 22 years since the business cycle trough of November 1982, the economy has been in recession for only 14 months, or a mere 5 per cent, of the time. During the period 1945–1982, the economy was in recession for 22 per cent of the time. Recessions were more common before the 1980s because rising inflation forced the Federal Reserve to hike interest rates in order to restore price stability. Since the 1980s, the economy has enjoyed a prolonged period of low inflation or disinflation, which has lessened the pressure on the Federal Reserve to play an actively restrictive role.

CYCLICAL STABILITY

There is a general consensus on Wall Street that the economy will enjoy 3.5–4.0 per cent growth during 2005 compared with some 4.3 per cent in 2004, largely because inflationary threats are seen as well contained:

● The Blue Chip survey of 50 forecasters is projecting output growth of 3.5 per cent during 2005 and an inflation rate of 2.4 per cent compared with 4.4 per cent output growth in 2004 and an inflation rate of 2.6 per cent. The forecasters also expect corporate profits to rise by 10.5 per cent in 2005 compared with a gain of 15.7 per cent in 2004.

● The Business Roundtable CEO confidence index was at 98.9 in early December compared with a previous peak of 101.7 in September and 67.7 during October 2003.

Analysts are optimistic because they believe inflation will average only about 2.4 per cent in 2005 compared with 2.7 per cent in 2004. If inflation remains subdued, the Federal Reserve will be able to continue its policy of incremental tightening rather than risking a highly restrictive policy. The core personal consumption expenditures (PCE) inflation rate index in the 12 months through to October 2004 was 1.5 per cent compared with 1.1 per cent at the end of 2003. There is little doubt that inflation has begun to accelerate but the rate of gain is still very modest. There is evidence that productivity growth has begun to decline – if this trend persists, it will increase the risk of either a contraction of profit margins or higher inflation.

STRUCTURAL QUESTIONS

Uncertainties centre instead on structural imbalances. The personal savings rate has dropped to an unprecedented low of 0.2 per cent because the household sector has been enjoying steady gains in house prices during the past five years and an upturn in the equity markets since 2002. Households also have significantly expanded their use of mortgage debt to finance consumption. Since the end of the recession in 2001, over 90 per cent of the increase in total household debt has been due to the growth of mortgage borrowing, which has increased by 25 per cent after adjusting for inflation. In contrast, consumer credit (eg credit cards and automobile loans) increased by only 4 per cent over the same period. Mortgage debt has grown from 32 per cent of GDP in 1980 to 60 per cent today (and consumer credit from 13 per cent to 18 per cent). Yet while debt has increased, household assets have increased to nearly US$50 trillion, or a level five times as large as total GDP. House prices rose 13 per cent during the third quarter, the largest gain in more than 25 years.

Low personal savings and a federal fiscal deficit close to 4 per cent of GDP have driven the current account deficit to 6 per cent of GDP, and it could expand to 7 per cent during 2005. Because the federal deficit looks unlikely to fall sharply during the next few years, the current account deficit has become a central concern for markets, fuelling dollar weakness. The Bush administration has been relaxed about the dollar's decline because it has not yet produced a large increase in US bond yields. If the bond market finally experiences a major correction that drives up mortgage rates, the administration could change the tone of its comments. However, short of reducing the federal deficit, there is little it can do other than acquiesce in trading partners' reserve accumulations – which it has largely done to the present.

POLICY AGENDA

The Bush administration plans to introduce proposals for social security privatization, tort reform and tax reform during 2005. The major concern in the financial markets about social security privatization is that it could add US$100 billion or more to the federal deficit. Business supports tort reform because it is estimated that the current tort rules cost US firms some US$250 billion per annum. The administration may create a commission to introduce new tax reform proposals. They are likely to focus on eliminating the alternative minimum tax, further reducing taxation of capital and, perhaps, introducing a national consumption tax in order to lessen the role of income tax. It is doubtful that the tax reform proposals will come in time to influence the economy during 2005 but they could be important in later years. The social security reforms could boost long interest rates if they set the stage for a major expansion of the fiscal deficit.

The markets will become increasingly concerned during 2005 about the pending retirement of Federal Reserve Chairman, Alan Greenspan. The financial media has focused on several possible replacements, including Professor Martin Feldstein of Harvard University, Professor Glen Hubbard of Columbia University, John Taylor of the US Treasury and Roger Ferguson, the current Federal Reserve vice-chairman. It is doubtful that the administration will make a decision before the fourth quarter of 2005. Because market volatility has increased in the past after the appointment of a new Federal Reserve chairman, investors will be watching the issue closely. The greatest risk would be the administration turning to an unknown business leader, such as happened with the appointment of G William Miller in 1977. It would take such a candidate several months to establish credibility in the markets and win the confidence of investors.

EXPENDITURE SOURCES

Capital spending will need to be a growth locomotive during 2005. US firms have experienced a significant recovery in profitability and have balance sheets with high levels of liquidity. Most econometric models suggest that capital spending has increased by far less since 2002 than traditional cyclical factors would have warranted. Greenspan attributes this weakness to corporate concern about the regulatory climate and policy changes such as Sarbanes-Oxley. Although concerns about Sarbanes-Oxley have not gone, they are waning, in which case investment should accelerate during 2005, assuming Greenspan's hypothesis is correct. There should also be a stronger contribution from net exports, which itself would encourage corporate spending.

CONCLUSION

The economy appears to be heading for another year of moderate output growth with stable inflation. The markets are concerned about large structural imbalances such as low household savings rate and large current account deficit. This will keep dollar weakness on the front burner, but it is difficult to imagine either factor destabilizing the economy during 2005 without a major crisis in the financial markets.

Year of Rising Risk for Argentina

Experts from Oxford Analytica, Oxford

2

Strong 2004 growth will provide the impetus for continued, albeit lower, expansion in 2005. However, lack of structural reforms, poor policy making and persistent uncertainties surrounding debt restructuring and relations with the IMF raise serious questions over medium-term prospects. Macroeconomic figures for 2004 remain strong, with an estimated growth of 8 per cent, inflation below 6 per cent and record exports and tax collection figures.

KEY INSIGHTS

→ Growth will remain at respectable levels in 2005, although difficulties in resolving the pending issues of debt restructuring and negotiations with the IMF will curtail access to credit and limit growth sustainability.

→ Poor policy making and the heavy concentration of decision making in the hands of the president will represent a more significant obstacle to economic development as recovery slows.

→ Social demands and opposition to the government will rise as popular expectations become more negative, while President Nestor Kirchner's efforts to sustain his approval ratings will militate against unpopular but needed structural reforms.

However, unemployment remains at around 14.8 per cent (not including some 1.5 million jobless heads of household who receive a monthly subsidy of US$50), while some 48.5 per cent of employment is 'informal', according to government figures. Over 44 per cent of the population remains below the poverty line.

High unemployment, poverty and insecurity are key concerns, which the government of President Nestor Kirchner has yet to address effectively – and which will prove more difficult to tackle as recovery slows. Kirchner, who has confined decision making to himself and a small circle of close advisers, continues to use populist rhetoric and nationalist language to bolster his still considerable popularity. This has played well at home. However, his constant criticisms of the IMF, members of the G7 and foreign holders of defaulted debt; his platform of increased state involvement in the economy; and his confrontational attitude towards some foreign investors do not favour credibility and economic stability. Moreover, rhetoric and highly publicized announcements (rarely translated into action) have largely taken the place of policy making.

ECONOMIC PROSPECTS

The 2005 budget foresees GDP growth of 4 per cent and inflation of 7.8 per cent, both probably understated. Given the inertial effect of strong 2004 growth, GDP may well expand by up to 5 per cent in 2005.

Inflation forecasts do not include the impact of any increase in utilities' tariffs. Rising wage claims will affect both costs and consumer demand if successful, while lack of idle capacity will also push prices up if new investment does not increase.

Projections of a 12 per cent rise in revenues may be over-optimistic, given the fall in growth and record tax collection levels in 2004. This may force public spending constraints, given significant maturities of performing debt falling due in 2005, as well as possible payouts on restructured debt and payments to multilateral lenders.

However, economic prospects are contingent upon three other issues in particular, the outcomes of which are currently uncertain:

1. Debt restructuring. Plans to launch the bond swap outlined in the government's 'final offer' faced a series of delays, putting paid to the government's intention of completing the swap by end-2004. Completion is now scheduled for the end of February 2005. However, further delays are probable, and the level of acceptance remains in doubt and may not greatly exceed the government's stated minimum of 55 per cent. This would leave pending an arrangement with the remaining creditors, and would delay any future return to international financial markets.

The restructuring process has also caused considerable friction between Economy Minister Roberto Lavagna and Kirchner. Lavagna is likely to leave the ministry in 2005, probably leaving economic policy in the hands of Kirchner confidants whose economic competence has yet to be demonstrated. Restructuring has been the one key economic issue for the government in the past year, and its poor performance here does not lead to optimism – nor does widespread budget under-spending, attributed to over-centralized decision making and intracabinet infighting.

2. IMF talks. The renewal of talks with the IMF, following the suspension of the standby agreement in August 2004 was scheduled for January 2005. As this is contingent upon resolution of the restructuring process, this too will be delayed, at least until the second quarter. Argentina will thus be forced, in the meantime, to meet payments due to the Fund from reserves. Moreover, the IMF has called for acceptance of the bond swap by at least 80 per cent of creditors, unlikely to be attained.

Argentina has yet to advance in areas of key concern to the Fund, including banking reform, reform of the revenue-sharing agreement with the provinces and the renegotiation of privatized utilities' contracts. Only limited advances can be expected in 2005. The government has recently announced that export taxes and the financial transactions tax on cheques will be retained, despite IMF pressures to eliminate them. The Fund is unlikely to soften its line on these issues, and may indeed press additional demands.

3. Utilities negotiations. There has been little progress on the renegotiation of utilities' tariffs since the January 2002 devaluation. Recent moves to define a new regulatory framework have raised concerns of increased government interference, while decisions to rescind some public service concessions (including the postal service and some railways) have raised fears that renationalization may be on the cards. Although this is highly implausible, such unease will continue to affect investments. Lack of investment in the electricity sector in particular may worsen energy shortages in 2005.

POLITICAL PROSPECTS

While the Peronists will retain control over both houses in 2005, prickly relations with Eduardo Duhalde, Kirchner's predecessor, and a growing sense of inertia will characterize the year ahead.

■ Elections

Legislative elections in October 2005 render it yet more unlikely that the government will undertake unpopular reforms in the meantime. The Peronist party will maintain its majority in both houses – not least owing to the continuing disarray of the other political parties – although many of its representatives will not be supporters of Kirchner himself. Kirchner's poor relations with Congress will continue to favour the use of decrees bypassing the legislature. The likely Senate candidacy of Kirchner's wife in Buenos Aires province will worsen already shaky relations with Duhalde, still the party's most influential figure.

■ **Foreign policy**

Poor relations with Duhalde, now president of the Mercosur Permanent Commission, are also a factor in the government's erratic foreign policy, with Duhalde often acting as virtual foreign minister and conciliator, and Kirchner taking an adversarial position. Kirchner's frequent last-minute decisions to avoid summit meetings and poor relations with most of the region (apart from Venezuela) contrast with Duhalde's positive image in Latin America. The likely departure of Foreign Minister Rafael Bielsa in 2005 will have no impact on foreign policy failings.

■ **Growing opposition**

Kirchner's 60 per cent approval ratings will not be sustained indefinitely in the face of government inertia, the failure to combat corruption and the inevitable growth slowdown. Although lack of economic policy making has been accepted during the upturn, a slowdown will create demands for a more proactive role. Indeed, a negative shift in expectations may lead to increased opposition, particularly given pending wage demands – above all in the public sector, where no wage increases are envisaged in 2005 – and a rise in strike action. Failure to define economic and social policy initiatives may create a perception of indecisiveness and inertia, such as that surrounding former President Fernando de la Rua – although a similar dramatic outcome is highly unlikely.

CONCLUSION

Debt restructuring and IMF negotiations will be more protracted than the government had anticipated, curtailing investment and growth levels. Slowing growth and worsening expectations may lead to an increase in social demands, undercutting Kirchner's political support and increasing instability

2

The Range of Country @ratings in the Americas

Sylvia Greisman and Olivier Oechslin

Coface Country Risk and Economic Studies Department, Paris

COUNTRY @RATING SCALE

The regional rating is the average of the country risk@ratings weighted according to the share of each country in the regional GDP.

Country @ratings measure the average level of short-term non-payment risk associated with companies in individual countries. A rating reflects the influence of a particular country's economic, financial and political outlook on financial commitments of local companies. It is thus complementary to @rating credit opinions on companies.

Quality of risk in North American companies has remained good. The strength of economic activity in the United States (A1) has reinforced the financial situation of companies and led to a further drop in non-payment incidents. The present economic slowdown and rising interest rates should not significantly affect the solvability of these companies in 2005. However, while the expected average level of credit risk remains low, it is likely now to have bottomed out.

In Latin America, corporate risk is generally high owing to the fragile economic, financial and political environment in which companies operate. Risk quality did, however, improve in 2004. This upturn can be explained by healthy export trade combined with improved political stability, stringent budget and monetary policies and renewed confidence on the part of lenders and investors in the region. Chile, for instance, already the region's highest scorer, has been upgraded to A2. Brazil (B) is positively watchlisted. Among higher-risk countries, Venezuela, Uruguay, Paraguay and Ecuador have been upgraded from D to C. This improvement in risk quality means that corporate payment behaviour should remain good in 2005, notwithstanding major upheavals such as a sudden US interest rate hike, which would undermine the financial situation in countries that are highly dependent on financial markets.

North and South America had exceptional years in 2004 with both robust demand and favourable financing terms supporting growth. In the US, there has been a corresponding increase in the twin deficits. Conversely, Latin America has benefited significantly not only from trade with China, but also from the improved financial situation in many of its constituting countries. In Brazil, for instance, growth has resumed without adversely affecting the country's external accounts.

The most likely scenario in North America for 2005 is a moderate slowdown in the United States due to a gradual rise in interest rates and a falloff in household demand.

Despite this less favourable context, Latin American countries should still benefit from strong

PAYMENT INCIDENTS INDEX
(12 months moving average - base 100 : World 1995)

2

demand from both their North American neighbours and more distant clients in China. Buoyant trading in commodities, strong internal demand, a more stable political environment and positive sentiment in financial markets vis-à-vis emerging countries should all contribute to sustaining growth. A slowdown seems nonetheless inevitable. Increased inflation, partly due to oil prices, and the emergence of bottlenecks in infrastructures has led central banks to increase domestic interest rates, which could well dampen internal demand. The slowdown could be moderate, but only if US interest rates remain at reasonable levels.

■ Countries rated A1
Very stable political and economic conditions favourably influence generally good corporate payment behaviour. Moreover, a satisfactory legal framework offers protection for creditors and efficient debt collection procedures. This generally favourable environment does not, however, exclude the possibility of growth disparities or occasional risks of payment default.

In the United States, despite a second quarter slowdown, 2004 was a year of strong growth thanks to buoyant domestic and foreign demand. Household consumption benefited from rising employment and income, interest rates that remained low and a wealth effect. A weaker dollar and improvements in the global economy permitted companies to increase exports. In 2005, activity will slow slightly as household consumption falls amid rising interest rates and the waning effects of tax breaks. Corporate investment will also fall off slightly, with a corresponding slowdown in profits.

In this still-favourable economic environment, profitability should suffer only moderately, with lower corporate debt making it possible for companies to withstand the effects of rising interest rates. Payment behaviour should remain generally good, although there may be some deterioration in the course of the year.

■ Countries rated A2
Default probability is still weak even in the case when one country's political and economic environment or the payment record of companies is not as good as in A1-rated countries.

Economic growth in Chile (rating upgraded in 2004) was among the healthiest in Latin America. That is attributable to the high price of copper and excellent performance of its other exports coupled with buoyant domestic demand. Mining and agriculture have remained the most robust sectors. The signing of free trade agreements with its main trading partners and a sound economic base, essentially due to healthy public finances and very moderate public debt, contributed to sustaining a level of growth that should persist in 2005.

■ Countries rated A4
An already patchy payment record could be further worsened by a deteriorating political and economic environment. Nevertheless, the probability of a default is still acceptable.

After three years of stagnation, Mexico's economy has at last regained momentum buoyed by US demand for manufactured products combined with increased levels of consumption and investment. The peso depreciation has permitted reduced market-share losses, particularly those resulting from competition from Asia. Nevertheless, some sectors such as textiles, metallurgy and foodstuffs are still suffering from competitiveness-related problems, which in turn have given rise to corporate behaviour involving frequent non-payment incidents. There is a need for fresh investment in both the productive sector and infrastructure – essential for increasing productivity – as well as a need for structural reforms. Although there is broad political consensus regarding the necessity for continued austerity measures, votes on structural reform still meet with opposition from parliament.

■ **Countries rated B**

An unsteady political and economic environment is likely to affect further an already poor payment record.

In Brazil (a positively watchlisted country), sharp increases in exports and domestic demand have spurred a marked economic upturn. All sectors are involved, with foodstuffs and steel benefiting, among other things, from strong demand from China. Corporate payment behaviour has thus improved considerably. Although that

COFACE MAP OF COUNTRY @RATINGS

CANADA

Ottawa

UNITED STATES OF AMERICA

Washington

ATLANTIC OCEAN

HAITI Port-au-Prince

MEXICO

Havana
CUBA

Mexico City

DOMINICAN REPUBLIC

JAMAICA
Kingston

Santo Domingo

GUATEMALA Guatemala

EL SALVADOR San Salvador

VENEZUELA   TRINIDAD AND TOBAGO
Caracas   Port of Spain

HONDURAS Tegucigalpa

GUYANA
Georgetown

NICARAGUA Managua

COLOMBIA
Bogota

COSTA RICA San Jose

SURINAME
Paramaribo

PANAMA Panama

ECUADOR Quito

PERU
Lima

BRAZIL

BOLIVIA
La Paz

Brasilia

PARAGUAY
Asunción

CHILE

PACIFIC OCEAN

Santiago

Buenos Aires

URUGUAY
Montevideo

ARGENTINA

ATLANTIC OCEAN

A1
A2
A3
A4
B
C
D

growth has doubtless spurred inflationary pressures, it has not generated current account deficit, paving the way for a virtuous circle that could result in durable reductions in debt ratios. Nevertheless, Brazil achieved that performance in an international context highly favourable to emerging countries. Any sudden trend reversal would deal a heavy blow to this country, which has remained dependent on financial market sentiment due to its large financing needs and still-excessive public sector debt.

In Colombia growth has been strong thanks to lively exports and an upturn in domestic demand. Improved security has helped create an environment more conducive to consumption and investment. Potential for growth is nonetheless still

COFACE MAP OF MEDIUM- AND LONG-TERM COUNTRY RISK

2

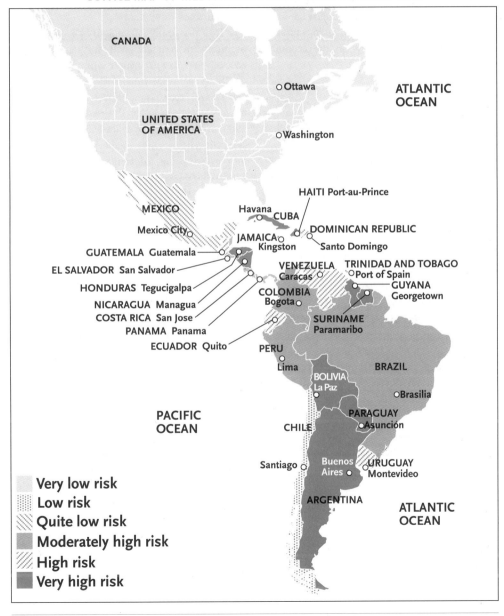

CANADA

Ottawa

ATLANTIC OCEAN

UNITED STATES OF AMERICA

Washington

HAITI Port-au-Prince

MEXICO

Havana
CUBA

Mexico City

DOMINICAN REPUBLIC

JAMAICA
Kingston

Santo Domingo

GUATEMALA Guatemala

EL SALVADOR San Salvador

VENEZUELA
Caracas

TRINIDAD AND TOBAGO
Port of Spain

HONDURAS Tegucigalpa

COLOMBIA
Bogota

GUYANA
Georgetown

NICARAGUA Managua

COSTA RICA San Jose

SURINAME
Paramaribo

PANAMA Panama

ECUADOR Quito

PERU
Lima

BRAZIL

BOLIVIA
La Paz

Brasilia

PACIFIC OCEAN

CHILE

PARAGUAY
Asunción

Santiago

Buenos
Aires

URUGUAY
Montevideo

Very low risk

Low risk

Quite low risk

Moderately high risk

High risk

Very high risk

ARGENTINA

ATLANTIC OCEAN

limited by the debt burden, despite a policy of austerity intended to re-establish financial orthodoxy. Moreover, the political situation has remained shaky with the level of violence still extremely high.

In 2004, for the third year running, the mineral sector's rapid development has considerably buoyed growth in Peru. Robust export trade, particularly in gold and copper, has permitted reducing the current account deficit and improving debt-to-export ratios. The very tense political environment has, however, been in sharp contrast to that undeniable improvement in the economic situation.

■ **Countries rated C**

A very unsteady political and economic environment could deteriorate an already bad payment record.

In Ecuador (upgraded in 2004), the exceptionally favourable oil situation has spurred a growth upturn, a sharp rise in fiscal revenues and a reduction of public debt. Continuation of that trend will nonetheless be highly dependent on rising oil prices with the domestic economy insufficiently diversified. The political situation has also remained very shaky.

In Venezuela, also upgraded in 2004, the economic situation has improved. Following the 2002–2003 crisis, rising market prices and resumption in oil production have spurred renewed growth since 2004. Moreover, although they penalize some private companies, exchange controls have permitted reducing capital flight and replenishing cash reserves. However, heavy regulations and exchange controls have put pressure on the business environment and affected corporate payment behaviour. Although President Chavez' victory in the August referendum reinforced the legitimacy of the country's leadership, the political situation still has a negative effect on its economic outlook.

■ **Countries rated D**

The high risk profile of a country's economic and political environment will further worsen a generally very bad payment record.

In Argentina (positively watchlisted), a dynamic recovery has meant that economic activity has reached levels close to those attained during the 1999 production peak. Industries have regained competitiveness thanks to the peso depreciation. Moreover, strong demand from China for commodities (especially soy beans) has increased exports. However, bottlenecks in both infrastructure and industry should hamper the economy in 2005. In some sectors with production capacity utilization rates already high, companies have been finding it difficult to invest due to insufficient financing. Although a substantial credit recovery will be essential to ensure durable growth, that will be impeded by difficulties in the banking sector and the reluctance of foreign investors and lenders to return to the country given the substantial debt cancellations they have to grant.

Argentina

Population (million inhabitants)	36
GDP (US$ million)	102,042

Coface analysis

Short-term: **D**

Medium-term:
Very high risk

2

STRENGTHS

- Endowed with abundant mineral and farming resources, the country has been benefiting from strong Chinese demand.
- The low peso exchange rate has buoyed exports, particularly with local production gaining an edge on foreign competition.
- The work force is skilled.

WEAKNESSES

- The debt restructuring and substantial cancellation of claims should deter the return of foreign capital.
- The financial system has remained weakened by the 2002 crisis and the presence of many non-performing loans.
- Authorities have had little fiscal room for manoeuvre.
- Although declining, unemployment and poverty have remained very high, substantially above their pre-crisis levels.
- How the political situation will evolve has remained very uncertain due to substantial dissension within the party in power.

RISK ASSESSMENT

The strength of the 2003–2004 recovery has permitted economic activity to nearly return to the production peak reached in 1999. Industrialists have been benefiting from renewed competitiveness thanks to the peso depreciation with strong Chinese demand for raw materials – notably soy beans – buoying exports. Moreover, expansionary monetary and fiscal policy and reduced political uncertainty have been spurring a domestic demand recovery.

Bottlenecks in both infrastructure and industry should slow the economy in 2005. With capacity utilization rates already high in some sectors, companies lacking financing have been having difficulty investing to increase capacity. The virtual absence of domestic or international bank credit is attributable to the substantial cancellation of claims imposed on creditors and especially to the lack of far-reaching financial system reform. A substantial resumption of lending will nonetheless be essential to establish sustainable growth. However, the reforms needed to establish a more hospitable environment for creditors and investors could trigger severe popular discontent. Although certainly still very popular at this juncture, President Kirchner has to contend with the strong rivalries within his party blocking the adoption of reforms.

MAIN ECONOMIC INDICATORS						
US$ billions	2000	2001	2002	2003	2004[(e)]	2005[(f)]
Economic growth (%)	−0.8	−4.4	−10.9	8.8	8.8	3.3
Inflation (%)	−0.7	−1.5	41.0	3.7	6.8	10.8
Public sector balance (%GDP)	−7.1	−8.2	−12.3	−9.1	−4.3	−5.7
Exports	26.4	26.6	25.7	29.6	33.1	34.1
Imports	23.9	19.2	8.5	13.1	21.2	24.8
Trade balance	2.5	7.5	17.2	16.4	12.0	9.3
Current account balance	−8.9	−3.9	9.1	7.8	3.9	2.5
Current account balance (%GDP)	−3.1	−1.5	9.0	6.1	2.8	1.6
Foreign debt (%GDP)	51.3	54.5	146.8	121.1	112.5	84.5
Debt service (%Exports)	75.6	76.1	49.1	57.3	39.8	37.1
Foreign exchange reserves (in months of imports)	6.3	4.3	5.4	5.7	5.9	5.7

e = estimate, f = forecast

CONDITIONS OF ACCESS TO THE MARKET

■ **Market overview**

Between 1998 and 2002, Argentina suffered a severe economic crisis, accompanied in January 2002 by the country's withdrawal from the currency board, a massive 70 per cent devaluation of the peso and a liquidity crisis in the banking sector. The risk of collapse of the banking system forced the Argentine government to introduce exchange controls and restrictions on foreign currency transfers. These have now been relaxed in respect of foreign trade transactions. Exporters, however, are required to convert their foreign exchange earnings from exports on the Argentine currency market as well as pay export duties amounting to as much as 23.5 per cent of the FOB value.

Following the peso's devaluation, the Argentine economy has become highly competitive. In 2003, Argentine exports increased by 14 per cent to US$29.3 billion on the back of improved terms of trade and higher international commodity prices.

Argentine labour is one of the cheapest in Latin America. The average monthly wage in 2003 was US$500 (US$700 in Buenos Aires). Social security contributions have also fallen since 1999. They currently stand at 23 per cent of wages up to 2,500 euros for employers and 17 per cent of wages up to 1,500 euros for employees.

■ **Means of entry**

The opening-up of borders, privatization and the pegging of the peso to the dollar were the main pillars of government economic policy in the 1990s. In 2002, the government introduced an economic and financial emergency law abolishing the convertibility system and establishing a free currency market.

Although the founding treaty of Mercosur enshrines the principle of free movement of goods, the four member countries maintain customs barriers for certain products which they have undertaken gradually to lift. In 2004, Argentina adopted measures, and encouraged the Argentine and Brazilian private sector, to reduce imports of electrical appliances from Brazil.

Since January 1995, goods from non-Mercosur countries have been subject to the common external tariff (CET), which ranges from 0 per cent to 28 per cent (average 11 per cent). Imports are also liable to 0.5 per cent statistical tax on the CIF value, 21 per cent VAT (CIF value + customs duties + statistical tax), 9 per cent additional VAT on goods intended for sale as opposed to those directly used by the importer and 30 per cent tax on profits (CIF value + customs duties + statistical tax). Special procedures, eg clearance from the competent ministry, also apply to pharmaceutical and agri-food imports.

■ Attitude towards foreign investors

The legal arrangements governing foreign investment in Argentina appear to be very liberal. Decree 1853/93 defines the investment framework and lays down the principles of equal treatment of domestic and foreign investors and free repatriation of capital and profits. Foreigners may invest – on the same terms as local investors – in virtually any branch of the economy without seeking prior approval. Nevertheless, the stability of the legal and tax environment for foreign investment could not be taken for granted, especially under the economic and financial emergency which was due to remain in force until 31 December 2004. The emergency could be extended by another year, but with reduced powers of delegated legislation. In this connection, 31 companies have filed a suit before ICSID, the World Bank's arbitration board, for breach of obligations by the Argentine government. Investors should also note that the Argentine trade and companies registration authorities (IGJ) have brought in a series of measures to tighten incorporation procedures for foreign companies established in Buenos Aires since 10 October 2003. New rules have been introduced in respect of composition of capital, designation of activity and multiple shareholdings. Some of the changes complicate the daily operation of foreign companies.

2

PAYMENT INCIDENTS INDEX
(12 months moving average - base 100 : World 1995)

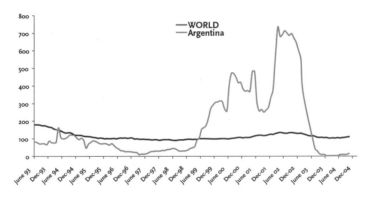

OPPORTUNITY SCOPE

Breakdown of domestic demand (%GDP + imports)

Private consumption	54
Public consumption	11
Investment	11

Exports: 28% of GDP

Imports: 13% of GDP

MAIN DESTINATIONS OF EXPORTS

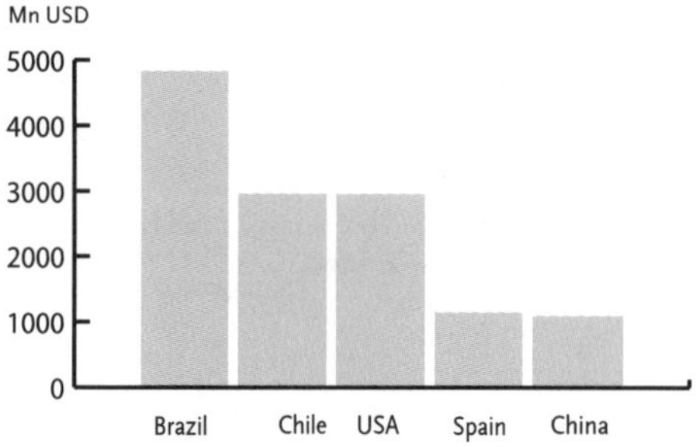

Mn USD
5000
4000
3000
2000
1000
0
Brazil
Chile
USA
Spain
China

MAIN ORIGINS OF IMPORTS

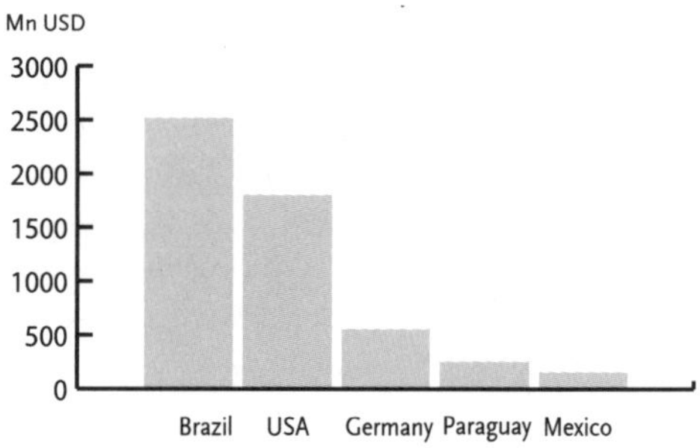

Mn USD
3000
2500
2000
1500
1000
500
0
Brazil
USA
Germany
Paraguay
Mexico

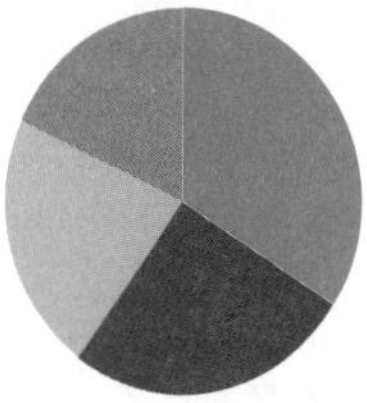

EXPORTS by products

- Processed food items 34%
- Manufactured goods 26%
- Agricultural products 22%
- Fuels 18%

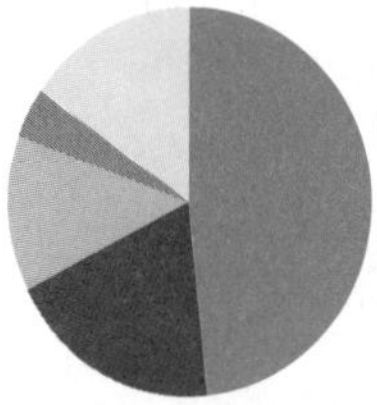

IMPORTS by products

- Intermediate goods 48%
- Capital goods and transport equipment 19%
- Consumer goods 13%
- Fuels 4%
- Miscellaneous 15%

STANDARD OF LIVING / PURCHASING POWER

Indicators	Argentina	Regional average	DC average
GNP per capita (PPP dollars)	10190	7925	4601
GNP per capita (USD)	4220	3467	1840
Human Development Index	0.853	0.782	0.684
Wealthiest 10% share of national income	38.9	44	32
Urban population percentage	88	78	45
Percentage under 15 years old	27	30	30
Number of telephones per 1000 inhabitants	219	172	120
Number of computers per 1000 inhabitants	82	69	37

Bolivia

Population (million inhabitants)	9
GDP (US$ million)	7,801

Coface analysis

Short-term: **D**

Medium-term:
Very high risk

2

STRENGTHS

- The country has substantial hydrocarbon resources and mineral wealth.
- Public sector creditors have granted concessional treatment for Bolivia's debt.
- Its association with Mercosur has improved the country's access to the Brazilian and Argentine markets.

WEAKNESSES

- Exports rest on a limited number of staple commodities with soy beans, zinc, gold and natural gas representing half of sales.
- Bolivia has remained heavily in debt despite the HIPC programme for highly indebted poor countries.
- This landlocked country's degree of development ranks among Latin America's lowest.
- The extensive dollarization will constitute a weakness in case of panic on deposits.
- The political and social climate has remained very tense.

RISK ASSESSMENT

Economic activity has been improving, buoyed mainly by hydrocarbon, mineral product and soy bean exports. However, consumer spending and FDI have remained sluggish. The dynamism of sales abroad coupled with weak domestic demand has been generating external account surpluses.

The country is nonetheless still financially shaky. Despite the reductions granted, debt ratios have remained high in relation to currency earnings. Furthermore, the banking sector's extensive dollarization would be a major source of vulnerability in a crisis of confidence.

Politically, tensions have remained very high with the population benefiting little from a recovery limited to capital intensive sectors. President Carlos Mesa's popularity has doubtless remained relatively high, bolstered by his success last 18 July in the referendum on the legal environment of gas exploitation. He will nonetheless have to reach a difficult compromise between the Indian movements demanding nationalization of underground resources and foreign multinationals, which have been threatening to leave the country. The president enjoys little room for manoeuvre, much like his predecessor who had to resign in June 2002 under pressure from the people.

MAIN ECONOMIC INDICATORS

US$ billions	2000	2001	2002	2003	2004(e)	2005(f)
Economic growth (%)	2.4	1.2	2.8	2.5	3.8	4.5
Inflation (%)	3.4	0.9	2.4	3.3	3.9	3.5
Public balance (%GDP)	−3.7	−6.9	−8.9	−8.1	−6.0	−5.2
Exports	1.2	1.3	1.3	1.6	2.0	2.1
Imports	1.8	1.7	1.8	1.6	1.8	1.8
Trade balance	−0.6	−0.4	−0.5	0.0	0.2	0.3
Current account balance	−0.4	−0.3	−0.3	0.0	0.2	0.1
Current account balance (%GDP)	−5.3	−3.4	−4.1	0.3	2.7	0.9
Foreign debt (%GDP)	69.0	58.5	62.5	67.7	70.4	72.2
Debt service (%Exports)	24.5	28.1	22.4	25.4	19.4	18.3
Foreign exchange reserves (in months of imports)	7.0	6.5	5.0	5.6	5.8	6.8

e = estimate, f = forecast

CONDITIONS OF ACCESS TO THE MARKET

■ **Market overview**

A small landlocked state surrounded by powerful neighbours, Bolivia set great store in the 1990s by the opening-up of its borders and trade integration with the other countries of the region. Since 1995, the five-tier Common External Tariff of the Andean Community of Nations (ACN) (0 per cent, 5 per cent, 10 per cent, 15 per cent and 20 per cent) has been in force in the country. The other ACN members have allowed Bolivia to apply *de facto* 10 per cent flat-rate *ad valorem* customs duty on all imports from non-ACN countries, excluding some capital goods, which are liable to a reduced rate of duty. FDI has fallen since 2000, due partly to the completion of the investment programme involving capitalized companies and partly to the resurgence of social and political conflicts.

Unskilled Bolivian labour is widely available and cheap. Wages can be fairly high for positions of responsibility. Employment of foreign staff is, in principle, limited to 15 per cent of a company's workforce.

■ **Means of entry**

Foodstuffs and crop and animal products require health certificates that comply with standards laid down by the ACN and approved by Bolivia. The National agency, Senasag, is responsible for administering all health standards relating to imports. All imports are subject to random checks by Bolivian customs. However, the growth in parallel markets is causing concern among legal traders.

Documentary credit is the most widely used means of payment for both cash and deferred settlements. Delivery against payment is also used, but is far less widespread. Where business relations are well established, payments are usually made by bank transfer. Corporate defaults have surged since 2000. Against this background, irrevocable and confirmed documentary credit is strongly recommended if there is any doubt whatsoever about the buyer's creditworthiness.

■ **Attitude towards foreign investors**

Although foreign investment before October 2003 was granted the same terms as investment by Bolivian nationals, in actual fact there has been an increase in the number of complaints against the latter. Moreover, the proposed reform of the oil and gas bill could call into question the country's legal certainty.

■ **Foreign exchange regulations**

There are no foreign exchange controls and no restrictions on the buying and selling of currency or capital transfers. Bolivia is a highly dollarized economy. In July 2004, however, the government introduced a two-year 0.3 per cent tax on bank transfers of foreign currency in excess of US$1,000. As a result, people have transferred most of their dollar holdings into local currency accounts in a bid to avoid this tax. Companies, on the other hand, have kept their accounts in dollars. Before July 2004, over 95 per cent of bank deposits were denominated in dollars.

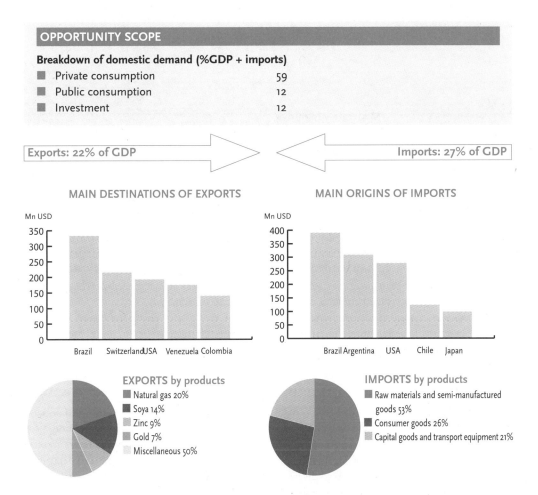

OPPORTUNITY SCOPE

Breakdown of domestic demand (%GDP + imports)

- Private consumption — 59
- Public consumption — 12
- Investment — 12

Exports: 22% of GDP   Imports: 27% of GDP

MAIN DESTINATIONS OF EXPORTS

Mn USD

Brazil, Switzerland, USA, Venezuela, Colombia

MAIN ORIGINS OF IMPORTS

Mn USD

Brazil, Argentina, USA, Chile, Japan

EXPORTS by products
- Natural gas 20%
- Soya 14%
- Zinc 9%
- Gold 7%
- Miscellaneous 50%

IMPORTS by products
- Raw materials and semi-manufactured goods 53%
- Consumer goods 26%
- Capital goods and transport equipment 21%

STANDARD OF LIVING / PURCHASING POWER

Indicators	Bolivia	Regional average	DC average
GNP per capita (PPP dollars)	2390	7925	4601
GNP per capita (USD)	900	3467	1840
Human Development Index	0.681	0.782	0.684
Wealthiest 10% share of national income	32	44	32
Urban population percentage	63	78	45
Percentage under 15 years old	39	30	30
Number of telephones per 1000 inhabitants	68	172	120
Number of computers per 1000 inhabitants	23	69	37

Brazil

Population (million inhabitants)	174
GDP (US$ million)	460,800

Coface analysis

Short-term: **B**

Medium-term:
Moderately high risk

STRENGTHS

- Brazil has abundant natural resources and a relatively diversified economy.
- Chinese demand has been benefiting exported products (food, minerals, airplanes).
- Fiscal and monetary policy has been prudent and pragmatic.
- The domestic market potential and the low cost of labour are attractive to foreign investors.
- The real's current level has permitted Brazilian companies to enjoy good competitiveness.
- The country benefits from international financial community backing.

WEAKNESSES

- The public debt burden is still heavy with maturities too short.
- The country's debt burden and external financing needs have remained excessive.
- Brazil continues to be vulnerable to a trend reversal on raw materials.
- The low savings rate, mainly absorbed by the government's financing needs, has been limiting private investment.
- The coalition in power has been limiting the room for manoeuvre to make progress on reforms.

RISK ASSESSMENT

A marked increase in exports and domestic demand has underpinned a notable economic upturn. All sectors have been involved, with food and steel particularly benefiting from strong world demand. Company payment behaviour has thus improved significantly.

Although growth has clearly triggered inflationary pressures, it has not generated current account deficits, which has prompted hopes for a virtuous circle that would permit durably reducing debt ratios. Nonetheless, the country has achieved those results in a favourable economic context with rising raw material prices and strong world demand coupled with good financial conditions for emerging countries. A sudden trend reversal would weaken the country, which has remained dependent on financial market sentiment due to its substantial financing needs and excessive public sector debt.

Growth is still impeded by economic bottlenecks (insufficient credit for companies and deficient infrastructure) that could re-ignite structural inflation. Moreover, the need to continue exercising restraint and pursuing structural reforms over a long period could ultimately spell trouble in an often volatile political climate.

MAIN ECONOMIC INDICATORS

US$ billions	2000	2001	2002	2003	2004[e]	2005[f]
Economic growth (%)	4.4	1.3	1.9	−0.2	5.1	4.0
Inflation (%)	5.3	9.4	14.7	10.4	8.0	6.1
Public sector balance (%GDP)	−3.6	−3.6	−4.6	−5.2	−3.8	−3.8
Exports	55.1	58.2	60.4	73.1	92.1	101.7
Imports	55.8	55.6	47.2	48.3	60.9	73.0
Trade balance	−0.7	2.6	13.1	24.8	31.2	28.7
Current account balance	−24.2	−23.2	−7.7	4.0	8.3	4.4
Current account balance (%GDP)	−4.0	−4.6	−1.7	0.8	1.5	0.7
Foreign debt (%GDP)	39.5	44.7	49.6	47.9	39.5	37.2
Debt service (%Exports)	101.1	88.8	65.3	67.8	53.3	42.3
Foreign exchange reserves (in months of imports)	4.2	4.5	5.4	6.9	6.0	6.3

e = estimate, f = forecast

CONDITIONS OF ACCESS TO THE MARKET

■ Market overview

Brazil's working population, according to the latest official figures published in 2003, is 86 million out of a total of 140 million persons over 10 years old, ie an activity rate of 61.3 per cent. The minimum monthly wage is currently 260 reals (about 72 euros). Employer social security and compulsory benefit contributions amount to about 50 per cent of gross wages. Pension and tax reforms could result in reduced contributions mainly in the export sectors.

■ Means of entry

The average rate of customs duty is approximately 10.8 per cent and the top rate is 35 per cent. The country is bound by Mercosur's Common External Tariff, which is subject to numerous exceptions. Brazil maintains a number of non-tariff barriers to imports, including import licences, customs valuation inspections and prior product registration. The most widely used means of payment are down payments, pre-payments, cash against documents, acceptance bills and irrevocable letters of credit confirmed by a Brazilian or foreign bank. There are restrictions on the employment of foreigners and two types of work permit – permanent and temporary – both of which are awarded on a fairly restricted basis. One of the

conditions people applying for a permanent visa must satisfy is that they should invest US$50,000.

■ Attitude towards foreign investors

Foreign investors have to register with the central bank and declare the amount, origin and purpose of the investment. All companies or individuals not domiciled in Brazil who hold or wish to acquire property in the country must register with CNPJ (companies register) or CPF (natural persons register). Foreign investment is banned in certain sectors. Shareholdings in financial institutions are subject to government approval. Investors may set up a wholly-owned subsidiary without being subject to legal restrictions of any kind. Foreigners must have a permanent visa to be appointed director of a subsidiary in the country, while foreign investors must be represented by a lawyer. Overseas transfers (capital repatriation, reinvestment, profit and dividend repatriation) are authorized provided

PAYMENT INCIDENTS INDEX
(12 months moving average - base 100 : World 1995)

the capital is registered. Apart from requiring central bank permission, such transfers have to be handled by financial institutions trading on the currency market. Profit and dividend transfers are not taxed.

■ **Foreign exchange regulations**
The new government formed after the October 2002 elections has honoured its pledge to maintain the flexible exchange rate system of 1999. The central bank intervenes only occasionally, when required, to ensure liquidity in the market, but not to shift rates. Its sole aim is to control inflation in a manner that does not undermine growth.

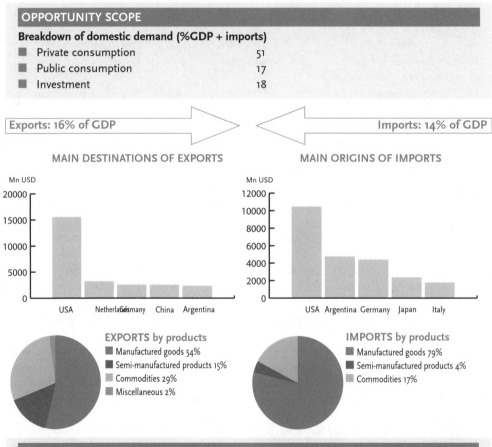

OPPORTUNITY SCOPE

Breakdown of domestic demand (%GDP + imports)

■ Private consumption	51
■ Public consumption	17
■ Investment	18

Exports: 16% of GDP → ← Imports: 14% of GDP

MAIN DESTINATIONS OF EXPORTS

Mn USD (USA, Netherlands, Germany, China, Argentina)

MAIN ORIGINS OF IMPORTS

Mn USD (USA, Argentina, Germany, Japan, Italy)

EXPORTS by products
■ Manufactured goods 54%
■ Semi-manufactured products 15%
■ Commodities 29%
■ Miscellaneous 2%

IMPORTS by products
■ Manufactured goods 79%
■ Semi-manufactured products 4%
■ Commodities 17%

STANDARD OF LIVING / PURCHASING POWER

Indicators	Brazil	Regional average	DC average
GNP per capita (PPP dollars)	7450	7925	4601
GNP per capita (USD)	2830	3467	1840
Human Development Index	0.775	0.782	0.684
Wealthiest 10% share of national income	46.7	44	32
Urban population percentage	82	78	45
Percentage under 15 years old	28	30	30
Number of telephones per 1000 inhabitants	223	172	120
Number of computers per 1000 inhabitants	75	69	37

Canada

Population (million inhabitants)	31.6
GDP (US$ million)	856,600
GDP per capita (US$)	27,100

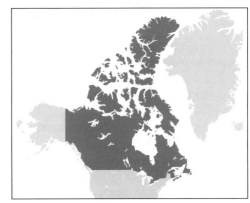

Coface analysis   Short-term: **A1**

2

RISK ASSESSMENT

In 2004, Canada benefited from robust growth spurred by firm domestic demand and exports. However, a marked slowdown developed toward year-end that should persist in 2005.

The Canadian dollar's appreciation against the US dollar and the economic slowdown in the United States (Canada's main trading partner) have had a negative effect not only on exporting companies but also on companies finding themselves in competition in their home market with more competitive American products. The resulting earnings decline could cause a drop in investment and employment.

Notwithstanding essentially expansionary fiscal policy and continued low interest rates despite tightening monetary policy, households should moderate their spending. Residential investment should begin sagging in the second half of the year although remaining at good levels. Meanwhile, with public sector accounts in surplus, public investment in health, education and infrastructure should remain robust.

The corollary effects of the favourable conditions in 2004 included increased company earning, a continued decline of bankruptcies (down 8 per cent in 2004) and a Coface payment incident index below the world average. Although the situation should remain good in the staple commodity-producing western provinces, it could prove shakier in the other provinces, notably for exporting companies contending with unfavourable exchange rates.

MAIN ECONOMIC INDICATORS						
%	2000	2001	2002	2003	2004(e)	2005(f)
Economic growth	5.2	1.8	3.4	2.0	2.7	2.4
Consumption (var.)	4.0	2.7	3.4	3.1	3.3	3.0
Investment (var.)	6.0	1.0	−6.0	3.4	7.2	5.7
Inflation	2.7	2.5	2.2	2.8	1.9	2.0
Unemployment rate	6.8	7.2	7.6	7.6	7.2	7.1
Short-term interest rate	5.7	4.0	2.6	3.0	2.3	2.6
Public sector balance (%GDP)	3.0	1.4	0.8	1.0	0.9	0.9
Public sector debt (%GDP)	82.0	81.0	77.8	75.6	74.0	74.0
Exports (var.)	8.9	−2.8	1.1	−2.4	7.1	4.9
Imports (var.)	8.1	−5.0	1.4	3.8	8.0	6.9
Current account balance (%GDP)	2.7	2.3	2.0	2.0	3.1	2.9

e = estimate, f = forecast

PAYMENT AND COLLECTION PRACTICES

A heritage of Canada's colonial past, its dual legal system comprises that used by nine of the ten provinces making up the federal state, which is inspired by British common law and that used by Quebec whose legal traditions are based on the codified principles of the Napoleonic code. Lower Canada's civil code, dating from 1 January 1866, was completely revised and implemented on 1 January 1994 as the Quebec Civil Code.

Under the British North America Act of 29 March 1867, Canada was the first British colony to exercise executive and legislative powers as a federal state. The Confederation of Canada came into effect as a dominion on 1 July 1867.

■ Payment

A single law governs bills of exchange, promissory notes and cheques throughout Canada, however this law is frequently interpreted according to common law precedents in the nine provinces or according to the civil code in Quebec. As such, sellers are well advised to accept such payment methods except in cases where long-term commercial relations, based on mutual trust, have been established with buyers.

Centralized accounts, which greatly simplify the settlement process by centralizing settlement procedures between locally based buyers and sellers, are also used within Canada.

SWIFT bank transfers are the most commonly used payment method for international transactions. The majority of Canadian banks are connected to the SWIFT network, offering a rapid, reliable and cost-effective means of payment, notwithstanding the fact that payment is dependent upon the client being in good faith insofar as only the issuer takes the decision to order payment.

The letter of credit (L/C) is also frequently used.

■ Debt collection

Canada's constitution divides judicial authority between the federal and provincial governments. Thus, each province is responsible for administering justice, organizing provincial courts

and enacting the rules of civil proceedings in its territory. Although the names of courts vary between provinces, the same legal system applies throughout the country, bar Quebec.

Within each province, provincial courts hear most disputes of all kinds concerning small claims, and superior courts hear large claims; for example, the Quebec superior court hears civil and commercial disputes exceeding C\$70,000 and jury trials of criminal cases. Canadian superior courts comprise two distinct divisions: a court of first instance and a court of appeal.

At federal level, the Supreme Court of Canada, in Ottawa, and only with leave of the Court itself (leave is granted if the case raises an important question of law), hears appeals against decisions handed down by the provincial appeal courts, or by the Canadian Federal Court (stating in appeal division), which has special jurisdiction in matters concerning maritime law, immigration, customs and excise, intellectual property, disputes between provinces, and so on.

The right of final recourse before the Privy Council, in London, was abolished in 1949.

The collection process begins with the issuance of a final notice, or 'seven-day letter', reminding the debtor of his obligation to pay together with any contractually agreed interest penalties.

Ordinary legal action – even if the vocabulary used to describe it may vary within the country – proceeds in three phases: the writ of summons whereby the plaintiff files his/her claim against the defendant with the court; the examination for discovery, which outlines the claim against the defendant and takes into account the evidence to be submitted by each party to the court; and, finally, the trial proper during which the judge hears the adverse parties and their respective witnesses, who are subject to examination and cross-examination by their respective legal counsels, to clarify the facts of the case before making a ruling.

The Quebec civil code reform, in effect since 1 January 2003, is intended to speed up and foster, by devolving a broader role on the court, smoother court proceedings, by, for example, instituting a standard 'originating petition' (*requête introductive d'instance*), introducing a 180-day time limit by which the proceedings must be scheduled for 'investigation and hearings' and promoting recourse to conciliation procedures during the trial.

PAYMENT INCIDENTS INDEX
(12 months moving average - base 100 : World 1995)

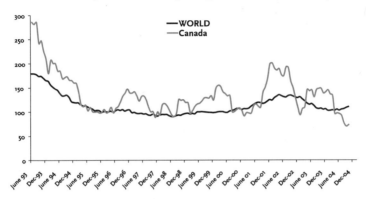

2

Chile

Population (million inhabitants)	16
GDP (US$ million)	64,153

Coface analysis

Short-term: **A2**

Medium-term:
Low risk

STRENGTHS

- The political environment has been stable with a consensus on maintaining fundamental macroeconomic equilibriums.
- The banking system is the soundest in the region.
- The country has succeeded in diversifying its exports (fruit, fish, wood, wood pulp, etc), even though copper still represents over a third of sales abroad.

WEAKNESSES

- The Chilean economy has remained too dependent on commodities or low value-added products.
- The high stock of FDI has been causing large foreign currency outflows.
- Some private companies have been carrying high foreign debt.
- Substantial social inequalities still mark the country.

RISK ASSESSMENT

Chile's economic growth has been among the strongest in Latin America, buoyed by high copper prices and very good performance for other exports, as well as robust domestic demand. The most dynamic sectors still include mining, farming and services (notably electricity, gas and water distribution). Moreover, the peso appreciation has helped reduce inflation and has offset inflationary pressures generated by strong domestic demand and high prices for oil products.

Signature of free trade agreements with its main trading partners coupled with good fundamentals, essentially sound public sector finances and very moderate public debt, will all be factors conducive to growth that is likely to remain strong in 2005.

For the long haul, however, the economy has remained too dependent on commodity exports. Diversification and transformation of production toward higher value-added products will thus be essential.

MAIN ECONOMIC INDICATORS						
US$ billions	2000	2001	2002	2003	2004[(e)]	2005[(f)]
Economic growth (%)	4.2	3.1	2.1	3.2	5.9	4.5
Inflation (%)	4.5	2.6	2.8	1.1	2.0	3.0
Public sector balance (%GDP)	0.1	−0.3	−0.8	−0.9	0.2	0.2
Exports	19.2	18.3	18.2	21.0	26.1	28.1
Imports	17.1	16.4	15.9	18.0	21.4	23.1
Trade balance	2.1	1.8	2.3	3.0	4.7	5.0
Current account balance	−0.9	−1.1	−0.9	−0.6	0.4	0.8
Current account balance (%GDP)	−1.2	−1.6	−1.3	−0.8	0.5	0.8
Foreign debt (%GDP)	49.7	57.0	61.9	62.0	51.1	51.8
Debt service (%Exports)	20.4	19.8	22.3	19.3	21.4	18.5
Foreign exchange reserves (in months of imports)	6.9	6.9	7.5	6.9	6.4	6.3

e = estimate, f = forecast

CONDITIONS OF ACCESS TO THE MARKET

■ Market overview

The Chilean market is secure and stable. The country's sound political and economic situation, good infrastructure and stable legislative and regulatory framework create an attractive business environment, especially for small and medium-sized companies. Chile has limited tariff protection and pursues unilateral measures to cut import duties, backed by bilateral and regional trade agreements. From 1 January 2003, standard customs duty on all products is 6 per cent. Moreover, ratification by Chile's parliament of the free trade agreement with the EU, in force since 1 February 2003, has led to the abolition of customs duties on 99.8 per cent of industrial goods.

■ Means of entry

Non-tariff barriers are few and far between. For food products, however, a number of food produce regulations, similar at times to non-tariff barriers, are in place (type approval and sampling procedures, variable levies on edible oils, sugar, wheat and wheat flour, super milk levy, etc).

Compared with the other countries of the region, Chile provides generally satisfactory protection of intellectual property rights despite the inadequacy of some laws and institutional arrangements (three-year delay in harmonizing local legislation with TRIPS, with the bill still under discussion in Congress) and the absence of public awareness. Chilean trademark and designation of origin laws are not yet fully WTO-compliant.

■ Attitude towards foreign investors

There is equal treatment of foreign and local investors. Foreigners are not required to tie up with a local partner. Foreign investment status within the meaning of Decree-Law 600 applies to deals in excess of US$5 million. Capital inflows below this figure but above US$10,000 must be declared to the central bank. Some regulations have been relaxed though; for example, the compulsory reserve requirement (*Encaje*) has been scrapped. The utilities privatization and concession programme continues to offer foreign investors start-up opportunities, even though most of the lucrative concessions have already been awarded. Corporation tax is 15 per cent, but there is a 24.85 per cent surtax on profits repatriated abroad. Moreover, some regions benefit from investment incentives (VAT exemption, etc) under regional development aid programmes. Labour legislation is not burdensome in terms of social security contributions. Employer social security contributions are extremely low and limited to industrial accident protection, despite the introduction of unemployment benefits in 2002 and the increase in severance pay under the recently revised labour code.

To counter the decline in foreign investment inflows in 2002, the government is looking to provide incentives for foreign start-ups in the country. One such initiative is the investment platform act adopted in 2002, which aims to turn Chile into a regional investment springboard. Provided they meet a number of strict criteria, foreign companies investing from Chile in neighbouring countries are exempt from tax on profits generated outside.

■ Foreign exchange regulations

The central bank abandoned the peso's crawling peg in September 1999. The exchange rate has since been determined solely by the market, with the monetary authorities intervening only on an exceptional basis.

All common means of payment are used.

PAYMENT INCIDENTS INDEX
(12 months moving average - base 100 : World 1995)

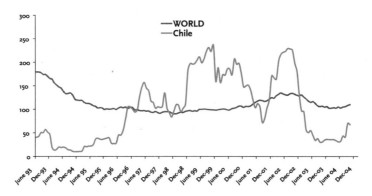

OPPORTUNITY SCOPE

Breakdown of domestic demand (%GDP + imports)
- Private consumption   46
- Public consumption   9
- Investment   17

Exports: 36% of GDP   →   ←   Imports: 32% of GDP

2

MAIN DESTINATIONS OF EXPORTS

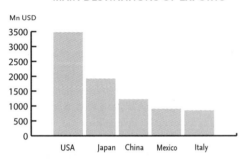

MAIN ORIGINS OF IMPORTS

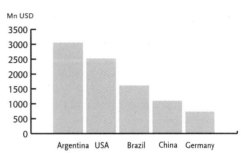

EXPORTS by products
- Copper 36%
- Fresh fruit 8%
- Paper and cellulose 6%
- Miscellaneous 51%

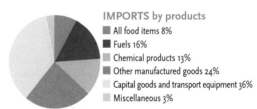

IMPORTS by products
- All food items 8%
- Fuels 16%
- Chemical products 13%
- Other manufactured goods 24%
- Capital goods and transport equipment 36%
- Miscellaneous 3%

STANDARD OF LIVING / PURCHASING POWER

Indicators	Chile	Regional average	DC average
GNP per capita (PPP dollars)	9420	7925	4601
GNP per capita (USD)	4250	3467	1840
Human Development Index	0.839	0.782	0.684
Wealthiest 10% share of national income	47	44	32
Urban population percentage	86	78	45
Percentage under 15 years old	27	30	30
Number of telephones per 1000 inhabitants	230	172	120
Number of computers per 1000 inhabitants	119	69	37

Colombia

Population (million inhabitants)	44
GDP (US$ million)	80,925

Short-term: **B**

Coface analysis

Medium-term:
Moderately high risk

STRENGTHS

- Colombia boasts abundant natural wealth (agriculture, hydrocarbons and minerals), which has permitted it to benefit from the high raw material prices.
- The country has nonetheless succeeded in reducing its traditional dependence on those resources by developing other export sectors.
- Colombia has thus become the Andean community's leading manufacturing power.
- President Alvaro Uribe has enjoyed broad popular support in his campaign against insecurity.
- Outside the Middle East, the country has been the primary beneficiary of American aid, intended to combat 'narco-terrorism'.

WEAKNESSES

- The presence of Latin America's most powerful guerrilla movement and an exceptional level of violence have been deterring foreign investment.
- Marked social inequalities along with geographic constraints have been responsible for the country's lack of cohesiveness.
- The government has had little leeway in managing public sector finances due to the debt interest burden, increased security spending and the rising cost of pension-related charges.
- Foreign debt has remained excessive in relation to currency earnings.
- The absence of support to aid the rehabilitation of former coca producers and the persistence of strong American demand have spurred doubts in the medium term about the current successes in the campaign against cocaine production.

RISK ASSESSMENT

Growth has been dynamic, buoyed by robust exports and a domestic demand upturn. Reduction of insecurity has also fostered a climate more conducive to consumption and investment. The country's growth potential has nonetheless remained limited by the debt burden, which has generated substantial financing needs and made Colombia vulnerable to a possible crisis of confidence vis-à-vis lenders, notwithstanding the economic austerity policy intended to restore financial orthodoxy. Moreover, although the president has remained very popular and obtained a constitutional amendment permitting him to run in the next elections in 2006, the political situation has remained shaky amid an exceptional level of violence. Total victory over the guerrillas will be unlikely in the near term since they remain entrenched in difficult-to-reach regions. A lack of solid results in that campaign could jeopardize Alvaro Uribe's re-election. The commitment to reform will nonetheless constitute something of a guarantee of economic policy implementation.

MAIN ECONOMIC INDICATORS

US$ billions	2000	2001	2002	2003	2004	2005(f)
Economic growth (%)	2.9	1.4	1.6	3.6	3.6	3.6
Inflation (%)	8.8	7.7	7.0	6.5	6.1	3.6
Public sector balance (%GDP)	–3.8	–3.8	–4.1	–2.8	–2.5	–2.6
Exports	13.6	12.8	12.3	13.0	13.7	14.4
Imports	11.1	12.3	12.1	13.0	13.8	14.5
Trade balance	2.5	0.5	0.2	0.0	–0.1	–0.1
Current account balance	0.6	–1.3	–1.6	–1.7	–1.9	–2.1
Current account balance (%GDP)	0.7	–1.5	–2.0	–2.2	–2.3	–2.5
Foreign debt (%GDP)	36.5	39.1	42.0	39.5	39.4	39.2
Debt service (%Exports)	43.3	43.2	47.9	55.7	41.9	41.1
Foreign exchange reserves (in months of imports)	6.0	6.3	6.9	6.7	6.6	6.5

f = forecast

CONDITIONS OF ACCESS TO THE MARKET

■ Market overview
The most buoyant sectors are mining (spurred by the rise in raw material prices), construction (propped by low interest rates as well as tax exemptions introduced by the previous government), manufacturing, energy and financial services.

■ Means of entry
The few barriers to trade that remain arise mainly from the legal uncertainty created by frequent parliamentary changes as well as the plethora of government bodies and players operating without unified standards. This is especially true of taxation. It should be noted that the bill to remedy the situation and promote legal stability for both foreign and domestic investment has been rejected by Congress.

■ Attitude towards foreign investors
All sectors of the economy are open to foreign investment, except for defence and the processing of toxic, hazardous or radioactive waste not produced in the country. Investment in financial services, oil and gas, and mining is subject to prior government approval.

■ Foreign exchange regulations
Under the floating exchange rate system adopted at the end of September 1999, the peso fell sharply until the end of the first quarter of 2003, losing 29 per cent of its value to almost 3,000 pesos to the dollar. The currency has since appreciated to around 2,500 pesos to the dollar. Efforts by the central bank to counter the dollar's sharp decline and so release some of the pressure on Colombian exports should see a reversal of this trend in 2005.

PAYMENT INCIDENTS INDEX
(12 months moving average - base 100 : World 1995)

OPPORTUNITY SCOPE

Breakdown of domestic demand (%GDP + imports)
- Private consumption   55
- Public consumption   17
- Investment   12

Exports: 20% of GDP   Imports: 21% of GDP

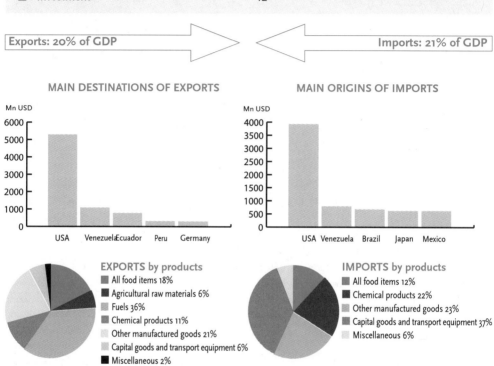

MAIN DESTINATIONS OF EXPORTS

Mn USD — USA, Venezuela, Ecuador, Peru, Germany

MAIN ORIGINS OF IMPORTS

Mn USD — USA, Venezuela, Brazil, Japan, Mexico

EXPORTS by products
- All food items 18%
- Agricultural raw materials 6%
- Fuels 36%
- Chemical products 11%
- Other manufactured goods 21%
- Capital goods and transport equipment 6%
- Miscellaneous 2%

IMPORTS by products
- All food items 12%
- Chemical products 22%
- Other manufactured goods 23%
- Capital goods and transport equipment 37%
- Miscellaneous 6%

STANDARD OF LIVING / PURCHASING POWER

Indicators	Colombia	Regional average	DC average
GNP per capita (PPP dollars)	6150	7925	4601
GNP per capita (USD)	1820	3467	1840
Human Development Index	0.773	0.782	0.684
Wealthiest 10% share of national income	46.5	44	32
Urban population percentage	76	78	45
Percentage under 15 years old	32	30	30
Number of telephones per 1000 inhabitants	179	172	120
Number of computers per 1000 inhabitants	49	69	37

Costa Rica

Population (million inhabitants)	3.9
GDP (US$ million)	16,837
GDP per capita (US$)	4,317

Short-term: **B**

Medium-term:

Coface analysis **Moderately high risk**

2

RISK ASSESSMENT

After three poor years, the economy has resumed strong growth since 2003, buoyed by tourism and a revival of demand for high technology products. Moreover, the country has remained attractive to investors with enviable social indicators, a good education level and political stability. Meanwhile, foreign debt, although increasing, has remained moderate, particularly for the region.

The public finance situation is nonetheless still precarious with the effects of the slowdown in recent years exacerbating fiscal imbalances and increasing public domestic debt. Costa Rica's current political landscape will not be conducive to adopting essential tax and pension reforms. Finally, the increasing number of dollar deposits and loans in relation to the very insufficient level of currency reserves will constitute another major risk.

MAIN ECONOMIC INDICATORS						
US$ billions	2000	2001	2002	2003	2004^(e)	2005^(f)
Economic growth (%)	2.2	0.9	2.8	5.6	4.0	4.0
Inflation (%)	11.0	11.3	9.2	9.5	11.1	8.4
Public sector balance (%GDP)	−3.7	−3.8	−5.0	−3.9	−4.0	−4.0
Exports	5.8	4.9	5.3	6.1	6.2	6.6
Imports	6.0	5.7	6.8	7.2	7.4	7.8
Trade balance	−0.2	−0.8	−1.5	−1.1	−1.3	−1.2
Current account balance (%GDP)	−4.4	−4.6	−5.8	−5.5	−5.5	−5.4
Foreign debt (%GDP)	28.2	28.5	30.4	33.0	34.0	35.8
Debt service (%Exports)	10.0	11.3	9.7	12.2	8.1	8.6
Foreign exchange reserves (in months of imports)	1.5	1.7	1.8	2.1	1.9	1.7

e = estimate, f = forecast

Cuba

Population (million inhabitants)	11
GDP (US$ million)	25,104

Coface analysis

Short-term: **D**

Medium-term:
Very high risk

STRENGTHS

- Cuba boasts real economic potential thanks to extensive resources in several areas: minerals (mainly nickel), agriculture (sugar, tobacco), fishing (langoustes) and especially tourism.
- Its labour force is well trained and its social indicators enviable in comparison with other Greater Antilles islands.

WEAKNESSES

- The country has been vulnerable to external shocks due to its dependence on tourist revenues and raw material exports (sugar, nickel).
- The economy's centralized structure has deterred foreign investment.
- Arrears on the debt have caused Cuba to be denied access to foreign financing.
- Hostile relations with the United States have remained a major obstacle to Cuba's integration into world trade.

RISK ASSESSMENT

Despite stiffer US sanctions, growth accelerated in 2004, buoyed by tourist sector dynamism and increased sugar and nickel exports. The tourist and sugar sectors should continue to drive the economy in 2005.

The country's substantial external vulnerability has nonetheless been clouding those prospects. High oil prices have notably weakened a country where energy purchases represent a quarter of imports and which lacks access to external financing. The currency shortage has resulted in distortions between the official and unofficial peso exchange rates with uneven access to foreign currency also spurring corruption. In response to those monetary tensions, the government has banned dollar transactions within the island since November 2004.

Cuba's isolation has thus limited its prospects while the country will need foreign capital to exploit its development potential. Its assets include vast tourist potential, mineral wealth and a relatively well-trained population. Reconciliation with the international community nonetheless still appears unlikely in the near term and relations with the United States should remain very tense due to the political situation.

MAIN ECONOMIC INDICATORS						
US$ billions	2000	2001	2002	2003	2004[(e)]	2005[(f)]
Economic growth (%)	5.6	3.0	1.1	2.6	3.3	3.5
Inflation (%)	−2.3	−1.4	3.9	4.5	6.5	2.2
Public sector balance (%GDP)	−2.2	−2.3	−3.1	−3.4	−3.0	−3.0
Exports	1.8	1.8	1.6	1.7	2.1	2.3
Imports	4.9	4.8	4.6	4.6	5.2	5.5
Trade balance	−3.1	−3.1	−3.0	−3.0	−3.1	−3.2
Current account balance	−0.8	−0.6	−0.8	−0.2	−0.2	−0.1
Current account balance (%GDP)	−3.2	−2.2	−1.5	−0.4	−0.3	−0.3
Foreign debt (%GDP)*	49.4	46.5	48.2	48.1	46.2	46.0
Debt service (%Exports)	15.0	15.0	15.3	15.7	14.0	14.0
Foreign exchange reserves (in months of imports)	1.0	1.1	0.9	1.0	1.0	1.0

*excluding debt to Russia   e = estimate, f = forecast

CONDITIONS OF ACCESS TO THE MARKET

■ Means of entry

Cuba is one of the founding members of the WTO and maintains trade relations with all the countries of the world, except the United States, which has maintained a trade embargo against it for the last 40 years. The Helms-Burton and Torricelli Acts drive up the price of imports. However, since late 2001 the US government has authorized a few agricultural and pharmaceutical goods to be traded against cash. The country's import regulations are very restrictive, with the government exercising tight controls (licences, import boards by product and sector, etc) and determining priority sectors. Price and funding are essential criteria, although quality, guarantees and after-sales service are gaining importance. Customs duties on the whole are fairly low but in 2003 they were raised on a number of products.

The country has severe payment problems. As Cuba is not eligible for funding from international institutions (World Bank, IDB), it is forced to seek short-term loans (12–24 months) at rates that are 3–12 per cent higher than Libor. Payments are delayed due to the shortage of foreign currency. The preferred means of payment for foreign trade is the irrevocable documentary credit confirmed by a leading bank. As foreign payments cannot legally be made in dollars, other convertible currencies (euro, yen, etc) are used. Exchange controls in force since July 2003 require Cuban firms and agencies to seek central bank approval for foreign trade payments.

■ Attitude towards foreign investors

Cuba has only encouraged foreign investment for the last 11 years and has concluded bilateral investment promotion and protection agreements with 53 countries. Sectors that have attracted FDI include tourism, basic industry, energy, telecommunications, foodstuffs and banking. Education, health care and services in general are closed to foreigners. Bureaucratic and restrictive procedures regulate foreign investment, which must meet strict technology transfer, capital contribution and export development criteria. Economic difficulties, red tape and the Helms-Burton Act hamper foreign investment in the island. In fact, investment has greatly declined in the last few years. The government reserves the right to grant, renew or refuse without explanation licences to foreign operators (representations, branches, mixed enterprises, economic associations, etc).

The tax system does not discriminate against foreign investors and offers a number of incentives. Free zones award companies exemptions from business and labour taxes, customs duties and corporation tax. Labour on the whole is skilled, but it is expensive and lacks motivation. The employing entity, necessarily Cuban, can decide pay rises unilaterally and lay off essential employees. Severance payments are compulsory and exorbitant.

■ Foreign exchange regulations

The exchange rate has steadied over the last three years at 26 pesos to the dollar (non-convertible Cuban pesos (CUPs)). From July 2003, domestic commercial transactions previously conducted in dollars are carried out in convertible pesos (CUCs; these are not recognized internationally) at the rate of one CUC to the US dollar. The convertible Cuban peso has, since November 2004, replaced the dollar for cash transactions and payments in all commercial entities across Cuba (shops, stores, hotels, restaurants, taxi companies, car hire, etc). A 10 per cent tax is now levied by banks on the sale of US dollars against CUCs. This tax is not applied to all the other freely convertible currencies recognized by the Cuban government (euro, Swiss franc, sterling, Canadian dollar).

OPPORTUNITY SCOPE

Breakdown of domestic demand (%GDP + imports)

- Private consumption — 59
- Public consumption — 19
- Investment — 8

Exports: 16% of GDP ⟹ ⟸ Imports: 18% of GDP

2

MAIN DESTINATIONS OF EXPORTS

MAIN ORIGINS OF IMPORTS

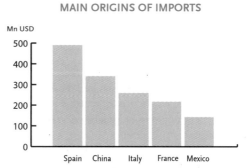

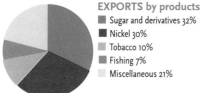

EXPORTS by products
- Sugar and derivatives 32%
- Nickel 30%
- Tobacco 10%
- Fishing 7%
- Miscellaneous 21%

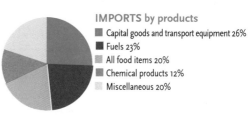

IMPORTS by products
- Capital goods and transport equipment 26%
- Fuels 23%
- All food items 20%
- Chemical products 12%
- Miscellaneous 20%

STANDARD OF LIVING / PURCHASING POWER

Indicators	Cuba	Regional average	DC average
GNP per capita (PPP dollars)	n/a	7925	4601
GNP per capita (USD)	n/a	3467	1840
Human Development Index	0.809	0.782	0.684
Wealthiest 10% share of national income	n/a	44	32
Urban population percentage	76	78	45
Percentage under 15 years old	21	30	30
Number of telephones per 1000 inhabitants	51	172	120
Number of computers per 1000 inhabitants	32	69	37

Dominican Republic

Population (million inhabitants)	8.6
GDP (US$ million)	21,651
GDP per capita (US$)	2,518

Short-term: **C**

Coface analysis

Medium-term:
High risk

STRENGTHS

- The Dominican Republic has become the most popular Caribbean tourist destination with this sector still enjoying substantial development potential.
- The country also boasts significant resources both natural (nickel, gold) and farm (sugar, tobacco).
- It has taken advantage of its proximity to the North American market to develop exports of manufactured products from customs-free areas.
- Remittances from the many expatriates residing in the United States have been a major source of foreign currency.

WEAKNESSES

- The country has remained one of the poorest in the Caribbean with social indicators below the regional average.
- The social climate has been very tense due to the austerity policy coupled with high inflation and frequent power failures.
- The Baninter bank failure in 2003 and a very high degree of dollarization have destabilized the financial system.
- Debt ratios that were moderate before the crisis have increased sharply since then due to the peso's collapse.
- Insufficient currency reserves have been a major source of weakness.

RISK ASSESSMENT

The country has been attempting to come back from the grave banking crisis of 2003 that triggered the peso collapse and a recession. The recession would have been worse, however, without the satisfactory performance of exports and especially of tourism, which allowed growth to resume from the second quarter of 2004. The leeway available to the new president Leonel Fernandez will nonetheless be very limited. Although lacking a parliamentary majority and with the social climate remaining very tense, he must meet commitments made to the IMF. High oil prices have been affecting external accounts, spurring inflation and, in particular, exacerbating the decline of household purchasing power.

The government has no financial room for manoeuvre with debt ratios having deteriorated sharply. The amount of short-term debt in relation to the low level of currency reserves and the extensive dollarization of the banks have made the country vulnerable to sudden capital flight. However, the country has mainly been contending with a liquidity crisis. Rescheduling under Paris Club auspices has eased its external financial situation and restructuring bond debt in agreement with creditors should have a similar effect. If confidence gradually comes back, the country will have assets to exploit, primarily its tourist potential and customs free areas in proximity to the North American market.

MAIN ECONOMIC INDICATORS						
US$ billions	2000	2001	2002	2003	2004(e)	2005(f)
Economic growth (%)	7.3	2.9	4.1	−1.3	1.5	2.5
Inflation (%)	7.7	8.9	5.2	27.5	52.4	11.5
Public sector balance (%GDP)	−1.7	−1.9	−2.3	−2.7	−1.0	n/a
Exports	5.7	5.3	5.2	5.4	5.6	5.6
Imports	9.5	8.8	8.8	7.9	7.9	8.5
Trade balance	−3.7	−3.5	−3.7	−2.4	−2.3	−2.9
Current account balance (%GDP)	−5.2	−3.4	−3.7	5.5	8.3	3.4
Foreign debt (%GDP)	23.3	23.4	29.6	44.0	50.2	49.9
Debt service (%Exports)	5.2	4.9	6.1	7.4	5.5	9.9
Foreign exchange reserves (in months of imports)	0.6	1.2	0.6	0.3	0.9	1.4

e = estimate, f = forecast

2

Ecuador

Population (million inhabitants)	13
GDP (US$ million)	24,311

Coface analysis

Short-term: **C**

Medium-term:
High risk

STRENGTHS

- With Ecuador possessing oil reserves, the new pipeline's construction should permit developing hydrocarbon exports in the short term.
- The country has been trying to diversify exports, notably via sales of shrimp and flowers.
- The dollarization process has contributed to stabilizing the economy and the banking sector's situation.

WEAKNESSES

- External accounts and public finances have remained dependent on oil prices.
- Dollarization has undermined the competitiveness of agriculture and industry.
- Debt ratios have remained high despite the restructuring accomplished.
- Insufficient investment in the oil sector has been preventing the country from benefiting fully from the opening of the second pipeline.
- Opposition between coastal and mountain regions has been undermining the country's cohesiveness with substantial political instability impeding implementation of reforms.

RISK ASSESSMENT

Ecuador has been benefiting from the exceptional oil market conditions, which have spurred a growth recovery, a sharp increase in fiscal revenues and reduction of public sector debt. Continuation of that trend will nonetheless be very dependent on how oil prices evolve with the economy not very diversified (except for the banana and shrimp sectors) due to poor competitiveness.

The very precarious level of currency reserves would afford little room for manoeuvre should export earnings decline. In such case, the country would have difficulty covering its financing needs lacking access to capital markets since the 1999 crisis due to persistence of excessive debt and particularly to a very shaky political situation.

President Lucio Gutierrez must contend with a parliament dominated by traditional conservative parties with the government coalition representing only a small minority. The history of a country having known five presidents since 1996, including two compelled to step down before the end of their term, coupled with great social unrest has tended to deter foreign investors.

MAIN ECONOMIC INDICATORS						
US$ billions	2000	2001	2002	2003	2004[(e)]	2005[(f)]
Economic growth (%)	2.3	5.1	3.4	3.0	6.0	4.2
Inflation (%)	91.0	22.4	9.5	6.1	4.8	4.0
Public sector balance (%GDP)	1.5	−0.5	1.0	1.7	2.2	2.2
Exports	5.1	4.8	5.2	6.1	6.6	7.0
Imports	3.7	5.2	6.2	6.3	6.5	6.8
Trade balance	1.4	−0.4	−1.0	−0.2	0.1	0.2
Current account balance	0.9	−0.5	−1.2	−0.2	0.1	0.2
Current account balance (%GDP)	5.8	−2.6	−4.8	−0.8	0.4	0.5
Foreign debt (%GDP)	85.1	68.5	66.6	63.1	56.3	51.3
Debt service (%Exports)	23.4	20.5	20.5	20.0	24.1	24.3
Foreign exchange reserves (in months of imports)	1.8	1.3	0.9	1.1	1.0	1.0

e = estimate, f = forecast

CONDITIONS OF ACCESS TO THE MARKET

■ Market overview

Ecuador is a founding member of the Andean Community of Nations (ACN) and follows, in principle, WTO rules since becoming a member in 1996. Although trade between Ecuador and its three 'main' ACN partners – Colombia, Bolivia and Venezuela – has been fully exempt from customs duties since 1994, a host of ad hoc tariff and non-tariff barriers hamper intra-ACN trade. With regard to non-ACN tariff barriers, in 2002 Ecuador brought out a rehash of the old customs tariff, maintaining the same rates of duty (0, 3, 5, 15, 20 and 35 per cent), but changing some tariff item numbers to reflect the creation of new tariff subitems. The deadline for the introduction of ACN's new common external tariff, due to come into force in December 2003, has been pushed back to May 2005. As well as the above rates of duty, there is 12 per cent VAT and a 5, 15 or 77.25 per cent special consumer tax (ICE) on a number of so-called 'luxury' products. Moreover, from April blonde cigarettes are liable to 98 per cent ICE (official journal 319 of 22 April 2004). The 2–10 per cent surtax known as the 'safeguard

clause' has been abolished. Despite the introduction of a standard import declaration form (DUI: *Documento unico de importación*), replaced by the DAU (standard customs declaration), import procedures remain lengthy and constitute a major stumbling block to the free flow of trade. Ecuador runs a highly complex system of controls, prohibitions, authorizations and permits. Moreover, frequent changes in legislation create a high degree of legal uncertainty.

■ Attitude towards foreign investors

In theory, non-discrimination between domestic and foreign investors is the norm, except in so-called strategic sectors (ban on property ownership along the borders). In practice, however, this liberalism is negated by the extreme complexity of the legal and judicial system, which breeds uncertainty. The high concentration of political, economic and financial power can also distort application of the law.

■ Foreign exchange regulations

The widespread use of the dollar provides a certain degree of monetary stability.

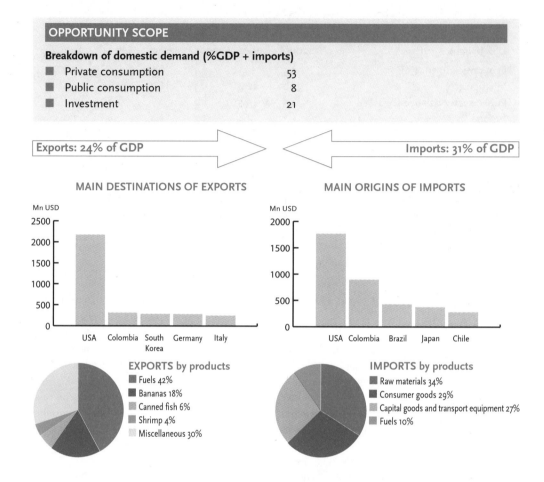

OPPORTUNITY SCOPE

Breakdown of domestic demand (%GDP + imports)
- ■ Private consumption — 53
- ■ Public consumption — 8
- ■ Investment — 21

Exports: 24% of GDP   Imports: 31% of GDP

MAIN DESTINATIONS OF EXPORTS

Mn USD

USA · Colombia · South Korea · Germany · Italy

EXPORTS by products
- ■ Fuels 42%
- ■ Bananas 18%
- ■ Canned fish 6%
- ■ Shrimp 4%
- ■ Miscellaneous 30%

MAIN ORIGINS OF IMPORTS

Mn USD

USA · Colombia · Brazil · Japan · Chile

IMPORTS by products
- ■ Raw materials 34%
- ■ Consumer goods 29%
- ■ Capital goods and transport equipment 27%
- ■ Fuels 10%

STANDARD OF LIVING / PURCHASING POWER

Indicators	Ecuador	Regional average	DC average
GNP per capita (PPP dollars)	3340	7925	4601
GNP per capita (USD)	1490	3467	1840
Human Development Index	0.735	0.782	0.684
Wealthiest 10% share of national income	41.6	44	32
Urban population percentage	64	78	45
Percentage under 15 years old	33	30	30
Number of telephones per 1000 inhabitants	110	172	120
Number of computers per 1000 inhabitants	31	69	37

El Salvador

Population (million inhabitants)	6.4
GDP (US$ million)	14,284
GDP per capita (US$)	2,232

Short-term: **B**

Medium-term:

Coface analysis **Moderately high risk**

2

RISK ASSESSMENT

Unlike most emerging countries, El Salvador's economy was not very dynamic in 2004, affected by the uncertainties surrounding the first-half electoral period and then by repercussions of high oil prices during the year. Moreover, an inflation rate too high for a dollarized economy has hampered export development by undermining competitiveness, especially for the factories that produce goods for export (*maquilas*) (mainly textile), in relation to neighbouring countries. Only a marked increase in remittances by expatriates (one Salvadoran in three) permitted sustaining demand and partially offsetting the large trade imbalance. Economic activity could strengthen somewhat in 2005 thanks

to prospective integration beside the United States in a free trade area with Central America.

Low investment has limited economic expansion in recent years to levels barely exceeding population growth. Meanwhile, a very narrow tax base has not permitted the country to meet its large social and infrastructure needs. Although the new President, Antonio Saca, (ARENA, the right-wing party in power for 15 years), elected 21 March 2004 is aware of that situation, he must nonetheless contend with a divided parliament. He does, however, benefit from a public sector debt burden that has remained moderate for the region despite a recent increase.

MAIN ECONOMIC INDICATORS

US$ billions	2000	2001	2002	2003	2004[(e)]	2005[(f)]
Economic growth (%)	2.2	1.7	2.1	2.0	2.1	2.7
Inflation (%)	2.3	3.8	1.8	2.1	4.5	4.4
Public sector balance (%GDP)	−3.0	−4.3	−4.6	−3.4	−3.0	n/a
Exports	2.9	2.9	3.0	3.2	3.2	3.5
Imports	4.6	4.8	4.9	5.4	5.9	6.1
Trade balance	−1.7	−1.9	−1.9	−2.3	−2.6	−2.6
Current account balance (%GDP)	−3.3	−1.4	−2.7	−4.9	−5.4	−5.2
Foreign debt (%GDP)	30.4	31.3	41.5	42.9	46.3	48.7
Debt service (%Exports)	9.6	10.3	11.9	11.1	10.8	11.4
Foreign exchange reserves (in months of imports)	4.5	4.1	3.5	3.2	2.5	2.5

e = estimate, f = forecast

171

Guatemala

Population (million inhabitants)	12
GDP (US$ million)	23,277

Short-term: **B**

Medium-term:
High risk

Coface analysis

STRENGTHS

- Prospects of joining the United States in the Central American free trade area will provide the country with major opportunities.
- Tourist potential is substantial.
- Fiscal deficits have been moderate.
- Public sector debt has remained at reasonable levels.
- Guatemala has been benefiting from international financial aid.

WEAKNESSES

- Exports are still too concentrated on a few traditional farm products, mainly coffee and bananas, with volatile prices.
- The tax base has been too narrow to permit the government to meet its financial commitments, notably those made concerning the Indians in the 1996 peace agreements.
- The country has remained very inegalitarian with Indians often marginalized although representing half of the population.

RISK ASSESSMENT

Growth improved slightly in 2004, buoyed mainly by increased transfers from emigrants that benefited the construction and financial services sectors and consumer spending in general. High oil prices have nonetheless affected household purchasing power and stoked inflationary pressures.

President Oscar Berger (conservative), elected 28 December 2003, has restored his predecessors' orthodox economic policy after some pre-electoral slippage. Debt levels have thus remained moderate for the region. Amid substantial demographic growth, however, economic expansion has been grossly insufficient to meet the population's enormous needs. The lack of an absolute parliamentary majority has been seriously impeding implementation of necessary reforms. The country must undertake the transformations needed to free the economy from its excessively dual structure where the textile industry and large export-oriented landowners coexist with subsistence farming. The rural conflict over land ownership could trigger an escalation of violence in a country still scarred by the aftermath of 30 years of civil war.

MAIN ECONOMIC INDICATORS

US$ billions	2000	2001	2002	2003	2004[(e)]	2005[(f)]
Economic growth (%)	3.6	2.2	2.2	2.1	2.6	3.1
Inflation (%)	6.0	8.9	6.3	5.9	7.0	5.0
Public sector balance (%GDP)	–2.2	–2.3	–0.8	–2.9	–2.0	n/a
Exports	3.1	2.9	2.6	2.8	2.9	3.1
Imports	5.2	5.6	6.1	5.7	6.1	6.5
Trade balance	–2.1	–2.7	–3.5	–3.0	–3.1	–3.4
Current account balance	–1.0	–1.2	–1.2	–1.1	–1.4	–1.5
Current account balance (%GDP)	–5.4	–5.9	–5.1	–4.5	–5.3	–5.6
Foreign debt (%GDP)	23.8	21.4	20.7	20.3	22.9	23.1
Debt service (%Exports)	9.4	8.2	8.8	10.0	10.3	10.1
Foreign exchange reserves (in months of imports)	3.4	4.2	3.9	4.5	4.4	4.5

e = estimate, f = forecast

2

CONDITIONS OF ACCESS TO THE MARKET

■ Means of entry

Under the Common External Tariff (CET) of the Central American Common Market (CACM), the rate of duty on commodities and capital goods is 0 per cent, on finished goods 15 per cent, and on semi-finished goods between 5 and 10 per cent. A certain degree of tariff protection remains in place for some agricultural products or locally manufactured goods, along with a system of temporary exceptions introduced under the state of emergency. The average customs tariff is 7.6 per cent, compared with the WTO's consolidated rate of 40 per cent. Import licences are not required. The new health regulations on wine and alcohol labelling are restrictive, but applied in a non-discriminatory manner. The two leading audit companies – SGS and Bureau Veritas – operate on a non-compulsory contractual basis at the request of the importer or exporter. In spite of the shaky banking sector, there are no difficulties with payments. Interest rates are very high. Letters of credit are the most widely used means of payment. Transfers are usually carried out in a timely manner.

■ Attitude towards foreign investors

Foreign investors benefit from non-discriminatory treatment and the most-favoured nation clause and are subject to more or less the same procedures as national investors. But it is felt these formalities are particularly lengthy and bureaucratic in comparison with the other countries of the region. An investment promotion and simplification agency 'Invest in Guatemala' was set up in September 2004 in a bid to lift obstacles to the establishment of foreign businesses.

There are no restrictions on investment, other than in the so-called strategic sectors, such as defence. Post-establishment difficulties derive from the sociocultural and political environment prevalent in Central America, rather than from actual discrimination against foreign investors. Costs arising from physical insecurity are extremely high. On the employment front, at least 90 per cent of a firm's staff must be made up of Guatemalans and wages paid to foreigners may not exceed 15 per cent of the total payroll. In principle, the legal system offers identical safeguards to foreign and national investors, but corruption and opaque administrative procedures often place foreigners at a disadvantage.

■ Foreign exchange regulations

There are no restrictions on capital, dividend and currency transfers, nor any exchange controls. The so-called 'Free Currency Trading' Act has legalized the circulation of the dollar within the economy and allows people to open dollar-denominated accounts and make all types of payment in that currency. There are no restrictions on repatriation by foreign investors exercising their shareholder rights of capital invested or their share of retained earnings.

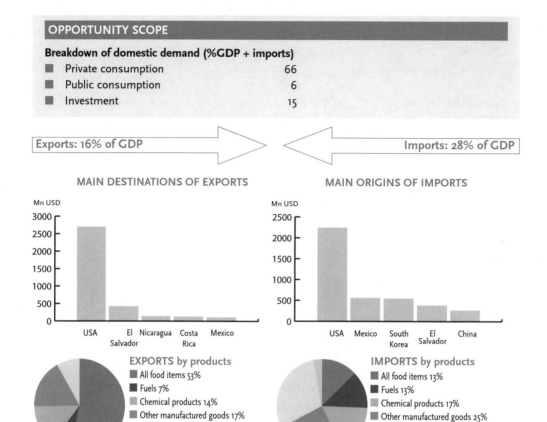

OPPORTUNITY SCOPE

Breakdown of domestic demand (%GDP + imports)
- Private consumption — 66
- Public consumption — 6
- Investment — 15

Exports: 16% of GDP ⟹ ⟸ Imports: 28% of GDP

MAIN DESTINATIONS OF EXPORTS

Mn USD

USA | El Salvador | Nicaragua | Costa Rica | Mexico

MAIN ORIGINS OF IMPORTS

Mn USD

USA | Mexico | South Korea | El Salvador | China

EXPORTS by products
- All food items 53%
- Fuels 7%
- Chemical products 14%
- Other manufactured goods 17%
- Miscellaneous 8%

IMPORTS by products
- All food items 13%
- Fuels 13%
- Chemical products 17%
- Other manufactured goods 25%
- Capital goods and transport equipment 30%
- Miscellaneous 3%

STANDARD OF LIVING / PURCHASING POWER

Indicators	Guatemala	Regional average	DC average
GNP per capita (PPP dollars)	4030	7925	4601
GNP per capita (USD)	1760	3467	1840
Human Development Index	0.649	0.782	0.684
Wealthiest 10% share of national income	48.3	44	32
Urban population percentage	40	78	45
Percentage under 15 years old	43	30	30
Number of telephones per 1000 inhabitants	71	172	120
Number of computers per 1000 inhabitants	14	69	37

Haiti

Population (million inhabitants)　　8.3
GDP (US\$ million)　　3,435
GDP per capita (US\$)　　414

Coface analysis

Short-term: **D**

Medium-term:
Very high risk

2

RISK ASSESSMENT

The situation has remained critical despite the departure into exile at the end of February 2004 of President Aristide, who was succeeded by a transition government that, unlike its predecessors, enjoys international community backing. However, social tensions have not only persisted, but have been exacerbated by the severe floods that devastated the country in 2004, contributing to a worsening of the climate of violence. The slow pace of disarmament implementation has been dimming prospects for easing political tensions. In those conditions, renewed combat between former soldiers insisting on re-establishment of the army disbanded by President Aristide in 1995 and the former regime's armed militias is still possible. Neither UN forces (Minustah) nor the government have the means to restore order.

Haiti's socioeconomic and political situation is thus not yet conducive to implementing stable economic policies capable of restoring foreign investor confidence. Due to the meagre resources of Latin America's poorest country and the very inadequate level of its currency reserves, Haiti has remained totally dependent on international aid and emigrant transfers.

MAIN ECONOMIC INDICATORS						
US\$ millions	2000	2001	2002	2003	2004[(e)]	2005[(f)]
Economic growth (%)	0.9	−1.0	−0.5	0.4	−5.0	3.0
Inflation (%)	15.3	16.8	8.7	32.5	28.3	17.5
Public sector balance (%GDP)*	−2.5	−2.8	−3.2	−3.7	−5.0	−2.1
Exports	331	305	273	330	338	418
Imports	1,087	1,055	983	1,116	1,081	1,170
Trade balance	−756	−750	−709	−785	−743	−752
Current account balance	−259	−224	−145	−141	−70	−79
Current account balance (%GDP)	−7.1	−6.3	−4.2	−3.6	−1.5	−1.4
Foreign debt (%GDP)	33	39	40	32	28	24
Debt service (%Exports)	3.7	3.8	4.3	4.0	4.0	2.9
Foreign exchange reserves (in months of imports)	1.4	1.0	0.5	0.3	0.2	0.3

* excluding donations　　　　　　　　　　　　e = estimate, f = forecast

Honduras

Population (million inhabitants)	6.8
GDP (US$ million)	6,564
GDP per capita (US$)	965

Short-term: **C**

Medium-term:

Coface analysis   **Very high risk**

RISK ASSESSMENT

The growth rate has been accelerating since 2004, driven essentially by export dynamism, mainly coffee and bananas but also *maquiladora* products, primarily textiles. The substantial increase in sales abroad and expatriate remittances, now representing 15 per cent of GDP, has been offsetting the rising cost of oil. High hydrocarbon prices have nonetheless been rekindling recurrent inflationary pressures and reducing purchasing power, which, in conjunction with the tight fiscal policy necessitated by the size of the public debt, has been stirring popular discontent.

Prospective partial cancellation of the foreign debt under the HIPC programme for highly indebted poor countries has improved the outlook for the country, which is one of Central America's poorest. The outlook will nonetheless depend on the capacity of government authorities to meet their commitments notably on public sector reform. The run-up to the elections scheduled for November 2005 could make it more difficult to implement unpopular measures. However, the population has readily accepted the drastic action taken against criminal gangs (the *maras* fomenting terror in the country) despite fears of breaches of civil liberties.

MAIN ECONOMIC INDICATORS						
US$ billions	2000	2001	2002	2003	2004(e)	2005(f)
Economic growth (%)	5.7	2.6	2.7	3.2	3.8	4.0
Inflation (%)	10.1	8.8	8.1	6.8	8.0	6.0
Public balance (%GDP)	−0.8	−3.2	−3.6	−5.1	−3.0	−2.5
Exports	1.4	1.4	1.4	1.4	1.6	1.6
Imports	2.7	2.8	2.8	3.1	3.7	3.8
Trade balance	−1.2	−1.4	−1.5	−1.7	−2.1	−2.2
Current account balance (%GDP)	−9.2	−10.5	−3.1	−3.7	−6.2	−3.6
Foreign debt (%GDP)	92.9	78.1	82.1	80.7	80.1	77.8
Debt service (%Exports)	18.8	19.8	19.0	17.9	11.1	10.8
Foreign exchange reserves (in months of imports)	4.3	4.4	5.1	4.5	4.6	4.7

e = estimate, f = forecast

Jamaica

Population (million inhabitants)	2.6
GDP (US$ million)	7,871
GDP per capita (US$)	3,027

Short-term: **C**

Medium-term:

Coface analysis **High risk**

2

RISK ASSESSMENT

The economy has finally begun showing signs of recovery after 10 years of sluggish growth. Large needs for alumina and bauxite along with a tourism rebound have been fuelling foreign demand. Conversely, very restrictive fiscal and monetary policy, necessitated by the poor public finance situation and high inflation rate, has continued to undermine domestic demand.

Public sector debt, although mostly domestic, ranks among the world's highest, behind that of Lebanon and ahead of Argentina's. It has reached 150 per cent of GDP with interest on the debt alone absorbing 20 per cent. The extreme fiscal and monetary austerity necessitated by that situation has resulted in drastic reductions in capital and education spending, durably undermining the island's development prospects. Moreover, insecurity and a lack of training have been undermining its regional competitiveness. The country has also remained vulnerable to internal and external shocks due mainly to its dependence on tourism, the government's substantial financing needs and the very insufficient level of currency reserves.

MAIN ECONOMIC INDICATORS						
US$ billions	2000	2001	2002	2003	2004$^{(e)}$	2005$^{(f)}$
Economic growth (%)	1.1	1.0	1.9	2.0	2.5	2.5
Inflation (%)	8.2	8.0	6.5	12.9	11.5	7.9
Public balance (%GDP)*	−0.9	−5.6	−7.6	−7.0	−3.5	0.1
Exports	1.6	1.4	1.3	1.4	1.6	1.6
Imports	3.0	3.0	3.3	3.3	3.7	3.8
Trade balance	−1.4	−1.6	−2.0	−1.9	−2.1	−2.2
Current account balance (%GDP)	−4.6	−9.4	−14.8	−11.0	−14.3	−13.9
Foreign debt (%GDP)	59.3	65.5	65.3	67.3	72.3	71.7
Debt service (%Exports)	13.5	14.0	16.7	14.8	17.5	18.6
Foreign exchange reserves (in months of imports)	2.5	4.4	2.7	3.2	2.6	2.8

* March of year t and April of year t+1

e = estimate, f = forecast

Mexico

Population (million inhabitants)	101
GDP (US$ million)	637,203

Coface analysis

Short-term: **A4**

Medium-term:
Quite low risk

STRENGTHS

- Mexico has become a major manufacturing power thanks notably to its inclusion in the North American free trade area.
- Healthier fundamentals and more moderate foreign debt than most regional countries have been reassuring to international investors.
- Bank balance sheets and foreign currency reserves have improved markedly since the 1994–1995 crisis with the country now much less vulnerable to a financial crisis.

WEAKNESSES

- Lacking sufficient investment, Mexico has been suffering from competitiveness problems against rivals like China.
- The banking sector has not been fulfilling its role of financing the economy.
- Public finances have remained dependent on oil revenues.
- Progress has been slow on essential structural reforms.

RISK ASSESSMENT

After three years of stagnation, economic growth has resumed, buoyed not only by US demand for manufactured goods but also by consumption and investment. The peso's decline has permitted stemming the loss of markets notably to Asian competition. Nonetheless, some sectors – particularly textiles, metallurgy and food – are still suffering from competitiveness problems, reflected by company payment behaviour marked by frequent payment incidents. To offset Mexico's much higher labour costs compared with China, company and infrastructure modernization will be essential. Among other obstacles, a low savings rate

and insufficient bank credit for companies have impeded that modernization. To spur investment in the productive sector and infrastructure, structural reforms will be essential. However, although there is a consensus in the political class on the need to maintain the austerity policy, adoption of structure reforms has come up against parliamentary opposition.

Mexico's financial situation has nonetheless been sound. Foreign debt has been moderate. Prudent public financial management has permitted preserving market confidence. Moreover, banks are well capitalized. Finally, the economy is diversified with reduced dependence on oil.

MAIN ECONOMIC INDICATORS

US$ billions	2000	2001	2002	2003	2004[(e)]	2005[(f)]
Economic growth (%)	6.6	−0.1	0.7	1.3	4.0	3.7
Inflation (%)	9.5	6.4	5.0	4.5	4.5	4.7
Public sector balance (%GDP)	−3.7	−3.7	−3.3	−3.1	−3.1	−2.6
Exports	166.5	158.4	160.8	164.9	187.5	197.0
Imports	174.5	168.4	168.7	170.5	193.3	208.1
Trade balance	−8.0	−10.0	−7.9	−5.6	−5.8	−11.1
Current account balance	−18.2	−18.2	−13.8	−8.9	−9.9	−14.5
Current account balance (%GDP)	−3.1	−2.9	−2.1	−1.4	−1.5	−2.2
Foreign debt (%GDP)	27.4	25.6	24.9	26.3	25.6	24.8
Debt service (%Exports)	19.8	16.4	13.3	16.7	18.3	11.7
Foreign exchange reserves (in months of imports)	2.0	2.6	3.0	3.5	3.2	3.1

e = estimate, f = forecast

CONDITIONS OF ACCESS TO THE MARKET

■ Means of entry

Since the entry into force of the North American Free Trade Association (NAFTA) agreement, Mexico offers incentives to foreign companies looking to gain a strategic foothold on the American continent. These include gradual elimination of tariff barriers, industrial property protection and free movement of capital. In all, Mexico has also signed 12 free-trade agreements with 33 countries. The last, signed in September 2004, was with Japan, making Mexico the only country in the world to have, at one and the same time, free trade agreements with the EU, United States and Japan. The free trade agreement with the EU, in force since 1 July 2000, makes it easier for EU countries to win back market share and step up investment, both of which have been declining under the impact of NAFTA and competition from Asian products. All EU manufactured goods now bear 0–5 per cent customs duty, with all tariffs due to be abolished by 2007.

Government-licensed independent inspection companies are responsible for checking product compliance with Mexican Official Standards (NOM) and issuing certificates of conformity. The services of these companies are widely used but fairly expensive. The most common invoicing currency is the US dollar. Payments are made within 30–45 days, which is fairly quick considering the high level of interest rates and shortage of credit. Documentary credit is the safest means of payment for export firms, but expensive for the buyer.

■ Attitude towards foreign investors

The economy today is open to foreign investment, although a number of strategic sectors are closed and remain the preserve of Mexican companies. Foreigners may invest in these sectors only through a 'neutral investment' scheme (without decision-making powers). Foreign investment in open sectors is subject to the approval of the National Commission on Foreign Investment if it falls above a certain threshold (currently 14 million euros).

PAYMENT INCIDENTS INDEX
(12 months moving average - base 100 : World 1995)

Provided this threshold is not crossed, foreigners may acquire 100 per cent of a Mexican firm without the Commission's approval. Since 1999, there is no capital ceiling on foreign investment in commercial and merchant banks.

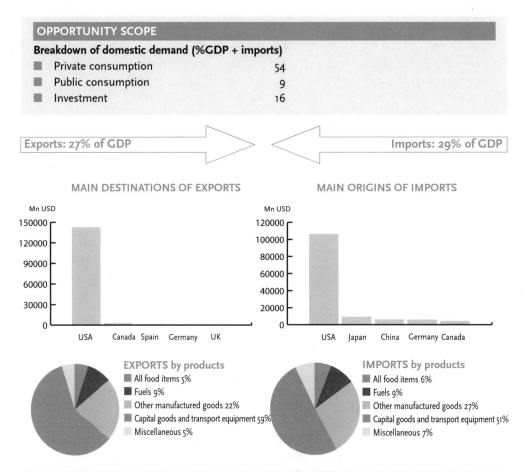

OPPORTUNITY SCOPE

Breakdown of domestic demand (%GDP + imports)
■ Private consumption	54
■ Public consumption	9
■ Investment	16

Exports: 27% of GDP → ← Imports: 29% of GDP

MAIN DESTINATIONS OF EXPORTS

Mn USD

USA · Canada · Spain · Germany · UK

MAIN ORIGINS OF IMPORTS

Mn USD

USA · Japan · China · Germany · Canada

EXPORTS by products
- ■ All food items 5%
- ■ Fuels 9%
- ■ Other manufactured goods 22%
- ■ Capital goods and transport equipment 59%
- ■ Miscellaneous 5%

IMPORTS by products
- ■ All food items 6%
- ■ Fuels 9%
- ■ Other manufactured goods 27%
- ■ Capital goods and transport equipment 51%
- ■ Miscellaneous 7%

STANDARD OF LIVING / PURCHASING POWER

Indicators	Mexico	Regional average	DC average
GNP per capita (PPP dollars)	8800	7925	4601
GNP per capita (USD)	5920	3467	1840
Human Development Index	0.802	0.782	0.684
Wealthiest 10% share of national income	43.1	44	32
Urban population percentage	75	78	45
Percentage under 15 years old	33	30	30
Number of telephones per 1000 inhabitants	147	172	120
Number of computers per 1000 inhabitants	82	69	37

Nicaragua

Population (million inhabitants)	5.3
GDP (US$ million)	4,003
GDP per capita (US$)	755

Short-term: **D**

Medium-term:

Coface analysis **Very high risk**

2

RISK ASSESSMENT

A recovery emerged in 2004. Improvement in coffee prices and increased expatriate transfers have been underpinning demand and reducing external imbalances. High oil prices have nonetheless had a negative impact on inflation and purchasing power. The discontent of a population also facing high unemployment led to the first victory in 14 years by the left-wing Sandinistas in local elections last 7 November.

That victory should make leading the country even more difficult in the run-up to presidential elections in 2006. The fratricidal conflict within the ruling party (Liberal constitutional party, right-

wing) has been dragging on since the imprisonment of former president, Arnaldo Aleman, who still claims many supporters in parliament. The current head of state, Enrique Bolaños, is threatened himself with impeachment. Still-excessive public debt, despite substantial cancellation under the HIPC programme for heavily indebted poor countries, along with extensive dollarization and the financial system's weakness would remain major sources of vulnerability in case the political crisis worsens. Moreover, that very unstable environment has contributed to deterring international investors and lenders.

MAIN ECONOMIC INDICATORS						
US$ billions	2000	2001	2002	2003	2004[(e)]	2005[(f)]
Economic growth (%)	4.2	3.0	1.0	2.3	3.7	3.8
Inflation (%)	7.4	7.4	4.0	5.2	7.6	4.9
Public sector balance (%GDP)	−9.5	−13.4	−10.5	−9.7	−7.0	−5.3
Exports	0.6	0.6	0.6	0.6	0.7	0.7
Imports	1.6	1.6	1.6	1.7	1.9	2.0
Trade balance	−1.0	−1.0	−1.1	−1.1	−1.3	−1.3
Current account balance (%GDP)	−23.5	−22.9	−20.3	−19.6	−20.6	−19.4
Foreign debt (%GDP)	174.5	159.4	151.8	141.8	75.4	74.9
Debt service (%Exports)	28.1	33.1	42.0	25.6	25.2	24.5
Foreign exchange reserves (in months of imports)	2.6	2.0	2.5	2.7	2.8	2.9

e = estimate, f = forecast

Panama

Population (million inhabitants)	2.9
GDP (US$ million)	12,296
GDP per capita (US$)	4,240

Coface analysis

Short-term: **A4**

Medium-term:
Moderately high risk

RISK ASSESSMENT

Since 2003, the Panamanian economy has registered a significant recovery driven mainly by external demand and public consumption linked to infrastructure projects and pre-election spending. However, the resulting budgetary slippage will compel the new president, Martin Torrijos, elected last 2 May, to tighten public sector finances, which should affect growth in 2005.

The head of state will have to tackle reduction of poverty and corruption as he has promised. He must also initiate unavoidable social security and pension reforms. The main focus will nonetheless be the project to enlarge the Panama Canal, the country's main resource far ahead of tourism and banks. Larger ships and increased traffic, notably between Asia and the eastern seaboard of the United States, will necessitate heavy investments likely to total at least US$8 billion. Financing the project will be a major challenge. Despite a relatively sound external financial situation, the project's cost will exceed the government's financing capacity with public sector debt exceeding 60 per cent of GDP.

MAIN ECONOMIC INDICATORS						
US$ billions	2000	2001	2002	2003	2004$^{(e)}$	2005$^{(f)}$
Economic growth (%)	3.3	0.3	0.8	4.1	6.0	3.7
Inflation (%)	1.4	0.3	1.0	1.4	2.1	2.3
Public sector balance (%GDP)	−0.7	−2.4	−1.9	−2.4	−2.0	−2.0
Exports*	1.0	1.1	1.0	1.0	1.1	1.2
Imports*	2.7	2.3	2.4	2.5	2.7	2.7
Trade balance	−1.7	−1.2	−1.4	−1.5	−1.6	−1.5
Current account balance (%GDP)	−6.2	−1.6	−0.8	−3.5	−2.1	−1.3
Foreign debt (%GDP)	59.3	64.2	65.0	65.3	62.2	58.7
Debt service (%Exports)	15.2	21.8	29.2	15.3	15.6	15.3
Foreign exchange reserves (in months of imports)	1.8	2.9	3.3	3.2	3.2	3.2

* excluding Colon customs-free area

e = estimate, f = forecast

Paraguay

Population (million inhabitants)	6
GDP (US$ million)	5,508

Short-term: **C**

Medium-term:
Very high risk

Coface analysis

STRENGTHS

- Endowed with extensive arable land, the country enjoys substantial farming potential.
- Rapid development of soy bean exports to China has been generating substantial currency earnings.
- The country also boasts extensive hydroelectric resources.
- Paraguay is located in the heart of Mercosur.

WEAKNESSES

- The economy has traditionally been very dependent on farm-product price fluctuations and, recently, on Chinese demand.
- Hemmed in between Argentina and Brazil, Paraguay has been vulnerable to economic trends in those two countries.
- With that geographic situation, Paraguay has also been a hub for smuggling and drug trafficking.
- The public sector is bloated and highly susceptible to corruption.
- Extreme inequality in land distribution associated with severe rural poverty has been a source of tension.
- Legal insecurity, widespread corruption and chronic political instability have deterred foreign investors.

RISK ASSESSMENT

After being in recession and on the verge of defaulting on its debt, Paraguay's economic situation has improved markedly since early 2003. Development of raw material exports, mainly soy beans (over half of sales abroad), has permitted the country to begin growing again and increase trade balance surpluses. Inflation has fallen and currency reserves have increased. Moreover, public finances have improved thanks to higher revenues.

The country has nonetheless remained structurally very weak. Severe political instability in the 1990s, serious governance problems, a financial system undermined by a series of crises, very low productivity attributable to deficiencies in the education system and public services explain the past 20 years of sluggish economic growth, which is below demographic growth on average. Although President Nicanor Duarte Frutos, elected in August 2003, has certainly undertaken ambitious reforms (budget, financial sector, public companies) and obtained IMF backing, he has nonetheless lacked a majority in parliament and past attempts at reform have always met with stiff resistance.

MAIN ECONOMIC INDICATORS						
US$ billions	2000	2001	2002	2003	2004[(e)]	2005[(f)]
Economic growth (%)	−0.4	2.7	−2.3	2.6	2.6	2.7
Inflation (%)	8.9	7.3	10.5	14.2	5.4	5.8
Public sector balance (%GDP)	−1.0	−3.3	−3.1	0.1	1.2	n/a
Exports	2.3	1.9	1.9	2.0	2.1	2.2
Imports	2.9	2.5	2.1	2.3	2.4	2.6
Trade balance	−0.5	−0.6	−0.2	−0.3	−0.3	−0.4
Current account balance	−0.2	−0.3	0.1	0.2	0.1	−0.1
Current account balance (%GDP)	−2.1	−3.9	2.4	2.7	1.5	−2.2
Foreign debt (%GDP)	40.1	40.8	50.7	51.8	51.5	54.8
Debt service (%Exports)	11.2	12.6	17.0	14.1	14.0	13.2
Foreign exchange reserves (in months of imports)	3.0	3.3	3.5	4.9	5.1	4.2

e = estimate, f = forecast

CONDITIONS OF ACCESS TO THE MARKET

■ Market overview

In general, Paraguay has a very open trade policy as its nascent industrial sector is unable to meet domestic demand. Membership of Mercosur in 1991 has forced it to raise customs duties on most products in line with the Common External Tariff gradually phased in by the four member countries. The privatization of three utilities (fixed telephones – Antelco, water/waste management – Corposana, and railways – FCP-CAL), launched in October 2000 and due to be completed by 2002, has been indefinitely postponed by Law 1932/02 of 5 June 2002. The new government, in power since 15 August 2003, is proposing either to recapitalize them or to open them partially to private investors. The most widely used invoicing currency is the US dollar. Documentary credit is only used for little-known importers, occasional sales or relatively large amounts.

■ Means of entry

An import ban is in place for certain products. The most restrictive non-tariff barrier is that erected by Law 194 providing for unfair protection of the interests of Paraguayan agents, representatives and importers. Although mandatory inspections of goods exported to Paraguay by an approved inspection firm were abolished in 1999, export documents must first be cleared with the Paraguayan consulate in the country of origin of the goods or the nearest consulate, and the relevant stamp duty paid.

The introduction of a new customs code in January 2005 (in line with a law voted in August 2004) should facilitate trade transactions, increase state revenues and reduce corruption. Copyright infringement and smuggling are rife in Paraguay. Despite repeated assurances from the government, the country's new intellectual property legislation lacks bite.

■ Attitude towards foreign investors

There is no discrimination between national and foreign investors, except in the case of contractual relationships (Law 194). Foreign investment is not subject to approval or compulsory registration, except that covered by Law 60/90 on tax incentives, to be be revised downwards under the new tax adequacy law voted in July 2004, and by the so-called 'Maquilla Act' (No. 1064 of 3 July 1997). Disputes between foreign investors and the government are heard by local courts. A new 'Arbitration and Mediation Act' (No. 1879/02) was passed in April 2002 in line with the model proposed by Unsitral, which handles both domestic and international arbitration. The Act replaces Book V of the Code of Civil Procedure relating to commercial disputes in particular. Launched in

May 2004, the Mercosur arbitration court is based in the Paraguayan capital.

■ **Foreign exchange regulations**

There are no exchange controls. The guarani rose by 13 per cent against the US dollar in 2003, after having fallen by 50 per cent against the same currency in the previous year. In 2004, it continued its upward trend against the dollar.

OPPORTUNITY SCOPE

Breakdown of domestic demand (%GDP + imports)
- ■ Private consumption — 59
- ■ Public consumption — 6
- ■ Investment — 14

2

Exports: 31% of GDP → ← Imports: 43% of GDP

MAIN DESTINATIONS OF EXPORTS

Mn USD

Brazil | Argentina | Chile | Bermuda | Netherlands

MAIN ORIGINS OF IMPORTS

Mn USD

Brazil | USA | Argentina | Uruguay | Hong Kong

EXPORTS by products
- ■ Soy beans 19%
- ■ Meat 2%
- ■ Cotton 2%
- ■ Miscellaneous 77%

IMPORTS by products
- ■ All food items 12%
- ■ Fuels 17%
- ■ Chemical products 17%
- ■ Other manufactured goods 24%
- ■ Capital goods and transport equipment 28%
- ■ Miscellaneous 2%

STANDARD OF LIVING / PURCHASING POWER

Indicators	Paraguay	Regional average	DC average
GNP per capita (PPP dollars)	4590	7925	4601
GNP per capita (USD)	1170	3467	1840
Human Development Index	0.751	0.782	0.684
Wealthiest 10% share of national income	43.6	44	32
Urban population percentage	57	78	45
Percentage under 15 years old	39	30	30
Number of telephones per 1000 inhabitants	47	172	120
Number of computers per 1000 inhabitants	35	69	37

Peru

Population (million inhabitants)	27
GDP (US$ million)	56,517

Short-term: **B**

Medium-term:

Coface analysis **Moderately high risk**

STRENGTHS

- Peru boasts enormous mineral wealth (including gold, copper and zinc) that has permitted it to benefit from currently high raw material prices.
- It has also benefited from particularly abundant fishing resources.
- Debt ratios have been declining in relation to currency earnings thanks to rapid export development.
- Monetary and fiscal policy has been prudent.
- Currency reserves have been increasing steadily, reaching very comfortable levels (nearly ten months of imports).

WEAKNESSES

- The country has remained vulnerable to a downturn of world raw material prices or a sharp worsening of weather conditions (*El Niño*).
- Although declining, foreign debt ratios are still too high.
- Peru has a dual economy with a relatively modern sector in the coastal plains and a subsistence sector inland.
- The president has to govern with a minority party in Congress and cannot rely on the support of a population not benefiting from the economic growth's positive effects.

RISK ASSESSMENT

In 2004, and for the third consecutive year, the mineral sector's rapid development has been strongly driving growth. Export dynamism, notably for gold and copper, has also permitted substantially reducing the current account deficit and debt ratios in relation to currency earnings. Domestic demand has also strengthened. Finally, continued strict fiscal and monetary discipline and IMF backing have bolstered lender confidence. The banking sector's extensive dollarization would, nonetheless, be a major source of vulnerability should a crisis of confidence develop.

The political context has been in sharp contrast with the undeniable improvement in the economic situation. President Toledo has been very unpopular, with the poorest population segment, mainly Indian, not benefiting from the good economic conditions deriving from mineral exports. Although the president should certainly remain in office until the 2006 elections, fears about a possible renewal of populism after that and the severe social unrest have been impeding diversification of investment towards sectors other than capital-intensive mineral extraction industries.

MAIN ECONOMIC INDICATORS

US$ billions	2000	2001	2002	2003	2004[(e)]	2005[(f)]
Economic growth (%)	2.8	0.2	4.9	3.8	5.0	4.3
Inflation (%)	3.7	−0.1	1.5	2.5	3.5	2.8
Public sector balance (%GDP)	−3.3	−2.5	−2.3	−1.8	−1.3	n/a
Exports	7.0	7.0	7.7	9.0	12.0	12.2
Imports	7.4	7.2	7.4	8.3	9.4	10.3
Trade balance	−0.4	−0.2	0.3	0.7	2.6	1.9
Current account balance	−1.6	−1.2	−1.1	−1.1	−0.2	−0.6
Current account balance (%GDP)	−2.9	−2.2	−2.0	−1.7	−0.3	−0.8
Foreign debt (%GDP)	53.3	51.5	50.8	49.5	46.1	42.7
Debt service (%Exports)	37.8	35.0	31.8	27.1	24.4	24.3
Foreign exchange reserves (in months of imports)	8.5	9.1	9.5	8.9	9.4	10.0

e = estimate, f = forecast

2

CONDITIONS OF ACCESS TO THE MARKET

■ **Market overview**

Key sectors include:

● The Camisea gas field, where a US$1.4 billion gas development project commissioned in August 2004 along with a US$3 billion LNG export scheme, should help foster the development of a large petrochemicals industry in the medium term. From 2005, Camisea will account for 1 per cent of GDP.

● Mining, which continues to grow on the back of Antamina, the world's largest copper and zinc mine commissioned in 2001, the recent concession of the Las Bambas copper and gold mine, and firm gold and copper prices.

● Construction, whose recovery is driven by a vast programme of low-cost housing and whose medium-term prospects will be further boosted by the award of the road network concessions.

● Textiles, which benefit from the inclusion of apparel in the generalized system of preferences (ATPDEA) granted by the US to four Andean countries over a four-year period (2002–2006) that could be extended under a forthcoming free trade agreement.

■ **Means of entry**

The market is open and there are no payment difficulties in respect of imports.

The average rate of customs duty is 10.9 per cent. An Andean Community of Nations common external tariff has been agreed for 62 per cent of tariff categories (four rates of duty: 0, 5,10 and 20 per cent), but Peru has asked for it to be replaced by a more open system.

■ **Attitude towards foreign investors**

Peru's legislation offers foreign investors a wide range of incentives and safeguards, including equal rights with domestic investors, the option of signing legal stability agreements, unrestricted transfer of profits, dividends and capital, freedom of enterprise, freedom to import and export, etc. Foreign investment is not subject to prior approval. However, investors seeking the benefit of legal stability agreements must be registered with Proinversion. Peru has signed the founding charter of the Multilateral Investment Guarantees Agency

PAYMENT INCIDENTS INDEX
(12 months moving average - base 100 : World 1995)

(MIGA) as well as the original act of the International Centre for Settlement of Investment Disputes (ICSID). It has also ratified the New York Convention on the Recognition and Enforcement of Arbitral Awards. In the field of taxation, Peru already has three dual taxation agreements (Sweden, Canada, Chile) and since late September 2003 has been engaged in talks to conclude a similar agreement with France.

There is no difficulty in obtaining a work or residence permit in connection with an investment.

■ **Foreign exchange regulations**
Peru has a floating, but managed, exchange rate.

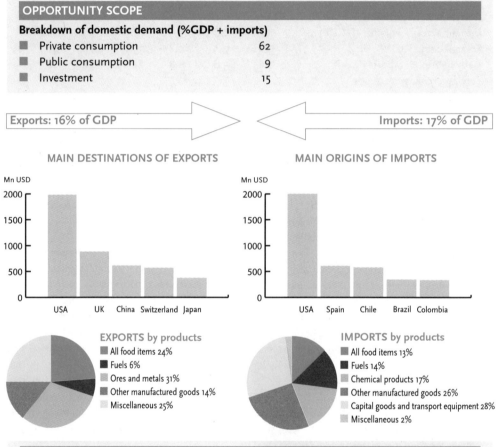

OPPORTUNITY SCOPE

Breakdown of domestic demand (%GDP + imports)
- Private consumption 62
- Public consumption 9
- Investment 15

Exports: 16% of GDP   Imports: 17% of GDP

MAIN DESTINATIONS OF EXPORTS

Mn USD

USA, UK, China, Switzerland, Japan

MAIN ORIGINS OF IMPORTS

Mn USD

USA, Spain, Chile, Brazil, Colombia

EXPORTS by products
- All food items 24%
- Fuels 6%
- Ores and metals 31%
- Other manufactured goods 14%
- Miscellaneous 25%

IMPORTS by products
- All food items 13%
- Fuels 14%
- Chemical products 17%
- Other manufactured goods 26%
- Capital goods and transport equipment 28%
- Miscellaneous 2%

STANDARD OF LIVING / PURCHASING POWER

Indicators	Peru	Regional average	DC average
GNP per capita (PPP dollars)	4880	7925	4601
GNP per capita (USD)	2020	3467	1840
Human Development Index	0.752	0.782	0.684
Wealthiest 10% share of national income	37.2	44	32
Urban population percentage	73	78	45
Percentage under 15 years old	32	30	30
Number of telephones per 1000 inhabitants	66	172	120
Number of computers per 1000 inhabitants	43	69	37

United States

Population (million inhabitants)   294
GDP (US$ million)   10,933,500
GDP per capita (US$)   37,600

2

Coface analysis   Short-term: **A1**

STRENGTHS

- The predominance of the US dollar and economy has facilitated financing public sector and current account deficits.
- High immigration rates, great geographic mobility and flexible labour legislation have been conducive to balancing labour supply and demand.
- The high level of research and development and the cooperation between the private and public sectors have permitted universities and companies to attract talent.
- The reactivity and flexibility of companies and public officials have permitted rapid adjustments to fluctuations in economic conditions.
- Strong growth potential has held foreign investor interest over the long haul.

WEAKNESSES

- The scale of the twin deficits could lead to sudden economic and financial adjustments.
- Restructuring has been inadequate in many industrial sectors, which has affected their competitiveness and prevented them from fully exploiting the dollar's weakness.
- Unequal access to education and the social safety net has exacerbated the increasing dispersion of incomes. Wealthy states can devote more resources to education and prosperous companies can offer supplementary retirement and health insurance benefits.
- The ultimately aging population has been jeopardizing the survival of the federal Medicare and Social Security programmes intended to cover the health and retirement of those aged 65 and over.

RISK ASSESSMENT

Despite a second-quarter slowdown, 2004 was a year of robust growth fuelled by dynamic domestic and foreign demand. Household consumption benefited from employment and income growth, still-low interest rates and increased net worth. Companies benefited from the weak dollar and world recovery to increase exports. In that context, the capital goods investment recovery and restocking process gained momentum.

Economic activity will slow moderately in 2005. Household consumption, representing 70 per cent of GDP, and housing spending should sag somewhat amid rising prices, notably for energy, higher interest rates and the waning effects of tax breaks. Despite a weak dollar, export growth should be less robust due to stabilization of world demand. That situation will also give rise to a slight investment slowdown by companies, also confronted with slower earnings growth.

In that favourable economic environment, company profitability has generally continued to improve as evidenced by the Coface payment incident index trend, which stabilized at a good

MAIN ECONOMIC INDICATORS						
%	2000	2001	2002	2003	2004[(e)]	2005[(f)]
Economic growth	3.6	0.8	1.9	3.0	4.4	3.2
Consumption (var.)	4.6	2.5	3.1	3.3	3.6	3.0
Investment (var.)	8.7	−4.5	−8.9	3.3	10.2	8.0
Inflation	3.4	2.8	1.6	2.3	2.7	2.6
Unemployment rate	4.0	4.8	5.8	6.0	5.5	5.3
Short-term interest rate	6.5	3.7	1.8	1.2	2.2	3.1
Public sector balance (%GDP)	1.6	−0.5	−3.8	−4.6	−3.9	−3.1
Public sector debt (%GDP)	58.7	58.7	60.8	62.5	61.0	60.0
Exports (var.)	8.7	−5.4	−2.3	1.9	8.8	7.8
Imports (var.)	13.1	−2.7	3.4	4.4	10.0	6.8
Current account balance (%GDP)	−4.2	−3.8	−4.5	−4.8	−5.6	−6.0

e = estimate, f = forecast

level. Companies have recovered some control over their prices, particularly timely in a context of rising costs. Having reduced their debt, they should be able to cope with interest increases. The impact of higher raw material prices should not be too negative, except in certain sectors like airlines whose situation has already not been very bright and, to a lessor extent, automobile parts manufacturers due to sagging demand. Although margins will doubtless shrink for road and air freight, chemicals, paper, metallurgy, mechanical engineering and construction material manufacturers, those sectors should nonetheless be able to cope provided demand for their products continues to trend up. For entirely different reasons linked notably to the intensity of domestic or foreign competition, the situation in telecommunications and textiles will remain difficult.

MAIN ECONOMIC SECTORS

■ Distribution

Despite Wal-Mart's invasive presence, the health of players in the sector has improved. Nonetheless, amid increased competition, the concentration process continued with the merger of K-Mart and Sears. Persistence of a high level of household consumption in 2005 should ensure continuation of favourable business conditions.

■ Car industry

In a stable market, and despite costly promotions, US vehicle manufacturers' production and sales declined in 2004 to the benefit of Asian manufacturers. They relied on certain segments (like sport utility vehicles (SUVs)) or secondary activities (financing) to bring their books into balance. Japanese manufacturers have continued to increase their car market share and are now attacking SUV markets, whereas Korean manufacturers have been penetrating the market by cutting prices. That situation should persist in 2005 with little change in sales or production.

■ Steel

Driven by Chinese demand, steel prices continued to rise in 2004. Producers have fully benefited from that trend, thereby substantially offsetting increased raw material prices. Distributors and processors have had greater difficulty passing those increases on in their sales prices, which led to some restructuring. With steady world demand, the 2005 landscape should be similar to that of 2004.

Telecommunications

The telecommunications market expanded slightly in 2004, thus consolidating the recovery that began in 2003. Equipment manufacturers strengthened their financial situation by launching latest generation handsets. The telephony market situation, however, remained uneven with fixed telephony going downhill – its competitive landscape, among other things, being transformed due to regulatory changes (unbundling) – and mobile telephony still dynamic. Although the telecommunications market should continue to expand in 2005, it could be difficult for operators lacking a complete product and service offer (fixed, mobile, internet).

Computer equipment

The computer equipment market was dynamic in 2004, thus bearing out the recovery begun in 2003. Growth should stay firm at least in the first months of 2005. The PC market, particularly for laptops, has benefited from widespread equipment renewal by companies and from aggressive pricing. That dynamism has nonetheless not extended to high-end solutions (servers, graphics). The sector's consolidation, already extensive in 2004, should continue in 2005 in a still very competitive context.

Textiles

Against all expectations, domestic production held its own in 2004. Cost cutting and delocalization programmes stopped the recent haemorrhaging. The scheduled end of protectionist solutions nonetheless augurs for continued downward pressure on retail prices and a continued strong position for distributors. To survive, the sector will have to refocus on its strengths – quality, reactivity to customer requirement – by basing its growth on innovation.

Paper

Paper/cardboard demand recovered moderately in 2004. The dynamic economy and weak dollar contributed to reviving demand. Despite increased raw material prices, producers were able to take advantage of the demand to improve their financial situation. The sector's firming up will depend on the economic trend in 2005.

PAYMENT AND COLLECTION PRACTICES

Payment

Exporters should be wary about the provisions of sales contracts payable on credit and ensure that the payment terms they obtain are appropriate to the context. Cheques and bills of exchange are very basic payment devices that do not allow creditors to bring actions for recovery in respect of exchange law (*droit cambiaire*).

Cheques are widely used but, as they are not required to be covered at their issue, offer relatively limited guarantees. Account holders may stop payment on a cheque by submitting a written request to the bank within 14 days of the cheque's issue. Moreover, in the event of default, payees must still provide proof of claim. Although more difficult to obtain, bank cheques drawn directly on a bank's own account provide greater security as they constitute a direct undertaking to pay from the bank.

Bills of exchange and promissory notes are less commonly used and offer no specific proof of debt.

SWIFT transfers are widespread and the majority of American banks are connected to the system. SWIFT funds transfers are fairly quick and easy to make and are particularly suitable where trust exists between the contracting parties, as the seller is dependent on the buyer acting in good faith and ordering the transfer of funds (open account system).

Debt collection

Owing to the complexity and expensive nature of the US legal system, exporters are advised, wherever possible, to negotiate and settle out of court with clients. Parties can seek mediation through the relatively informal system of Alternative Dispute Resolution (ADR) and in so doing avoid costly and lengthy court cases.

The judicial system comprises two basic types of court: district courts, which fall under the federal court system; and circuit courts or county courts, which fall within the jurisdiction of the state. The vast majority of proceedings are heard by state courts, which apply state and federal law to disputes falling within their jurisdictions (ie legal actions concerning persons domiciled or resident in the state).

Federal courts, on the other hand, rule on disputes involving state governments, cases involving interpretations of the constitution or federal treaties, and claims above US$75,000 between citizens of different US states or between a US citizen and a foreign national or foreign state body or, in some cases, between plaintiffs and defendants from foreign countries.

A key feature of the US judicial system is the pre-trial 'discovery' phase whereby each party may demand evidence and testimonies relating to the dispute from the adversary before the court hears the case. During the trial itself, judges give plaintiffs and their lawyers considerable leeway to produce pertinent documents at any time and conduct the trial in general (prosecution-orientated procedure).

The 'discovery' phase can last several months, even years, entail high costs due to each adversary's insistence on constantly providing pertinent evidence (argued by each party), and involve various means, such as examinations, requests to provide supporting documents or testimony of witnesses, before submitting them for court approval.

Another feature of the US procedural system is that litigants may request a civil or criminal case to be heard by a jury – usually made up of 12 ordinary citizens not familiar with legal aspects, ('*twelve good men and true*'... was the popular expression for the jury) – whose task is to deliver a verdict based overall on the facts of the case.

For especially complex, lengthy or expensive litigation, as in the case of insolvency actions, courts have been known to allow creditors to hold the professionals (eg auditors) counselling the defaulting party liable, where such advisors have demonstrably acted improperly.

PAYMENT INCIDENTS INDEX
(12 months moving average - base 100 : World 1995)

Uruguay

Population (million inhabitants)	3
GDP (US$ million)	12,129

Coface analysis

Short-term: **C**

Medium-term:
High risk

2

STRENGTHS

- Uruguay boasts rich farmland.
- The country benefits from international financial community backing.
- Despite two brief interludes, Uruguay has been one of Latin America's most stable democracies and its social and education indicators have been high.

WEAKNESSES

- The 2002 banking crisis durably compromised Montevideo's role as a financial centre.
- Exports are still not very diversified and have remained centred on farming.
- Debt has become very heavy, leaving the new president, Tabare Vazquez, with little room for manoeuvre to meet the aspirations of his electors.
- High unemployment has prompted some skilled workers to emigrate.

RISK ASSESSMENT

After four recession years and a currency collapse (which caused a 50 per cent drop in GDP per capita in US dollars), the economy has finally been registering a robust recovery. Exports have been growing strongly thanks to increases in prices and world demand for products like beef, soy beans, wool, rice and leather. Domestic demand has also improved, buoyed by both consumption and investment.

The country has nonetheless remained very shaky financially and a downturn could develop if raw material prices decline or financial conditions become less favourable for emerging countries. Since the 2002 crisis, Uruguay's debt ratios have been among the highest for emerging countries.

Nonetheless, successful restructuring of bond debt with the support of international financial institutions and in agreement with creditors has permitted capital to begin flowing back into the country. The new left-wing president elected last November, Tabare Vazquez, should pursue the same pragmatic policy of cooperation with multilateral financial institutions much like President Lula in Brazil.

MAIN ECONOMIC INDICATORS						
US$ billions	2000	2001	2002	2003	2004[e]	2005[f]
Economic growth (%)	−1.4	−3.4	−11.0	2.5	8.0	3.5
Inflation (%)	5.1	3.6	25.9	10.2	9.2	6.0
Public sector balance (%GDP)	−4.1	−4.3	−4.1	−3.2	−2.9	−2.9
Exports	2.4	2.1	1.9	2.3	2.9	3.1
Imports	3.3	2.9	1.9	2.1	2.8	3.2
Trade balance	−0.9	−0.8	0.0	0.2	0.1	−0.1
Current account balance	−0.6	−0.5	0.3	0.1	0.0	−0.2
Current account balance (%GDP)	−2.8	−2.6	2.6	0.7	−0.4	−1.4
Foreign debt (%GDP)	72.7	83.5	104.8	127.1	121.2	114.0
Debt service (%Exports)	26.0	44.1	48.7	34.2	28.0	53.1
Foreign exchange reserves (in months of imports)	5.9	8.1	3.2	7.8	6.5	6.3

e = estimate, f = forecast

CONDITIONS OF ACCESS TO THE MARKET

■ Market overview

Following the grave financial crisis of 2002, the government has restored the country's finances and undertaken courageous reforms. The economy rallied in mid-2003 and industrial production rose across all sectors. Private sector investment has picked up and infrastructure projects are beginning to resurface. Growth sectors include agri-foods, services (in particular support) and new technologies such as software.

■ Means of entry

The Uruguayan market is open, although complex customs clearance procedures and high duties stem the flow of imported luxury products. Goods can be freely imported into the country, with the exception of military equipment, second-hand vehicles and spare parts, meat, livestock, etc. A number of non-tariff barriers – such as strict health inspections of all foodstuffs – persist but should gradually be lifted within the framework of Mercosur, whose customs union currently applies to 85 per cent of tariff categories (excluding automobiles, spare parts and sugar). Customs duties and levies are calculated on the CIF value and vary between 0 per cent and 23 per cent. There is also a raft of levies, including a port tax, a fee payable to the Bank of the Republic of Uruguay, VAT and an ad hoc levy on non-essential goods (IMESI). It is advisable to use the documentary credit for payments.

■ Attitude towards foreign investors

Foreign investment is unrestricted and not subject to a declaration. All sectors are open to foreign investment, except for oil refining, fixed telephony and electricity generation. The Foreign Investment Act 1998 offers important financial incentives, including exemption from tax and customs duties. Free zones open to Mercosur members are starting to develop their activities.

■ Foreign exchange regulations

There are no restrictions on currency inflows or outflows. The US dollar is the de facto benchmark currency, with 85 per cent of loans and deposits denominated in dollars. The peso has been floating freely since July 2002. There are no exchange controls for import payments, but all foreign exchange transactions above US$10,000 must be declared. No authorization is required for capital and profit transfers.

OPPORTUNITY SCOPE

Breakdown of domestic demand (%GDP + imports)
- ■ Private consumption — 61
- ■ Public consumption — 11
- ■ Investment — 10

Exports: 22% of GDP — Imports: 20% of GDP

2

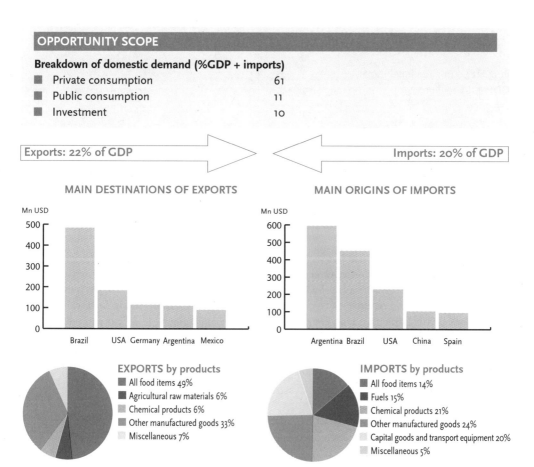

MAIN DESTINATIONS OF EXPORTS

Mn USD

Brazil   USA   Germany   Argentina   Mexico

MAIN ORIGINS OF IMPORTS

Mn USD

Argentina   Brazil   USA   China   Spain

EXPORTS by products
- ■ All food items 49%
- ■ Agricultural raw materials 6%
- ■ Chemical products 6%
- ■ Other manufactured goods 33%
- ■ Miscellaneous 7%

IMPORTS by products
- ■ All food items 14%
- ■ Fuels 15%
- ■ Chemical products 21%
- ■ Other manufactured goods 24%
- ■ Capital goods and transport equipment 20%
- ■ Miscellaneous 5%

STANDARD OF LIVING / PURCHASING POWER

Indicators	Uruguay	Regional average	DC average
GNP per capita (PPP dollars)	7710	7925	4601
GNP per capita (USD)	4340	3467	1840
Human Development Index	0.833	0.782	0.684
Wealthiest 10% share of national income	33.5	44	32
Urban population percentage	92	78	45
Percentage under 15 years old	25	30	30
Number of telephones per 1000 inhabitants	280	172	120
Number of computers per 1000 inhabitants	110	69	37

Venezuela

Population (million inhabitants)	25
GDP (US$ million)	94,340

Coface analysis

Short-term: **C**

Medium-term:
High risk

STRENGTHS

- Venezuela boasts extensive oil, gas and mineral resources with North America constituting the main market for its oil exports.
- The foreign debt burden has been moderate.

WEAKNESSES

- The economy has been overly dependent on oil, which represents over 70 per cent of goods and services exports and half of fiscal revenues.
- The rapid growth of deficits and public sector debt in a context of high oil prices has been a source of concern.
- Institution of exchange controls limiting access to foreign currency has severely hampered private companies.
- Political tensions have had a negative effect on investment and confidence in business circles.

RISK ASSESSMENT

The economic situation has improved. Although the 2002–2003 political crisis doubtless undermined the economy, Venezuela has resumed economic growth since 2004 thanks notably to increased oil prices and a production upturn for that raw material. Meanwhile, although hampering some private companies, exchange controls have permitted stemming capital outflows and replenishing currency reserves. Moreover, the oil wealth and relatively modest foreign debt level have remained positive factors that bolster the country's financial situation.

There are nonetheless still some problems. The cumbersome regulations and exchange controls weighing on the business environment are hardly favourable to the non-oil sector and can cause late payments.

The political situation is still clouding the outlook. Although President Chavez's August referendum victory and dissension within the opposition have certainly bolstered the incumbent government's legitimacy, the after-effects of the 2002–2003 social and political conflict should be long in dissipating considering the extent of the gap between the two parties. The main risk will be continuation of extravagant public financial policy, which could prove disastrous should oil prices drop suddenly.

MAIN ECONOMIC INDICATORS

US$ billions	2000	2001	2002	2003	2004[(e)]	2005[(f)]
Economic growth (%)	3.2	2.8	–8.9	–9.2	17.5	5.5
Inflation (%)	16.2	12.4	22.5	31.1	23.7	31.3
Public sector balance (%GDP)	–2.5	–6.3	–6.0	–7.3	–5.8	–6.6
Exports	33.2	26.3	26.7	25.8	38.7	43.7
Imports	16.6	18.7	13.6	10.7	17.3	20.8
Trade balance	16.6	7.6	13.0	15.0	21.4	22.8
Current account balance	12.1	2.1	7.4	9.6	14.8	15.2
Current account balance (%GDP)	9.9	1.6	7.9	11.3	14.7	14.3
Foreign debt (%GDP)	28.9	27.1	36.2	41.4	34.7	34.0
Debt service (%Exports)	15.2	17.1	16.3	14.3	13.5	13.9
Foreign exchange reserves (in months of imports)	6.1	4.0	4.5	9.9	10.5	10.6

e = estimate, f = forecast

2

CONDITIONS OF ACCESS TO THE MARKET

■ Market overview

Exchange and price controls have been in force since 5 February 2003, but their application has improved to such an extent that they no longer obstruct the normal flow of imports or economic activity. On the other hand, maximum retail prices for foodstuffs, consumer goods, cement and waste processing remain more or less at 2002 levels, even though inflation between end-2002 and end-2004 approached 50 per cent. Intellectual property protection remains patchy, especially for textiles and pharmaceuticals.

■ Means of entry

Apart from exchange controls, a number of tariff and non-tariff measures remain in place: multiple licensing procedures and discretionary licence awards (in particular for cheese and milk powder), reduction in the number of licences awarded, stringent health restrictions on apples and potatoes, compulsory product labelling with mention of origin, discrimination against imported products and special treatment under foreign exchange rules for South American products traded within the framework of the Latin American Integration Association (LAIA). Such an environment is conducive to corruption. In the field of government procurement, preferential measures have been adopted in favour of local companies that show a domestic value added rate of over 20 per cent. This device is tantamount to knocking 20 per cent off the value a local bid before comparing with foreign bids.

■ Attitude towards foreign investors

The 2000 constitution gives foreign and domestic investors equal rights and duties. The only sectors to have seen major investment in the past three years are oil and gas, alumina, banking and telecoms. But for a few notable exceptions, the poor law and order situation, the hesitations over utilities' privatization and longstanding political uncertainty combine to deter investors.

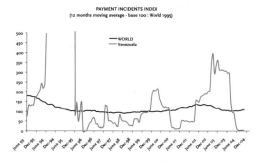

PAYMENT INCIDENTS INDEX
(12 months moving average - base 100 : World 1995)

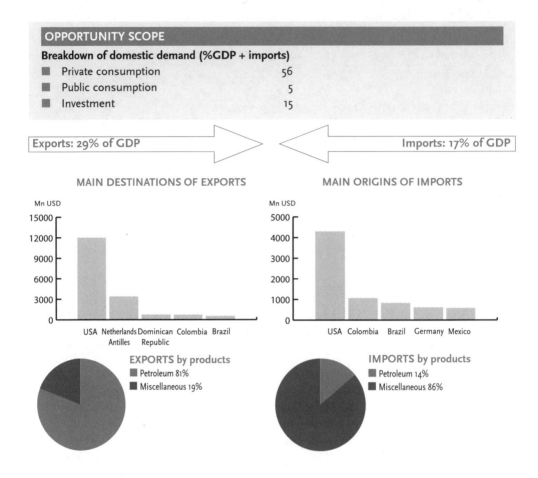

OPPORTUNITY SCOPE

Breakdown of domestic demand (%GDP + imports)

- Private consumption 56
- Public consumption 5
- Investment 15

Exports: 29% of GDP → ← Imports: 17% of GDP

MAIN DESTINATIONS OF EXPORTS

Mn USD

USA, Netherlands Antilles, Dominican Republic, Colombia, Brazil

EXPORTS by products
- Petroleum 81%
- Miscellaneous 19%

MAIN ORIGINS OF IMPORTS

Mn USD

USA, Colombia, Brazil, Germany, Mexico

IMPORTS by products
- Petroleum 14%
- Miscellaneous 86%

STANDARD OF LIVING / PURCHASING POWER

Indicators	Venezuela	Regional average	DC average
GNP per capita (PPP dollars)	5220	7925	4601
GNP per capita (USD)	4080	3467	1840
Human Development Index	0.778	0.782	0.684
Wealthiest 10% share of national income	36.3	44	32
Urban population percentage	87	78	45
Percentage under 15 years old	33	30	30
Number of telephones per 1000 inhabitants	113	172	120
Number of computers per 1000 inhabitants	61	69	37

Asia

3

Uninterrupted Growth for China

Experts from Oxford Analytica, Oxford

The economy appears to have survived the worst effects of the over-investment bubble of 2003 and early 2004 and, barring external shocks, is headed for a soft landing, with GDP growth of 8.5 per cent in 2005. The major short-term risk is higher inflation, the major long-term risk a period of deflation and lower growth rates as the excess capacity built up over the past two years is wrung out. Beijing's top policy makers concluded their annual economic work conference on 5 December 2004 with an apparent determination to keep the current set of policies in place until the middle of next year.

KEY INSIGHTS

→ Growth should be 8.5 per cent in 2005, following 9.5 per cent in 2004.

→ Macroeconomic controls are likely to remain in place until the middle of 2005.

→ Interest and exchange rate changes do not appear to be the main levers of policy in 2005.

They did so despite a flurry of market rumours about a change in the exchange rate, hikes in interest rates and an end to administrative controls on lending and investment. This suggests that a widening of the trading band around the renminbi, which as recently as November seemed to be likely during the first half of 2005, will now not take place until much later in the year, if then.

MACRO-CONTROLS

Administrative controls on investment and lending, in place since spring 2004, appear to be having an effect. Loan growth has decelerated dramatically, from 20.7 per cent year-on-year in February 2004 to 10.9 per cent in October – well below the government's target for the year of 16 per cent. The decrease has been so sharp that there is some evidence of a selective easing of credit policy in November and December 2004, which could bring the full-year loan growth rate back up somewhat. Such an increase will be a temporary adjustment, not an indication that the macroeconomic control programme is ending. Officials have been unanimous in stating that there is still excessive investment, especially in basic materials and property, and controls will be required for several more months. A lesson seems to have been learned from the mid-1990s when a premature relaxation of macro-controls allowed inflation to peak at over 24 per cent in 1994.

Tightening has begun to have some impact on physical indicators in recent months. Growth in industrial value-added, which peaked at 19.4 per cent year-on-year in March, declined steadily to 14.8 per cent in November. Aggregate investment in fixed assets grew by 27.7 per cent in the first three quarters over the comparable year-earlier period, down from a mid-year figure of 31 per cent. Given the time lag between monetary and physical indicators, it is likely that industrial production and fixed-asset investment will continue to decline over the next several months. Taken together, trends in monetary and physical indicators suggest full-year GDP growth of around 9.5 per cent in 2004. With a continuation of present policies, this suggests 8.5 per cent growth in 2005.

MONETARY POLICY

Interest rate moves are unlikely to be a large part of the policy mix unless consumer-price inflation takes off again. The People's Bank of China (PBoC) raised one-year deposit and lending rates by about 0.25 per cent on 29 October 2004 as a precautionary measure against CPI inflation which was above 5 per cent from June through to September. CPI inflation slowed to 4.3 per cent in October and 2.8 per cent in November, on the back of moderating food price growth. PBoC Governor Zhou Xiaochuan, in a November speech, warned that future interest rate rises could threaten the financial health of businesses. There remains some risk that CPI inflation will rise again in the first half of 2005, lagging this year's rapid rise in raw materials prices (in double digits since April). However, producer-price inflation (for both raw materials and industrial goods) appeared to peak in October and began to descend in November. If this trend continues, CPI inflation is likely to remain under 4 per cent and interest rates are unlikely to rise further.

FISCAL POLICY

Fiscal policy will continue a gradual tightening that began in 2004. After six consecutive years of increased budget deficits, the 2004 deficit was held at the same level as the previous year's, at 320 billion renminbi (US$40 billion). The intent for 2005 seems to be to keep the deficit steady at that level or perhaps reduce it slightly. Moreover, the central government's stimulative infrastructure bond issues, which averaged over 140 billion renminbi per year from 1998 through to 2003, were cut to 110 billion renminbi in 2004 and look likely to fall further in 2005. In an article in the *People's Daily* published at the conclusion of the work conference in early December 2004, Finance Minister Jin Renqing said he would 'appropriately decrease' both the fiscal deficit and the infrastructure bond issues, although both would continue 'at a certain scale'.

The intent of fiscal policy is to reduce the government's explicit domestic debt from the end-year 2003 level of 24 per cent of GDP to 20 per cent by 2008. This is achievable if the deficit is capped in nominal terms, real GDP growth continues at an annual rate of 8 per cent and inflation runs at 3 per cent per annum. Capping or even reducing the deficit is a highly plausible goal – even with large expenditure increases – given the strong growth in government revenue. In the first ten months of 2004, government revenues rose by nearly 25 per cent over the year-earlier period, about double the nominal GDP growth rate.

REFORMS AHEAD

The government's explicit debt is not very high by international standards but Beijing wants to reduce it to make room for massive implicit liabilities, namely bad loans in the banking system, which are 30–45 per cent of GDP. Ultimately, the government will have to pay for some non-recoverable proportion of those loans, and this will increase its debt burden. Not surprisingly, then, the financial sector remains the top reform priority. Strengthening the state banks will minimize the ultimate fiscal hit resulting from bad loans. More importantly, the government recognizes that the long-term cure to China's main economic disease – over-investment fuelled by cheap money – is a better system of capital allocation.

Market rumours suggest that the Industrial and Commercial Bank of China (ICBC), the nation's largest bank with assets of US$640 billion, will soon get a US$45 billion capital injection, equal to the combined amount injected into the Bank of China and China Construction Bank at the beginning of 2004. China's banks are subject to tough new capital rules, in force since March 2004, which require them to meet international capital adequacy standards by the end of 2006. Enforcing these rules will be the major focus of bank regulators over 2005 and 2006.

3

CONCLUSION

Macroeconomic controls are likely to remain in place until the middle of 2005 as Beijing continues its effort to restrain excess investment. Interest rates are unlikely to be raised again unless CPI inflation reignites in the second quarter on the back of higher raw materials prices. Fiscal policy will be moderately tighter in 2005 as the budget deficit is held steady in nominal terms and the issuance of stimulative infrastructure bonds is reduced further. The net result should be a 'soft landing', with official GDP growth of 8.5 per cent.

The Range of Country @ratings in Asia

Sylvia Greisman and Pierre Paganelli
Coface Country Risk and Economic Studies Department, Paris

COUNTRY @RATING SCALE

PAYMENT INCIDENTS INDEX
(12 months moving average - base 100 : World 1995)

The regional rating is the average of the country risk@ratings weighted according to the share of each country in the regional GDP.

Country @ratings measure the average level of short-term non-payment risk associated with companies in individual countries. A rating reflects the influence of a particular country's economic, financial and political outlook on financial commitments of local companies. It is thus complementary to the @rating credit opinion on a company.

Quality of company risk in emerging Asian countries continued to improve in 2004. Coface has thus upgraded Hong Kong to A1, Thailand to A2, India to A3 and Indonesia to B. Only the Philippines' A4 rating has been negatively watchlisted because of deterioration of the country's financial situation. Overall, Asia presents the lowest risk level of all emerging countries. Thus, despite a moderate falloff in growth in 2005, company solvency in most regional countries should remain satisfactory.

In Japan, although companies benefited from cashflow buoyed by a good year in 2004, companies now face the prospect of more sluggish external demand combined with a loss of competitiveness resulting from the yen appreciation against the US dollar. However, that trend has not jeopardized the average A1 rating for companies in Japan.

The economic slowdown in Japan contrasts with the dynamism of emerging Asian countries, which still make up the strongest area of economic growth in the world thanks to the booming Chinese economy. The diversification of the economies and international financial aid should help offset the negative impact of the tragic December 2004 tsunami on the hardest-hit emerging countries in the region. Economic activity should, however, slow somewhat this year due to less buoyant worldwide demand, a slowdown in the electronics sector and a soft landing for the Chinese economy.

Although China's growing involvement in regional trade represents an opportunity, it is also

203

a key challenge. Besides the vulnerability of local economies to fluctuations in Chinese growth, they must foster complementarity to avoid head-to-head competition. In that regard, discontinuation of the Multifibre Arrangement in 2005 and the move upmarket of Chinese products will necessitate real restructuring efforts both in countries most involved in the textile sector and in those at the forefront of new technologies.

However, access of private companies to financing is often limited with banking sectors continuing to suffer from an excessive number of non-performing loans and with significant public debt causing an eviction effect. Monetarily, pressure for revaluation of the Chinese yuan could lead to an overall appreciation of emerging-country currencies in the region, exacerbating the constraints that affect their competitiveness.

COFACE MAP OF COUNTRY @RATINGS

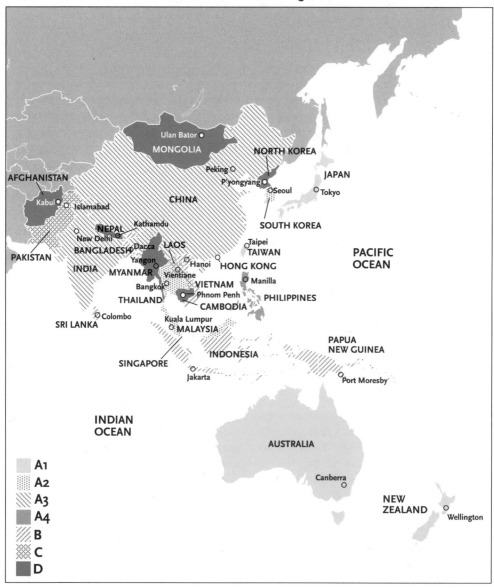

However, those weaknesses should not obscure generally healthy economic fundamentals, sustained dynamism and good company payment behaviour in the region.

■ **Countries rated A1**

Very stable political and economic conditions favourably influence generally good company payment behaviour. Moreover, a satisfactory legal framework ensures protection of creditors and the effectiveness of collection procedures. That generally favourable environment nonetheless does not exclude either disparities in growth or occasional risks of payment default

In Japan (upgraded in 2004), growth should decelerate to a level more consistent with economic fundamentals. Faced with a slowdown in the United States and certain regional economies, and with the yen's re-appreciation, exports will be unable to progress at the same rate. Concomitantly,

COFACE MAP OF MEDIUM- AND LONG-TERM COUNTRY RISK

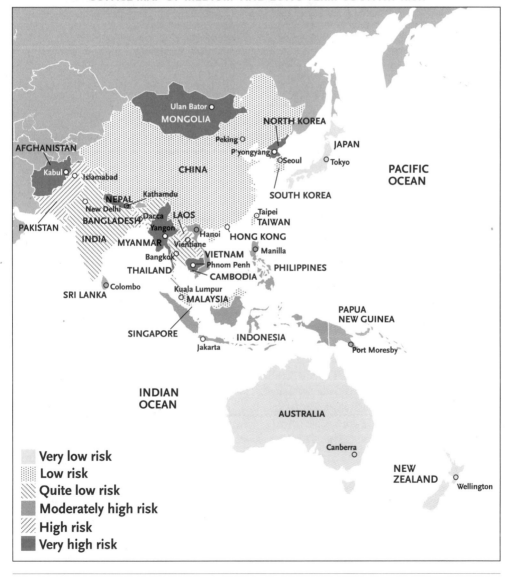

Very low risk
Low risk
Quite low risk
Moderately high risk
High risk
Very high risk

investment and industrial production will be slowing. The economy will thus grow more slowly in 2005, provided that external demand remains buoyant and the yen does not appreciate too much. Restructuring and last year's economic upturn nonetheless allowed many companies to post higher earnings. Industries exporting intermediate products, high-tech products and capital goods benefited most. Conversely, construction, commerce and smaller companies in general continued to have problems.

Taiwan will have to cope with the effects of economic slowdowns in the United States and China as well as a less dynamic electronics cycle. However, the island benefits from good positioning in technology and from the reactivity of its companies. By continuing to delocalize production, especially to China, they have been improving their earnings and solvency. Despite its solid foundations, the economy still suffers from two handicaps: public accounts in chronic deficit and a banking sector weakened by the presence of too many banks. Politically, following the victory of the opposition (which has a more conciliatory stance with respect to China) in the December 2004 general elections, the risk of deadlock with President Chen Shui-bian has re-emerged. However, the status quo with China should be preserved, thanks mainly to increasing economic ties.

Growth should slow in Hong Kong (upgraded in 2004) following last year's sharp recovery, due to slackening world demand and slower Chinese expansion. Companies here generally cope well with economic fluctuations, although some that only trade locally are still penalized by high costs. Moreover, the scope of the free trade agreement with China has been extended. Hong Kong has thus been adapting its positioning and maintaining its advance, thanks notably to the quality of its infrastructure, legal framework and financial system. Finally, after the opposition's modest gains in the September general elections, the local executive, with its ties to China, can look forward to a relatively trouble-free period through to the end of its term in office in 2007.

Growth in Singapore can also be expected to slacken, following a sharp recovery in 2004, due to more sluggish worldwide demand for electronic products (a sector that accounts for almost two-thirds of the country's exports). This slowdown should not, however, affect the satisfactory payment behaviour of most companies. Moreover, the banking system remains one of the most robust in Asia, despite an appreciable proportion of non-performing loans. However, Singapore's re-exporter role has been waning. Also, to enhance the city-state's attractiveness and foster diversification of its economy, authorities have been offering many incentives to companies.

■ Countries rated A2

Default probability is still weak even in the case when one country's political and economic environment or the payment record of countries is not as good as in A1-rated countries.

In South Korea, exports (especially to China) are still the mainstay of the economy with the persistent slackness of private consumption its main shortcoming. The country has robust public finances, large external account surpluses and a comfortable external financial situation. However, there is still progress to be made in the banking sector and in the modernization of certain conglomerates. In this context, companies trading solely in the domestic market have been more vulnerable than exporting companies to non-payment incidents. Moreover, the return of political stability should facilitate resumption of dialogue with North Korea. The government is adopting a more pragmatic approach in the economic domain with a narrow parliamentary majority limiting its room for manoeuvre.

In Malaysia, domestic consumption, a private investment upturn and robust exports are still driving the economy. In the political arena, the new Prime Minister Badawi has consolidated his power more rapidly than expected, which should facilitate implementation of reforms. Fiscal deficit reduction has also been scheduled with large external account surpluses persisting and debt ratios improving. Moreover, the ringgit's continued US dollar peg has protected the country from an exchange crisis.

Although the banking sector's consolidation has made good headway, the high number of non-performing loans has continued to undermine it. Company payment behaviour has nonetheless remained generally satisfactory, despite frequent cases of poor earnings performance and high debt.

In Thailand (upgraded to A2), the performance of both investment and exports will sustain growth in 2005. The Thai economy's size, its diversification and international aid should offset the adverse effects (especially on tourism) of the tragic tsunami in late December 2004. Moreover external accounts are still in surplus with the country continuing to reduce its foreign debt and short-term debt ratios remaining satisfactory. The use of public banks as a vector for economic support policy could, however, cause difficulties. Company solvency is progressing, but an improvement in the legal environment for business is still needed. Finally, despite problems with the Muslim minority in southern Thailand, T. Shiwanatra's government continues to enjoy a good deal of popular support and won the general elections in February 2005.

■ Countries rated A3

Adverse political or economic circumstances may lead to a worsening payment record that is already lower than the previous categories, although the probability of a payment default is still low.

In China, the prospect of a soft landing seems likely. Overheating in some sectors has led the authorities to take corrective steps, but expansion should continue. Although it is easier to obtain financial data on companies, their reliability should not be taken for granted and the legal environment is not very conducive to debt collection. Moreover, the present transitional phase does not encourage the elimination of imbalances, as the support given to state companies in deficit continues to fuel significant flows of non-performing loans through public banks. Restructuring costs also affect public accounts, but external debt ratios are satisfactory and exchange reserves continue to grow. In this framework, the question remains of a move towards increased exchange rate flexibility.

In India (upgraded to A3), buoyant economic activity is being fuelled by the emergence of rapidly expanding sectors such as computers, pharmaceuticals and the car industry. This development has stimulated demand from a generally urban middle class employed in these same sectors and has also prompted improvement in company solvency and payment behaviour. Moreover, the economy's diversification should allow the country to cope with the economic repercussions of the December 2004 tsunami. However, public debt remains too high and structural reforms are insufficient. In politics, the coalition in power should maintain its position, but only at the price of compromise and a relative lack of action. Relations with Pakistan have eased, but talks are expected to produce few meaningful results on sensitive issues such as Kashmir.

■ Countries rated A4

An already patchy payment record could be further worsened by a deteriorating political and economic environment. Nevertheless, the probability of a default is still acceptable.

The Philippines has been negative watchlisted since June 2004 because of deterioration of the financial situation in the country, which remains one of the most vulnerable in Asia. Activity is still fuelled by private demand sustained by expatriate transfers, but structural problems have impeded more balanced growth. The state of public finances has been a source of concern, and public debt has reached excessive levels. Moreover, insufficient local savings and foreign investment mean that the country has remained dependent on financial markets. In addition, the rise in interest rates worldwide could complicate the reimbursement of the country's high external debt. Despite this, the level of non-payment incidents remains reasonable, large local groups and subsidiaries of foreign companies being less vulnerable. The political situation remains problematic, due in particular to the authorities' difficulty in implementing reforms.

3

■ **Countries rated B**

An unsteady political and economic environment is likely to affect further an already poor payment record.

In Indonesia (upgraded to a B rating in 2004), the victory of ex-general Susilo in the September 2004 presidential election has not meant a significant change in economic policy; macroeconomic stability and structural reform programmes have been maintained. Despite the very high human cost, the economic impact of the tragic tsunami in late December 2004 should be relatively limited because of the economy's size, its diversification and the presence of international financial aid. Nonetheless, activity is expected to slow in 2005, due in particular to a falloff in exports. In addition, the country has made use of concessional loans to cover its rising external financing needs, as it fails to attract significant numbers of foreign investors. Despite this, Indonesia should continue to reduce its still high external debt, while the moderate level of its short-term debt and the satisfactory level of its exchange reserves will help limit the risk of a possible liquidity crisis.

Economic expansion is still buoyant in Vietnam, fuelled by brisk domestic demand and dynamic private and export sectors. In addition, reform programmes are set to intensify in view of the country's accession to the WTO in 2005. However, the public industrial and banking sector is the economy's weak link and the high cost of overhauling it has increased a public sector debt burden nonetheless covered by abundant local savings and international financial institutions. Moreover, the modernization of the economy has increased imports and added to the current account deficit without raising financing issues, thanks to the amount of FDI. Nevertheless, the country's low currency reserves may lead to liquidity problems.

Australia

Population (million inhabitants) 19.9
GDP (US$ million) 518,700
GDP per capita (US$) 25,900

Coface analysis Short-term: **A1**

3

RISK ASSESSMENT

Strong growth again marked 2004, buoyed by unremitting internal demand dynamism and upward-trending farm and mineral commodity markets. Continued easing of unemployment and still relatively accommodating monetary policy spurred household spending. Saturated production capacity, notably in the mineral sector, bolstered company investment.

Growth will remain robust in 2005. Farm and mineral commodity exports and tourism revenues will continue to benefit from Chinese and North American demand with sales of industrial products remaining hampered by the Australian dollar's persistent strength. Company investment will

remain dynamic. Domestic demand should decline, however, due to still-high energy prices, increased financial charges resulting from higher interest rates and a waning wealth effect resulting from the weakening of the property market. That slowdown will nonetheless be limited amid rising employment and wages. Furthermore, the excellent health of public finances will permit maintaining expansionary fiscal policy, which will result in increased public spending and further tax cuts.

Bankruptcies declined slightly in 2004. Amid excellent economic conditions, the company financial situation should remain good in all sectors as borne out by the low Coface payment incident index.

MAIN ECONOMIC INDICATORS						
%	2000	2001	2002	2003	2004 (e)	2005 (f)
Economic growth	3.3	2.7	3.6	3.3	3.6	3.4
Consumption (var.)	3.1	2.9	4.0	4.1	5.2	3.5
Investment (var.)	−0.9	0.6	15.2	8.2	7.5	6.6
Inflation	4.5	4.4	3.0	2.8	2.4	2.6
Unemployment rate	6.3	6.8	6.4	6.0	5.7	5.3
Short-term interest rate	6.2	4.9	4.7	4.9	5.2	5.4
Public sector balance (%GDP)	0.6	−0.8	0.3	0.8	0.5	0.5
Public sector debt (%GDP)	25.2	22.1	20.7	19.6	18,6	16.7
Exports (var.)	10.9	1.8	0.3	−2.6	5.8	7.8
Imports (var.)	7.5	−4.2	11.9	11.0	15.0	6.7
Current account balance (%GDP)	−4.0	−2.3	−4.1	−5.9	−5.5	−4.5

e = estimate, f = forecast

PAYMENT AND COLLECTION PRACTICES

As a former colony of the British crown, Australia's legal system and legal precepts are broadly inspired by British 'common law' and the British court system. On 1 January 1901, the six British colonies formed the dominion of Australia as an independent federated union within the Commonwealth.

■ Payment

Bills of exchange and promissory notes are not widely used in Australia and are considered, above all, to authenticate the existence of a claim. Cheques, defined as 'bills of exchange drawn on a bank and payable on presentation', are commonly used for domestic and international transactions.

SWIFT bank transfers are the most commonly used payment method for international transactions. The majority of Australian banks are connected to the SWIFT network, offering a rapid, reliable and cost-effective means of payment. Moreover, the handling of payments via the client bank's internet site is becoming increasingly commonplace.

■ Debt collection

The collection process starts with service of an order to pay via a registered 'seven-day letter', reminding the client of his or her obligation to pay the amount due plus any contractually agreed interest penalties or, lacking such a penalty clause, interest at the legal rate applicable in each state.

In cases of absent payment by the debtor company and if the creditor's claim is due for payment, uncontested and over A$2,000 (or after a ruling has been made), the creditor may issue a summons demanding payment within 21 days. Unless the debtor settles the claim within the required timeframe, the creditor may lodge a petition for the winding-up of the debtor's company, considered insolvent (statutory demand under section 459E of the Corporations Act 2001).

Under ordinary proceedings, once a statement of claim (summons) has been filed and where debtors have no grounds on which to dispute claims, creditors may solicit a fast-track procedure enabling them to obtain an executory order by issuing the debtor with an application for summary judgement. This petition must be accompanied by an affidavit (a sworn statement by the plaintiff attesting to the claim's validity) along with supporting documents authenticating the unpaid claim.

For more complex or disputed claims, creditors must instigate standard civil proceedings, an arduous, often lengthy process lasting up to two years given the fact that court systems vary from one state to the next.

During the preliminary phase, the proceedings are written insofar as the court examines the case documents authenticating the parties' respective claims. During the subsequent 'discovery phase' the parties' lawyers may request their adversaries to submit any proof or witness testimony that is relevant to the matter and duly examine the case documents thus submitted. Before handing down its judgement, the court examines the case and holds an adversarial hearing of the witnesses who may be cross-examined by the parties' lawyers.

Besides local courts, which hear minor claims not exceeding A$50,000 on average, claims for amounts up to A$750,000 in New South Wales, A$250,000 in Queensland and Western Australia, or A$200,000 in Victoria, for example, are heard either by a county court or a district court, depending on the state. Claims exceeding the aforementioned amounts are heard by the supreme court in each state.

As a general rule, appeals lodged against supreme court decisions, where a prior ruling in appeal instance has been handed down by a panel of judges, are heard by the High Court of Australia, in Canberra, which may decide, only with 'leave' of the court itself, to examine cases of important legal subject. The right of final recourse before the Privy Council, in London, was abolished in 1986.

Lastly, although the Australian legal system does not have commercial courts per se, in certain states, such as New South Wales, commercial sections of the district or supreme courts offer fast-track proceedings for commercial disputes.

Since 1 February 1977, federal courts have been created alongside the state courts and established in each state capital. The federal courts have wide powers to hear civil and commercial cases (like company law, winding up proceedings) in addition to matters concerning fiscal, maritime, intellectual property, consumer law, and so on. In certain cases, the jurisdictional boundaries between state and federal courts may be indistinct and this may lead to conflicts depending on the merits of each case.

Arbitration and mediation proceedings may also be used to resolve disputes and obtain out-of-court settlements, often at a lower cost than through the ordinary adversarial procedure.

PAYMENT INCIDENTS INDEX
(12 months moving average - base 100 : World 1995)

3

Bangladesh

Population (million inhabitants)	135.7
GDP (US$ million)	47,563
GDP per capita (US$)	351

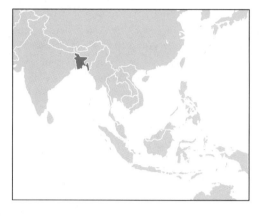

Short-term: **B**

Medium-term:
High risk

Coface analysis

RISK ASSESSMENT

Tensions between the party leading the government coalition, the BNP (Bangladesh Nationalist Party), and the main opposition grouping Awami League – which has refused to recognize the ruling party's legitimacy – have continued to trigger frequent strikes and recurring violent confrontations. Moreover, the tensions could heighten in the run-up to the 2006 legislative elections.

Economically, growth has remained robust with the summer flooding ultimately having only a limited impact on demand, thanks notably to support measures for the farm sector, which has remained crucial for the population as it employs 65 per cent of the work force. Although the external financial situation has been stable, the country's very high poverty rate has made it dependent on bilateral and multilateral aid. Extensive corruption and poor infrastructure, moreover, have tended to impede improvement of economic performance.

The textile sector's size (75 per cent of the country's exports with two-thirds of clothing products destined for the European market) has raised fears of possible harmful consequences from elimination of quotas with the end of the Multifibre Arrangement in 2005. Current account imbalances should worsen slightly amid an expected export decline. The country's specialization – highly focused on low value-added products – could come up against competition from China. Moreover, Bangladesh does not produce the cotton it uses. Further out, however, the country will nonetheless retain some assets, including very low-cost labour.

MAIN ECONOMIC INDICATORS

US$ millions	2000/01	2001/02	2002/03	2003/04	2004/05(e)	2005/06(f)
Economic growth (%)	5.3	4.4	5.3	5.5	5.3	5.2
Inflation (%)	1.6	2.8	4.4	5.9	6.0	5.0
Public sector balance (%GDP)	−5.1	−4.7	−3.4	−3.8	−4.3	−4.2
Exports	6,477	5,929	6,492	7,353	7,566	7,429
Imports	9,524	7,697	8,699	10,071	10,690	11,027
Trade balance	−3,047	−1,768	−2,207	−2,718	−3,124	−3,598
Current account balance (%GDP)	−2.4	0.5	0.6	−0.2	−1.0	−1.4
Foreign debt (%GDP)	33.5	34.4	31.9	29.9	29.1	27.7
Debt service (%Exports)	7.1	6.1	5.5	5.4	5.8	6.5
Foreign exchange reserves (in months of imports)	1.6	2.5	3.5	3.1	3.4	3.3

e = estimate, f = forecast

Cambodia

Population (million inhabitants)	12.5
GDP (US$ million)	4,005
GDP per capita (US$)	320

Short-term: **D**

Medium-term:
Very high risk

Coface analysis

RISK ASSESSMENT

After a year-long political deadlock following the July 2003 elections, Prime Minister Hun Sen will continue as the head of a new government coalition between his party (Cambodian People's Party) and the royalist Funcipec led by Prince Ranariddh, with Prince Sihamoni succeeding his father Sihanouk on the royal throne in October 2004.

The economy has suffered from the predominant agricultural sector's low productivity. Moreover, the end of the textile sector's Multifibre Arrangement will affect the growth of one of the world's poorest countries. From 2005, that sector, which has been the economy's growth engine, will have to contend with increased competition notably from China. Increased competitiveness and diversification will be all the more necessary since

development of the tourism sector will not permit completely cushioning that shock.

In that context, Cambodia will remain very dependent on international aid to finance the chronically large deficits of its public sector finances and external accounts.

Meanwhile, an ASEAN member since 1999, the country joined the WTO in October 2004, which should facilitate its economic transformation. However, there are still major structural obstacles and a deficient business environment and pervasive corruption have been deterring many foreign investors. Moreover, the lagging pace of economic and legal reforms along with continued deforestation and illegal trafficking could affect donor country sentiment.

3

MAIN ECONOMIC INDICATORS						
US$ millions	2000	2001	2002	2003	2004[(e)]	2005[(f)]
Economic growth (%)	7.0	5.7	5.5	5.2	4.3	2.0
Inflation (%)	−0.8	−0.6	3.2	1.3	3.2	2.8
Public sector balance (%)	−4.9	−5.5	−6.7	−7.0	−6.1	−6.0
Exports	1,401	1,571	1,749	2,076	2,230	2,026
Imports	1,939	2,094	2,314	2,613	2,922	2,839
Trade balance	−538	−523	−565	−537	−692	−813
Current account balance (%GDP)	−11.7	−9.4	−9.0	−10.2	−10.8	−11.7
Foreign debt (%GDP)	67	67	68	71	46	49
Debt service (%Exports)	8.7	3.4	3.1	3.2	2.2	2.5
Foreign exchange reserves (in months of imports)	2.9	3.0	3.3	3.3	3.2	3.3

e = estimate, f = forecast

China

Population (million inhabitants)   1,292
GDP (US$ million)   1,299,000

Short-term: **A3**

Medium-term:

Coface analysis   **Low risk**

STRENGTHS

- China has continued the structural reform process associated with its admission to the WTO.
- External account surpluses have persisted thanks to export sector dynamism and competitiveness.
- Foreign debt has been negligible in relation to GDP and currency reserves that are the world's second largest after Japan.
- The savings and investment rates have been high.
- Relatively well trained, the work force is still not very costly.

WEAKNESSES

- Public sector restructuring has only been making slow progress with the banking sector still hampered by the extent of its non-performing loans with state-owned enterprises.
- Great disparities between the wealthy coastal provinces and poor provinces have persisted.
- Establishment of a genuine social safety net has proven necessary amid increasing inequality and unemployment.
- Durable development will depend on sustainable mitigation of environmental problems.
- Relations with Taiwan have remained problematic.

RISK ASSESSMENT

Although the expansion has continued, overheating in some sectors has prompted authorities to take corrective measures. A soft landing for the economy in 2005 should be facilitated by economic regulation combining continued strong private consumption and exports with resumption of more moderate investment rates. Moreover, greater integration of China into the WTO has contributed to the ongoing process of opening the country, with foreign investors remaining attracted by this growth magnet.

The current transition phase has not been conducive to the elimination of imbalances, with the support given to unprofitable state-owned enterprises sustaining the flow of non-performing loans, which have remained at particularly high levels in the portfolios of state banks. Meanwhile, although financial information on companies has become easier to obtain, its reliability is still subject to caution with the legal environment being not very conducive to claim collection.

Financially, although extra-budgetary commitments and restructuring costs have weakened China's public accounts, foreign debt ratios have been satisfactory with foreign exchange reserves continuing to grow. In that framework, the question of evolving towards a more flexible foreign exchange regime has yet to be answered.

Authorities seem to desire more balanced economic development, while remaining focused on continued strong growth and structural reforms.

MAIN ECONOMIC INDICATORS						
US$ billions	2000	2001	2002	2003	2004[(e)]	2005[(f)]
Economic growth (%)	8.0	7.5	8.0	9.3	9.5	8.5
Inflation (%)	0.4	0.7	−0.8	1.2	3.8	2.9
Public sector balance (%GDP)	−2.8	−2.6	−2.9	−2.5	−2.4	−2.7
Exports	249.1	266.1	325.7	438.3	571.0	764.0
Imports	214.7	232.1	281.5	393.6	543.0	729.0
Trade balance	34.5	34.0	44.2	44.7	28.0	35.0
Current account balance	20.5	17.4	35.4	45.9	37.0	34.0
Current account balance (%GDP)	1.9	1.5	2.7	3.3	2.3	1.9
Foreign debt (%GDP)	16.2	14.3	13.4	13.8	12.8	11.7
Debt service (%Exports)	8.2	7.5	7.1	4.5	3.2	2.6
Foreign exchange reserves (in months of imports)	7.3	8.6	9.9	10.4	10.1	9.4

e = estimate, f = forecast

3

CONDITIONS OF ACCESS TO THE MARKET

■ Means of entry

Access to the Chinese market is cluttered with obstacles that block, slow down or mark up imports. As a full-time WTO member for the last three years, China has undertaken to open up its market. The average customs tariff was cut from 12.7 per cent to about 11.5 per cent in 2003 and 10.4 per cent in 2004. Import licences and quotas will be phased out by 2005. Restrictive and often discriminatory health and technical standards, however, continue to be applied to some imported goods (foodstuffs, cosmetics etc), while a safety certification procedure (CCC) restricts the entry of vehicles, electrical appliances and electronic goods. In compliance with its WTO commitments, China has opened up the import–export sector to all Chinese law companies, including foreign-held ones, and is set to lift all remaining restrictions on distribution. In future, foreign companies will at last be able to form purely trading subsidiaries in China.

■ Attitude towards foreign investors

The opening up of the Chinese market to FDI has been skilfully handled by the government, with the pace of change quickening markedly since WTO entry.

There are four categories of FDI – encouraged, tolerated, restricted and prohibited – by sector. The main legislation in this field was amended in March 2002 to take account of China's WTO obligations. While FDI is prohibited in basic postal services, air traffic control, publishing and media, sectors such as telecommunications, construction, town gas and water supply and tourism have been opened up. Every FDI scheme is subject to government approval. The tier of government from which approval is required – municipal, provincial or central – is determined by the size of an investment. There is a trend towards granting more powers to local authorities, which are more flexible in the enforcement of national legislation, with the centre retaining the right to vet locally approved projects. FDI projects are generally carried out via a foreign investment company (FIC), a somewhat unsophisticated entity eligible for tax incentives. There has been a flurry of acquisitions (asset purchases, buy-ins) of Chinese enterprises, especially state-owned ones. Because of the principle of public ownership of land, which can only be acquired leasehold (50 years for an industrial plant), investors are advised to check the status of land offered to them by the local authority. In principle, foreign investment companies are required to hire local labour, but may employ foreigners on an exceptional basis. The statutory working week is 40 hours and the duration of paid leave varies from 5 to 15 business days per year. China does not yet have a unified social welfare system.

■ **Foreign exchange regulations**

The yuan is freely convertible only for ordinary business transactions. Although it remains pegged to the US dollar (around 8.28 yuan to the dollar) for the time being, a revaluation in the future cannot be totally ruled out.

OPPORTUNITY SCOPE

Breakdown of domestic demand (%GDP + imports)

Private consumption	34
Public consumption	10
Investment	32

Exports: 29% of GDP

Imports: 26% of GDP

MAIN DESTINATIONS OF EXPORTS

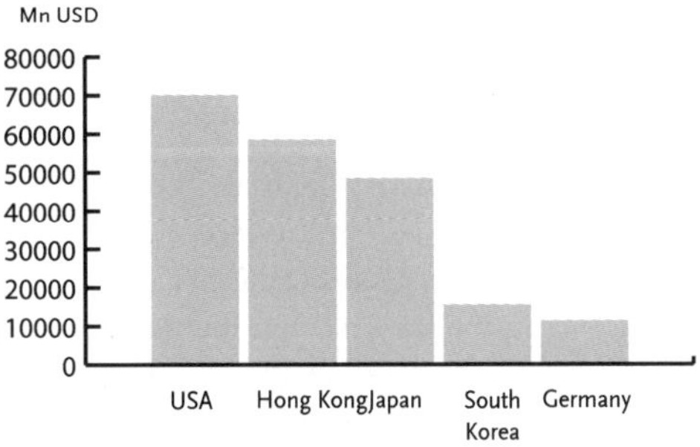

Mn USD
80000
70000
60000
50000
40000
30000
20000
10000
0
USA
Hong Kong
Japan
South Korea
Germany

MAIN ORIGINS OF IMPORTS

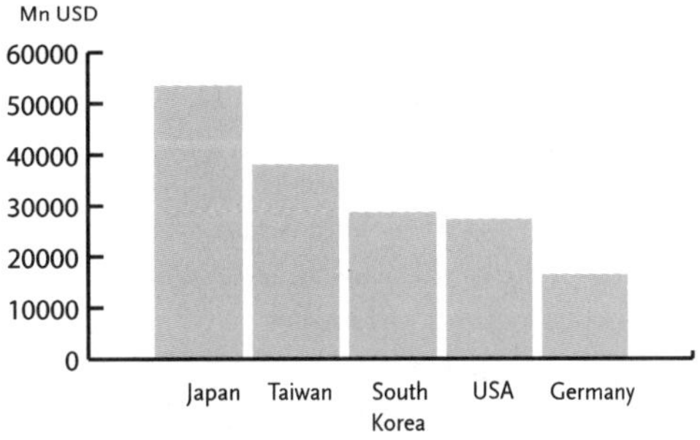

Mn USD
60000
50000
40000
30000
20000
10000
0
Japan
Taiwan
South Korea
USA
Germany

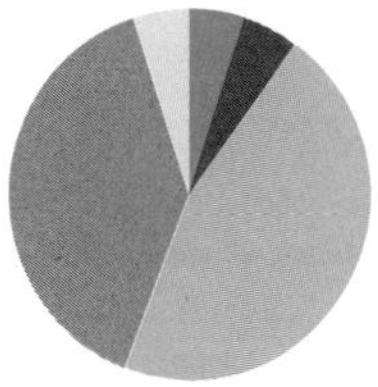

EXPORTS by products

- All food items 5%
- Chemical products 5%
- Other manufactured goods 46%
- Capital goods and transport equipment 39%
- Miscellaneous 5%

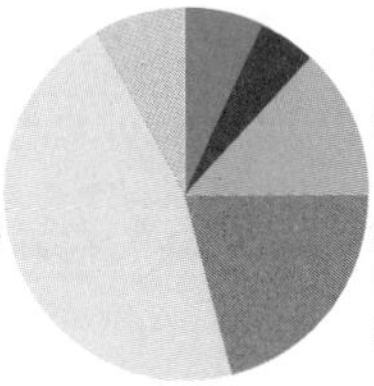

IMPORTS by products

- Fuels 7%
- Ores and metals 5%
- Chemical products 13%
- Other manufactured goods 21%
- Capital goods and transport equipment 46%
- Miscellaneous 8%

STANDARD OF LIVING / PURCHASING POWER

Indicators	China	Regional average	DC average
GNP per capita (PPP dollars)	4520	3923	4601
GNP per capita (USD)	960	996	1840
Human Development Index	0.745	0.678	0.684
Wealthiest 10% share of national income	33.1	30	32
Urban population percentage	38	36	45
Percentage under 15 years old	24	29	30
Number of telephones per 1000 inhabitants	167	106	120
Number of computers per 1000 inhabitants	28	29	37

Hong Kong

Population (million inhabitants)	6.8
GDP (US$ million)	161,531

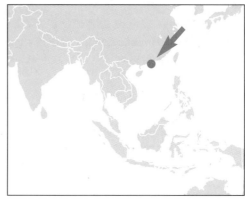

Coface analysis

Short-term: **A1**

Medium-term:
Low risk

STRENGTHS

- Hong Kong has remained a privileged intermediary between continental China and the rest of the world thanks to its expertise and advance in logistics and finance.
- The Special Administrative Region has been counting on greater integration with China to permit developing its complementarity, notably via the CEPA (Closer Economic Partnership Agreement) bilateral free trade agreement that went into effect in 2004.
- Asia's second financial centre and stock market behind Japan, Hong Kong has benefited from a good legal environment and very sound banking system.
- The territory has continued to diversify, focusing on development of tourism and high technology.
- Preservation of Hong Kong's economic specificity and of the 'one country, two systems' principle will be in the interests of central Chinese authorities.

WEAKNESSES

- Hong Kong will have to improve its positioning and competitiveness in the face of increased competition from continental China.
- With its very open economy, the territory has also remained particularly dependent on international economic conditions.
- Hong Kong's alignment with US monetary policy (resulting from the local currency's US dollar peg) could constitute a handicap.
- The outlook for Hong Kong's political autonomy in relation to China has raised some questions.

RISK ASSESSMENT

After a marked recovery in 2004, attributable notably to a domestic demand upturn, Hong Kong's economy – traditionally focused on exports to industrialized countries – should register a growth slowdown due to sagging world demand and weaker expansion in China. Companies have generally coped effectively with economic fluctuations, as evidenced by the Coface payment

incident index trend, even if some companies that operate exclusively in the domestic market have been hampered by high costs.

The scope of the CEPA bilateral free trade agreement in effect with China since early 2004 has been broadened. Hong Kong has thus been adjusting its positioning to allow it to take fuller advantage of the continental economy's ascendancy. Meanwhile, the territory's substantial fiscal reserves

MAIN ECONOMIC INDICATORS

US$ billions	2000	2001	2002	2003	2004[(e)]	2005[(f)]
Economic growth (%)	10.2	0.5	2.3	3.3	8.2	4.6
Inflation (%)	−3.7	−1.6	−3.0	−2.6	−0.4	0.4
Public sector balance (%GDP)	−0.6	−5.0	−4.9	−4.1	−3.2	−2.0
Exports	202.7	190.9	200.3	224.7	269.1	316.5
Imports	210.9	199.3	205.4	230.4	277.6	326.5
Trade balance	−8.2	−8.3	−5.1	−5.7	−8.5	−10.0
Current account balance	8.6	12.1	13.9	15.8	14.1	13.0
Current account balance (%GDP)	5.2	7.4	8.7	10.1	8.8	8.1
Foreign debt (%GDP)	25.7	35.4	35.9	36.9	42.4	44.9
Debt service (%Exports)	1.6	2.4	3.0	3.1	2.7	2.3
Foreign exchange reserves (in months of imports)	4.5	5.0	5.0	4.8	4.2	3.8

e = estimate, f = forecast

3

have permitted it to cushion the impact of the chronic public sector financial deficit linked to its narrow tax base. That major hub has also bolstered its advance based notably on the quality of its infrastructure, legal environment and financial system.

Politically, after modest gains by the pro-democracy opposition in the September 2004 legislative elections, the local executive, linked to China, seems to be assured that the end of his term in office (through 2007) will be free of major problems.

CONDITIONS OF ACCESS TO THE MARKET

■ Means of entry

Hong Kong's reputation is built on the effectiveness and transparency of its free trade legislation and regulations. It is unquestionably the most open market in Asia and one of the most open in the world, even in the field of government procurement. Hong Kong's return to China on 1 July 1997 and its new status as a Special Administrative Region, which has allowed the former colony to keep its economic and legal system, has not affected its openness to international trade. Hong Kong has also remained a free port. There are no customs duties; indirect taxes are levied on only a small number of products such as cigarettes, wines and spirits, fuel and cars. Non-tariff barriers are scarce. A few foodstuffs require a health certificate. For most imports, the only requirement is an import declaration. In some cases, it is possible to make a monthly declaration, rather than one with each shipment. Hong Kong's standards are in line with,

or similar to, international standards. It is the second largest financial centre after Tokyo and boasts a highly internationalized banking sector. Payments are usually made by ordinary letter of credit, but it is advisable to insist on payment by irrevocable letter of credit when dealing with small and medium-sized businesses.

■ Attitude towards foreign investors

The territory's free trade principles, inherited from the British, are upheld by the government of the Administrative Region without any meddling by China in the territory's legal, financial and economic affairs. In keeping with its free market traditions, Hong Kong does not place any restrictions on the activities of foreign investors. There are no prior notification or approval formalities, but by the same token there are no government incentives or subsidies for foreign investors. On the ground, local monopolies have succeeded in driving out foreign competitors. In the absence of competition law, the authorities only intervene when distortions damage consumer interests.

The legal system is simple and company incorporation formalities rapid. Tax laws too are simple and tax rates fairly low. The marginal rate of income tax is 16 per cent (since 1 April 2004) and corporation tax is 17.5 per cent (since 1 April 2003). On the other hand, the rules for the award of permanent work permits have been considerably tightened. The substantial fall in office property prices and the modest decline in nominal wages has in the last few months given way to a sharp upturn in the property market and wage stabilization marked by small wage increases. Hong Kong continues to impose high start-up costs on potential investors.

■ Foreign exchange regulations

There are no exchange controls. The Hong Kong dollar is pegged to the US dollar at the rate of 7.8 Hong Kong dollars to the US dollar. This rate is guaranteed by a currency board system, which automatically links Hong Kong's foreign currency reserves to the monetary base.

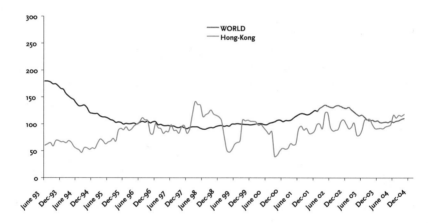

PAYMENT INCIDENTS INDEX
(12 months moving average - base 100 : World 1995)

OPPORTUNITY SCOPE

Breakdown of domestic demand (%GDP + imports)
- Private consumption   24
- Public consumption   4
- Investment   10

Exports: 151% of GDP   Imports: 142% of GDP

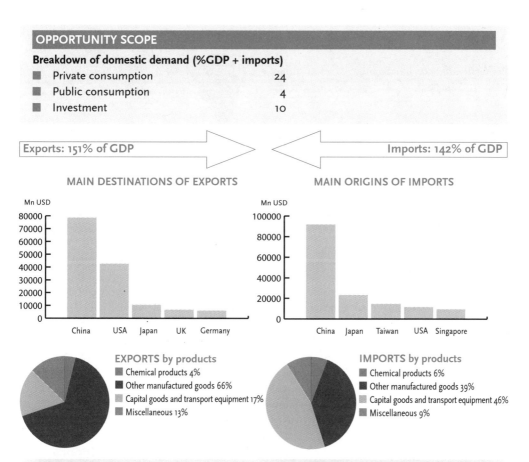

MAIN DESTINATIONS OF EXPORTS

Mn USD — China, USA, Japan, UK, Germany

MAIN ORIGINS OF IMPORTS

Mn USD — China, Japan, Taiwan, USA, Singapore

3

EXPORTS by products
- Chemical products 4%
- Other manufactured goods 66%
- Capital goods and transport equipment 17%
- Miscellaneous 13%

IMPORTS by products
- Chemical products 6%
- Other manufactured goods 39%
- Capital goods and transport equipment 46%
- Miscellaneous 9%

STANDARD OF LIVING / PURCHASING POWER

Indicators	Hong Kong	Regional average	DC average
GNP per capita (PPP dollars)	27490	3923	4601
GNP per capita (USD)	24690	996	1840
Human Development Index	0.903	0.678	0.684
Wealthiest 10% share of national income	34.9	30	32
Urban population percentage	100	36	45
Percentage under 15 years old	16	29	30
Number of telephones per 1000 inhabitants	565	106	120
Number of computers per 1000 inhabitants	422	29	37

India

Population (million inhabitants)	1,049
GDP (US$ million)	510,177

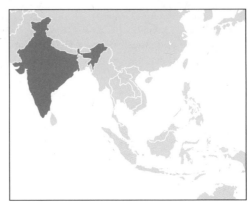

Coface analysis

Short-term: **A3**

Medium-term:
Quite low risk

STRENGTHS

- Great market potential with over one billion inhabitants.
- Rapid development of industries in the information technology and communications sectors.
- Growing foreign currency reserves thanks to revenues from services and to inward private transfers.
- High but manageable foreign debt.
- Gradual progress on structural reforms concerning the banking sector, exchange liberalization and taxation.

WEAKNESSES

- A poor public finance situation and high domestic debt.
- An insufficient level of investment due to poor financial intermediation and inadequate infrastructure.
- Very inegalitarian growth apt to generate great social discontent.
- Difficult negotiations with Pakistan despite current progress.

RISK ASSESSMENT

Emergence of rapidly growing sectors like high technology, pharmaceuticals and the car industry has been driving a dynamic economy. That trend has been spurring demand from an essentially urban middle class employed in those sectors. The economy has thus become relatively less dependent on the agricultural sector. (A diversified economy should allow India to manage the economic impact of the December 2004 tsunami.) Indian company payment behaviour has improved as evidenced by the marked decline of the Coface payment incident index. The company situation nonetheless continues to be marked by insufficient financial transparency and still limited possibilities for recourse in case of non-payment.

Exports have continued to grow strongly and inward private transfers have remained high, which has permitted currency reserves to increase and foreign debt ratios to improve. Conversely, public debt has remained too high with structural reforms (taxation, privatization) still insufficient to reduce public sector imbalances. Deficit financing by banks has caused an eviction effect on private sector credit.

Politically, although the government coalition is heterogeneous, it should retain power via compromises that may result in relative immobilism. Although relations with Pakistan have eased, any meaningful results of the current talks are likely to be limited on delicate questions like Kashmir.

MAIN ECONOMIC INDICATORS·

US$ millions	2001/02	2002/03	2003/04[e]	2004/05[f]	2005/06[f]
Economic growth (%)	5.8	4.0	8.1	7.0	7.5
Inflation (%)	1.7	6.0	4.7	5.0	4.5
Public sector balance (%GDP)	−10.1	−10.7	−9.9	−9.2	−9.2
Exports	44.9	52.5	61.5	72.0	85.0
Imports	51.9	58.9	71.2	84.6	97.5
Trade balance	−6.9	−6.4	−9.7	−12.6	−12.5
Current account balance	0.8	4.1	5.5	0.9	0.0
Current account balance (%GDP)	0.2	0.8	0.9	0.1	0.0
Foreign debt (%GDP)	23.8	23.0	21.4	20.3	18.9
Public debt (%GDP)	76.3	80.9	81.6	84.0	85.0
Debt service (%Exports)	14.6	13.5	14.6	8.6	10.8
Foreign exchange reserves (in months of imports)	7.7	9.4	12.4	11.7	10.8

e = estimate, f = forecast

3

CONDITIONS OF ACCESS TO THE MARKET

■ Means of entry

Customs duties, although still high, are trending downwards. In 2004, the median rate of duty was cut to 20 per cent and the special additional duty of 4 per cent abolished, but the tax burden remained heavy due to the maintenance of 16 per cent general additional duty. The year also saw the introduction of a 2 per cent special education levy. Numerous products, especially foodstuffs, continue to attract high rates of duty (wine: 140–254 per cent; spirits: 209–525 per cent). Conversely, certain products regarded as essential to the country's economic development benefit from reduced rates of duty (textile and computer equipment and semi-finished goods, certain uncut gems, drinking water treatment equipment). Overall, India is taking action to reduce customs duties. Under the information technologies agreement, it has cut the rate of duty for 217 products to 0 per cent and is due to reduce and rationalize import duties over the next few years.

Complex non-tariff barriers not only remain in place but have multiplied since the complete abolition of quantitative restrictions on 1 April 2001. Each shipment of imported foodstuffs is, in principle, subject to systematic inspections. Moreover, prior to import pre-packaged goods must bear the maximum retail price (including local taxes and transport costs) on their label. Finally, for certain goods product certification rules of the Bureau of Indian Standards are applied in a manner that places importers at a disadvantage (eg requirement to open a subsidiary or a liaison office and to pay ad hoc duties).

■ Attitude towards foreign investors

In contrast to the policy of economic self-sufficiency pursued by the government since independence, from 1991 India has been actively involved in opening up its economy to foreign investment – mainly via the adoption of a 'negative list' of sectors, which makes automatic approval of FDI the norm. Nevertheless, a number of obstacles remain. These include restrictions on the manufacture of 675 goods, which remain the preserve of local small industry; ceilings on foreign shareholdings in a variety of sectors; and closure of the retail sector to foreign investors. Moreover, a foreign company already based in India via a joint venture agreement may not open a subsidiary without the written consent of its Indian partner. Corporation tax for foreign law companies is 41.82 per cent, compared with 36.59 per cent for Indian companies. Indirect taxation is both complex and opaque. Nevertheless, the reform programme continues apace under the present government as it did under the previous one with the focus primarily on higher ceilings for foreign investment in the few remaining sectors concerned, setting up of a foreign investment commission, greater transparency in approval procedures for foreign investment applications, adaptation of intellectual property legislation and convertibility of the rupee for ordinary business transactions.

PAYMENT INCIDENTS INDEX
(12 months moving average - base 100 : World 1995)

OPPORTUNITY SCOPE

Breakdown of domestic demand (%GDP + imports)
- Private consumption 56
- Public consumption 11
- Investment 20

Exports: 15% of GDP → ← Imports: 16% of GDP

MAIN DESTINATIONS OF EXPORTS

Mn USD

USA, UK, Hong Kong, Germany, UAE

MAIN ORIGINS OF IMPORTS

Mn USD

USA, Belgium, China, Singapore, UK

EXPORTS by products
- Construction materials (incl. iron and steel) 21%
- Gems and jewellery 18%
- Textiles 11%
- Ready-made garments 10%
- Chemical products 11%
- Miscellaneous 29%

IMPORTS by products
- Petroleum products 27%
- Capital goods and transport equipment 13%
- Refined petroleum products 10%
- Precious and semi-precious stones 9%
- Chemical products 8%
- Miscellaneous 33%

STANDARD OF LIVING / PURCHASING POWER

Indicators	India	Regional average	DC average
GNP per capita (PPP dollars)	2650	3923	4601
GNP per capita (USD)	470	996	1840
Human Development Index	0.595	0.678	0.684
Wealthiest 10% share of national income	27.4	30	32
Urban population percentage	28	36	45
Percentage under 15 years old	33	29	30
Number of telephones per 1000 inhabitants	40	106	120
Number of computers per 1000 inhabitants	7	29	37

Indonesia

Population (million inhabitants)	217
GDP (US$ million)	203,820

Short-term: **B**

Medium-term:

Coface analysis   **Moderately high risk**

STRENGTHS

- Indonesia boasts enormous natural resources (agriculture, energy, minerals).
- The country has recovered its macroeconomic and financial stability.
- External account surpluses have persisted with foreign currency reserves at satisfactory levels.
- Indonesia's first presidential election by universal suffrage, in July/September 2004, strengthened the democratic process.

WEAKNESSES

- Growth has been below the country's potential due notably to underinvestment and competitiveness problems.
- With the external debt burden still heavy, the country has remained dependent on international lenders.
- Progress has been lagging on efforts to improve the business environment and on the campaign against extensive corruption.
- Modernizing infrastructure, reducing poverty and raising the education level will be essential for future development.
- The cohesiveness of the world's largest Muslim country has remained shaky amid terrorist and separatist movements and risks of conflict in some parts of the archipelago.

RISK ASSESSMENT

Former General Susilo Bambang Yudhoyono's victory in the September 2004 presidential election, over the incumbent Megawati Sukarnoputri, will not result in significant changes in the established economic policy, since it is based on a programme whose main targets are to maintain macroeconomic stability and continue structural reforms.

Despite its high human cost, the economic impact of the December 2004 tsunami should be relatively limited due to the economy's size and diversification and to massive international financial aid. Economic activity should nonetheless sag in 2005 due particularly to a slowdown of exports, affected by a decline in oil production and expiration of the Multifibre Arrangement.

Meanwhile, the country has been relying on concessional loans to cover its growing financing needs as it has not been successful in attracting significant foreign investment. However, foreign debt reduction should nonetheless continue and remain a priority with debt ratios still high. Finally, the moderate level of short-term debt and satisfactory currency reserves will help limit any liquidity crisis with efforts to consolidate the banking sector continuing.

MAIN ECONOMIC INDICATORS

US$ billions	2000	2001	2002	2003	2004[e]	2005[f]
Economic growth (%)	4.9	3.8	4.3	4.5	4.7	4.5
Inflation (%)	3.7	11.5	11.9	6.7	6.5	7.2
Public sector balance (%GDP)	−1.5	−2.4	−1.2	−1.6	−1.5	−1.1
Exports	65.4	57.4	59.2	63.3	68.0	66.6
Imports	40.4	34.7	35.7	39.5	45.4	47.1
Trade balance	25.0	22.7	23.5	23.7	22.6	19.5
Current account balance	8.0	6.9	7.8	7.3	5.5	3.0
Current account balance (%GDP)	4.8	4.2	3.8	3.0	2.1	1.1
Foreign debt (%GDP)	85.9	81.2	64.5	55.2	48.2	43.7
Debt service (%Exports)	31.3	35.1	34.9	31.2	28.6	27.3
Foreign exchange reserves (in months of imports)	5.1	5.5	6.0	6.6	5.6	5.4

e = estimate, f = forecast

CONDITIONS OF ACCESS TO THE MARKET

■ Means of entry

Indonesia pursues a liberal trade policy and since the Marrakech agreement has gradually dismantled customs duties. Of tariff items, 72 per cent are liable to 0–5 per cent duty. There are tariff peaks for imported cars, iron and steel, certain chemicals and wines and spirits. As well as cutting customs duties, Indonesia is gradually lifting non-tariff barriers on all items except priority products such as rice and sugar. A number of products, especially consumer goods, must have a licence or certificate before being released on the market. Moves to liberalize trade in line with WTO commitments have been backed by measures to open trade further with the country's ASEAN partners. The objective of AFTA is to cut duties on manufactured goods to between 0 and 5 per cent.

■ Attitude towards foreign investors

The Indonesian government is extremely open to foreign investment. BKPM, the government investment promotion and coordination agency, performs its role actively, albeit with limited powers. The government is keen to revive declining foreign investment after years of crisis. It regards FDI as vital to technology transfer and job creation. Indonesia has signed investment protection and guarantee agreements with 56 countries that are binding on it. The country's economic situation does not allow it to grant a range of extremely attractive tax incentives, except for companies operating in a limited number of priority free zones such as Batam Island near Singapore. There is temporary tax relief for raw materials and initial equipment purchased by foreign manufacturing companies. Foreign investors may repatriate profits upon payment of local tax. Despite the initiatives announced by successive governments to simplify start-ups in Indonesia, the procedure for approving investments used by BKPM remains tedious and finicky. Projects in the banking, financial services and insurance sectors are overseen by the Ministry of Finance, whereas those in mining and oil and gas are the responsibility of the Ministry of Energy. The negative list – which bars foreign investors from a limited number of sectors or activities and regulates access to sectors deemed sensitive by the government – is under review and a new investment law is expected to be passed shortly.

PAYMENT INCIDENTS INDEX
(12 months moving average - base 100 : World 1995)

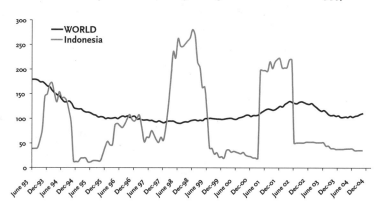

3

OPPORTUNITY SCOPE

Breakdown of domestic demand (%GDP + imports)

Private consumption	55
Public consumption	6
Investment	11

Exports: 35% of GDP

Imports: 29% of GDP

MAIN DESTINATIONS OF EXPORTS

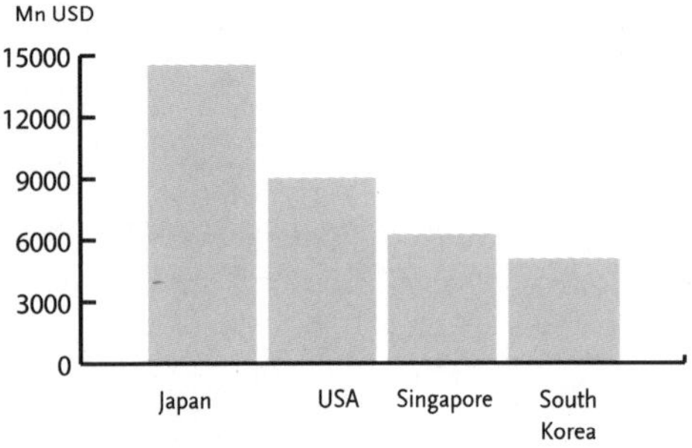

Mn USD
15000
12000
9000
6000
3000
0
Japan
USA
Singapore
South Korea

MAIN ORIGINS OF IMPORTS

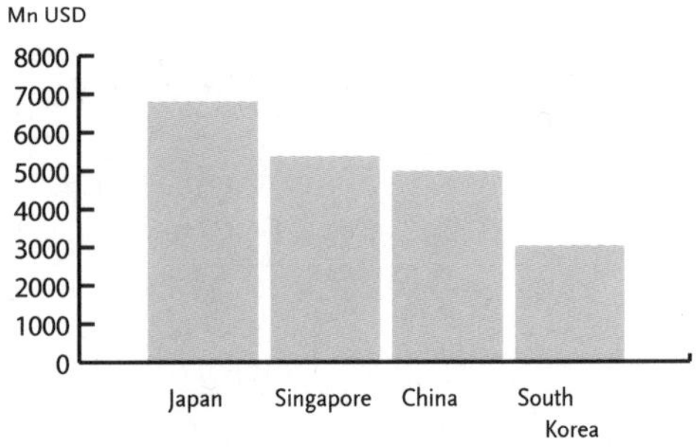

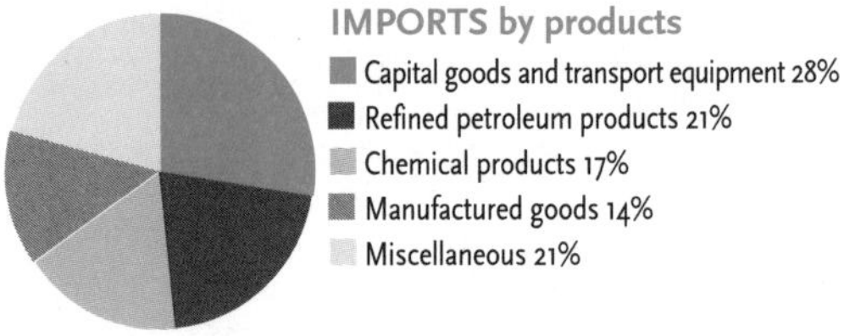

Mn USD
8000
7000
6000
5000
4000
3000
2000
1000
0
Japan
Singapore
China
South Korea

EXPORTS by products
Petroleum and gas 22%
Textiles and clothing 12%
Wood and by-products 5%
Miscellaneous 61%

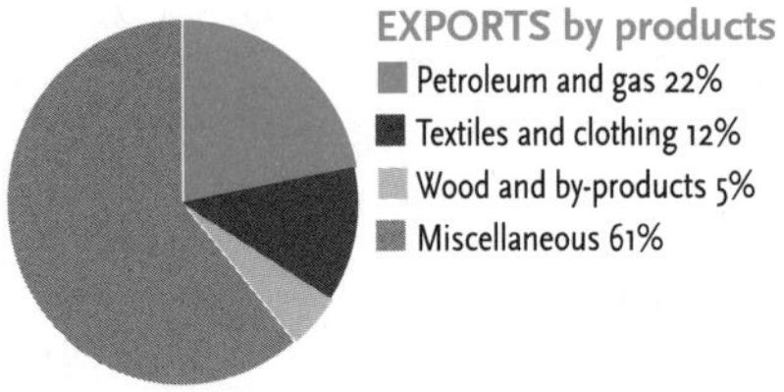

IMPORTS by products
Capital goods and transport equipment 28%
Refined petroleum products 21%
Chemical products 17%
Manufactured goods 14%
Miscellaneous 21%

STANDARD OF LIVING / PURCHASING POWER

Indicators	Indonesia	Regional average	DC average
GNP per capita (PPP dollars)	3070	3923	4601
GNP per capita (USD)	710	996	1840
Human Development Index	0.692	0.678	0.684
Wealthiest 10% share of national income	28.5	30	32
Urban population percentage	43	36	45
Percentage under 15 years old	30	29	30
Number of telephones per 1000 inhabitants	37	106	120
Number of computers per 1000 inhabitants	12	29	37

Japan

Population (million inhabitants)	127.6
GDP (US$ million)	4,300,900
GDP per capita (US$)	33,700

Coface analysis   Short-term: **A1**

3

STRENGTHS

- The very dynamic regional environment has benefited Japan.
- Confronted with international competition, multinationals have managed to remain competitive by restructuring and delocalizing operations.
- Consolidation of bank balance sheets should permit resumption of lending to companies, even if regional banks have continued to lag behind.
- Substantial household savings have constituted reserves for consumption.
- Emergence of a credible political opposition with the Democratic Party of Japan's breakthrough and the Japan Post's ultimate privatization could contribute to greater transparency in relations between the political, government-service and economic spheres.

WEAKNESSES

- The economy has remained relatively closed to the outside with foreign trade contributing little to total production and FDI still limited.
- The rapidly aging population will constitute a major challenge that will necessitate reducing the public debt and deficit, with the recently revamped retirement insurance system satisfying no-one.
- The social safety net has proven to be too limited with family and professional solidarity waning amid increasingly precarious employment and growing social and regional disparities.
- A too-rigid education system has proven ill-suited to meet the economic and social needs of today.
- Although easing, deflationary pressures have persisted.

RISK ASSESSMENT

After 2004 began exceptionally well, growth soon declined to a rate more consistent with the economy's fundamentals. Confronted with economic slowdowns in the region and the United States and with a new yen appreciation, exports have been unable to sustain their explosive growth. Concomitantly, investment and industrial production also declined. Conversely, household spending increased thanks notably to a drop in savings.

In 2005, the economy will expand very moderately provided foreign demand remains strong and the yen does not appreciate too much. Despite a marked slowdown, exports should nonetheless continue to grow with industrial investment shadowing that trend. However, service companies (and more so a public sector grappling with massive debt and deficits) will further reduce capital spending. The continued decline of wages in services and small businesses along with increased pension contributions will prompt households to

MAIN ECONOMIC INDICATORS

%	2000	2001	2002	2003	2004(e)	2005(f)
Economic growth	2.8	0.4	−0.3	2.5	2.8	1.8
Consumption (var.)	1.0	1.7	0.9	0.8	2.0	2.0
Investment (var.)	9.6	1.1	−7.2	9.7	7.0	4.4
Inflation	−0.7	−0.7	−0.9	−0.3	−0.1	0.1
Unemployment rate	4.7	5.0	5.4	5.3	4.7	4.5
Short-term interest rate	0.2	0.1	0.1	0.0	0.0	0.1
Public sector balance (%GDP)	−7.4	−6.1	−7.9	−8.0	−7.5	−6.9
Public sector debt (%GDP)	133.1	141.5	147.3	157.3	162.0	162.0
Exports (var.)	12.4	−6.1	8.0	10.1	13.0	5.5
Imports (var.)	9.2	0.1	1.9	5.0	8.5	6.5
Current account balance (%GDP)	2.5	2.2	2.8	3.1	3.7	3.2

e = estimate, f = forecast

reduce spending despite easing unemployment. Deflationary pressures should fade and, for the first time since 1998, a symbolic price rise should develop.

Restructuring and economic recovery have permitted many companies to post higher earnings. Industries exporting intermediate products, high technology and capital goods, along with their subcontractors, have particularly benefited from that favourable context. However, construction, retail and small companies in general have continued to experience difficulties. The Coface payment incident index has been stable, below the world average. Bankruptcies have declined for the second consecutive year (down about 17 per cent in 2004) with public financial assistance not completely unrelated to that trend.

MAIN ECONOMIC SECTORS

■ Car industry

Domestic motor vehicle production has faintly augmented in 2004 to reach 10.5 million units. However, the production of subsidiaries located abroad surged, notably in Asia, buoyed by growth of demand in emerging countries. It also rose in Europe and the United States thanks to substantial market share gains. With the stabilization of traditional markets, the Japanese car industry will again turn to emerging Asian countries to find new sources of growth in 2005.

■ Steel

With tonnage of about 110 million in 2004, Japanese steel has just posted its fifth consecutive high-production year. Strong demand from carmakers, shipbuilders and electrical manufacturers offset weak demand from the building sector. Moreover, investment dynamism bolstered demand from the industrial equipment manufacturing sector. Exports, driven by demand from other Asian countries – primarily South Korea and China – rose further. Despite an expected slowdown of domestic market outlets, continued strong external demand should contribute to sustaining production, prices and earnings in 2005.

■ Construction

As in the past five years, investment in the construction sector declined 3.5 per cent for the 2004 financial year. That decline is essentially attributable to the 10 per cent drop in public sector investment. Companies, however, particularly in manufacturing, increased their property investments. Demand from individuals rose slightly thanks to the low interest rates and tax credits benefiting new home buyers. In 2005, based on stabilization in the public sector, construction investment should at last increase, albeit at a slow rate (up 1 per cent).

■ Household appliances and consumer electronics

Household appliance manufacturing underwent a structural decline in Japan due to delocalization of production to other Asian countries. That downward trend has also been apparent in the consumer electronics market for products like televisions, camcorders and CD reader/writers. At the other extreme, production of new high value-added products (like plasma and liquid-crystal television screens, DVD video player/recorders) has been growing strongly, permitting Japanese consumer electronics companies to return to

equilibrium after years of restructuring. The electronic component and computer equipment market has been faring well thanks to generalization of digital technology.

■ Distribution

After seven years of weak growth, household consumption rose about 2 per cent in 2004. That upturn has not benefited everyone with supermarket and megastore sales declining in 2004 for the seventh consecutive year. With the government planning to cancel some tax breaks and increase pension contributions, consumption should increase more moderately in 2005. However, the already well-advanced restructuring process, particularly the closing of unprofitable stores, should prevent the sales decline from eating into profits.

PAYMENT AND COLLECTION PRACTICES

■ Payment

Japan has ratified the international conventions of June 1930 on bills of exchange and promissory notes, and of March 1931 on cheques. As a result, the validity of these instruments in Japan is subject to the same rules as in Europe. The bill of exchange and the widely used promissory note, when unpaid, allow creditors to initiate debt recovery proceedings via a fast-track procedure, subject to certain conditions. The fast-track procedure is available for unpaid cheques as well, although the use of cheques is far less common.

Clearing houses play an important role in the collective processing of the money supply arising from these instruments. The penalties for payment default act as a powerful deterrent. A debtor who, twice in six months, fails to honour a bill of exchange, a promissory note or a cheque liable to be settled in Japan, is barred for a period of two years from undertaking business-related banking transactions (current account, loans) with financial establishments attached to the clearing house. In other words, the debtor is reduced to a *de facto* state of insolvency.

These two measures normally result in the calling in of any bank loans granted to the debtor.

Over the past few decades, bank transfers have become increasingly prominent in all fields of economic trade, thanks to the widespread use of electronic transfer systems by banks.

■ Debt collection

In principle, to avoid certain disreputable practices employed in the past by specialized companies, only lawyers (*bengoshi*) may undertake debt collection. However, the law of 16 October 1998, which came into force on 1 February 1999, established the profession of 'servicer' to foster debt securitization and facilitate collection of non-performing loans (NPL debts) held by financial institutions. Servicers are debt collection companies licensed by the Ministry of Justice to provide collections services but only for certain types of debt (bank loans, loans by designated institutions, loans contracted under leasing arrangements, credit card repayments, and so on).

Out-of-court settlement is always preferable and involves obtaining a signature from the debtor on a notarized deed that includes a clause acknowledging compulsory enforcement, which, in the event of continued default, is directly enforceable without requiring a prior court judgment.

The standard practice is for the creditor to send debtor a registered letter with acknowledgement of receipt (*Naïyo Shomeï*), the content of which must be written in Japanese letters and certified by the post office. The effect of this letter is to set back the statute of limitation by six months (which is five years for commercial debts). If the debtor still fails to respond, the creditor must start legal action during this period in order to retain the benefit of interruption of the limitation period.

Summary proceedings (*Shiharaï Meireï*), comparable to an injunction to pay, apply to undisputed claims and allow creditors to obtain a court order within about six months. Court fees, payable by the plaintiff in duty stamps, vary according to the size of the claim. In the event of a dispute, these proceedings are converted into ordinary proceedings.

Ordinary proceedings are brought before the summary court (*kan-i saibansho*) for claims under 1,400,000 yen and before the district court (*chiho saibansho*) for claims above this amount. These proceedings, consisting of written and oral submissions, can take from one to three years and generate significant legal costs. Court fees, payable in duty stamps, depend on the size of the claim.

With the 1 January 1998 revision of the civil procedure code undertaken to reduce the duration of legal procedures, the new amendment adopted 1 April 2004 is notably intended to speed up the submission of evidence to both the adverse party and judge during the preliminary examination phase.

The importance attached to conciliation represents the chief characteristic of the Japanese legal system. Under a conciliation procedure (*chotei*) – conducted under court supervision – a panel of mediators, usually comprising a judge and two assessors, attempts to resolve civil and commercial disputes amicably. While avoiding lengthy and costly proceedings, any transaction obtained through such conciliation becomes enforceable once approved by the court.

Similarly, disputes can be resolved via arbitration (*chusai*), an approach well appreciated locally and not involving excessive formalism.

PAYMENT INCIDENTS INDEX
(12 months moving average - base 100 : World 1995)

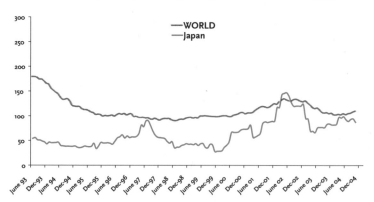

Malaysia

Population (million inhabitants)	24.5
GDP (US$ million)	95,200

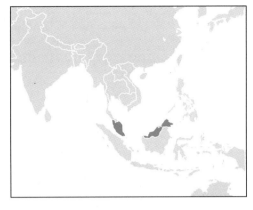

Short-term: **A2**

Medium-term:
Coface analysis   **Low risk**

3

STRENGTHS

- Endowed with good infrastructure, the country lies at the junction of the Malaysian, Chinese and Indian worlds.
- Efforts of education and technological development have contributed to the economy's diversification and competitiveness.
- The country has benefited from a high savings rate.
- The external financial situation has been satisfactory with sustainable debt and growing currency reserves.
- The business environment has been improving.

WEAKNESSES

- The substantial specialization of exports in electric and electronic equipment has remained a source of vulnerability.
- The country must broaden the move upmarket of its products and services.
- Although declining, public sector domestic debt has remained high.
- The banking sector has remained weakened by the extent of non-performing loans.
- With social stability rooted in striking a balance between ethnic communities, Islamic fundamentalists have nonetheless been generating a persistent risk of unrest.

RISK ASSESSMENT

Export dynamism along with sustained domestic consumption and a private investment recovery has been driving the economy. Malaysia was barely hit by the tragic tsunami of late December 2004. The country will nonetheless have to focus more on higher value-added products and services, particularly by opening more to FDI.

Meanwhile, favourable economic conditions and high oil and gas revenues have facilitated planned fiscal deficit reductions. In any case, abundant domestic savings have been financing public sector debt. Furthermore, large external account surpluses have persisted with debt ratios improving especially in relation to exports. Moreover, the modest level of short-term debt in relation to currency reserves and maintenance of the ringgit–US dollar peg have protected the country from a currency crisis. Despite good progress on consolidation of the banking sector, it has remained affected by the high level of non-performing loans, resulting notably from unfinished industrial restructuring. Nonetheless, company payment behaviour has generally remained satisfactory despite often poor profitability and substantial debt.

Politically, the new prime minister Abdullah Badawi consolidated his power base sooner than expected after the government coalition's victory in the March 2004 early legislative elections, which should facilitate implementation of more reform-oriented economic policy.

MAIN ECONOMIC INDICATORS

US$ billions	2000	2001	2002	2003	2004(e)	2005(f)
Economic growth (%)	8.9	0.3	4.1	5.3	7.2	6.0
Inflation (%)	1.5	1.4	1.8	1.1	1.3	2.5
Public sector balance (%GDP)	−4.5	−4.9	−4.3	−4.7	−4.4	−3.8
Exports	98.4	88.0	93.4	105.0	122.8	137.5
Imports	77.6	69.6	75.2	79.3	97.6	112.5
Trade balance	20.8	18.4	18.1	25.7	25.3	25.0
Current account balance	8.4	7.3	7.2	13.4	11.0	8.5
Current account balance (%GDP)	9.3	8.3	7.6	12.9	9.8	7.0
Foreign debt (%GDP)	46.9	51.9	51.6	47.9	47.0	46.1
Debt service (%Exports)	6.1	6.5	·7.8	7.7	4.8	4.6
Foreign exchange reserves (in months of imports)	3.3	3.8	4.0	4.9	5.3	5.2

e = estimate, f = forecast

CONDITIONS OF ACCESS TO THE MARKET

■ Means of entry

A WTO member and signatory to the AFTA free trade agreement, Malaysia pursues a free trade policy. The average rate of customs duty for all goods is below 8 per cent; over 99 per cent of tariff lines bear 0–5 per cent duty under AFTA rules and duties on imports from the five other founding members of ASEAN (Brunei, Philippines, Singapore, Indonesia, Thailand) will be cut to below 0.5 per cent for 99 per cent of tariff lines. Tariff peaks remain for cars, steel and alcoholic beverages. The Malaysian government regulates the import and export of certain goods (17 per cent of tariff lines) through automatic and non-automatic licensing. This measure is not very restrictive in practice and mainly concerns forestry, agriculture, construction, chemicals, cars and metallurgical products. The automotive sector faces a combination of high customs duties, excise duties, quotas and compulsory licensing prior to import.

■ Attitude towards foreign investors

The Malaysian government welcomes foreign investment, especially if it generates export income and does not compete with Malaysian companies. Government policy aims to encourage greater involvement of Malays in the country's economic growth, by guaranteeing them a minimum stake of 30 per cent in companies operating in certain sectors. However, faced with a slowdown in foreign investment, in May 2003 the government announced a series of measures designed to relax the rules on foreign shareholdings. Foreigners may now acquire a 100 per cent stake in manufacturing and high-tech companies. The only exceptions are the so-called strategic sectors (telecommunications, transport, defence, electricity and water supply) where foreign shareholdings are subject to a 30 per cent ceiling.

The government has introduced tax incentives to encourage the establishment of foreign businesses (Pioneer Status, Investment Tax Allowance, International Procurement Centre Status, Operational Headquarters Status). Malaysia has an offshore financial site at Labuan in the east of the country and 14 tax- and duty-free zones.

PAYMENT INCIDENTS INDEX
(12 months moving average - base 100 : World 1995)

■ Foreign exchange regulations

In September 1998, the government pegged the ringgit at 3.8 ringgits to the US dollar and introduced exchange and capital controls, which were relaxed for the first time in September 1999. Transfers are subject to the approval of the central bank, but this requirement – which too has been eased since – has not hampered business transactions and FDI.

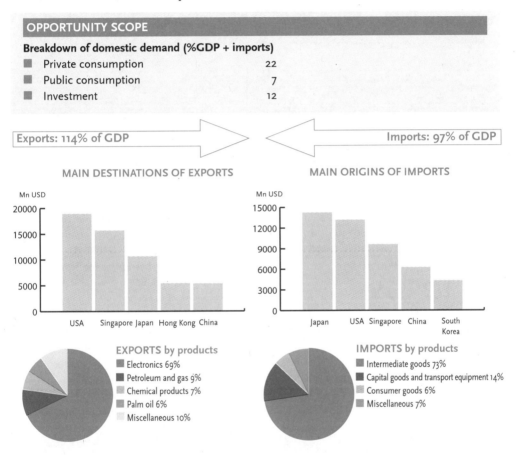

OPPORTUNITY SCOPE

Breakdown of domestic demand (%GDP + imports)

■ Private consumption	22
■ Public consumption	7
■ Investment	12

Exports: 114% of GDP

Imports: 97% of GDP

3

MAIN DESTINATIONS OF EXPORTS

Mn USD

USA · Singapore · Japan · Hong Kong · China

MAIN ORIGINS OF IMPORTS

Mn USD

Japan · USA · Singapore · China · South Korea

EXPORTS by products
- ■ Electronics 69%
- ■ Petroleum and gas 9%
- ■ Chemical products 7%
- ■ Palm oil 6%
- ■ Miscellaneous 10%

IMPORTS by products
- ■ Intermediate goods 73%
- ■ Capital goods and transport equipment 14%
- ■ Consumer goods 6%
- ■ Miscellaneous 7%

STANDARD OF LIVING / PURCHASING POWER

Indicators	Malaysia	Regional average	DC average
GNP per capita (PPP dollars)	8500	3923	4601
GNP per capita (USD)	3540	996	1840
Human Development Index	0.793	0.678	0.684
Wealthiest 10% share of national income	38.4	30	32
Urban population percentage	59	36	45
Percentage under 15 years old	33	29	30
Number of telephones per 1000 inhabitants	190	106	120
Number of computers per 1000 inhabitants	147	29	37

Mongolia

Population (million inhabitants)	2.4
GDP (US$ million)	1,119
GDP per capita (US$) .	466

Coface analysis

Short-term: **D**

Medium-term:
Very high risk

RISK ASSESSMENT

The People's Revolutionary Party, in power since 2001, suffered a setback in the June 2004 legislative elections having failed to sufficiently reduce poverty. A coalition thus had to be formed with the liberal opposition (baptised the Motherland Democratic Coalition) with presidential elections scheduled for May 2005.

The mining sector has remained the main growth driver with industrial production nonetheless remaining firm, farming benefiting from better weather conditions, and tourism beginning to develop. The economic situation has thus remained linked to swings in world prices for its raw material exports (copper, gold, coal, cashmere) with imports of the capital equipment needed by the mining sector negatively affecting external accounts.

Moreover, the size of the fiscal deficits (whose reduction has nonetheless been planned) and public foreign debt (whose amount approximates the GDP) has limited the authorities' room for manoeuvre. At the end 2003, however, they resolved the problem of reducing debt contracted with Russia before 1991. Under IMF aegis, meanwhile, the authorities have been pursuing reform of land ownership and the public and social sectors, as well as privatization of banks and public companies.

Mongolia has nevertheless remained very dependent on international financial aid. Except for the growing mineral sector, foreign investors are still reluctant due to the domestic market's narrowness and the country's landlocked situation. However, Mongolia has been striving to derive benefit from its Chinese neighbour's booming economy.

MAIN ECONOMIC INDICATORS

US$ millions	2000	2001	2002	2003	2004(e)	2005(f)
Economic growth (%)	1.1	1.0	4.0	5.6	6.0	5.5
Inflation (%)	11.6	6.3	1.0	5.0	9.0	5.0
Public sector balance (%GDP)	−7.7	−5.4	−6.0	−4.2	−4.0	−5.0
Exports	536	523	524	627	721	762
Imports	676	693	753	827	901	948
Trade balance	−140	−170	−229	−200	−180	−186
Current account balance (%GDP)	−15.8	−16.6	−15.9	−12.9	−10.9	−10.9
Foreign debt (%GDP)	86.3	88.7	88.1	96.4	96.3	96.1
Debt service (%Exports)	5.2	5.1	4.1	4.3	3.9	4.1
Foreign exchange reserves (in months of imports)	2.9	3.0	3.4	3.0	3.1	3.2

e = estimate, f = forecast

Myanmar

Population (million inhabitants)	49
GDP (US$ million)	7,659

Short-term: **D**

Coface analysis

Medium-term:
Very high risk

3

STRENGTHS

- Myanmar boasts substantial energy, mineral and agricultural resources, as well as tourist potential based on an interesting cultural heritage.
- The country has benefited from its enviable geographic situation in a dynamic region near China and India.
- Myanmar has derived benefit from its ASEAN membership since 1997, which has allowed it to avoid total diplomatic isolation.

WEAKNESSES

- The strengthening in 2003 of economic sanctions, adopted in 1989 by Western countries due to human rights violations, has deprived Myanmar of market outlets and the backing of international financial institutions.
- Deficiencies in infrastructure and energy production have been preventing the economy of one of the world's poorest countries from taking off.
- A lack of coherent economic policy and structural reforms has also been undermining development prospects.
- Ethnic minorities in conflict with the central government have constituted a chronic source of instability.

RISK ASSESSMENT

The military junta (State Peace and Development Council) was reshuffled at the end of October 2004 after dismissal of the prime minister. The concentration of power in favour of the head of state, Commander-in-chief Than Shwe, reflects a hardening of the regime after the 'roadmap' intended to start the junta on the path of democracy had inspired some hope. The continued house arrest of Aung San Suu Kyi, leader of the National League for Democracy, means that negotiations with the democratic opposition are no longer on the agenda. Western economic sanctions have thus not changed the military regime's approach, especially since Myanmar has been benefiting from economic aid from China and India, as well as from backing by ASEAN of which it will assume the rotating presidency mid-2006.

Economic activity has depended solely on gas and oil exports, mainly to Thailand, with authorities having limited rice exports. Manufactured product exports, especially textiles, have suffered from the sales prohibition in the United States, and external accounts have been deteriorating. Furthermore, major macroeconomic imbalances have persisted with economic policy lacking coherence. Thus, due notably to monetization of the fiscal deficit, inflation has remained high and the local currency has continued to depreciate. Moreover, serious structural

237

MAIN ECONOMIC INDICATORS						
US$ millions	2000	2001	2002	2003[(e)]	2004[(f)]	2005[(f)]
Economic growth (%)	5.0	5.4	5.2	−1.0	−1.5	1.3
Inflation (%)	11.4	21.1	57.1	42.1	14.5	26.5
Public sector balance (%GDP)	−8.3	−5.9	−4.1	−4.5	−5.9	−5.0
Exports	1,619	2,225	2,886	2,560	2,255	2,221
Imports	2,135	2,625	2,184	1,898	2,057	2,109
Trade balance	−516	−400	702	662	198	112
Current account balance (%GDP)	−3.3	−4.0	1.2	−0.5	−3.2	−4.1
Foreign debt (%GDP)	60.7	78.1	68.9	57.4	57.1	56.1
Debt service (%Exports)	16.1	9.9	10.3	14.0	15.5	15.5
Foreign exchange reserves (in months of import)	1.0	1.4	2.0	2.5	2.2	2.2

e = estimate, f = forecast

deficiencies, the grey economy's weight, and insecurity have been preventing the economy from really taking off.

CONDITIONS OF ACCESS TO THE MARKET

■ Means of entry

The increase in duties on imported products in June 2004 constituted yet another barrier to trade, already hampered by non-tariff barriers and the local business climate. The country, altogether devoid of transparency, is governed by obsolete, unsuitable, changeable and unpredictable regulations, often announced *a posteriori* in the absence of an official journal. A restrictive system of import licences – the sort of non-tariff barrier typically found in an impoverished country – is in place complete with product lists, which classify goods as essential, non-essential or prohibited (wines and spirits). These regulations are not enforced with any zeal. Instead they are circumvented by way of a thriving border trade with mainly Thailand and China, as attested by the ready availability of contraband goods in most Rangoon shops. The export assistance policy pursued by the government since 1998 requires private sector importers to use export earnings for all import transactions. In other words, they must generate or 'purchase' from an export firm the equivalent in hard currency of the amount payable for the imported item. In March 2002, the government toughened its stance by suspending the import–export licences of foreign firms and granting import licences only to Burmese export companies.

■ Attitude towards foreign investors

The Foreign Investment Law of 1991, highly investment-friendly on paper, provides the legal framework for the majority of foreign-held companies in Myanmar. But its somewhat restrictive and rigid interpretation by the Myanmar Investment Commission, coupled with lengthy approval formalities (two years on average), contradicts its very spirit and explains why, in the last few years, growing numbers of rogue Asian investors have decided to circumvent it altogether.

Apart from a few notable exceptions such as Total and airlines, foreign companies are barred by the Myanmar Investment Commission from 12 sectors of the country's economy. Burmese intellectual property legislation is woefully inadequate. The present law – a legacy of the colonial past (the Burma Copyright Act 1914 for copyright protection and the Indian Patent Act 1911 for trademark and patent protection) – provides no safeguards or remedies, especially for foreign rights.

As a result of the US embargo and European sanctions, Myanmar has not received any international aid for the past 15 years. Its hand-to-mouth existence forces it to adopt expedients that move it closer to its Asian neighbours, who have accounted for 60 per cent of FDI in the country since 1988. China, India and Thailand, which between them accounted for more than 60 per cent of Myanmar's trade in 2003, undoubtedly see their neighbour as a cheap source of raw materials for their own fast-growing economies as well as a potential outlet for their manufactured goods, although in this case financing is usually required.

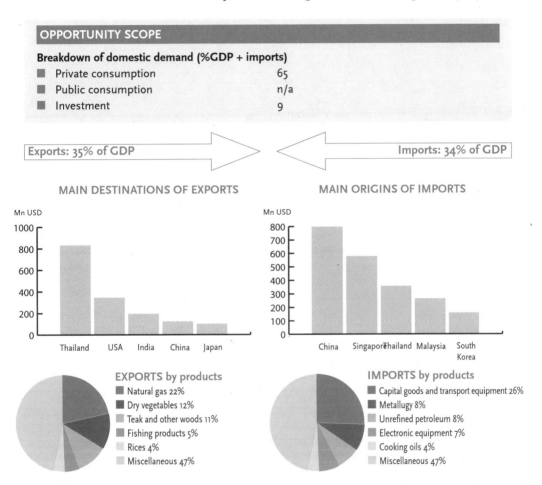

OPPORTUNITY SCOPE

Breakdown of domestic demand (%GDP + imports)
- Private consumption — 65
- Public consumption — n/a
- Investment — 9

Exports: 35% of GDP → ← Imports: 34% of GDP

3

MAIN DESTINATIONS OF EXPORTS

Mn USD — Thailand, USA, India, China, Japan

MAIN ORIGINS OF IMPORTS

Mn USD — China, Singapore, Thailand, Malaysia, South Korea

EXPORTS by products
- Natural gas 22%
- Dry vegetables 12%
- Teak and other woods 11%
- Fishing products 5%
- Rices 4%
- Miscellaneous 47%

IMPORTS by products
- Capital goods and transport equipment 26%
- Metallugy 8%
- Unrefined petroleum 8%
- Electronic equipment 7%
- Cooking oils 4%
- Miscellaneous 47%

STANDARD OF LIVING / PURCHASING POWER

Indicators	Myanmar	Regional average	DC average
GNP per capita (PPP dollars)	n/a	3923	4601
GNP per capita (USD)	156	996	1840
Human Development Index	0.551	0.678	0.684
Wealthiest 10% share of national income	n/a	30	32
Urban population percentage	29	36	45
Percentage under 15 years old	32	29	30
Number of telephones per 1000 inhabitants	7	106	120
Number of computers per 1000 inhabitants	5	29	37

Nepal

Population (million inhabitants)	24.1
GDP (US$ million)	5,549
GDP per capita (US$)	230

Coface analysis

Short-term: **D**

Medium-term:
Very high risk

RISK ASSESSMENT

The political situation has remained very tense with substantial risk of escalation in the conflict opposing the government and Maoist insurgents. The civil war has now lasted nine years and claimed about 10,000 victims. The rebels now control large swaths of the country and, despite the lifting of the Kathmandu blockade in summer 2004, an improvement in the situation now appears unlikely. The king appointed SB Deuba as the new prime minister in June 2004 with the task of managing the peace process with the Maoists and preparing legislative elections for April 2005. The Maoists, however, seeking a constitutional amendment to abolish the monarchy, have not appeared ready to pursue the dialogue.

The conflict has had major economic consequences. Temporary company shutdowns, frequent work stoppages and various forms of extortion have been among the many constraints on economic activity. Poverty has spread with 40 per cent of the Nepalese now living below the poverty line. The tourism revenues essential to the country's economy have been flat due to the political situation. Growth will thus be weak in 2005, particularly with the economy dependent on the farm sector, which has represented 40 per cent of GDP and remained subject to weather conditions. Although inward transfers by expatriate workers and an IMF programme have been buoying the external financial situation, a worsening of the political climate could brutally undermine the debt's sustainability.

MAIN ECONOMIC INDICATORS

US$ millions	2000/01	2001/02	2002/03	2003/04	2004/05(e)	2005/06(f)
Economic growth (%)	4.8	−0.6	3.1	3.5	3.0	3.0
Inflation (%)	3.4	3.5	6.1	2.0	5.5	4.5
Public sector balance (%GDP)	−6.2	−5.8	−3.7	−3.9	−5.3	−4.9
Exports	945	754	653	737	788	1,023
Imports	1,710	1,448	1,556	1,796	2,075	2,384
Trade balance	−765	−694	−903	−1,059	−1,287	−1,361
Current account balance (%GDP)	2.9	1.9	0.3	0.1	−2.2	−2.2
Foreign debt (%GDP)	49.9	53.2	51.5	46.5	43.7	42.0
Debt service (%Exports)	4.7	5.3	5.6	6.0	6.3	6.3
Foreign exchange reserves (in months of imports)	7.2	7.0	6.7	7.3	6.8	6.1

e = estimate, f = forecast

New Zealand

Population (million inhabitants)	4
GDP (US$ million)	79,000
GDP per capita (US$)	19,600

Coface analysis   Short-term: **A1**

RISK ASSESSMENT

Economic activity strengthened in 2004, driven by strong domestic demand, a dynamic tourism sector and an export recovery. Inflation rose, reflecting higher oil prices, alcohol taxes and property prices. To avoid overheating, the central bank had to raise interest rates several times during the year.

Growth will be more moderate in 2005. Domestic activity should weaken, notably in residential housing, currently faced with high interest rates and sagging demand. Moreover, exports will grow at a less robust pace with investment thus slowing although remaining at a high level. Continued low unemployment (about

4 per cent) could trigger tension in the labour market with companies anticipating difficulties in filling vacant positions. That situation will nonetheless keep upward pressure on wages and, inflation notwithstanding, on purchasing power. Despite increased social spending by the government in 2005, public sector finances will remain largely in surplus.

The economy's good health has benefited companies as evidenced by their satisfactory payment behaviour with the Coface payment incident index below the world average and trending down in recent months.

MAIN ECONOMIC INDICATORS

%	2000	2001	2002	2003	2004[(e)]	2005[(f)]
Economic growth	3.6	2.7	4.5	3.2	4.5	2.1
Consumption (var.)	2.1	2.2	4.4	4.8	5.5	1.1
Investment (var.)	19.0	−0.4	6.0	13.4	16.0	10.0
Inflation	2.6	2.6	2.7	1.8	2.8	2.6
Unemployment rate	6.0	5.3	5.2	4.6	4.1	4.0
Short-term interest rate	6.5	5.7	5.7	5.4	6.1	5.9
Public sector balance (%GDP)	1.5	2.0	2.7	3.1	2.8	3.0
Public sector debt (%GDP)	45.1	42.8	40.5	38.4	35.0	35.0
Exports (var.)	6.0	2.5	6.3	1.7	7.5	6.2
Imports (var.)	0.3	1.7	8.4	9.2	14.9	4.9
Current account balance (%GDP)	−4.8	−2.4	−3.1	−4.2	−4.6	−3.9

e = estimate, f = forecast

PAYMENT AND COLLECTION PRACTICES

As a former British colony in the 19th century, New Zealand's legal code and precepts are largely inspired by British 'common law' and the British court system.

New Zealand became a dominion within the Commonwealth on 26 September 1907.

■ **Payment**

Bills of exchange or promissory notes are not frequently used for commercial transactions in New Zealand and mainly serve to authenticate the existence of claims.

Conversely, cheques are relatively widely used for domestic transactions.

Wire transfers or SWIFT bank transfers are the most commonly used payment method for domestic and international transactions. Most of the country's banks are connected to the SWIFT network, which offers a rapid, cost-efficient means of effecting payments.

■ **Debt collection**

The collection process starts with the serving of final notice by recorded delivery of a 'seven-day letter' whereby the creditor notifies the debtor of his payment obligations.

Without payment by the debtor company of an uncontested payable claim exceeding NZ$1,000 (or after obtaining a ruling), the creditor may summon the debtor to settle his debt within 15 days or face a winding-up petition with his company considered insolvent (statutory demand under section 289 of the 1993 Companies Act).

Under ordinary proceedings, once a statement of claim (summons) has been filed and where debtors have no grounds on which to dispute claims, creditors may solicit a fast-track procedure enabling them to obtain an executory order by issuing the debtor with an application for summary judgment. This petition must be accompanied by an affidavit (a sworn statement by the plaintiff attesting to the claim's existence) along with supporting documents authenticating the unpaid claim.

For more complex or disputed claims, creditors must instigate standard civil proceedings, an arduous, often lengthy process lasting up to two years. Proceedings are heard by the District Courts, or by the High Courts for claims exceeding NZ$200,000.

Appeals against the decisions handed down by the Court of Appeal, located in Wellington, concerning claims for NZ$5,000 and more are lodged as of 1 January 2004, and after leave on its part, with the recently established Supreme Court of New Zealand, also located in Wellington. Such recourse was previously sought via the Privy Council in London.

In addition, the High Court may hold summary proceedings for commercial disputes concerning, for example, the fields of insurance, banking, finance, intellectual property, goods transport, and which are enumerated in its 'commercial list'.

During the preliminary phase, proceedings are written insofar as the Court examines the case documents authenticating the parties' respective claims. During the subsequent 'discovery phase', the parties' lawyers may request their adversaries to submit any proof or witness testimony that is relevant to the case and duly examine the case documents thus submitted. Before handing down its judgement, the Court examines the case and holds an adversarial hearing of the witnesses who may be cross-examined by the parties' lawyers.

Arbitration and mediation proceedings may also be used to resolve disputes and obtain out-of-court settlements, often at a lower cost than through the ordinary adversarial procedure.

PAYMENT INCIDENTS INDEX
(12 months moving average - base 100 : World 1995)

Pakistan

Population (million inhabitants)	145
GDP (US$ million)	59,071

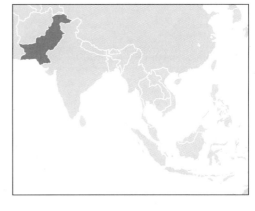

Short-term: **C**

Medium-term:

Coface analysis **High risk**

STRENGTHS

- The financial situation has benefited from debt rescheduling and grants-in-aid as well as from an upsurge of inward private transfers.
- Several structural reforms, like restructuring public companies and overhauling the tax system, have been progressing under IMF auspices.
- The country's nuclear-power status and the risk of it falling into an anti-Western camp have made Pakistan a key American strategic priority.
- A dialogue with India is under way.

WEAKNESSES

- The economy is still very dependent on low value-added sectors (textiles, cotton).
- Foreign investment has been slow to pick up the slack for official financing due to political risk.
- Pakistan's role in nuclear proliferation will be a potential source of conflict with the United States.
- Foreign policy options have been far from generating a consensus among the population and the elite.

RISK ASSESSMENT

Investment and consumer spending dynamism has been buoying economic conditions, bolstered by a structural reform programme initiated under IMF auspices. The country's financial situation has stabilized thanks to a steady current account and a limited debt-service level. Although still high, public sector debt ratios have been declining progressively with the improvement in sovereign risk underpinned by prudent fiscal policy and tax reform.

However, Pakistan's specialization has remained focused on low value-added goods even if the end of the Multifibre Arrangement in early 2005 will be unlikely to substantially reduce textile exports. Its human development indicators, meanwhile, have been well below those of other regional economies.

Political risk has remained high with the country contending with a rash of inter-religious confrontations and a substantial risk of increased terrorism. Although Pervez Musharraf's position has been shaky, the army is still very powerful, so much so that a scenario of a break-off with current pro-Western strategy seems highly unlikely. Although relations with India have been progressively improving, the debate over the thorny Kashmir question has little chance of producing a viable solution in the near term.

MAIN ECONOMIC INDICATORS

US$ billions	2000/01	2001/02	2002/03	2003/04	2004/05[f]	2005/06[f]
Economic growth (%)	2.2	3.4	5.1	6.4	6.0	5.7
Inflation (%)	4.4	2.7	3.1	4.1	5.0	4.0
Public sector balance (%GDP)	−5.2	−5.2	−4.5	−4.0	−4.0	−4.5
Exports	8.9	9.1	10.9	15.1	16.4	17.7
Imports	10.2	9.4	11.3	14.0	15.6	17.2
Trade balance	−1.3	−0.3	−0.4	1.1	0.8	0.5
Current account balance	0.3	0.1	3.2	4.2	3.2	2.6
Current account balance (%GDP)	0.6	0.2	4.6	4.9	3.0	2.6
Foreign debt (%GDP)	60.1	60.2	51.1	45.8	40.9	39.9
Debt service (%Exports)	24.8	21.9	16.9	13.4	12.5	11.7
Foreign exchange reserves (in months of imports)	1.1	3.7	6.9	7.0	6.4	5.7

e = estimate, f = forecast

CONDITIONS OF ACCESS TO THE MARKET

■ Means of entry

The country's economy is gradually opening up. Customs duties in the industrial sector are trending downwards. The maximum rate of custom duty is 25 per cent *ad valorem* (CIF value), except for products subject to a separate system of taxation, such as cars. The maximum rate of duty in the service sector is 10 per cent. As a rule, Pakistan customs follow the World Customs Organization's harmonized international nomenclature and recommendations. However, the practice of reclassifying imported goods in a higher duty category places local importers at a disadvantage and sometimes leads to disputes. Excise duty of 2–3 per cent and 25 per cent maximum general sales tax is levied on all goods and transactions on top of customs duties. Capital transfers are not subject to major restrictions. The central bank now permits full convertibility and unrestricted capital transfers and there is a free currency market. In a crisis, however, the bank may intervene to regulate foreign currency flows with foreign countries.

■ Attitude towards foreign investors

Foreign investment is governed by special legislation. The Pakistan government takes an extremely positive view of foreign investment and hopes to attract investors by creating a far more investment-friendly legal environment. FDI, although small in volume terms, rose by 19 per cent in the period from 2003 to 2004. There are no restrictions on the type of company incorporated by foreign investors or on foreign property rights, nor any requirement for foreigners to tie up with a local partner, except for projects in the service and agricultural sectors. Foreign shareholdings in farm projects are capped at 60 per cent. In services, foreign investors must tie up with a local partner after five years and reduce their stake to 60 per cent or less. In agriculture, services and public works, they are required to make a minimum capital contribution of US$0.3 million.

Once established, resident firms are liable to the same taxation as local enterprises. In 2004–2005, corporation tax in the banking sector was 41 per cent and general corporate taxation 39 per cent, down from 44 per cent and 41 per cent respectively a year ago. Moreover, the Pakistan government has signed bilateral investment protection treaties with 36 countries, including France, designed to offer investors effective safeguards against nationalization or unlawful expropriation, and unrestricted capital and profit repatriation rights. French companies looking to do business in Pakistan can get in touch with the honorary counsellor for investments, Mr Tahir M Bhatti, 80 rue Réaumur, 75002 Paris (phone: +33 142361054; fax: +33 142362756).

Pakistan has signed, ratified and implemented the Convention on the Settlement of Investment Disputes and is a signatory to the founding treaty of the Multilateral Investment Guarantee Agency (MIGA), an arm of the World Bank.

3

OPPORTUNITY SCOPE

Breakdown of domestic demand (%GDP + imports)
- Private consumption — 62
- Public consumption — 9
- Investment — 13

Exports: 19% of GDP → ← Imports: 19% of GDP

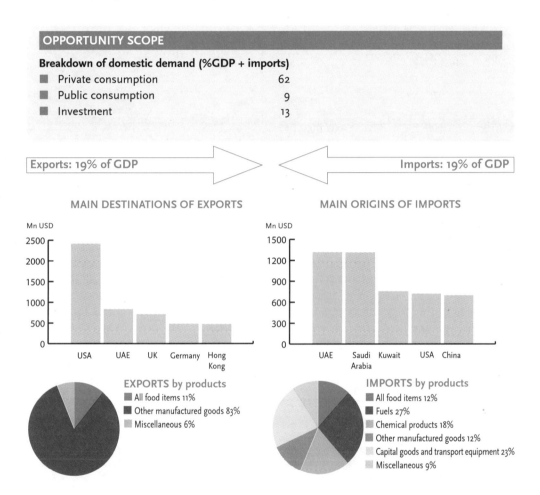

MAIN DESTINATIONS OF EXPORTS

EXPORTS by products
- All food items 11%
- Other manufactured goods 83%
- Miscellaneous 6%

MAIN ORIGINS OF IMPORTS

IMPORTS by products
- All food items 12%
- Fuels 27%
- Chemical products 18%
- Other manufactured goods 12%
- Capital goods and transport equipment 23%
- Miscellaneous 9%

STANDARD OF LIVING / PURCHASING POWER

Indicators	Pakistan	Regional average	DC average
GNP per capita (PPP dollars)	1960	3923	4601
GNP per capita (USD)	420	996	1840
Human Development Index	0.497	0.678	0.684
Wealthiest 10% share of national income	28.3	30	32
Urban population percentage	34	36	45
Percentage under 15 years old	41	29	30
Number of telephones per 1000 inhabitants	25	106	120
Number of computers per 1000 inhabitants	4	29	37

Papua New Guinea

Population (million inhabitants)	5.4
GDP (US$ million)	2,814
GDP per capita (US$)	521

Short-term: **B**

Medium-term:

Coface analysis **Moderately high risk**

RISK ASSESSMENT

Fragmented geographically, ethnically and linguistically, the country has also suffered from inadequate infrastructure. To benefit from sustainable development, it must also diversify its economy and reduce its vulnerability to fluctuations in world prices for exported raw materials. The vagaries of weather, depletion of natural resources and deficiencies in the business environment have continued to undermine growth. Nonetheless, the production start-up of new oil fields as well as the start of operations of the Kainantu gold mine in 2004 and Ok Tedi copper mine in 2005 should bolster economic activity, even before the possible development of a gas pipeline to Australia.

Moreover, the restoring of macroeconomic stability, particularly consolidation of public sector finances, is now under way with external accounts remaining in surplus and foreign debt declining. Structural reforms have nonetheless been lagging, although continuation of the essential backing provided by the main donor countries and international financial institutions will depend on progress achieved on that score. However, with a ten-party government coalition, it has been difficult to implement an 'improvement and development' programme focused on export sectors, a public sector reform plan and an economic policy of 'stabilization with growth'.

MAIN ECONOMIC INDICATORS						
US$ millions	2000	2001	2002	2003	2004[(e)]	2005[(f)]
Economic growth (%)	−1.2	−2.3	−0.8	1.8	2.3	2.2
Inflation (%)	10.0	10.3	11.7	11.8	3.5	7.3
Public sector balance (%GDP)	−1.4	−4.1	−5.5	−2.0	−1.7	−1.5
Exports	2,215	1,878	1,646	2,213	2,330	2,280
Imports	1,490	1,326	1,292	1,431	1,610	1,710
Trade balance	725	552	354	782	720	570
Current account balance (%GDP)	8.7	6.9	−0.7	10.1	4.5	2.3
Foreign debt (%GDP)	73.7	87.7	88.3	72.4	62.5	57.3
Debt service (%Exports)	16.9	23.9	25.6	20.7	20.4	20.7
Foreign exchange reserves (in months of imports)	1.8	2.9	2.3	3.1	2.7	2.5

e = estimate, f = forecast

Philippines

Population (million inhabitants)	78.6
GDP (US$ million)	77,954

Short-term: **A4**

Medium-term:

Coface analysis **Moderately high risk**

STRENGTHS

- The country represents a large and open market in a favourable regional economic environment.
- The labour force's skills, productivity and adaptability constitute assets, particularly for multinational companies.
- Competitiveness has been satisfactory in electronics and services (call centres, administrative management), particularly in the special economic zones.
- External account surpluses have persisted thanks notably to the extent of expatriate worker financial transfers.

WEAKNESSES

- Growth has remained insufficient in relation to the country's demographic development and has not permitted reducing the substantial social inequality.
- Reducing the structural fiscal deficits will necessitate greater political commitment with the question of the public debt's sustainability now posed.
- With insufficient domestic savings, the country has been dependent on international markets to cover its financing needs.
- The business environment is not very satisfactory.
- Banking sector reform has only been making slow progress.
- Insecurity, notably due to the Islamist rebellion in the south of the archipelago, has had a dissuasive effect on foreign investment and tourism.

RISK ASSESSMENT

Private demand, notably buoyed by expatriate transfers, has been driving the economy. However, the slowdown of international demand, high oil prices and progressive interest rate increases could affect weakened growth.

Moreover, structural problems have been impeding more balanced development. Thus, with the accumulation of large fiscal deficits, public debt has reached excessive levels (about 110 per cent of GDP). However, the inadequacy of domestic savings – unlike other Asian countries – and of FDI, deterred by an unfavourable business climate, has made the country dependent on financial markets and vulnerable to market sentiment. Rising world interest rates could hinder reimbursement of the high foreign debt burden. The limited amount of short-term financing will nonetheless mitigate near-term liquidity-crisis risk. Meanwhile, efforts will still be necessary to strengthen the banking sector and improve oversight. Despite that context, the level of payment incidents has remained limited,

MAIN ECONOMIC INDICATORS						
US$ billions	2000	2001	2002	2003	2004[(e)]	2005[(f)]
Economic growth (%)	6.0	1.8	4.3	4.7	5.9	4.4
Inflation (%)	4.3	6.1	3.1	2.9	5.6	6.3
Public sector balance (%GDP)	−4.7	−4.6	−5.5	−5.6	−4.5	−4.0
Exports	37.3	31.2	34.4	34.8	37.9	39.2
Imports	33.5	32.0	34.0	36.1	38.6	40.1
Trade balance	3.8	−0.7	0.4	−1.3	−0.7	−0.9
Current account balance	6.3	1.3	4.4	3.3	3.4	3.5
Current account balance (%GDP)	8.2	1.9	5.7	4.2	4.0	3.8
Foreign debt (%GDP)	74.5	80.6	77.9	79.1	71.8	65.1
Debt service (%Exports)	16.7	22.0	17.1	19.8	16.3	16.2
Foreign exchange reserves (in months of imports)	3.6	4.0	3.8	3.8	3.5	3.4

e = estimate, f = forecast

with large local groups and subsidiaries of foreign companies less vulnerable than other companies.

Politically, the situation has remained problematic due to the difficulties encountered by authorities in implementing reforms, reducing the extent of poverty and corruption and resolving insecurity problems.

CONDITIONS OF ACCESS TO THE MARKET

■ Market overview

On the whole, the market is very open and whatever import restrictions there are consist mainly of non-tariff barriers. It is difficult, even impossible, for foreigners to enter certain sectors (utilities) protected by the constitution. Imports of certain products are subject to stringent regulatory restrictions involving the award of certificates by an inefficient and often corrupt administrative service. The government has already met its tariff reduction targets for 2003, agreed with the WTO, in respect of 85 per cent of tariff items. Accordingly, duty on finished products has been cut to 10 per cent and on commodities to 3 per cent. By 2004, a single rate of 5 per cent applied, although some exceptional protective tariffs remain in force. At present, there are six rates of duty: 0, 3, 5, 10, 15 and 20 per cent. Products subject to preferential tariff quotas, such as agricultural goods, are taxable outside the quota system at rates as high as 45, 50 or even 60 per cent.

Payment by irrevocable documentary letter of credit is strongly recommended.

While a legal framework has been set in place to enhance intellectual property protection, the slowness of administrative procedures and the lack of resources at the disposal of judges for the enforcement of legal decisions limit its effectiveness.

■ Attitude towards foreign investors

A 'one-stop action centre' is responsible for disseminating practical information and facilitating registration formalities. Foreign companies are advised to use the services of a local lawyer. The Security and Exchange Commission, a government agency, has responsibility for the registration, regulation and monitoring of all companies and partnerships established in the Philippines. Registration with the SEC can take anything from one to four weeks. A fast-track system, based on the filing of applications in English, allows registration formalities to be completed within three days against cash payment of the invoice. By easing foreign investment regulations, the Foreign Investments Act of 1991, amended in 1996 and again in 1998, has greatly boosted investment over the last ten years. Foreign investors interested in infrastructure development can avail themselves of certain provisions of the Build-Operate-Transfer Act (1990). Another law allows foreign investors to lease land for the purposes of establishing a manufacturing facility. The Philippines constitution also allows foreign businesses to repatriate their investment, together with any profits earned, in the original currency, and to raise loans on the local financial market. Foreign firms are provided with safeguards against expropriation and confiscation of their investment. Various types of incentive are also available. The Philippines is one of the most open countries in the region, even though some sectors of activity remain the preserve of local investors.

■ Foreign exchange regulations

There are no exchange controls, but all imports in excess of US$1,000 are subject to a foreign exchange application being filed by the importer. Similarly, when the currency is under strong pressure, local banks may, on the instructions of the central bank, require clients to document their request for foreign currency. The exchange rate is floating.

3

PAYMENT INCIDENTS INDEX
(12 months moving average - base 100 : World 1995)

OPPORTUNITY SCOPE

Breakdown of domestic demand (%GDP + imports)

Private consumption	46
Public consumption	8
Investment	13

Exports: 49% of GDP

Imports: 49% of GDP

MAIN DESTINATIONS OF EXPORTS

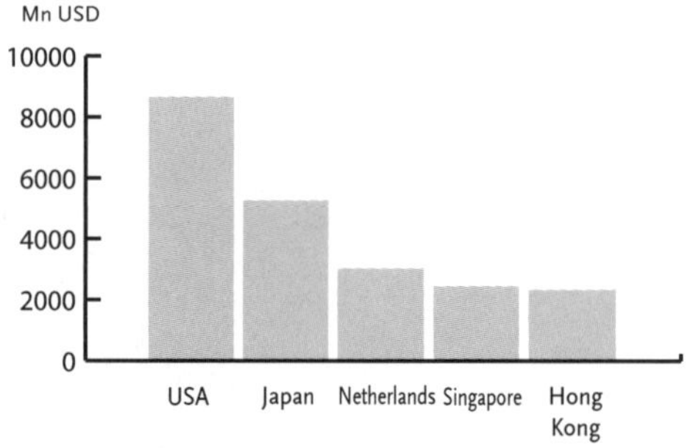

Mn USD
10000
8000
6000
4000
2000
0
USA
Japan
Netherlands
Singapore
Hong Kong

MAIN ORIGINS OF IMPORTS

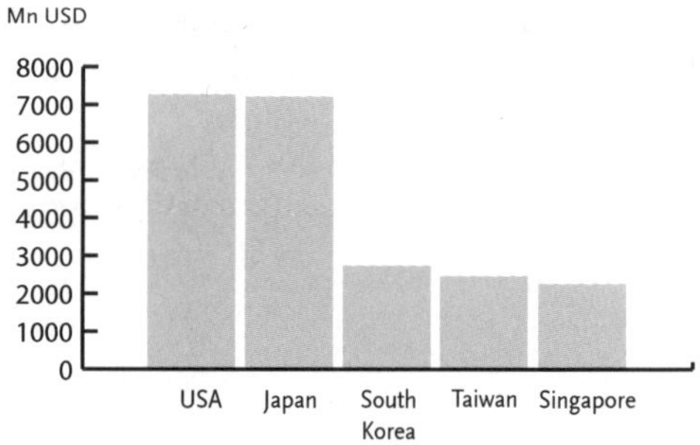

Mn USD
8000
7000
6000
5000
4000
3000
2000
1000
0
USA
Japan
South Korea
Taiwan
Singapore

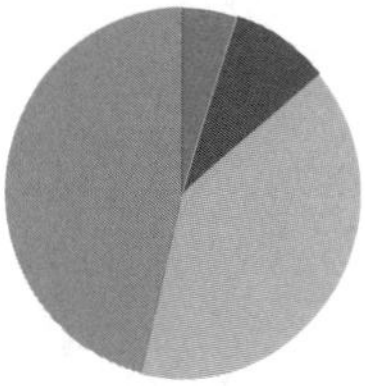

EXPORTS by products

- All food items 5%
- Other manufactured goods 9%
- Capital goods and transport equipment 40%
- Miscellaneous 46%

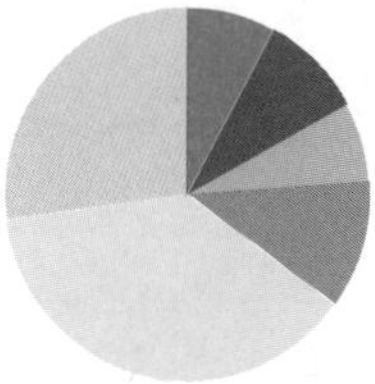

IMPORTS by products

- All food items 8%
- Fuels 9%
- Chemical products 7%
- Other manufactured goods 11%
- Capital goods and transport equipment 38%
- Miscellaneous 27%

STANDARD OF LIVING / PURCHASING POWER

Indicators	Philippines	Regional average	DC average
GNP per capita (PPP dollars)	4450	3923	4601
GNP per capita (USD)	1030	996	1840
Human Development Index	0.753	0.678	0.684
Wealthiest 10% share of national income	36.3	30	32
Urban population percentage	60	36	45
Percentage under 15 years old	37	29	30
Number of telephones per 1000 inhabitants	42	106	120
Number of computers per 1000 inhabitants	28	29	37

Singapore

Population (million inhabitants) 4.2
GDP (US$ million) 88,300

Short-term: **A1**

Medium-term:

Coface analysis **Very low risk**

3

STRENGTHS

- A strategic regional hub, Singapore has attracted investors thanks to the quality of its infrastructure and financial system.
- The workforce is very well trained and highly skilled.
- Economic fundamentals have been particularly good.
- The business environment has been very favourable.
- Political continuity has been remarkable.

WEAKNESSES

- The economy's specialization in electronics has tended to increase its exposure to shifts in world economic conditions.
- The diversification under way, notably in services, should be accelerated to bolster the economy's competitiveness in a regional environment undergoing profound change.
- Reforms are still needed to foster entrepreneurial spirit and innovation as well as modernization of the education system.

RISK ASSESSMENT

After the robust economic recovery in 2004, growth should become more moderate amid a likely slowdown of world demand for electronic products, with that sector representing nearly two-thirds of Singapore's exports. That slowdown should nonetheless not jeopardize the satisfactory payment record of most companies.

Moreover, public sector accounts should show a slight deficit only, with the persistence of substantial external account deficit only, limited foreign debt and comfortable foreign exchange reserves. Furthermore, the banking system has remained one of Asia's soundest, despite stiff domestic competition and an appreciable proportion of non-performing loans.

However, Singapore's re-export activity has been sagging and the current development model has reached its limits. To offset that trend, the city-state has been working to improve its positioning. To enhance Singapore's attractiveness compared with other regional countries, government authorities have been reducing taxes on companies and increasing the number of incentives available to them. They have also been progressively privatizing state-owned enterprises. Finally, while diversifying its industry toward petrochemical and pharmaceutical products, the city-state has been focusing on high value-added services, biotechnology development and advanced research.

MAIN ECONOMIC INDICATORS						
US$ billions	2000	2001	2002	2003	2004(e)	2005(f)
Economic growth (%)	9.4	−2.4	2.2	1.1	8.1	4.2
Inflation (%)	1.4	1.0	−0.4	0.5	1.7	1.6
Public sector balance (%GDP)	2.0	1.6	−1.8	0.1	−1.2	−0.8
Exports	138.9	122.5	128.4	153.8	195.5	207.1
Imports	127.5	109.6	109.8	128.5	163.9	180.2
Trade balance	11.4	12.9	18.5	25.3	31.6	26.9
Current account balance (%GDP)	17.2	21.1	21.4	29.5	29.8	26.2
Foreign debt (%GDP)	14.9	19.9	20.1	19.4	15.7	15.7
Debt service (%Exports)	0.6	0.8	0.9	0.9	0.8	0.8
Foreign exchange reserves (in months of imports)	6.0	6.4	6.8	7.1	6.3	6.5

e = estimate, f = forecast

CONDITIONS OF ACCESS TO THE MARKET

■ Market overview

A fervent advocate of multilateral trade through international institutions such as the WTO, of which it has been a member since 1995, and regional bodies such as ASEAN and APEC, Singapore is engaged in a series of ambitious free trade talks aimed at strengthening its links with the most vibrant markets. The city-state has so far signed a total of six free trade agreements: with New Zealand in 2000; with Japan and EFTA in 2002; with the United States and Australia in 2003 and with Jordan in 2004. Agreements with another ten countries, including Canada, India, Mexico and South Korea, are under negotiation. The failure of the Cancun conference has led Singapore to speed up the negotiation of bilateral and regional free trade agreements.

■ Means of entry

Singapore's openness to the outside world is one of the keys to its economic success, with foreign trade accounting for 298 per cent of GDP in 2003. The country is a free port and its economy is to a large extent centred around storage and warehousing. Regardless of the international economic situation, Singapore continues to pursue liberal trade and investment policies, without the slightest inclination towards protectionism. Singapore's trade policy is characterized by the absence of all but a few tariff and non-tariff barriers. With a few exceptions, customs duties are zero.

■ Attitude towards foreign investors

Singapore keenly welcomes foreign investment and offers a very open and well-planned economic and political environment. The government uses FDI to develop priority sectors (electronics, chemicals, biotechnology). The aim is to encourage the growth of high value-added activities and turn the island into a regional hub for foreign investors looking to do business in Asia. The Economic and Development Board (EDB) is a key actor in the development and promotion of investment in Singapore. However, certain sectors (media, legal and financial services, energy generation and distribution, water supply) are only partially open to foreign investment. The government is starting to open them up, but progress is slow.

PAYMENT INCIDENTS INDEX
(12 months moving average - base 100 : World 1995)

■ **Foreign exchange regulations**

The exchange rate is the key instrument of government monetary policy. The main feature of this policy is a flexible exchange rate within an adjustable fluctuation band. Since 2001, the declared aim of the Monetary Authority of Singapore (MAS) has been to steady the Singapore

dollar's nominal effective exchange rate against a basket of currencies of its main trading partners, the main component of which is the US dollar. On 12 April 2004, however, the government decided to revert to its traditional policy of modest and gradual appreciation of the Singapore dollar.

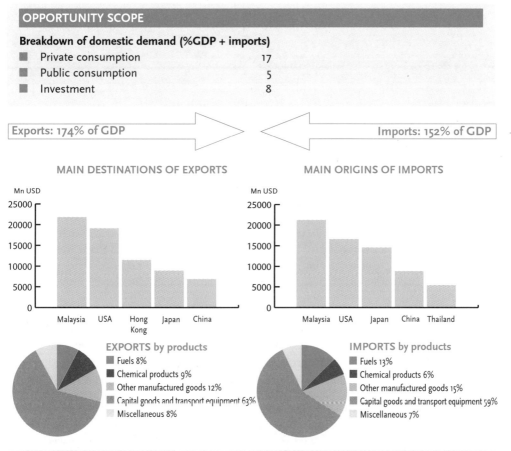

OPPORTUNITY SCOPE

Breakdown of domestic demand (%GDP + imports)
- Private consumption — 17
- Public consumption — 5
- Investment — 8

Exports: 174% of GDP   Imports: 152% of GDP

MAIN DESTINATIONS OF EXPORTS (Mn USD): Malaysia, USA, Hong Kong, Japan, China

MAIN ORIGINS OF IMPORTS (Mn USD): Malaysia, USA, Japan, China, Thailand

EXPORTS by products
- Fuels 8%
- Chemical products 9%
- Other manufactured goods 12%
- Capital goods and transport equipment 63%
- Miscellaneous 8%

IMPORTS by products
- Fuels 13%
- Chemical products 6%
- Other manufactured goods 15%
- Capital goods and transport equipment 59%
- Miscellaneous 7%

STANDARD OF LIVING / PURCHASING POWER

Indicators	Singapore	Regional average	DC average
GNP per capita (PPP dollars)	23730	3923	4601
GNP per capita (USD)	20690	996	1840
Human Development Index	0.902	0.678	0.684
Wealthiest 10% share of national income	32.8	30	32
Urban population percentage	100	36	45
Percentage under 15 years old	21	29	30
Number of telephones per 1000 inhabitants	463	106	120
Number of computers per 1000 inhabitants	622	29	37

South Korea

Population (million inhabitants)	48
GDP (US$ million)	546,934

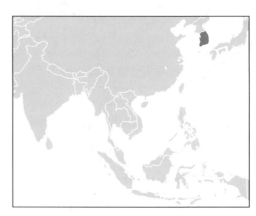

Short-term: **A2**

Coface analysis

Medium-term:
Low risk

STRENGTHS

- The country has been diversifying an already competitive and effective industrial apparatus.
- It has been focusing more on high value-added products thanks to progress made on education and research and development.
- The objective has also been to become Northeast Asia's major business platform.
- The external account and foreign debt situation has remained very satisfactory.
- Authorities have continued to intervene to support the financial system.

WEAKNESSES

- Improvement in the governance of certain conglomerates (*chaebols*) and in labour relations, and strengthening of the legal system will be essential in modernizing the economy.
- Banking oversight is still inadequate with the sector's consolidation still incomplete.
- The very export-oriented economy has remained exposed to possible external shocks.
- North Korea's uncertain future has continued to affect South Korea with the peninsula's ultimate reunification seeming ineluctable.

RISK ASSESSMENT

Exports have remained the main growth driver due notably to robust sales in China (now South Korea's first trading partner). The main weakness is still the persistent sluggishness of private consumption, with inflation fuelled by high farm and oil prices. In that context, companies operating in the domestic market have been more prone than exporting companies to payment incidents.

Public sector finances have been sound despite the substantial burden of bank restructuring costs. Large external account surpluses have persisted and the external financial situation has remained comfortable. The relative foreign debt burden has remained moderate, while currency reserves are at satisfactory levels and the won's situation is good. Nonetheless, progress still has to be made in the banking sector, the loan diversification strategy in favour of consumer credit having met with serious problems. Moreover, the question of improving transparency and governance of certain conglomerates and easing social tensions have persisted.

The return of political stability could facilitate resumption of the dialogue with North Korea. Meanwhile, the government has adopted a more pragmatic approach on economic matters with its room for manoeuvre limited by a slim parliamentary majority.

MAIN ECONOMIC INDICATORS

US$ billions	2000	2001	2002	2003	2004[(e)]	2005[(f)]
Economic growth (%)	8.5	3.8	7.0	3.1	4.8	4.0
Inflation (%)	2.3	4.1	2.8	3.5	3.9	4.0
Public sector balance (%GDP)	−1.4	−1.7	0.7	0.2	−0.7	−1.0
Exports	176.2	151.5	163.4	197.6	265.0	322.0
Imports	159.3	138.0	148.6	175.5	229.0	278.0
Trade balance	17.0	13.5	14.8	22.2	36.0	44.0
Current account balance	12.4	8.2	5.4	12.3	26.0	32.0
Current account balance (%GDP)	2.4	1.7	1.0	2.0	3.9	4.6
Foreign debt (%GDP)	29.0	27.1	26.3	26.6	25.7	25.4
Debt service (%Exports)	11.2	14.3	9.5	9.9	6.8	7.0
Foreign exchange reserves (in months of imports)	5.7	6.9	7.5	8.3	7.6	7.4

e = estimate, f = forecast

3

CONDITIONS OF ACCESS TO THE MARKET

■ Means of entry

South Korea's import arrangements are fairly open, with the vast majority of imports having been liberalized over recent years, in particular since OECD membership in 1996. The average rate of customs duty is 8 per cent, although tariff peaks remain in place, especially in the agricultural sector. Obstacles to trade placed in the way of foreign companies consist mainly of non-tariff barriers. These usually take the form of technical standards (as for cars) or health norms (particularly for new food products).

Intellectual property remains poorly protected and there is widespread abuse despite reforms aimed at harmonizing legislation with international standards. The legal system may seem satisfactory today, but there are shortcomings in the way laws are sometimes enforced. Business relations with a Korean partner are not quite as difficult as they are made out to be. For ordinary business transactions, it is customary for the exporter, at least early on in a relationship, to ask for partial or total payment before shipment. In any case, for small buyers the irrevocable letter of credit is recommended.

■ Attitude towards foreign investors

Since joining the OECD in 1996, South Korea has pursued a particularly dynamic FDI promotion strategy and opened up almost all sectors to foreign investment. The few restrictions that remain are often also found in the legislation of other OECD countries (utilities, defence, agriculture). FDI inflows increased eightfold to US$15.7 billion between 1995 and 2000, but seem to have dried up since. President Ron Moo-hyun's government, which came to power in February 2003, is taking measures to enhance South Korea's attractiveness to foreign investors and, ultimately, to turn the country into a hub of Northeast Asia. The measures announced so far include the setting up of special economic areas designed to attract foreign investment in an environment governed by exceptions to common law. FDI in the first nine months of 2004 totalled US$8.4 billion, way above the US$6.4 billion received in 2003.

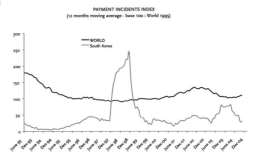

PAYMENT INCIDENTS INDEX
(12 months moving average - base 100 : World 1995)

■ **Foreign exchange regulations**

The parity of the won is determined by the currency market and since January 2001 – when exchange controls introduced in the wake of the 1997 financial crisis were abolished – the currency is fully convertible and freely transferable. Korean residents, however, are required to declare capital exports. In addition, approval must be obtained for certain transactions. The exchange system will be fully liberalized in phases by 2011.

OPPORTUNITY SCOPE

Breakdown of domestic demand (%GDP + imports)

■	Private consumption	45
■	Public consumption	8
■	Investment	19

Exports: 40% of GDP   Imports: 39% of GDP

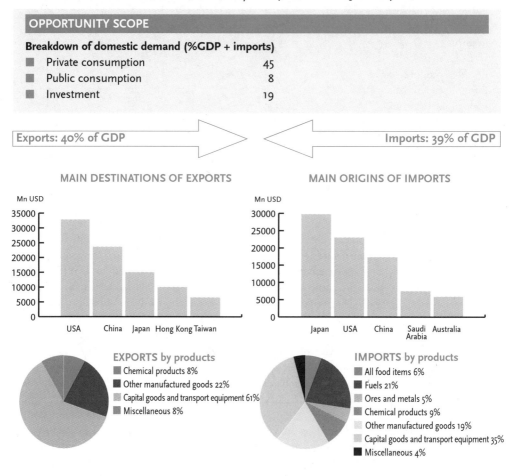

MAIN DESTINATIONS OF EXPORTS

MAIN ORIGINS OF IMPORTS

EXPORTS by products
■ Chemical products 8%
■ Other manufactured goods 22%
■ Capital goods and transport equipment 61%
■ Miscellaneous 8%

IMPORTS by products
■ All food items 6%
■ Fuels 21%
■ Ores and metals 5%
■ Chemical products 9%
■ Other manufactured goods 19%
■ Capital goods and transport equipment 35%
■ Miscellaneous 4%

STANDARD OF LIVING / PURCHASING POWER

Indicators	South Korea	Regional average	DC average
GNP per capita (PPP dollars)	16960	3923	4601
GNP per capita (USD)	9930	996	1840
Human Development Index	0.888	0.678	0.684
Wealthiest 10% share of national income	22.5	30	32
Urban population percentage	83	36	45
Percentage under 15 years old	21	29	30
Number of telephones per 1000 inhabitants	489	106	120
Number of computers per 1000 inhabitants	556	29	37

Sri Lanka

Population (million inhabitants)	19
GDP (US$ million)	16,567

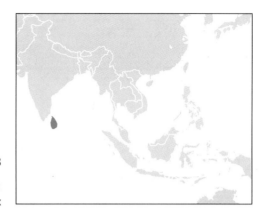

Short-term: **B**

Medium-term:

Coface analysis   **Moderately high risk**

3

STRENGTHS

- The country has emerged from 20 years of civil war between the Tamil Tigers and Singhalese authorities, which left 60,000 dead.
- Sri Lanka's health and education indicators have been far above the average for South Asia.
- Diversification of the economy has been progressing with manufacturing and services playing an increasingly important role in growth.
- The country boasts substantial tourism potential.

WEAKNESSES

- The economy has remained very dependent on weather with agriculture representing 19 per cent of GDP and hydroelectricity producing 70 per cent of the country's energy.
- The international specialization has centred on textiles, a sector subject to stiff competition from China and India.
- Deterioration of public accounts has caused a rise of the public debt burden, whose high proportion of securities has been a source of vulnerability.

RISK ASSESSMENT

The peace talks begun with the Tamil Tigers in 2002 have stalled since the new majority resulting from the early legislative elections of April 2004 took power. Some components of the coalition have been opposed to making concessions to the independence movement. The political uncertainties and the precarious nature of the peace process have not been conducive to a more marked improvement in the economic situation.

The economy has nonetheless continued to demonstrate some dynamism with construction and services posting high growth. If the tsunami of the end of 2004 could have a negative impact on the rebound of tourism, its consequences on overall activity could be limited thanks to the diversification of the economy. However, the size of the fiscal deficit has led to excessive public sector debt (95 per cent of GDP). An adjustment of spending (especially military) and disciplined policy under an IMF programme must be continued to reduce public sector debt. The current account deficit could widen due to elimination of textile quotas in 2005, which could lead to slower growth of exports (half of which involve textiles). Clothing, a very concentrated sector that sells mainly to the American market, could then suffer from competition from countries with lower labour costs. The country's external financial situation has nonetheless not been a source of concern due to the concessional nature of foreign debt.

MAIN ECONOMIC INDICATORS						
US$ billions	2000	2001	2002	2003	2004[(e)]	2005[(f)]
Economic growth (%)	6.0	−1.5	4	5.9	5.4	5.8
Inflation (%)	6.2	14.2	9.6	6.3	6.0	5.5
Public sector balance (%GDP)	−9.9	−10.8	−8.9	−8.1	−7.9	−7.6
Exports	5.5	4.8	4.7	5.1	5.3	6.0
Imports	7.3	6.0	6.1	6.6	7.2	7.9
Trade balance	−1.8	−1.2	−1.4	−1.4	−1.9	−1.9
Current account balance (%GDP)	−6.4	−1.5	−1.6	−1.0	−5.7	−6.0
Foreign debt (%GDP)	60.8	61.8	59.9	55.2	52.1	52.8
Debt service (%Exports)	14.7	13.3	13.2	12.0	12.0	12.0
Foreign exchange reserves (in months of imports)	1.3	1.9	2.6	3.2	3.3	3.6

e = estimate, f = forecast

CONDITIONS OF ACCESS TO THE MARKET

■ Means of entry

With the opening of 80 per cent of its economy (which nevertheless leaves it exposed to international economic developments), Sri Lanka enthusiastically welcomes foreign investment – clearly the key to its development – as it grapples with the problem of modernizing its infrastructure and plant. Its simplified customs tariff structure and trade practices modelled on the UK make the island a fairly free and attractive market.

Sri Lanka is ideally placed to serve as a gateway to the Indian subcontinent, especially since the ratification in 2000 of a free trade agreement with India. Moves are under way to sign free trade agreements with Pakistan, the United States and Egypt.

Numerous investment opportunities exist not only in the agri-food sector but also in manufacturing (seeking greater diversification), infrastructure construction (financed by international aid) and the fast-growing service sector (hotels, tourism, ICT).

■ Attitude towards foreign investors

Sri Lanka is open to foreign investment despite restrictions in several sectors. Its liberal regulations, laws and constitution provide adequate investment safeguards. The country maintains a policy of non-discrimination between foreigners and nationals (investors should nevertheless note the reappearance of the 100 per cent tax on the acquisition of property by non-nationals) and, as a founding member of the Multilateral Investment Guarantee Agency (MIGA), provides safeguards against expropriation and non-commercial and political risks. Sri Lanka has also entered into bilateral investment protection agreements with many countries, including France, which protect investors against possible nationalization and provide for full compensation if necessary, free repatriation of profit and capital, and the settlement of disputes under the aegis of the International Convention of the Settlement of Investment Disputes (ICSID).

The Board of Investment (BOI) is responsible for promoting and monitoring investment. It offers much-needed assistance with a whole raft of administrative formalities relating to start-up as well as numerous tax incentives.

OPPORTUNITY SCOPE

Breakdown of domestic demand (%GDP + imports)
- Private consumption   54
- Public consumption   6
- Investment   15

Exports: 36% of GDP   Imports: 43% of GDP

MAIN DESTINATIONS OF EXPORTS

Mn USD

USA   UK   Belgium   Germany   India

MAIN ORIGINS OF IMPORTS

Mn USD

India   Hong Singapore   South   Taiwan
        Kong   Korea

EXPORTS by products
- All food items 21%
- Other manufactured goods 69%
- Capital goods and transport equipment 5%
- Miscellaneous 6%

IMPORTS by products
- All food items 14%
- Capital goods and transport equipment 18%
- Chemical products 9%
- Other manufactured goods 41%
- Fuels 14%
- Miscellaneous 5%

STANDARD OF LIVING / PURCHASING POWER

Indicators	Sri Lanka	Regional average	DC average
GNP per capita (PPP dollars)	3510	3923	4601
GNP per capita (USD)	850	996	1840
Human Development Index	0.740	0.678	0.684
Wealthiest 10% share of national income	28	30	32
Urban population percentage	23	36	45
Percentage under 15 years old	26	29	30
Number of telephones per 1000 inhabitants	47	106	120
Number of computers per 1000 inhabitants	13	29	37

Taiwan

Population (million inhabitants)	22.4
GDP (US$ million)	281,131

Coface analysis

Short-term: **A1**

Medium-term:
Low risk

STRENGTHS

- The industrial fabric comprises flexible and reactive companies capable of adjusting quickly to preserve their technological advance.
- Taiwan has been expanding research and development efforts to acquire the best capacity for innovation, already benefiting from an excellent level of education.
- The country has benefited from relatively high savings and productive investment rates.
- The various external debt ratios have been satisfactory, particularly in relation to the country's very large foreign exchange reserves (third in the world after Japan and China).
- A consensus exists on consolidation of established democratic principles and practices.

WEAKNESSES

- Relations with the People's Republic of China are still the main source of uncertainty despite the requisite pragmatism exercised by Taiwanese and Chinese leaders.
- The banking sector has remained weakened by the persistence of an excessive number of institutions.
- The public sector financial situation will necessitate tax reform, although financing public debt has not been a real problem.
- The country has been somewhat dependent on electronic exports and energy imports.

RISK ASSESSMENT

Taiwan will have to contend with less robust external demand, notably resulting from an economic slowdown in the United States and China and from a less buoyant electronic cycle. The island has benefited from its good positioning on dynamic technology market segments and the reactivity of Taiwanese companies. Constantly evolving and pursuing relocation of their production, particularly to China, the companies have been improving their earnings performance and solvency as evidenced by their good payment record.

The economy has nonetheless continued to suffer from two handicaps: a chronic public sector financial deficit that will mainly necessitate broadening the tax base and a banking sector weakened by an excessive number of institutions despite progress made on consolidating the system. The economy's foundations are nonetheless still solid with Taiwan remaining protected from market crisis by its enormous currency reserves, much larger than its foreign debt.

After the close re-election of incumbent president, Chen Shui-bian, the success of an opposition more conciliatory toward the People's Republic of China marked the December 2004 legislative elections. Although that situation could rekindle risks of domestic gridlock, it should permit preserving the status quo with the continent, based notably on increasing economic ties.

MAIN ECONOMIC INDICATORS

US$ billions	2000	2001	2002	2003	2004(e)	2005(f)
Economic growth (%)	5.9	−2.2	3.6	3.3	5.9	4.3
Inflation (%)	1.3	0.0	−0.2	−0.3	1.8	1.7
Public sector balance (%GDP)	−4.5	−6.6	−4.3	−2.8	−2.7	−2.5
Exports	147.6	122.1	129.9	143.5	171.1	180.8
Imports	133.9	102.2	105.7	118.6	154.6	164.8
Trade balance	13.7	19.9	24.2	24.9	16.5	16.0
Current account balance	8.8	17.9	25.6	28.6	20.2	19.7
Current account balance (%GDP)	2.9	6.4	9.1	10.0	6.4	5.8
Foreign debt (%GDP)	11.8	12.6	16.0	18.7	21.5	22.0
Debt service (%Exports)	2.0	3.2	2.5	2.9	2.9	3.3
Foreign exchange reserves (in months of imports)	7.8	11.2	14.1	16.2	15.1	15.0

e = estimate, f = forecast

3

CONDITIONS OF ACCESS TO THE MARKET

■ Market overview

The Taiwanese market has no major barriers to the import of foreign goods and services. For the last 10 years, the Taiwanese government has focused on widening market access and harmonizing its regulations with international standards to pave the way for WTO membership. The country's accession to the organization on 1 January 2002 gives foreign companies an added incentive to invest there. Under the terms of accession, customs duties – low in comparison with other countries in the region – will be slashed and tariff barriers dismantled even further. The average nominal tariff rate was cut from 8.25 per cent prior to accession to 7.2 per cent on 1 January 2002, and will be lowered to 5.5 per cent by 2005. Tariff reductions for almost 4,500 imported products will be spread over a 10-year period from 2002 to 2011. The first series of cuts became effective on 1 January 2002. The biggest reductions concern agricultural products. In 2002, their average tariff was cut from 20.02 per cent to 14.01 per cent. By 2005, it will be reduced to 12.9 per cent.

The obstacles identified by certain European firms concern the tightly regulated nature of certain sectors (agri-foods, pharmaceuticals) and the business practices prevalent in sectors little orientated towards export (construction, environment, utilities). Numerous businesspersons point to the inadequacies of the legal environment,

especially in matters of public procurement and intellectual property. Local business practices also leave a lot to be desired when it comes to observance of agreements and follow-up of commitments.

The letter of credit generally valid for 180 days is the most widely used means of payment in Taiwan. To a lesser degree, open accounts are also used for settlements between companies. Instruments other than the letter of credit should be used with caution because of the difficulties in enforcing court rulings against defaulters. Taiwan is neither a member of major international organizations nor a signatory to international treaties and so applies the principle of bilateral reciprocity, especially in matters of enforcement.

■ Attitude towards foreign investors

Foreign companies encounter few administrative obstacles to establishment. Most are engaged in marketing and so look to open a sales office or branch in the country. Those involved in a heavier activity such as manufacturing set up subsidiaries in

PAYMENT INCIDENTS INDEX
(12 months moving average - base 100 : World 1995)

the form of capital companies having their own legal personality and commercial capacity. Taiwan's company law contains discriminatory provisions against foreign-held subsidiaries, which can be waived by obtaining foreign investment approval.

■ **Foreign exchange regulations**
In theory, the Taiwanese currency (new Taiwanese dollar or NTD) has a floating exchange rate. In practice, however, the central bank intervenes very actively on the currency market to control the currency's value. Investors should note that Taiwan's foreign exchange regulations are fairly strict, although the foreign investment approval requirement was relaxed in 2003.

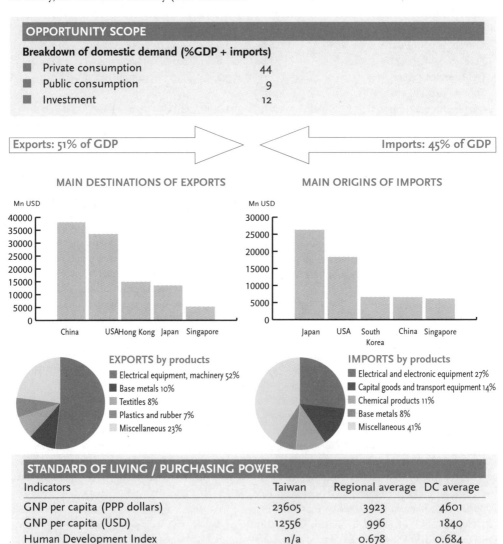

OPPORTUNITY SCOPE

Breakdown of domestic demand (%GDP + imports)
- Private consumption — 44
- Public consumption — 9
- Investment — 12

Exports: 51% of GDP → ← Imports: 45% of GDP

MAIN DESTINATIONS OF EXPORTS

Mn USD
(China, USA, Hong Kong, Japan, Singapore)

MAIN ORIGINS OF IMPORTS

Mn USD
(Japan, USA, South Korea, China, Singapore)

EXPORTS by products
- ■ Electrical equipment, machinery 52%
- ■ Base metals 10%
- ■ Textitles 8%
- ■ Plastics and rubber 7%
- ■ Miscellaneous 23%

IMPORTS by products
- ■ Electrical and electronic equipment 27%
- ■ Capital goods and transport equipment 14%
- ■ Chemical products 11%
- ■ Base metals 8%
- ■ Miscellaneous 41%

STANDARD OF LIVING / PURCHASING POWER

Indicators	Taiwan	Regional average	DC average
GNP per capita (PPP dollars)	23605	3923	4601
GNP per capita (USD)	12556	996	1840
Human Development Index	n/a	0.678	0.684
Wealthiest 10% share of national income	n/a	30	32
Urban population percentage	n/a	36	45
Percentage under 15 years old	n/a	29	30
Number of telephones per 1000 inhabitants	573	106	120
Number of computers per 1000 inhabitants	n/a	29	37

Thailand

Population (million inhabitants)	62.2
GDP (US$ million)	126,905

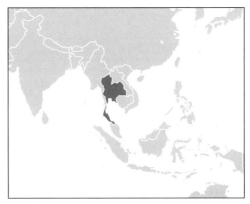

Short-term: **A2**

Medium-term:

Coface analysis   **Quite low risk**

3

STRENGTHS

- The economy has benefited from the performance of agriculture (notably rice and fish farming), certain industrial sectors (food, car industry, electronics) and tourism.
- The savings rate has remained high and external accounts in surplus.
- The foreign debt reduction programme has been actively going forward.
- A regional hub, the country benefits from ethnic and religious cohesiveness and a democratic political system.

WEAKNESSES

- Production will have to move upmarket to overcome competitiveness problems, notably in textiles.
- Structural reforms have been meeting resistance with the economy insufficiently open to foreign investment.
- Modernization of the banking sector, weakened by its burden of non-performing loans, has been lagging.
- Progress still needs to be made on the business legal framework, training and rural development.
- The country has remained dependent on oil imports and the economic fortunes of its main trading partners, the United States and Japan.

RISK ASSESSMENT

The growth outlook has dimmed slightly although an upward trend has persisted for investment and for farm and manufacturing product exports. In any case, the size of the Thai economy, its diversification and international aid should offset the negative effects, notably on tourism, of the tragic tsunami of late December 2004.

Economic fundamentals have remained solid: abundant domestic savings have covered the financing of public debt, external accounts have remained in surplus, and the country has continued to reduce its foreign debt. Short-term debt ratios have been satisfactory, notably in relation to currency reserves, although the baht has remained volatile. However, use of state-owned banks as policy vectors to stimulate the economy could cause problems for the whole banking sector.

As for the company situation, the low Coface payment incident index reflects improving solvency. However, improvement will be necessary in the business environment, notably bankruptcy law, to permit better protection of creditor rights.

Finally, despite the lagging pace of implementation of certain structural reforms and problems involving the Muslim minority in

MAIN ECONOMIC INDICATORS

US$ billions	2000	2001	2002	2003	2004[(e)]	2005[(f)]
Economic growth (%)	4.8	2.1	5.4	6.8	6.0	5.0
Inflation (%)	1.6	1.7	0.6	1.8	2.8	3.3
Fiscal balance (%GDP)	−4.1	−3.3	−3.0	0.9	0.9	0.7
Exports	67.9	63.1	66.1	78.4	94.1	108.3
Imports	56.2	54.6	57.0	66.8	83.8	99.2
Trade balance	11.7	8.5	9.1	11.6	10.3	9.1
Current account balance	9.3	6.2	7.0	8.0	5.8	4.0
Current account balance (%GDP)	7.6	5.4	5.5	5.6	3.6	2.3
Foreign debt (%GDP)	65.0	58.4	48.0	37.8	30.4	26.3
Debt service (%Exports)	12.9	19.3	17.5	9.9	7.9	5.5
Foreign exchange reserves (in months of imports)	5.0	5.2	5.8	5.5	4.7	4.2

e = estimate, f = forecast

southern Thailand, Prime Minister Thaksin Shiwanatra benefited from strong popular support, which allowed him to obtain a landslide victory in the February 2005 legislative elections and become the first head of a Thai government to win a second consecutive term in office.

CONDITIONS OF ACCESS TO THE MARKET

■ Means of entry

In compliance with its WTO commitments, Thailand is gradually reducing import quotas and replacing them with tariff quotas and customs duties, which are fairly high for consumer goods, especially foodstuffs. However, the government has decided to cut customs duties on many semi-finished and capital goods. Thailand's active involvement in the construction of the ASEAN's free trade area (AFTA) has led it to slash customs duties on goods traded with its ASEAN partners.

■ Attitude towards foreign investors

The government's legal reform programme continues apace. The purpose of the reforms is to improve the business environment in the country. Although government rhetoric vacillates between protectionism and liberalization, Thailand's multiple strengths continue to attract investors. The government's investment promotion agency, the Board of Investment, is responsible for facilitating foreign start-ups, particularly in the NICT, automotive and fashion industry sectors, and granting them incentives (total or partial exemption from corporation tax and import duties for inputs) based on sector of activity and place of establishment. The tax exemptions, however, are due to be abolished in accordance with WTO requirements.

■ Foreign exchange regulations

From the onset of the Asian crisis on 2 July 1997, the baht has been floating against the US dollar. Anxious to maintain the stability of the local currency as well as its foreign currency reserves, the central bank only intervenes on an ad hoc basis to cushion sharp fluctuations and limit offshore transactions of the baht. While Thai legislation does not restrict foreign currency transactions linked to the trade of goods and services, it has recently been tightened to prevent purely speculative movements.

PAYMENT INCIDENTS INDEX
(12 months moving average - base 100 : World 1995)

OPPORTUNITY SCOPE

Breakdown of domestic demand (%GDP + imports)

- Private consumption — 37
- Public consumption — 7
- Investment — 15

Exports: 65% of GDP   Imports: 57% of GDP

MAIN DESTINATIONS OF EXPORTS

Mn USD

USA Japan Singapore Hong Kong China

MAIN ORIGINS OF IMPORTS

Mn USD

Japan USA China Malaysia Singapore

EXPORTS by products
- Mechanical appliances 14%
- Electrical circuits 13%
- Computer parts 10%
- Electrical appliances 8%
- Miscellaneous 55%

IMPORTS by products
- Electrical equipment 12%
- Capital goods and transport equipment 11%
- Refined petroleum 11%
- Base metals 8%
- Miscellaneous 59%

STANDARD OF LIVING / PURCHASING POWER

Indicators	Thailand	Regional average	DC average
GNP per capita (PPP dollars)	6890	3923	4601
GNP per capita (USD)	2000	996	1840
Human Development Index	0.768	0.678	0.684
Wealthiest 10% share of national income	33.8	30	32
Urban population percentage	20	36	45
Percentage under 15 years old	23	29	30
Number of telephones per 1000 inhabitants	105	106	120
Number of computers per 1000 inhabitants	40	29	37

Vietnam

Population (million inhabitants)	80.3
GDP (US$ million)	35,086
GDP per capita (US$)	

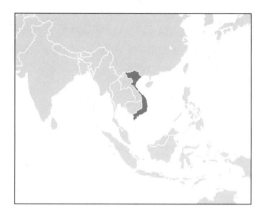

Short-term: **B**

Medium-term:

Coface analysis **Moderately high risk**

STRENGTHS

- Vietnam boasts good farm potential, substantial natural resources and a skilled low-cost labour force, which has permitted attracting foreign companies.
- The reform of economic structures has progressed since the 2001 Communist Party leadership changes, with the country engaged in an irreversible process.
- Private sector dynamism has been contributing to the economic boom.
- Already an ASEAN member, Vietnam's new objective is joining WTO by the end of 2005.
- Vietnam's economic relations with the United States have developed since the signing of a bilateral trade agreement – in force since end 2001.

WEAKNESSES

- Bureaucratic red tape and foot-dragging are still impeding progress on reforms.
- Government debt has continued to grow due to the public sector restructuring.
- The external account deficit has been widening with foreign exchange reserves remaining insufficient.
- Much progress is still needed on improving the country's administrative and legal environment and adapting it to foreign investor needs.
- Increasing social and geographic inequalities could constitute a source of tension.
- Per capita income has been among the lowest in Asia.

RISK ASSESSMENT

Robust domestic demand, buoyed by steady farm earnings and investment, along with private sector and export dynamism will be conducive to continued high growth. Speeding up the transition process has remained a priority. On that score, the country will have to further intensify reform efforts, already bolstered by trade liberalization, in the run-up to WTO admission by the end of 2005.

In that context, the business environment has been slowly improving with companies making notable efforts on financial transparency. However, claims collection has remained problematic.

Meanwhile, the public industrial and banking sector has been the economy's weak link with banks remaining burdened by non-performing loans. The high cost of consolidating that sector has increased public sector debt, which has nonetheless remained covered by abundant domestic savings and international financial institutions.

Moreover, modernization of the economy has spurred the country's imports and widened its current account deficit, without posing financing problems thanks notably to the extent of FDI. However, Vietnam's limited currency reserves, amid deterioration of external accounts, could cause liquidity problems.

MAIN ECONOMIC INDICATORS

US$ billions	2000	2001	2002	2003	2004[(e)]	2005[(f)]
Economic growth (%)	6.8	6.9	7.0	7.2	7.0	6.9
Inflation (%)	−1.7	−0.4	3.8	3.1	8.0	6.8
Public sector balance (%GDP)	−2.8	−2.9	−1.9	−2.6	−3.5	−4.1
Exports	14.4	15.0	16.7	19.9	23.7	26.5
Imports	14.1	14.4	17.6	21.9	26.2	29.8
Trade balance	0.4	0.6	−0.9	−2.0	−2.5	−3.3
Current account balance	1.1	0.8	−0.5	−1.6	−2.2	−2.8
Current account balance (%GDP)	3.5	2.5	−1.4	−4.2	−5.0	−6.0
Foreign debt (%GDP)	41.2	38.2	37.7	36.3	35.2	35.3
Debt service (%Exports)	7.1	6.1	5.4	4.9	4.6	3.9
Foreign exchange reserves (in months of imports)	2.3	2.4	2.3	2.9	2.5	2.4

e = estimate, f = forecast

3

CONDITIONS OF ACCESS TO THE MARKET

■ Means of entry

There is no doubt that Vietnam has been striving for several years to liberalize trade. The first step was membership of AFTA in 1995 as part of the country's regional commitments to ASEAN. In December 2001, Vietnam committed itself to a broader programme of liberalization under a bilateral trade agreement with the United States. The EU–Vietnam cooperation agreement slots in nicely alongside these two agreements to pave the way for Vietnam's WTO accession in 2005, despite the failure of the Cancun ministerial conference.

Vietnam's membership of AFTA is the driving force behind the country's tariff reductions. Since July 2003, most ASEAN products are liable to less than 20 per cent customs duty (with the notable exception of agri-foods and cars). Tariff reductions are due to continue, with the rate of duty being cut to below 5 per cent by end-2005. The finalization of a bilateral trade agreement with the EU (designed to facilitate Vietnam's accession to the WTO) has also led to another round of across-the-board cuts in customs duties. The abolition of minimum pricing is a significant step forward in the process of integrating the country's economy into world trade.

■ Attitude towards foreign investors

The legal environment is in a state of flux. The country's basic law sets out very investment-friendly principles. The Constitution, amended in 1992, encourages private investment and recognizes free enterprise as private ownership of the means of production, with the exception of land and mineral resources. Moreover, the country's foreign investment law, amended on several occasions and most importantly in 2000, is one of the most liberal in the region.

However, the government exercises *de facto* control over investment via the prior approval requirement for all foreign investment projects. The legal framework may be attractive and relatively liberal, but it is incomplete, unstable and ambiguous. Investments in the form of joint ventures are often difficult to manage if the Vietnamese partner proves to be uncooperative. As for the settlement of disputes, in addition to questions of legal process and jurisdiction, there is no guarantee that court decisions will be properly enforced. National arbitration is limited and there is little or no recourse to international arbitration. Yet foreign investment during the first nine months of 2004 rose by 5.3 per cent to US$2.37 billion compared with the same period in 2003. Ongoing investment projects increased funding by US$870 million. The main investors in 2004 were Asian (Taiwan, Japan, Singapore).

■ **Foreign exchange regulations**

Foreign-held companies may acquire foreign exchange from commercial banks in connection with their business. There are no admissible cash guarantees, but the law provides for government guarantees in respect of 'very important' projects. Foreign-held companies may now open a foreign account. In the past, central bank permission was required for these accounts, which could only be used for foreign loans repayments. In addition, a major change in currency legislation has lifted the provision under which companies were required to convert a proportion of their foreign currency earnings into local currency.

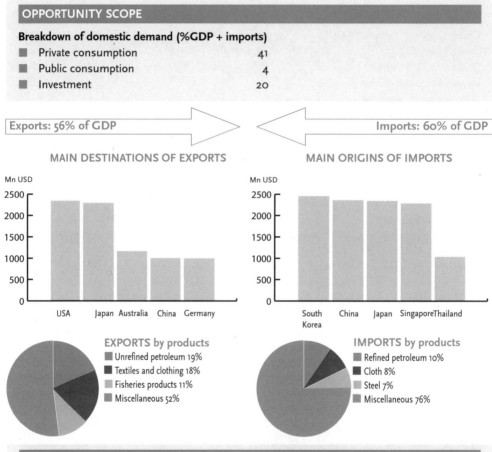

OPPORTUNITY SCOPE

Breakdown of domestic demand (%GDP + imports)

■ Private consumption	41
■ Public consumption	4
■ Investment	20

Exports: 56% of GDP → ← Imports: 60% of GDP

MAIN DESTINATIONS OF EXPORTS

Mn USD

USA, Japan, Australia, China, Germany

MAIN ORIGINS OF IMPORTS

Mn USD

South Korea, China, Japan, Singapore, Thailand

EXPORTS by products
- ■ Unrefined petroleum 19%
- ■ Textiles and clothing 18%
- ■ Fisheries products 11%
- ■ Miscellaneous 52%

IMPORTS by products
- ■ Refined petroleum 10%
- ■ Cloth 8%
- ■ Steel 7%
- ■ Miscellaneous 76%

STANDARD OF LIVING / PURCHASING POWER

Indicators	Vietnam	Regional average	DC average
GNP per capita (PPP dollars)	2300	3923	4601
GNP per capita (USD)	430	996	1840
Human Development Index	0.691	0.678	0.684
Wealthiest 10% share of national income	29.9	30	32
Urban population percentage	25	36	45
Percentage under 15 years old	31	29	30
Number of telephones per 1000 inhabitants	48	106	120
Number of computers per 1000 inhabitants	10	29	37

The Middle East and North Africa

4

Saudi Regime to Weather Insurgency

Experts from Oxford Analytica, Oxford

The continuing insurgency poses no immediate threat to the regime. However, the fear generated by it, coupled with the confidence induced by high oil prices, is leading to a scaling back of tentative reform efforts. Following insurgent attacks in Riyadh, Al-Khobar, Yanbu and most recently Jeddah over the past 18 months, analysts in the US government and commentators outside it question the stability of the Saudi regime.

KEY INSIGHTS

→ Elections to municipal councils will be the first real test of public opinion in decades. If a clear Islamist trend were to emerge, it could tilt Saudi politics even further away from the kinds of reforms outsiders are urging.

→ If there are more than two or three spectacular insurgent attacks next year, it would indicate that the regime, contrary to current indications, does not have the upper hand.

→ If either Abdallah or Sultan falls ill, at the very least, decision making – never swift in the best of Saudi circumstances – will slow down.

→ Average oil prices over US$30 per barrel (OPEC basket) in 2005 should give the regime a comfortable revenue cushion to maintain its patronage networks and dampen discontent. Should there be an oil market crash, with prices falling below US$20 per barrel, the Saudis will face a serious fiscal crisis.

STABLE OUTLOOK

Despite the spectacular nature of the attacks by al-Qaida and its confederates, they pose no immediate threat to the regime:

● The attacks show no signs of mobilizing large numbers of Saudis to support the opposition.
● With oil prices high, the rulers have plenty of grease to lubricate the wheels of governance.
● While family dynamics could change with the death of a senior prince, the al-Saud are currently united enough to prevent debilitating factional infighting.
● Relations with the United States, unsettled since the 9/11 attacks, look to be steady and supportive with the re-election of President George Bush.

The most interesting question in 2005 is whether the Saudis will continue their very cautious efforts at political and economic reform, or take the insurgency as a reason or excuse to scale them back. There will be indicators in both directions, but the overall tendency will be against change and reform.

TERRORIST THREAT

The regime faces a serious but limited violent opposition, either directed or inspired by al-Qaida. It scored a number of successes against that opposition in 2004, killing or capturing 17 opponents from its 'most wanted' list. Those opponents did launch a number of gruesome and successful attacks in 2004, but most in the first half of the year. The attack in early December 2004 on the US consulate in Jeddah, although professional and damaging, killed no Americans and was ended by Saudi security forces within three hours.

If the insurgents are able to maintain or increase the pace of attacks, it would indicate that the Saudi security forces have not turned the corner in their fight against them. However, it would not mean that the regime was crumbling. Islamist insurgencies took years to pacify in Syria, Algeria and Egypt, with much more violence than has been seen in Saudi Arabia. There will be more violence in 2005 in Saudi Arabia, but not enough to shake the regime.

OIL PRICE IMPACT

Political stability is strengthened by high oil prices. With every indication that oil prices will find a new equilibrium above US$30 per barrel in 2005, the regime has plenty of money to spread around. The fiscal situation is improved, some of the government debt acquired in the 1990s is being retired and patronage networks can be well maintained. Moreover, because general economic indicators in the country closely match oil prices, the overall economy is in decent shape, while the stock market has boomed. Long-term problems of youth unemployment and demographic pressures on the infrastructure remain, but the short-term economic picture for 2005 is positive. This reduces the pressure on the government to undertake structural reforms and helps to stabilize the political situation.

AL-SAUD SPLIT?

The most serious threat to immediate political stability is a split within the ruling family that leads either to wider political conflict or stasis in decision making. Although there are differences among the senior princes, they are not of a magnitude to lead to open family conflict. It is possible that 2005 will finally see the death of the infirm King Fahd, but succession should be smooth, as Crown Prince Abdallah has been managing governmental affairs for some time. As long as he is willing to appoint Defence Minister Prince Sultan as crown prince, there should be no significant family squabbles over succession.

POLITICAL REFORM

There will be municipal elections in early 2005, spread out by region from February until April. This is a significant but limited step. Only half of the members of the municipal councils will be elected; the others appointed by the government. The powers of these municipal councils remains unclear. Parties are still illegal, and it does not appear that partisan lists will be allowed to campaign together or that country-wide political trends will emerge from these local contests.

The combination of the fear generated by the insurgency and confidence induced by increased oil prices has led the government to put limits on the tentative steps towards political liberalization of 2003 and early 2004. A number of prominent liberals were arrested for advocating political reform, and those who did not recant remain on trial. The more open political atmosphere of that period, with petitions circulated and greater press freedoms, has been curtailed. With the democratic experiment in Iraq experiencing such problems, it does not seem that regional events will pressure the Saudis to be more open to real reform.

ISLAMIST ALLIES

Islamists are a more important constituency for the rulers than liberals. Separating Islamist activists from the violent insurgents has been key to limiting the latter's appeal. Since 2001, the al-Saud have been very successful at coopting their Islamist critics. However, in November 2004 a number of these important Islamist critics issued a fatwa supporting the Iraqi insurgency and the participation of Saudis in it. This judgment was rejected by the government and its religious officials, but if it marks the beginning of a split between the government and the Islamists, it could presage problems for the government. Although not accepting their view of Iraq, the government will do what it can to keep the Islamists on its side.

US RELATIONS

Although US public and elite opinion has been strongly anti-Saudi since the 9/11 attacks, the Bush administration has worked to protect the relationship from damage, while pressing the

4

Saudis to cooperate more fully on terrorism. Since the emergence of their own violent opposition in 2003, the Saudis have been more forthcoming, stabilizing the relationship. Although the Saudis will be subject to occasional rhetorical pressure from Washington on human rights and political reform, the administration evinces little desire to push them towards fundamental political change. With oil prices high and Iraq a continuing problem, Washington has little leverage on Riyadh. Bush will most likely exempt the Saudis from any serious pressures he may seek to place on other Arab regimes for democratic reform.

CONCLUSION

Despite the inevitability of more violent confrontations between security forces and the violent Islamist opposition in 2005, the regime should weather the year well, bolstered by continuing high oil prices and a steady relationship with the United States.

The Range of Country @ratings in the Middle East and North Africa

Sylvia Greisman and Catherine Monteil

Coface Country Risk and Economic Studies Department, Paris

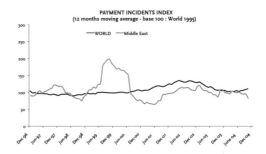

The regional rating is the average of the country risk@ratings weighted according to the share of each country in the regional GDP.

Country @ratings measure the average level of short-term non-payment risk associated with companies in individual countries. A rating reflects the influence of a particular country's economic, financial and political outlook on financial commitments of local companies. It is thus complementary to the @rating credit opinion on a company.

The quality of risk has improved on companies across the region. High oil prices, tourism dynamism, good harvests and, in some cases, a manufacturing recovery prompted the upgrading or positive watchlisting of several countries in 2004. The main changes thus concerned the positive watchlisting of the B ratings for Turkey and Algeria and the removal from negative watchlist status of the ratings for Tunisia (A4), Israel (A4) and Egypt (B). Iran's rating was upgraded from C to B.

Those positive trends would suggest that the expected slowdown of oil revenues and growth in 2005 should not jeopardize the improved company solvency provided, but that regional geopolitical tensions remain limited. The risk level for regional companies has nonetheless remained above the emerging-country average.

Soaring oil prices undeniably strengthened the economic and financial situation of exporting countries in 2004. The large increase in their fiscal revenues, moreover, allowed them to pursue expansionary economic policies thereby spreading the growth to other economic sectors. Companies benefited from more buoyant demand and greater liquidity in stock markets (whose capitalization, incidentally, has remained very limited). Most non-oil countries also benefited indirectly from that abundant liquidity with tourism and an export recovery spurring an economic upturn. In 2005, sagging oil demand and better compliance with OPEC production quotas should slow the growth of the most oil-dependent economies. However, the likely stabilization of prices at a continued high level should allow governments to pursue expansionary fiscal policy. For regional non-oil economies, growth should remain at a level comparable to that registered last year, although Mediterranean textile industries may have to contend with competition exacerbated by discontinuation of the Multifibre Arrangement.

That still generally bright outlook should not obscure the severe geopolitical tensions that have been gripping the region and that will remain a major risk factor notably affecting the social climate and implementation of structural reforms.

In Iraq, the electoral process and work preliminary to adoption of a constitution could further exacerbate tensions in the country due to political, ethnic, religious and tribal cleavages. Until the political situation is normalized, substantial risks of civil war will persist and they could have repercussions in the region.

Regional peace will also depend on the situation in the Palestinian Territories. With Yasser Arafat gone, the new authorities may be able to resume negotiations with Israel and revive the peace process.

Meanwhile, although Libya, by abandoning its arms of mass destruction programmes, has clearly

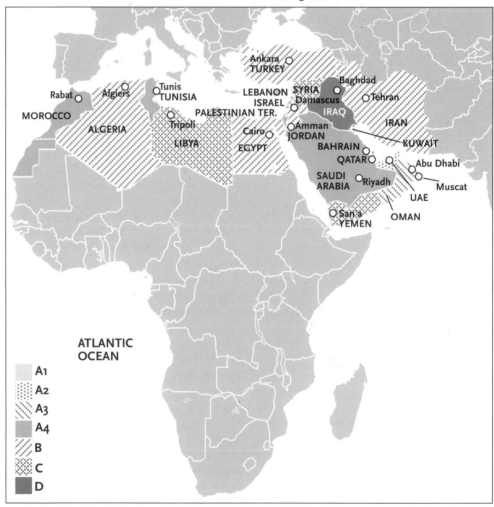

COFACE MAP OF COUNTRY @RATINGS

ATLANTIC
OCEAN

A1
A2
A3
A4
B
C
D

demonstrated its commitment to restoring relations with the international community, Syria and Iran still have strained relations with the United States. With Tehran, the nuclear issue has particularly been a source of concern.

■ Countries rated A2

Default probability is still weak even in the case of when one country's political and economic environment or the payment record of companies is not as good as in A1-rated countries.

Besides its oil and gas wealth concentrated in Abu Dhabi, the United Arab Emirates boasts one

of the region's most open and diversified economies, thanks notably to Dubai's dynamism, which has permitted the country to cope more effectively with oil shocks. It has nonetheless remained dependent on the oil sector with oil revenues predominant in both the fiscal budget and external accounts. The Federation's economic equilibrium has thus largely depended on Abu Dhabi. Politically, despite an uncertain regional environment, liberal economic policy has reassured investors and attracted capital.

In Qatar the economic and financial outlook has remained excellent due to increased production

COFACE MAP OF MEDIUM- AND LONG-TERM COUNTRY RISK

ATLANTIC
OCEAN

Low risk
Quite low risk
Moderately high risk
High risk
Very high risk

4

capacity for gas and derivative industries. The economy should thus continue to post high growth rates. Outside hydrocarbons, expansionary fiscal policy and low interest rates have been spurring consumption and investment.

■ Countries rated A3

Adverse political or economic circumstances may lead to a worsening payment record that is already lower than the previous categories, although the probability of a payment default is still low.

In the Sultanate of Oman, despite increased gas production, poor oil-sector performance due to aging oil fields has continued to impede growth. However, continued high oil prices are still permitting the country to offset the production constraint. Domestic demand, buoyed by abundant market liquidity and low interest rates, contributing to good performance by most economic sectors, should continue to be the main economic driver.

■ Countries rated A4

An already patchy payment record could be further worsened by a deteriorating political and economic environment. Nevertheless, the probability of a default is still acceptable.

Saudi Arabia has continued to reap profits from very favourable economic conditions that have allowed it to increase production with barrel prices soaring. The expected slowdown of external oil demand should slow growth in 2005 with the non-oil sector and public spending then buoying the economy. Stabilization of barrel prices at a high level should continue to generate fiscal and external surpluses with market liquidity remaining beneficial to company solvency.

Meanwhile, regional geopolitical instability and exacerbation of anti-American sentiment have spurred the activism of Islamic extremists and amplified their capacity for destabilization. In that context, social tensions have been severe, reducing the authorities' room for manoeuvre and impeding the reform programme and investment.

In Israel, mainly high technology content exports and increased North American demand have been driving the recovery. Economic growth in 2005 should be comparable to that posted in 2004 thanks to buoyant private consumption.

Insecurity has nonetheless been affecting consumption, tourism and investment. Further out, the country's development will essentially depend on resolution of the conflict with the Palestinians, but the chances for a successful conclusion still appear uncertain. Consolidation of public sector finances has, moreover, remained a major challenge with the accumulation of deficits generating high debt that could undermine government spending in the long term. With the United States' guarantee nonetheless limiting sovereign default risk, Israel has enjoyed privileged access to capital markets.

In Morocco increased farm production, the dynamism of the civil engineering, mining and tourism sectors, along with expansion of public and private investment, have contributed to sustaining robust economic growth. The outlook remains positive for 2005, provided that weather conditions are good and the tourist season satisfactory. In that context, company payment behaviour should continue to improve even if some sectors, such as textiles, may suffer from the opening of the country's borders and discontinuation of the Multifibre Arrangement. External account surpluses should nonetheless persist with tourism revenues and expatriate remittances offsetting a worsening trade deficit. The public sector deficit is still too high, however, due to the extent of current spending and the negative impact on fiscal revenues of reducing customs duties.

Tunisia has continued to benefit from a stable macroeconomic and political framework. Good weather conditions as well as tourism recovery and the dynamism of the telecommunications, mechanical engineering and electrical industries have been buoying economic growth. Continued expansion of those sectors will be essential to offset the stagnation of textile industries, which should suffer from discontinuation of the Multifibre Arrangement. Those good economic conditions have led to a reduction of payment incident frequency, which has nonetheless remained above the world average, due notably to the textile sector's difficulties.

The favourable economic context has also allowed deficit reduction in a public sector continuing to suffer from rigidities. External financing needs, meanwhile, have remained moderate.

■ **Countries rated B**

An unsteady political and economic environment is likely to affect further an already poor payment record.

In Turkey (positively watchlisted) growth is still high despite the slowdown expected in 2005. Renewed financial market operator confidence and multilateral institutional backing have bolstered economic conditions. The public sector financial situation has been gradually improving thanks to continued fiscal discipline. Company solvency and payment behaviour have remained good.

Financially, the country has nonetheless remained very vulnerable to intrinsically volatile market confidence. With the current account weakened by booming domestic demand, extensive foreign currency financing needs have compelled the country to assume massive debt. The growing current account deficit has also generated substantial foreign exchange risk. Furthermore, the increased short-term debt carried by companies has kept liquidity crisis risk at a high level. However, the possibility of initiating EU accession negotiations will be conducive to maintaining confidence and going forward with political and economic reforms.

In Algeria (positively watchlisted), the economic and financial environment has benefited from very favourable oil-market conditions allowing the country to use its production capacity fully, with barrel prices remaining high. Increased oil revenues have provided authorities with the means to pursue fiscal policy supporting non-oil sector expansion. In that context, the economy has sustained robust growth. Currency earnings have reached unprecedented levels, strengthening the external financial situation and contributing to the accumulation of reserves. Moreover, foreign debt has continued to decline. That upward economic trend should continue in 2005 considering the extension of gas production capacity, whereas stricter OPEC discipline may limit oil production.

That environment has continued to buoy the company financial situation. The private sector has remained underdeveloped, however, hampered by red tape and banking sector deficiencies as well as by competition from an unprofitable public industrial sector.

In Egypt, the return of tourism, spurred by the pound depreciation, led to improvement in external accounts and an economic recovery after a slowdown lasting several years. The upward trend of exports, investment and household consumption (spurred by lower interest rates) should drive stronger economic growth in 2005. A decline in payment incident frequency, reflecting increased company solvency, has accompanied the improvement in the economic environment.

Despite that upturn, FDI has remained limited and external accounts vulnerable to the regional context. Moreover, the country has continued to accumulate large budget deficits due notably to interest on a public sector debt representing over 100 per cent of GDP.

In Iran, sagging external demand for oil should lead to a slowdown of growth, which would then depend on the non-oil sector. With oil revenues nonetheless still high, government authorities will again have the means to pursue expansionary fiscal policy spurring domestic demand, household consumption and investment. That favourable economic trend should again particularly benefit the manufacturing and construction sectors. However, the economic support policy based on public spending in conjunction with market liquidity will keep inflation high.

■ **Countries rated C**

A very unsteady political and economic environment could deteriorate an already bad payment record.

In Lebanon, buoyant tourism, a dynamic construction sector, capital inflows and lower interest rates have contributed to improving the economic situation and reducing large external and fiscal imbalances. Moreover, the international aid mobilized at the end of 2002 gave the country some breathing space allowing it to meet due dates and reschedule loans at low interest rates.

4

Sovereign risk has remained very high, however, amid excessive public sector debt (185 per cent of GDP). In the long term, servicing that debt could undermine government finances and generate increasing debt. The risk could become unsustainable if the economy slows down, interest rates rise or Lebanon's main source of financing – namely, commercial banks – dries up.

■ **Countries rated D**

The high risk profile of a country's economic and political environment will further worsen a generally very bad payment record.

Despite the insecurity in Iraq, an oil production recovery drove the economy in 2004. The chaotic situation and political uncertainties were not conducive, however, to setting up the financing needed for reconstruction.

In 2005, excluding debt service, the financial equilibrium will continue to rest on oil revenues, the country's financial holdings abroad and donations from the United States. The debt will nonetheless be unsustainable, even if cancellation of 80 per cent of Iraq's commitments to Paris Club member-country creditors constituted an important initial measure. However, the country will still remain long dependent on international aid, itself subordinate to normalization of the country's political and legal situation.

Algeria

Population (million inhabitants)   31
GDP (US$ million)   55,914

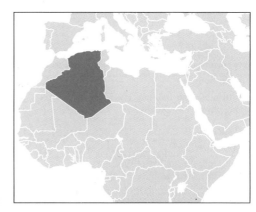

Short-term: **B**

Medium-term:

Coface analysis   **Moderately high risk**

STRENGTHS

- The country boasts substantial natural wealth (oil, gas).
- Considering the foreign interests in the hydrocarbon sector and Europe's energy dependence on its oil and gas, Algeria can rely on Western country backing.
- An oil stabilization fund is intended to permit the country to cope with a trend reversal in the oil market.
- The country has engaged in an economic liberalization and diversification process.

WEAKNESSES

- The economy has remained very dependent on the hydrocarbon sector and, concerning agriculture, on weather conditions.
- The equilibrium of fiscal accounts, strained by spending rigidities (wages and debt service), has been very dependent on oil revenues.
- The high unemployment rate has been stoking social tensions and severely hampering the economy.
- Red tape and the banking system's deficiencies have been impeding investment.

RISK ASSESSMENT

The economic and financial environment has continued to benefit from extremely favourable oil market conditions, permitting the country to fully exploit its production capacity while oil prices have remained high. The increased oil earnings have given government authorities the means to pursue fiscal policy in support of the non-oil sector. In that context, the economy has been posting strong growth rates. Currency earnings have reached unprecedented levels, bolstering the foreign financial situation and helping to build up reserves. Moreover, foreign debt has continued to decline.

While oil production could be constrained due to a stricter observation of the OPEC quotas, higher gas production capacity should continue to spur growth in 2005. This environment remains conducive to the financial situation of companies. However the private sector is still insufficiently developed, hampered by red tape, banking system ineffectiveness and competition from an unprofitable public industrial sector.

Structural reforms intended to diversify the economy and modernize the productive apparatus have progressed little in recent years. The process could continue to lag due to social and political resistance.

MAIN ECONOMIC INDICATORS						
US$ billions	2000	2001	2002	2003	2004[e]	2005[f]
Economic growth (%)	2.2	2.6	4.1	6.8	4.6	4.5
Inflation (%)	0.3	4.2	1.4	2.6	4.3	4.4
Public sector balance (%GDP)	9.7	3.4	0.2	5.1	5.7	5.0
Exports	21.7	19.1	18.7	24.5	31.1	31.8
Imports	9.4	9.5	12.0	13.3	15.6	16.6
Trade balance	12.3	9.6	6.7	11.1	15.5	15.2
Current account balance	9.1	7.1	4.4	8.9	12.6	12.7
Current account balance (%GDP)	16.7	13.0	7.8	13.4	15.8	15.3
Foreign debt (%GDP)	46.4	41.1	40.5	35.3	26.1	22.3
Debt service (%Exports)	20.5	20.8	17.8	15.1	14.2	12.8
Foreign exchange reserves (in months of imports)	9.8	15.1	16.0	20.2	23.0	26.8

e = estimate, f = forecast

CONDITIONS OF ACCESS TO THE MARKET

■ Market overview

Algeria has substantially reformed its customs tariff, streamlining and slashing customs duties (three rates are now applicable: 30 per cent, 15 per cent and 5 per cent) and abolishing the administered prices system. The new tariff, which came into force in January 2002, lowers the average weighted rate of duty to below the 9 per cent mark. Duties are levied on the transaction value in line with the most favoured nation principle, pending enforcement of the association agreement with the EU signed in April 2002. Certain branches of the country's manufacturing industry will continue to enjoy extra protection via an additional duty (24 per cent in 2004) due to be abolished by 2006. There are no special import restrictions, licences or quotas, except for pharmaceuticals, where imports are subject to a commitment to invest subsequently in production. Close to 66 per cent of Algeria's imports come from the EU.

Given the low capitalization of many recently established Algerian companies, the lack of transparency of balance sheets hampers the work of the few audit firms in the marketplace. The most widely recommended means of payment is the bill of exchange and, in its absence, the documentary bill. People doing business with Algeria should check the reputation of their customer's bank. The country's cumbersome banking procedures continue to pose problems.

■ Attitude towards foreign investors

Algeria does not discriminate between local and foreign investment in manufacturing and services (development, extension of capacity, privatization-related buy-ins or buy-outs) or investments made in connection with the award of concessions and/or licences (Decree No. 01–03 of 20 August 2001). Similar tariff preferences and tax concessions to encourage investment are granted to locals and foreigners. Wholly foreign-held subsidiaries are permitted to operate in most sectors open to private investment, including financial services. The law guarantees repatriation of all capital invested and earnings. A certain number of sectors (telecommunications, sea and air transport, electricity and gas supply, mining) have been opened to private investment. As a rule, investment in manufacturing is welcome. Conversely, trade and retail are not eligible for investment. Fee transfers relating to services and intangible investments (royalties, etc) continue to pose problems. Investment in the oil and gas sector is subject to specific regulations.

■ **Foreign exchange regulations**

The dinar is fully convertible for the import of goods and equipment. However, exchange controls are in place for the settlement of service contracts invoiced in foreign currency for which permission from the central bank is required.

OPPORTUNITY SCOPE

Breakdown of domestic demand (%GDP + imports)

■ Private consumption   35
■ Public consumption   12
■ Investment   25

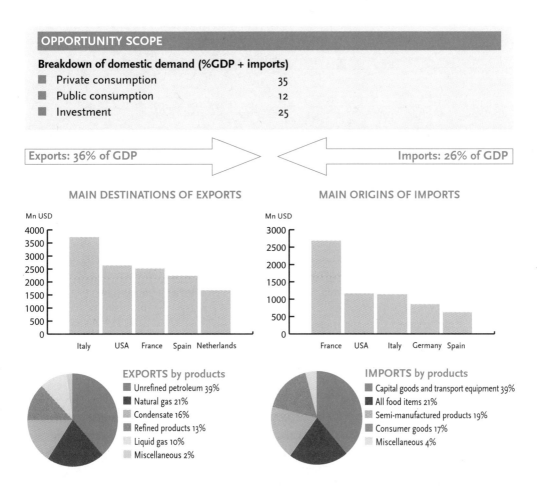

Exports: 36% of GDP   Imports: 26% of GDP

MAIN DESTINATIONS OF EXPORTS

Mn USD
Italy, USA, France, Spain, Netherlands

MAIN ORIGINS OF IMPORTS

Mn USD
France, USA, Italy, Germany, Spain

EXPORTS by products
■ Unrefined petroleum 39%
■ Natural gas 21%
■ Condensate 16%
■ Refined products 13%
■ Liquid gas 10%
■ Miscellaneous 2%

IMPORTS by products
■ Capital goods and transport equipment 39%
■ All food items 21%
■ Semi-manufactured products 19%
■ Consumer goods 17%
■ Miscellaneous 4%

STANDARD OF LIVING / PURCHASING POWER

Indicators	Algeria	Regional average	DC average
GNP per capita (PPP dollars)	5530	6086	4601
GNP per capita (USD)	1720	7569	1840
Human Development Index	0.704	0.705	0.684
Wealthiest 10% share of national income	26.8	30	32
Urban population percentage	58	61	45
Percentage under 15 years old	35	33	30
Number of telephones per 1000 inhabitants	61	156	120
Number of computers per 1000 inhabitants	8	47	37

Bahrain

Population (inhabitants)	698,000
GDP (US$ million)	8,450

Coface analysis

Short-term: **A3**

Medium-term:
Quite low risk

STRENGTHS

- The economy is open and diversified (hydrocarbons, aluminium, financial services and tourism).
- Bahrain has become the region's leading financial centre thanks to offshore banks including rapidly developing Islamic banks.
- The archipelago has benefited from financial aid granted by neighbouring countries.
- A free trade agreement with the United States has paved the way for exports to that country.
- The country has initiated a democratization process.

WEAKNESSES

- With its own oil reserves very limited, the country has depended on crude oil donations from Saudi Arabia.
- Despite its diversification, the economy has remained very dependent on hydrocarbon-sector revenues.
- Foreign debt has been increasing.
- The country's Shi'ite majority has been a destabilizing factor with the Sunni minority controlling the monarchy.
- Rising unemployment has been stoking tensions.

RISK ASSESSMENT

The economy has been posting strong growth and the upward trend should persist in 2005. Oil revenues should continue to underpin public investment spending. Furthermore, low interest rates should still stimulate private consumption and investment. That favourable environment should notably benefit the construction and manufacturing sectors with financial services spurred by a buoyant regional environment likely to continue to drive growth.

Firm oil revenues should permit the country to run a current account surplus. The foreign debt burden has represented a moderate constraint at this stage and the financial situation will be unlikely to constitute a source of difficulties with the kingdom enjoying access to financial markets and relying on foreign investment. A decline in oil prices, meanwhile, would particularly affect public sector finances and impede investments.

In that regard, the economy has remained vulnerable to an oil price downturn with the growing foreign debt burden constituting a source of weakness. Bahrain's liberal policies and structural reform programme have reassured investors. However, regional instability could affect economic activity and the social climate.

MAIN ECONOMIC INDICATORS

US$ billions	2000	2001	2002	2003	2004[(e)]	2005[(f)]
Economic growth (%)	5.3	4.6	5.1	5.7	5.5	6.5
Inflation (%)	−0.7	−1.2	−0.5	1.6	1.8	1.3
Public sector balance (%GDP)	9.9	0.8	−3.9	−2.0	1.2	0.2
Exports	6.2	5.6	5.8	6.6	8.0	8.7
Imports	4.4	4.1	4.7	5.1	5.8	6.0
Trade balance	1.8	1.5	1.1	1.5	2.2	2.7
Current account balance	0.8	0.1	−0.6	−0.1	0.3	0.7
Current account balance (%GDP)	9.8	1.8	−7.3	−1.5	2.6	6.5
Foreign debt (%GDP)	47.1	46.8	47.6	57.4	63.2	70.0
Debt service (%Exports)	3.9	4.4	5.5	5.6	6.1	7.0
Foreign exchange reserves (in months of imports)	1.5	2.0	2.2	2.4	2.3	2.3

e = estimate, f = forecast

CONDITIONS OF ACCESS TO THE MARKET

■ **Market overview**

The Kingdom of Bahrain pursues a liberal trade policy designed to attract maximum FDI, diversify the country's economy and reduce its dependence on oil and gas. A WTO member from the outset and by virtue of its long trading tradition, Bahrain is one of the most open countries in the Gulf. It has demonstrated this on several occasions since 2001 by taking measures to free up trade before its GCC neighbours. These include permission for foreign companies to acquire a 100 per cent stake in a Bahraini company, introduction of anti-money laundering regulations and harmonization of customs duties with the GCC common external tariff from 2003.

Customs duties on imports from non-GCC countries are 5 per cent for all but 53 duty-free products, and alcohol and cigarettes, which are liable to 125 per cent and 100 per cent duty respectively. Imports of goods intended for local manufacture are exempt from duty. Under the GCC free trade agreement, any product with a 40 per cent GCC component is admitted duty-free by member countries. The Sheikh Khalifa bin Salman port, currently undergoing privatization, is a free zone providing duty-free access to all GCC markets for goods intended for re-export and imported machinery and equipment intended for manufacture.

Under the decree of 13 March 1998, foreign companies may use the services of several agents in Bahrain. The country remains the financial centre of the region, facilitating the establishment of financial institutions, banks and insurance companies by means of highly flexible regulations and attractive tax laws, administered by the central bank or Bahrain Monetary Agency. A single GCC currency pegged to the US dollar will be introduced in 2010.

■ **Attitude towards foreign investors**

Bahrain offers foreign companies a highly attractive legal and tax environment, including:

● no corporation tax, income tax, fund transfer tax or VAT;
● unrestricted foreign investment in projects;
● up to 100 per cent foreign ownership of local companies in certain sectors (information and communication technologies, health care, tourism, training, services, manufacturing);
● easy movement of persons (simplified visa formalities, free social customs);
● duty-free access for goods intended for re-export and for manufacturing equipment and machinery);
● possibility for foreigners to acquire land.

As well as these benefits, in 2001 the foreign investment-friendly Bahrain government set up an

4

Economic Development Board to facilitate and speed up administrative formalities. Acting in cooperation with the Business Affairs Department and agencies attached to the Ministry of Trade and Industry, the EDB has set in place a fast-track registration procedure for companies.

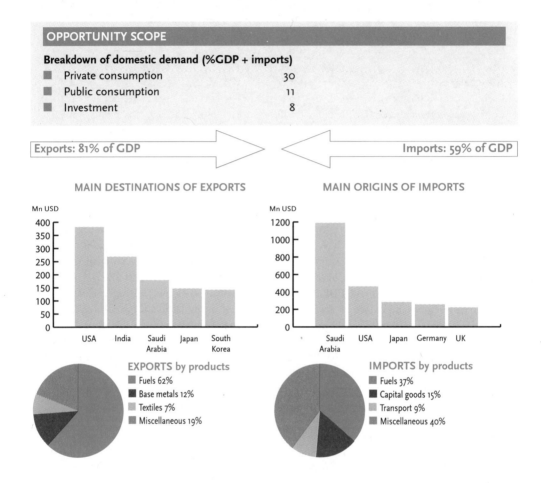

OPPORTUNITY SCOPE

Breakdown of domestic demand (%GDP + imports)
- Private consumption — 30
- Public consumption — 11
- Investment — 8

Exports: 81% of GDP → ← Imports: 59% of GDP

MAIN DESTINATIONS OF EXPORTS

Mn USD — USA, India, Saudi Arabia, Japan, South Korea

MAIN ORIGINS OF IMPORTS

Mn USD — Saudi Arabia, USA, Japan, Germany, UK

EXPORTS by products
- Fuels 62%
- Base metals 12%
- Textiles 7%
- Miscellaneous 19%

IMPORTS by products
- Fuels 37%
- Capital goods 15%
- Transport 9%
- Miscellaneous 40%

STANDARD OF LIVING / PURCHASING POWER

Indicators	Bahrain	Regional average	DC average
GNP per capita (PPP dollars)	16190	6086	4601
GNP per capita (USD)	10500	7569	1840
Human Development Index	0.843	0.705	0.684
Wealthiest 10% share of national income	n/a	30	32
Urban population percentage	92	61	45
Percentage under 15 years old	29	33	30
Number of telephones per 1000 inhabitants	267	156	120
Number of computers per 1000 inhabitants	144	47	37

Egypt

Population (million inhabitants)	66
GDP (US$ million)	89,854

Short-term: **B**

Medium-term:

Coface analysis **High risk**

4

STRENGTHS

- Egypt enjoys diversified sources of foreign currency including the Suez Canal, tourism and inward private transfers with the possibility of gas ultimately picking up the slack for declining oil production.
- Since 1991, the country has been pursuing a structural reform programme intended to consolidate the conditions for economic growth.
- Thanks to reductions granted by the Paris Club, the debt burden has remained moderate.
- With its regional mediator role, Egypt can rely on political and financial backing from Western countries.

WEAKNESSES

- A bloated and not very profitable public sector is still predominant with restructuring only progressing slowly.
- Fiscal spending rigidities (wages and interest on the debt) have been undermining public sector finances.
- Tourism, an essential source of revenues in the current account balance, is vulnerable to regional uncertainties.
- The investment rate is still low in relation to infrastructure needs.
- Uncertainties surrounding exchange policy have been deterring FDI with foreign exchange controls hurting companies.

RISK ASSESSMENT

Resumption of tourism, buoyed by the pound's depreciation, has permitted improvement in external accounts and an economic recovery after a slowdown of several years. The upward trends on exports, investment and household spending, spurred by lower interest rates, should result in higher growth in 2004–2005. With that improvement in the economic environment, the Coface payment incident index has fallen, attesting to improved company solvency.

Despite those favourable conditions, FDI has remained low with external accounts vulnerable to

the regional context. Furthermore, the country has continued to accumulate fiscal deficits due notably to interest payments on the public debt, which has represented over 100 per cent of GDP. Reforms have remained necessary, particularly to consolidate public finances and attract investors. Government authorities have thus been striving to re-energize the reform process. However, political resistance and consideration given to the social cost could again impede pursuit of reforms.

MAIN ECONOMIC INDICATORS (financial year ending June 30th)						
US$ billions	1999/00	2000/01	2001/02	2002/03	2003/04[e]	2004/05[f]
Economic growth (%)	5.1	3.5	3.2	3.1	3.7	4.5
Inflation (%)	2.8	2.4	2.4	3.2	5.2	5.7
Public sector balance (%GDP)*	−4.4	−5.9	−6.9	−6.8	−6.6	−5.5
Exports	6.4	7.1	7.1	8.2	10.5	11.0
Imports	17.9	16.4	14.6	14.8	17.9	19.0
Trade balance	−11.5	−9.4	−7.5	−6.6	−7.4	−8.0
Current account balance**	−2.1	−0.8	−0.5	1.3	2.9	1.8
Current account balance (%GDP)	−2.1	−0.8	−0.6	1.6	4.3	2.4
Foreign debt (%GDP)	27.9	27.6	33.6	35.9	43.8	40.6
Debt service (%Exports)	8.5	8.0	10.5	10.4	9.4	9.5
Foreign exchange reserves (in months of imports)	7.1	6.9	8.3	8.7	7.4	7.2

*excluding donations **excluding official transfers   e = estimate, f = forecast

CONDITIONS OF ACCESS TO THE MARKET

■ Market overview

Wide-ranging tariff reforms were introduced in 2004 under presidential decree 300/2004 of 7 September 2004. The new law provides for a 35 per cent reduction in customs duties on average and a simpler tariff nomenclature. Measures to simplify tariffs include adoption of the 2002 harmonized international nomenclature (6,000 tariff items under SH6 compared with 13,000 items under SH8 previously) and reduction of the number of duty categories from 27 to six (2, 5, 12, 22, 32 and 40 per cent), except for goods such as wines and spirits, cigarettes and cars over 1600cc. This reform is fully in line with the policy of modernizing the Egyptian economy pursued by the government of Ahmed Nazif, who was appointed in July 2004. In fact, the reform goes beyond Egypt's WTO commitments with which it has complied since 1994, when it started to slash customs tariffs. Further reductions in duties are due to be made by summer 2005.

However, actual rate setting is often haphazard and arbitrary and the definition of product categories questionable. Moreover, the basis for customs valuations remains arbitrary, despite the Customs Valuation Act of 25 June 2001, which aims to align procedures with international standards.

■ Means of entry

Numerous non-tariff barriers remain in place, despite a programme to streamline customs organization financed by the EU and USAID. Government departments and agencies are required to meet their procurement requirements through local suppliers for a number of products (telephone equipment, furniture, cars, tyres, bulbs, pipes, etc), as imported goods may be purchased only where there is no local substitute. The merging, in 2000, of the various inspection agencies into the General Organization for Import and Export Control (GOEIS), responsible for coordinating import and export inspection procedures, as well as the approval granted recently to international certification firms, should undoubtedly help to simplify procedures. Exporters and importers can also qualify for simplified inspections by applying for registration on 'white lists'. The commitments contracted by Egypt to the WTO as well as the association agreement with the EU, which came into force on 1 June 2004, should also speed up the opening of numerous sectors in the medium term.

■ Attitude towards foreign investors

Law No. 8/1997 guarantees the transfer and repatriation of capital and offers investors longer-term tax incentives if their businesses are located in a new industrial town or in the high or middle Nile Valley. Plans are under way to privatize a number of sectors, including telecommunications and banking. In connection with the application of investment law 8/1997, the prime minister promulgated a decree (OJ No. 39a of 27/9/2001) on 24 September 2001 setting up a new interministerial committee for the settlement of investor disputes. The committee is charged with resolving disputes relating to the application of the investment act and ensuring coordination between the various ministries and General Authority for Investment (GAFI). A circular issued in 2001 significantly raises the equity threshold for foreign managers and partners of an Egyptian-based company applying for a work permit in Egypt.

■ Foreign exchange regulations

The Egyptian pound is officially convertible. There are no legal restrictions on the repatriation by foreign companies of income and profits, although access to the currency market has often been restricted in the recent past. The depreciation and successive devaluations of the pound (which has lost 50 per cent of its value against the US dollar in the last two years) have not eroded demand for hard currency on the unofficial market against a background of economic and regional political uncertainty. For payments, the irrevocable and confirmed documentary letter of credit is both recommended and widely used in Egypt.

4

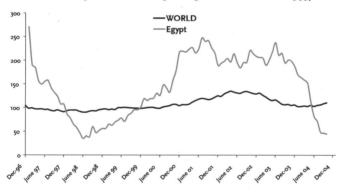

PAYMENT INCIDENTS INDEX
(12 months moving average - base 100 : World 1995)

— WORLD
— Egypt

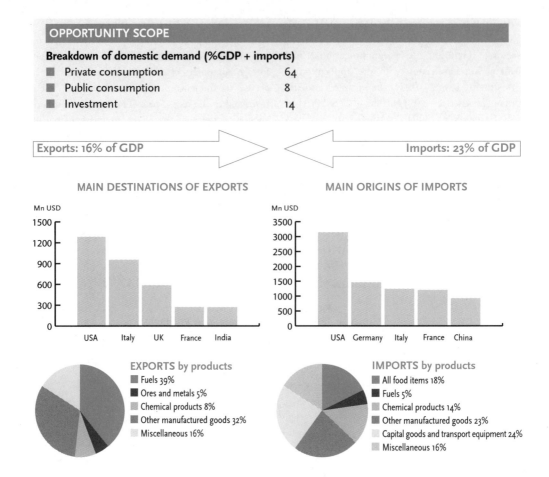

OPPORTUNITY SCOPE

Breakdown of domestic demand (%GDP + imports)
- Private consumption — 64
- Public consumption — 8
- Investment — 14

Exports: 16% of GDP → ← Imports: 23% of GDP

MAIN DESTINATIONS OF EXPORTS

Mn USD

USA, Italy, UK, France, India

EXPORTS by products
- Fuels 39%
- Ores and metals 5%
- Chemical products 8%
- Other manufactured goods 32%
- Miscellaneous 16%

MAIN ORIGINS OF IMPORTS

Mn USD

USA, Germany, Italy, France, China

IMPORTS by products
- All food items 18%
- Fuels 5%
- Chemical products 14%
- Other manufactured goods 23%
- Capital goods and transport equipment 24%
- Miscellaneous 16%

STANDARD OF LIVING / PURCHASING POWER

Indicators	Egypt	Regional average	DC average
GNP per capita (PPP dollars)	3810	6086	4601
GNP per capita (USD)	1470	7569	1840
Human Development Index	0.653	0.705	0.684
Wealthiest 10% share of national income	29.5	30	32
Urban population percentage	43	61	45
Percentage under 15 years old	34	33	30
Number of telephones per 1000 inhabitants	110	156	120
Number of computers per 1000 inhabitants	17	47	37

Iran

Population (million inhabitants)   66
GDP (US$ million   115,800

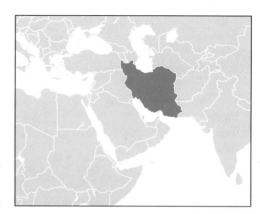

Short-term: **B**

Medium-term:

Coface analysis   **Moderately high risk**

STRENGTHS

- Iran is the second OPEC oil producer and, after Russia, boasts the world's largest gas reserves.
- Structural reforms implemented progressively in recent years, including exchange rate unification, have spurred non-oil sector development.
- Foreign debt has been limited.

WEAKNESSES

- The economy has remained very dependent on the oil sector, the country's main source of foreign and fiscal revenues.
- The constitutional and political framework is still not very conducive to privatization or FDI in some sectors with the public sector remaining predominant.
- Iran has remained under embargo by the United States, which may continue to oppose its WTO candidacy.
- The nuclear issue has been complicating relations with the international community.
- The country has been exposed to regional tensions.

4

RISK ASSESSMENT

Sagging external demand for oil could lead to a slowdown of growth then mainly driven by the dynamism of the non-oil sector. With oil price forecasts for 2005–2006 remaining high, government authorities will still have the means to pursue expansionary fiscal policy to stimulate domestic demand, household spending and investment. That favourable trend is notably benefiting manufacturing sectors and construction. However, economic expansionary policy based on public spending coupled with high market liquidity is spurring inflation.

Despite sharp growth of fiscal spending and imports associated with the economic expansion, good oil-market income should continue to generate external and fiscal surpluses and permit foreign exchange reserves to build up.

Further out, the economy will remain vulnerable to a decline in barrel prices. Notwithstanding the progress made, reforms are still necessary to consolidate the conditions for growth. In this respect the influence lost by reformers may slow the process.

MAIN ECONOMIC INDICATORS (fiscal year ending March 20th)						
US$ billions	2000/01	2001/02	2002/03	2003/04[e]	2004/05[f]	2005/06[f]
Economic growth (%)	5.1	3.7	7.5	6.6	6.6	5.2
Inflation (%)	12.6	11.4	15.8	15.6	14.9	13.0
Public sector balance (%GDP)	8.7	1.8	−2.4	−0.2	4.2	3.0
Exports	28.5	23.9	28.2	33.8	43.8	43.2
Imports	15.1	18.1	22.0	28.8	33.8	36.0
Trade balance	13.4	5.8	6.2	5.0	10.0	7.2
Current account balance	12.8	6.1	3.6	2.1	6.4	3.8
Current account balance (%GDP)	13.5	6.1	3.1	1.5	4.0	2.1
Foreign debt (%GDP)	8.4	7.2	8.1	8.7	8.3	8.9
Debt service (%Exports)	12.1	7.5	3.9	4.8	5.2	6.9
Foreign exchange reserves (in months of imports)	8.1	9.4	9.1	8.3	8.7	9.0

e = estimate, f = forecast

CONDITIONS OF ACCESS TO THE MARKET

■ Market overview

Iran's customs tariff, whose *raison d'être* remains the protection of local producers, has in the last two years been adjusted to switch from a non-tariff to a tariff system that eventually complies with WTO rules. Launched on 21 March 2002, this process has involved the unification of exchange rates resulting, in some cases, to a reduction in duties. It is still forbidden to import non-Islamic products (wines and spirits, non-halal meat, etc). Payments for imported goods are primarily made by documentary credit issued through Iranian banks.

■ Attitude towards foreign investors

The law on attracting foreign investment (FIPPA), passed in 2002, maintains the requirement to obtain government approval for all investment. The sole body in charge of foreign investment is OIATEI (Iranian Economic and Technical Assistance and Investment Organization), headed by the Deputy Minister of Economic Affairs. The vetting of investment applications is the responsibility of an inter-ministerial body called the Foreign Investment Commission. Foreign investment can take the form of direct investment in areas open to the private sector, or buy-back and BOT contracts in other cases. To prevent the creation of monopolies, the law sets a ceiling on foreign operations in the country. The total value of goods and services delivered by foreign investment may not exceed 25 per cent and 35 per cent market share respectively of the sector and sub-sector in question. However, a foreign investor may now hold a 100 per cent stake in an Iranian company. With regard to taxation, the reforms undertaken in 2002 slashed corporation tax from 54 per cent to 25 per cent and offer a great deal of encouragement to local and foreign firms.

■ Foreign exchange regulations

On 21 March 2002, the two exchange rates were unified into a single market rate (US$1 = 8,800 rials). The administered exchange rate has been abolished. Subsidies are now included in the accounts of beneficiary firms.

OPPORTUNITY SCOPE

Breakdown of domestic demand (%GDP + imports)
- Private consumption   39
- Public consumption   10
- Investment   27

Exports: 31% of GDP   Imports: 29% of GDP

MAIN DESTINATIONS OF EXPORTS

Mn USD

Japan   China   Italy   South   Turkey
                          Korea

EXPORTS by products
- Fuels 86%
- All food items 8%
- Manufactured goods 5%
- Miscellaneous 1%

MAIN ORIGINS OF IMPORTS

Mn USD

Germany France   Italy   South   China
                          Korea

IMPORTS by products
- All food items 34%
- Agricultural raw materials 13%
- Fuels 13%
- Ores and metals 40%

STANDARD OF LIVING / PURCHASING POWER

Indicators	Iran	Regional average	DC average
GNP per capita (PPP dollars)	6690	6086	4601
GNP per capita (USD)	1720	7569	1840
Human Development Index	0.732	0.705	0.684
Wealthiest 10% share of national income	33.7	30	32
Urban population percentage	65	61	45
Percentage under 15 years old	31	33	30
Number of telephones per 1000 inhabitants	187	156	120
Number of computers per 1000 inhabitants	75	47	37

Iraq

Population (million inhabitants)	24
GDP (US$ million)	n/a

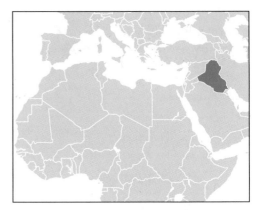

Short-term: **D**

Medium-term:

Coface analysis   **Very high risk**

RISK ASSESSMENT

Despite the insecurity, the recovery of oil production, which has returned to its pre-conflict level, has been the main economic driver. The chaotic situation and political uncertainties have nonetheless not been conducive to setting up the financing needed for reconstruction.

Financially, supposing that debt servicing will remain suspended until end-2005, oil revenues, Iraq's financial holdings abroad and grants from the United States will ensure equilibrium. Once those funds are used up, oil revenues alone will not be sufficient to cover the government's operating expenses, finance reconstruction and service the debt beyond 2005. In that regard, cancellation of

80 per cent of Iraq's commitments to creditors belonging to the Paris Club represented a major step forward. The country will nonetheless be long dependent on international aid, which will remain subject to normalization of Iraq's political and legal situation.

The latter has constituted the main source of uncertainty and 2005 could prove to be a major turning point. Work preparatory to adoption of a constitution could exacerbate tensions in the country due to the political, ethnic, religious and tribal cleavages. Until the political situation is normalized, risks of civil war will remain substantial.

MAIN ECONOMIC INDICATORS						
US$ billions	2000	2001	2002	2003	2004[(e)]	2005[(f)]
Economic growth (%)	4.0	−6.0	−6.5	−21.8	51.7	16.7
Inflation (%)	n/a	29.0	15.0	36.3	7.0	15.0
Public sector balance (%GDP)	n/a	n/a	n/a	−42.0	−42.9	−27.7
Exports	20.6	15.8	12.5	9.3	16.5	17.6
Imports	11.1	10.8	9.4	7.3	21.7	25.5
Trade balance	9.5	5.0	3.1	2.0	−5.1	−7.9
Current account balance	5	1	0	2	−4	−4
Current account balance (%GDP)	22.7	3.3	−2.5	20.8	−17.8	−18.2
Foreign debt (%GDP)	455	550	724	974	588	473

e = estimate, f = forecast

Israel

Population (million inhabitants)   7
GDP (US$ million)   103,689

Coface analysis

Short-term: **A4**

Medium-term:
Quite low risk

STRENGTHS

- The economy is diversified and open.
- Development of advanced technology industries has been a growth factor, nonetheless dependent on a cyclical US market.
- Israel can count on political and financial support from the United States and the diaspora.

WEAKNESSES

- The security situation has been affecting economic activity, deterring tourism and straining the budget.
- The accumulation of fiscal deficits has inflated public sector debt, now exceeding 100 per cent of GDP.
- Unemployment, fiscal retrenchment and insecurity have been undermining the social climate.

4

RISK ASSESSMENT

High-technology content exports benefiting from increased North American demand have been mainly responsible for driving the recovery. Private consumption has also been recovering buoyed by interest rate and tax reductions. In 2005, the economy should grow at a rate comparable to that posted in 2004 thanks to increasing private consumption and despite an export slowdown and reduced public spending. In that context, the business climate has been gradually improving as evidenced the decline in the Coface payment incident index.

The climate of insecurity affecting consumption, tourism and investment has nonetheless been impeding economic activity. In the long term, the country's development will mainly depend on resolution of the conflict with the Palestinians, a goal with uncertain chances of success.

Consolidating public finances has remained a major challenge since the accumulation of deficits has generated high debt that could durably affect government spending. It will depend on austerity measures and a privatization programme, which could prove difficult to implement rapidly, however, due to their social impact. Fiscal slippage and political tensions linked to the implemention of unpopular measures could thus develop. The United States' guarantee, which has provided Isreal with privileged access to capital markets, will nonetheless mitigate government default risk.

MAIN ECONOMIC INDICATORS						
US$ billions	2000	2001	2002	2003	2004[(e)]	2005[(f)]
Economic growth (%)	7.5	−0.9	−0.8	1.3	3.6	3.5
Inflation (%)	1.1	1.1	5.7	0.7	−0.3	1.4
Public sector balance (%GDP)	−0.7	−4.4	−3.8	−5.6	−3.5	−3.4
Exports	31.0	27.8	27.3	30.2	34.4	37.4
Imports	34.0	31.0	31.2	32.3	37.1	40.4
Trade balance	−3.0	−3.2	−3.9	−2.2	−2.7	−3.0
Current account balance	−1.7	−2.1	−1.8	0.2	−0.2	−0.6
Current account balance (%GDP)	−1.5	−1.9	−1.8	0.1	−0.2	−0.5
Foreign debt (%GDP)	55.8	57.5	65.0	65.1	66.8	65.9
Debt service (%Exports)	13.3	17.5	15.7	16.4	12.0	11.6
Foreign exchange reserves (in months of imports)	4.9	5.5	5.9	6.2	5.7	5.3

e = estimate, f = forecast

CONDITIONS OF ACCESS TO THE MARKET

■ Market overview

With per capita GDP of around 15,000 euros, the Israeli market is sizeable. The market offers now and in the future significant export and joint venture opportunities to the vast majority of European firms, both big and small, regardless of sector. The Israeli economy is highly liberalized, with the government pursuing a major programme of structural reforms (reduction of the public sector, reform of the pensions system, private sector involvement in the development of public infrastructure, etc).

■ Means of entry

Israel is one of the rare countries in the world to have a free trade agreement with both the EU and the United States. Similar agreements have been passed with Turkey, Canada, the Czech Republic, Poland, Hungary and Mexico. Except for some agricultural products, goods covered by the major free trade agreements may be imported into Israel duty-free. They remain, however, liable to 17 per cent VAT. A variable sales tax is levied on some consumer goods. Under the Public Tender Act, foreign bidders are often subject to offsetting arrangements that amount to at least 30 per cent of the tender's total value.

■ Attitude towards foreign investors

Israeli legislation contains various measures designed to encourage investment, whether local or foreign. Foreign investment is unrestricted (subject to the filing of an application to claim any existing benefits) except in protected sectors such as defence and some utilities. There are no restrictions on commercial payments between Israel and foreign countries, nor on the transfer or repatriation of profits, dividends and financial receivables, after payment of Israeli taxes. In fact, the tax system has been adjusted for the purposes of foreign investment. However, regulations in respect of foreign workers are now more restrictive. The cost of living in Israel, while comparable to the European average, remains below that level today mainly due to the sharp rise in the euro/shekel parity over the last two years.

PAYMENT INCIDENTS INDEX
(12 months moving average - base 100 : World 1995)

— WORLD
— Israel

OPPORTUNITY SCOPE

Breakdown of domestic demand (%GDP + imports)
- Private consumption   40
- Public consumption   21
- Investment   12

Exports: 37% of GDP   Imports: 46% of GDP

MAIN DESTINATIONS OF EXPORTS

Mn USD

USA   Belgium   Hong Kong   UK   Germany

MAIN ORIGINS OF IMPORTS

Mn USD

USA   Belgium   Germany   UK   Switzerland

EXPORTS by products
- Chemical products 13%
- Other manufactured goods 51%
- Capital goods and transport equipment 29%
- Miscellaneous 7%

IMPORTS by products
- All food items 6%
- Fuels 9%
- Chemical products 10%
- Other manufactured goods 40%
- Capital goods and transport equipment 31%
- Miscellaneous 3%

STANDARD OF LIVING / PURCHASING POWER

Indicators	Israel	Regional average	DC average
GNP per capita (PPP dollars)	19000	6086	4601
GNP per capita (USD)	16020	7569	1840
Human Development Index	0.908	0.705	0.684
Wealthiest 10% share of national income	28.2	30	32
Urban population percentage	92	61	45
Percentage under 15 years old	28	33	30
Number of telephones per 1000 inhabitants	467	156	120
Number of computers per 1000 inhabitants	243	47	37

4

Jordan

Population (million inhabitants)	5
GDP (US$ million)	9,301

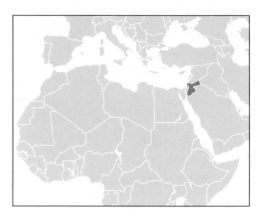

Coface analysis

Short-term: **B**

Medium-term:
Moderately high risk

STRENGTHS

- Development of customs-free areas and a free trade agreement with the United States has buoyed manufactured product exports and attracted investors.
- Government authorities have been actively managing foreign debt, benefiting moreover from successive reliefs granted by the Paris Club.
- Jordan enjoys political and financial backing from the international community.

WEAKNESSES

- The country has limited natural resources (phosphate and potassium) and a narrow industrial base.
- The unstable regional environment has been affecting tourism and investment.
- The social climate has been tense amid high levels of poverty and unemployment affecting a mostly Palestinian population.
- The country continues to depend on international aid to cover its internal and external financing needs.

RISK ASSESSMENT

Domestic demand along with a foreign demand and tourism rebound have been underpinning the economy. That trend has been benefiting most sectors (manufactured products, construction, transportation, hotels, water and electricity), which should permit company solvency to improve. However, the recovery has been accompanied with a sharp increase in imports affected, moreover, by oil prices. That has contributed to increasing the current account deficit despite favourable trends on tourism and exports of goods, notably textile products headed for the United States. Debt reliefs granted by the Paris Club and official transfers have nonetheless permitted limiting external financing needs.

Fiscal deficit reduction and the country's dependence on international aid have remained the main policy focus for Jordanian authorities. That will necessitate a speed-up of company restructuring and pursuit of austerity policy – two objectives difficult to implement in a social context marked by high levels of poverty and unemployment. Moreover, uncertainties continue to cloud the region's geopolitical outlook, which could affect tourism and investment.

MAIN ECONOMIC INDICATORS						
US$ billions	2000	2001	2002	2003	2004[(e)]	2005[(f)]
Economic growth (%)	4.1	4.2	4.8	3.3	5.8	6.2
Inflation (%)	0.7	1.8	1.8	2.3	3.4	2.6
Public sector balance (%GDP)*	−8.9	−8.0	−10.1	−13.3	−14.0	−11.0
Exports	1.9	2.3	2.8	3.1	3.8	4.2
Imports	4.1	4.3	4.5	5.0	6.4	6.7
Trade balance	−2.2	−2.0	−1.7	−1.9	−2.6	−2.5
Current account balance**	−0.3	−0.5	−0.1	−0.2	−0.9	−0.6
Current account balance (%GDP)**	−4.1	−5.2	−1.0	−2.1	−8.2	−5.3
Foreign debt (%GDP)	93.4	86.5	89.7	85.4	74.4	66.3
Debt service (%Exports)	18.4	13.0	14.0	14.5	11.0	9.8
Foreign exchange reserves (in months of imports)	6.3	5.7	7.2	8.8	7.6	7.7

* excluding donations **excluding official transfers   e = estimate, f = forecast

CONDITIONS OF ACCESS TO THE MARKET

■ Means of entry

The banking system is generally solid and is made up of many first-rate financial institutions, which continued to improve profitability in 2004. However, with 24 banks the system remains oversized in relation to the market. The central bank is striving to encourage mergers without much success. Since the introduction of the new Banking Act in 2000, the Bank of Issue has strengthened prudential measures mainly by raising bad debt provisions (90 days instead of 180) and improving bank capitalization. By 2007, the minimum capital requirements for banks will be 40 million dinars (approximately US$56.4 million), compared with 20 million dinars today.

In the hotel sector, where investment has been particularly heavy, Jordan's role as regional platform, especially in the provision of supplies for Iraq, has helped boost occupancy as European tourists return to the country.

Caution is called for when dealing with private Jordanian customers. Although bankruptcies remain few and far between, cases of late payment have been reported. Also, information on the creditworthiness of local firms remains scarce. For example, there is still no system for informing bankers in real time about all the banking commitments of a given client; however, there have been moves towards greater transparency. In 2002, Jordan's credit insurer merged its database with that of the Coface @rating network. The central bank too collates the information provided by banks far more effectively. Nevertheless, exporters should check the credit history of potential customers and gather key information about them from local market sources so as to avoid unreasonable risk.

■ Attitude towards foreign investors

Apart from the first wave of privatizations that saw France become Jordan's leading foreign investor in volume terms, recent moves to open up other sectors of the economy (banking, retail, potassium, mobile telephony) have facilitated the influx of new players who have a stabilizing and market-leading function. The rule is equality of treatment between foreign and local investors. Moreover, Jordan's membership of the WTO, the implementation of a free trade agreement with the United States and an association agreement with the EU together with the structural reforms undertaken to modernize the economy (Amman Stock Exchange, introduction of VAT, intellectual property protection) are helping to bring the country in line with Western standards. The deteriorating regional political situation has, if anything, led Jordan to redouble efforts to attract foreign investors via tax benefits and preferential access to the US and European markets.

4

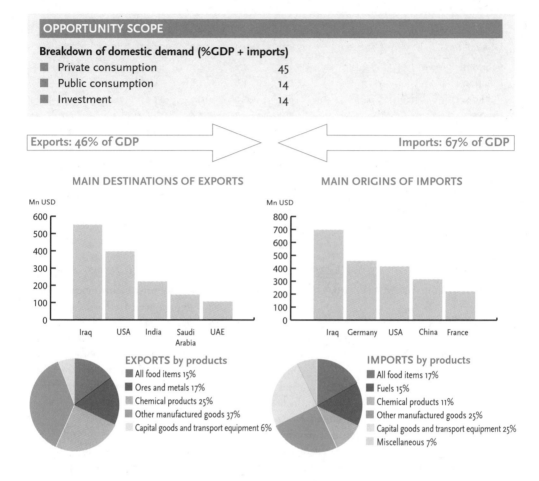

OPPORTUNITY SCOPE

Breakdown of domestic demand (%GDP + imports)
- Private consumption   45
- Public consumption   14
- Investment   14

Exports: 46% of GDP   Imports: 67% of GDP

MAIN DESTINATIONS OF EXPORTS

Mn USD

Iraq   USA   India   Saudi Arabia   UAE

EXPORTS by products
- All food items 15%
- Ores and metals 17%
- Chemical products 25%
- Other manufactured goods 37%
- Capital goods and transport equipment 6%

MAIN ORIGINS OF IMPORTS

Mn USD

Iraq   Germany   USA   China   France

IMPORTS by products
- All food items 17%
- Fuels 15%
- Chemical products 11%
- Other manufactured goods 25%
- Capital goods and transport equipment 25%
- Miscellaneous 7%

STANDARD OF LIVING / PURCHASING POWER

Indicators	Jordan	Regional average	DC average
GNP per capita (PPP dollars)	4180	6086	4601
GNP per capita (USD)	1760	7569	1840
Human Development Index	0.750	0.705	0.684
Wealthiest 10% share of national income	29.8	30	32
Urban population percentage	79	61	45
Percentage under 15 years old	38	33	30
Number of telephones per 1000 inhabitants	127	156	120
Number of computers per 1000 inhabitants	38	47	37

Kuwait

Population (million inhabitants)	2
GDP (US$ million)	35,369

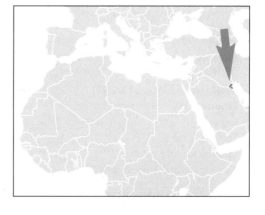

Short-term: **A2**

Coface analysis

Medium-term:
Low risk

STRENGTHS

- Kuwait boasts very large oil reserves.
- Its financial position has been sound with oil surpluses permitting it to amass considerable financial holdings.
- Foreign debt has been moderate.
- The banking system is efficient and well supervised.
- The country enjoys strategic alliances not only with the United States but also with France, the United Kingdom and Russia.

WEAKNESSES

- With little diversification, the economy has remained dependent on the oil sector.
- Despite the fall of Saddam Hussein's regime, political instability in Iraq could affect investment.
- Growth of the working population could jeopardize the welfare state's durability.
- Political cleavages have been impeding reforms.

4

RISK ASSESSMENT

Sagging external demand for oil could lead to stagnation of oil GDP and a slowdown of growth then mainly driven by the non-oil sector. The latter should still benefit from the government's expansionary and redistribution policy that has been spurring domestic demand. Meanwhile, low interest rates should continue to buoy household consumption and investment. Moreover, the economy benefits from increased trade with Iraq. The outlook for companies is thus bright.

With a still high level of oil revenues, external and fiscal accounts should continue to run large surpluses and permit accumulating more funds for future generations.

In the long term, the oil-export income redistribution system will have its limits. The country needs to create jobs and reform a bloated public sector. That will require undertaking structural reforms and privatiztions. Progress could be slow, however, considering the capacity for obstruction of a parliament that has remained conservative. Moreover, the unstable situation in Iraq will continue to affect development of foreign investment.

MAIN ECONOMIC INDICATORS (fiscal year ending March 31st)						
US$ billions	2000/01	2001/02	2002/03	2003/04[e]	2004/05[e]	2005/6[f]
Economic growth (%)	1.9	0.6	−0.4	9.1	4.3	3.3
Inflation (%)	1.8	1.7	1.4	1.2	1.5	1.4
Public sector balance (%GDP)	38.2	21.4	24.8	23.2	27.3	25.3
Exports	19.5	16.2	15.4	21.0	26.2	26.1
Imports	6.5	7.0	8.1	9.7	11.2	12.5
Trade balance	13.0	9.2	7.2	11.3	15.1	13.6
Current account balance	14.7	8.3	4.2	7.6	11.0	10.2
Current account balance (%GDP)	−39.6	24.5	12.0	18.1	22.7	20.8
Foreign debt (%GDP)	26.9	32.6	35.1	34.5	26.9	28.6
Debt service (%Exports)	8.2	8.3	9.1	7.5	7.0	7.4
Foreign exchange reserves (in months of imports)	6.1	7.9	6.7	4.8	4.4	4.4

e = estimate, f = forecast

CONDITIONS OF ACCESS TO THE MARKET

■ Means of entry

Kuwait is a free market with one of the highest import to consumption ratios in the world (90 per cent). In line with the decision by the six member countries of the Gulf Cooperation Council to standardize their customs duties, Kuwait applies customs duty at a standard rate of 5 per cent *ad valorem*, with duty-free admission for numerous imported goods, including pharmaceuticals and food staples.

Per capita income is high and demand for capital and consumer goods disproportionately large for a country of its size. But Kuwait is a much coveted market demanding special knowledge and perseverance, backed by close contact with ordering customers. Companies exporting to Kuwait are not required to have a sole local partner and may sell directly to several Kuwaiti importers. Since the restoration of relations with Iraq, Kuwait has regained its role as a hub serving both the vast Iraqi market with its 25 million consumers and Iran, with its large towns facing the Kuwaiti coast.

■ Attitude towards foreign investors

Since the implementation, in 2003, of FDI Act No. 8/2001, the government has introduced 100 per cent foreign ownership of companies and ten-year tax exemption for foreigners. It has also drawn up a positive list of sectors open to FDI, with the exception of oil exploration and production, which remain closed. Sectors that are open include light processing industries, tourism, hotels, leisure (foreigners may acquire real estate for their projects), culture, information, marketing, livestock breeding and farming, banking (BNP Paribas is the first foreign bank authorized to operate in the country), investment management and securities brokering, insurance and information technology. At the same time, cuts in corporation tax for foreign companies from 55 per cent to 25 per cent have been announced under the government's tax reform programme. Moreover, the government is seriously contemplating privatizing a certain number of public enterprises as part of its policy of openness. Already moves are under way to set up a private company responsible for the management of state-owned petrol stations, while there are plans to form another company to oversee the opening of upstream activities to international oil companies.

The third-largest Gulf economy, with GDP of US$42 billion in 2003, Kuwait is a lucrative and solvent market attracting renewed investor interest due to robust growth, a buoyant economy and institutional stability.

OPPORTUNITY SCOPE

Breakdown of domestic demand (%GDP + imports)
- ▪ Private consumption — 40
- ▪ Public consumption — 19
- ▪ Investment — 6

Exports: 48% of GDP → ← Imports: 40% of GDP

MAIN DESTINATIONS OF EXPORTS

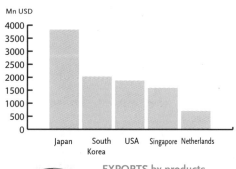

MAIN ORIGINS OF IMPORTS

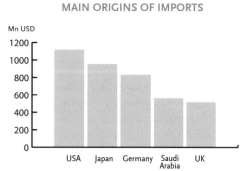

EXPORTS by products
- ▪ Unrefined petroleum 89%
- ▪ Miscellaneous 11%

IMPORTS by products
- ▪ Consumer goods 45%
- ▪ Intermediate goods 40%
- ▪ Capital goods and transport equipment 15%

STANDARD OF LIVING / PURCHASING POWER

Indicators	Kuwait	Regional average	DC average
GNP per capita (PPP dollars)	17780	6086	4601
GNP per capita (USD)	16340	7569	1840
Human Development Index	0.838	0.705	0.684
Wealthiest 10% share of national income	n/a	30	32
Urban population percentage	96	61	45
Percentage under 15 years old	25	33	30
Number of telephones per 1000 inhabitants	204	156	120
Number of computers per 1000 inhabitants	121	47	37

4

Lebanon

Population (million inhabitants)	4.4
GDP (US$ million)	17,294

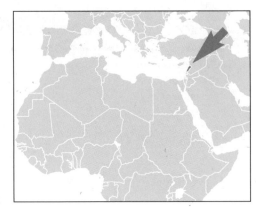

Short-term: **C**

Medium-term:

Coface analysis **Very high risk**

STRENGTHS

- Financial support provided by the diaspora and Arab capital has permitted cushioning the country's economic and financial difficulties.
- Tourism and financial services have continued to play a major role in the economy.
- Despite its exposure to sovereign risk, the banking sector has remained solid, benefiting from abundant deposits by the diaspora and Gulf countries.

WEAKNESSES

- Public sector debt has been very high.
- The economy's dependence on imported products has caused a profound trade imbalance.
- The domestic political landscape has impeded speedy implementation of economic policies that would permit bringing accounts back into balance.
- Uncertainties linked to the regional environment have affected the country's economic outlook and, thus, its capacity to attract FDI.

RISK ASSESSMENT

Steady tourism performance, a dynamic construction sector, capital inflows and the decline of interest rates have contributed to improving the economic situation and easing major external and fiscal imbalances. Moreover, the international aid mobilized at the end of 2002 gave Lebanon some breathing space that permitted it to meet due dates and reschedule loans at low interest rates.

However, sovereign risk has remained very high due to excessive public sector debt (185 per cent of GDP). In the long term, servicing that debt could undermine government accounts and generate increasing debt. That risk could become unsustainable in case of an economic slowdown, interest rate increase or drying up of the main source of financing – namely, commercial banks. Although currently well capitalized, liquid and profitable, those banks are nonetheless still vulnerable due to their sovereign risk exposure. Meanwhile, the external account situation has remained precarious and vulnerable to a crisis of investor confidence. Appreciable debt rescheduling risk has persisted.

Finally, political tensions have been running high. Syria has continued to exercise oversight authority, which the international community has attempted to bring to an end. After prolongation of President Lahoud's mandate, the arrival of a new government team has initiated a period of uncertainty that could undermine the confidence of investors and potential donor countries.

MAIN ECONOMIC INDICATORS

US$ billions	2000	2001	2002	2003	2004$^{(e)}$	2005$^{(f)}$
Economic growth (%)	−0.5	2.0	2.0	3.0	5.0	4.0
Inflation (%)	−0.4	−0.4	1.8	1.3	2.0	3.0
Public sector balance (%GDP)	−24.6	−18.9	−15.1	−14.6	−8.2	−6.7
Exports	0.7	0.9	1.0	1.4	1.8	2.0
Imports	5.8	6.8	6.0	6.7	8.2	8.7
Trade balance	−5.1	−5.9	−5.0	−5.2	−6.4	−6.7
Current account balance	−2.8	−3.6	−2.4	−2.4	−2.4	−2.1
Current account balance (%GDP)	−17.3	−21.5	−13.8	−13.1	−12.2	−10.0
Foreign debt (%GDP)	79.3	79.2	93.0	115.9	109.3	97.5
Debt service (%Exports)	69.4	57.9	50.6	47.5	42.5	40.7
Foreign exchange reserves (in months of imports)	8.2	5.2	6.1	10.9	9.8	9.6

e = estimate, f = forecast

CONDITIONS OF ACCESS TO THE MARKET

■ Market overview

Against a background of political instability and financial disequilibrium, Lebanon is struggling to implement structural reforms, rendered all the more vital by its increasing international exposure (ratification of the association agreement in December 2002, implementation of the Arab free trade agreement in January 2005, WTO accession scheduled for 2005). The Paris II conference held in November 2002 was followed by steep cuts in lending rates to debtors, thereby offering the private sector, which accounts for 80 per cent of GDP, new growth prospects. A 17 million euro industrial assistance package was signed in July 2004 under a MEDA programme.

■ Means of entry

Lebanon stands out from its neighbours by virtue of a highly developed and reliable banking system competently managed by the Bank of Lebanon, full currency convertibility, a free currency market, a dollarized economy and the absence of restrictions on capital movements. In late 2000, the rates of customs duty were slashed from the 6–105 per cent range to the 0–70 per cent range. A new customs code based on the Brussels Nomenclature was adopted in April 2001 in line with WTO and World Customs Organization criteria. The customs service has also adopted an automated customs control and clearance system, which complies with international standards. However, the cuts in customs duties introduced in 2002 for a large number of products have been accompanied by a strengthening of both tariff (rejection of amounts declared and their revaluation by reference to local transaction values) and non-tariff barriers (inspections, etc) in respect of imports. The latter consist mainly of an import ban on some 326 products or product categories, import licences and permits for 261 other product categories, and technical inspections based on changing specifications.

Health regulations, while based on somewhat vague legal principles, are fairly liberal and comply with the recommendations of leading international organizations. All means of payment are accepted, although the irrevocable and confirmed letter of credit (L/C), denominated in euros or US dollars, is the most widely used instrument to guarantee payment of imported goods.

Exporters should note that the central bank requires a bank guarantee in cash equal to 15 per cent of the L/C's value. Late payment, especially in connection with the short-term contracts, is fairly rare. In the event of default, companies usually avoid litigation due to the unpredictability of the legal system and the lack of transparency of procedures that continue to mar the investment

4

303

environment. The problem of bad debt is often sorted out amicably. For large contracts, the best way to deal with disputes is through international arbitration outside Lebanon. Lebanese legislation has provided for international arbitration of commercial disputes since 1983. The reform of civil procedure on 1 August 2002 has extended legislation to include agreements signed with the state.

■ Attitude towards foreign investors

The country has, over the years, developed a legal system that protects the rights and assets of both Lebanese and foreign investors and that contains few obstacles to the establishment of foreign businesses in the country, other than nationality requirements and permits. Foreign joint ventures are automatically subject to common law in matters of taxation, labour relations, etc. They are eligible for benefits under the country's Investment Promotion Act of August 2001, which, among other things, empowers the government one-stop shop, IDAL (Investment Development Authority in Lebanon), to handle and facilitate investor formalities in certain sectors or specially designated underprivileged regions. Liable to fairly low ordinary taxation (15 per cent), foreign companies can also obtain tax exemptions in respect of investments having a recognized economic, social and environmental impact.

On the subject of unfair competition, holders of intellectual property rights are known to face difficulties arising primarily from the slowness of the judicial system dealing with 'economic' offences and the absence of a proactive anti-infringement policy, even though the customs service seems more determined than before to enforce intellectual property laws. Moreover, the decree law of 1967 continues to offer a high degree of protection to domestic sales agents by maintaining the exclusive agency system.

OPPORTUNITY SCOPE

Breakdown of domestic demand (%GDP + imports)
- Private consumption 67
- Public consumption 10
- Investment 13

Exports: 14% of GDP → ← Imports: 41% of GDP

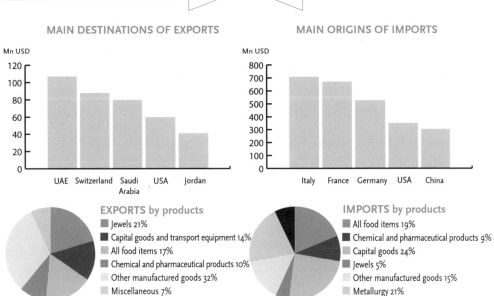

MAIN DESTINATIONS OF EXPORTS

Mn USD

UAE Switzerland Saudi Arabia USA Jordan

MAIN ORIGINS OF IMPORTS

Mn USD

Italy France Germany USA China

EXPORTS by products
- Jewels 21%
- Capital goods and transport equipment 14%
- All food items 17%
- Chemical and pharmaceutical products 10%
- Other manufactured goods 32%
- Miscellaneous 7%

IMPORTS by products
- All food items 19%
- Chemical and pharmaceutical products 9%
- Capital goods 24%
- Jewels 5%
- Other manufactured goods 15%
- Metallurgy 21%
- Miscellaneous 7%

STANDARD OF LIVING / PURCHASING POWER

Indicators	Lebanon	Regional average	DC average
GNP per capita (PPP dollars)	4600	6086	4601
GNP per capita (USD)	3990	7569	1840
Human Development Index	0.758	0.705	0.684
Wealthiest 10% share of national income	n/a	30	32
Urban population percentage	90	61	45
Percentage under 15 years old	31	33	30
Number of telephones per 1000 inhabitants	199	156	120
Number of computers per 1000 inhabitants	81	47	37

Libya

Population (million inhabitants)	5.5
GDP (US$ million)	19,131

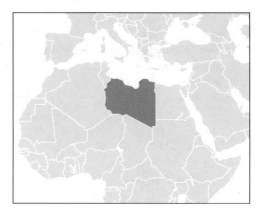

Short-term: **C**

Medium-term:
High risk

Coface analysis

STRENGTHS

- The country boasts substantial natural oil and gas resources.
- Dismantlement of arms of mass destruction programmes has paved the way for Libya's international rehabilitation.
- Recognizing the need to attract foreign investment, government authorities have manifested their commitment to reforms.
- The financial situation has been comfortable.
- Tourism potential has constituted a development focus.

WEAKNESSES

- The unpredictability of economic policy and lack of an adequate legal and financial framework have been deterring investors.
- The economy has been dependent on the oil sector and thus vulnerable to external shocks.
- A bloated and inefficient public sector has constituted a constraint in developing the private sector.
- Centralized management and years of international embargo (lifted in 2003) have weakened the country.

RISK ASSESSMENT

The economy has benefited from the good conditions in the hydrocarbon sector, which have generated fiscal surpluses and spurred growth. The oil wealth has also benefited external accounts, which have been running large surpluses, and permitted Libya to amass foreign exchange reserves. That trend should continue in 2005 with oil prices remaining high.

However, growth has been very dependent on the oil sector, which is vulnerable to external shocks and whose production capacity has remained constrained. The country needs foreign investment to increase hydrocarbon production and diversify its productive apparatus. The choices made by authorities to permit Libya's reintegration into the international community should encourage investors. Structural reforms will nonetheless also be necessary to ensure the transition to a market economy. Although that will take time, the country's candidacy for WTO membership should facilitate the process.

However, the opacity of data has made it difficult to analyze risks with the system's unpredictability constituting the main source of uncertainty. Progress on that score will depend on effective implementation of the announced reforms.

MAIN ECONOMIC INDICATORS						
US$ billions	2000	2001	2002	2003	2004[e]	2005[f]
Economic growth (%)	2.3	0.5	−0.2	4.6	4.9	4.3
Inflation (%)	−3.0	−8.8	−9.8	2.8	2.9	3.2
Public sector balance (%GDP)	9.5	−0.3	3.9	10.3	10.0	n/a
Exports	14.3	12.0	11.6	14.5	20.6	20.1
Imports	4.1	5.3	7.4	6.3	7.2	8.6
Trade balance	10.2	6.7	4.2	8.2	13.4	11.5
Current account balance	9.2	5.5	3.1	6.6	11.9	9.8
Current account balance (%GDP)	26.9	19.4	16.1	23.0	33.2	23.8
Foreign debt (%GDP)	15.3	19.1	29.1	19.6	15.6	13.7
Debt service (%Exports)	6.0	6.1	6.0	5.2	3.9	4.5
Foreign exchange reserves (in months of imports)	25.8	24.3	18.1	28.0	31.8	31.9

e = estimate, f = forecast

CONDITIONS OF ACCESS TO THE MARKET

■ Market overview

Foreign investment is encouraged by the amendments to Law No. 5, which provide for foreign majority ownership of joint ventures in the agricultural, fisheries, services, industrial and tourism sectors as well as in state-owned industries undergoing privatization (cement works, agri-foods, etc). Significant investment programmes have been launched to improve transport infrastructure and equipment (air, land, rail), telecommunications (extension of the landline network from one million to 2.5 million and of the GSM network to 3 million subscribers), electricity production (extension of generating capacity from 4,500 MW to 10,000 MW over five years), oil and gas production and exploration (award of new licences with a view to increasing output to 3 million barrels daily by 2010), large-scale river development (water supply), desalination (installation of 11 desalination plants), environment, radio and television (digitization of equipment and training) and food supply.

Libya, therefore, offers a host of new business opportunities, despite the widespread system of state controls, characterized by cumbersome, slow and inconsistent administrative practices.

■ Means of entry

Since early 2003, licences are no longer required to import goods into the country. However, all shipments must be accompanied by a certificate of origin. Libya switched its customs tariff to the simplified harmonized nomenclature in January 1998. An import ban is in place on so-called 'luxury' and locally manufactured products, a list of which is available. Sales contracts are settled exclusively by irrevocable letter of credit, which can take six months or more to open. The law governing contracts with Libyan government agencies requires foreign suppliers to pay 2 per cent stamp duty on the total value of the contracts (1 per cent for subcontracting agreements). Companies should factor in the cost of this duty when preparing bids. The Libyan market should only be approached by financially solid companies used to long and arduous negotiations. SMEs can usefully engage in ordinary business that does not require funding. Firms wishing to sell goods in Libya must henceforth sign a representation agreement with a Libyan agent responsible for after-sales service.

■ Foreign exchange regulations

The country's foreign exchange regulations, far more flexible than in the past, are overseen by the Exchange Control Department, an arm of the central bank. Since 16 June 2003, the Libyan government has succeeded in setting a single and free exchange rate on the capital market by abolishing the tax on external financial and currency transactions and carrying out a 15 per cent devaluation of the Libyan dinar. The current exchange rate is 1.6 dinars to the euro.

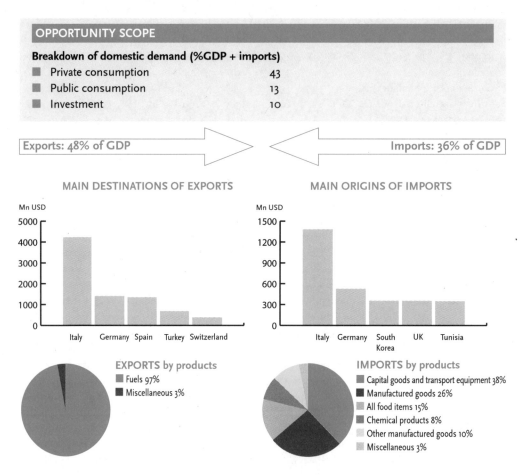

OPPORTUNITY SCOPE

Breakdown of domestic demand (%GDP + imports)

- Private consumption — 43
- Public consumption — 13
- Investment — 10

Exports: 48% of GDP → ← Imports: 36% of GDP

MAIN DESTINATIONS OF EXPORTS

Mn USD — Italy, Germany, Spain, Turkey, Switzerland

MAIN ORIGINS OF IMPORTS

Mn USD — Italy, Germany, South Korea, UK, Tunisia

EXPORTS by products
- Fuels 97%
- Miscellaneous 3%

IMPORTS by products
- Capital goods and transport equipment 38%
- Manufactured goods 26%
- All food items 15%
- Chemical products 8%
- Other manufactured goods 10%
- Miscellaneous 3%

STANDARD OF LIVING / PURCHASING POWER

Indicators	Libya	Regional average	DC average
GNP per capita (PPP dollars)	n/a	6086	4601
GNP per capita (USD)	n/a	7569	1840
Human Development Index	0.794	0.705	0.684
Wealthiest 10% share of national income	n/a	30	32
Urban population percentage	88	61	45
Percentage under 15 years old	33	33	30
Number of telephones per 1000 inhabitants	118	156	120
Number of computers per 1000 inhabitants	23	47	37

Morocco

Population (million inhabitants)	30
GDP (US$ million)	36,093

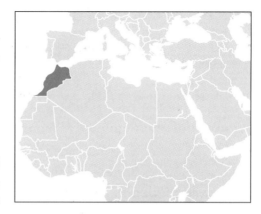

Coface analysis

Short-term: **A4**

Medium-term:
Moderately high risk

STRENGTHS

- The country's economic potential and the significant progress made on structural reforms (privatizations, banking reform, the labour code) have been attracting investors.
- The investment rate, both public and private, has permitted progressively diversifying the economy.
- Morocco has benefited from its political, economic and financial proximity to the EU and from support by financial backers.
- Its external constraint has been moderate.

WEAKNESSES

- The Moroccan economy has remained too dependent on farming (16 per cent of GDP, 40 per cent of the working population) and, thus, on weather conditions.
- The public sector financial situation has been delicate.
- Demographic pressure, the unemployment rate and high poverty (especially among the young) could exacerbate social tensions and will constitute a major challenge for the government.
- The unresolved West Sahara problem has continued to affect relations with Algeria and other African countries.

4

RISK ASSESSMENT

Increased farm production, the dynamism of the civil engineering, mineral and tourism sectors, and expansion of public and private investment have contributed to sustaining robust growth. The outlook has remained positive for 2005 provided weather conditions are good and the tourist season satisfactory. External account surpluses have persisted with tourism revenues and inward expatriate transfers permitting Morocco to offset a widening trade deficit.

In that context, the country's financing needs have been limited, which has permitted reducing the foreign debt burden. However, the public sector financial deficit has remained excessive due to the extent of current spending and negative impact of

reduced customs duties on fiscal revenues. With that deficit largely covered by recourse to borrowing, domestic debt has tended to increase, which has ultimately reduced the authorities' fiscal leeway.

However, fiscal room for manoeuvre will be essential to speed up the economy's modernization with growth remaining insufficient to reduce unemployment and poverty, which could exacerbate social tensions and spur political extremism. Such tensions would moreover have a negative impact on FDI and tourism revenues and undermine the country's stability.

The steady economic conditions have contributed to improvement in company solvency and the payment incident index has moved

MAIN ECONOMIC INDICATORS

US$ billions	2000	2001	2002	2003	2004(e)	2005(f)
Economic growth (%)	1.0	6.3	3.2	5.2	4.8	4.7
Inflation (%)	1.9	0.6	2.8	1.2	2.0	2.0
Public sector balance (%GDP)	−6.4	−11.1	−4.5	−5.7	−5.7	−5.0
Exports	7.4	7.1	7.8	8.7	9.6	10.4
Imports	10.7	10.2	10.9	13.0	14.9	16.4
Trade balance	−3.2	−3.0	−3.1	−4.3	−5.4	−6.0
Current account balance	−0.5	1.6	1.5	1.3	0.9	0.6
Current account balance (%GDP)	−1.4	4.7	4.1	2.9	1.8	1.1
Foreign debt (%GDP)	55	50	47	39	33	31
Debt service (%Exports)	17.1	16.0	17.1	18.1	12.3	11.0
Foreign exchange reserves (in months of imports)	4.2	7.6	8.4	8.8	9.5	9.3

e = estimate, f = forecast

significantly close to the world average. Certain sectors, like textiles, could suffer from the opening of the borders and the end of the Multifibre Arrangement in January 2005.

CONDITIONS OF ACCESS TO THE MARKET

■ Market overview

Customs duties range from 0 to 50 per cent. Tariff peaks remain in place for agriculture and agri-foods, in particular food staples. *Ad valorem* customs duty can be as high as 376 per cent. Variable customs duty can be levied on some farm products. Five years on from the implementation of the association agreement with the EU on 1 March 2000, zero-rated customs duty is applied to half the tariff categories (raw materials, spare parts, inputs and goods not produced in Morocco). Under this agreement, a free trade area is due to be established by 2012.

The last few years have seen wide-ranging reforms aimed at stabilizing the business environment. The measures include a new Trade Code (1996); an SA (public limited company) law (in force since 2001); a SARL (private limited liability company) Partnership and Joint Venture Law (1997); new government procurement legislation modelled on the French code (1998); a new Customs Code (2000) that crowns the modernization programme so ably conducted by the government; a Competition and Price Act; an Intellectual and Industrial Property Protection Act,

due to come into force on 18 December 2004; and a Literary and Artistic Property Act, in force since 1 January 2001. After a lengthy committee stage, the Insurance Bill was passed by parliament in November 2002 pending enactment of its implementing decrees. Finally, the labour law has been reformed, with a new labour code coming into force in June 2004.

■ Attitude towards foreign investors

The setting up of sixteen regional investment centres (CRI), overseen by *walis* (prefects), significantly simplifies start-up procedures by offering a one-stop shop to investors. Long awaited by the business community, this measure shortens start-up formalities to under a week. The general provisions of the investment charter are also quite favourable.

PAYMENT INCIDENTS INDEX
(12 months moving average - base 100 : World 1995)

■ **Foreign exchange regulations**

A supervised foreign exchange market remains in place. The exchange rate is set by the central bank, Bank Al Maghrib, on the basis of a basket of currencies. A currency convertibility system, set up in 1992, encourages hard currency investment in Morocco by guaranteeing profit repatriation.

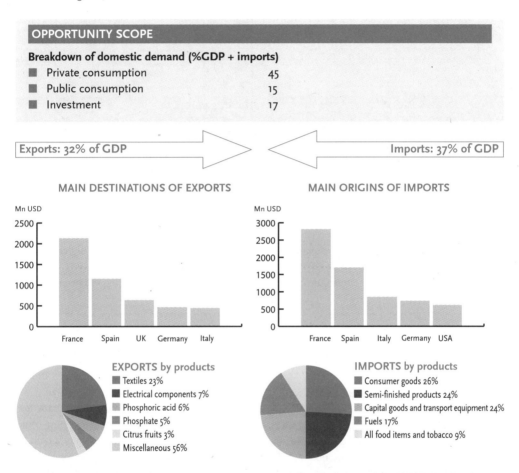

OPPORTUNITY SCOPE

Breakdown of domestic demand (%GDP + imports)
- ■ Private consumption   45
- ■ Public consumption   15
- ■ Investment   17

Exports: 32% of GDP   Imports: 37% of GDP

MAIN DESTINATIONS OF EXPORTS

Mn USD

France, Spain, UK, Germany, Italy

MAIN ORIGINS OF IMPORTS

Mn USD

France, Spain, Italy, Germany, USA

EXPORTS by products
- ■ Textiles 23%
- ■ Electrical components 7%
- Phosphoric acid 6%
- Phosphate 5%
- Citrus fruits 3%
- Miscellaneous 56%

IMPORTS by products
- ■ Consumer goods 26%
- ■ Semi-finished products 24%
- Capital goods and transport equipment 24%
- ■ Fuels 17%
- All food items and tobacco 9%

STANDARD OF LIVING / PURCHASING POWER

Indicators	Morocco	Regional average	DC average
GNP per capita (PPP dollars)	3730	6086	4601
GNP per capita (USD)	1170	7569	1840
Human Development Index	0.620	0.705	0.684
Wealthiest 10% share of national income	30.9	30	32
Urban population percentage	57	61	45
Percentage under 15 years old	34	33	30
Number of telephones per 1000 inhabitants	38	156	120
Number of computers per 1000 inhabitants	24	47	37

4

Oman

Population (million inhabitants)	2.5
GDP (US$ million)	20,309

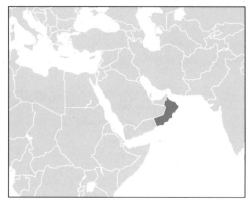

Coface analysis

Short-term: **A3**

Medium-term:
Quite low risk

STRENGTHS

- The country enjoys natural wealth (gas and oil) but with relatively limited reserves.
- The economy is diversified (gas, petrochemicals, aluminium, tourism) and open to domestic or foreign private investment.
- The country holds financial assets abroad managed in a reserve fund for future generations.
- Foreign debt has remained limited.

WEAKNESSES

- Despite diversification, the economy is still dependent on oil revenues and vulnerable to a drop in barrel prices and declining crude production capacity.
- Oil production costs have been high due to the age of the oil fields.
- Wage and defence spending has been straining public accounts.
- Outward transfers by foreign labour have been undermining the invisibles balance.

RISK ASSESSMENT

Despite increased gas production, the oil sector's poor performance due to the ageing of crude extraction fields has continued to hamper growth. High oil prices, nonetheless, still permit offsetting the production constraint. Economic activity should thus continue to depend mainly on domestic demand buoyed by abundant market liquidity and low interest rates, which have contributed to the good performance of most economic sectors.

The external financial situation should continue to benefit from steady foreign currency earnings with the debt burden remaining moderate. However, the growth of investment spending could have a negative effect on public accounts should oil prices decline with fiscal revenue sources still not very diversified. Politically, the situation has been stable despite continuing uncertainty about the succession of Sultan Qaboos.

MAIN ECONOMIC INDICATORS

US$ billions	2000	2001	2002	2003	2004[(e)]	2005[(f)]
Economic growth (%)	5.5	7.5	1.7	1.4	2.5	3.6
Inflation (%)	−1.1	−1.0	−0.7	−0.4	−0.1	−0.2
Public balance (%GDP)	9.3	3.4	3.1	5.0	4.2	0.0
Exports	11.3	11.1	11.2	11.7	13.5	13.2
Imports	4.6	5.3	5.6	6.1	6.8	7.3
Trade balance	6.7	5.8	5.5	5.6	6.7	5.9
Current account balance	3.4	2.0	1.8	1.4	2.3	1.2
Current account balance (%GDP)	16.9	10.0	8.7	6.7	9.8	5.0
Foreign debt (%GDP)	29.9	27.1	22.3	19.5	22.2	26.6
Debt service (%Exports)	7.2	14.3	11.3	10.6	9.3	9.3
Foreign exchange reserves (in months of imports)	3.3	2.9	3.8	3.9	4.0	4.0

e = estimate, f = forecast

4

CONDITIONS OF ACCESS TO THE MARKET

■ Market overview

Oman remains highly dependent on the oil sector. The government continues to pursue its five-year plan, which focuses on economic diversification via industrial development, in particular the development of natural gas as a source of energy or raw material for large-scale industrial schemes and the promotion of the private sector's role in the economy through privatization of state-owned companies and utilities. The last plank of government policy concerns the Omanization of jobs.

■ Means of entry

For private contracts, exporters of consumer goods that do not demand any after-sales service are not required to have a local agent. For public tenders open to foreign companies, the foreign supplier must have a local office or be represented by an Omani company. General customs duty for the majority of products is 5 per cent of the CIF value. However, a prior licence is mandatory for some products on grounds of health, religion or protection of local manufacture. There are no exchange controls and foreign currency may be sold freely. There are no restrictions on the transfer of corporate profits and no barriers to the free movement of capital.

■ Attitude towards foreign investors

Omani legislation tends to encourage foreign investment but has kept in place a number of restrictions in order to channel funds into industrial and infrastructure projects, especially those linked to the country's privatization programme. As a result, foreigners can now acquire a stake in manufacturing, trading and service companies, whereas in the past they were rarely allowed to own shares in the last two. From 2000, foreign companies that have operated for more than ten years and possess at least three foreign subsidiaries may open a local sales office without local sponsorship.

Tax incentive schemes have been introduced to reduce discrimination against foreign companies and encourage local companies to open their capital to foreigners.

OPPORTUNITY SCOPE

Breakdown of domestic demand (%GDP + imports)

- Private consumption — 32
- Public consumption — 17
- Investment — 10

Exports: 57% of GDP → ← Imports: 50% of GDP

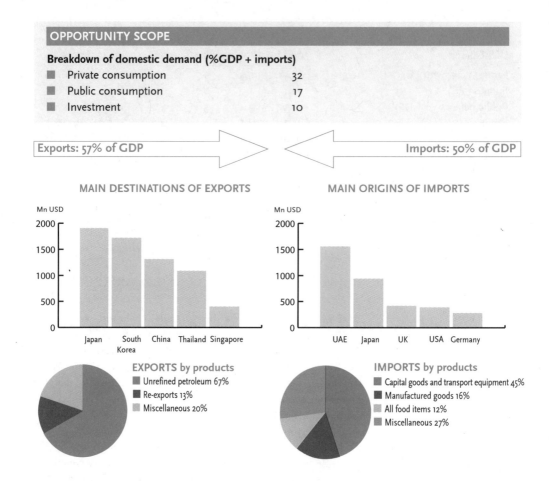

MAIN DESTINATIONS OF EXPORTS

Mn USD

Japan, South Korea, China, Thailand, Singapore

MAIN ORIGINS OF IMPORTS

Mn USD

UAE, Japan, UK, USA, Germany

EXPORTS by products
- Unrefined petroleum 67%
- Re-exports 13%
- Miscellaneous 20%

IMPORTS by products
- Capital goods and transport equipment 45%
- Manufactured goods 16%
- All food items 12%
- Miscellaneous 27%

STANDARD OF LIVING / PURCHASING POWER

Indicators	Oman	Regional average	DC average
GNP per capita (PPP dollars)	13000	6086	4601
GNP per capita (USD)	7830	7569	1840
Human Development Index	0.770	0.705	0.684
Wealthiest 10% share of national income	n/a	30	32
Urban population percentage	77	61	45
Percentage under 15 years old	42	33	30
Number of telephones per 1000 inhabitants	84	156	120
Number of computers per 1000 inhabitants	35	47	37

Palestinian Territories

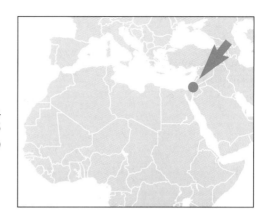

Population (million inhabitants)	3.4
GDP (US$ million)	3,396
GDP per capita	999

Coface analysis

RISK ASSESSMENT

The economy, which collapsed after the launching of the Intifada in September 2000, has been running at a slow pace. Travel difficulties, jobs lost in Israel and insecurity have been impeding economic activity and deterring investment. Donor countries have thus reduced aid for infrastructure and development projects. In that context, the unemployment rate has remained high with strong demographic growth tending to exacerbate deterioration of the standard of living. Nearly half of the population has been living below the poverty line. The administration is the largest employer, but the growth of spending on wages has been generating large fiscal deficits despite resumption since 2003 of payment of taxes collected by Israel. International community donations, recalibrated as emergency fiscal aid, have been recently covering those deficits.

Although that situation will not be sustainable, an economic recovery and reconstruction of the Territories will depend on an easing of tensions and the authorities' capacity to resume peace negotiations with Israel.

4

MAIN ECONOMIC INDICATORS						
US$ billions	1999	2000	2001	2002	2003	2004[e]
Economic growth (%)	8.9	−5.6	−14.8	−10.1	6.1	1.6
Inflation (%)	5.5	2.8	1.2	5.7	4.4	3.0
Public sector balance (%GDP)	−5.3	6.6	−25.4	−24.4	−18.0	−19.0
Unemployment rate (%)	11.9	14.5	25.5	31.4	25.7	28.7
Exports	3.8	3.4	3.2	2.8	3.0	n/a
Imports	0.9	0.9	0.5	0.4	0.5	n/a
Trade balance	−2.9	−2.5	−2.7	−2.4	−2.5	n/a
Current account balance (%GDP)	−34.9	−25.2	−23.4	−5.6	n/a	n/a

315

e = estimate

Qatar

Population (inhabitants)	710,000
GDP (US$ million)	18,700

Short-term: **A2**

Medium-term:

Coface analysis   **Low risk**

STRENGTHS

- Immense gas resources (Qatar's reserves rank third in the world) represent substantial development potential.
- Diversification toward high-energy content export industries (steel and petrochemicals) has continued.
- The emirate has benefited from backing by the United States.

WEAKNESSES

- Financing gas and industrial projects has generated heavy foreign debt with the resulting constraint nonetheless appearing less severe in relation to the size of the economy and currency earnings.
- Fiscal revenues have remained very dependent on oil market conditions.
- Statistical data have tended to lack transparency.

RISK ASSESSMENT

Qatar's investment strategy has borne fruit. Rising living standards and the options pursued by the government in undertaking a process of economic liberalization and democratization have been fostering political stability and an investment-friendly environment despite regional geopolitical uncertainties. In that regard, the presence of the US army has been guaranteeing the country's protection.

The economic and financial outlook has remained excellent, thanks to the increased production capacity of gas and derivative industries. The economy should thus continue to post high growth rates. Outside the hydrocarbon sector, expansionary fiscal policy and low interest rates will buoy consumption and investment.

Despite increased spending, public sector accounts should remain in surplus thanks to steady oil revenues. The country should also consolidate its external financial situation with large current account surpluses, allowing it to cover its financing needs and accumulate foreign exchange reserves and financial assets.

MAIN ECONOMIC INDICATORS

US$ billions	2000	2001	2002	2003	2004[(e)]	2005[(f)]
Economic growth (%)	9.3	6.8	5.7	5.2	7.0	7.3
Inflation (%)	1.7	1.5	0.2	2.3	2.8	2.0
Public sector balance (%GDP)	8.0	3.5	8.5	10.1	11.4	9.6
Exports	11.1	11.4	11.4	13.6	17.9	19.5
Imports	4.1	4.6	4.7	5.5	6.3	7.2
Trade balance	7.0	6.8	6.7	8.1	11.6	12.3
Current account balance	3.1	3.5	3.4	5.7	8.9	9.2
Current account balance (%GDP)	17.7	20.5	18.0	26.5	34.2	33.5
Foreign debt (%GDP)	91.7	86.0	79.0	62.0	59.1	61.0
Debt service (%Exports)	14.7	17.7	19.8	16.0	10.3	10.4
Foreign exchange reserves (in months of imports)	1.6	1.7	2.0	3.4	3.0	3.0

e = estimate, f = forecast

CONDITIONS OF ACCESS TO THE MARKET

■ Market overview

The Qatari market is free and open to trade, except for imports of live cattle and bovine products of European origin (due to the BSE crisis). Other imported goods are governed by rules of origin that vary from country to country. The distribution and marketing of imported goods is subject to a local sponsorship requirement, except in the case of public tenders. Trademark and intellectual property protection legislation is relatively recent. Qatar has been a signatory to the Geneva Convention (industrial property) and the Bern Convention (intellectual property) only since 5 July 2000. Consequently, the country still lacks the means to enforce and implement this legislation on a systematic basis.

■ Means of entry

Since 1 January 2003, all goods are liable to 5 per cent *ad valorem* duty under the GCC customs union, except for products directly competing with local manufacture (steel: 20 per cent), products taxed on grounds of health (cigarettes: 100 per cent) or those banned by Islam (wines and spirits: 100 per cent). Exporters are advised to demand an irrevocable and confirmed letter of credit, the most widely used means of payment in Qatar, for transactions with local customers.

■ Attitude towards foreign investors

Regulations governing foreign investment were relaxed under a new law passed on 16 October 2000. Foreign investors are now permitted to own 100 per cent of a company in the agricultural, manufacturing, healthcare, education, tourism and energy sectors, subject to the approval of the Ministry of Economic Affairs and Trade. The only precondition is that the foreign investment complies with the government's development plans. Sectors falling outside the scope of this legislation include banking, insurance, property and retail. Foreigners investing in these sectors are required to have a majority Qatari partner who holds at least a 51 per cent stake. Foreign investors may acquire leaseholds of up to 50 years, which are renewable, but are barred from acquiring freehold property except in the building complex under construction on the artificial island known as Pearl Island.

Disputes between foreign investors and local parties are brought before local or international arbitration. Foreigners are required to have a Qatari sponsor when applying for a residence permit linked to a work permit. Moves are under way to open foreign access to the Doha Stock Exchange via

4

mutual funds, following the announcement by the government on 1 July 2003 to allow foreigners to own up to 25 per cent of listed companies. The Ministry of Finance, Economic Affairs and Trade grants wholly foreign-funded projects ten-year tax relief, together with exemption from customs duties for imported equipment, raw materials and semi-finished goods not available locally.

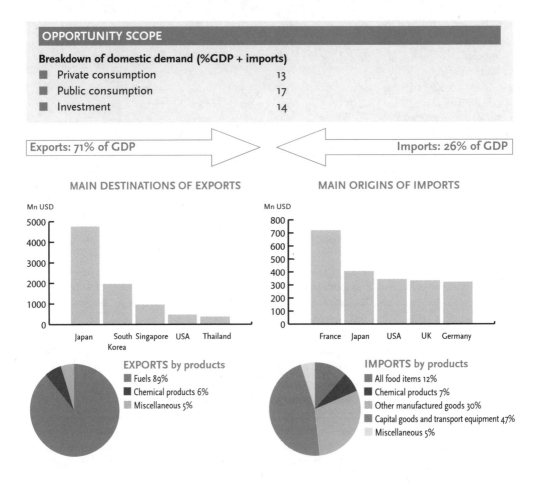

OPPORTUNITY SCOPE

Breakdown of domestic demand (%GDP + imports)
- Private consumption — 13
- Public consumption — 17
- Investment — 14

Exports: 71% of GDP   Imports: 26% of GDP

MAIN DESTINATIONS OF EXPORTS

Mn USD

(Japan, South Korea, Singapore, USA, Thailand)

MAIN ORIGINS OF IMPORTS

Mn USD

(France, Japan, USA, UK, Germany)

EXPORTS by products
- Fuels 89%
- Chemical products 6%
- Miscellaneous 5%

IMPORTS by products
- All food items 12%
- Chemical products 7%
- Other manufactured goods 30%
- Capital goods and transport equipment 47%
- Miscellaneous 5%

STANDARD OF LIVING / PURCHASING POWER

Indicators	Qatar	Regional average	DC average
GNP per capita (PPP dollars)	n/a	6086	4601
GNP per capita (USD)	n/a	7569	1840
Human Development Index	0.833	0.705	0.684
Wealthiest 10% share of national income	n/a	30	32
Urban population percentage	93	61	45
Percentage under 15 years old	27	33	30
Number of telephones per 1000 inhabitants	275	156	120
Number of computers per 1000 inhabitants	169	47	37

Saudi Arabia

Population (million inhabitants)	22
GDP (US$ million)	188,479

Short-term: **A4**

Medium-term:

Coface analysis **Quite low risk**

STRENGTHS

- World leading oil exporting country and leader of OPEC, Saudi Arabia holds a strategic position in oil markets.
- Development of the gas industry will enhance economic diversification and growth prospects.
- Foreign debt has been limited.
- The prospect of imminent admission to the WTO has been spurring reform efforts with Saudi Arabia gradually opening to foreign investment.
- The country has continued to enjoy a privileged relationship with the United States in the region, even though relations have become more complicated since 11 September 2001.

WEAKNESSES

- Very dependent on oil revenues, the economy has remained vulnerable to external shocks.
- Spending rigidities (subsidies, wages and interest on domestic debt) have been straining public finances.
- High demographic growth and an ineffective education system have been contributing to a high unemployment rate that jeopardizes the social climate.
- The terrorist risk has been undermining the economic and political environment.
- Ultimately, the succession of King Fahd and Prince Abdallah could spawn a period of uncertainty.

4

RISK ASSESSMENT

In 2004, the country continued to reap profits from very favourable oil-market conditions permitting it to increase production while oil prices soared. Those good conditions have generated solid external and fiscal surpluses that have contributed to consolidating its economic and financial situation. Those surpluses have permitted Saudi Arabia to amass foreign exchange reserves, increase public spending and reduce domestic debt. In spite of a possible slackening of the oil income in 2005, economic growth should remain sustained and the market liquidity beneficial to company finances.

However, the economy is still dependent on the oil sector and any brutal market reversal would necessarily affect the activity as well as fiscal and external accounts. Meanwhile, regional political instability and growing anti-American sentiment have been spurring the activism of Islamic extremists and increasing their capacity for destabilization. In that context, social tensions have been running high. This situation has been limiting the authorities' room for manoeuvre and weighing on the reform programme and investment.

319

MAIN ECONOMIC INDICATORS

US$ billions	2000	2001	2002	2003	2004[(e)]	2005[(f)]
Economic growth (%)	4.9	0.5	0.1	7.2	4.0	3.5
Inflation (%)	−1.1	−1.1	0.2	0.6	1.1	1.0
Public sector balance (%GDP)	3.2	−3.9	−2.9	3.7	6.5	3.8
Exports	77.5	68.0	72.5	95.2	113.3	111.0
Imports	27.7	28.6	29.6	33.9	37.9	41.4
Trade balance	49.8	39.4	42.8	61.4	75.4	69.7
Current account balance	14.3	9.4	11.9	29.7	41.0	32.9
Current account balance (%GDP)	7.6	5.1	6.3	13.8	17.3	13.5
Foreign debt (%GDP)	21.1	19.7	19.9	17.1	15.6	16.4
Debt service (%Exports)	8.2	8.4	7.2	5.6	4.9	5.0
Foreign exchange reserves (in months of imports)	3.3	3.2	3.6	3.7	3.8	3.9

e = estimate, f = forecast

CONDITIONS OF ACCESS TO THE MARKET

■ Market overview

Saudi households spend the bulk of their income on non-durable goods. Consumer demand for such goods is strong, fuelled by years of abundant cash. With 22 million inhabitants and per capita GDP of around US$10,000 in 2004, the Kingdom is one of the main markets of the Middle East. However, the Saudization of jobs (5 per cent a year is the official target) remains a problem as local manpower is inadequately trained to meet the needs of business. Rising unemployment (estimated at 15–20 per cent among men) has a destabilizing effect on the 200,000 young Saudis who arrive on the job market each year. Spending on education and vocational training is therefore a government priority in every budget.

■ Means of entry

Although member states of the Gulf Cooperation Council (Saudi Arabia, Bahrain, United Arab Emirates, Kuwait, Oman and Qatar) introduced a customs union on 1 January 2003, Saudi Arabia continues to apply differential duties on 750 or so products over a transition period that is due to expire in 2006. Actual customs duty on basic foodstuffs and staple commodities is 0 per cent, on 80 per cent of imported goods 5 per cent, on some locally produced goods 12 per cent or 20 per cent, on various fruit and vegetables 25 per cent, and on milk, wheat, cigarettes and dates 100 per cent.

Import bans are in force on mostly religious grounds. Variable and reduced rates of duty are levied on products from Jordan, Egypt, Morocco and Syria. All public procurement contracts are subject to the national preference rule. Entry and residence requirements for foreigners are very strict (compulsory Saudi sponsor). The legal environment is fairly unstable and intellectual property protection inadequate. In general, government agencies are slow to pay (7–30 months), but defaults remain rare.

■ Attitude towards foreign investors

A new Investment Code was adopted in April 2000. Its key features include: issue of licences within 30 days, establishment of a one-stop shop for processing applications (SAGIA), freehold ownership of staff facilities and accommodation, self-sponsorship for foreign companies and access

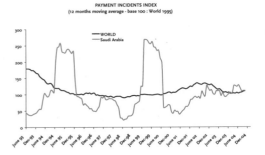

PAYMENT INCIDENTS INDEX
(12 months moving average - base 100 : World 1995)

to concessional Saudi financing. However, given the monopoly barring foreigners from directly holding shares in the country, foreign companies may only operate through Saudi law subsidiaries incorporated as private limited liability companies or branches. A negative list of sectors from which foreign investors are barred was drawn up in February 2001 and cut in February 2003. The marginal rate of corporation tax for foreign companies has been cut to 20 per cent. Losses can now be carried forward over a limited number of years.

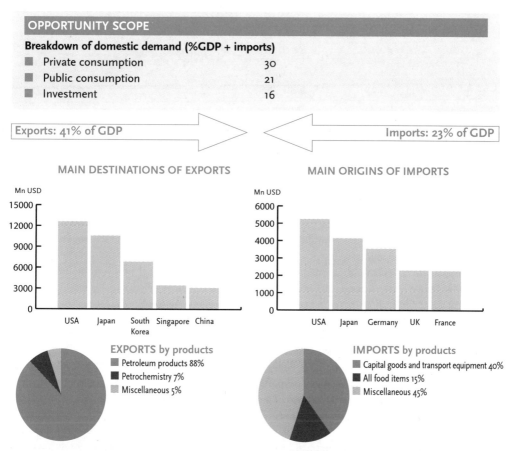

OPPORTUNITY SCOPE

Breakdown of domestic demand (%GDP + imports)
■ Private consumption   30
■ Public consumption   21
■ Investment   16

Exports: 41% of GDP   Imports: 23% of GDP

MAIN DESTINATIONS OF EXPORTS

Mn USD

(USA, Japan, South Korea, Singapore, China)

MAIN ORIGINS OF IMPORTS

Mn USD

(USA, Japan, Germany, UK, France)

EXPORTS by products
■ Petroleum products 88%
■ Petrochemistry 7%
■ Miscellaneous 5%

IMPORTS by products
■ Capital goods and transport equipment 40%
■ All food items 15%
■ Miscellaneous 45%

STANDARD OF LIVING / PURCHASING POWER

Indicators	Saudi Arabia	Regional average	DC average
GNP per capita (PPP dollars)	12660	6086	4601
GNP per capita (USD)	8530	7569	1840
Human Development Index	0.768	0.705	0.684
Wealthiest 10% share of national income	n/a	30	32
Urban population percentage	87	61	45
Percentage under 15 years old	40	33	30
Number of telephones per 1000 inhabitants	144	156	120
Number of computers per 1000 inhabitants	130	47	37

4

Syria

Population (million inhabitants)	17
GDP (US$ million)	20,783

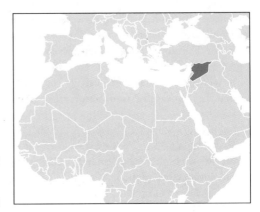

Short-term: **C**

Medium-term:

Coface analysis **Very high risk**

STRENGTHS

- Although Syria has initiated a process to liberalize its economy and thereby foster investment to spur growth and create jobs, progress has been slow.
- The tourism sector offers substantial development potential.
- Increased gas production should permit prolonging oil production.
- Efforts made to clean up payment arrears should permit Syria to restore its image with international financial backers (debt owed to the former USSR is nonetheless still pending).

WEAKNESSES

- Government has retained extensive control over the entire economy, including banks, which has been impeding emergence of a dynamic private sector with progress on reforms lagging.
- With dwindling oil reserves, the economy has nonetheless remained dependent on both the farm and oil sectors, which are vulnerable to exogenous shocks.
- Sanctions adopted by the United States have had a negative effect on the country's image.
- Regional instability has been undermining tourism and investment.

RISK ASSESSMENT

The sharp increase in barrel prices spurred exports and buoyed economic activity in 2004. It also offset losses resulting from discontinuation of Iraqi oil supplies on concessional terms. Growth should remain strong. Tax revenues, underpinned by still buoyant exports, could prompt government authorities to pursue stimulatory fiscal policy via public spending. The interest rate decline should, moreover, spur household consumption and investment. Meanwhile, tourism has been demonstrating some dynamism and trade with Iraq has been gradually resuming.

Expansionary fiscal policy will not be sustainable, however, since it will generate increasing debt, especially if oil prices decline. The external financial situation will also be vulnerable to a decline in oil revenues with debt ratios remaining high.

Reforms will be necessary to consolidate public sector finances, diversify the economy and foster private sector development; government authorities have been heading in that direction. However, the transition process to a market economy will take time considering the internal 'foot-dragging'. That situation has prompted investors to adopt a wait-and-see stance, accentuated by regional tensions.

CONDITIONS OF ACCESS TO THE MARKET

■ **Means of entry**

Syria has carried out customs reforms and gradually liberalized its foreign trade. It has entered into numerous free trade negotiations and agreements with countries of the region (Lebanon, Iraq, United Arab Emirates, Jordan and Saudi Arabia). A

MAIN ECONOMIC INDICATORS						
US$ billions	2000	2001	2002	2003	2004[(e)]	2005[(f)]
Economic growth (%)	0.6	3.4	3.2	2.5	3.6	3.5
Inflation (%)	−3.9	3.0	0.6	4.3	4.0	4.0
Public sector balance (%GDP)	−1.4	2.4	−1.6	−3.5	−2.0	−2.5
Exports	5.1	5.7	6.7	5.9	6.4	6.2
Imports	3.7	4.3	4.5	4.2	4.6	5.1
Trade balance	1.4	1.4	2.2	1.7	1.8	1.1
Current account balance	1.1	1.2	1.4	1.1	1.1	0.5
Current account balance (%GDP)	5.6	6.1	7.1	5.0	5.0	2.0
Foreign debt (%GDP)	114.6	107.8	105.9	100.3	94.6	88.6
Debt service (%Exports)	37.6	34.6	30.7	35.7	34.3	35.3
Foreign exchange reserves (in months of imports)	5.0	5.8	6.7	7.7	7.4	7.0

e = estimate, f = forecast

signatory to GAFTA (Greater Arab Free Trade Area), it will have full and free access to the Arab market from 1 January 2005.

Syria and the EU finalized an association agreement on 19 October 2004 after a series of negotiations commencing in 1996. Under the terms of the agreement, trade between Europe and Syria will be exempt from customs duties at the end of a period of gradual tariff reductions that is due to run until 2015. There are ten rates of customs duty ranging from 1 per cent for agricultural and industrial raw materials to 150 per cent for cars (down from 300 per cent). A significant piece of legislation to reform the customs nomenclature was introduced on 1 September 2004. The new law announces steep cuts in tariff rates for agri-food and industrial inputs and a number of chemicals and textiles. It also combines the various levies (war levy, port charges) in a uniform duty included in the customs tariff. As part of its customs reform policy, the Syrian government issued a series of decrees in December 2002 in order to facilitate customs clearance, free up certain imports and classify banned products into eight customs categories. Syria follows the EU's tariff nomenclature.

The means of payment normally used in transactions between foreign suppliers and Syrian buyers from both the public and private sectors is the letter of credit. Most Syrian private import firms have funds with foreign banks, especially in Lebanon. The arrival of private banks on the Syrian market in January 2004 has changed practices, with more and more transactions being carried out in Syria. Export credit agencies are gradually resuming their mid-term guarantees for Syria.

■ **Attitude towards foreign investors**

In 1991, Syria introduced a series of tax and legal regulations, collectively known as Law No. 10, to encourage investment, regardless of the origin of funds or the nationality of investors. This law was subsequently relaxed by a raft of measures, including:

- a decree passed in June 2000 authorizing the transfer of principal after five years of business and extending the tax exemption period, although only companies earning foreign exchange may transfer their profits;
- an amendment to Law No. 10 in 2001 offering private investors greater incentives and encouraging long-term projects. This amendment also grants investors property ownership rights in connection with their business.

A specific law governing investment in tourism offers numerous tax incentives and authorizes property ownership. There are also seven free zones in Syria, plus one run jointly by Syria and Jordan, offering highly attractive tax breaks. The main restrictions relate to trade with Israel or with Israeli-held companies under Arab boycott legislation.

4

■ Foreign exchange regulations

The Syrian pound's exchange rate is pegged to the US dollar. There are three rates in force, the most widespread being the floating rate set by the Commercial Bank of Syria (55 pounds to the US dollar at 30 October 2004). The Syrian pound is a non-convertible currency. Since the opening of private banks, foreign currency accounts are authorized, but transfers are limited to foreign currency brought into the country from abroad.

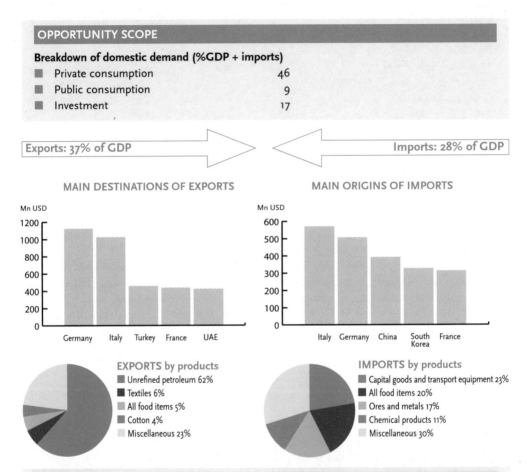

OPPORTUNITY SCOPE

Breakdown of domestic demand (%GDP + imports)
- ■ Private consumption — 46
- ■ Public consumption — 9
- ■ Investment — 17

Exports: 37% of GDP → ← Imports: 28% of GDP

MAIN DESTINATIONS OF EXPORTS

Mn USD
(Germany, Italy, Turkey, France, UAE)

MAIN ORIGINS OF IMPORTS

Mn USD
(Italy, Germany, China, South Korea, France)

EXPORTS by products
- ■ Unrefined petroleum 62%
- ■ Textiles 6%
- ■ All food items 5%
- ■ Cotton 4%
- ■ Miscellaneous 23%

IMPORTS by products
- ■ Capital goods and transport equipment 23%
- ■ All food items 20%
- ■ Ores and metals 17%
- ■ Chemical products 11%
- ■ Miscellaneous 30%

STANDARD OF LIVING / PURCHASING POWER

Indicators	Syria	Regional average	DC average
GNP per capita (PPP dollars)	3470	6086	4601
GNP per capita (USD)	1130	7569	1840
Human Development Index	0.710	0.705	0.684
Wealthiest 10% share of national income	n/a	30	32
Urban population percentage	52	61	45
Percentage under 15 years old	39	33	30
Number of telephones per 1000 inhabitants	123	156	120
Number of computers per 1000 inhabitants	19	47	37

Tunisia

Population (million inhabitants)   10
GDP (US$ million)   21,024

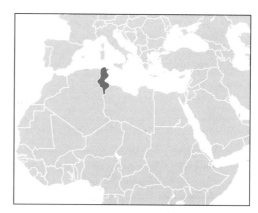

Short-term: **A4**

Medium-term:
Quite low risk

Coface analysis

STRENGTHS

- Diversification of the economic fabric and the improvement under way of the business environment together with the private sector's capacity to adapt (company upgrading) have strengthened Tunisia's ability to withstand economic shocks.
- Partnership with the EU and support from the international community have facilitated that policy.
- Access to education and a developed social system have helped reduce inequalities and limit the social cost of the adjustment.
- Social and political stability have attracted investment and facilitated access to international capital markets.

WEAKNESSES

- Economic activity has remained dependent on exogenous factors (weather conditions, European demand, tourism).
- The end of the Multifibre Arrangement on 1 January 2005 and the complete opening of the economy to European products from 2008 will necessitate improving industrial product competitiveness and increasing efforts on investment.
- The banking system situation has remained shaky and the insufficient transparency of company accounts has hampered development of a veritable financial market.
- The social constraints linked to unemployment, particularly of youth, have remained severe.

RISK ASSESSMENT

Tunisia has continued to enjoy a stable macroeconomic and political framework with the results of the October 2004 presidential and legislative elections bearing out its political stability. Growth has benefited not only from good weather but also from a tourism recovery and the dynamism of the telecommunications, mechanical engineering and electrical sectors. Continued expansion of those sectors will be essential to offset the stagnation of textile industries, which should moreover suffer from the end of the Multifibre Arrangement. Those good conditions have permitted improving the payment incident index, which has nonetheless remained above the world average due to the difficulties in textiles.

That favourable context has permitted reducing public financial deficits still hampered by substantial rigidity (with the public sector and interest on public debt absorbing 53 per cent and 11 per cent of tax revenues respectively).

External financing needs have remained moderate thanks to tourism revenues and expatriate remittances, which have been offsetting a growing trade deficit. That deficit could worsen due to uncertainties linked to textile export behaviour in Europe. It has nonetheless remained covered by FDI inflows and debt, which has remained sustainable, benefiting from the country's good signature in international capital markets.

4

MAIN ECONOMIC INDICATORS

US$ billions	2000	2001	2002	2003	2004[(e)]	2005[(f)]
Economic growth (%)	4.7	4.9	1.7	5.5	5.7	5.6
Inflation (%)	3.0	1.9	2.7	2.8	3.5	2.4
Public sector balance (%GDP)	−3.7	−3.8	−3.5	−3.5	−2.8	−2.8
Exports	5.8	6.6	6.9	8.0	9.0	9.7
Imports	8.1	9.0	9.0	10.3	11.6	12.4
Trade balance	−2.3	−2.4	−2.1	−2.3	−2.5	−2.7
Current account balance	−0.8	−0.9	−0.7	−0.7	−0.8	−0.8
Current account balance (%GDP)	−4.2	−4.3	−3.5	−2.9	−2.6	−2.5
Foreign debt (%GDP)	57.2	59.4	64.3	62.3	56.6	54.9
Debt service (%Exports)	19.8	13.6	15.1	13.1	15.0	13.4
Foreign exchange reserves (in months of imports)	2.1	2.1	2.4	2.7	2.9	3.0

e = estimate, f = forecast

CONDITIONS OF ACCESS TO THE MARKET

■ Means of entry

Ninety per cent of foreign goods can be freely imported. Authorization must be obtained from the Ministry of Trade or the competent ministry to import products considered sensitive on grounds of security, public order, health, hygiene and morality, or essential for the protection of wildlife, plants and cultural heritage. Despite the conclusion of a free trade agreement with the EU, the average level of tariff protection in Tunisia remains high. Consequently, the effective rate of duty on a large number of foodstuffs exceeds 100 per cent, as do the rates of duty on imported products that compete with local manufacture and so-called luxury goods. Duties on these items have gradually been lowered since January 2000 and should be abolished by 2008.

Tunisian import firms are able to pay their suppliers directly in foreign exchange and hold hard currency accounts for that purpose. Since 1993, payments for ordinary transactions have been handled by approved financial institutions (banks) without the need for central bank permission. Disputes over contracts entered into with Tunisian companies are usually brought before Tunisian courts.

■ Attitude towards foreign investors

Under the Investment Incentive Code (CII) of December 1993, foreigners are free to invest in all sectors, except mining, energy, local trade and financial services – all of which are governed by specific regulations. Local trade by foreigners is governed by the decree law of 1961. Foreigners may not invest in industries in which the state has a monopoly (water supply, post office, cigarettes) unless they are awarded a concession. This area has been opened up since the deregulation of electricity generation, mobile telephone services and, more recently, banking. Foreign investment is treated on an equal footing with domestic investment. However, prior authorization must be obtained for certain service activities that are not entirely export related and in which the foreign interest exceeds 50 per cent. Investments that are totally export related are granted tax incentives. The acquisition by foreigners of marketable securities with attached

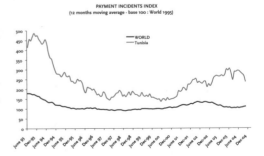

PAYMENT INCIDENTS INDEX
(12 months moving average - base 100 : World 1995)

voting rights or of shareholdings in existing Tunisian companies is subject to the approval of the Higher Investment Commission where the overall foreign interest exceeds 49 per cent. Foreigners are barred from owning farmland.

A number of sectors face only limited administrative formalities, as do offshore banks, totally export-orientated firms and non-profit organizations. Yet administrative formalities usually take longer than expected, in spite of a one-stop shop for foreign investors. On the whole, attitudes towards foreign businesspersons are open. However, investors should give serious attention to the management of risks relating to wider issues of governance (legal stability, legal certainty, clarity of administrative procedures).

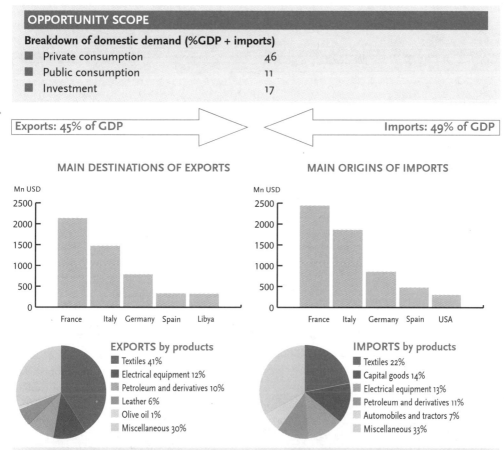

OPPORTUNITY SCOPE

Breakdown of domestic demand (%GDP + imports)
- Private consumption — 46
- Public consumption — 11
- Investment — 17

Exports: 45% of GDP　　　Imports: 49% of GDP

MAIN DESTINATIONS OF EXPORTS

Mn USD (France, Italy, Germany, Spain, Libya)

MAIN ORIGINS OF IMPORTS

Mn USD (France, Italy, Germany, Spain, USA)

EXPORTS by products
- Textiles 41%
- Electrical equipment 12%
- Petroleum and derivatives 10%
- Leather 6%
- Olive oil 1%
- Miscellaneous 30%

IMPORTS by products
- Textiles 22%
- Capital goods 14%
- Electrical equipment 13%
- Petroleum and derivatives 11%
- Automobiles and tractors 7%
- Miscellaneous 33%

STANDARD OF LIVING / PURCHASING POWER

Indicators	Tunisia	Regional average	DC average
GNP per capita (PPP dollars)	6440	6086	4601
GNP per capita (USD)	1990	7569	1840
Human Development Index	0.745	0.705	0.684
Wealthiest 10% share of national income	31.5	30	32
Urban population percentage	67	61	45
Percentage under 15 years old	28	33	30
Number of telephones per 1000 inhabitants	117	156	120
Number of computers per 1000 inhabitants	31	47	37

Turkey

Population (million inhabitants)	70
GDP (US$ million)	183,665

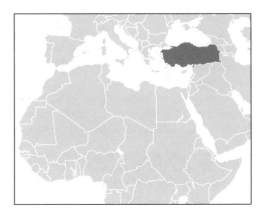

Short-term: **B**

Medium-term:
Moderately high risk

Coface analysis

STRENGTHS

- Diversified and dynamic, the private sector has proven capable of adapting quickly to an unstable environment.
- Despite continued high risk, banking reforms have progressed.
- With its NATO membership and European partner status, Turkey has benefited from international community backing.
- Recent adoption of several laws linked to the country's efforts to join the EU has improved the political framework.

WEAKNESSES

- Debt-related interest expenses, whose weight depends on financial market confidence, have sustained public sector financial imbalances.
- The risk of a foreign currency liquidity crisis will be substantial considering the current increase in short-term debt.
- The Cyprus-status issue and minority Kurd situation (with the possible emergence of an autonomous Kurdish state in Iraq) are still potential sources of conflict with the secularism debate ultimately capable of destabilizing the Turkish political situation.
- The debate over Turkey's candidacy for EU membership has been influencing market operator confidence.

RISK ASSESSMENT

Growth has been very high, buoyed by a spectacular investment rebound. The economy has benefited from the renewed confidence of market operators and renewal of multilateral institution backing, which has ensured coverage of foreign financing needs in the short term. The public sector financial situation has been gradually improving thanks to continued fiscal austerity with the public debt burden declining in consequence. Turkish performance has benefited from appreciable achievements on structural reform, although privatization has still not gone far enough. Company payment behaviour has continued to improve with the Coface payment incident index now below the world average.

Financially, the country has nonetheless remained vulnerable. The extent of foreign financing needs with the current account weakened by booming demand has compelled the country to assume massive debt in the markets. That dependence has made the financial situation very vulnerable to swings in intrinsically volatile confidence levels. The higher current account deficit has also made exchange risk a major factor. With companies carrying more short-term debt, liquidity crisis risk has remained high.

Politically, the country has been enjoying unprecedented stability. The possibility of beginning membership negotiations with the EU sustains the pursuit of political and economic reforms and confidence levels.

MAIN ECONOMIC INDICATORS

US$ billions	2000	2001	2002	2003	2004(f)	2005(f)
Economic growth (%)	7.4	−7.4	7.8	5.8	10.1	5.8
Inflation (%)	39.0	68.4	29.8	18.4	9.9	7.5
Public sector deficit (%GDP)	−17.8	−19.0	−14.5	−11.7	−7.8	−5.0
Exports	31.7	35.3	39.8	51.2	69.4	85.0
Imports	54.0	39.7	48.2	65.2	94.5	112.9
Trade balance	−22.4	−4.5	−8.4	−14.0	−25.1	−27.9
Current account balance	−9.8	3.4	−1.5	−7.9	−15.3	−15.0
Current account balance (%GDP)	−5.0	2.3	−0.8	−3.4	−5.1	−4.7
Foreign debt (%GDP)	61.6	79.4	73.7	65.7	56.7	56.8
Debt service (%Exports)	41.7	62.5	56.5	42.9	31.2	32.1
Foreign exchange reserves (in months of imports)	4.0	4.2	5.2	5.0	3.8	3.3

e = estimate, f = forecast

CONDITIONS OF ACCESS TO THE MARKET

■ Means of entry

The Turkish market is on the whole open to foreign goods and services. The country's economic system is largely harmonized with that of the EU, except for some agricultural products. Turkish companies are particularly keen to conclude partnership agreements and joint ventures. All means of payment are used and accepted. Documentary credit is strongly recommended for initial transactions and during periods of economic instability. It should preferably be opened with a French or foreign bank, although Turkish companies generally favour their own banks. Acceptance credit letters are the most widely used means of payment but, because of their cost, cash against documents or payment against goods are usually preferred by Turkish importers. Several inspection companies of international standing have offices in Turkey.

■ Attitude towards foreign investors

On 5 June 2003, Turkey's Grand National Assembly voted a law regulating FDI in Turkey. The law relaxes administrative restrictions and authorizations, while protecting the rights of foreign investors. Article 1 of the law aims to encourage FDI, protect the rights of foreign investors, harmonize the definitions of investment and

investor with international standards and replace the system of prior authorizations and approvals with a new information system. Another provision waives the obligation foreign investors were under to contribute a minimum of US$50,000 in equity and to obtain prior approval from the Directorate General for Foreign Investment (DGIE) at the Office of the Under-Secretary of State for the Treasury. This last formality has been replaced by a duty to inform the competent authorities. However, the opening of a branch office remains subject to the approval of the DGIE. FDI fell to US$1 billion in 2002 from US$3.26 billion in 2001 in the wake of the financial crisis, but then climbed to US$1.56 billion in 2003. By the end of the third quarter of 2004, it had risen to US$2.28 billion. Despite this improvement, FDI accounts for less than 1 per cent of GDP, thereby making Turkey less attractive to foreign investors than other emerging economies.

4

PAYMENT INCIDENTS INDEX
(12 months moving average - base 100 : World 1995)

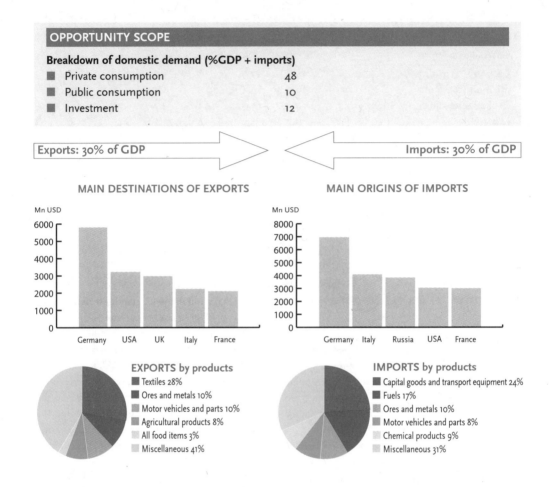

OPPORTUNITY SCOPE

Breakdown of domestic demand (%GDP + imports)
- Private consumption   48
- Public consumption   10
- Investment   12

Exports: 30% of GDP   Imports: 30% of GDP

MAIN DESTINATIONS OF EXPORTS

Mn USD

Germany   USA   UK   Italy   France

MAIN ORIGINS OF IMPORTS

Mn USD

Germany   Italy   Russia   USA   France

EXPORTS by products
- Textiles 28%
- Ores and metals 10%
- Motor vehicles and parts 10%
- Agricultural products 8%
- All food items 3%
- Miscellaneous 41%

IMPORTS by products
- Capital goods and transport equipment 24%
- Fuels 17%
- Ores and metals 10%
- Motor vehicles and parts 8%
- Chemical products 9%
- Miscellaneous 31%

STANDARD OF LIVING / PURCHASING POWER

Indicators	Turkey	Regional average	DC average
GNP per capita (PPP dollars)	6300	6086	4601
GNP per capita (USD)	2490	7569	1840
Human Development Index	0.751	0.705	0.684
Wealthiest 10% share of national income	30.7	30	32
Urban population percentage	67	61	45
Percentage under 15 years old	28	33	30
Number of telephones per 1000 inhabitants	281	156	120
Number of computers per 1000 inhabitants	45	47	37

United Arab Emirates

Population (million inhabitants)	3
GDP (US$ million)	70,960

Short-term: **A2**

Medium-term:

Coface analysis **Low risk**

STRENGTHS

- The economy is open and diversified.
- Dubai has been aggressively developing the non-oil sector (aluminium, financial services, tourism).
- Abu Dhabi boasts large oil and gas reserves.
- Efforts to attract foreign investment have been sustained.
- Considerable holdings abroad constitute a guarantee of the Federation's financial soundness.

WEAKNESSES

- Public sector accounts are still opaque.
- Although diversified, the economy has remained dependent on Abu Dhabi oil revenues and exposed to external shocks.
- Transfers abroad by foreign workers have been affecting external accounts.
- Disagreement has persisted with Iran over that country's occupation of the Lesser Tumbs, Greater Tumbs and Abu Mousa islands since 1971.

4

RISK ASSESSMENT

High hydrocarbon price and production levels have been benefiting the Federation's economic and financial situation. Those good conditions have generated high growth rates and comfortable external and fiscal surpluses that have permitted increasing holdings abroad, which guarantee the country's financial solidity. Moreover, debt has remained moderate.

Besides its oil and gas wealth concentrated in Abu Dhabi, the economy is among the most open and diversified in the region, thanks to Dubai's dynamism, which permits it to better withstand shocks. It has nonetheless remained dependent on the oil sector, whose revenues continue to have a predominant impact on the fiscal situation and external accounts. The Federation's economic equilibrium has thus largely depended on Abu Dhabi.

Politically, despite the uncertain regional environment, the liberal economic policy has been reassuring to investors and has attracted capital.

MAIN ECONOMIC INDICATORS						
US$ billions	2000	2001	2002	2003	2004[(e)]	2005[(f)]
Economic growth (%)	12.3	3.5	1.9	7.0	4.8	4.8
Inflation (%)	1.4	2.7	2.9	3.1	3.4	3.1
Public sector balance (%GDP)	12.5	−0.4	10.8	14.4	18.9	16.1
Exports	49.6	48.4	51.2	65.8	77.6	82.6
Imports	30.8	32.8	37.5	45.7	52.1	58.8
Trade balance	18.8	15.6	13.7	20.1	25.6	23.8
Current account balance	12.2	7.3	2.5	6.3	11.4	9.8
Current account balance (%GDP)	17.4	10.6	3.5	7.9	12.6	10.3
Foreign debt (%GDP)	25.9	28.0	23.5	21.0	21.9	22.9
Debt service (%Exports)	7.4	7.0	6.2	5.7	5.5	5.4
Foreign exchange reserves (in months of imports)	3.7	3.7	3.5	2.9	3.1	3.1

e = estimate, f = forecast

CONDITIONS OF ACCESS TO THE MARKET

■ Market overview

In spite of a number of restrictive practices (local majority partner requirement, closure of certain sectors to foreigners, local agent requirement, local sponsorship requirement for obtaining a residence visa), the United Arab Emirates' market is very open and thus highly competitive. In the last ten years, UAE imports have grown at an average rate of 6 per cent per annum.

The UAE is a member of the WTO and, through the Gulf Cooperation Council, party to talks on a free trade agreement with the EU.

■ Means of entry

Customs duties in force in the UAE as of 1 January 2003, the date of introduction of the customs union of the Gulf Cooperation Council, are 0 per cent for 417 customs nomenclatures and 5 per cent of the CIF value for other goods.

The UAE's standards policy is based on that of the GCC. In the first six months of 2003, a national agency – ESMA (Emirates Authority for Standardization and Metrology) – was set up to establish nationwide standards and, above all, to play an active role in the harmonization of regulations within the GCC.

All modern means of payment are available in the UAE, but the cheque, documentary credit collection, promissory note and bill of exchange are not recommended.

■ Attitude towards foreign investors

The Emirate of Abu Dhabi has actively sought FDI both to develop the oil and gas sector and, more recently, to improve management of some of its public services. The Emirate of Dubai, in the face of gradual depletion of its resources, is striving to attract foreign investment aimed at stepping up and consolidating economic diversification, particularly in the property, tourism and service sectors.

The absence in the UAE of direct taxation of companies (except banks, oil companies and telecommunications operators) and people, of exchange controls and of restrictions on the repatriation of capital acts as a magnet for investment. On the whole, the country's legislation and legal practices (adoption of new intellectual property protection laws, progress in Dubai on ownership of land by foreigners) are investment friendly. However, a number of obstacles to FDI remain. These include the requirement for foreign companies outside the free zones to have a local majority partner in a joint venture, stringent restrictions on property ownership by foreigners and a sponsorship requirement for non-nationals residing in the Emirates.

■ Foreign exchange regulations

There are no exchange controls in the UAE. The UAE dirham enjoys fixed parity with the US dollar (3.6725 dirhams to the dollar). There are no restrictions on capital transfers.

OPPORTUNITY SCOPE

Breakdown of domestic demand (%GDP + imports)
- Private consumption — 29
- Public consumption — 11
- Investment — 16

Exports: 72% of GDP   Imports: 60% of GDP

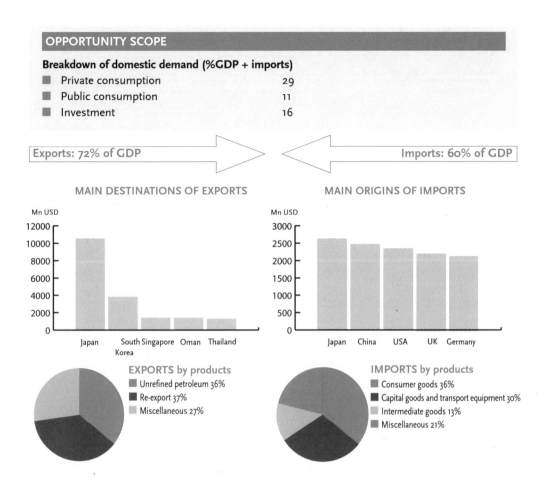

MAIN DESTINATIONS OF EXPORTS

Mn USD

Japan | South Korea | Singapore | Oman | Thailand

EXPORTS by products
- Unrefined petroleum 36%
- Re-export 37%
- Miscellaneous 27%

MAIN ORIGINS OF IMPORTS

Mn USD

Japan | China | USA | UK | Germany

IMPORTS by products
- Consumer goods 36%
- Capital goods and transport equipment 30%
- Intermediate goods 13%
- Miscellaneous 21%

STANDARD OF LIVING / PURCHASING POWER

Indicators	United Arab Emirates	Regional average	DC average
GNP per capita (PPP dollars)	24030	6086	4601
GNP per capita (USD)	n/a	7569	1840
Human Development Index	0.824	0.705	0.684
Wealthiest 10% share of national income	n/a	30	32
Urban population percentage	88	61	45
Percentage under 15 years old	26	33	30
Number of telephones per 1000 inhabitants	314	156	120
Number of computers per 1000 inhabitants	129	47	37

4

Yemen

Population (million inhabitants)	19
GDP (US$ million)	9,984

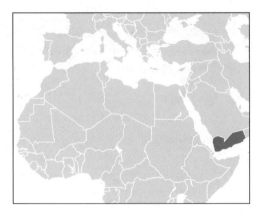

Short-term: **C**

Medium-term:

Coface analysis **Very high risk**

STRENGTHS

- Yemen boasts major but still little-exploited natural gas reserves.
- It has benefited from backing by the international community, which has nonetheless continued to monitor progress on reforms.
- Foreign debt has constituted a mild constraint thanks to reliefs granted by the Paris Club.
- Expatriate worker remittances have been bolstering the invisibles balance.
- The country has strengthened its cooperation with the United States and Saudi Arabia.

WEAKNESSES

- The economy has remained dependent on an oil sector with declining reserves.
- Subsidies on oil products have not only promoted waste, smuggling and corruption, they have also contributed to public sector financial imbalances.
- Structural reforms will be essential.
- Insecurity has affected investment and tourism.

RISK ASSESSMENT

In 2004, economic activity suffered from a major oil production decline attributable to the aging of the fields, with GDP growth mainly driven by public spending. Soaring oil prices led to sharp subsidy increases that generated a new fiscal deficit. Restoration of oil production will buoy recovery in 2005 and also contribute to reducing the fiscal deficit. The external financial situation, meanwhile, is not a cause for concern in the near term considering the relatively limited debt burden in relation to currency earnings and the comfortable level of official foreign exchange reserves.

Further out, the economy will be vulnerable to an oil price and production decline. It will thus be imperative to implement reforms to achieve lasting growth and consolidate public sector accounts. However, the climate of insecurity, social tensions and corruption could continue to weigh on the process and deter foreign investment.

Politically, the cooperation with the United States in combating terrorism could strengthen opposition movements.

MAIN ECONOMIC INDICATORS

US$ billions	2000	2001	2002	2003	2004[(e)]	2005[(f)]
Economic growth (%)	4.4	4.6	3.9	3.1	1.9	5.6
Inflation (%)	4.6	11.9	12.3	10.8	11.3	12.1
Public sector balance (%GDP)	6.7	2.3	−2.8	−3.3	−2.1	−1.5
Exports	3.8	3.4	3.6	3.9	5.0	5.2
Imports	2.6	2.8	2.6	3.6	3.7	3.9
Trade balance	1.2	0.6	1.0	0.4	1.3	1.3
Current account balance	1.2	0.5	0.8	0.1	0.8	0.8
Current account balance (%GDP)	12.6	5.2	8.2	1.3	5.7	5.3
Foreign debt (%GDP)	50.8	53.1	51.5	53.0	47.2	45.9
Debt service (%Exports)	4.6	5.1	3.6	5.1	3.7	3.8
Foreign exchange reserves (in months of imports)	7.6	9.6	11.7	10.6	10.8	10.7

e = estimate, f = forecast

CONDITIONS OF ACCESS TO THE MARKET

■ Market overview
Yemen can be called a free market economy, as there are few restrictions and no discrimination between supplier countries.

■ Means of entry
There are several types of levy on imported goods: 'duties and taxes' on all authorized imports based on the CIF value (5, 10, 15 and 25 per cent), a freight tax calculated on the volume and length of storage and a tax on net trading profits (1 per cent). Customs tariff reforms are under review. Exporters are advised to use either irrevocable and confirmed letters of credit, guaranteed by a first rate (preferably foreign) bank or advance payments, as some Yemeni traders have financial assets abroad and can use them to pay for imports into the country. If a letter of credit is opened with CALYON (formerly Crédit Agricole Indosuez) – the only Western financial institution with branches in Yemen – it does not need to be confirmed, as long as the seller is prepared to cover the risk of non-transfer. Some foreign inspection companies (eg SGS, but not Véritas) are represented in Yemen, although they do not have offices there. As a result, caution is called for in matters of inspection and verification.

■ Attitude towards foreign investors
Foreign investment is governed by law No. 22 of 2002. There are also ad hoc laws offering special terms for oil exploration and production, and public works. Generally, investors are granted tax breaks and exemptions from customs duty. Capital invested and profits can be freely repatriated at the market rate. The law enshrines the principle of equality between Yemenis and foreigners. Foreigners can hold a majority, even a 100 per cent, stake in local companies. The Labour Code, written in Arabic, covers key issues, but its interpretation can be a source of confusion. As social protection is poor, some companies take out private insurance cover for their employees.

■ Foreign exchange regulations
The rial has been fairly stable against the US dollar for a year. In October 2004, the exchange rate was 185 rials to the dollar.

4

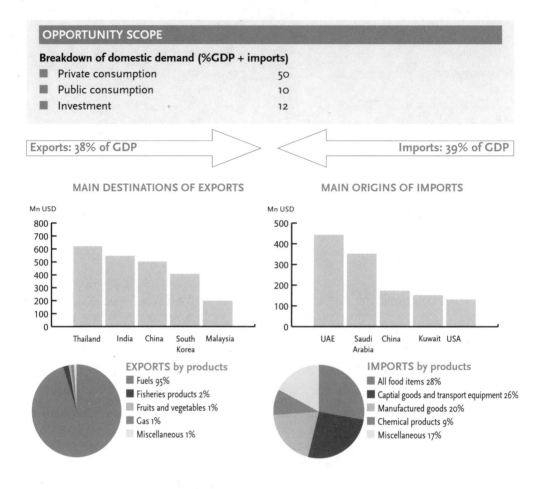

OPPORTUNITY SCOPE

Breakdown of domestic demand (%GDP + imports)
- Private consumption — 50
- Public consumption — 10
- Investment — 12

Exports: 38% of GDP → ← Imports: 39% of GDP

MAIN DESTINATIONS OF EXPORTS

Mn USD

Thailand, India, China, South Korea, Malaysia

MAIN ORIGINS OF IMPORTS

Mn USD

UAE, Saudi Arabia, China, Kuwait, USA

EXPORTS by products
- Fuels 95%
- Fisheries products 2%
- Fruits and vegetables 1%
- Gas 1%
- Miscellaneous 1%

IMPORTS by products
- All food items 28%
- Captial goods and transport equipment 26%
- Manufactured goods 20%
- Chemical products 9%
- Miscellaneous 17%

STANDARD OF LIVING / PURCHASING POWER

Indicators	Yemen	Regional average	DC average
GNP per capita (PPP dollars)	800	6086	4601
GNP per capita (USD)	490	7569	1840
Human Development Index	0.482	0.705	0.684
Wealthiest 10% share of national income	25.9	30	32
Urban population percentage	25	61	45
Percentage under 15 years old	46	33	30
Number of telephones per 1000 inhabitants	28	156	120
Number of computers per 1000 inhabitants	7	47	37

Sub-Saharan Africa

5

Succession Dominates in South Africa

Experts from Oxford Analytica, Oxford

South Africa's politics in 2005 will be shaped by the emerging struggle for the succession to President Thabo Mbeki and by the local elections campaign. Economically, barring major global upheavals or policy misjudgements, the current expansionary phase will continue. Although it is less than eight months since President Thabo Mbeki led the tripartite ANC–South African Communist Party (SACP)–Congress of South African Trade Unions (Cosatu) alliance to a near-comprehensive general election victory, virtually all political developments in South Africa are already viewed through the prism of the succession to the presidency of the ANC.

KEY INSIGHTS

→ With increased spending by government and private industry, growth of at least 3.5 per cent is expected for 2005. However, a widening current account deficit could pose challenges in the future.

→ The strengthening rand will put pressure on the manufacturing sector, which may prompt the South African Reserve Bank to lower interest rates.

→ Pretoria's policy of 'quiet diplomacy' with regard to Zimbabwe will continue to leave it at odds with the international community, especially in light of the forthcoming Zimbabwean parliamentary elections in March.

→ As the ANC prepares to elect a new presidential candidate in 2007, the question of succession will increasingly dominate political developments.

→ Despite internal tensions within the ANC-led alliance, the ruling partnership will continue its strategic collaboration and will maintain its overwhelming dominance in the 2005 local elections.

ECONOMIC OUTLOOK

South Africa's economy is approaching 2005 with the main indicators positive. In addition, revised GDP data have raised the average annual growth rate in the period 2000–2004 from 2.7 per cent to 3.0 per cent. With private gross fixed investment by domestic firms also rising steeply, and government still rolling out its programmes of infrastructure investment and public works, much of the demand-side for growth of at least 3.5 per cent in 2005 is in place. However, continuing skills shortages will preclude a significant rise in employment. The main weaknesses in this optimistic scenario revolve around the potential for international developments to impinge on the balance of payments and domestic monetary policy (and their interactions).

BALANCE OF PAYMENTS

Despite buoyant demand and higher dollar prices for South Africa's key commodity exports, the current account has moved strongly into deficit in the past two years. From a surplus of 0.6 per cent of GDP in 2002, the 2004 deficit ratio is expected to reach 2.5 per cent. This widening gap between import payments and export earnings has been comfortably financed to date by inflows of portfolio capital, attracted by the still substantial real interest-rate premiums payable in South Africa, the attractiveness of local stock prices and the strength of the rand. This scenario should remain sustainable well into 2005, provided the current benign global outlook for growth and inflation remains undisturbed.

However, the rand's continuing strength will pose its own problems. Manufactured exports are being severely squeezed, while commodity price increases are not compensating fully for the dollar's weakness. Falling profits and mounting job losses in the export-oriented and import-competing sectors will increase the pressure on the monetary authorities to lower interest rates and, thereby, the exchange rate. The danger is that domestic demand would also spiral higher, triggering a vicious circle of rising inflationary expectations and too sharp a depreciation in the exchange rate. However, this outcome would be ameliorated if still scarce foreign direct investment (FDI) inflows were to increase significantly.

Mbeki's successor within the ANC will not be elected until the end of 2007, and the next general election is not due until 2009, but the absence of an apparent heir points to the probability of a hotly contested, protracted and potentially divisive process.

SUCCESSION STRUGGLES

The claim of the current vice-president and front-runner, Jacob Zuma, to Mbeki's crown has been rendered indecisive by the widespread perception that the party hierarchy is undermining his plans for succession. In August 2003, the Director of Public Prosecutions announced that that there was a *prima facie* case for Zuma to answer in connection with corruption allegations linked to a major arms deal, but maintained that no charges would be brought against him. Zuma's name has also cropped up repeatedly during the current trial of his financial adviser, Shabir Shaik, on related corruption charges, and his position could be undermined further if Shaik is convicted. Despite the dented image, Zuma's grass-roots popularity is unlikely to be diminished, and it may require a criminal conviction and formal debarment from political office to

prevent him from standing. However, the ANC has not yet developed a culture of competitive elections (as opposed to consensual endorsement by the leadership) for its presidency, and if historical precedent prevails, Zuma's rank-and-file support base may prove irrelevant even if he does stand.

LOCAL ELECTIONS

The third round of fully democratic local elections is due in 2005. A repeat of the ANC-led alliance's overwhelming victory can be expected, and the elections will be of more interest for the performance of some of the opposition parties:

- The ANC is likely to make gains in Kwa-Zulu Natal, confirming that the power base of the country's main black opposition party, the Zulu-based Inkatha Freedom Party, has begun to erode.
- The recently established Independent Democrats, led by former Pan African Congress stalwart Patricia De Lille, should make further inroads against Tony Leon's Democratic Alliance, still seen by many blacks as the protector of white privilege. However, the effect will be further fragmentation of the centre-right opposition to the ANC.

INTRA-ALLIANCE POLITICS

The long-standing tensions between the ANC and its SACP and Cosatu partners have deteriorated further in recent months, with Zimbabwe, black economic empowerment (BEE), HIV/AIDS policy and economic policy all in the frame. However, the strategic and electoral utility of the alliance to all partners will continue to preclude a fundamental schism in the year ahead.

RACE-BASED POLITICS

The government's hypersensitivity to criticism, both within and outside its own ranks, appears undiminished. The growing criticism from all quarters of the BEE process, which is proving embarrassingly narrowly based, will force the government to consider mechanisms for broadening the range of beneficiaries.

5

FOREIGN POLICY

The crisis in Zimbabwe will be brought sharply into focus internationally by the parliamentary elections, expected in March. Without more effective leverage over both government and opposition in Zimbabwe, which might lead to a more open and inclusive electoral process, Mbeki's 'quiet diplomacy' strategy threatens to leave South Africa at odds with much of the international community over the validity and outcome of the elections.

By contrast, Pretoria's active diplomacy in the negotiations surrounding several of Africa's other key conflicts, including Burundi, Congo, Ivory Coast and Sudan, shows no sign of abating. However, South Africa's capacity to contribute further to peacekeeping operations will be stretched. Mbeki will use this extensive engagement with Africa to bolster the standing of the African Union and to press Pretoria's claim for a seat at the UN Security Council should any of the recent proposals for expansion of that body be accepted.

CONCLUSION

Tensions within the ANC-led alliance over succession and policy issues will remain, but the government's unassailable electoral position will be confirmed by the local elections. The gradual structural transformation of the post-apartheid economy has yet to address the balance of payments constraint and the problem of jobless growth.

The Range of Country @ratings in Sub-Saharan Africa

Sylvia Greisman and Bernard Lignereux

Coface Country Risk and Economic Studies Department, Paris

COUNTRY @RATING SCALE

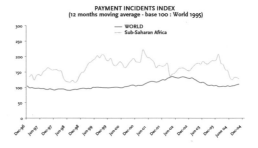

PAYMENT INCIDENTS INDEX
(12 months moving average - base 100 : World 1995)

A regional country risk @rating represents an average of country @ratings weighted according to their contribution to the region's production.

Country @ratings measure the average level of short-term non-payment risk associated with companies in individual countries. A rating reflects the influence of a particular country's economic, financial and political outlook on financial commitments of local companies. It is thus complementary to the @rating credit opinion on a company.

Sub-Saharan Africa is still characterized by the vulnerability of its companies to an unstable economic, financial and political environment. The level of risk in the region has been considerably higher than the emerging-country average. With the exception of Botswana (A2), South Africa (A3), Mauritius (A3) and Namibia (A3), most regional countries are rated B, C or D.

The anticipated improvement of risk in 2005 mainly reflects the upgrading of South Africa to A3,

as this country represents more than 40 per cent of the region's GDP. Only two other countries were upgraded last year: Tanzania (upgraded to B) and Madagascar (upgraded to C).

The growth rate accelerated in 2004 (4.5 per cent). Sub-Saharan Africa benefited from steady raw materials prices, both for oil and minerals (gold, platinum and copper) and certain agricultural products (cotton and cocoa). In addition, beyond the traditional specialization in primary products, sectors with high added value such as textiles, timber or farm product processing and telecommunications services have performed very well. The structural reforms and diversification efforts made for several years in certain countries thus appear to be bearing fruit.

Forecasts for 2005 assume ongoing sustained growth (4.7 per cent). However, economic activity has remained vulnerable to political, ethnic and social tensions, as shown by recent events in Ivory Coast and the Democratic Republic of Congo. Exogenous shocks, like extreme weather conditions and other natural disasters, regularly compound those risks. Moreover, except for South Africa and a few other countries in the south of the continent, dependence on international aid remains high. Despite the international financial community's efforts, particularly, substantial debt relief via the HIPC initiative reserved for heavily indebted poor countries, external account imbalances have persisted in most of those countries.

These weaknesses have been responsible for wide fluctuations in company solvency and the payment incident index, which has remained above the world average. In that regard, the improvement registered in 2004, although doubtless reflecting better payment behaviour in some countries is also attributable to the collapse of trade flows with Ivory Coast, formerly a major trade partner in West Africa.

■ **Countries rated A3**

Adverse political or economic circumstances may lead to a worsening payment record that is already lower than the previous categories, although the probability of a payment default is still low.

Economic activity in South Africa (upgraded in 2004) has picked up, a trend that should gain moment in 2005. Global recovery and, above all, domestic demand have spurred growth in all sectors, including manufacturing (a sector otherwise penalized by the South African currency appreciation). Interest rate levels have been conducive to private investment, and the authorities' tight fiscal policy gives them sufficient leeway to undertake public investment programmes. That favourable context has buoyed the financial situation of local companies with their payment behaviour index remaining excellent.

COFACE MAP OF COUNTRY @RATINGS

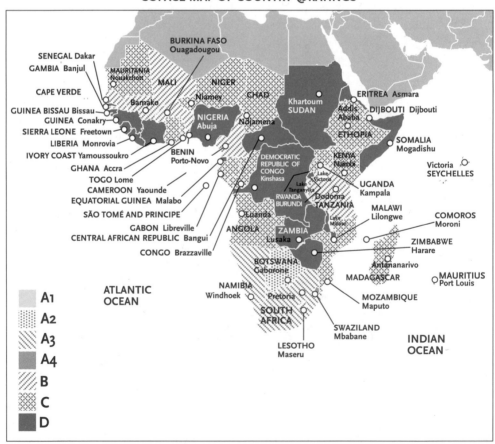

Moreover, the country's external financing needs have remained moderate and its debt burden correspondingly low. Although the level of short-term debt has been a source of weakness, the ongoing capital account surplus reflected by a two-fold increase in currency reserves, would enable the country to cope more effectively with a crisis of confidence in financial markets.

In Mauritius, investment levels and service industry performance have been fuelling strong growth; this should not obscure the challenges involved in restructuring the sugar and textile sectors with discontinuation of the Multifibre Arrangement in January 2005 and of preferential European market access for sugar by 2007. Company payment behaviour has been reflecting the favourable economic conditions.

An ambitious investment policy and structural reductions in customs revenue have, however, undermined public finances and contributed to increase internal debt. Conversely, the good performance of the island's external accounts thanks to a services balance surplus and limited foreign debt has afforded government authorities ample room for manoeuvre.

■ Countries rated B

A precarious economic environment could affect company payment behaviour, which is often poor. Growth should remain buoyant in Senegal, with the difficulties encountered in 2004 in the farm sector partly offset by good performance in services, extraction and manufacturing industries, as well as by improvement in electrical power production.

5

COFACE MAP OF MEDIUM- AND LONG-TERM COUNTRY RISK

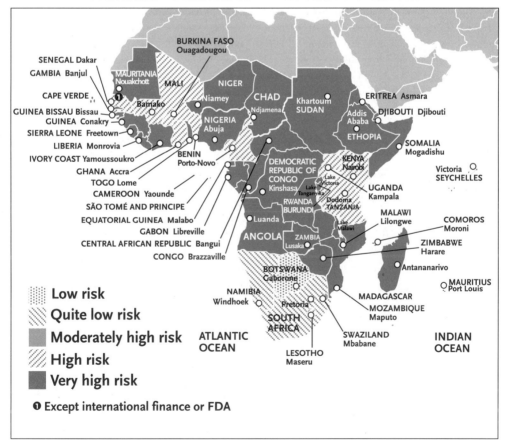

Low risk
Quite low risk
Moderately high risk
High risk
Very high risk

❶ Except international finance or FDA

Moreover, the country's public investment programme has benefited the construction and public works sector. Economic policy objectives established in the three-year programme concluded with the IMF in 2003 have been met, enabling the country to reach the completion point under the HIPC initiative for heavily indebted poor countries in April 2004. In this favourable context, though Senegal's company payment incident index has stabilized at a relatively high level, it reflects payment delays more than actual defaults.

In Mali, too, the outlook for 2005 is bright, even with the level of economic activity remaining vulnerable to unforeseeable problems in farm production, which suffered from locust swarms in 2004. Cotton production and processing (despite sectoral restructuring problems), gold production (the nation's primary export revenue source) and the telecommunications and transport sectors should enable Mali to sustain a satisfactory growth rate. Although the debt burden has been reduced via the HIPC initiative for heavily indebted poor countries since 2003, external financing needs have remained high and are being met by concessional loans and grants, and a new three-year programme was concluded with the IMF in June 2004.

The Tanzanian economy (rating upgraded in 2004) remains one of contained inflation and dynamic growth fuelled by the strong performance of farm production and mining and by the emergence of a manufacturing sector. These results have been consolidated by the pursuance of structural and institutional reforms and by improvements in the business environment. Significant weaknesses have persisted, however. The country's narrow tax base has made it impossible to reduce public sector financial deficits, despite tight policy. Similarly, the economy's structure has impeded reduction of external account imbalances, despite expanding agricultural and gold exports. In that context, the country has remained dependent on international aid, benefiting from substantial debt relief as early as 2001 via the HIPC initiative for heavily indebted poor countries.

The outlook for Cameroon (negative watchlisted) is more mixed. Although growth accelerated slightly in 2004, the tight fiscal policy expected in 2005 is likely to affect economic activity. Insufficiently rigorous management of public finances has prevented the country from cancelling its public external debt via the HIPC initiative for heavily indebted poor countries. Moreover, although high oil prices have kept the country's financing needs relatively low, the significant external debt burden has nevertheless made debt reduction measures necessary. In this context there has been a resurgence of non-payment incidents.

■ **Countries rated C**

A very unsteady political and economic environment could deteriorate an already bad payment record.

Although encouraging, Kenya's outlook has remained shaky despite the signing of a new agreement with the IMF, promises of financial support from the international community and new debt rescheduling granted by the Paris Club in January 2004. Tensions within the coalition in power have been hindering implementation of structural reforms and consolidation of public finances. In this context, disbursement of promised financing has often been postponed, which has affected investment and economic activity levels. Moreover, external financing needs have been increasing due to rising oil prices and Kenya's still inadequate export capacity.

The economic situation in Madagascar (upgraded in 2004) has continued to stabilize. The return of investor confidence has facilitated the recovery of the industrial free trade zone. Tourism has resumed, although remaining below the country's potential. Renewed political stability, implementation of structural reforms and international community backing enabled Madagascar to reach the 'completion point' in the HIPC programme for heavily indebted poor countries in October 2004. Nevertheless, with the external account situation likely to remain fragile and the debt burden high, the island will continue to depend on international aid. Those encouraging results should not, however, mask the economy's structural vulnerability to weather conditions.

■ **Countries rated D**

The high risk profile of a country's economic and political environment will further worsen a generally bad payment record.

In Nigeria high oil prices, increased gas production and good harvests have had a positive impact on growth, despite social tensions and troubles in the Niger Delta. Thanks to hydrocarbon production and the dynamism of private investment, the outlook remains positive for 2005. Oil revenues have also considerably improved the country's public sector and external account situation. Despite that favourable context, the country has continued to accumulate payment arrears. Although President Obasanjo, re-elected in 2003, has a mandate that affords him more leeway to accelerate structural reforms designed to modernize the economy, their implementation still meets with strong resistance.

In Ivory Coast, the political situation has been deadlocked since the September 2002 events ended in the country's partition, despite efforts by the international community and African states to implement the Marcoussis agreement signed in January 2003. In that context, the cocoa sector's good performance has enabled the government to continue to function adequately in the south (although at the price of accumulating debt repayment arrears), while the economic situation in the north has become even more precarious. Although economic stabilization will depend on how the political situation evolves, the lack of confidence between the various parties has made the prospects for ending the crisis highly uncertain.

5

Angola

Population (million inhabitants)   13
GDP (US$ million)   11,248

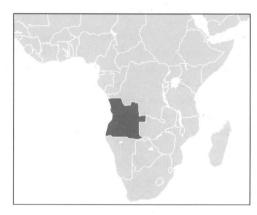

Short-term: **C**

Coface analysis

Medium-term:
Very high risk

STRENGTHS

- Sub-Saharan Africa's second oil-producing country (980,000 barrels a day) and attracting substantial FDI, Angola also represents a strategic interest for Western countries.
- It boasts other natural resources including diamonds, various minerals, as well as hydroelectricity, farming and fishing potential.
- Since the signature of a peace treaty with UNITA in 2002, Angola has been able to redeploy resources to infrastructure development and the war against poverty.

WEAKNESSES

- The oil sector's dynamism has not been spreading throughout the economy, whose restructuring has been progressing very slowly.
- The civil war's aftermath has continued to weigh heavily on the country's demographic, economic and financial outlook.
- Without support, the country would lack the resources needed to rebuild infrastructure and cope with severe social deficiencies.
- Foreign investment has remained very limited outside the hydrocarbon sector due to very high levels of corruption and a deficient legal system.

RISK ASSESSMENT

The strong growth in 2004 and 2005 reflects higher oil production and prices. However, the macroeconomic situation, although improving, has remained unstable amid continued high inflation, persistently large public sector deficits and an overvalued exchange rate. This situation, coupled with the slow pace of structural reform implementation, has complicated matters in setting up an international financial community support programme. However, that support will be essential in consolidating external accounts undermined by the weight of imports, a high invisibles balance deficit and heavy debt contracted on unfavourable terms. Relations with the IMF have nonetheless improved recently due to government efforts to make public finances more transparent.

Meanwhile, uncertainties surrounding the date and organization of legislative and presidential elections to be held mid-2006 could unsettle the political calm spell that began with the end of the civil war (except in the Cabinda enclave).

MAIN ECONOMIC INDICATORS						
US$ millions	2000	2001	2002	2003[(e)]	2004[(e)]	2005[(f)]
Economic growth (%)	3.0	3.2	9.7	2.4	13.2	11.9
Inflation (%)	325.0	153.0	109.0	98.2	45.8	48.1
Public sector balance (%GDP)	−8.6	−3.7	−9.0	−8.9	−8.9	−8.9
Exports	7,921	6,534	8,359	9,310	12,120	11,430
Imports	3,040	3,179	3,709	4,080	4,488	4,824
Trade balance	4,881	3,355	4,650	5,230	7,632	6,606
Current account balance	796	−1,430	−644	−1,035	−572	−598
Current account balance (%GDP)	9.0	−15.1	−5.8	−8.2	−4.2	−3.9
Foreign debt (%GDP)	115	101	94	87	83	79
Debt service (%Exports)	38.7	48.8	25.1	21.5	16.0	16.9
Foreign exchange reserves (in months of imports)	1.9	1.1	0.5	0.6	1.1	1.5

e = estimate, f = forecast

CONDITIONS OF ACCESS TO THE MARKET

■ Means of entry

The country is highly import-orientated, being dependent for 90 per cent of its consumption and investment on imported goods. There is no protectionist customs barrier, and duties range from 5 to 30 per cent. The simplification of import procedures (establishment of a single customs document) has not yielded the desired results and the country still remains one of the most bureaucratic in the world. Red tape, mainly at ports, hampers the development of trade. Angola does not apply a preferential customs tariff to countries belonging to the Southern Africa Development Community (SADC) of which it is a member. However, tax exemptions are granted to imports intended for investment projects undertaken in priority areas.

Exporters are strongly advised to check the existence of funding and the solvency of partners. They should demand cash payment with their order or payment by irrevocable documentary credit confirmed by a leading bank. As far as public tenders are concerned, investors should only bid for those financed by multilateral institutions.

■ Attitude towards foreign investors

Reform of the investment code is under way, yet it still does not offer all the guarantees for which foreign investors might hope. The system has been liberalized and brought into line with that in other SADC member countries, but it remains complex and short on incentives. The National Foreign Investment Agency (ANIP) – a one-stop shop – seeks to bring together the main government departments, but is unwieldy. Formalities are lengthy and each step of the approval process has to be followed up by a local partner. At all echelons of the administration, investors face practices that are incompatible with those of a modern state.

Despite the innovative language, the genuine attempts to open the country to trade and the reforms undertaken in the last two years, ideological archaisms survive in the form of administrative obstacles, patronage at all levels of government, widespread corruption and lack of transparency in public accounting. Legally established foreign enterprises are subject, more than their national counterparts, to untimely tax audits and inspections by the employment and health departments. Furthermore, the legal system is incapable of providing all the guarantees required of it.

Because of large-scale offshore and inland oil production by 50 or so foreign companies, Angola is the largest beneficiary of FDI in Africa, along with Egypt and Nigeria.

5

■ **Foreign exchange regulations**

The kwanza (the country's non-convertible currency) has stabilized over the last few months and in November 2004 stood at around 85–90 kwanzas to the US dollar. The securities exchange set up in 2004 is still at an embryonic stage.

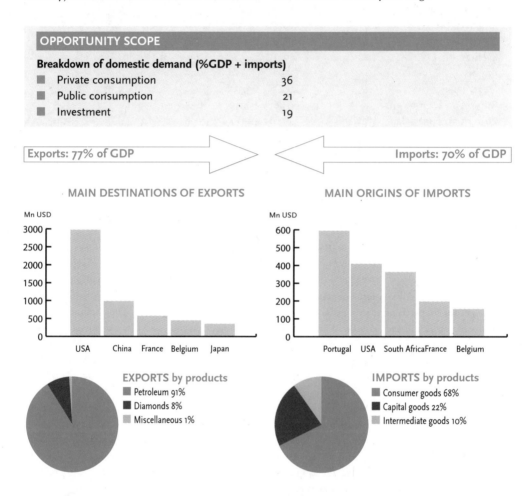

OPPORTUNITY SCOPE

Breakdown of domestic demand (%GDP + imports)
- ■ Private consumption   36
- ■ Public consumption   21
- ■ Investment   19

Exports: 77% of GDP   Imports: 70% of GDP

MAIN DESTINATIONS OF EXPORTS

Mn USD — USA, China, France, Belgium, Japan

MAIN ORIGINS OF IMPORTS

Mn USD — Portugal, USA, South Africa, France, Belgium

EXPORTS by products
- ■ Petroleum 91%
- ■ Diamonds 8%
- ■ Miscellaneous 1%

IMPORTS by products
- ■ Consumer goods 68%
- ■ Capital goods 22%
- ■ Intermediate goods 10%

STANDARD OF LIVING / PURCHASING POWER

Indicators	Angola	Regional average	DC average
GNP per capita (PPP dollars)	1840	2342	4601
GNP per capita (USD)	710	658	1840
Human Development Index	0.381	0.489	0.684
Wealthiest 10% share of national income	n/a	39	32
Urban population percentage	35	42	45
Percentage under 15 years old	48	42	30
Number of telephones per 1000 inhabitants	6	22	120
Number of computers per 1000 inhabitants	2	17	37

Benin

Population (million inhabitants)	6.6
GDP (US$ million)	2,695
GDP per capita (US$)	408

Short-term: **B**

Medium-term:

Coface analysis **High risk**

RISK ASSESSMENT

The country has benefited from its position at the crossroads of West Africa and from substantial farm potential that should permit diversifying an economy still very dependent on the cotton sector. With its transit-trade specialization, it is also subject to trade policy changes by neighbours, particularly Nigeria.

Restrictions on imports from Benin in conjunction with a cotton production decline thus explain the growth slowdown in 2004. In that context, the drop in customs revenues has increased the public sector deficit and large current account deficits have persisted. With the expected completion of cotton industry restructuring and regularization of trade relations with Nigeria, growth should nonetheless rebound in 2005. Uncertainties linked to the presidential elections looming in March 2006 should not undermine those forecasts.

To cover its deficits, the country will continue to depend on support from financial backers. In 2003, it qualified for debt cancellation by reaching the completion point in the HIPC programme. Meanwhile, a new triennial programme under negotiation with the IMF is intended to speed up structural reforms and free up more resources for infrastructure investments.

5

MAIN ECONOMIC INDICATORS

US$ millions	2000	2001	2002	2003	2004(e)	2005(f)
Economic growth (%)	5.8	5.0	6.0	4.8	3.0	5.0
Inflation (%)	4.2	4.0	2.4	1.5	2.6	3.0
Public sector balance (%GDP)	−3.5	−4.2	−3.5	−4.6	−5.5	−5.2
Exports	189	210	196	269	323	346
Imports	447	467	510	654	745	794
Trade balance	−258	−256	−313	−385	−423	−448
Current account balance	−223	−244	−301	−371	−410	−440
Current account balance (%GDP)	−9.9	−10.2	−11.1	−10.7	−10.1	−9.3
Foreign debt (%GDP)	69	70	68	47	42	39
Debt service (%Exports)	13.7	13.7	14.4	7.5	5.9	5.8
Foreign exchange reserves (in months of imports)	8.4	10.2	9.8	6.4	4.3	4.0

e = estimate, f = forecast

Botswana

Population (million inhabitants)	2
GDP (US$ million)	5,273

Short-term: **A2**

Medium-term:
Low risk

Coface analysis

STRENGTHS

- The country's political stability, low level of corruption and good infrastructure are attractive to foreign investors.
- Botswana has made major efforts to diversify and increase the value of domestic production (textiles, automobile assembly, financial sector development).
- The country boasts abundant mineral resources including diamonds (second world producer), copper and nickel.
- It has little debt and satisfactory levels of currency reserves.

WEAKNESSES

- The AIDS pandemic afflicting a third of the adult population has affected growth and fiscal spending (health, social) and will ultimately cause major demographic and economic imbalances.
- Diamond extraction (60 per cent of fiscal revenues, 75 per cent of export earnings) has remained the country's economic focal point, which makes it vulnerable to external shocks.
- The high unemployment rate (30 per cent) could trigger a new upsurge of social tensions.
- The country has suffered from the narrowness of its domestic market, remaining very commercially dependent on South Africa.

RISK ASSESSMENT

Despite services sector dynamism, economic activity slowed slightly in 2004 due to the modest rise of diamond extraction with the overall growth rate still dependent on diamond price and production trends.

This dependence reflects not only on external accounts but also on public finances. Strained by large increases in health and social spending linked to the AIDS pandemic, public finances have been running deficits that should nonetheless remain limited. Conversely, external accounts have been posting large surpluses, which explain the country's low foreign debt and high currency reserves. Furthermore, graded well by rating agencies, Botswana can benefit from easy access to international capital markets.

Politically, the incumbent President Festus Mogae's victory in the October 2004 legislative elections consolidated the country's stability. In the longer term, the AIDS pandemic's social and health consequences could impede Botswana's economic development and diversification.

MAIN ECONOMIC INDICATORS

US$ millions	2000	2001	2002	2003[e]	2004[e]	2005[f]
Economic growth (%)	8.4	2.3	5.5	5.4	4.6	5.7
Inflation (%)	8.5	6.6	8.0	9.3	5.7	6.0
Public sector balance (%GDP)	9.1	−3.3	−4.3	−1.3	−1.7	−0.8
Exports	2,682	2,326	2,376	3,038	3,160	3,200
Imports	1,778	1,612	2,040	2,372	1,776	2,488
Trade balance	904	714	335	666	1,384	711
Current account balance	548	599	97	425	1,158	512
Current account balance (%GDP)	10.4	11.5	11.6	11.0	6.4	5.7
Foreign debt (%GDP)	19.6	22.8	23.0	16.7	17.0	16.7
Debt service (%Exports)	3.4	3.8	3.5	2.6	3.1	2.8
Foreign exchange reserves (in months of imports)	31.9	36.3	26.0	21.6	28.3	21.9

e = estimate, f = forecast

CONDITIONS OF ACCESS TO THE MARKET

■ Market overview

Botswana is a member of the Southern Africa Customs Union (SACU), which also comprises Lesotho, Swaziland, Namibia and South Africa. *Ad valorem* common external tariffs and excise duties are applicable to third countries. The renewed Lomé Convention, the Generalized System of Preferences and the extension of the Trade, Development and Cooperation Agreement between the EU and South Africa to SACU member countries grant Botswanan products preferential access to European and North American markets in line with AGOA rules. In October 2002, Botswana teamed up with other SACU members to sign a fresh customs protocol establishing a new system for resolving commercial disputes and setting customs duties. Botswana is also an active member of the South African Development Community (14 countries in Southern Africa), headquartered in the capital Gaborone. The local market, however, remains narrow and mainly concentrated in towns to the east of the country.

■ Means of entry

Botswana's customs regulations grant duty-free admission to raw materials and machinery imported for the manufacture of products intended for export.

Other tax measures include exemption from sales tax on raw materials used in exported products.

Sales agents of any nationality are allowed to operate, though local agents and representatives predominate. Public invitations to tender and large-scale works contracts comply with internationally recognized standards. Imports are usually invoiced in rands, US dollars or pounds sterling. The euro is starting to gain acceptance as legal tender in trade, albeit to a limited degree. Botswana uses similar means of payments to those used in Europe and the United States.

■ Attitude towards foreign investors

Botswana possesses numerous investment-grade assets and is one of the most competitive countries in Africa. It has a liberal economy, no exchange controls, a convertible currency, attractive tax laws (15 per cent corporation tax for manufacturing companies and 25 per cent for others, 10 per cent VAT from July 2002) and peaceful social relations. The Botswana Export Development and Investment Authority (BEDIA) encourages investment in the country, especially through export-related projects and import substitution. The focus is on industrial diversification to reduce the country's dependence on the mining sector (diamonds) and on partnerships between foreign investors and local players with a view to facilitating technology

5

transfers. Priority sectors include manufacturing (glass, tanneries, textiles, etc), information and communication technologies, tourism and financial services (international financial centre).

Botswana's legal system is founded on the principles of common law. Consequently, its judicial procedures are highly liberal and similar to those in developed countries.

As the country is a signatory to both the World Bank's MIGA Agreement and the OPIC Agreement with the United States, it provides investment safeguards.

■ Foreign exchange regulations

Botswana's foreign exchange reserves – over US$5 billion or nearly 100 per cent of GDP – enable it to pursue a highly flexible foreign exchange policy. There are no exchange controls. The fully convertible local currency, the pula, was introduced after the country's withdrawal from the rand area in 1976. There are no restrictions on the repatriation of capital by non-residents. Both dividends and capital can be freely transferred by a foreign investor upon payment of 15 per cent withholding tax.

OPPORTUNITY SCOPE

Breakdown of domestic demand (%GDP + imports)
- Private consumption 20
- Public consumption 24
- Investment 18

Exports: 51% of GDP   Imports: 37% of GDP

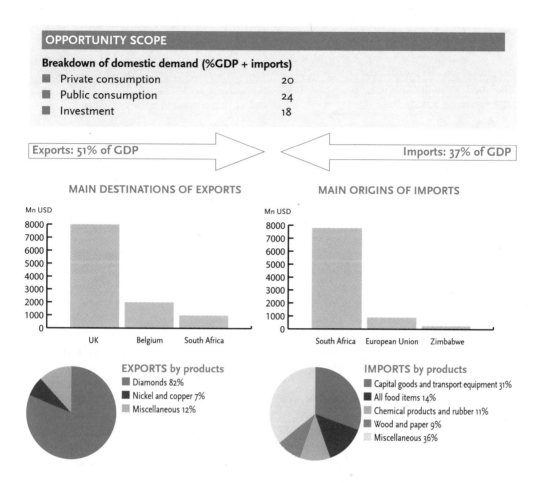

MAIN DESTINATIONS OF EXPORTS

Mn USD

UK   Belgium   South Africa

EXPORTS by products
- Diamonds 82%
- Nickel and copper 7%
- Miscellaneous 12%

MAIN ORIGINS OF IMPORTS

Mn USD

South Africa   European Union   Zimbabwe

IMPORTS by products
- Capital goods and transport equipment 31%
- All food items 14%
- Chemical products and rubber 11%
- Wood and paper 9%
- Miscellaneous 36%

5

STANDARD OF LIVING / PURCHASING POWER

Indicators	Botswana	Regional average	DC average
GNP per capita (PPP dollars)	7740	2342	4601
GNP per capita (USD)	3010	658	1840
Human Development Index	0.589	0.489	0.684
Wealthiest 10% share of national income	56.6	39	32
Urban population percentage	50	42	45
Percentage under 15 years old	42	42	30
Number of telephones per 1000 inhabitants	87	22	120
Number of computers per 1000 inhabitants	41	17	37

Burkina Faso

Population (million inhabitants)	11.8
GDP (US$ million)	3,127
GDP per capita (US$)	265

Short-term: **B**

Medium-term:

Coface analysis **High risk**

RISK ASSESSMENT

The robust growth of 2004 should continue in 2005 despite tensions linked to the upcoming presidential elections and regional instability. Effects of the crisis in the Ivory Coast, which constituted Burkina's main seaport outlet, have been limited, with companies adapting rapidly by redirecting merchandise shipments towards ports in Ghana and Benin.

Despite those favourable conditions, the country's financial imbalances have nonetheless persisted. Sharp export growth, spurred by increased cotton production and prices, has not sufficed to offset the expansion of imports, resulting in large external account deficits. Moreover, the public sector deficit has remained high due to the low level of fiscal revenues linked to the country's narrow tax base. To cover its financing needs, Burkina has thus had to depend on international aid. By implementing structural reforms, meanwhile, the country reached the completion point under the HIPC programme in 2002 and thus benefited from substantial foreign debt reduction.

Further, it will nonetheless remain dependent on an insufficiently productive primary sector with a lack of infrastructure and limited human capital impeding a take-off by the industrial sector. Meanwhile, mineral resources (gold, zinc, manganese) have remained underexploited even if the recent mining code reform could foreshadow a gold production recovery.

MAIN ECONOMIC INDICATORS						
US$ millions	2000	2001	2002	2003	2004[e]	2005[f]
Economic growth (%)	1.6	4.6	4.4	6.5	6.0	6.2
Inflation (%)	−0.3	4.9	2.3	2.0	2.5	2.5
Public sector balance (%GDP)	−10.9	−11.3	−10.2	−9.2	−9.6	−9.1
Exports	238	231	224	280	373	396
Imports	599	606	538	594	770	877
Trade balance	−361	−376	−314	−315	−397	−481
Current account balance	−452	−472	−392	−425	−535	−626
Current account balance (%GDP)	−14.7	−13.5	−12.3	−12.2	−11.8	−11.2
Foreign debt (%GDP)	57	61	60	69	57	46
Debt service (%Exports)	16.6	13.1	17.6	8.4	6.6	6.3
Foreign exchange reserves (in months of imports)	4.5	4.4	4.9	4.3	3.9	3.7

e = estimate, f = forecast

Burundi

Population (million inhabitants)	7.1
GDP (US$ million)	719
GDP per capita (US$)	101

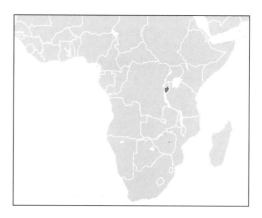

Short-term: **D**

Medium-term:

Coface analysis **Very high risk**

RISK ASSESSMENT

Under the supervision of the UN and African countries, the political transition implemented via the 2000 Arusha Accords to end ten years of turmoil is in its final stages. A new constitution, which must be approved by referendum, went into force on 1 December 2004. Elections (local, legislative, then presidential in April 2005) should put the finishing touches to normalization of the political landscape.

The coming period will nonetheless remain sensitive. The power-sharing agreement intended to guarantee that the Tutsi minority's institutional representation has been subject to reservations by that same minority. The process of disarming and integrating the former militias could take longer than expected with one militia that did not sign the accords still conducting guerrilla actions. Meanwhile, a deteriorating situation in the Great Lakes region could undermine the process. Moreover, returning refugees could pose major problems concerning land.

In that context, economic activity will depend on continuation of the peace process, the impact of weather conditions on harvests and reconstruction work financed by international aid. Considering the scale of its financial imbalances, Burundi has qualified for the HIPC programme and will remain dependent on that support.

5

MAIN ECONOMIC INDICATORS						
US$ millions	2000	2001	2002	2003	2004$^{(e)}$	2005$^{(f)}$
Economic growth (%)	−0.9	2.1	4.5	−1.0	5.1	5.3
Inflation (%)	24.3	9.3	−1.3	10.3	6.4	5.2
Public sector balance (%GDP)	−4.9	−7.2	−5.7	−9.9	−9.8	−8.9
Exports	49	39	31	47	33	45
Imports	108	108	104	128	140	146
Trade balance	−59	−69	−73	−81	−108	−102
Current account balance	−104	−107	−117	−141	−169	−149
Current account balance (%GDP)	−14.6	−16.1	−18.6	−23.5	−26.1	−21.7
Foreign debt (%GDP)	155	163	182	204	182	178
Debt service (%Exports)	77	91	138	76	157	71
Foreign exchange reserves (in months of imports)	0.7	0.5	1.4	1.2	1.9	1.4

e = estimate, f = forecast

Cameroon

Population (million inhabitants)	16
GDP (US$ million)	9,060

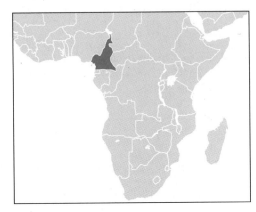

Short-term: **B**

Medium-term:

Coface analysis   **High risk**

STRENGTHS

- The country boasts substantial resources – agriculture, timber and energy (oil, gas, hydroelectricity) – and its economy is one of Central Africa's most diversified.
- The expected speed-up on structural reforms and Cameroon's political stability represent positive factors for foreign investors.
- The completion of the Chad–Cameroon oil pipeline should strengthen regional integration and improve the country's economic outlook.
- Franc-zone membership has contributed to its monetary stability.

WEAKNESSES

- Cameroon is still dependent on exogenous factors (weather, world commodity prices).
- Proven oil reserves have been declining.
- Implementation of disciplined fiscal policy has remained problematic, which has been a source of discord with financial backers.
- The business environment has remained difficult.
- The weaknesses of neighbouring countries (Central African Republic and Nigeria) could affect Cameroon.
- Combating poverty has continued to represent a major challenge for government authorities.

RISK ASSESSMENT

Driven by household consumption and increased public spending, growth rose slightly in 2004. However, the restrictive fiscal policy expected in 2005 should dampen the economy. Insufficiently strict public sector financial management has prevented cancellation of public external debt under the HIPC programme for highly indebted poor countries.

Although the country's financing needs have remained all the more moderate amid high oil prices, the significant external debt burden has made debt reduction measures necessary with FDI remaining insufficient.

The prospective speed-up of structural reforms and resulting strengthening of Cameroon's economic potential could enhance its attractiveness to investors. Moreover, the country has enjoyed political stability. The dispute with Nigeria over the Bakassi peninsula should come to a peaceful conclusion and the incumbent President Biya's re-election in October 2004 reflects that stability.

MAIN ECONOMIC INDICATORS						
US$ millions	2000	2001	2002	2003	2004$^{(e)}$	2005$^{(f)}$
Economic growth (%)	4.2	5.3	4.4	4.3	4.6	4.2
Inflation (%)	−2.1	4.5	2.8	0.6	1.0	2.0
Public sector balance (%GDP)	2.5	1.4	1.7	2.5	1.8	1.6
Exports	2,318	1,929	1,884	2,247	2,445	2,378
Imports	1,380	1,863	1,902	2,121	1,979	2,097
Trade balance	938	66	−18	126	466	281
Current account balance	510	−504	−631	−505	−149	−350
Current account balance (%GDP)	5.7	−5.9	−6.6	−4.2	−1.1	−2.3
Foreign debt (%GDP)	104	97	89	69	62	57
Debt service (%Exports)	17.9	12.6	13.6	9.2	9.2	9.5
Foreign exchange reserves (in months of imports)	1.0	1.3	2.3	2.2	2.2	2.3

e = estimate, f = forecast

CONDITIONS OF ACCESS TO THE MARKET

■ Market overview

The Cameroon market is open to imports and the authorities apply no special protectionist measures or tariff barriers. Customs duties on imports from within the CEMAC area range from 5 per cent for staple commodities and 10 per cent for raw materials and capital goods to 20 per cent for semi-finished and miscellaneous products and 30 per cent for certain consumer goods. There is 18.7 per cent VAT, from which staple commodities are exempt, as well as excise duty on so-called luxury products. Red tape, however, remains a problem, with customs clearance taking several weeks. Foreign companies are strongly advised to demand cash payment upon confirmation of the order, or payment by irrevocable letter of credit confirmed by a first rate bank.

■ Attitude towards foreign investors

A developing country heavily dependent on foreign capital, Cameroon has an open policy towards foreign investment. The Investment Code was replaced in 2002 by an Investment Charter. Broadly similar in content to the CEMAC charter, this law was supplemented with sector codes – 40 or so sectors have been defined – by April 2004. However, the only codes passed so far concern gas,

mining and oil. A new law introduced in July 2004 provides for the extension of the current investment code and industrial free zone legislation. The new transition period expires in April 2007. The investment code of 1990 remains *de facto* in force. Revised in 1994 as part of the tax and customs reform of the Central African Economic and Customs Union, the 1990 code offers some tax incentives. These privileges are subject to the usual conditions, ranging from the hiring of local staff and the export of a proportion of turnover to joint ventures with local partners.

The tax structure has been simplified. The country also has an Investment Code Management Unit designed to promote investment and inform and assist investors. In actual fact a number of factors, in particular rampant corruption (the country is the second most corrupt African country after Nigeria, according to Transparency International) at all levels of the economy, hamper foreign investment. The inadequacy of the country's transport infrastructure and deficient electricity production are major obstacles to the development of the private sector. Moreover, foreign companies operating in the country have to cope with a heavy tax burden and a largely ineffectual legal and judicial system characterized by widespread circumvention of laws and regulations.

5

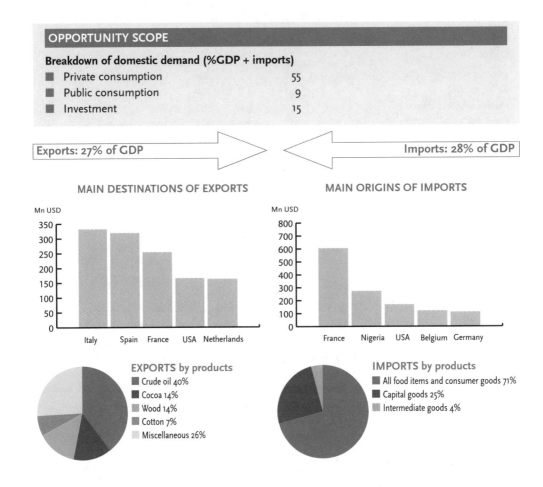

OPPORTUNITY SCOPE

Breakdown of domestic demand (%GDP + imports)

- Private consumption — 55
- Public consumption — 9
- Investment — 15

Exports: 27% of GDP → ← Imports: 28% of GDP

MAIN DESTINATIONS OF EXPORTS

Mn USD

(bar chart: Italy, Spain, France, USA, Netherlands)

MAIN ORIGINS OF IMPORTS

Mn USD

(bar chart: France, Nigeria, USA, Belgium, Germany)

EXPORTS by products
- Crude oil 40%
- Cocoa 14%
- Wood 14%
- Cotton 7%
- Miscellaneous 26%

IMPORTS by products
- All food items and consumer goods 71%
- Capital goods 25%
- Intermediate goods 4%

STANDARD OF LIVING / PURCHASING POWER

Indicators	Cameroon	Regional average	DC average
GNP per capita (PPP dollars)	1910	2342	4601
GNP per capita (USD)	550	658	1840
Human Development Index	0.501	0.489	0.684
Wealthiest 10% share of national income	35.4	39	32
Urban population percentage	50	42	45
Percentage under 15 years old	41	42	30
Number of telephones per 1000 inhabitants	7	22	120
Number of computers per 1000 inhabitants	6	17	37

Cape Verde

Population (inhabitants)	500,000
GDP (US$ million)	588
GDP per capita (US$)	1,284

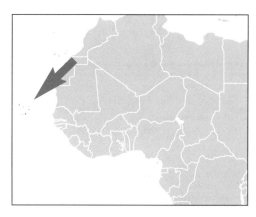

Coface analysis

Short-term: **C**

Medium-term:
Very high risk

RISK ASSESSMENT

Dynamic growth has persisted, buoyed by increased tourism revenues and public sector investments. The economy has nonetheless remained hampered by weak farm production and its energy dependence. Large external account imbalances have thus persisted, financed by transfers from the diaspora, international aid and massive reliance on debt and accumulation of arrears.

The triennial IMF programme (Poverty Reduction and Growth Facility) instituted in 2002 has permitted bringing the public deficit under control. Public finances have nonetheless remained largely in deficit and dependent on international aid, which has represented a third of fiscal revenues. Structural reforms (privatizations) have been making progress, albeit slow, but the opposition's ascendancy after the March 2004 local elections could impede their implementation. The refusal of government authorities to move up legislative elections scheduled for 2006 could increase domestic tensions.

The country's economic dynamism will depend on FDI inflows to the tourist and light industry sectors. The country also boasts substantial seaport potential and fishing resources. The local currency's euro peg and prospects for signature of an agreement on association with the EU could, moreover, attract investors.

MAIN ECONOMIC INDICATORS						
US$ millions	2000	2001	2002	2003	2004[(e)]	2005[(f)]
Economic growth (%)	6.6	4.7	4.9	5.3	5.5	5.5
Inflation (%)	−2.4	3.8	1.9	1.2	1.0	2.0
Public sector balance (%GDP)	−25.9	−10.5	−11.1	−8.7	−9.9	−8.5
Exports	40	37	47	59	62	71
Imports	233	232	316	384	395	458
Trade balance	−81	−81	−124	−133	−139	−166
Current account balance	−194	−196	−269	−325	−333	−387
Current account balance (%GDP)	−14.7	−14.6	−17.6	−14.3	−14.6	−14.9
Foreign debt (%GDP)	65.4	94.7	84.4	74.6	69.4	64.4
Debt service (%Exports)	5.9	17.4	8.1	5.7	5.8	5.6
Foreign exchange reserves (in months of imports)	1.0	1.4	1.9	1.7	1.9	2.0

e = estimate, f = forecast

5

Central African Republic

Population (million inhabitants)	3.8
GDP (US$ million)	1,046
GDP per capita (US$)	275

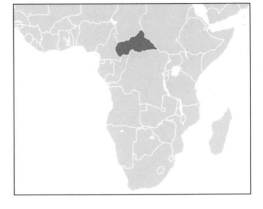

Short-term: **D**

Medium-term:

Coface analysis **Very high risk**

RISK ASSESSMENT

The economic situation has been slowly improving after years of turmoil resulting in a coup by General Bozizé in March 2003. The recovery, which has remained modest, could ultimately be consolidated by the accompanying implementation of reforms: timber industry reform, a new mining code permitting consolidation of the diamond sector together with road and waterway remediation to open up the country.

Difficulties have persisted. Consolidating public sector finances (undermined by a very narrow tax base, an insolvent parapublic sector and payment arrears) will require unpopular spending cuts. External account deficits have persisted along with an unsustainable debt burden. The country has thus remained dependent on international aid. In that regard, the IMF granted an initial loan under a post-conflict programme in July 2004, preliminary to initiation of a procedure under the HIPC programme reserved for highly indebted poor countries.

The extent of the support will depend on the success of the political transition. After the December 2004 referendum on the new constitution, the elections scheduled for February 2005 should complete the process. However, the security situation is still uncertain.

MAIN ECONOMIC INDICATORS						
US$ millions	2000	2001	2002	2003	2004[e]	2005[f]
Economic growth (%)	1.8	0.3	−0.6	−7.5	2.3	4.4
Inflation (%)	3.2	3.8	2.3	4.2	0.8	2.5
Public sector balance (%GDP)	−6.6	−4.3	−5.0	−4.6	−3.7	−2.6
Exports	156	142	146	118	159	197
Imports	119	107	122	114	132	159
Trade balance	37	35	24	4	27	38
Current account balance	−69	−56	−63	−88	−70	−66
Current account balance (%GDP)	−7.2	−5.8	−6.3	−7.3	−5.0	−4.4
Foreign debt (%GDP)	94	85	107	107	102	96
Debt service (%Exports)	20.6	18.8	23.1	27.7	25.1	25.0
Foreign exchange reserves (in months of imports)	6.2	6.3	6.2	6.6	6.1	5.5

e = estimate, f = forecast

Chad

Population (million inhabitants)	8.3
GDP (US$ million)	2,002
GDP per capita (US$)	241

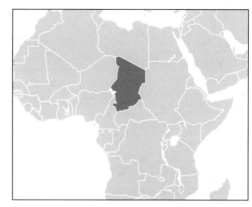

Short-term: **C**

Medium-term:

Coface analysis   **Very high risk**

RISK ASSESSMENT

With the start-up of the pipeline carrying Chadian oil from Doba to the Cameroonian port Kribi in July 2003, Chad became a member of the oil exporter club. The 225,000 barrel-a-day production increase underlies the exceptional economic growth posted in 2004.

Management of that wealth under World Bank auspices should ultimately facilitate consolidation of public sector finances even if government authorities regret the slow pace of payments. The new export earnings should also permit a marked improvement in external accounts and debt ratios after the imbalances run in recent years linked to capital goods imports.

The country's situation has nonetheless remained shaky. The production of other economic sectors will not permit significantly reducing poverty. Agriculture (35 per cent of GDP and 72 per cent of the working population) has suffered from difficulties in the cotton industry and Chad's landlocked condition. An insufficient energy supply and inadequate infrastructure have been hampering industry. A new triennial programme has thus been announced for early 2005 intended to speed up structural reforms and ultimately permit debt cancellation under the HIPC initiative. Politically, meanwhile, the oil could stir up rivalries, with Darfour refugees contributing to heightened tensions along the Sudanese border.

CONDITIONS OF ACCESS TO THE MARKET

■ **Market overview**

With the commissioning of its oil production facilities, Chad's economic growth climbed from 10.5 per cent in 2003 to nearly 40 per cent in 2004. Yet, owing to bureaucratic mismanagement of oil revenues and the suspension of the bulk of funding earmarked by donor countries following the failure of the sixth review of the Poverty Reduction and Growth Facility programme, Chad is facing a growing cash squeeze that is detrimental to economic stability. The volume of FDI – meagre until the arrival of the oil scheme – soared in 2002 and, to a lesser extent, in 2003 on the back of the construction of the oil pipeline; this, however,

should dry up by 2005. Customs duties on imports within the Economic and Monetary Community of Central Africa range from 5 per cent for basic staples to 30 per cent for consumer goods (raw materials and capital goods 10 per cent, semi-finished goods and miscellaneous products 20 per cent). Exporters are strongly advised to demand cash payment with the order or payment by irrevocable documentary credit confirmed by a leading bank, or to take out short-term cover against default.

■ **Attitude towards foreign investors**

In theory, the country is open to FDI. Its political will in this matter is demonstrated by its regional and international commitments and business-

5

MAIN ECONOMIC INDICATORS						
US$ millions	2000	2001	2002	2003	2004[(e)]	2005[(f)]
Economic growth (%)	0.6	9.5	9.9	10.0	37.9	13.3
Inflation (%)	3.8	12.4	5.2	−1.0	3.0	3.0
Public sector balance (%GDP)	−12.3	−10.7	−12.3	−12.0	−12.2	−9.1
Exports	177	186	183	465	1,621	1,888
Imports	237	510	867	886	706	663
Trade balance	−60	−324	−684	−421	914	1,225
Current account balance	−188	−615	−1,146	−1,067	−508	−324
Current account balance (%GDP)	−16	−38	−55	−45	−19	−11
Foreign debt (%GDP)	75	76	72	61	42	37
Debt service (%Exports)	12.3	14.0	20.1	12.8	4.0	3.3
Foreign exchange reserves (in months of imports)	3.0	1.7	1.8	1.6	1.6	2.0

e = estimate, f = forecast

friendly regulations (no obligation to buy local products, no discrimination between local and foreign capital, unrestricted access to foreign exchange, no export obligation). In practice, however, the country is fraught with risk as well as being unattractive. Foreign investors face geographical obstacles arising from the country's land-locked situation, together with sociological barriers (no business culture or medium- to long-term planning) and climatic uncertainties. Moreover, the country has a tiny financial sector: seven banks for ordinary transactions with only one possessing an international network, no domestic stock exchange and an unoperational regional stock exchange based in Libreville. There is virtually no basic infrastructure (roads, water, electricity, telecommunications) and one part of the country remains a hotbed of rebellion. The overall situation forces both domestic and foreign investors to adopt, because of lack of security and visibility, a strategy of short-term gains incompatible with the objectives of sustained development.

Congo

Population (million inhabitants)	3.7
GDP (US$ million)	3,017
GDP per capita (US$)	815

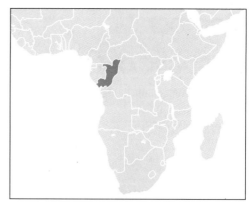

Short-term: **C**

Medium-term:

Coface analysis

Very high risk

RISK ASSESSMENT

After years of internal conflict, a process of political stabilization has firmed up despite the after-affects of that period that still mark the economic situation. Moreover, the age of the oil fields has limited prospects for expanding the industry with non-oil sector dynamism impeded by the inadequacy of structural reforms and of transport and energy supply infrastructure.

In those conditions, public finances and external accounts have been in a precarious state despite the excess oil revenues accumulated with high prices. With its financing needs remaining substantial, the country has been assuming debt

and accumulating arrears. The foreign debt burden, partly contracted on unfavourable terms with the debt secured by oil revenues, has thus become unsustainable.

Restructuring that debt will require implementing a programme with the IMF, which has proven very critical of late due to the opacity of oil revenue management and public finances. The progress registered in that area, along with the speed-up on reforms, nonetheless permitted the country to conclude an agreement with the IMF in December 2004 and to benefit from a new debt rescheduling agreement.

5

MAIN ECONOMIC INDICATORS						
US$ millions	2000	2001	2002	2003	2004(e)	2005(f)
Economic growth (%)	8.2	3.6	3.5	1.0	3.6	3.7
Inflation (%)	0.4	0.8	3.1	1.2	2.0	2.0
Public sector balance (%GDP)	0.8	−0.9	−8.2	−0.1	−7.0	−8.4
Exports	2,456	2,055	2,249	2,539	2,668	2,682
Imports	597	681	706	812	916	1,003
Trade balance	1,859	1,374	1,543	1,727	1,752	1,679
Current account balance	245	−82	−4	17	−217	−275
Current account balance (%GDP)	7.6	−3.0	−0.1	0.5	−5.4	−7.0
Foreign debt (%GDP)	209	236	218	214	203	209
Debt service (%Exports)	24.9	39.8	33.3	25.8	34.3	34.8
Foreign exchange reserves (in months of imports)	1.2	0.4	0.2	0.2	0.1	0.2

e = estimate, f = forecast

Democratic Republic of Congo

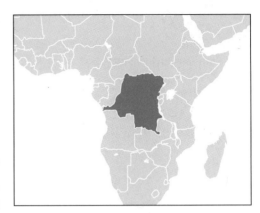

Population (million inhabitants)	51.6
GDP (US$ million)	5,707
GDP per capita (US$)	111

Short-term: **D**

Medium-term:

Coface analysis   **Very high risk**

RISK ASSESSMENT

Formation in June 2003 of a national unity government comprising almost all the country's political, civil and military power forces marked a positive turning point after six years of conflict. The forming of the unity government accompanied signature of accords with Rwanda and Uganda. Still, the political situation has nevertheless remained volatile. The process of disarming the militias and reunifying the army has made little progress; the central government's authority has not been restored throughout the country and it is weakened by divisions which could sharpen in the run-up to the elections scheduled in 2005. Furthermore, the eastern border provinces have remained areas of persistent instability despite the presence of UN peacekeepers.

The substantial aid promised, and partly delivered, by the international financial community under the triennial programme concluded with the IMF in 2002 should facilitate reviving the economy. However, although economic recovery has been perceptible, the challenges facing the government will be immense with the outlook remaining very uncertain. A very narrow tax base, notably attributable to a very large grey economy, has been hampering public sector accounts with needs remaining enormous. Moreover, exploitation of the country's vast natural resources has been lagging due to difficulties with implementation of structural reforms and inadequate infrastructure. In those conditions, external accounts have remained in deficit despite the external debt restructuring agreement concluded with the Paris Club and international aid will continue to cover the country's financing needs.

MAIN ECONOMIC INDICATORS						
US$ millions	2000	2001	2002	2003	2004(e)	2005(f)
Economic growth (%)	−7.0	−2.0	3.5	5.6	6.3	7.0
Inflation (%)	550	357	25	13	5	5
Public sector balance (%GDP)	−6.0	−1.7	−2.4	−5.9	−10.1	−15.0
Exports	892	880	1,076	1,281	1,413	1,485
Imports	680	807	1,093	1,404	1,873	2,265
Trade balance	212	73	−17	−123	−460	−780
Current account balance	−409	−518	−568	−459	−900	−1,367
Current account balance (%GDP)	−9.5	−11.0	−5.3	−7.5	−12.0	−15.8
Foreign debt (%GDP)	259	258	192	189	176	165
Debt service (%Exports)	73.9	74.2	2.9	8.0	5.1	7.0
Foreign exchange reserves (in months of imports)	0.4	0.2	0.5	0.6	0.9	1.2

e = estimate, f = forecast

Djibouti

Population (inhabitants)	700,000
GDP (US$ million)	576
GDP per capita (US$)	831

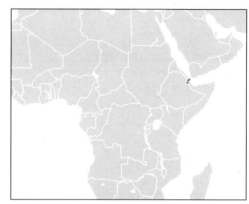

Short-term: **C**

Coface analysis

Medium-term:
Very high risk

RISK ASSESSMENT

Lacking natural resources and having limited diversification potential, the country's economic situation has remained precarious. The economic growth rate, particularly in relation to demographic growth, has been insufficient to reduce poverty and the unemployment affecting 50 per cent of the population. That situation, along with increased current capital spending, has been undermining public finances marked by large deficits financed not only through recourse to debt but also via donations and transfers linked to the presence of French and, since 2000, US military bases.

That income has also contributed to covering high external financing needs linked to a very large structural trade deficit, offset nonetheless by revenues from services related to port and transport activities towards Ethiopia. Although high, the foreign debt burden – contracted on concessional terms – has not been enough to permit the country to benefit from the HIPC programme for highly indebted poor countries.

In those conditions, and although the April 2005 presidential elections should bolster the country's political stability, it will be necessary to speed up structural reforms to energize the economy.

5

MAIN ECONOMIC INDICATORS						
US$ millions	2000	2001	2002	2003	2004[(e)]	2005[(f)]
Economic growth (%)	0.7	1.9	2.6	3.5	3.2	3.9
Inflation (%)	2.4	1.8	0.6	2.0	2.8	2.2
Public sector balance (%GDP)	−8.4	−6.3	−9.4	−8.4	−7.5	−9.7
Exports	75	76	83	89	90	116
Imports	270	263	287	338	373	413
Trade balance	−195	−187	−204	−249	−283	−297
Current account balance	−100	−71	−84	−95	−127	−130
Current account balance (%GDP)	−18.0	−12.3	−14.3	−15.2	−19.1	−18.8
Foreign debt (%GDP)	67	50	56	63	61	72
Debt service (%Exports)	6.3	5.7	6.1	5.2	4.9	4.5
Foreign exchange reserves (in months of imports)	2.2	2.4	2.4	2.8	2.4	2.4

e = estimate, f = forecast

Eritrea

Population (million inhabitants)	4.3
GDP (US$ million)	642
GDP per capita (US$)	149

Coface analysis

Short-term: **D**

Medium-term:
Very high risk

RISK ASSESSMENT

Economic activity has continued to suffer from both a long, dry spell, which has profoundly affected farm production, and the aftermath of the conflict with Ethiopia. In that context, infrastructure projects financed with international aid are still driving the economy. Very high public sector deficits – resulting from the inadequacy of tax revenues in relation to the scale of military spending and reconstruction programmes – have been responsible for the unsustainable level of public sector debt.

Moreover, to cope with structural external-account imbalances, the country has remained dependent on international aid whose volume will continue to depend on how the regime evolves. Relations with Western countries, notably the EU, have been strained due to increased repression of the opposition and the press as well as the indefinite postponement of general elections originally scheduled for 2001.

Although the country boasts mineral wealth and substantial tourism potential, persistent tensions with Ethiopia over the border between the two countries have increased risks of renewed hostilities.

MAIN ECONOMIC INDICATORS

US$ millions	2000	2001	2002	2003	2004(e)	2005(f)
Economic growth (%)	−13.1	9.2	0.7	3.0	1.8	0.7
Inflation (%)	19.9	14.6	16.9	22.7	21.5	20.5
Public sector balance (%GDP)	−60.8	−53.8	−42.4	−34.8	−46.2	−33.9
Exports	31	26	46	12	13	15
Imports	422	393	400	456	426	370
Trade balance	−391	−368	−355	−444	−413	−355
Current account balance	−172	−111	−95	−212	−211	−172
Current account balance (%GDP)	−27.1	−16.5	−15.0	−36.5	−33.9	−23.6
Foreign debt (%GDP)	51	61	79	105	85	65
Debt service (%Exports)	3.8	5.3	15.1	12.9	10.8	16.4
Foreign exchange reserves (in months of imports)	0.8	1.1	0.7	0.3	0.3	0.4

e = estimate, f = forecast

Ethiopia

Population (million inhabitants)	67.2
GDP (US$ million)	6,059
GDP per capita (US$)	90

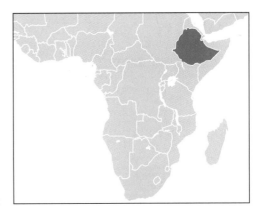

Short-term: **C**

Medium-term:

Coface analysis **Very high risk**

RISK ASSESSMENT

The economic recovery in 2004 is mainly attributable to improved weather conditions and the more favourable situation of farming after two years of drought that undermined the macroeconomic environment. Growth prospects for 2005 are still good although dependent on precipitation patterns. Although improving under the effect of tight fiscal policy, public sector finances have nonetheless remained a source of concern. Severe external-account imbalances have been generating large financing needs.

In that context, the country has remained dependent on international financial community backing, which notably permitted a substantial cancellation of foreign debt in April 2004 under the HIPC programme for highly indebted poor countries.

The support of financial backers will nonetheless depend on continuation of structural reforms. Furthermore, relations with Eritrea have remained tense since the war ended in December 2000 as Ethiopian authorities still reject the border decided on in April 2002 by an ad hoc commission. The catastrophic health situation in the country's eastern region could moreover spur severe social and ethnic tensions.

5

MAIN ECONOMIC INDICATORS						
US$ millions	2000	2001	2002	2003	2004[(e)]	2005[(f)]
Economic growth (%)	5.4	7.7	1.2	−3.9	11.6	5.7
Inflation (%)	4.2	−5.2	−7.2	15.1	9.6	5.4
Public sector balance (%GDP)	−14.8	−9.6	−14.0	−17.7	−12.6	−10.5
Exports	486	441	452	483	552	609
Imports	1,611	1,556	1,696	1,940	2,415	2,394
Trade balance	−1,125	−1,115	−1,244	−1,457	−1,863	−1,785
Current account balance	−626	−658	−782	−1,340	−1,050	−1,114
Current account balance (%GDP)	−9.8	−9.7	−12.9	−12.8	−13.0	−12.6
Foreign debt (%GDP)	86	90	103	99	69	69
Debt service (%Exports)	36.9	16.6	12.5	14.8	11.2	3.9
Foreign exchange reserves (in months of imports)	1.8	2.0	3.8	4.5	5.1	4.9

e = estimate, f = forecast

Gabon

Population (million inhabitants)	1.2
GDP (US$ million)	4,971

Short-term: **C**

Medium-term:

Coface analysis   **Very high risk**

STRENGTHS

- Gabon has abundant mineral wealth (second world manganese producer, oil) as well as extensive hydroelectric and forest resources.
- Oil revenues have permitted financing infrastructure development.
- Diversification of the economy toward higher value-added production is under way (notably in wood processing).
- The country's political stability has attracted foreign investment.

WEAKNESSES

- The economy has been very sensitive to price trends for oil (which represents 42 per cent of GDP, 54 per cent of tax revenues and nearly 80 per cent of export earnings) with proven reserves tending to decline.
- Foreign debt is high and financing needs are large.
- The country has depended on imports for its food supply with its farm potential underexploited.
- With 1.2 million inhabitants, Gabon represents a narrow market.

RISK ASSESSMENT

Economic growth should remain weak in 2005 with the gradual decline of oil production continuing to affect the growth rate despite the increased dynamism of non-oil sectors (manganese, wood). Moreover, to deal with the public sector debt burden and permit the country to obtain additional support from the international financial community, government authorities have adopted more restrictive fiscal policy that has limited their capacity to stimulate the economy.

Meanwhile, the domestic financial situation has improved under the effect of high oil prices and the disciplined fiscal policy pursued under IMF auspices. Moreover, that improvement has permitted speeding up payment of arrears and

reducing public sector dept. Company payment behaviour, often affected by fiscal arrears, has also improved.

Despite improved external accounts, new IMF commitments and rescheduling granted by the Paris Club in June 2004, the foreign debt burden has nonetheless remained substantial. Authorities have been hoping for at least partial debt cancellation even if the country cannot benefit from the HIPC programme reserved for highly indebted poor countries.

Meanwhile, a political situation characterized by great stability, which the implementation of austerity policy will be unlikely to jeopardize, has continued to attract the foreign investment needed to continue diversifying the economy.

MAIN ECONOMIC INDICATORS

US$ millions	2000	2001	2002	2003	2004(e)	2005(f)
Economic growth (%)	−1.9	2.0	0.0	2.8	1.5	0.7
Inflation (%)	0.4	2.1	0.2	2.1	2.0	2.0
Public sector balance (%GDP)	11.6	3.2	3.4	7.4	8.0	9.6
Exports	3,354	2,574	2,888	3,623	4,221	4,364
Imports	806	835	1,063	1,211	1,303	1,469
Trade balance	2,548	1,740	1,825	2,412	2,918	2,895
Current account balance	997	501	274	646	787	781
Current account balance (%GDP)	19.9	10.8	5.0	9.5	11.4	10.8
Foreign debt (%GDP)	98.3	82.6	87.4	71.0	72.3	77.2
Debt service (%Exports)	18.0	28.6	22.3	16.9	15.6	15.6
Foreign exchange reserves (in months of imports)	1.0	0.1	0.7	0.8	1.6	2.6

e = estimate, f = forecast

CONDITIONS OF ACCESS TO THE MARKET

■ Market overview

The Gabonese market is very open. The country's customs tariff system is the same as that used throughout the Economic and Monetary Community of Central Africa (CEMAC). Its main features include duty-free admission of goods from other CEMAC countries (although the volume of goods traded is extremely limited), zero rate of duty on certain products such as medical equipment and stationary, 6 per cent on staple commodities, 11 per cent on raw materials and capital goods, 21 per cent on semi-finished goods and 31 per cent on consumer goods.

The most strongly recommended means of payment is the irrevocable and confirmed letter of credit. Documentary collection upon presentation of a complete set of bills of lading and bills of exchange should only be used if the customer is well known to the exporter. Bank transfers and cheques, for which the customer incurs no liability, should be avoided. Exporters should be cautious when dealing with government agencies. For all public sector orders, it is necessary to obtain a copy of the official purchase order issued by the Budget Expenditure Office at the Ministry of Finance. Contracts and orders placed by the government with a foreign supplier must be countersigned by the Director General of Public Accounts. Suppliers are advised to check the relevant tax clauses with the departments concerned.

■ Attitude towards foreign investors

The legislative and regulatory environment is extremely liberal and the attitude of government officials generally positive. Investors enjoy free trade through CEMAC, modern instruments of business law through OHADA (Organization for the Harmonization of Business Law in Africa), investment security through the Multilateral Investment Guarantee Agency (MIGA) and a guaranteed appeals procedure through the International Centre for the Settlement of International Disputes (ICSID). The country's Investment Charter provides for freedom of enterprise, the right to property (including intellectual property), unrestricted access to foreign currency, free movement of capital, etc. It is gradually being supplemented with special laws (Forestry Code, Investment Code, Mining Act, Oil Act, Labour Code, Competition Act). Recently the government set up a Competition Directorate and a National Commission Against Illicit Gain at the Ministry of Commerce and a Public Procurement Directorate at the Ministry of Economic Affairs, Finance, Budget and Privatization. Moreover, the Private Investment Promotion Agency (APIP) – a one-stop shop set up in 2002 – provides investors with practical information and a steadily improving

5

service, especially with regard to the time required to obtain administrative documents. The Gabonese Employers Federation (CPG) gives entrepreneurs proper support and is proactive rather than reactive.

Customs duties and VAT are negotiable for large industrial schemes. New VAT-related tax provisions were introduced in summer 2004 (see economic mission website: www.missioneco.org/gabon). In 2005, the Mandji Free Zone (Port-Gentil) is due to open its doors to companies engaged in the processing of natural resources, the provision of services and the assembly and distribution of finished goods. These companies will be eligible for extremely attractive tax incentives and capital transfer provisions (ten-year tax exemption, investment- and job-related tax

credits, etc). Wood processing under the new Forestry Code offers interesting investment opportunities. Libreville too offers real comparative advantages for the development of services on a regional scale, especially as a site for the regional headquarters of international companies.

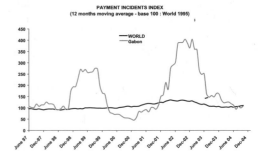

PAYMENT INCIDENTS INDEX
(12 months moving average - base 100 : World 1995)

OPPORTUNITY SCOPE

Breakdown of domestic demand (%GDP + imports)
- Private consumption   37
- Public consumption   7
- Investment   20

Exports: 59% of GDP   Imports: 39% of GDP

MAIN DESTINATIONS OF EXPORTS

Mn USD

USA   France   China   Trinidad and Tobago   Singapore

MAIN ORIGINS OF IMPORTS

Mn USD

France   USA   Netherlands   UK   Italy

EXPORTS by products
- Crude oil 81%
- Wood 11%
- Manganese 5%
- Miscellaneous 4%

IMPORTS by products
- Capital goods 20%
- All food items 16%
- Consumer goods 14%
- Miscellaneous 51%

5

STANDARD OF LIVING / PURCHASING POWER

Indicators	Gabon	Regional average	DC average
GNP per capita (PPP dollars)	5530	2342	4601
GNP per capita (USD)	3060	658	1840
Human Development Index	0.648	0.489	0.684
Wealthiest 10% share of national income	n/a	39	32
Urban population percentage	83	42	45
Percentage under 15 years old	40	42	30
Number of telephones per 1000 inhabitants	25	22	120
Number of computers per 1000 inhabitants	19	17	37

Ghana

Population (million inhabitants)	20
GDP (US$ million)	6,160

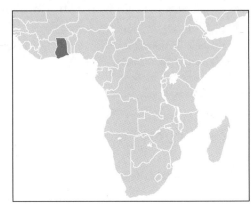

Coface analysis

Short-term: **C**

Medium-term:
High risk

STRENGTHS

- Political stability coupled with development of regional economic and monetary integration within ECOWAS, the Economic Community of West African States, should enhance the country's attractiveness to investors.
- With implementation of structural reforms, the country has earned international financial community backing.
- Under the HIPC initiative for highly indebted poor countries, Ghana reached the point of completion in July 2004 permitting it to benefit from substantial public foreign-debt reduction.

WEAKNESSES

- With the economy insufficiently diversified, gold and cocoa still represent nearly two-thirds of export revenues making the country vulnerable to exogenous factors (weather, world prices).
- Past public finance imbalances have generated heavy debt and high inflation.
- The country has remained dependent on international aid.

RISK ASSESSMENT

Growth remained strong in 2004, buoyed by high cocoa prices and increased gold production. The economy should remain dynamic in 2005, despite a poorer cocoa harvest. Deterioration of the situation in Ivory Coast, meanwhile, has spurred transport infrastructure development due to rerouting of merchandise flows from the Sahel now transiting more through Ghana. Nonetheless, the consolidation of public finances still represents a formidable challenge considering the heavy public domestic debt with inflationary pressures remaining problematic.

Meanwhile, external account imbalances have persisted with the trade deficit growing under the effect of robust domestic demand. Ghana has nonetheless reached the point of completion in the HIPC programme for highly indebted poor countries, thereby qualifying the country for cancellation of its public foreign debt.

In that context, characterized by international financial community backing and political stability that the December 2004 general elections should not jeopardize, the country should be able to attract more foreign investment, which will permit accelerating the modernization and diversification of the economic fabric.

MAIN ECONOMIC INDICATORS						
US$ millions	2000	2001	2002	2003	2004[e]	2005[f]
Economic growth (%)	3.7	4.2	4.5	5.2	5.4	4.9
Inflation (%)	25.2	32.9	14.8	26.7	13.0	16.5
Public sector balance (%GDP)	−10.0	−14.6	−8.1	−8.0	−5.2	−2.8
Exports	1,936	1,867	2,057	2,562	2,789	2,677
Imports	2,759	2,831	2,714	3,233	3,657	3,848
Trade balance	−823	−964	−657	−671	−868	−1,171
Current account balance	−389	−433	−261	−173	−315	−568
Current account balance (%GDP)	−7.8	−8.2	−4.3	−2.4	−4.1	−7.0
Foreign debt (%GDP)	141	138	115	108	97	93
Debt service (%Exports)	18.4	14.9	14.1	8.7	9.0	4.5
Foreign exchange reserves (in months of imports)	0.9	1.1	2.2	3.7	3.9	4.2

e = estimate, f = forecast

CONDITIONS OF ACCESS TO THE MARKET

■ Market overview

There are no import licences or exchange controls. The country has comprehensive copyright protection laws, although these are not properly enforced. Industrial property is better protected. Trademarks and company logos receive proper and adequate protection, provided they have been registered beforehand.

Customs duties vary between 0 and 25 per cent. Some products from the Economic Community of West African States (ECOWAS) are exempt from customs duty. Products from non-ECOWAS countries are subject to 0.5 per cent duty (ECOWAS levy). A new 0.5 per cent tax has also been introduced to provision the Export Development Investment Fund (EDIF). Since 1 April 2000, goods inspections at the point of entry have been carried out by GSBV (a Bureau Véritas/Ghana Standards Board joint venture) and by Gateway Services Limited (GSL), a Cotecna/Ghanian Customs joint venture. GSBV inspects goods at airports and land borders, whereas GSL conducts inspections at the ports of Tema and Takoradi.

VAT is applicable at a flat rate of 12.5 per cent on the customs value of goods, in addition to customs duties and levies. Since 1 August 2004, a national health tax of 2.5 per cent is applicable, together with VAT, to all imported goods and services. It is levied by the tax department responsible for VAT collection. Foreign companies, however, face a number of difficulties, including a stifling bureaucracy, a somewhat arbitrary legal and judicial system subject to outside interference (even if it can be said to be adequate for the job) and poor financing (the banking system is not interested in industrial and business investment).

■ Attitude towards foreign investors

To set up a joint venture with a local partner, a minimum investment of US$10,000 is required. The equity requirement is five times greater for wholly foreign-owned companies. Purchasing and sales groups are required to invest US$300,000 and employ at least ten local staff. These conditions do not apply to investment or fund management firms or to companies engaged in the export of Ghanian products.

5

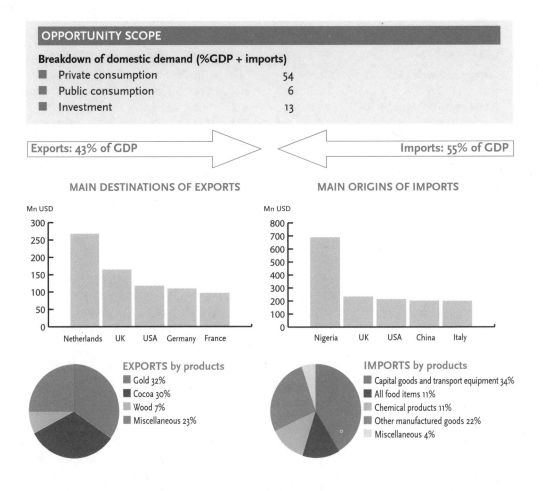

OPPORTUNITY SCOPE

Breakdown of domestic demand (%GDP + imports)
- Private consumption — 54
- Public consumption — 6
- Investment — 13

Exports: 43% of GDP   Imports: 55% of GDP

MAIN DESTINATIONS OF EXPORTS

Mn USD

Netherlands   UK   USA   Germany   France

MAIN ORIGINS OF IMPORTS

Mn USD

Nigeria   UK   USA   China   Italy

EXPORTS by products
- Gold 32%
- Cocoa 30%
- Wood 7%
- Miscellaneous 23%

IMPORTS by products
- Capital goods and transport equipment 34%
- All food items 11%
- Chemical products 11%
- Other manufactured goods 22%
- Miscellaneous 4%

STANDARD OF LIVING / PURCHASING POWER

Indicators	Ghana	Regional average	DC average
GNP per capita (PPP dollars)	2080	2342	4601
GNP per capita (USD)	270	658	1840
Human Development Index	0.568	0.489	0.684
Wealthiest 10% share of national income	30	39	32
Urban population percentage	37	42	45
Percentage under 15 years old	43	42	30
Number of telephones per 1000 inhabitants	13	22	120
Number of computers per 1000 inhabitants	4	17	37

Guinea

Population (million inhabitants)	8
GDP (US$ million)	3,213

Coface analysis

Short-term: **D**

Medium-term:
Very high risk

STRENGTHS

- Guinea boasts abundant mineral resources (a third of world bauxite reserves, iron, gold and diamonds) and considerable hydroelectric, farming (coffee, cocoa, cotton) and tourist potential.
- The country's prospective economic and monetary integration into ECOWAS, the Economic Community of West African States, will ultimately constitute an asset for investors.

WEAKNESSES

- Regional instability (Sierra Leone, Liberia, Ivory Coast) has had grave repercussions on the country (refugees, guerrillas and smuggling).
- The troubled political context and a strained domestic financial position have been deterring foreign investment.
- Electricity shortages, inadequate infrastructure and corruption have made the business environment relatively unattractive.
- The economy's dependence on farming and mineral exports has made the country vulnerable to external shocks.

RISK ASSESSMENT

Growth remained weak in 2004. Electricity shortages limited industrial activity and poor weather conditions undermined farm production. That situation should deteriorate further in 2005 with the internal and external political context remaining uncertain and deterring foreign investment.

Domestically, the poor health of President Conté, nonetheless re-elected in December 2003 with the opposition boycotting the vote, will pose the problem of his succession. Rising farm prices and poverty have been exacerbating social tensions and structural reforms have stalled. For that reason, with the situation of external accounts and public sector finances remaining poor and the country already in default on debt repayment, it no longer enjoys the support of its main financial backers and the Poverty Reduction and Growth Facility programme expired in May 2004.

MAIN ECONOMIC INDICATORS						
US$ millions	2000	2001	2002	2003	2004[e]	2005[f]
Economic growth (%)	1.9	4.0	4.2	1.2	2.6	1.0
Inflation (%)	6.8	5.4	3.0	12.9	16.6	20.0
Public sector balance (%GDP)	−5.5	−7.5	−6.2	−7.9	−4.1	−3.9
Exports	667	723	709	725	733	774
Imports	583	562	496	578	578	619
Trade balance	83	161	212	146	155	155
Current account balance	−252	−137	−81	−147	−130	−118
Current account balance (%GDP)	−7.2	−4.8	−5.6	−4.0	−3.7	−3.3
Foreign debt (%GDP)	112	113	102	88	87	82
Debt service (%Exports)	21.6	22.7	20.6	25.5	23.6	20.5
Foreign exchange reserves (in months of imports)	1.8	2.6	2.4	1.8	1.2	1.5

e = estimate, f = forecast

CONDITIONS OF ACCESS TO THE MARKET

■ **Means of entry**

Average import duty (excluding internal levies) is 16.5 per cent. The minimum rate is 2 per cent, the maximum 32 per cent and there is 18 per cent VAT.

■ **Attitude towards foreign investors**

The main priority of the Guinean government is to come up with innovative tax solutions that would enable the state and strategic foreign investors to share revenues from mining in an equitable manner. However, rigid administrative practices do not make life any easier for foreign investors as they grapple with an environment where domestic concerns hold sway. Although Guinea has ratified the OHADA treaty, set up an arbitration board and overhauled the investment code, in practice the legal system offers few safeguards, with appeals difficult to obtain and rarely successful. Industrial property protection is non-existent in the face of unfair competition from products imported on the informal market.

■ **Foreign exchange regulations**

Guinea is not a member of the franc area and the Guinean franc is not convertible. Since 1999, its official rate against the US dollar (the invoicing currency for Guinean mining exports) has been fixed via a mechanism operated by the central bank in coordination with banks, bureaux de change and international institutions. Pressure on foreign exchange reserves has led to a series of devaluations and the emergence of a parallel market. There are no restrictions on transfers.

OPPORTUNITY SCOPE

Breakdown of domestic demand (%GDP + imports)
- Private consumption 63
- Public consumption 5
- Investment 13

Exports: 24% of GDP   Imports: 30% of GDP

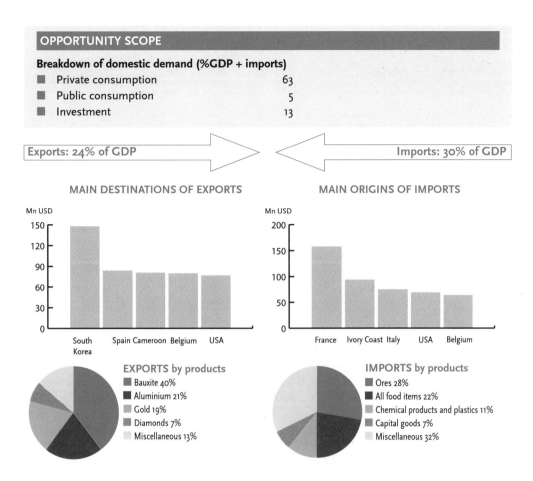

MAIN DESTINATIONS OF EXPORTS

Mn USD

South Korea | Spain | Cameroon | Belgium | USA

MAIN ORIGINS OF IMPORTS

Mn USD

France | Ivory Coast | Italy | USA | Belgium

EXPORTS by products
- Bauxite 40%
- Aluminium 21%
- Gold 19%
- Diamonds 7%
- Miscellaneous 13%

IMPORTS by products
- Ores 28%
- All food items 22%
- Chemical products and plastics 11%
- Capital goods 7%
- Miscellaneous 32%

5

STANDARD OF LIVING / PURCHASING POWER

Indicators	Guinea	Regional average	DC average
GNP per capita (PPP dollars)	2060	2342	4601
GNP per capita (USD)	410	658	1840
Human Development Index	0.425	0.489	0.684
Wealthiest 10% share of national income	32	39	32
Urban population percentage	28	42	45
Percentage under 15 years old	44	42	30
Number of telephones per 1000 inhabitants	3	22	120
Number of computers per 1000 inhabitants	6	17	37

Ivory Coast

Population (million inhabitants)	17
GDP (US$ million)	11,682

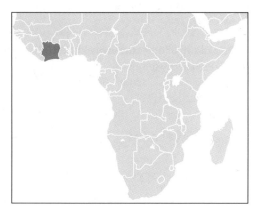

Coface analysis

Short-term: **D**

Medium-term:
Very high risk

STRENGTHS

- The Ivory Coast economy's resources are diversified – besides farming capacity, it boasts significant mineral and industrial potential and good financial, transportation and telecommunications infrastructure.
- The country has traditionally served as a corridor to landlocked Sahel countries.
- Membership in UEMOA, the West African economic and monetary union, has remained a factor of monetary stability despite the turmoil buffeting the country.

WEAKNESSES

- Recurrent political tensions since the December 1999 coup, exacerbated by the country's partition in September 2002, have seriously affected the economy.
- The durability of the country's regional role (finance, transit, commercial base) is now in jeopardy.
- The country's dependence on its farm production – cocoa (world leading producer), coffee, cotton – and thus on weather conditions and world prices has consequently been increasing.
- Relations with financial backers have been suspended with structural reforms falling increasingly far behind.

RISK ASSESSMENT

The political situation has been deadlocked since the events of September 2002 that resulted in the country's partition despite the efforts of the international community and African states to implement the Marcoussis accords signed in January 2003. Prospects for the settlement envisioned with the Accra accords in July 2004 have fizzled with parliament failing to adopt legislative reforms in time and the disarmament process not getting off the ground.

The escalation of military and political tensions in November 2004, prompting the departure of 9,000 foreign residents, further undermined the pacifying process. Although South African mediation has been a positive factor, the chances for success and the holding of elections in 2005 are still very uncertain considering the mutual lack of confidence among the various parties.

In that context, the cocoa sector's good performance has permitted the government in the south to maintain an acceptable operating level but at the cost of accumulating arrears on debt repayment. The economic situation in the north, on the other hand, has become much shakier. Although economic stabilization will depend on political stabilization, a recovery will remain improbable until the country restores relations with the international financial community.

MAIN ECONOMIC INDICATORS						
US$ billions	2000	2001	2002	2003	2004[e]	2005[f]
Economic growth (%)	−2.3	0.1	−1.6	−3.8	−1.2	0.2
Inflation (%)	2.5	4.4	3.1	3.3	1.4	3.2
Public sector balance (%GDP)	−1.7	0.4	−2.0	−2.4	−1.1	n/a
Exports	3.8	3.7	5.7	5.8	5.0	5.0
Imports	2.3	2.3	2.6	3.2	3.3	3.2
Trade balance	1.4	1.5	3.1	2.7	1.7	1.8
Current account balance	−0.9	−1.5	0.8	0.1	−1.3	−1.4
Current account balance (%GDP)	−3.5	−3.9	6.5	3.8	−1.2	−1.8
Foreign debt (%GDP)	121	119	111	106	100	n/a
Debt service (%Exports)	36.4	32.1	25.7	25.5	29.9	n/a
Foreign exchange reserves (in months of imports)	1.7	2.7	3.9	4.1	3.7	n/a

e = estimate, f = forecast

CONDITIONS OF ACCESS TO THE MARKET

■ Means of entry

From 1 January 2000, the date of introduction of the common external tariff, all WAEMU countries have the same customs procedures. Member states enjoy total exemption from customs duties, while non-members are liable to four rates of duty: 0, 5, 10 and 20 per cent. There is also a statistical tax (1 per cent of the CIF value), a community solidarity tax (1 per cent), an ECOWAS community levy (0.5 per cent) and 18 per cent flat-rate VAT. Special taxes are levied ad hoc on a number of products such as alcoholic beverages, tobacco and cigarettes, tomato paste and petroleum products, while a limited number of products are liable to temporary sliding-scale duties. Protectionist measures include an import licence for cottons and 100 per cent cotton products (eg wax and bazin). Products are quantity- and quality-controlled by Bivac and Cotecna prior to shipment.

Under the law of 2 April 2002, a certificate of conformity is required to commercialize 80 or so products from 2 June 2003. Nevertheless, conformity checks have been temporarily suspended by the Ministry of Industry and Private Sector Development. With regard to exchange controls, the flow of capital between the Ivory Coast and non-ECOWAS member states (excluding France) is subject to the approval of the Ministry of Economic Affairs and Finance (Finex Department). There are no restrictions in principle on the movement of capital between Ivory Coast and other member countries (including France).

■ Attitude towards foreign investors

Introduced in 1995, Ivory Coast's new Investment Code is generally considered investment-friendly. The Code provides for two separate schemes and five- or eight-year tax exemptions based on the size and type of investment. Under the approval scheme (investment of more than 762,000 euros), investors are liable to 5 per cent flat-rate import duty on machinery, equipment and first batch of spares. The Code does not differentiate between origin of investment and applies to both local and foreign investment. However, legal uncertainty and poor customs and tax administration continue to cause concern among companies. Although there are no special restrictions on the employment of foreign workers in Ivory Coast, foreigners can be hired only if a vacancy has been advertized for one month and approval obtained from the Ministry of Labour.

5

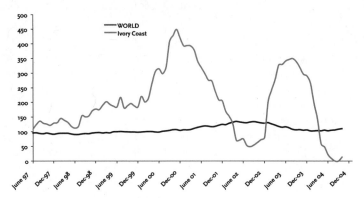

PAYMENT INCIDENTS INDEX
(12 months moving average - base 100 : World 1995)

OPPORTUNITY SCOPE

Breakdown of domestic demand (%GDP + imports)
- Private consumption   46
- Public consumption   8
- Investment   8

Exports: 48% of GDP   Imports: 30% of GDP

MAIN DESTINATIONS OF EXPORTS

Mn USD — France, Netherlands, USA, Germany, Mali

MAIN ORIGINS OF IMPORTS

Mn USD — France, Nigeria, China, Italy, Belgium

EXPORTS by products
- Cocoa 44%
- Petroleum 12%
- Processed wood 5%
- Other foodstuffs 4%
- Miscellaneous 35%

IMPORTS by products
- Intermediate goods 42%
- All food items 24%
- Other consumer goods 21%
- Capital goods 14%

5

STANDARD OF LIVING / PURCHASING POWER

Indicators	Ivory Coast	Regional average	DC average
GNP per capita (PPP dollars)	1450	2342	4601
GNP per capita (USD)	620	658	1840
Human Development Index	0.399	0.489	0.684
Wealthiest 10% share of national income	35.9	39	32
Urban population percentage	44	42	45
Percentage under 15 years old	42	42	30
Number of telephones per 1000 inhabitants	20	22	120
Number of computers per 1000 inhabitants	9	17	37

Kenya

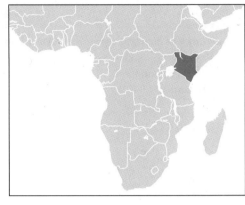

Population (million inhabitants)	31
GDP (US$ million)	2,330

Short-term: **C**

Medium-term:

Coface analysis **High risk**

STRENGTHS

- Besides farming (tea, coffee) and tourism resources, Kenya boasts a more diversified economy than most African countries.
- The country has played a role as an economic, financial and political platform for East Africa (eg its role in peace negotiations between Sudan and Somalia).
- The strengthening of regional integration, notably with implementation of a customs union within the East African Community, will represent an additional asset.

WEAKNESSES

- The slow pace of structural reforms, along with extensive corruption, has been undermining the country's economic potential.
- Erratic relations with the international financial community have had a negative impact on investment.
- Inadequate infrastructure has thus hampered an economy still very dependent on weather conditions.
- With the country unable to attract adequate external financing, the public domestic debt burden has been substantial.
- Authorities must meet major challenges, such as combating poverty, unemployment and the AIDS pandemic.

RISK ASSESSMENT

Hopes raised by the political changeover resulting from the December 2002 general elections have been slow to materialize. Although favourable, the outlook is still shaky despite signature of a new IMF agreement, promises of support by the international financial community and new debt rescheduling granted by the Paris Club in January 2004.

Tensions within the ruling coalition have been impeding implementation of structural reforms (financial and public sectors, privatizations) with the mere announcement of the reforms spurring severe social tensions. In that context, the release of promised financing has often been postponed, which has affected investment and economic activity despite a tourism recovery and the steadiness of the transport and telecommunication sectors.

Consolidation of public finances burdened by heavy domestic debt could take longer than expected. Moreover, with external financing needs growing under the effect of increased oil prices and Kenya's still-insufficient exporting capacity, the country will have to intensify efforts to attract more foreign investment.

MAIN ECONOMIC INDICATORS

US$ millions	2000	2001	2002	2003	2004[(e)]	2005[(f)]
Economic growth (%)	−0.2	1.1	1.0	1.5	2.2	3.5
Inflation (%)	10.0	5.7	2.0	9.8	10.0	7.5
Public sector balance (%GDP)	−5.1	−3.1	−5.5	−6.2	−5.8	−4.0
Exports	1,782	1,891	2,169	2,411	2,730	3,060
Imports	3,044	3,238	3,159	3,590	4,210	4,860
Trade balance	−1,262	−1,347	−990	−1,179	−1,480	−1,800
Current account balance	−199	−339	−10	−227	−430	−750
Current account balance (%GDP)	−1.9	−3.0	−0.1	−1.7	−3.0	−5.1
Foreign debt (%GDP)	60.1	51.4	49.3	47.4	49.5	51.3
Debt service (%Exports)	16.0	14.1	10.4	13.6	8.4	7.9
Foreign exchange reserves (in months of imports)	2.7	3.1	3.4	3.9	3.9	3.9

e = estimate, f = forecast

CONDITIONS OF ACCESS TO THE MARKET

■ **Market overview**

Kenya has a free market economy open to investment and imported capital and consumer goods that meet the country's standards. Only some products (arms, pesticides, animal and plant seed, etc) are banned or restricted. The few protectionist measures in place consist essentially of restrictions on the acquisition of land by foreigners, on the liberalization or privatization of utilities and on the running of investment management and reinsurance businesses. There are also tariff barriers in the form of temporary surcharges on import duties (suspended duties) aimed at protecting local industry (vehicle assembly) and agricultural products (maize, sugar, wheat, rice, natural fibres such as cotton, etc) These vary between 20 and 60 per cent and apply in addition to other duties and levies.

As well as reduced import duty on products processed locally, there are duty-free import arrangements and tax exemptions for export industries based in the free zone. The structure of customs duties has been gradually simplified to facilitate assessment and collection. Customs duties are due to be aligned to the EAC's common external tariff shortly. As of July 2003, the standard rate of VAT is 16 per cent.

The heads of state of three East African countries (Kenya, Uganda and Tanzania) have in fact signed a customs union agreement, which provides for a common external tariff of 0, 10 and 25 per cent as well as asymmetrical intraregional duties.

■ **Means of entry**

The US dollar and the pound sterling are the traditional units of account, although the euro has rapidly gained ground as the EU is the country's largest trading partner and biggest lender. Some formalities, such as pre-inspection of imported goods prior to shipment to Kenya, must be complied with. Administrative formalities remain fairly cumbersome at the various points of entry and the country employs local standards (labelling in English, weights and measures, etc). In any case, it is advisable to take certain precautions with regard to payments and to use tested procedures such as presentation of documents against payment, guaranteed bank cheques, international transfers and confirmed letters of credit.

■ **Attitude towards foreign investors**

That Kenyan government is looking to attract new investment to create the 500,000 jobs a year that it has set itself as a target. However, it still has to deal with discontent among local people who do not

5

always take kindly to the domination of the economy by Kenyans of Indian and British origin as well as multinationals.

Foreign investment is welcomed by the government, especially where it helps to promote exports, technology transfers and jobs. Growth sectors include agriculture (horticulture),

telecommunications, energy and utilities earmarked for privatization (roads, electricity generation and supply, railways, port terminal). Other than ad hoc decisions to limit access to specific sectors and stricter conditions for obtaining work permits, there are few restrictive or discriminatory measures.

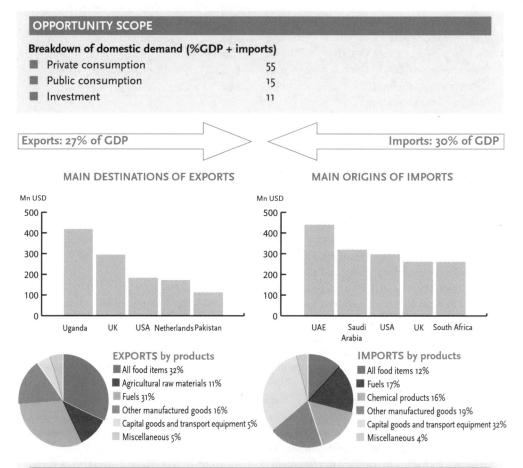

OPPORTUNITY SCOPE

Breakdown of domestic demand (%GDP + imports)
- Private consumption — 55
- Public consumption — 15
- Investment — 11

Exports: 27% of GDP   Imports: 30% of GDP

MAIN DESTINATIONS OF EXPORTS
Mn USD — Uganda, UK, USA, Netherlands, Pakistan

MAIN ORIGINS OF IMPORTS
Mn USD — UAE, Saudi Arabia, USA, UK, South Africa

EXPORTS by products
- All food items 32%
- Agricultural raw materials 11%
- Fuels 31%
- Other manufactured goods 16%
- Capital goods and transport equipment 5%
- Miscellaneous 5%

IMPORTS by products
- All food items 12%
- Fuels 17%
- Chemical products 16%
- Other manufactured goods 19%
- Capital goods and transport equipment 32%
- Miscellaneous 4%

STANDARD OF LIVING / PURCHASING POWER

Indicators	Kenya	Regional average	DC average
GNP per capita (PPP dollars)	1010	2342	4601
GNP per capita (USD)	360	658	1840
Human Development Index	0.488	0.489	0.684
Wealthiest 10% share of national income	36.1	39	32
Urban population percentage	35	42	45
Percentage under 15 years old	43	42	30
Number of telephones per 1000 inhabitants	10	22	120
Number of computers per 1000 inhabitants	6	17	37

Madagascar

Population (million inhabitants)	16.4
GDP (US$ million)	4,400
GDP per capita (US$)	268

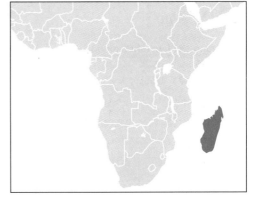

Short-term: **c**

Medium-term:

Coface analysis **Very high risk**

RISK ASSESSMENT

The economic situation has continued to stabilize since the 2002 crisis. The return of investor confidence has facilitated the recovery of the export processing zone, which has benefited the services sector. Moreover, tourism has recovered although remaining below Madagascar's potential.

The return of political stability, implementation of structural reforms and international community backing permitted the country to reach, in October 2004, the completion point in the HIPC programme reserved for highly indebted poor countries. However, with the external account situation likely to remain shaky and with high debt,

Madagascar will continue to depend on international aid.

Those encouraging results should not obscure the economy's structural vulnerability to weather conditions. The early-year cyclones thus, among other damage, exacerbated a rice shortfall that contributed to deterioration of external accounts and depreciation of the currency. Inflation, which increased as a result, has fanned social tensions. Measures taken to ease those tensions have widened the deficits of public sector accounts already undermined by reconstruction spending and a too-narrow tax base.

5

MAIN ECONOMIC INDICATORS

US$ millions	2000	2001	2002	2003	2004[e]	2005[f]
Economic growth (%)	4.8	6.0	-12.7	9.8	5.3	6.5
Inflation (%)	11.9	7.0	16.3	-1.7	10.1	7.6
Public sector balance (%GDP)	-6.4	-8.2	-7.7	-9.3	-11.3	-10.0
Exports	829	965	486	854	874	1,079
Imports	932	950	603	1,109	1,291	1,366
Trade balance	-103	15	-118	-254	-418	-287
Current account balance	-251	-90	-273	-471	-593	-465
Current account balance (%GDP)	-6.5	-2.0	-6.1	-8.6	-13.2	-10.1
Foreign debt (%GDP)	106	104	95	89	70	73
Debt service (%Exports)	12.5	10.7	20.9	13.1	4.2	5.5
Foreign exchange reserves (in months of imports)	2.2	3.1	3.8	2.6	2.8	3.0

e = estimate, f = forecast

Malawi

Population (million inhabitants)	10.7
GDP (US$ million)	1,901
GDP per capita (US$)	178

Short-term: **D**

Medium-term:

Coface analysis   **Very high risk**

RISK ASSESSMENT

The improvement in economic conditions has remained tentative and, in any case, insufficient to reduce poverty in the country with the government's incapacity to consolidate public finances and implement a reform programme having led financial backers to withdraw support. In the absence of that backing, the country has been covering its financing needs by assuming debt that has become unsustainable.

President Mutharika's election in May 2004 could prove to be a turning point. Work on structural reforms has resumed and the government has announced a zero-tolerance policy on corruption and adopted an austerity budget.

Authorities have thus been able to restore relations with the international financial community and obtain promises of new support. In that regard, Malawi concluded an interim agreement with the IMF in 2004, which should result in the extension of new loans within a year.

Obstacles to the implementation of that programme have nonetheless remained substantial. Growth is still dependent on the farm sector and, thus, on weather conditions. The consolidation of public finances has remained uncertain with the political tensions generated by that policy, notably within the majority party, limiting the government's room for manoeuvre.

MAIN ECONOMIC INDICATORS

US$ millions	2000	2001	2002	2003	2004(e)	2005(f)
Economic growth (%)	1.7	−4.1	1.9	4.4	3.9	4.2
Inflation (%)	29.6	27.2	14.9	9.6	14.9	15.0
Public sector balance (%GDP)	−15.0	−14.8	−19.0	−19.7	−15.9	−12.2
Exports	406	427	421	402	476	484
Imports	563	585	727	630	703	693
Trade balance	−157	−158	−306	−228	−227	−209
Current account balance	−219	−214	−457	−304	−289	−482
Current account balance (%GDP)	−14.2	−12.6	−24.5	−17.8	−16.2	−13.9
Foreign debt (%GDP)	159	162	146	160	158	150
Debt service (%Exports)	21.2	22.3	19.7	25.5	27.1	22.1
Foreign exchange reserves (in months of imports)	3.8	3.3	1.4	1.9	1.3	1.3

e = estimate, f = forecast

Mali

Population (million inhabitants)	11.4
GDP (US$ million)	3,364
GDP per capita (US$)	295

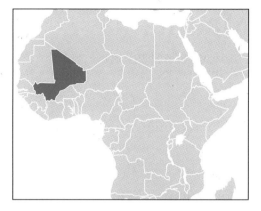

Short-term: **B**

Medium-term:
High risk

Coface analysis

RISK ASSESSMENT

Economic activity has remained subject to the vagaries of farm production, which suffered from locust swarms in 2004. The outlook is nonetheless still bright for 2005. Cotton production and processing (despite difficulties in restructuring the industry) and gold production (the country's primary source of export revenues), along with the telecommunications and transport sectors should permit restoring strong growth, the continuing Ivory Coast crisis notwithstanding.

Although benefiting from debt reduction since 2003 under the HIPC programme for highly indebted poor countries, Mali has been relying on concessional loans and grants to cover its still-high financing needs. Moreover, with the country facing the challenge of reducing the poverty still affecting two-thirds of the population, public finances have been deteriorating despite markedly improved fiscal discipline. Reflecting increased spending on education and health, however, that trend has not jeopardized Mali's relations with the IMF with a new triennial programme concluded in June 2004.

The May 2004 local elections consolidated support for the authorities elected in 2002. A broad political consensus should facilitate implementation of reforms essential to continued diversification and modernization of the country's economic fabric.

5

MAIN ECONOMIC INDICATORS						
US$ millions	2000	2001	2002	2003	2004$^{(e)}$	2005$^{(f)}$
Economic growth (%)	−3.2	12.1	4.3	6.0	4.7	6.1
Inflation (%)	−0.7	5.2	5.0	−1.3	2.5	2.5
Public sector balance (%GDP)	−7.7	−7.0	−7.3	−5.1	−7.5	−7.3
Exports	545	729	899	1,082	1,263	1,343
Imports	592	739	709	970	1,099	1,322
Trade balance	−47	−10	190	112	164	20
Current account balance	−319	−379	−144	−319	−281	−503
Current account balance (%GDP)	−12.0	−12.5	−4.3	−6.5	−5.1	−6.3
Foreign debt (%GDP)	99	96	84	59	58	52
Debt service (%Exports)	11.6	5.8	5.7	4.8	5.0	5.3
Foreign exchange reserves (in months of imports)	4.5	3.1	5.4	5.9	5.7	5.0

e = estimate, f = forecast

Mauritania

Population (million inhabitants)	3
GDP (US$ million)	969

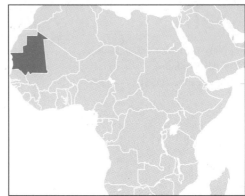

Coface analysis

Short-term: **C**

Medium-term:
Very high risk

STRENGTHS

- Abundant mineral resources (eg oil, copper, diamonds and potential in oil) have attracted foreign investors.
- The country has undertaken structural reforms and benefits from international financial community backing.
- That backing resulted in debt cancellation in 2002 under the HIPC programme.
- The strengthening of regional cooperation (Morocco, Senegal) will be an asset for the country.

WEAKNESSES

- Mauritania has remained very dependent on a small number of sectors with iron and fishing generating 99 per cent of export revenues.
- Its resources are still underexploited due to deficient infrastructure.
- Due to geographic and weather constraints (desert), the food supply has depended on imports.
- Mauritania's market is narrow.
- Recurrent intercommunity tensions and a high poverty rate are risk factors.

RISK ASSESSMENT

Economic results have been mixed. Growth has continued at a significant pace (despite a slight slowdown in 2004 due to the locust invasion's impact on farm production) thanks to steady investment, both public (infrastructure) and private (notably oil and mineral exploration). Moreover, implementation of structural reform programmes in recent years has spurred foreign investor interest in the country. For several years, foreign investment has been covering a large portion of the country's financing needs. However, foreign debt has remained high despite debt cancellation granted under the HIPC programme for highly indebted poor countries.

The country, nonetheless, still suffers from major weaknesses and external account imbalances will persist until its first oil revenues begin flowing in 2006. Those imbalances have been undermining the national currency and spurring inflationary pressures despite the coverage of financing needs provided by FDI inflows.

Moreover, the functioning of the banking system and foreign exchange system has been a source of difficulty for companies.

Above all, political tensions have increased since 2003 with coup attempts (June 2003, August and September 2004) and the turmoil that marred the November 2003 presidential elections won by the incumbent.

MAIN ECONOMIC INDICATORS						
US$ millions	2000	2001	2002	2003	2004[e]	2005[f]
Economic growth (%)	5.2	4.0	3.3	5.4	3.0	5.5
Inflation (%)	3.3	4.7	3.9	6.4	9.0	9.0
Public sector balance (%GDP)	-4.4	-5.5	6.2	-2.1	-2.7	-2.9
Exports	345	339	330	341	368	393
Imports	336	372	418	472	500	538
Trade balance	9	-34	-88	-131	-133	-145
Current account balance	-89	-180	-116	-309	-325	-417
Current account balance (%GDP)	-5.8	-10.4	-0.6	-9.5	-8.0	-7.1
Foreign debt (%GDP)	208	204	183	151	142	134
Debt service (%Exports)	33.6	31.6	14.9	12.3	12.8	12.1
Foreign exchange reserves (in months of imports)	7.0	6.1	7.8	5.8	5.0	4.3

e = estimate, f = forecast

CONDITIONS OF ACCESS TO THE MARKET

■ **Attitude towards foreign investors**

The legal environment is fairly well endowed in terms of both the quantity and quality of the country's laws (trade code, investment code, taxation code, etc). Property ownership laws, however, tend to be fairly vague in some cases and need to be improved in respect of urban areas, industrial areas, ports, airports and their surroundings, and land adjacent to major roads. A foreign company can win an action against a local partner belonging to the dominant tribe. It is even possible to win an action against the government and have the ruling enforced. On the other hand, it may be difficult, even impossible, for a foreigner to enforce a ruling against a business person belonging to the dominant Smacid tribe or an allied tribe (Ouled Bousba or Idawali).

There exists a double taxation treaty about which nobody has complained so far. However, the relationship between parent and subsidiary companies should be re-examined as there appear to be cases of double taxation that could be detrimental to investment.

The financial environment gives the greatest cause for concern. Mauritanian banks perform none of the functions normally expected of a banking system: savings collection, provision of credit for investment, etc. Their only role is to serve a limited number of interest groups as providers of foreign exchange and, lately, the national currency. Business persons not linked to these groups turn to bureaux de change to meet their foreign currency requirements in the exercise of their activities, but have to pay a surcharge for this service. As both business and non-business people keep cash savings in the local currency at home or at their workplace, there is a thriving grey market.

5

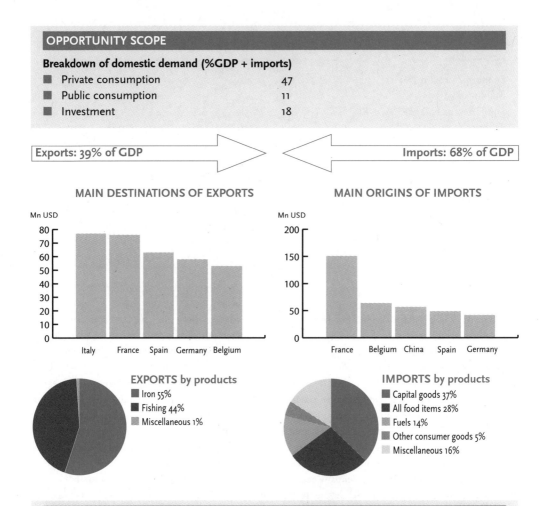

OPPORTUNITY SCOPE

Breakdown of domestic demand (%GDP + imports)
- Private consumption 47
- Public consumption 11
- Investment 18

Exports: 39% of GDP   Imports: 68% of GDP

MAIN DESTINATIONS OF EXPORTS

Mn USD

Italy, France, Spain, Germany, Belgium

MAIN ORIGINS OF IMPORTS

Mn USD

France, Belgium, China, Spain, Germany

EXPORTS by products
- Iron 55%
- Fishing 44%
- Miscellaneous 1%

IMPORTS by products
- Capital goods 37%
- All food items 28%
- Fuels 14%
- Other consumer goods 5%
- Miscellaneous 16%

STANDARD OF LIVING / PURCHASING POWER

Indicators	Mauritania	Regional average	DC average
GNP per capita (PPP dollars)	1790	2342	4601
GNP per capita (USD)	280	658	1840
Human Development Index	0.465	0.489	0.684
Wealthiest 10% share of national income	29.5	39	32
Urban population percentage	60	42	45
Percentage under 15 years old	43	42	30
Number of telephones per 1000 inhabitants	12	22	120
Number of computers per 1000 inhabitants	11	17	37

Mauritius

Population (million inhabitants)	1
GDP (US$ million)	4,533

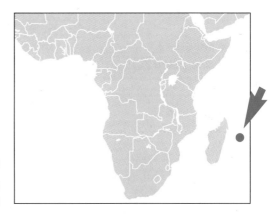

Short-term: **A3**

Coface analysis

Medium-term:
Quite low risk

STRENGTHS

- Mauritius is one of Africa's most advanced countries (GDP per capita, human development index).
- The economy has been turning to high value-added activities (new technologies, finance), which tend to attract foreign investment.
- External financing needs, and thus foreign debt, have been moderate.
- Beyond good economic and financial relations with Western countries and Africa, Mauritius has been developing relations with India and China.

WEAKNESSES

- The economy's growth rate has remained sensitive to sugar sector trends.
- The country has been suffering from competitiveness problems that the end of the Multifibre Arrangement in January 2005 should exacerbate.
- The growing unemployment level reflects the labour force's lack of technical skills.
- The investment needed for skills development (education, professional training) has been straining public accounts that are already squeezed by a narrow tax base.

RISK ASSESSMENT

Mauritius' economy will have to meet major challenges with profound restructuring of the textile and sugar sectors necessitated by the end of the Multifibre Arrangement in January 2005 and of the agreement on preferential access for sugar to the European market by 2007. Those sectors have already been suffering from a loss of competitiveness that has caused increased unemployment. Nonetheless, the level of investment and steadiness of the services sector (finances, information technology and telecommunications with tourism flat) have permitted the country to sustain strong growth.

Company payment behaviour has been reflecting the favourable economic conditions.

However, an ambitious public sector investment policy (education, infrastructure) and the decline of duty revenues have been straining public finances and contributing to the growth of public domestic debt. Consolidation of public sector finances has been a factor in political and social tensions with legislative elections coming between August and October 2005.

Conversely, the steadiness of the country's external accounts due to the services balance surplus and the very limited foreign debt burden with no hint of default risk have been affording government authorities ample room for manoeuvre.

5

MAIN ECONOMIC INDICATORS						
US$ millions	2000	2001	2002	2003	2004[(e)]	2005[(f)]
Economic growth (%)	2.7	7.6	4.3	2.7	4.7	4.5
Inflation (%)	5.3	4.4	6.4	5.1	4.5	4.7
Public sector balance (%GDP)	−3.8	−5.7	−5.9	−6.2	−5.5	−4.7
Exports	1,523	1,639	1,593	1,844	1,995	1,967
Imports	2,007	1,892	1,798	2,129	2,226	2,218
Trade balance	−484	−253	−205	−286	−231	−251
Current account balance	−69	154	248	136	235	247
Current account balance (%GDP)	−1.6	3.4	5.4	2.6	3.9	3.7
Foreign debt (%GDP)	42.3	45.8	45.0	41.3	35.4	32.7
Debt service (%Exports)	12.0	14.9	13.1	11.1	11.3	11.4
Foreign exchange reserves (in months of imports)	4.0	5.0	5.4	6.9	7.5	7.9

e = estimate, f = forecast

CONDITIONS OF ACCESS TO THE MARKET

■ Market overview

Mauritius has been a full member of the WTO since the 1994 Marrakech Summit. It signed the New York Convention on International Arbitration in June 1996 and ratified it in October 2002. Tariff barriers have been dismantled under a series of regional agreements (SADC, COMESA, IOC). A 10 per cent flat-rate VAT was introduced in 1998, but raised to 15 per cent in the 2002–2003 budget. Import licences remain in force for only three product categories: prohibited goods (dangerous items such as arms and explosives, vehicle spare parts), supervised goods subject to government approval (foodstuffs, energy and pharmaceuticals) and unrestricted or formality-free goods.

Adopted in 1994, the system of customs duties differentiates between exporting countries benefiting from a preferential tariff (EU, United States, COMESA, SADC) and the 25 or so countries that are subject to a general tariff. Customs duties vary between 0 and 80 per cent. Regional agreements permit tariff reductions on certain products with a view to establishing free trade areas. Excise duties are levied on four categories of imported and/or locally manufactured goods (alcoholic beverages, cigarettes, petrol and motor vehicles). They range from 15 to 400 per cent *ad valorem* for imported products and can be as high as 255 per cent for locally manufactured products (eg cigarettes). Some products (food staples and pharmaceuticals) and services (education, transport, electricity and water) are exempt from VAT. All imported products face 0–80 per cent customs duty. There have been fairly sizeable reductions in duty since 1998.

Non-tariff barriers such as import licences and price controls apply to staples, 30 of which are also subject to either administered pricing or profit control. Government monopolies enjoy exclusive powers to import so-called 'strategic' products. There are two main monopolies: State Trading Corporation (STC) and Agricultural Marketing Board (AMB). STC imports almost all the rice ration (other types of rice may be imported freely), wheat flour (but not special packaged flour), petroleum products and cement (up to 25 per cent of requirements) – rice, moreover, enjoys a subsidy. AMB holds an import monopoly for onions, garlic, potato seeds, saffron and cardamoms. However, since early 1998 AMB has relinquished some of its monopoly powers and permits potatoes to be imported free from price controls by approved private agents subject to certain conditions. The purpose of AMB is to regulate markets and protect local producers.

■ Attitude towards foreign investors

While Mauritius has, over the years, sought to attract the largest possible number of foreign investors – one just has to look at the numerous incentive schemes offered by the Board of Investment (a one-stop shop set up in 2001 for investments of 300,000 euros or more) and the investment protection agreements entered into with the country's main trading partners – it remains very selective about FDI, ensuring that the funds are channelled only into certain sectors. The country's laws and regulations reflect this will to direct FDI flows towards specific sectors.

■ Foreign exchange regulations

There are no exchange controls in Mauritius. The Mauritian rupee is fully convertible against the main currencies and may be transferred without restriction upon the sender providing proof of the origin of funds.

PAYMENT INCIDENTS INDEX
(12 months moving average - base 100 : World 1995)

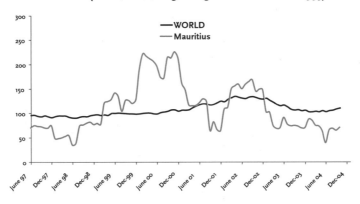

5

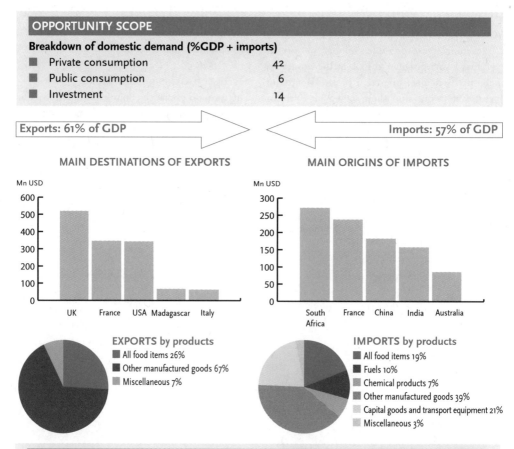

Breakdown of domestic demand (%GDP + imports)
- Private consumption — 42
- Public consumption — 6
- Investment — 14

Exports: 61% of GDP   Imports: 57% of GDP

MAIN DESTINATIONS OF EXPORTS

Mn USD

UK   France   USA   Madagascar   Italy

EXPORTS by products
- All food items 26%
- Other manufactured goods 67%
- Miscellaneous 7%

MAIN ORIGINS OF IMPORTS

Mn USD

South Africa   France   China   India   Australia

IMPORTS by products
- All food items 19%
- Fuels 10%
- Chemical products 7%
- Other manufactured goods 39%
- Capital goods and transport equipment 21%
- Miscellaneous 3%

STANDARD OF LIVING / PURCHASING POWER

Indicators	Mauritius	Regional average	DC average
GNP per capita (PPP dollars)	10820	2342	4601
GNP per capita (USD)	3860	658	1840
Human Development Index	0.785	0.489	0.684
Wealthiest 10% share of national income	n/a	39	32
Urban population percentage	42	42	45
Percentage under 15 years old	25	42	30
Number of telephones per 1000 inhabitants	270	22	120
Number of computers per 1000 inhabitants	117	17	37

Mozambique

Population (million inhabitants)	18
GDP (US$ million)	3,599

Coface analysis

Short-term: **C**

Medium-term:
Very high risk

STRENGTHS

- The country boasts natural resources (coal, hydroelectricity, gas, bauxite) and tourist potential that, although insufficiently exploited, have been attracting foreign investors.
- Mozambique has also benefited from its economic and financial relations with South Africa.
- With an ambitious structural reform programme, the country has earned continued international financial community backing, which has permitted it to substantially reduce its foreign debt via the HIPC programme after reaching the completion point in 2002.

WEAKNESSES

- The economy still bears the scars of 30 years of civil war: refugees, displaced persons, extreme poverty.
- The predominant farm sector employs 80 per cent of the population and represents 34 per cent of GDP, making the country very dependent on weather conditions.
- The inadequacy of infrastructure and the business environment has undermined the country's attractiveness.
- Economic development has focused on Maputo, which could exacerbate the severe social tensions simmering since the civil war ended in 1994.
- The country has remained very dependent on international aid.

RISK ASSESSMENT

Growth remained strong in 2004, buoyed by dynamic private investment, good harvests and increased aluminium production. Although foreign investment has continued to spur growth, it has remained too geographically concentrated and dependent on large projects. In the longer term, infrastructure problems will undermine development prospects.

Although improving, public sector finances still suffer from major imbalances. External accounts have also remained very out of balance, even if completion of large projects (MOZAL aluminium factory, gas pipeline) generating notable increases in gas and aluminium export revenues has helped reduce the deficits. The country's solvency has thus continued to depend on international community backing and cancellation of claims granted under the programme for highly indebted poor countries.

Despite increased domestic tensions, the December 2004 general elections should not jeopardize the relative political stability.

MAIN ECONOMIC INDICATORS						
US$ millions	2000	2001	2002	2003	2004[(e)]	2005[(f)]
Economic growth (%)	1.5	13.0	7.4	7.1	8.4	6.8
Inflation (%)	12.7	9.0	16.8	13.5	12.9	7.8
Public sector balance (%GDP)	−14.0	−21.4	−19.7	−15.4	−13.1	−11.6
Exports	364	703	679	880	1,257	1,311
Imports	1,163	1,063	1,351	1,445	1,446	1,712
Trade balance	−799	−360	−672	−565	−189	−401
Current account balance	−1,042	−966	−877	−803	−646	−887
Current account balance (%GDP)	−28.9	−28.1	−24.3	−18.6	−12.4	−15.6
Foreign debt (%GDP)	198	130	141	127	110	105
Debt service (%Exports)	2.5	3.5	4.5	4.5	4.8	4.5
Foreign exchange reserves (in months of imports)	4.9	4.4	5.0	5.8	5.1	4.4

e = estimate, f = forecast

CONDITIONS OF ACCESS TO THE MARKET

■ **Market overview**

Customs duties currently range from 0 per cent for pharmaceuticals, 2.5 per cent for commodities, 5 per cent for capital goods and 7.5 per cent for semi-finished goods to 25 per cent for luxury and similar products. Different rates of duty may apply to one and the same product category (eg vegetables and private vehicles). Duties on passenger cars, for instance, vary between 5 and 25 per cent. According to foreign companies based in Mozambique, the existence of a thriving parallel economy not subject to import duties, levies or VAT hampers fair competition and exports of their products. Customs procedures are so long-winded and complex that it is essential to hire the services of a special Mozambican agent (*despachante*) in addition to a shipping agent.

For payments, other than credit from international lenders, the irrevocable and confirmed documentary letter of credit is strongly recommended. Even where central bank and Ministry of Finance approval is obtained, foreign capital may be repatriated only if the investment project has been authorized beforehand by the Investment Promotion Centre (CPI). Since 1998, customs management has been satisfactorily handled by Crown Agents of the United Kingdom and goods inspection by the UK firm Intertek Testing Services (ITS).

■ **Attitude towards foreign investors**

The Investment Promotion Centre (CPI) was set up to facilitate and coordinate the direct investment decision-making process. While there is no legal requirement to consult this body, foreign investors are strongly recommended to do so. The government guarantees legal certainty and protection of property and other rights. A tax benefits code and industrial free zone legislation offer many FDI incentives. While the country's legislation provides for the establishment of wholly foreign-owned businesses, joint ventures with local partners are encouraged by the government. Living conditions for expatriates are highly satisfactory in the capital and major towns, but hygiene remains a concern in some regions.

■ **Foreign exchange regulations**

An interbank currency market regulating purchases and sales of foreign currency has been launched. This market is closed to everyone but the central bank and approved financial institutions. The value of the metical is determined daily on the basis of supply and demand. Foreigners are strongly advised to carry out all foreign exchange transactions via approved banks and bureaux de change. Banks may carry out currency transactions up to the value of their hard currency holdings. There are no restrictions on capital transactions.

OPPORTUNITY SCOPE

Breakdown of domestic demand (%GDP + imports)
- Private consumption   43
- Public consumption   8
- Investment   33

Exports: 24% of GDP   Imports: 38% of GDP

MAIN DESTINATIONS OF EXPORTS

Mn USD

Belgium   South Africa   Netherlands   Spain   UK

MAIN ORIGINS OF IMPORTS

Mn USD

South Africa   Portugal   USA   India   Australia

EXPORTS by products
- Aluminium 52%
- Electricity 15%
- Shrimp 9%
- Cotton 3%
- Miscellaneous 21%

IMPORTS by products
- Capital goods and transport equipment 39%
- All food items 22%
- Other manufactured goods 22%
- Fuels 11%
- Miscellaneous 6%

STANDARD OF LIVING / PURCHASING POWER

Indicators	Mozambique	Regional average	DC average
GNP per capita (PPP dollars)	990	2342	4601
GNP per capita (USD)	200	658	1840
Human Development Index	0.354	0.489	0.684
Wealthiest 10% share of national income	31.7	39	32
Urban population percentage	34	42	45
Percentage under 15 years old	43	42	30
Number of telephones per 1000 inhabitants	5	22	120
Number of computers per 1000 inhabitants	5	17	37

5

Namibia

Population (million inhabitants)	2
GDP (US$ million)	2,904
GDP per capita (US$)	1,452

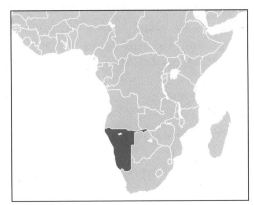

Short-term: **A3**

Medium-term:

Coface analysis **Quite low risk**

RISK ASSESSMENT

Growth has remained strong, buoyed by dynamic mineral sectors. Current account surpluses have persisted thanks to increased exports of zinc, diamonds and uranium. Foreign debt has thus remained low.

Besides abundant mineral resources, good quality infrastructure and substantial tourism potential, the country has benefited from relative political stability, bolstered by the November 2004 re-election of the party in power.

A process of economic diversification is under way, buoyed by foreign investment inflows to the communications, transportation and energy sectors. Although unlikely at this stage, radicalization of the land redistribution policy could, however, jeopardize those inflows.

Weaknesses have nonetheless persisted. With the public sector deficit continuing to grow, financing it by increasing domestic debt could ultimately prove nettlesome. Moreover, fishing and mineral extraction have been generating most export revenues making Namibia vulnerable to external shocks. Finally, the challenges facing the authorities, such as combating poverty and AIDS, have remained grave.

MAIN ECONOMIC INDICATORS

US$ millions	2000	2001	2002	2003	2004[(e)]	2005[(f)]
Economic growth (%)	3.3	2.4	2.3	3.1	4.8	5.2
Inflation (%)	9.3	9.3	11.3	7.3	5.5	6.2
Public sector balance (%GDP)	−1.0	−4.8	−4.4	−4.9	−6.0	−6.0
Exports	1,313	1,142	1,162	1,157	1,352	1,443
Imports	1,432	1,325	1,190	1,361	1,435	1,506
Trade balance	−119	−183	−28	−204	−83	−63
Current account balance	227	67	195	19	140	160
Current account balance (%GDP)	6.5	2.1	2.1	2.7	4.3	2.8
Foreign debt (%GDP)	4.6	12.3	19.5	23.9	22.4	22.9
Debt service (%Exports)	1.4	3.9	2.3	5.0	5.2	5.1
Foreign exchange reserves (in months of imports)	1.8	1.7	2.5	3.4	3.8	3.7

e = estimate, f = forecast

Niger

Population (million inhabitants)	11.4
GDP (US$ million)	2,171
GDP per capita (US$)	190

Short-term: **C**

Medium-term:

Coface analysis **Very high risk**

RISK ASSESSMENT

Economic growth has remained dependent on performance of the mineral sector (uranium and, since 2004, gold), agriculture (affected in 2004 by locust swarms) and infrastructure projects financed by international aid. Although encouraging, the growth rate has nonetheless not been sufficient to significantly reduce poverty and combat desertification.

In that difficult context, government authorities will have to continue consolidating public sector finances and discharging fiscal arrears, which have been sources of recurring social tension. Meanwhile, to cover external financing needs largely due to a structural trade deficit, the country

has depended on international community backing. That backing resulted in the cancellation of foreign debt in April 2004 granted via the HIPC initiative and in negotiation with the IMF of a new triennial programme for the 2005–2007 period. That programme should lead to implementation of structural reforms, some of which (notably privatization of public services for electricity, oil distribution) have been lagging.

President Tandja's re-election in December 2004 should facilitate that policy, which could attract more foreign investment, limited thus far to the uranium and gold sectors due to Niger's landlocked condition and inadequate infrastructure.

5

MAIN ECONOMIC INDICATORS						
US$ millions	2000	2001	2002	2003	2004(e)	2005(f)
Economic growth (%)	−1.4	7.1	3.0	5.3	4.1	4.2
Inflation (%)	2.9	4.0	2.7	−1.6	0.4	2.0
Public sector balance (%GDP)	−8.1	−7.9	−7.7	−7.5	−8.3	−7.0
Exports	283	274	280	350	390	490
Imports	330	334	372	474	569	647
Trade balance	−48	−60	−92	−125	−179	−157
Current account balance	−95	−119	−184	−249	−359	−313
Current account balance (%GDP)	−7.9	−6.6	−7.8	−7.8	−7.9	−6.4
Foreign debt (%GDP)	99	80	88	74	66	66
Debt service (%Exports)	28.3	34.0	37.2	31.2	15.7	10.6
Foreign exchange reserves (in months of imports)	2.2	2.9	3.2	2.2	2.1	2.0

e = estimate, f = forecast

Nigeria

Population (million inhabitants)	133
GDP (US$ million)	43,540

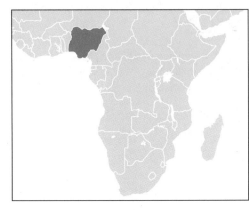

Coface analysis

Short-term: **D**

Medium-term:
Very high risk

STRENGTHS

- The country boasts extensive oil and hydroelectric resources, substantial farming and industrial potential and a large domestic market representing half the population of West Africa.
- It is thus expected to play a leading political and economic role regionally and on the African continent.
- It has initiated structural reforms.
- Prospective economic and monetary integration within the Economic Community of West African States (ECOWAS) will ultimately represent an asset for investors.

WEAKNESSES

- The economy is still insufficiently diversified with hydrocarbons representing 98 per cent of exports and 75 per cent of fiscal revenues.
- High foreign debt has been severely straining public sector finances affected by recurrent imbalances.
- Ethnic and religious conflicts, inequalities between north and south, poverty and unemployment have been constantly stoking strong domestic tensions.
- Implementation of reforms demanded by financial backers has been a delicate matter due to the constitutional and political context.
- A difficult business climate has deterred investment flows.

RISK ASSESSMENT

High oil prices, increased gas production and the good level of farm production have had a positive impact on growth despite social tensions and unrest in the Niger Delta. Thanks to hydrocarbon production and private investment dynamism, the outlook for 2005 has remained positive with persistent inflationary pressures still a source of concern.

Oil revenues have sharply improved the situation of public sector finances and external accounts. Despite that favourable context, the country has been accumulating payment arrears for several years on its debt with the Paris Club and still does not intend to settle all payments due in 2005, hoping for a substantial reduction of its debt. Government authorities have based that expectation on Nigeria's greater prominence on the world scene and leading role on the African continent.

Although President Obasanjo's new term in office since his re-election in 2003 has afforded him more room for manoeuvre to speed up structural reforms intended to modernize the economy, their implementation has nonetheless met with substantial resistance with recurrent strike threats.

MAIN ECONOMIC INDICATORS						
US$ billions	2000	2001	2002	2003	2004[e]	2005[f]
Economic growth (%)	4.1	3.3	1.4	10.9	4.1	4.5
Inflation (%)	6.9	18.0	13.7	14.4	16.5	11.5
Public sector balance (%GDP)	6.4	−3.3	−5.3	−1.3	5.3	3.8
Exports	21.4	19.6	17.7	27.4	31.5	30.9
Imports	11.1	11.5	13.3	16.9	17.5	19.0
Trade balance	10.3	8.1	4.3	10.5	14.0	11.9
Current account balance	4.2	1.3	−5.1	−1.6	0.7	−1.6
Current account balance (%GDP)	9.9	2.6	−11.1	−2.7	1.0	−2.3
Foreign debt (%GDP)	71.8	64.2	69.5	58.3	49.7	46.9
Debt service (%Exports)	14.9	13.9	13.7	9.5	8.8	9.2
Foreign exchange reserves (in months of imports)	5.7	6.3	4.1	3.5	5.8	7.0

e = estimate, f = forecast

The persistence of severe domestic intercommunity tensions and a difficult business climate have limited investor interest to the hydrocarbon sector despite the country's substantial potential for diversification.

CONDITIONS OF ACCESS TO THE MARKET

■ Market overview

The country is a member of the WTO but does not fully observe its rules. There is a huge variety of imported goods, customs duty on which ranges from 5 to 100 per cent of the CIF value. An import ban is in place for a growing number of products (currently around 40), including retreaded and second-hand tyres, second-hand clothes, cars over five years old, frozen foods, mineral water, pasta and biscuits. The Nigerian government has increased the number of protectionist measures in favour of local products, such as finished goods, but cut customs duties for raw materials and machinery. Labour is fairly cheap. A skilled worker earns about 150 euros a month, whereas an English-speaking local secretary gets 245 euros a month. Employees usually receive one month extra pay.

■ Attitude towards foreign investors

The Nigerian Investment Promotion Commission (NIPC), headquartered in Abuja, regularly publishes a list of priority investment sectors and incentives (financial, tax, etc) granted to companies by the government. The repatriation of capital, dividends and profit is unrestricted but extremely slow. Nigeria encourages oil companies to expand their exploration and production activities (long-term target: 4 million barrels daily). Accordingly, the country's deep-sea oil fields are under development and gas output is rising sharply. The oil majors are also involved in the development of the gas group NLNG, which is setting up new production facilities.

■ Foreign exchange regulations

The Central Bank of Nigeria (CBN) uses Dutch auctions to supply the local market with currency. Under this system, twice a week the CBN announces the volume of currency (dollars) it is prepared to sell against nairas and invites importers and foreign currency end-users to put in purchase bids for nairas through their banks.

Exporters are strongly advised to obtain payment for all orders before shipment either by irrevocable and confirmed letter of credit or in cash in a hard currency.

5

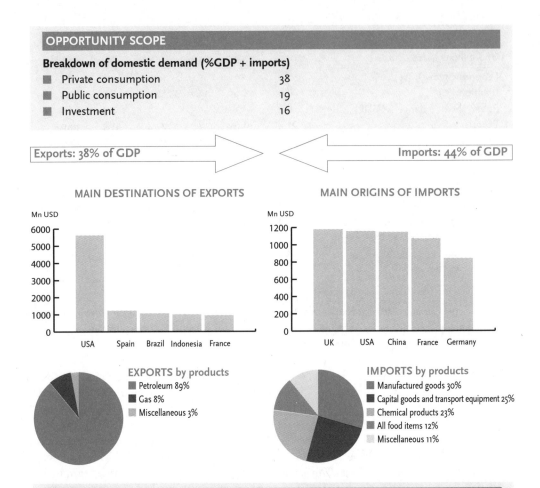

OPPORTUNITY SCOPE

Breakdown of domestic demand (%GDP + imports)

- Private consumption — 38
- Public consumption — 19
- Investment — 16

Exports: 38% of GDP

Imports: 44% of GDP

MAIN DESTINATIONS OF EXPORTS

Mn USD

(bar chart: USA, Spain, Brazil, Indonesia, France)

MAIN ORIGINS OF IMPORTS

Mn USD

(bar chart: UK, USA, China, France, Germany)

EXPORTS by products
- Petroleum 89%
- Gas 8%
- Miscellaneous 3%

IMPORTS by products
- Manufactured goods 30%
- Capital goods and transport equipment 25%
- Chemical products 23%
- All food items 12%
- Miscellaneous 11%

STANDARD OF LIVING / PURCHASING POWER

Indicators	Nigeria	Regional average	DC average
GNP per capita (PPP dollars)	800	2342	4601
GNP per capita (USD)	300	658	1840
Human Development Index	0.466	0.489	0.684
Wealthiest 10% share of national income	40.8	39	32
Urban population percentage	46	42	45
Percentage under 15 years old	44	42	30
Number of telephones per 1000 inhabitants	6	22	120
Number of computers per 1000 inhabitants	7	17	37

Rwanda

Population (million inhabitants)	8.2
GDP (US$ million)	1,732
GDP per capita (US$	211

Short-term: **D**

Medium-term:

Coface analysis **Very high risk**

RISK ASSESSMENT

A landlocked country subject to strong demographic pressures, Rwanda has been making a major effort to rebound from the 1994 genocide that devastated its human capital, institutions and infrastructure. Because of the crisis affecting the Great Lakes region, the country has also had to maintain high levels of military spending.

With the progress registered on structural reforms, economic stabilization is well under way but not complete. Although still vulnerable, Rwanda's economy should continue to grow at a respectable pace while remaining very dependent on farm sector performance despite the steadiness of services.

In that context, the tax base has remained narrow, resulting in persistently high public sector financial deficits. Similarly, external accounts have been structurally in deficit. The country has large financing needs. Having become unsustainable, its debt has depended on international financial community backing, which should notably result in debt cancellation under the programme for highly indebted poor countries.

The extent of that backing will depend on continuation of the political liberalization initiated with the holding of presidential and legislative elections in August and September 2003 (with President Kagamé winning 95 per cent of the votes in August and his party 74 per cent in September). Moreover, the persistence of high regional tensions has remained a serious handicap.

5

MAIN ECONOMIC INDICATORS						
US$ millions	2000	2001	2002	2003	2004[(e)]	2005[(f)]
Economic growth (%)	6.0	6.7	9.4	0.9	6.0	4.8
Inflation (%)	3.9	3.4	2.0	7.4	6.9	4.0
Public sector balance (%GDP)	−8.9	−9.5	−9.1	−10.5	−14.8	−14.9
Exports	90	94	67	63	77	80
Imports	240	238	235	244	260	280
Trade balance	−150	−144	−167	−181	−184	−201
Current account balance	−280	−271	−287	−324	−336	−361
Current account balance (%GDP)	−16.3	−15.9	−16.6	−19.2	−19.6	−19.8
Foreign debt (%GDP)	72	79	80	85	87	86
Debt service (%Exports)	50.6	12.8	19.8	13.7	12.6	18.5
Foreign exchange reserves (in months of imports)	1.9	1.8	2.7	2.3	2.0	2.2

e = estimate, f = forecast   403

São Tomé and Principe

Population (inhabitants)	200,000
GDP (US$ million)	47
GDP per capita (US$)	305

Short-term: **C**

Medium-term:

Coface analysis **Very high risk**

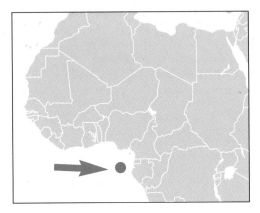

RISK ASSESSMENT

Political instability has increased since the July 2003 attempted coup. Corruption, tensions between President Menezes and the government and political infighting within the parties have been jeopardizing achievement of objectives agreed with the IMF to permit the country to ultimately benefit from cancellation of its foreign debt, which has reached unsustainable proportions (the previous agreement, signed in 2000, was suspended in 2001 due to grave public sector financial slippage).

That poor country's outlook has nonetheless improved. Not only have efforts been made to remedy the country's grave macroeconomic imbalances, but also the receipt of premium prices in the auctioning of offshore oil fields from 2004 should especially permit consolidating public sector finances. Although the marketing of the oil is not likely before 2007, profits on investments linked to exploitation have begun to affect the economy. Moreover, the country has adopted a law to ensure the transparency of future revenues and thus permit it to avoid the 'oil curse'.

With the country's strategic importance growing in consequence, it has earned the backing of the United States and has also developed closer cooperation with Angola and Nigeria.

MAIN ECONOMIC INDICATORS						
US$ millions	2000	2001	2002	2003	2004[(e)]	2005[(f)]
Economic growth (%)	3.0	4.0	4.1	4.5	6.5	6.5
Inflation (%)	11.0	9.5	9.2	9.6	13.3	14.5
Public sector balance (%GDP)	−30.5	−60.0	−40.4	−39.2	−41.0	−37.2
Exports	3	4	5	6	7	7
Imports	21	24	26	28	40	45
Trade balance	−18	−21	−20	−21	−33	−38
Current account balance	−25	−42	−35	−33	−56	−54
Current account balance (%GDP)	−52	−65	−51	−45	−68	−73
Foreign debt (%GDP)	588	650	619	555	500	521
Debt service (%Exports)	37.5	49.4	49.0	47.4	144.0	38.6
Foreign exchange reserves (in months of imports)	3.8	3.2	3.8	5.4	3.7	3.6

e = estimate, f = forecast

Senegal

Population (million inhabitants)   10
GDP (US$ million)   5,037

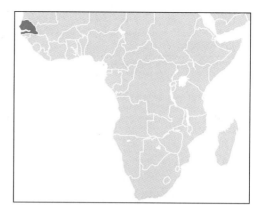

Coface analysis

Short-term: **B**

Medium-term:
High risk[1]

STRENGTHS

- The country has benefited from political stability and its good image.
- Implementation of major structural reforms (taxation, investment promotion, a new mining code) has improved the business climate.
- The economy has continued to diversify toward higher value-added sectors.
- Senegal can count on international community backing and, having reached the completion point in the HIPC programme for highly indebted poor countries, will benefit from cancellation of public sector foreign debt.

WEAKNESSES

- The economy is still dependent on agriculture (60 per cent of the work force and 20 per cent of GDP) and thus on exogenous factors.
- Demographic growth, unemployment and poverty affecting 57 per cent of the population with marked regional disparities have remained sources of weakness and social tension.
- With a structural trade imbalance, the country has remained dependent on expatriate remittances and the international community to cover its financing needs.
- Although Senegal's problem with the separatist southern Casamance province has eased, it is still unresolved.

RISK ASSESSMENT

Economic growth should remain strong, driven by household consumption and public spending. The steadiness of the services, extractive and manufacturing sectors as well as improvement in electric power production offset the difficulties met by the farm sector in 2004 (locusts, reorganization of the groundnut sector). Meanwhile, the public investment programme benefited the civil engineering sector.

Despite the worsening fiscal deficit in 2004, attributable to the cost of structural reforms and farm support, Senegal met the economic policy objectives set for the triennial programme agreed with the IMF in 2003, which permitted the country to reach the completion point under the HIPC initiative reserved for highly indebted poor countries in April 2004. Cancellation of the public sector's foreign debt will facilitate improving external account balances marked by high financing needs.

Despite repeated ministerial reshuffling, the absence of elections until 2006 should permit the authorities to continue to implement structural reforms.

The Coface payment incident index has stabilized but at a relatively high level. It is nonetheless more a reflection of late payments than actual defaults.

[1] Except international finance or FDA (French Development Association)

MAIN ECONOMIC INDICATORS						
US$ millions	2000	2001	2002	2003	2004(e)	2005(f)
Economic growth (%)	5.6	5.6	1.1	6.5	6.0	5.8
Inflation (%)	0.7	3.0	2.3	0.0	0.8	2.0
Public sector balance (%GDP)	−2.0	−3.9	−3.1	−3.4	−4.8	−3.6
Exports	920	1,009	1,069	1,488	1,661	1,785
Imports	1,337	1,437	1,608	2,270	2,453	2,586
Trade balance	−417	−428	−538	−782	−793	−801
Current account balance	−365	−295	−396	−595	−594	−594
Current account balance (%GDP)	−8.5	−6.5	−8.0	−8.3	−7.4	−6.8
Foreign debt (%GDP)	82.9	78.5	62.2	41.5	35.9	32.1
Debt service (%Exports)	11.6	9.3	11.5	5.6	4.5	4.0
Foreign exchange reserves (in months of imports)	2.4	2.8	3.1	2.9	3.1	3.0

e = estimate, f = forecast

CONDITIONS OF ACCESS TO THE MARKET

■ Means of access

The customs union established by the member states of the West African Economic and Monetary Union (WAEMU) is simple and non-discriminatory. Customs duties vary between 0 and 20 per cent according to product category. There are some token surtaxes (usually around 2.5 per cent), plus 18 per cent flat-rate VAT. All importers and exporters are required to register with the Foreign Trade Department (Comex) and to obtain a trading and import/export licence. Arms and drugs are banned.

The Senegalese government has appointed Swiss-based Cotecna Inspection to carry out goods inspections under the Import Verification Programme (PVI). Since 15 October 2001, imports with a CIF value of 1 million CFA francs or more. Since 15 October 2001, imports with a CIF value over 4,500 euros are subject to pre-shipment inspection.

■ Attitude towards foreign investors

The existence of a harmonized regional regulatory framework (OHADA, SYSCOA) and the action of the investment promotion agency, boosted by a new investment code, have led the Senegalese government to introduce a groundbreaking concession law in connection with an ambitious infrastructure programme involving strategic foreign partners. However, this scheme is undermined by a judiciary whose rulings are too unpredictable for the liking of many foreign investors as well as by a system of tax audits excessively concentrated on the formal sector, the impact of which is to strengthen unfair competition from the informal sector still exempt from taxation despite the introduction of a composite tax.

■ Foreign exchange regulations

There are no restrictions on business-related transfers within the franc area, provided they are handled by approved intermediaries such as banks. Fund transfers outside the franc area must be accompanied by an invoice, a pro forma, a contract or a documentary letter of credit. Dividend transfers are permitted, but must be supported by proof of entitlement.

PAYMENT INCIDENTS INDEX
(12 months moving average - base 100 : World 1995)

OPPORTUNITY SCOPE

Breakdown of domestic demand (%GDP + imports)
- Private consumption   54
- Public consumption   10
- Investment   14

Exports: 31% of GDP   Imports: 41% of GDP

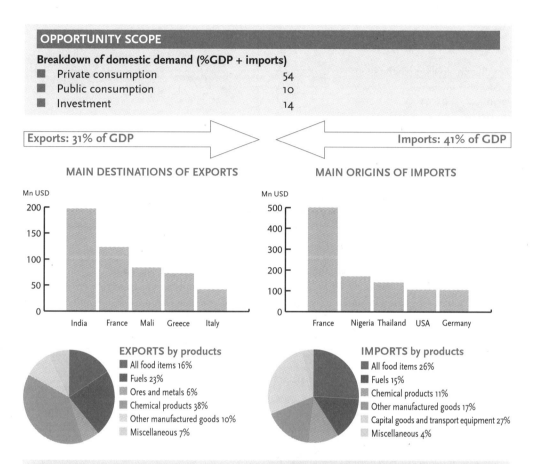

MAIN DESTINATIONS OF EXPORTS

Mn USD

India, France, Mali, Greece, Italy

MAIN ORIGINS OF IMPORTS

Mn USD

France, Nigeria, Thailand, USA, Germany

EXPORTS by products
- All food items 16%
- Fuels 23%
- Ores and metals 6%
- Chemical products 38%
- Other manufactured goods 10%
- Miscellaneous 7%

IMPORTS by products
- All food items 26%
- Fuels 15%
- Chemical products 11%
- Other manufactured goods 17%
- Capital goods and transport equipment 27%
- Miscellaneous 4%

STANDARD OF LIVING / PURCHASING POWER

Indicators	Senegal	Regional average	DC average
GNP per capita (PPP dollars)	1540	2342	4601
GNP per capita (USD)	470	658	1840
Human Development Index	0.437	0.489	0.684
Wealthiest 10% share of national income	33.5	39	32
Urban population percentage	49	42	45
Percentage under 15 years old	44	42	30
Number of telephones per 1000 inhabitants	22	22	120
Number of computers per 1000 inhabitants	20	17	37

5

Sierra Leone

Population (million inhabitants)	5.2
GDP (US$ million)	783
GDP per capita (US$)	151

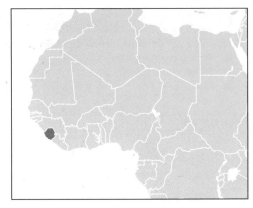

Short-term: **D**

Medium-term:
Very high risk

Coface analysis

RISK ASSESSMENT

Since its security situation improved, the country has enjoyed sustained growth buoyed by recovery of mining, farm production and infrastructure reconstruction financed by international aid.

That situation has nonetheless remained shaky with government authorities facing major challenges. Severe public sector financial imbalances have increased inflationary pressures. Despite the recovery of diamond and rutile exports, large external account deficits have persisted. Moreover, a still-difficult social situation (returning refugees, reintegration of former combatants, very high unemployment, corruption) and a still-unstable regional environment (Liberia, Guinea) have remained major risk factors.

In that context, the country's prospects will depend on international community backing currently manifested by the presence of UN forces and broad financial aid that includes foreign debt restructuring before cancellation scheduled for 2005 under the HIPC programme for highly indebted poor countries. However, delays incurred in effectively implementing anti-corruption measures and far-reaching reforms intended to improve the business environment could lead to reductions in the scale of that assistance.

MAIN ECONOMIC INDICATORS						
US$ millions	2000	2001	2002	2003	2004[(e)]	2005[(f)]
Economic growth (%)	3.8	5.4	6.6	6.5	6.0	5.0
Inflation (%)	−0.9	2.2	−3.1	7.6	12.0	15.0
Public sector balance (%GDP)	−17.3	−15.8	−19.7	−19.4	−20.1	−18.0
Exports	13	77	104	137	162	221
Imports	137	163	227	287	319	326
Trade balance	−124	−86	−124	−151	−157	−105
Current account balance	−113	−144	−201	−239	−250	−202
Current account balance (%GDP)	−18.1	−19.2	−27.4	−30.4	−31.3	−23.3
Foreign debt (%GDP)	181	155	156	146	109	209
Debt service (%Exports)	35.4	46.4	24.4	22.8	18.4	12.6
Foreign exchange reserves (in months of imports)	2.2	2.3	2.9	1.7	2.3	2.8

e = estimate, f = forecast

South Africa

Population (million inhabitants)	45
GDP (US$ million)	104,242

Coface analysis

Short-term: **A3**

Medium-term:
Quite low risk

STRENGTHS

- South Africa wields considerable economic clout on the continent with the country notably boasting 25 of the 30 largest African companies.
- Its mineral resources, diversified industry and high-performance tertiary sector (banks, telecommunications, transport) underpin the country's substantial economic potential.
- The macroeconomic framework has been conducive to the country's development with public sector finances under control and its financing needs and foreign debt both moderate.
- South Africa's role in seeking solutions to various conflicts (Democratic Republic of Congo, Burundi, Zimbabwe, Ivory Coast) has underscored its growing political importance.

WEAKNESSES

- Considering the scale of challenges such as combating poverty, unemployment and AIDS, an insufficient growth rate could exacerbate social and political tensions.
- Moreover, the country's social and economic dualism has remained a source of tension.
- The economy has suffered from an insufficiently skilled work force.
- Investors have had reservations about reforms intended to redistribute power and wealth in favour of the black majority (agrarian reform, economic emancipation programme).
- The country has remained vulnerable to a crisis of confidence in capital markets.

5

RISK ASSESSMENT

With inflation under control despite oil prices, economic growth has regained some dynamism, which should intensify in 2005. World recovery and, in particular, domestic demand have been driving growth in all sectors, including a manufacturing sector nonetheless hampered by the rand appreciation. The level of interest rates has been buoying private investment, and the tight fiscal policy pursued by authorities has given them substantial leeway to undertake public investment programmes. That favourable context has bolstered the financial situation of companies whose payment behaviour index has remained excellent.

Meanwhile, despite a worsening current account deficit, the country's external financing needs have remained moderate with debt thus remaining relatively low. Furthermore, the capital flow balance is still in surplus, which has resulted in a doubling of currency reserves that would permit the country to cope more effectively with a crisis of confidence in financial markets. Sources of weaknesses have nonetheless persisted on that score with short-term debt still high and FDI inflows insufficient.

MAIN ECONOMIC INDICATORS

US$ billions	2000	2001	2002	2003	2004^(e)	2005^(f)
Economic growth (%)	4.2	2.7	3.6	2.8	3.7	4.5
Inflation (%)	5.3	5.7	9.2	5.9	5.4	5.5
Public sector balance (%GDP)	−2.0	−1.6	−1.2	−2.1	−3.0	−3.1
Exports	31.9	30.8	31.3	38.5	42.6	45.3
Imports	27.3	25.7	26.6	34.7	40.5	44.2
Trade balance	4.6	5.1	4.6	3.8	2.1	1.1
Current account balance	−0.2	0.0	0.6	−1.3	−4.1	−5.9
Current account balance (%GDP)	−0.2	0.0	0.6	−0.8	−2.1	−2.9
Foreign debt (%GDP)	28.8	27.0	30.9	23.2	21.1	21.1
Debt service (%Exports)	13.6	15.7	13.7	13.0	11.1	8.5
Foreign exchange reserves (in months of imports)	1.8	1.9	1.9	1.6	2.5	2.5

e = estimate, f = forecast

CONDITIONS OF ACCESS TO THE MARKET

■ **Market overview**

South Africa's trade liberalization started in 1990 and has gathered pace since the country's membership of the WTO in 1995. South Africa uses the World Customs Organization's harmonized international nomenclature. Customs duties have been significantly reduced in the last five years, with tariff reforms being completed in late 1999.

■ **Means of entry**

Under the free trade agreement signed with the EU in October 1999, some 86 per cent of products imported from the EU will be exempt from customs duty by 2012. South Africa is not a signatory to the WTO agreement on the award of government procurement contracts. Until now, tenders have been overseen at the central level by the State Tender Board and at the local level by one of nine provincial tender boards. In the near future, however, a common service provider is due to replace the tender boards and put in place a uniform policy on government procurement under the State Tender Board Act. The Preferential Procurement Policy Framework Act, in force since February 2000, creates a points system that favours companies whose shareholders or managers are 'historically underprivileged people' (black, mixed race, Indian), women and the disabled. South

African public tender legislation consequently favours South African or foreign companies that team up with black partners (BEE – black economic empowerment). Where a public tender exceeds US$10 million, foreign companies are required to pay 30 per cent compensation on the total value of imports under the National Industrial Participation Programme. A Black Economic Empowerment Charter has been adopted by the financial services industry under which 25 per cent of a company's equity must be held by black people by 2010.

The South African Bureau of Standards (SABS) cooperates with a large number of similar international bodies to harmonize technical standards and regulations. International standards such as IEC and ISO are recognized by the Bureau but still need to be cleared by it.

■ **Attitude towards foreign investors**

Foreign companies are subject to numerous statutory provisions and orders (BEE, affirmative action) that limit their decision-making powers. The administrative environment in which they operate at times lacks transparency and predictability, as in the case of privatizations and public tenders. Invoicing of imported goods is generally done in US dollars. Also used are the euro, the pound sterling, the Japanese yen and the South African rand. The means of payment available in South Africa are similar to those in Europe and the United States.

■ Foreign exchange regulations

Exchange controls, which are governed by the 1961 Act and its manifold amendments, have been considerably relaxed in the last few years. The provisions governing capital transfers for ordinary business transactions have been liberalized. Currency traders believe there are no more *de facto* exchange controls for non-residents, with a few notable exceptions (borrowings in local currency, loans from a parent company to a South African subsidiary, etc). Measures designed to abolish restrictions on the amounts foreigners may invest were announced on 26 October 2004.

PAYMENT INCIDENTS INDEX
(12 months moving average - base 100 : World 1995)

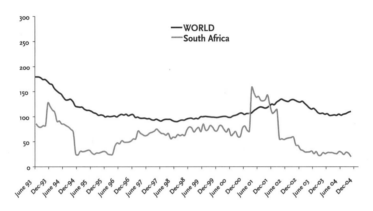

5

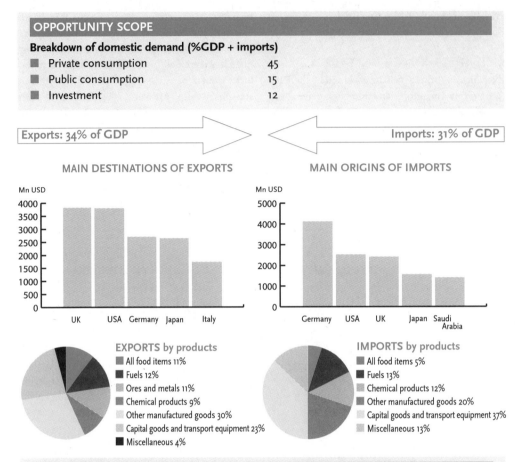

OPPORTUNITY SCOPE

Breakdown of domestic demand (%GDP + imports)
- Private consumption — 45
- Public consumption — 15
- Investment — 12

Exports: 34% of GDP   Imports: 31% of GDP

MAIN DESTINATIONS OF EXPORTS

Mn USD

UK   USA   Germany   Japan   Italy

MAIN ORIGINS OF IMPORTS

Mn USD

Germany   USA   UK   Japan   Saudi Arabia

EXPORTS by products
- All food items 11%
- Fuels 12%
- Ores and metals 11%
- Chemical products 9%
- Other manufactured goods 30%
- Capital goods and transport equipment 23%
- Miscellaneous 4%

IMPORTS by products
- All food items 5%
- Fuels 13%
- Chemical products 12%
- Other manufactured goods 20%
- Capital goods and transport equipment 37%
- Miscellaneous 13%

STANDARD OF LIVING / PURCHASING POWER

Indicators	South Africa	Regional average	DC average
GNP per capita (PPP dollars)	9810	2342	4601
GNP per capita (USD)	2500	658	1840
Human Development Index	0.666	0.489	0.684
Wealthiest 10% share of national income	46.9	39	32
Urban population percentage	58	42	45
Percentage under 15 years old	32	42	30
Number of telephones per 1000 inhabitants	107	22	120
Number of computers per 1000 inhabitants	73	17	37

Sudan

Population (million inhabitants)	32.8
GDP (US$ million)	13,516
GDP per capita (US$)	412

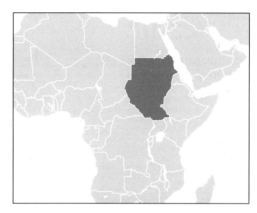

Short-term: **D**

Coface analysis

Medium-term:
Very high risk

RISK ASSESSMENT

Sudan's economic outlook appears bright. Oil revenues have permitted reducing the public sector financial deficit and financing implementation of major infrastructure projects that will facilitate diversifying the economy. In that context, strong growth has persisted and implementation of a vast structural reform programme has contributed to modernizing the economy's structure.

External account imbalances and a heavy foreign debt burden have nonetheless persisted. With its accumulated arrears, including to multilateral institutions, the country cannot benefit from debt reduction measures before sorting out its situation.

Moreover, the political situation is still unstable and could again tarnish the country's image. The

signing of various agreements with southern rebel factions since 2002 (notably agreements on sharing natural wealth and power during a six-year interim period intended to lead to the holding of a referendum on self-determination for the South) may augur the end of 20 years of internal war. However, emergence in 2003 of a new conflict in Darfur that revealed a deplorable humanitarian situation has again thrust Khartoum authorities into the spotlight and subjected them to criticism from the international community and UN. That situation has made the conclusion of final agreements with the South more uncertain, whereas possible implementation of international sanctions could impede the country's development.

MAIN ECONOMIC INDICATORS						
US$ millions	2000	2001	2002	2003	2004[e]	2005[f]
Economic growth (%)	6.9	6.1	6.0	6.0	6.6	7.6
Inflation (%)	8.0	4.9	8.3	7.7	6.5	6.0
Public sector balance (%GDP)	−0.8	−0.9	−0.8	1.0	−1.2	−0.7
Exports	1,864	1,699	1,949	2,577	3,001	3,197
Imports	1,634	2,031	2,153	2,536	3,032	3,268
Trade balance	230	−332	−204	41	−31	−71
Current account balance	−1,246	−1,554	−874	−727	−950	−1,077
Current account balance (%GDP)	−15.1	−16.2	−10.0	−8.6	−8.7	−7.9
Foreign debt (%GDP)	164	161	160	142	133	130
Debt service (%Exports)	68.6	49.4	28.5	25.3	22.8	22.5
Foreign exchange reserves (in months of imports)	0.5	0.1	0.8	1.6	2.0	2.5

e = estimate, f = forecast

413

Tanzania

Population (million inhabitants)	35.2
GDP (US$ million)	9,382

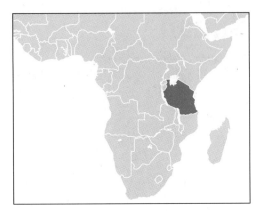

Coface analysis

Short-term: **B**

Medium-term:
High risk

RISK ASSESSMENT

Tanzania's economy has remained marked by contained inflation and sustained robust growth buoyed by steady farm production and mineral extraction and by the manufacturing sector's emergence. Continued far-reaching structural and institutional reforms and an improved business environment have consolidated the good economic results. Moreover, establishment of a customs union with Kenya and Uganda within the East African Community should make the country more attractive to investors.

Major sources of weakness have nonetheless persisted. Due to the narrow tax base, reducing public sector financial deficits has not been possible despite tight policy. Similarly, the economy's structure has made it too difficult to eliminate external-account imbalances despite increased farm and gold exports. External financing needs have remained substantial and foreign investment inflows, although growing, have not permitted covering them. In that context, the country is still very dependent on international aid, which resulted in substantial debt reduction as early as 2001 under the HIPC programme.

Politically, reforms and growth have not resulted in significant reductions of poverty and unemployment, which could affect the outcome of the general elections scheduled for October 2005. Meanwhile, the economic and political situation on the autonomous island of Zanzibar has remained tense.

MAIN ECONOMIC INDICATORS

US$ millions	2000	2001	2002	2003	2004[(e)]	2005[(f)]
Economic growth (%)	4.9	5.7	6.2	5.6	6.3	6.5
Inflation (%)	5.9	5.1	4.6	4.4	5.0	4.0
Public sector balance (%GDP)	−5.3	−5.6	−7.8	−9.6	−12.1	−11.0
Exports	715	816	1,010	1,173	1,277	1,453
Imports	1,439	1,554	1,660	2,101	2,457	2,595
Trade balance	−724	−738	−650	−927	−1,180	−1,142
Current account balance	−852	−832	−771	−1,127	−1,386	−1,356
Current account balance (%GDP)	−9.4	−8.9	−7.3	−10.9	−12.6	−11.2
Foreign debt (%GDP)	80	68	42	43	44	42
Debt service (%Exports)	30.2	5.9	4.7	5.0	5.8	5.2
Foreign exchange reserves (in months of imports)	5.2	6.0	7.9	7.7	7.3	7.8

e = estimate, f = forecast

Togo

Population (million inhabitants)	4.8
GDP (US$ million)	1,384
GDP per capita (US$)	288

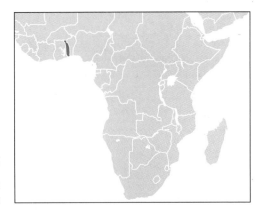

Short-term: **C**

Medium-term:

Coface analysis **Very high risk**

RISK ASSESSMENT

The political gridlock since the 1998 elections has affected the economy due to a substantial reduction in international financial community backing. The country has thus been undergoing a dose of austerity that has cut back the investment needed to modernize infrastructure and contributed to the accumulation of internal and external arrears.

However, increased cotton, cement and phosphate production, along with the steadiness of the transport sector, which has benefited from the Ivory Coast crisis, have tended to spur recovery. That recovery could firm up in 2005 with the announcement of a progressive lifting of the EU embargo.

A complete lifting of sanctions will depend on the continuation of efforts made in recent months to democratize the regime. In this case, Togo could benefit from new financial assistance. That would permit the country to cover structurally high external financing needs and reduce an unsustainable foreign debt burden before envisaging ultimate cancellation of its foreign debt under the HIPC programme. Nevertheless, uncertainties linked to the succession process of the late President Eyadema could open up a new period of tensions.

5

MAIN ECONOMIC INDICATORS						
US$ millions	2000	2001	2002	2003	2004[(e)]	2005[(f)]
Economic growth (%)	−0.8	−0.2	4.2	2.7	3.0	3.2
Inflation (%)	1.9	3.9	3.1	−0.9	1.0	2.0
Public sector balance (%GDP)	−5.1	−0.9	−0.8	0.8	−3.7	−0.5
Exports	326	352	404	460	495	702
Imports	564	564	597	678	856	939
Trade balance	−238	−212	−193	−218	−362	−237
Current account balance	−233	−231	−212	−237	−199	−169
Current account balance (%GDP)	−17.5	−17.4	−14.4	−12.9	−10.5	−8.4
Foreign debt (%GDP)	108	109	122	119	105	103
Debt service (%Exports)	15.5	17.6	13.1	13.6	13.7	7.8
Foreign exchange reserves (in months of imports)	2.5	2.1	3.2	2.4	2.8	2.5

e = estimate, f = forecast

Uganda

Population (million inhabitants)	25
GDP (US$ million)	5,803

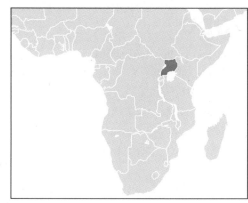

Coface analysis

Short-term: **C**

Medium-term:
High risk

STRENGTHS

- With effective implementation of structural reforms, diversification of Uganda's economic fabric is well under way.
- Via that policy, the country has earned international financial community backing and became one of the first beneficiaries of the HIPC programme.
- Uganda has made encouraging progress in several areas including education, the campaign against poverty and AIDS, and improving sanitary conditions for the population.

WEAKNESSES

- The country is still very dependent on farming, which represents 40 per cent of GDP and employs 80 per cent of the working population.
- Persistent regional and domestic tensions have been hampering Uganda's development.
- International aid is still essential to cover its financial needs.
- The business environment has remained difficult due notably to insufficient civil service capacity.

RISK ASSESSMENT

Economic growth has remained robust. Besides steady farm growth, nonetheless dependent on adequate precipitation, the manufacturing, construction and communications sectors should continue to buoy the economy.

Despite higher tax revenues, large public account imbalances have persisted due to the narrow tax base and extent of security spending. Moreover, increased exports, notably fish and tea, have not permitted offsetting low coffee prices. Large external account deficits have thus persisted.

In that context, with FDI inflows covering under 20 per cent of external financing needs, the country will remain dependent on international aid. However, the level of that backing will depend on continued but still uncertain easing of regional tensions (particularly in the Democratic Republic of Congo) and liberalization of the regime.

CONDITIONS OF ACCESS TO THE MARKET

■ Market overview

Piecemeal customs and tax (VAT) management is one of the main problems faced by importers and investors. Customs declarations must be supported by an import certificate, an invoice and a certificate of origin. Where applicable, a health certificate for live animals, a health certificate and import licence for plants (fresh fruits, vegetables and seeds) and a disinfection certificate for second-hand clothes, bedding and similar articles intended for sale must also be produced. Customs clearance takes about a week. Following cuts in customs duties, henceforth the lowest in East Africa, three rates of duty are applicable: 0, 7 and 15 per cent. COMESA

MAIN ECONOMIC INDICATORS						
US$ millions	2000	2001	2002	2003	2004[(e)]	2005[(f)]
Economic growth (%)	5.3	5.3	6.8	4.7	5.7	5.9
Inflation (%)	5.8	4.5	−2.0	5.7	5.1	3.5
Public sector balance (%GDP)	−15.5	−8.9	−12.2	−11.3	−11.2	−10.9
Exports	453	446	472	512	628	652
Imports	978	973	1,083	1,150	1,336	1,497
Trade balance	−525	−527	−611	−638	−708	−845
Current account balance	−767	−800	−787	−870	−795	−948
Current account balance (%GDP)	−13.0	−14.5	−13.9	−13.8	−11.7	−13.1
Foreign debt (%GDP)	59	59	67	71	63	61
Debt service (%Exports)	16.3	7.9	6.5	8.1	6.6	7.0
Foreign exchange reserves (in months of imports)	5.5	5.5	5.9	6.3	6.7	5.9

e = estimate, f = forecast

member countries are granted a preferential tariff also based on three rates: 0, 4 and 6 per cent. Production equipment and essential staples are admitted duty free. All duties are *ad valorem* and calculated on the CIF value of goods transported by road, and on the insured value of goods transported by air. In addition to customs duties and a 4 per cent levy calculated on the CIF value (warehousing duty), all imports are charged 0.8 per cent import duty on the FOB value (in respect of inspection fees), 2 per cent import levy on the CIF value (Import Licence Commission) and, where applicable,17 per cent VAT and excise duties.

An agreement establishing the EAC customs union between the three member states – Kenya, Tanzania and Uganda – was signed in March 2004. The EAC has adopted a three-tier common external tariff (0,10 and 25 per cent), which differs from Uganda's tariff structure of 0, 7 and 15 per cent. Some 426 products imported by Uganda from Kenya bear temporary duty at the initial rate of 10 per cent, which is to be reduced by two points each year.

■ Attitude towards foreign investors

Foreign direct investment in Uganda is governed by the 1991 investment code, which is restrictive on paper but liberal in its application. The Uganda Investment Authority (UIA) is responsible for processing investment proposals and offering

assistance and advice to investors. In a pragmatic move, the government has given it wide powers of initiative to reduce discrimination between foreigners and nationals, pending the introduction of a more liberal-minded code.

To obtain a licence, foreign investors must submit to the UIA a business plan along with a detailed financial statement of their company's activities. The accounts do not have to be infallibly accurate as licences for a minimum period of five years are granted automatically if the investment complies with the code. The UIA is required to draw up a report on each investment application within 30 days and reach its decision within a further 14 days.

The investment code does not guarantee foreign and local investors equal treatment. Foreigners face a number of obligations not applicable to domestic investors, including a minimum investment of US$100,000, staff training, use of local suppliers, respect for the environment, technology transfer, etc. No sector of the economy is closed to foreign investment.

Foreign investors are protected from forced sales. Where a company is subject to an expropriation measure, it is entitled to receive compensation based on the real value of its business within 12 months of the date of expropriation.

Property laws continue to pose problems for investors looking for land to start up in business. It

5

is therefore advisable to turn to specialist agencies, law firms or the UIA, all of whom can propose land with established landlords or carry out identity checks of landlords. Another problem facing investors is the fairly inconsistent manner in which the government hands out investment grants. For instance, the replacement of a five-year tax exemption with more favourable sliding-scale depreciation has actually sown confusion in investors' minds by giving the impression that the government does not honour its pledges.

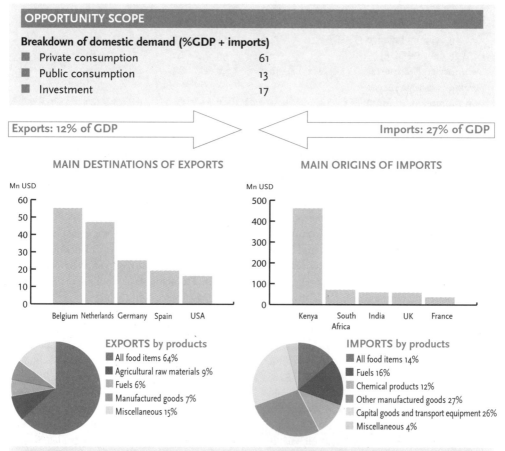

OPPORTUNITY SCOPE

Breakdown of domestic demand (%GDP + imports)
- Private consumption — 61
- Public consumption — 13
- Investment — 17

Exports: 12% of GDP | Imports: 27% of GDP

MAIN DESTINATIONS OF EXPORTS

Mn USD
Belgium, Netherlands, Germany, Spain, USA

EXPORTS by products
- All food items 64%
- Agricultural raw materials 9%
- Fuels 6%
- Manufactured goods 7%
- Miscellaneous 15%

MAIN ORIGINS OF IMPORTS

Mn USD
Kenya, South Africa, India, UK, France

IMPORTS by products
- All food items 14%
- Fuels 16%
- Chemical products 12%
- Other manufactured goods 27%
- Capital goods and transport equipment 26%
- Miscellaneous 4%

STANDARD OF LIVING / PURCHASING POWER

Indicators	Uganda	Regional average	DC average
GNP per capita (PPP dollars)	1360	2342	4601
GNP per capita (USD)	240	658	1840
Human Development Index	0.493	0.489	0.684
Wealthiest 10% share of national income	34.9	39	32
Urban population percentage	15	42	45
Percentage under 15 years old	49	42	30
Number of telephones per 1000 inhabitants	2	22	120
Number of computers per 1000 inhabitants	3	17	37

Zambia

Population (million inhabitants)	10
GDP (US$ million)	3,697

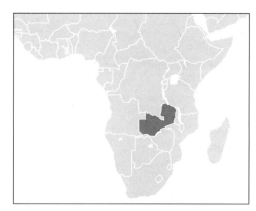

Coface analysis

Short-term: **D**

Medium-term:
Very high risk

STRENGTHS

- A major world producer of copper and cobalt, Zambia also has farming and tourism potential.
- Those assets and structural reforms undertaken could attract foreign investors.
- The country has benefited from international financial community backing and the debt reduction programme reserved for highly indebted poor countries.

WEAKNESSES

- With little diversification, the economy has remained vulnerable to exogenous shocks (copper prices, weather conditions).
- Structurally high external financing needs have resulted in unsustainable debt.
- The business environment has remained difficult (inadequate infrastructure, limited access to financing, corruption).
- Poverty has affected a large proportion of a population (73 per cent) that is also afflicted with the AIDS virus.

5

RISK ASSESSMENT

The economy has been growing at a satisfactory pace thanks to dynamic mineral (copper and cobalt) and farm sectors. That growth has nonetheless remained insufficient to meet the challenges of infrastructure modernization and poverty reduction.

The current account deficit has continued to shrink with copper exports increasing in both volume and value terms. Conversely, the public financial situation has remained shaky and the relative improvement registered in 2004 may prove ephemeral in the run-up to general elections in

2006. Further public sector financial slippage could jeopardize the backing granted by the international financial community.

Considering the extent of the country's financing needs and public sector external debt, that backing will be essential, notably to permit envisaging reduction of its foreign debt under the HIPC programme.

Meanwhile, although risks of social tensions increased recently with implementation of an austerity policy, the country has continued to benefit from relative political stability.

MAIN ECONOMIC INDICATORS						
US$ millions	2000	2001	2002	2003	2004(e)	2005(f)
Economic growth (%)	3.6	4.9	3.3	5.1	4.6	4.7
Inflation (%)	26.1	21.7	22.2	21.5	18.0	15.4
Public sector balance (%GDP)	−11.6	−13.0	−13.4	−12.9	−8.6	−9.8
Exports	746	884	916	1,134	1,537	1,596
Imports	978	1,253	1,204	1,393	1,513	1,634
Trade balance	−232	−369	−288	−259	24	−38
Current account balance	−633	−785	−681	−644	−378	−489
Current account balance (%GDP)	−19.2	−20.8	−17.3	−14.3	−11.4	−11.6
Foreign debt (%GDP)	193	200	172	153	143	139
Debt service (%Exports)	17.2	63.0	68.5	47.4	34.3	29.7
Foreign exchange reserves (in months of imports)	0.9	0.8	2.0	1.2	1.0	1.5

e = estimate, f = forecast

CONDITIONS OF ACCESS TO THE MARKET

■ Means of entry

Goods can be exchanged freely and some agricultural and mining products are exempt from import duties. ATA carnets are accepted. Customs clearance usually takes about 72 hours after presentation of the products, and consolidated import shipments are allowed. For preferential treatment of products, a COMESA or SADC certificate of origin is required. Excise duties vary between 5 and 125 per cent of the product's value and customs duties between 0 and 25 per cent. There is 17.5 per cent VAT as well as a refund scheme under the so-called duty drawback system. All means of payment are available, but documentary credit is recommended.

■ Attitude towards foreign investors

The Investment Act 1993, amended in 1998, guarantees freedom of investment in Zambia. Certain sectors – tourism, mining, air and road transport and financial services – require an additional operating licence. No regulations exist to restrict foreign shareholders and the Lusaka Stock Exchange is largely open to foreign investors. Corporate tax stands between 15 per cent and 45 per cent, depending on the nature of the business. There are no restrictions on the repatriation of profits. The free zones (EPZ) set up in 2003 provide foreign investors with tax breaks, including exemptions from corporation tax and excise duties. Zambia has mutual investment protection and double taxation agreements with numerous countries, including France. All disputes between foreign investors and local parties are subject to local or international arbitration (ICSIO and UNICITRAL). Zambian law makes it difficult to employ expatriates and 50 per cent of company directors must be Zambian.

■ Foreign exchange regulations

There are no exchange controls in Zambia. A foreign resident may open a foreign currency account with a local bank. However, there is no provision for exchange rate cover. Financial transaction costs are high.

OPPORTUNITY SCOPE

Breakdown of domestic demand (%GDP + imports)
- Private consumption — 59
- Public consumption — 8
- Investment — 12

Exports: 29% of GDP   Imports: 42% of GDP

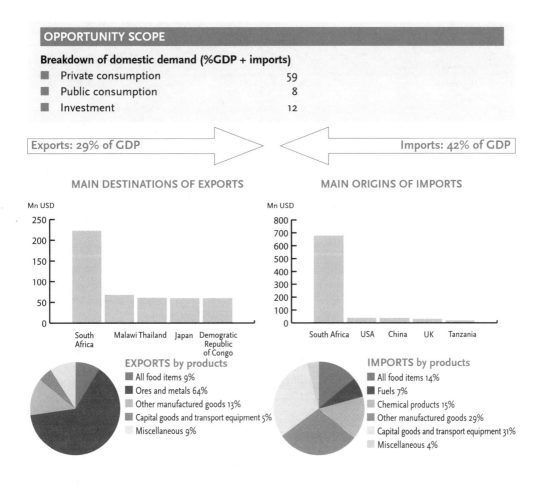

MAIN DESTINATIONS OF EXPORTS

Mn USD

South Africa, Malawi, Thailand, Japan, Demographic Republic of Congo

EXPORTS by products
- All food items 9%
- Ores and metals 64%
- Other manufactured goods 13%
- Capital goods and transport equipment 5%
- Miscellaneous 9%

MAIN ORIGINS OF IMPORTS

Mn USD

South Africa, USA, China, UK, Tanzania

IMPORTS by products
- All food items 14%
- Fuels 7%
- Chemical products 15%
- Other manufactured goods 29%
- Capital goods and transport equipment 31%
- Miscellaneous 4%

5

STANDARD OF LIVING / PURCHASING POWER

Indicators	Zambia	Regional average	DC average
GNP per capita (PPP dollars)	800	2342	4601
GNP per capita (USD)	340	658	1840
Human Development Index	0.389	0.489	0.684
Wealthiest 10% share of national income	41	39	32
Urban population percentage	40	42	45
Percentage under 15 years old	45	42	30
Number of telephones per 1000 inhabitants	8	22	120
Number of computers per 1000 inhabitants	8	17	37

Zimbabwe

Population (million inhabitants)	13
GDP (US$ million)	8,304

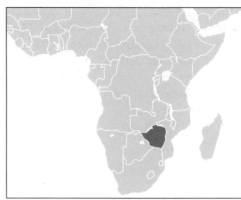

Short-term: **D**

Medium-term:

Coface analysis **Very high risk**

STRENGTHS

- Zimbabwe has benefited from extensive mineral and farm resources, a diversified industrial fabric and well-trained labour force.
- The quality of its transportation infrastructure and financial institutions could facilitate the country's recovery.
- With South Africa, Zimbabwe could be Southern Africa's economic and political engine.

WEAKNESSES

- The farm sector is still suffering from the speed-up of the agrarian reform initiated in 2000.
- The economic crisis has spurred strong social and political tensions.
- Zimbabwe is in default on payments to international financial organizations and creditors.
- It has been ostracized by the international community.
- The AIDS pandemic rate has been among the highest in Africa and the world.

RISK ASSESSMENT

After several recession years, the country is still mired in a grave economic crisis that has affected all economic sectors and, thus, personal income. Farm sector disorganization has amplified the effects of a drought, causing a food shortage. Meanwhile, a dearth of credit has been preventing companies from being supplied with energy and intermediate goods. Furthermore, inflation has remained very high.

Lacking currency earnings, the country has been unable to meet international commitments.

Moreover, it has been at odds with the IMF and the international financial community. In that context, the outlook for 2005 has remained gloomy and the country's deficits have been growing. Furthermore, preparations for legislative elections in March 2005 should exacerbate already severe political and social tensions.

In any case, the country's recovery will depend on international backing and that dependency will last for several years.

MAIN ECONOMIC INDICATORS

US$ millions	2000	2001	2002	2003	2004[(e)]	2005[(f)]
Economic growth (%)	−7.9	−2.8	−11.1	−13.2	−8.5	−3.3
Inflation (%)	56	77	140	432	353	448
Public sector balance (%GDP)	−21.6	−9.4	−3.9	−0.3	−9.7	−11.3
Exports	2,200	1,575	1,398	1,225	1,129	1,160
Imports	1,907	1,792	1,923	1,627	1,550	1,470
Trade balance	293	−217	−525	−402	−421	−310
Current account balance	−38	−497	−603	−421	−445	−334
Current account balance (%GDP)	−0.4	−5.9	−7.9	−6.0	−6.5	−12.8
Foreign debt (%GDP)	60.2	60.4	67.2	74.3	81.9	83.0
Debt service (%Exports)	22.9	31.4	35.1	35.4	35.3	30.9
Foreign exchange reserves (in months of imports)	0.1	0.1	0.1	0.1	0.1	0.1

e = estimate, f = forecast

CONDITIONS OF ACCESS TO THE MARKET

■ Market overview

Zimbabwe's economic and financial situation makes it a high risk country for foreign investors.

■ Means of entry

Goods can be freely exchanged, although a certificate of origin is required for imports. Customs duties vary between 0 and 138 per cent according to the type of import, except for goods from COMESA, which are exempt from duties on the basis of reciprocity. There is also a 15 or 25 per cent import levy – replaced by VAT from 1 January 2004 – plus a 10 per cent surtax. All means of payment are accepted, although credit cards are not widely used.

■ Attitude towards foreign investors

In principle, the 1989 Investment Act guarantees foreign investors unhindered market access. The government allows foreign majority stakes in mining and manufacturing, but no more than 70 per cent in services and 35 per cent in agricultural, armaments and water supply. Since 1 January 1995, all profits and dividends may be repatriated after payment of taxes. Disputes between a foreign investor and a local party are subject to local or international arbitration.

Corporation tax is 30 per cent, but foreign companies are also liable to 15 per cent tax on 56 per cent of the taxable income of their subsidiaries, plus a 3 per cent AIDS levy. Foreign enterprises can locate to any of the so-called 'export processing zones', which offer a number of incentives, including tax breaks and more flexible wage arrangements.

The stock exchange is open to foreign capital, but a listed company must not be more than 40 per cent foreign-held nor more than 10 per cent-owned by any single foreign shareholder. Investors can obtain a three-year work permit. It is possible to employ foreigners where equivalent local skills are unavailable.

■ Foreign exchange regulations

Foreign exchange transactions in Zimbabwe are subject to strict controls due to a shortage of hard currency. The official exchange rate is 824 Zimbabwean dollars to one US dollar. This rate only applies to exporters who are required to exchange 10 per cent of their export income at this rate through the Reserve Bank of Zimbabwe. A commercial rate has been in force since early 2004, (with an exchange rate of 6000 Zimbabwean dollars to the US dollar in February 2005).

5

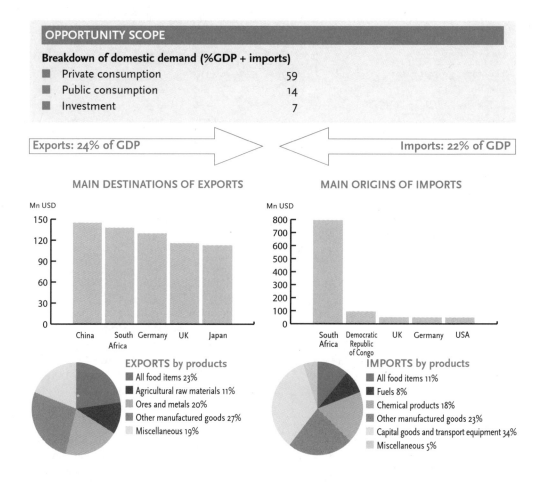

OPPORTUNITY SCOPE

Breakdown of domestic demand (%GDP + imports)
- Private consumption — 59
- Public consumption — 14
- Investment — 7

Exports: 24% of GDP   Imports: 22% of GDP

MAIN DESTINATIONS OF EXPORTS

Mn USD

China · South Africa · Germany · UK · Japan

MAIN ORIGINS OF IMPORTS

Mn USD

South Africa · Democratic Republic of Congo · UK · Germany · USA

EXPORTS by products
- All food items 23%
- Agricultural raw materials 11%
- Ores and metals 20%
- Other manufactured goods 27%
- Miscellaneous 19%

IMPORTS by products
- All food items 11%
- Fuels 8%
- Chemical products 18%
- Other manufactured goods 23%
- Capital goods and transport equipment 34%
- Miscellaneous 5%

STANDARD OF LIVING / PURCHASING POWER

Indicators	Zimbabwe	Regional average	DC average
GNP per capita (PPP dollars)	2180	2342	4601
GNP per capita (USD)	n/a	658	1840
Human Development Index	0.491	0.489	0.684
Wealthiest 10% share of national income	40.3	39	32
Urban population percentage	37	42	45
Percentage under 15 years old	44	42	30
Number of telephones per 1000 inhabitants	25	22	120
Number of computers per 1000 inhabitants	52	17	37

ACRONYM TABLE AND LEXICON

AFTA: Asian Free Trade Area

AKP (Turkey): The Justice and Development Party running the Turkish government since November 2002

BJP (India): Bharatiya Janata Party, the Indian nationalist party leading the coalition in power since 1999

BOT: Build Operate Transfer

CAEMC: Central African Economic and Monetary Community

CEPA (Hong Kong): Closer Economic Partnership Association (with mainland China)

CIS: Community of Independent States

COMESA: Common Market for Eastern and Southern Africa

Currency board: system whereby a country pegs its currency to a foreign currency (generally the US dollar or euro) with a currency board supplanting the central bank

EAC: East African Community

ECOWAS: Economic Community of West African States

FDI: foreign direct investment

FMLN and ARENA (El Salvador): major political parties – Frente Farabundo Marti para la Liberacion Nacional and Alianza Republicana Nacionalista

GDP: gross domestic product

GNP: gross national product

HIPC initiative or programme: a joint IMF/World Bank initiative in favour of heavily indebted poor countries, which can permit cancellation of their public external debt once they meet specified conditions and thus reach the HIPC 'completion point'

IDB: Inter-American Development Bank

ILSA (USA): Iran–Libya Sanctions Act approved by Congress in August 1996 to punish Iran and Libya notably via trade sanctions

IMF: International Monetary Fund

MERCOSUR: Mercado Común del Sur. A free trade agreement between Argentina, Brazil, Paraguay and Uruguay

NATO: North Atlantic Treaty Organization

NICT: new information and communication technologies

NAFTA: North American Free Trade Agreement

OHBLA: Organization for the Harmonization of Business Law in Africa

OPEC: Organization of Petroleum Exporting Countries

5

Paris Club: an informal group of official creditors devoted to finding sustainable solutions to payment difficulties experienced by debtor nations

Payment incidents index: payment default indices reflect the payment-incident trend on commercial transactions payable in the short term worldwide across a broad range of economic sectors. The monitoring of payment incidents is based on a composite of several sets of company-payment–capacity indicators available in Coface databases: those derived directly from its credit insurance, receivables management and company information activities, and those obtained from partners. Payment incidents are expressed as indices based on the average of incidents recorded over the world between 1995 and 2000. The resulting curves thus permit comparing a country's or sector's payment risk level with the world average as well as monitoring the trend of those risks

PPP: purchasing power parity

PRGF: Poverty Reduction and Growth Facility, the IMF's special low-interest lending programme for poor countries with structural balance-of-payments difficulties

R&D: research and development

SADC: Southern African Development Community

SWIFT: Society for Worldwide Interbank Financial Telecommunication, which runs a worldwide network whereby messages concerning financial transactions can be exchanged between banks and other financial institutions in 194 countries

UEOMA: (Union Economique et Monétaire Ouest Africaine) West African Economic and Monetary Union

UNITA (Angola): União para a Independência Total de Angola, rebel movement defeated in 2002 after nearly 30 years of civil war